LAW AND ECOLOGY

Ecology and Law in Modern Society

Series Editors:
Richard O. Brooks
Environmental Law Center, Vermont Law School, USA
and
Ross A. Virginia
Environmental Studies Program, Dartmouth College, USA

This series will present a legal and ecological perspective on important environmental issues such as declining biodiversity and the ecological significance of endangered species, the effects of pollution on natural and managed systems, the ecology of fragile ecosystems (mountains, grazed lands) pollution and its effects on ecosystem services. The scientific basis for understanding important areas of environmental law will be presented by experts in their fields. The formulating of environmental law to influence human activities will be analyzed by leading legal scholars. The central legal cases and challenges will be explored and the resulting success of the statutes considered. It is the intent of the series to provide a balance in the treatment of legal and ecological material not traditionally found in environmental law texts.

Law and Ecology

The rise of the ecosystem regime

RICHARD O. BROOKS
Environmental Law Center, Vermont Law School, USA

ROSS JONES
Environmental Studies Program, Dartmouth College, USA

ROSS A. VIRGINIA
Environmental Studies Program, Dartmouth College, USA

ASHGATE

Published by
Ashgate Publishing Limited
Gower House
Croft Road
Aldershot
Hants GU11 3HR
England

Ashgate Publishing Company
Suite 420, 101 Cherry Street
Burlington, VT 05401-4405 USA

Ashgate website: http://www.ashgate.com

British Library Cataloguing in Publication Data
Brooks, Richard Oliver
    Law and ecology : the rise of the ecosystem legal regime. -
    (Ecology and law in modern society)
    1. Environmental law - History 2. Environmental law 3. Ecology
    I. Title II. Jones, Ross III. Virginia, Ross A.
    344' .046

Library of Congress Control Number: 2002107427

ISBN 0 7546 2038 7 (Hbk)
ISBN 0 7546 2316 5 (Pbk)

Printed and bound in Great Britain by MPG Books Ltd, Bodmin, Cornwall

Contents

List of Figures

List of Tables
(Includes definitions and case examples)

List of Bridge Documents

Preface

On April 22, 1970, Earth Day arrived, a watershed date commemorating the recognition of an interconnected environment and human society. This day was also one more day in the gradual development of the science of ecology and its increasingly important role in the public policy of environmental protection as reflected in environmental law. By Earth Day [and even before], the field of ecosystem science had become a distinct part of ecology, although significant new developments were to take place between 1970 and the new millennium. Ecosystem science increasingly provided a systematic approach to the study of nature and suggested, by implication, a vision of a new relationship of humans and nature. In 1970 and immediately thereafter, some of the most important United States environmental laws were adopted including the National Environmental Policy Act and the Coastal Zone Management Act. These laws were the result of a unique coming together of a wide range of citizens creating a public culture of support for protecting ecosystems both to insure nature's own intrinsic value and the health and recreation of its present citizens and future generations.

For the past three decades since Earth Day, citizens and environmental leaders have sought to employ the insights of ecology to further the protection of nature and the sustainable use of natural resources. Lawyers and legal scholars have tried to craft laws which would incorporate the insights of ecology or reshape an understanding of ecology to fit the legal process and environmental laws already adopted. And ecologists would both pursue the inner logic of their own field and seek to make relevant some of their conclusions to society for the continual pursuit of environmental protection.

This book, and the series of books to follow, seek to explore the desirability and feasibility of placing the ecological study of ecosystems at the center of an understanding of environmental policy and law. *Our contention is that ecology is the heart of environmental law and policy. Only by accepting this premise and realizing this truth can the promise of Earth Day be realized and a satisfactory regime of environmental law be put in place.* To attain this ideal one must begin with the recognition that ecology itself is a "contested ground," where scientists debate, test and refine theories and practices aimed at improving the diversity and function of ecosystems. Debate continues over the centrality of the ecosystem concept as the core for reaching an understanding of nature. Even if the ecosystem is recognized to be the central organizing idea within ecology, the task remains of reconciling it with other aspects of ecology and framing its appropriate role within environmental law and policy. This task is difficult since environmental law and policy are responsive to a public culture which is largely unaware of the subtleties of the science of ecology and its concepts.

Ecologists have written extensively about their field. Cultural historians have discussed the impacts of ecology and nature writing upon our culture. Political and economic theorists have explored the relationship of ecology to the political and economic structure of our society. Legal scholars have described the environmental law regime and offered case studies of how ecology might (or might not) fit within the legal regime. Ethical philosophers have sought to lay bare the implications of ecology for ethical thought. We have sought to bring together these writings in our history of the relationships of ecology and law.

First we offer the reader a brief overview of the disciplines of ecology and environmental law. Following an introductory discussion of ecology and environmental law, we turn to an historical examination of the significant trends in the development of the two fields. We recognize and then explore the importance of the ecological study of ecosystems and its relationship to environmental law by analyzing the autonomous influence of four major historical factors: (1) "ecology," i.e., the developing science of ecology; (2) "public culture," i.e., the emergence of a public culture which increasingly embraces an ethos of nature and sustainability; (3) "public policy," i.e., local, state and federal policies, largely the result of the arousal of vigorous environmental movements and the emergence of "ecosystem regimes" as central players in the environmental policy debate; and (4) "environmental law," i.e., environmental constitutional provisions, legislation, regulation, court rulings, and international agreements, laws and treaties. Each one of these influences is the subject of one or more academic disciplines. Ecology is often viewed as a synthesis or emergent field drawing from several disciplines including biology, botany, zoology, soils, meteorology, chemistry, hydrology, and so on. Public culture and an ethos of nature is studied in environmental history, literature, sociology and ethics. The social movements and their resulting public institutions are studied in history, political science, and public policy courses. Environmental law is the subject of public policy and a myriad of law courses. As a consequence of the many disciplines contributing to ecosystem law, an immense literature has emerged. This literature supplies the subject matter for this book as well as for environmental studies programs across the world, as well as courses within more traditional disciplines.

Our historical account of the early origins of both ecology and environmental law is followed by a more specific discussion of its three modern phases: the mid-century period from 1950 to 1970, a period of testing the relationship from 1970 to 1990, and the "fruition" of the relationship since

1990. This fruition has taken the form of both a more integrated ecology with place-based and species-based ecosystem regimes and global regimes informed by a new earth systems science. In this introductory volume, we merely introduce the prospect of a future integrated ecology as part of ecosystem regimes. We neither dogmatically assert that such a proposal is inevitable, nor do we articulate the details of a hoped-for unification.

This history is introduced and illustrated by selected case studies of the interaction of environmental law and ecology. Although there have been other histories of both ecology and environmental law, we are not aware of any historical account of their relationship. We document that relationship by focusing upon linkage persons whose scholarship links law and ecology, "bridge documents" between the two fields, the migration of ecological concepts into environmental law, and the constitution of interdisciplinary frameworks which link ecology and law. Having set forth this history, we seek, in the conclusion of the book, to identify the key questions and problems which have emerged from this history of the two disciplines. It is this set of problems which we hope will stimulate and guide the future volumes of this series.

The specialization of the study of the environment and environmental law, has produced serious problems. Often one discipline (either law, ecology, the study of public policy or public culture) is adopted as the "dominant discipline" and the other disciplines are treated as ancillary contributors to that discipline. For example, one can find ecology books in which environmental law is either ignored or treated as an afterthought of the author. On the other hand, environmental law books often dismiss ecology after a brief introductory chapter where it is treated as an amusing introduction before the environmental law is set forth in completely legal terms, and in isolation from its ecological dimensions. When efforts are made to join disciplines, they often result in a total distortion or misstatement of each discipline. Since the disciplines of law and ecology and their objects are continually evolving, the forging of an interdisciplinary synthesis will be a difficult challenge since this evolution makes any effort to relate these disciplines, one to another, very difficult. It is our hope that we can stimulate a more harmonious treatment of law and ecology and their interactions through this series.

The inherent complexities of human constructs such as environmental law and the science of ecosystems has led to the emergence of a variety of interdisciplinary and/or multi-disciplinary conceptual frameworks which seek to understand their relationships. Thus the interdisciplinary frameworks of large scale modeling, risk analysis, resource and ecosystem regimes, and ecosystem management seek to encompass concern for ecology, public culture, public policy, and environmental law. These new inter-disciplinary or multi-disciplinary frameworks are themselves complex and abstract conceptual schema, difficult to relate to the specifics of the disciplines they propose to unify. We discuss briefly ecosystem regimes and ecosystem management. In short, this volume offers:

(1) A succinct description of law and ecology and their problematic relationship;

(2) A history of their relationship which includes illustrative cases and a concentration upon "bridge documents" and integrating concepts linking the two fields;

(3) A detailed inventory and taxonomy of the problems and questions which the history of the relationship of these two fields raise;

(4) A broad description of some of the different interdisciplinary intellectual frameworks through which the relationship of law and ecology may be understood;

(5) An agenda of future research within environmental law, ecology and about their relationship.

In future volumes of this series on topics such as ecotoxicology and the law, endangered species and ecology, fragile ecosystem management (e.g., mountains) and the law, we will probe more into the relations between these two fields, and provide a framework that we hope will improve our ecosystems and our legal system.

To carry out the admittedly ambitious agenda of this series, we have joined the faculty of two institutions together to plan, co-edit, or author these volumes. These institutions are the Environmental Law Center of Vermont Law School and the Environmental Studies Program at Dartmouth College.

Vermont Law School's Environmental Law Center [ELC] is located in South Royalton, Vermont, and administers two environmental law degree programs, an LL.M. in Environmental Law for attorneys seeking to specialize in this challenging field, and the Master of Studies in Environmental Law, open to both law and non-law students. It is the largest master's of law degree program in the nation with over 250 students currently enrolled. The ELC also conducts research, hosts symposia and workshops, sponsors a student-produced online journal, *Res Communes*, and assists local organizations and communities with environmental problems. The program adopts a multidisciplinary approach to environmental law, including in addition to law, the study of economics, ethics and ecology. Its array of courses allows students to choose from a series of concentrations in the field of environmental law. For example, the Law and Ecology concentration features courses in conservation biology, coastal systems, biodiversity protection, watershed management, and oceans law. Other concentrations include Pollution Prevention and Abatement, International Environmental Law, and Alternative Dispute Resolution.

Dartmouth College's Environmental Studies Program is located in Hanover, New Hampshire, and was among the nation's first such interdisciplinary programs founded in response to Earth Day. The program takes a broad view of what is meant by environment, and provides courses drawn from the sciences, social sciences and humanities and course-project activities oriented towards providing policy options and potential solutions to decisionmakers at the level of the College, community, adjoining communities, states, and federal government. Its programs include the Environmental Studies Major, Minor and Honors Program, an Off-Campus Program in Africa, the Dickey Center Institute of Arctic Studies, the Institute on International Environmental Governance, and faculty research programs in ecosystem science and global change, ecological and environmental economics, and the human dimensions of environmental issues.

This series also draws law faculty, attorneys, and ecological scientists from other institutions to co-edit and co-author other volumes in the series. The purpose of recruiting an interdisciplinary authorship is both to promote communication among the faculty within these two fields and insure the highest quality possible for this interdisciplinary effort. As the series extends to the laws of other nations, we hope to draw upon the expertise of law faculty and attorneys from these nations.

We do not propose to simply publish collections of interesting papers. The purpose of this publishing project requires carefully integrated volumes which carefully advance an understanding of the relations between ecology and environmental law and which identify and resolve the problems of those relations. The ultimate goal is to create an environmental law which is fully informed and guided by the best methods and conclusions which ecology has to offer.

Acknowledgments

The three authors would like to highlight their acknowledgment of Kathy Leonard's contribution to this volume. In addition to typing innumerable drafts, she reconciled the different drafts of the three authors, coordinated student contributions, proofread parts of the manuscript, constructed most of the tables, figures, and bridge documents, and brought the volume into compliance with the editorial requirements of Ashgate publishers. The resulting volume is as much the product of her work as it is the work of the three authors.

All three authors would also like to acknowledge student contributions to this volume. Vermont Law School student contributors included M.E. Rolle, 2001 LL.M. candidate, who provided substantial reviews of many chapters in this volume, Shawn Behrens, Kim Bryant, Bryan Dempsey, Erin Flynn, Rebecca Gonzalez, Dori Harris, Ed McNamara, Shannon Nutt, Tom Storrer, Amy Beiersdorfer, Jennifer Burkhardt, Stefania Fregosi, Albert Huang, Matthew Mattila, Robert Weisberg, Roger Fleming, Kirk Bloomer, Jason Brandeis, Tonya Jansen, Brian Maddox, Kelly Berfield, April Doughty, Kristin Shanley, Susanne Miller, Brett Rosenthal, Thomas Leary, and from Dartmouth College, Kathleen Stewart.

Richard Brooks

I would like to acknowledge the support of Vermont Law School, its Environmental Law Center and the Center's Director, Karin Sheldon. Also, comments on earlier versions of Chapter 1 by Patrick Parenteau and by Dartmouth College faculty, including Oran Young.

I drew inspiration from the works of Bruce Ackerman, Joe Sax, Robert Keiter, J.B. Ruhl, Michael Bean, Oran Young, Celia Campbell-Mohn, John Dryzek, Lakshman Guruswamy, Christopher Stone, Lynton Caldwell, Kristin Schrader-Frechette, A. Dan Tarlock, William Cronon, Jutta Brunée and Stephen Toope, Charles Wilkinson, Daniel Rohlf, Douglas L. Honnold, John Cairns, Russell Lande, and Oliver Houck.

Thanks, Mollie.

Ross Jones

I would like to acknowledge three ecologists/evolutionary biologists whose work has been particularly influential: Michael Soulé for being the guiding force behind the initial creation of a separate discipline of conservation biology – which to this point remains the most successful example of the interaction of ecology and law (at least in this author's opinion), Russell Lande for having the courage to try (mostly successfully) to show environmental lawyers and managers how ecology (particularly mathematical ecology) could be used to solve environmental issues (even in that most unscientific of settings - the courtroom), and David Culver, my major advisor, who taught me to be an evolutionary biologist and ecologist.

Most importantly, I wish to thank the two people without which this author could not have carried through on this project: my wife Anita and son Conlon. Their patience in enduring the time and, sometimes, frustration in completing this book is (as always) greatly, if far too often silently, appreciated.

Ross Virginia

I want to thank my colleagues Dick Brooks and Ross Jones for many thought provoking breakfast meetings at the Norwich Inn, where we challenged and reconciled our perspectives on environmental law, population ecology and ecosystem ecology. This book is the richer for these exchanges. My wife Sandy and my children Will and Emma deserve special recognition for enduring the long process of completing our book. Many people have influenced my development as an ecosystem ecologist and several have motivated me to explore the interdisciplinary connections between ecology, law and policy. My major advisor, C.C. Delwiche, among the first global systems scientists, gave me an appreciation for "systems" and the ways in which humans change them. James Reynolds, Diana Wall, Wesley Jarrell, William Schlesinger and Walt Whitford have greatly influenced my thinking on ecosystems and their functioning during great times conducting research together in hot desert, Arctic tundra, and Antarctic ecosystems.

My recent progress toward understanding the human dimensions of eco-systems has been guided by my friends in the Environmental Studies Program at Dartmouth College. Among them, Oran Young, Jim Hornig, the late Donella Meadows, Jack Shepherd, and Rich Howarth have been wonderful in guiding me to new perspectives. Finally I give a very special thanks to Dick Brooks. His vision that ecology should be the core discipline supporting environmental law and his intellectual leadership in exploring their connections made this book possible.

1   The Problem

There was a moment in the spring of 1979 when Mono Lake (California) environmental advocates seemed to be sweeping all before them. The lawsuit was underway. The Mono Lake Committee had a thousand members and was ready to incorporate in its own name. At the same time, the National Guard was about to blast a second moat in the land bridge, threatening breeding birds on a previously isolated island. A task force of government agencies was wrestling with the Mono problem, and in Sacramento a legislator had introduced a 'save-the-lake bill.' This high drama was but a stage in the struggle which began with the ancient Great Basin when water covered most of Nevada, or 15,000 years ago when the Great Basin Lakes were still scattered throughout the Utah, Nevada and Southern California range. But the human struggle began when, at the turn of the last century, Mulholland and Easton made a secret trip to Owens Valley and began to plan the drainage of Sierra Nevada lakes to slake the increasing thirst of a growing Los Angeles. Aqueducts were built, water sucked out and the slow decline of Mono Lake soon began.

– John Hart, *Storm Over Mono*[1]

There is a growing public recognition that one of the most important public uses of the tidelands – a use encompassed within the tidelands trust – is the preservation of those lands in their natural state, so that they may serve as ecological units for scientific study, as open space, and as environments which provide food and habitat for birds and marine life, and which favorably affect the scenery and climate of the area ... Mono Lake is a navigable waterway ... It supports a small local industry which harvests brine shrimp for sale as fish food, which endeavor probably qualifies the lake as a 'fishery' under the traditional public trust cases. The principal values plaintiffs seek to protect, however, are recreational and ecological – the scenic views of the lake and its shore, the purity of the air, and the use of the lake for nesting and feeding by birds ... [I]t is clear that protection of these values is among the purposes of the public trust.

– National Audubon v. city of Los Angeles[2]

Introduction

The story of Mono Lake and its protection symbolizes the coevolution of ecology and environmental law in America and the emergence of place-based ecosystem regimes. Mono Lake is a saline lake whose food chain dramatizes the workings of an ecosystem. The lowering of the water table through the Los Angeles [water] withdrawals dried up some of its tributaries, lowered the very level of the lake itself, exposing the previous water-based tufa towers, eradicating some aquatic plant life, and leaving an alkali band around the lake, producing dust storms and ultimately threatening the base of the lake's food chain, the brine shrimp themselves. As early as 1972, the first ecological study of the lake was completed to be followed by many more over the years, climaxed by a National Academy of Sciences study in 1987: *The Mono Basin Ecosystem: Effects of Changing Lake Level.*[3] This elegant study identifies terrestrial and aquatic species, projects their future population levels, estimates the critical level needed to support this wildlife population, describes the hydrology of Mono Lake, estimates the impact of water withdrawals on the populations and assesses the significance of changes in wildlife populations.[4]

The history of the Mono Lake case is the story of growing ecological sensitivity to continued exploitation of ecosystems and increasing awareness of ecological knowledge needed for the legal protection of this lake. What began as an environmentally insensitive water withdrawal spurred by the thirst of Los Angeles, leading to a series of ad hoc lawsuits, eventually led to a deep understanding of the ecology of the lake ecosystem. The public began to comprehend the profound ecological impacts of water withdrawal from a delicate arid zone lake. New ecologically-informed court opinions were handed down and new ecosystem legislation was adopted to protect the lake. In short, the political and ecological history of Mono Lake illustrates the gradual emergence of a public awareness of the values of this beautiful place, the slow creation of new institutions and modification of old ones to manage the Mono Lake ecosystem, and the availability and usefulness of the science of ecology to these efforts. All of these were infused into the resulting ecosystemic legal regime, which saved Mono Lake.

The Rise of the Ecosystemic Regime

The history of Mono Lake is one of many stories illustrating the history of the rise of an ecosystemic regime,[5] i.e., new social institutions or clusters of institutions designed to properly govern ecosystems. Within these regimes the science of ecology is applied through environmental laws which are part of the regimes.[6] The vision, method and conclusions of ecology are at the center of these ecological regimes, and hence embody ecological governance through law. Building upon our account of the history of ecosystem regimes, we introduce the idea of a "regime of ecosystemic law" in which law and ecology mutually inform each other's content, method and purpose. By "regime" we mean the cluster of rules and roles which govern our practices in regard to a given ecosystem. By "ecology" we mean the scientific study of the systematic interdependencies of the biotic and abiotic environment. *By "ecosystemic laws" is meant those laws which seek to regulate human activities with explicit awareness of the structure, function and integrity of the ecosystems and the biodiversity within those systems affected by those activities.*[7] *It is our contention that ecology is the central discipline for understanding both a viable environment and the modern threats to that environment.*

Table 1.1 ECOSYSTEMIC LEGAL REGIME

A cluster of rules and roles which

1. Originate out of a concern for human interventions in the structure and functioning of ecosystems;
2. Define their objectives in terms of the maintenance and/or restoration of these ecosystemic functions and structures;
3. Rest upon a public culture of awareness of the ecosystem, landscape or global system;
4. Provide for systematic collection of information about ecosystem, landscape and global systems, organizing that information in system terms, and projecting the future functioning of that system;
5. Define the geographic boundaries in terms of the different levels of ecosystems including specific ecosystems, landscape features, and global systems;
6. Establish management controls in terms of parameters of ecosystem functioning;
7. Provide for feedback evaluation about the effects of human activities within ecosystems and evaluation of efforts to manage those activities.

The growth of the ecosystemic legal regime has been underway for at least the past half-century.[8] Its early history was the result of the independent evolution of the discrete spheres of ecology, public culture, political theory, and environmental law. Since 1970, there has been an *episodic coevolution* of ecology and environmental law, along with changes in our public culture. Thus, ecology has informed and shaped important areas of environmental law including coastal management, endangered species protection, forest management and a variety of global pollution problems. For example, the environmental law effort to protect endangered species and more broadly, biodiversity, has led to the creation of the field of conservation biology which in turn has modified both the Endangered Species Act and other laws designed to protect biodiversity. The public's interest in laws mandating mitigation of environmental change and restoration of environmental sites has led to the creation of the discipline of restoration ecology. The legal regulation of estuaries has stimulated the development of estuarine science.[9]

The understanding of the relationship between ecology and modern law cannot be understood without a full understanding of the notion of regimes identified above. The study of regimes was introduced by Oran Young in the early 1980s to describe the institutional context in which decisionmakers make decisions about natural resources and ecosystems.[10] The 1980s and 1990s may be viewed as the history of the creation of a series of new environmental regimes, poetically described by one political theorist as "institutions for the earth."[11]

While the science of ecology was steadily emerging over the past century and a half, environmental law, as a body of law, assumed its present shape only in the mid-twentieth century in response to specific environmental problems of water and air pollution, harmful pesticides, clear-cutting of forests, dumping of hazardous and radioactive wastes and the public demand for the protection of national parks and endangered species. These early environ-mental laws were intended to reduce those ill-advised human interventions in the workings of the natural environment which resulted in obvious harms, but the laws were not formulated with a full understanding of how the environment functioned. The laws were ad hoc, pragmatic responses. Over time, states and communities were left a poorly organized collection of laws, many of which ignored a slowly growing wisdom about nature in the science of ecology. Yet, only through such an ecological understanding of nature was it possible to determine which human activities were compatible with the natural eco-systems in which we live and on which we depend.

The importance of ecology to an understanding of our environmental problems slowly ripened within the public culture from 1970-2000. As illustrated in the Mono Lake history, a growing ecological understanding helped to inform the public about the nature and extent of harms which en-vironmentally thoughtless activities created. Equally important, the ecological understanding contributed to devising sustainable solutions for these problems – solutions which did not simply displace the problem somewhere else or to another time. The ultimate contribution of ecology to societal welfare only emerges with the gradual public realization of our interdependence with nature. To be sure, this insight is not yet widespread enough to stop present careless interventions such as the unchecked use of fossil fuels or massive world financed development projects. Despite these problems, there has been progress during the 1980s and 1990s. With the growing understanding of the global problems of biodiversity reduction, ozone depletion, acid rain and global warming, the public has become more aware of the need to view our environmental problems, whether global or local, in ecological terms.[12]

In order to prepare the reader for the history and analysis which follows, we offer a brief introductory discussion of public culture, ecology, resource regimes and environmental law. Since our major focus will be upon ecology and environmental law, our introduction to these topics will be more extensive.

The Public Culture of Ecology and Environmental Law

The transition to an ecosystem legal regime requires a public culture which supports such a regime. By "public culture" we mean the values implicit in our public practices – the assumptions about nature, the threats to it and the role of government and other institutions in controlling those threats – assumptions which inform our public life. Such a culture is often referred to as an ethos, or public values, public opinion or public philosophy. Although such a public culture is the object of study of anthropology, history, political science, economics, geography, sociology, cultural studies, and critical moral philosophy, our study will only briefly discuss such a culture as a background to the history of ecology and environmental law.[13] In that discussion, we recognize that ecology and environmental law are both responses to the public culture and, like social movements, a shaper of that culture. For example, early ecologists' focus on mutualism as an important concept in ecology was influenced by the prevalent cultural embrace of nineteenth-century social Darwinism.[14] Conversely, key environmental court cases such as those involving the prohibition of DDT have shaped our environmental culture.

Although there have been general surveys of American values finding majority support of "environmental values" and the need for government regulation, the extent to which such environmentalism reflects a significant shift to those "post materialist" values which reflect on ecological perspective is debatable.[15] To find a public culture specifically supportive of ecosystemic regimes may require a culture which not only values the environment and its protection, but also views nature and formulates its values in ecologic terms. Specific studies of ecological history may be more suggestive of the public culture's increasing sympathy toward ecosystems and the regimes which manage them. For example, Roderick Nash's *Wilderness and the American Mind*[16] documents our changing attitudes toward wilderness and wetlands. Case studies of recent citizen efforts to protect unique places (such as Mono Lake study cited above, or the Mediterranean discussed below) further docu-ment the growing ecological awareness of the citizenry and more specialized "epistemic communities."

The shift in ecological awareness as part of our public culture is best reflected in the recent explosion of popular nature writing and the rise of a new field of environmental ethics. Our history below reveals how this ethos[17] has penetrated the legal world of statutes, court decisions and regulations.

Legislatures require the conservation of ecosystems, and at least some judges recognize the intrinsic value of such ecosystems – urging they be awarded legal standing. These modern developments are partly the outgrowth of the works of a group of nineteenth- and early twentieth-century "nature visionaries," who discovered the ecological essence of nature and guided their lives and their writing to reflect this vision. However, the views of these nature visionaries were clearly peripheral to a dominant public culture – a culture committed to economic growth.[18] Now we find a growing environmental ethos which is partly based upon the discoveries of ecology and which is particularly influential in guiding the formation of ecosystem regimes. This ethos[19] has been the object of study both by social scientists, and has been elaborated by scholars of ethics.[20]

Before the advent of the environmental age, traditional western ethics was primarily occupied with concerns of leading "the good life" (Aristotle), maximizing happiness (John Stuart Mill), and formulating universal ethical rules (Immanuel Kant). The classic ethic of the moral virtues, utilitarianism and Kantian moral autonomy have provided a basis for the three principal environmental ethical positions. Each of these three positions has been reformulated in light of the recognition of environmental problems and of the important role which a new understanding of nature contributes to ethical thought.

There has been, however, a deeper change in the ethical landscape which has been created by the ecological recognition of an interdependent nature and our place within that nature. This recognition has required a fundamental change in the traditional ethical positions which assumes – to a lesser or greater degree – an autonomy of human life.[21] A modern environmental ethos recognizes a newly formulated relationship between humans and nature: a fundamental interdependence.[22] Within the interdependence of humans and nature within environmental ethics, two very different formulations of that interdependence have been formulated. In one formulation, the identity of the autonomous self is retained intact, but is viewed as affected by nature's processes. This view rests upon the phenomenon of individual consciousness and the acts of the will. A second view of the human regards the self as momentary concretizations of components and processes of a large interdependent nature.[23]

Despite the importance of these issues of public culture and environmental ethics, in the chapters below we concentrate our sights upon the history of the science of ecology and environmental law, but we recognize that the public culture and its expression in ethical thought is an important aspect of this history, and in the final chapter we turn to identify the interdisciplinary frameworks of environmental thought which have emerged in the past century.

The Science of Ecology

Ecology is the study of the relationship of organisms and their environment.[24]
The environment includes other individuals in its population, other populations
of plants and animals with which an organism and its population interacts, and
the physical and chemical factors that influence life (i.e., the abiotic
environment). "Relationships" include such diverse subjects as the adaptation
of an individual's physiology to environmental extremes (e.g., low moisture and
high temperatures), the killing and eating of prey by predators, and the flow of
carbon through the living and non-living components of the environment. To
study such a diversity of natural phenomena, ecology takes an interdisciplinary
approach, drawing from biology, chemistry, physics, and the earth sciences to
achieve an understanding of how the natural world functions, and in so doing,
sustains human life.[25]

Because ecology encompasses so many conceivable relationships
between organisms and the environment, it is impossible for any one ecologist
to study more than a small fraction of the field.[26] As a result, ecologists have
divided themselves into subdisciplines defined by different objectives or
focusing on distinct levels of biological organization (e.g., individuals,
populations, and ecosystems) and a few of the various biological and physical
processes occurring at each level. This traditional division among ecological
disciplines affected how ecology has interacted with environmental law and with
different parts of ecology contributing to the various environmental laws in very
different ways.

The division of ecology that we will stress in this book is the one based
on the hierarchical scaling of nature from genes, individuals, populations,
communities, ecosystems, landscapes to, ultimately, the entire Earth. Each
progressively higher level contains the lower levels of ecological organization
as components. However, each level also contains its own set of processes
and/or interactions that distinguish it from the other scales. Historically,
ecologists confined their work to one ecological level and one, or very few,
ecological processes. However, there is a growing trend of ecologists expanding
their studies to look at the interactions among levels and processes; hence,
moving towards a new integrated ecology. Will this new integration within
ecology result in the change in how ecology interacts with en-vironmental law?
One possible outcome, discussed later in the book, is that environmental laws
themselves will become more integrated in response to this change within
ecology.

Finally, differing objectives among ecologists are most clearly seen in
the division between basic and applied ecology. Traditionally, an academic
ecologist strives to understand how natural systems are organized and function.

This understanding may or may not have short or even long term economic benefits to human society. The applied ecologist is interested in solving particular problems, ranging from the elimination of insect destruction of agricultural products to the design of large-scale natural reserves.[27] The boundary between basic and applied ecologists is blurring with the growing awareness by basic ecologists of the need to use their understanding of ecological relationships to solve growing environmental problems which, in turn, "test" the accuracy of the scientific understanding.

Stages of the History of Ecology

The history of ecology can be divided into two general stages. First, from its origin in the nineteenth century to the mid-twentieth, ecology gradually developed along two separate paths. The holistic view sought to understand how natural systems of plants and animal interacted with each other and with the physical environment to form communities. In contrast, most early animal ecologists focused on how the abundance and distribution of individual organisms and single populations were affected by changes in the environment.

Ecosystem ecology, which arose from the community centered holistic view of ecology, became a distinct branch of ecology in 1942 with the publication of Raymond Lindeman's classic paper, *The Trophic-Dynamic Aspects of Ecology.*[28] From this point, ecosystem ecology would begin its separate development as that part of ecology explicitly concerned with the function of relatively large systems of plants, animals, and their physical environment. The goal of the ecosystem ecologist would be the understanding of ecosystem structure and function, including what controls the energy (i.e., food) flow and nutrient (e.g., carbon and nitrogen) cycles through these systems.

During the late 1950s and into the 1960s, ecosystem ecology would itself divide into two sub-parts, the system ecology exemplified by the grassland study of the International Biological Program and championed by Eugene Odum, and the experimental approach of the Hubbard Brook study led by Gene Likens.[29] This division still persists today with empirical ecosystem ecologists concentrating on the measurement and manipulation of nutrient cycles and energy flows in relatively small manageable ecosystems and systems ecologists concentrating on the modeling of large-scale (landscape to global) fluxes in energy and nutrients.[30] However, while the initial separation of ecosystem ecology was due to conceptual differences in how best to understand ecosystems, the current division is mostly due to pragmatic considerations; very large-scale ecological systems are less amendable to the experimental approach.

During the 1960s, that part of ecology focusing on single populations and interacting groups of populations would also undergo a rapid revolution under the leadership of, among others, Robert MacArthur. Population ecologists, in sharp contrast to the ecosystem ecologists, would focus on those lower-level aspects of ecology and associated processes (e.g., a predator-prey system) which would allow for relatively small-scale experiments and simple mathematical models. This division between the "big science" ecosystem ecology and "small science" population ecology was partially a result in differences in government funding of science.[31]

By Earth Day 1970, practitioners of both ecosystem and population ecology had achieved a high degree of self-confidence (if not arrogance) about the level of maturity of their fields. Ecosystem ecologists believed that by combining their holistic approach of study with the logistic resources of "Big Science," that the structure and functions of ecosystems could be understood and catalogued.[32] Population ecologists believed that the factors controlling the observed patterns of species were relatively few (with competition among populations being the most important) and could be studied through the use of relatively simple mathematical models.[33] Many ecologists believed that the outcome of these early conflicts would be a Darwinian natural selection of one discipline of ecology that would achieve dominance by its ability to more accurately describe and model the real world.

During the 1980s and 1990s much of this self-confidence among ecologists was replaced with two different views of ecology. One was that there were no general rules in ecology to discover (at either the population or ecosystem level) and that ecology would only advance through a case by case cataloging of the ecology of individual populations, communities, or ecosystems.[34] In contrast, other ecologists continued to believe that there are general rules of how ecological systems evolve and function, but that they must be discovered through the use of new concepts and methods. However, both groups shared the view that a more integrated ecology, which combined methods and concepts from all of ecology with those of other disciplines (e.g., evolutionary biology and climatology), was necessary. The result is an early twenty-first century ecology that is a more unified science in which system ecologists, experimental ecosystem ecologists, population ecologists, and others all contribute to the understanding of the natural world.[35] To again borrow from Charles Darwin, while the 1960s and 1970s were a time of competition between ecological disciplines (with the result that some unsuccessful sub-disciplines have been lost and other have been strengthened) the 1980s and even more, the 1990s, were a time of mutualism in which the foundation of a unified ecology was laid.

Table 1.2 LEVELS AND PROCESSES IN ECOLOGY

INDIVIDUAL	POPULATION	COMMUNITY	ECOSYSTEM/LAND-SCAPE/BIOSPHERE

Genes
Natural selection
Physiology
Behavior
	Population genetics
	Demographics
	Intraspecific
	  competition
	Other density-dependent
	  factors
	Density-independent
	  factors (e.g. climate)
		Interspecific
		  competition
		Predation
		Mutualism
		Succession
		Trophic
		  dynamics
		Niche
		  diversification
			Similar functions over
			increasing spatial scales
			- Nutrient cycling
			- Energy flux
			- Climate change
			- Habitat
			    fragmentation

This table shows some of the relevant processes that occur at each level of ecology. Some, such as genetic variation and nutrient cycling, are critical processes at more than one level of organization.
Source: Brooks, Jones and Virginia

Levels of Ecology[36]

Everything in the universe exists at a particular scale, from the microscopic scale of subatomic particles to the super-macro scale of the entire universe. Biology, the study of life, is concerned with scales ranging from the components of cells (e.g., DNA) to the possibility of life on other planets. Within this range of scales, ecologists study individual organisms, populations of organisms, communities of different populations, ecosystems of communities interacting with the physical environment, and the interaction of all life on Earth with the global environment (i.e., the biosphere).[37] One important exception to this *ecological realm* is the growing interest over the last thirty years of how genetic variation helps individuals and populations adapt to the environment. This use of genetics has led to the creation of two distinct ecological sub-disciplines which combine the genetic level with either the individual or the population level; *Ecological Genetics* (the study of how particular genes help individuals adapt to the environment) and *Evolutionary Ecology* (the study of the interaction of genetics and ecology in the evolution of populations). The basis of all ecological systems is the *organism*. Physiological and behavioral ecologists study the variation in an organism's physiological or behavioral response to environmental variation. *Behavioral Ecology* is an important element of conservation biology applications (see below), including the recent controversy over the effect of logging on the endangered Northern Spotted Owl in the Pacific Northwest.[38] *Physiological Ecology* is one of the foundations of *Ecotoxicology*; the latter is another part of applied ecology.

Groups of interacting individuals of the same species that occupy a specific area at the same time form a *population*. *Population ecologists* seek to estimate the distribution and abundance of populations, as well as to discover the processes that control this distribution and abundance (see below).[39] A *habitat* is the place where specific organisms and their populations live (e.g., a coral reef for tropical fish or the African savanna for lions). Traditionally, population ecologists study interactions among populations and remain more strictly "biological," with their emphasis on the biotic component of the environment, than ecosystem ecologists who are concerned with large scale patterns of energy flow and nutrient cycling (see below).[40] However, one of the important changes in modern ecology has been the growing emphasis by population ecologists on studying the influence of the abiotic environment (e.g., climate variation, energy flows, nutrient cycles, etc.) on individual populations. Conservation biology was founded by and is still rooted in population ecology and the conservation of single populations, under the Endangered Species Act, remains a predominately population level concern.

Community Ecology is an important discipline of ecology, for the study of the formation of microbe, plant and animal associations (i.e., communities) is the link between the lower level study of individuals and populations and the high level study of ecosystems, landscapes, and the biosphere. Community ecologists tend to view a community as the sum of the various populations in a place and the interactions (i.e., community level processes) that bind these populations together. As we discuss in the next chapter, community ecology is one of the original areas of ecological research and today is the discipline where much of the integration of ecology is taking place. However, while some concepts from community ecology (e.g., food webs) have been incorporated into environmental law, it is only recently that community ecology has become an explicit part of the interaction of ecology and law.[41]

Central to the current use of ecology by environmental law is the concept of the *ecosystem*. An ecosystem "consists of all of the organisms in an area and the physical environment with which they interact."[42] Ecosystems are distinguishable from communities by the addition of the non-living, or abiotic component of the environment and by applying the concept of a system. At this level of organization, ecological research becomes a true multi-disciplinary field borrowing from both the natural and physical sciences.[43] The attempt to delineate the appropriate area, or boundaries, of specific ecosystems has driven much of the research in ecosystem ecology and has practical importance to management and law. Strictly speaking, the size (scale) of an ecosystem is defined by the objectives of the study. Most past research on ecosystems concentrated on relatively small systems such as small lakes, springs, or patches of isolated forest. This is due both to limitations in the techniques necessary to measure ecological variables as well as the belief that small systems are easier to understand.[44] Ecosystem research has used a holistic approach in which the ecosystem is studied as a functional and structural whole, and each plant and animal population within an ecosystem, along with each abiotic factor (e.g., hydrologic cycle) is treated as one component of a complex system.[45] The ideas of ecosystem ecology were important in stimulating the creation of many of the major environmental laws of the 1960s and 1970s (see Chapter 3) and are currently the scientific centerpiece of the new paradigm for environmental management, ecosystem management.

The *landscape* is the spatially organized set of habitats or ecosystems that define a particular region. *Landscape Ecology* has been an area of great growth in ecology due to satellite imaging and other techniques, such as Geographic Information Systems (GIS), which allows for the collection and analysis of large scale data (e.g., continental temperature gradients). While the landscape concept has been used for decades in land use law, the American variant of landscape ecology arose from ecosystem ecology as a way to study the interrelationship among multiple landscapes and has only relatively recently been used in the environmental management.[46] Landscape ecology, more than traditional ecosystem ecology, concentrates on spatial patterns and how these patterns affect lower levels of ecology. Landscape ecology is becoming a critical element in environmental law's use of ecology, especially linking ecology to concepts of place. In Chapter 8, we will discuss how it is being applied to such large-scale environmental management problems as the Florida Everglades and the Chesapeake Bay.

Global Ecology (the study of all the earth's life, the *biosphere*) has arisen directly from the relatively new understanding among both ecologists and environmental policy makers that large scale environmental problems such as climate change and biodiversity loss cannot be solved by focusing on single ecosystems or landscapes. Ecosystems and landscapes themselves interact on a global scale, and human perturbations now ripple through the entire earth system. We are beginning to understand how the linked marine ecosystems of the world interact to produce a healthy fishery or how the destruction of tropical rainforests influences the climate of northern temperate forests and the diversity of migratory songbirds.[47]

Processes of Ecology

While the division of ecology into separate sub-disciplines is mainly based on the hierarchy of nature, the actual work of ecologists focuses on the biological and physical processes that occur at each level. Some of these processes only occur at a single level while others, particularly the bio-geochemical processes, function at multiple levels.

The single most important process influencing life in ecological systems is *natural selection*. Natural selection, used by Darwin as the cornerstone of evolutionary theory, is the process whereby individual organisms with an adaptive advantage over others in its population are more likely to survive and reproduce. When the adaptive trait is at least partially controlled by an individual's genes the trait is more likely to be transferred to future generations where, because of the advantage it gives to individuals, it will increase in frequency among the population and genetic change (i.e., evolution) will occur.

The aggregation of individual level processes creates new higher-level processes that regulate populations. The most important *population-level processes* are the demographic factors that control population growth. These include density-dependent processes in which the rate and direction of change in the size of a population is dependent upon the density of a population. One of these processes is intra-specific competition, in which individuals of the same population compete for scarce resources (e.g., food or mates). These processes and others (e.g., age-dependent dispersal and the population's sex ratio) are all examples of the life-history of individuals and populations. Density-independent processes include climatic or other environmental factors that can affect population growth independent of population density. In Chapter 3 we will review how the study of the most basic processes of population ecology, the growth of a single population, was borrowed from the work of early human demography (the population ecology of humans).

Community-level processes are those that involve the interaction of two or more populations of plants and/or animals and are, along with ecosystem level processes, the core of what the public perceives as ecology. The study of competition in ecological systems has a long history and the role of competition in structuring biological communities is often debated in ecology. One critical concept arising from the role of population interactions in community formation is that of the *keystone species*; those species whose importance to a community's health or an ecosystem's function is greater than its population size would suggest. Recently the keystone concept has been one bridge concept serving to integrate community and ecosystem ecology.

Except for the protection of single species threatened with extinction (e.g., the Northern Spotted Owl and the Gray Wolf), most environmental problems are expressed at the scale of the ecosystem and higher. *Ecosystem-level processes* are very different from the biologically defined processes at the individual, population, and community level of organization because they include the physical environment. Ecosystem ecologists have traditionally focused on two general types of processes; *energy flow* and *nutrient cycling*. Energy flow is the one way flow of energy from the sun through various *trophic* (feeding) levels from photosynthetic (green) plants (producers) to herbivores and carnivores (consumers), and decomposers.

   Nutrient cycling refers to the cycling of elements essential to life (e.g., carbon, nitrogen, phosphorus) through the living environment and non-living environment. Nutrients released during the decomposition of organic matter (most often plant litter) sustain the functioning of most ecosystems. The cycling of organic matter is controlled by the biological community, especially the diversity of microorganisms found in soil and sediments, but is limited by such physical factors as temperature and moisture. Traditionally, ecosystem ecologists have concentrated on understanding energy transfers (trophic or food-web dynamics) and nutrient cycling processes by aggregating species into functional groups to reduce the number of species-environment interactions that must be considered. More recently the importance of individual species on ecosystem level processes has been recognized from the results of ecosystem experiments where biodiversity is manipulated and ecosystem variable such as productivity and nutrient flow are measured.

   Many of the *processes at the landscape and biosphere level* are the same as those at the community and ecosystem level, only on a much larger scale. Instead of the structure of biological communities within an ecosystem, landscape ecologists are concerned with the spatial patterns over multiple ecosystems. The flow of energy and cycling of nutrients among ecosystems on an ever-increasing scale is a prime focus of "large-scale" ecology. This is most obvious in the current concern over the effects of climate change on such "biosphere" level processes as the global carbon cycle.

Integrative Ecology

Today many ecologists are moving away from a focus on a single ecological level or process and towards carrying out research designed to understand how variation in processes at one level affect other levels of organization.[48] This change is obvious in the primary literature of ecology where there is an increased use of concepts from one ecological level by ecologists at other levels. It is also seen in the methodology and objectives of ecological research. The gradual breakdown of the "walls" that traditionally separated ecologists in the different sub-disciplines,[49] along with the technological advance in the methodologies used to measure ecological processes at all levels of organization, has produced a modern integrated ecology to support the development of ecosystem law.

   Ecosystem ecologists are now beginning to account for how population and community level processes affect energy flow and nutrient cycling. For example, certain species, termed keystone species, have a disproportionate influence (relative to their biomass) on ecosystem functioning.[50] Their loss may produce a chain-reaction of effects on the remainder of the ecosystem. An example of a keystone species is a predator that influences biodiversity by keeping a number of prey species populations at reduced levels so that a superior competitor does not increase in numbers and exclude the other species from the ecosystem. In this way, the predator maintains a multiple species community. The recognition of the significant influence that even minor species (in terms of abundance, biomass) may have on ecosystem processes has practical applications since keystone species and their habitats should receive high priority in conservation management plans.

More generally, ecosystem ecologists are beginning to ask; is biodiversity important to ecosystem function? This question is at the heart of an active debate among ecologists.[51] Many ecosystem scientists predict that the influence of biodiversity on ecosystem functioning should be large because ecosystem production and nutrient cycling are coupled by the biological interactions of organisms. In a widely cited study,[52] the response of a Minnesota grassland to a severe drought is purported to show the potential significance of biodiversity to ecosystem function and its response to dis-turbance or stress. During a long-term study of a grassland ecosystem a severe drought occurred. Experimental plots with high plant species diversity experienced about a 50 percent decline in productivity, whereas productivity in less diverse plots declined by more than 90 percent. Many ecologists are convinced that high species diversity can provide "insurance" to the ecosystem against unusual environmental conditions. In the case of the grassland study, the likelihood of drought-tolerant species being present in the community should be increased with higher diversity, thus ensuring relatively high productivity when the ecosystem experiences drought. This study showed that species diversity affects productivity and nutrient cycling.

In another recent study, Donald Zak and Kurt Pregitzer present data from preliminary studies and a protocol for future research that seeks to show how an ecosystem's Carbon Cycle is influenced by variation in the physiological ecology of individual trees. Traditional ecosystem ecology would have ignored the physiology of individual trees and focused on the total amount of carbon that enters and leaves the ecosystem. However, by combining the two levels of studies, Zak and Pregitzer found that variation in the life-history among plant populations results in differences in how carbon is allocated in plant. This variation proves to be a major factor in controlling the carbon cycle in some terrestrial ecosystems. Zak and Pregitzer suggest that this of study can be used in different types of ecosystems (e.g., aquatic) and for animal populations as well.[53]

Finally, in a recent review, Polis, Anderson, and Holt detail how movements of nutrients, prey, and predators, among ecosystems are some of the controlling factors of ecosystem function. In turn, this movement of population and community level factors (e.g., prey) is to a large degree controlled by landscape level variables such as the perimeter/area ratio of habitats and ecosystems and the degree of "permeability" of ecosystem boundaries (variation in permeability can result from geological factors such as mountain ranges or rivers which either facilitate or impede the movement and establishment of populations).[54]

These three examples are just some of the many examples of ways that modern ecologists are breaking away from the traditional bounds of academic and conceptual divisions. The figure below shows some of connections between the various ecological levels and processes. Where once the main object of ecology was an understanding of one process, today it is the connections between processes that is the focus of some of the most exciting progress in ecology.

Figure 1.1 SOME OF THE IMPORTANT LINKAGES BETWEEN THE SUBDISCIPLINES OF ECOLOGY[55]

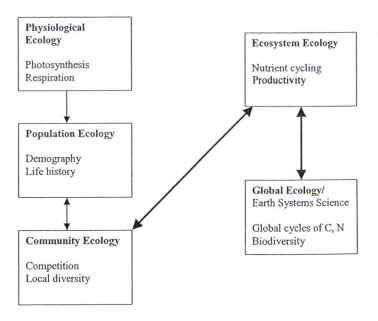

The bold arrows represent the interactions of most interest to environmental law; i.e., the relationships between community ecology and ecosystem ecology, and the linkages between ecosystem ecology and global ecology. *Source*: Brooks, Jones and Virginia

The Practice of Ecology

Modern ecology is a mathematical science. This is true whether the focus is a population, ecosystem, or the integration among levels and processes. The use of mathematics and statistics, coupled with the use of the hypo-deductive scientific method is what distinguishes ecology from natural history. Ecologists today do not simply observe, they collect data that is used to test hypotheses about how nature works. As a consequence, advances in computer capability and new mathematical techniques are being applied to all areas of ecology. These applications have led to recent advances in systems ecology and simulation modeling, which in turn have resulted in the growing awareness that most ecological systems are dynamic non-equilibrium systems.[56] There have also been tremendous advances in data collection techniques.[57] For example, ecologists use radioisotopes to follow the path of nutrients into, through, and out of an ecosystem. Molecular genetic techniques (DNA technology) are used in behavioral and physiological ecology to identify specific individuals within a family or population. At the landscape and global levels, satellite remote sensing and imaging techniques are being using to study the spatial patterns at the landscape and biosphere levels and to follow large-scale patterns of productivity. Another important advancement in modern ecology is the increased use of long-term studies of populations, ecosystems, landscapes, and the interaction between them.[58] Given that many ecological processes occur over years and decades, these long-term research programs attempt to provide a more accurate picture of ecosystem function than can be achieved through short-term (one to two year research) research on populations and communities.

Below are two examples of how these modern approaches to ecology are being used in research that is both of fundamental interest and applicable to current environmental problems. We pick these particular examples for two reasons. First, they are related to ongoing environmental problems covered by environmental law and, therefore amenable to treatment by an ecosystemic regime. Second, they involve problems that span multiple ecological levels and processes and are being studied through the use of an integrated ecology. They are also examples of ecological work that is already interacting with environmental law and policy in the management of specific environmental problems. Most importantly, they are examples of two broad categories of environmental problems among which we believe the interaction between law and ecology differs: (1) the preservation or restoration of natural resources and ecosystem services such as clean air and water; and (2) the protection of single endangered or threatened populations or the complete biodiversity of an ecosystem.

(1) Preservation and restoration of ecosystems: Mono Lake and Hubbard Brook. We began this chapter with a brief review of how the environmental restoration of Mono Lake was carried out, after decades of failed management, through the application of ecosystem ecology. The proper management of Mono Lake required the awareness that several different ecological levels and processes interacted with each other in ways whereby the alteration of one level or process affected other levels and processes. In Mono Lake, the central problem was the alteration of the community-level food chain that resulted both in harm to the component populations of the food chain (e.g., the gulls and shrimp) and in the interference with the ecosystem-level energy flow and nutrient cycles. The harm to populations and the ecosystem would then cause even more rapid destruction of the food web.

Mono Lake is a good example of a well defined environmental problem, the lake was originally mismanaged, and then restored as a result of the incorporation of ecosystem and community ecology into the management regime. The effects of acid rain on the northern forests is dissimilar in that the effects are not limited to a single well defined ecosystem (e.g., a single lake in California), but are seen throughout much of eastern North America. However, like Mono Lake, the full understanding of the problem, as well as the restoration of specifically damaged habitats and ecosystems requires proper attention to the ecological levels and processes that are affected.

The Hubbard Brook ecosystem project began in 1963 in the White Mountains of New Hampshire and is arguably the most recognized ecosystem study.[59] The research was originally designed to investigate forest recovery after harvest with an emphasis on understanding the processes of production and nutrient cycling and biotic controls on nutrient loss. However, one of the unexpected results of the Hubbard Brook study was the first North American report of acid rain. The identification of the presence and effects of acid rain was a result of one of the first major ecosystem ecology "experiments," in which energy flow and nutrient cycling in a patch of northern forest was studied. Once patterns of forest growth and nutrient cycling were quantified, all the trees from an entire watershed were removed (clear-cut) and regrowth was inhibited by herbicides. Clear-cutting the forest and preventing the reestablishment of plants had a large effect on ecosystem functioning. The amount of water leaving the watershed in streams increased because water use by plants had been nearly eliminated by the forest harvest. The previously "closed" or conservative nutrient cycle of the forest became "open" and nutrients were lost from the ecosystem in large amounts. Once the Hubbard Brook watershed was allowed to recover (regrow), nutrient losses to streams decline to near baseline levels. The Hubbard Brook ecosystem experiment has influenced the development of ecosystem science and also informed forest management practices. This research shows the consequences of breaking the linkages between plant and soil processes. In this case, an unsustainable rate of nutrient loss from the forest was the result. The Hubbard Brook study is not a clear example of environmental restoration, unlike the Mono Lake example. However, it might well be a more important example in other ways. Since most environmental problems are not isolated within a relatively small area and by relatively well defined boundaries (as with Mono Lake), but are more extensive and require the results of ecosystem level (and higher) studies to be applied over an entire region. Hubbard Brook has played a major role in the restoration of more sustainable nutrient cycles in forests by the regulation of anthropogenic inputs of nitrogen and other pollutants, accomplished through more informed environmental laws.

Other examples of how ecology is being used to preserve or restore ecosystems (which we will discuss in later chapters) are the Chesapeake Bay, the Florida Everglades, and the North Carolina coastal zone. All three are examples of large-scale collections of interacting ecosystems (i.e., landscapes) in which previous management strategies failed to include the full range of applicable ecological concepts and methods.

(2) Protection of biodiversity: the Salmon and Northern Spotted Owl of the Pacific Northwest. When the environmental issue is the protection of *biodiversity*, the ecology that is used depends upon what biodiversity we mean. Biodiversity can, among other things, refer to the number of different genes in a population, the number of individuals in a single population of a species listed as endangered or threatened by the Endangered Species Act or the number of species and habitats in some defined area (e.g., National Park or National Forest). When the problems is the protection of individual populations then individual, population, and community level ecological processes become the dominant factors in creating a proper management scheme.

One of the most important recent questions concerning how to integrate individual and population level ecology concerns how to define *species* and *populations* under the Endangered Species Act (ESA). For both Atlantic and Pacific Salmon the question is: what group of salmon can be defined as a "Distinct Population Segment," which is the smallest "part" of a species that can separately listed as endangered or threatened under the ESA. This question has led to the direct incorporation of population and ecological genetics into debates over the proper application of the ESA.[60]

Population genetics is concerned with measuring the level of genetic variation within and among populations and explaining the causes and effects of this variation.[61] For two populations to be different species or distinct population segments requires that they be separated by some amount of genetic variation. Therefore, assessing the genetic variation within and among species and populations has become important to environmental law and to endangered species management. The recent concept of Evolutionary Significant Units (ESUs) was created by ecologists at the U.S. Marine Fishery Service as a way to incorporate population genetics into the question of what specific salmon populations are entitled to protection under the ESA.[62] ESUs are related to the "Distinct Population Segments" identified as the smallest species division that can be listed as threatened or endangered under the Endangered Species Act.[63] Given the current fragmented distribution of most species, these "sub-species" levels of organization are becoming the focus of conservation plans for protecting species or regional biodiversity.[64]

While individual and population level genetics has been critical to the management of Pacific and Atlantic salmon, behavioral and population ecology has been the most important levels of ecology in relation to the protection of the Northern Spotted Owl. In the late 1980s ecologist Russell Lande published an article which showed how the then current U.S. Forest Service's management plan for Spotted Owls did not properly account for two critical elements of behavioral ecology, mating behavior and foraging for food and habitat. Nor did it account for the basic population demographics of the population. This and subsequent ecological studies became the foundation for the litigation strategy in a series of cases during the late 1980s and early 1990s by environmental groups against the Forest Service. The management of the Northern Spotted Owl also demonstrates how individual through community levels of ecology can be integrated in the management of specific populations; analogous to the way Hubbard Brook integrates ecosystem and higher levels of ecology.

Applied Ecology[65]

To this point our focus has been on providing an introduction to the concepts and methods of basic ecology and how these concepts and methods are being used to address environmental problems. In the Hubbard Brook and Salmon examples above, the relevant concepts and methods were taken directly from the academic side of ecology. However, as the remainder of our book will make clear, when ecology becomes part of the management strategy for a particular environmental problem it usually does so through an applied ecological discipline and not through the more academic form of ecology. All applied ecology disciplines are originally derived from or have recently merged with one or more of the basic ecological disciplines, but are now evolving independently and have their own practitioners, journals, and professional societies.

Most generally, applied ecology can be divided into two broad categories based upon both the objects that are being managed and the ethical basis for the management decision. First are those disciplines concerned with the restoration or preservation of ecosystems and the ecosystem functions considered most important to humans (i.e., ecosystem services). Usually, the object of management for these types of applied ecology are ecosystems (e.g., the Florida Everglades), but when populations take on economic importance, as with the commercial fishery, then the fish populations and their ecosystems become objects of preservation or restoration. The ethical motivation for the preservation of ecosystems and ecosystem services has traditionally been a utilitarian one, in which the economic, social, or cultural use of the ecosystem to humans is the reason for its protection.

Ecosystem functioning is a consequence of organisms and their life processes (production, consumption, and excretion) and the effects that these activities have on the environment. These functions are considered to be ecosystem services when they have economic or aesthetic value. Ecosystem services include the cycling and purification of water; the production of food, fuel and fiber; and the provision of organisms that provide products such as drugs and serve as biological control agents.[66] More and more, environmental issues are being cast in the vernacular of the ecosystem scientist.[67]

Table 1.3 EXAMPLES OF PROCESSES AND ECOSYSTEMS AND THEIR SOCIETAL RELEVANCE

PROCESSES	ECOSYSTEM FUNCTION	SOCIETAL INTERESTS
Photosynthesis Plant nutrient uptake	Primary production	Agriculture, forestry
Microbial respiration Soil food web dynamics	Decomposition	Carbon dioxide flux and climate
Decomposition Nitrogen fixation	Nitrogen cycling	Soil fertility, Nutrient retention
Plant transpiration Root activity	Hydrologic cycle	Water supply & quality
Mineral weathering Vegetation succession	Soil formation	Agriculture, forestry

Source: Ross A. Virginia & Diana H. Wall, Ecosystem function, principles of, in *Encyclopedia of Biodiversity* 345 (S.A. Levin, ed., 2001)

Within this first category of applied ecology are such fields as Restoration Ecology, Ecotoxicology, and Natural Resource Management (e.g., Silviculture and Fishery Management), all of which we will be returning to throughout this book.[68] Restoration Ecology has become an important recent area of ecological research by taking on the challenge of applying ecological principles to restoring (repairing) damaged ecological systems to their former or in some cases "original" state. Research on practices to repair damaged systems is providing basic insights on ecosystem functioning.[69] Increasingly, economic development of coastal and urban lands may proceed only if a mitigation plan provides for the set aside or restoration of land in another location.

Whether the goal is to restore a damaged ecosystem or manage a market fish species, these forms of applied ecology are concerned with pro-tecting services which are seen as being important to human survival or, more often, economics; a primary concern of the most current paradigm of environ-mental management; i.e., ecosystem management. The premise of ecosystem management is that the utilization of lands for sustained levels of ecosystem services[70] and natural resources requires an understanding of how ecosystems function, how they respond to disturbance, and the role of biodiversity in regulating their function and stability.[71]

The second broad category of applied ecology, conservation biology, focuses on the protection of biodiversity usually, as with the Spotted Owl, at the level of the single endangered or threatened species. However, one result of the integration of ecology has been the growing concern over the protection of other levels of biodiversity, including genetic diversity and ecosystem diversity (see above). Whichever level of biodiversity is being protected, the motivation for the protection, at least among conservation biologists, is the assumption that *biodiversity has inherent value*, beyond its value to humans. This is not to deny that biodiversity can have a utilitarian value, such as sources for food and medicine or as important components of ecosystem functions (e.g., replenishment of oxygen by green plants or control of prey populations by predators). However, for most conservation biologists, ecologists, and environmentalists, the ethical foundation for biodiversity protection is the biocentric view that the various levels of biodiversity possess value independent of their human use. In Chapters 7 and 9 we discuss the foundations of conservation biology, and in Chapter 10, the international approach to species protection. For the present purposes it is sufficient that many, if not most, conservation biologists would argue that protecting and preserving biodiversity does not require a showing that the particular population(s) in question have an instrumental or anthropocentric value.[72]

Conservation biology is guided by three basic principles: evolutionary change, the non-equilibrium nature of ecological systems, and that humans are part of the ecosystem and must be factored into conservation planning.[73] This third principle means that human actions, past, present, and future, must be considered in any management strategy designed to protect biodiversity. It is the third principle that is currently most discussed in relation to the interaction of ecology and environmental law. However, the realization that evolutionary change is a paradigm for all biological systems and the acceptance that ecological systems (e.g., populations, ecosystems and the entire earth) are dynamic are the core concepts in modern ecology.

Ecology and the Balance of Nature

Most, if not all, early ecologists shared a common view that the "preferred" state of an ecological system was equilibrium and that if an ecological system was left unaffected by human actions it would return to its "natural" state. It is this view of nature that is historically referred to as "Balance of Nature." For the person interested in preserving or restoring a national forest or a river system, this meant that if the source of human-made interference (logging or a polluting factory) was removed the system would also return to a natural state ("the balance of nature"). The success of environmental laws could then presumably be measured by the stability of the population or ecosystem being managed. In the next chapter we will discuss the historical foundation for this early belief in ecological stability.

However, even before the 1960s, many ecologists believed that some ecological systems were naturally dynamic and ever changing (i.e., in disequilibrium). This view has recently been generalized by some ecologists to a belief that most ecological systems are in a state of disequilibrium; even if it is at a time scale unobservable by the individual researchers. The changes that have taken place within the science of ecology have not gone unnoticed among the non-ecological environmental scholar and policy maker. Much of the recent legal scholarship that discusses ecology concerns what Daniel Botkin originally termed the "New Ecology."[74]

With the 1986 publication of Daniel Botkin's book, *Discordant Harmonies*, the layperson and legal scholar became aware of what many ecologists have been saying for decades; most, if not all populations and ecosystems, are in a state of constant change, with no single equilibrium point. Both the integration across ecological disciplines and the disequilibrium of nature are important to understanding ecology's future role in environmental law. The question that must be asked for all present and future environmental law is; if ecological stability is an illusion, how do we measure the success of our laws? Legal scholars have begun to study the implications of non-equilibrium systems and how they affect the adequacy of current environmental laws.[75]

The Theory of Regimes

The story of Mono Lake is the story of a group of cooperating (and conflicting) persons, associations and public institutions including the Mono Lake

Committee, Los Angeles Department of Water and Power, California Water Resources Control Board, Sierra Club, California Department of Water Resources and Fish and Game, Caltrans, U.S. Forest Service and Fish and Wildlife Services, National Academy of Science and federal and state courts. Although these groups frequently conflicted in court, they also joined together in cooperation, sometimes sealed by written agreements. Although not as well structured as many organizations and institutions held responsible for the management of an ecosystem, this cluster of organizations is usefully viewed as a single entity – an ecosystem regime and environmental law is usefully examined as part of that regime.[76]

The regimes may be aimed at the protection of a species or the conservation of a resource or may be explicitly organized along ecosystemic lines – lakes, rivers, watersheds, forests, coastal areas, wetlands, and so forth. As we shall see in Chapters 7, 9 and 10, ecosystem regimes may emerge within newly created regimes such as the Adirondacks Park Act, the ecological retrofit of laws such as the Endangered Species Act, or as more global regimes such as the international ozone depletion agreement (Montreal Protocol).

Since the late 1980s, scholars have recommended and federal and state agencies have rushed to adopt one or another ecosystem approach within environmental law. In response to the powerful notions of biodiversity, federal and international agencies have undertaken efforts to protect biodiversity both within existing domestic laws as well as internationally. These efforts have been followed by more recent legislation and proposals for legislation for biodiversity protection, and as we discussed above, ecosystem management. Animated in part by a powerful sense of place,[77] the federal government, the states and localities have undertaken regional ecosystem approaches in areas such as the Chesapeake Bay, the Pine Barrens, and Yellowstone Park. New areas are proposed for ecological management almost daily. Federal and state administrators of existing laws, such as the Endangered Species Act or the National Forest Management Act have undertaken the protection of bio-diversity as part of ecosystem planning and management. The federal government has sought to identify ecosystems throughout the nation, document the laws protecting those systems, and recommend new approaches to eco-system management. In a similar move, state governments have adopted ecosystemic laws and reorganized their agencies along ecosystem principles. Perhaps the most powerful stimulus towards adopting an ecosystemic approach to environmental law is the recognition of global environmental problems, such as ozone depletion and global warming. The seriousness of these problems promotes massive efforts to understand them. The understanding of these problems requires a comprehension of the interdependent nature of these global regimes.[78]

The theory of regimes envisages governance processes as applicable to a common resource or ecosystem.[79] Although the system in question may be composed of public, private and commons resources, it is regarded as a commons regime.[80] Viewing the ecosystem as commons permits the examination of its natural processes from the point of view of natural systems, facilitates the examination of the governance processes in a systematic way, and allows for the consideration of governance from the point of view of certain common values.

Oran Young, in his initial study of such regimes identified a series of common criteria by which such regimes may be evaluated in their effort to manage resources including: allocative efficiency, non-economic values, equity, transaction costs and feasibility. Environmental laws which are instruments of a regime's management might be evaluated along these and other criteria. In later work, Young has suggested mechanisms which might contribute the functioning of such a regime:[81]

Table 1.4   DESIGN PRINCIPLES ILLUSTRATED BY LONG-ENDURING COMMON-POOL RESOURCE (CPR) INSTITUTIONS

1. Clearly defined boundaries. Individuals or households who have rights to withdraw resource units from the CPR must be clearly defined, as must the boundaries of the CPR itself.

2. Congruence between appropriation and provision rules and local conditions. Appropriation rules restricting time, place, technology, and/or quantity of resource units are related to local conditions and to provision rules requiring labor, material, and/or money.

3. Collective-choice arrangements. Most individuals affected by the operational rules can participate in modifying operational rules.

4. Monitoring. Monitors, who actively audit CPR conditions and appropriate behavior, are accountable to the appropriators or are the appropriators.

5. Graduated sanctions. Appropriators who violate operational rules are likely to be assessed graduated sanctions (depending on the seriousness and context of the offense) by other appropriators, by officials accountable to these appropriators, or by both.

6. Conflict-resolution mechanisms. Appropriators and their officials have rapid access to low-cost local arenas to resolve conflicts among appropriators or between appropriators and officials.

7. Minimal recognition of rights to organize. The rights of appropriators to devise their own institutions are not challenged by external government authorities.

Source: Oran Young, et al., *Institutional Dimensions of Global Environmental Change* (1999)

The Pluralism of U.S. Environmental Law[82]

Environmental law is that body of law aimed at the protection and enhancement of the environment and the sustainable development of natural resources. The present environmental law of the United States is a com-pendium of federal and state statutes and local ordinances authorizing a myriad of federal, state, and local regulations.[83] This domestic law fits, somewhat uneasily, within treaties and protocols governing the more global environment. Like the Constitution, these statutes and regulations overlay a common law of property which establishes a system of private and public property, a law of contracts which governs transactions, and a tort law which provides remedies for intentional and unintentional harms. The complexity of environmental law is thus due to the unique nature of our nation's legal history of federalism and common law.[84] The slow accretion of environmental laws has been further complicated by two centuries of federal and state court decisions which not only establish the common law and interpret the constitution and statutes, but also extend this common law, constitution, and statutes in new directions.

Both environmental law and ecology have their own histories, but each is intertwined with the other. Our hypothesis is that at least after 1970, each field has episodically co-evolved.[85] In coevolution, evolution of one species or ecosystem over time produces an accompanying evolution in a related species or ecosystem and vice versa. Thus, ecology and its applications has influenced law and law has shaped the nature and application of some parts of ecology. At various times in their separate histories, the demands for the practical resolution of environmental problems, e.g., coastal pollution, have stimulated ecological research, e.g., estuarine science. Conversely, discoveries of ecology, e.g., conservation biology, have helped to shape parts of selected environmental laws. The history set forth in Chapters 2 through 10 of this book will focus upon selected episodes of interaction between law and ecology; first we briefly offer a thumbnail sketch of the broader history of environmental law in order to gain an initial understanding of this field.

The Stages of History of Environmental Law

The history of environmental law is part of a larger history of emerging environmental consciousness, prodded by the environmental movement of the 1970s. Key stages of the environmental movement mark our memories. Key events – environmental disasters, important court cases, and legislation – are associated with these stages, and historians weave them into a collective public narrative. Professional historians and legal scholars refine them further.[86] Consequently, there have been numerous histories of environmental law and policy written in the past twenty years. The following table outlines these stages:

Table 1.5 THE HISTORY OF THE STAGES OF U.S. ENVIRONMENTAL LAW[87]

I.	The Common Law of Response to Industrialism and Urbanization	1850–1970
II.	The Establishment of the Constitutional and Administrative Law Foundations for Modern Administrative Law	1900–1950
III.	The Emerging Outlines of the Modern Environmental Law Regime	1960–1970
IV.	The Parallel (but Unrelated) Development of Population Policy	1965–1976
V.	Earth Day: The Fork in the Road Between Media-Based Regulations and Ecology-Oriented Solutions; the Failure of Constitutional Reform and the Recognition of the Public Trust	1970 1970–1972
VI.	The Eruption of the Energy Crisis	1973–1980
VII.	The Greening of Natural Resources Law	1974–1977
VIII.	The Rediscovery of Waste and Hazardous Pollutants	1974–present
IX.	"The Season of Spoils" (The Reagan era)	1980–1988
X.	The Globalization of Environmental Law	1980–present
XI.	The Rediscovery of Ecology and the Fruition of Environmental Management and Conservation Biology	1990–2000
XII.	The Ecosystemic Environmental Law Regime	The future?

Source: Brooks' modification of William Futrell's "History of Environmental Law" in Campbell-Mohn, et al., *Environmental Law From Resources to Recovery* (1993)

In the first stage, United States law was responding to the large scale economic development of the country in which nature was regarded merely as a resource to be developed. This nineteenth century created a "development momentum" extending well into the twentieth century and resulting in the environmental abuses which our recent environmental law regime seeks to rectify.[88] Most of the environmentally related laws of this period were statutes facilitating the exploitation of nature. The common law era of environmental law which accompanied this exploration treated environmental disputes as if they were two-party private lawsuits. The courts struggled to provide remedies for persons harmed by environmental abuses. The nineteenth-century common law failed to protect the environment; hence, in the present environmental law regime, the common law has been largely replaced by statutes.[89] The first part of the twentieth century witnessed the establishment of the constitutional basis and structure of the administrative law regime, which both supported and constrained the fashioning of an ecologically-based federal environmental law. Pollutants and valuable ecosystems (lakes, rivers, airsheds) extended beyond state boundaries requiring a constitutional foundation for federal regulation rather than state-only action. At the same time, since the functioning of ecosystems does not respect the boundaries of constitutionally established private property rights, a new constitutional regime permitting the environmental regulation of private property rights was required. This administrative law system was more flexible than the courts, and permitted a more policy-oriented use of science. Nevertheless, at the time of its adoption in the early twentieth century, administrative law contained a series of provisions making the administrative recognition of persons harmed by the destruction of ecosystems difficult.[90] Environmental plaintiffs sought to gain access to the courts by asserting "legal standing" under appropriate environmental laws and their administrative counterparts.[91] The struggle for standing continues to this very day.[92]

In the third stage of U.S. environmental law, an increased awareness of ecosystems – or at least interconnected nature – took place. During the 1960s, in landmark legal decisions involving oil spills and DDT, the first effort was made to design specific laws or fashion legal doctrines to accommodate a growing national environmental awareness of ecosystems. At the end of the 1960s, the fourth "quiet stage" in the development of a comprehensive environmental law regime was the provision for federal aid for population research and control both nationally and internationally. The first public funding for population control was available in the mid 1960s and major legislation was then adopted in 1970 and 1976. However, despite the predictions of Paul and Anne Ehrlich of a "population bomb," the "environmentalization" of population policy did not begin until the 1990s, when environmental groups began to focus upon the need for population controls. Stage five, "Earth Day 1970," is often identified as the dawn of the modern age of environmentalism. It was also the origin of a basic split in the approaches to environmental law. One set of the laws – the "media laws" – the Clean Air Act and the Federal Water Pollution Act of 1972 – largely ignored the ecological vision and sought specific enforceable technology-based regulations. The other part of Earth Day's environmental law – the National Environmental Policy Act (impact-based) the Coastal Zone Management Act (place-based), and the Endangered Species Act (species-based) – adopted more ecologically sensitive approaches. *This dichotomy between technology-based enforcement laws and ecology-based regulation was to haunt environmental law history for the next thirty years.*

During the same period, other important legal developments were taking place. The federal courts refused to uphold claims for recognition of a federal constitutional right to a healthful environment. On the other hand, the successful recovery of the public trust doctrine from the mists of Roman and early English history created a new legal tool in the effort to protect ecosystems. More recent state efforts to establish constitutional environmental rights and development of the public trust doctrine open up the possibility of incorporating an ecological approach to environmental protection based upon broad constitutional and public trust legal doctrines.

In the sixth stage, the world energy crisis of 1974 struck the United States and Western Europe. It was both a distraction and an opportunity for the environmental movement. On the one hand, the need to secure a new fossil fuel supply tempted the nation to push aside environmental constraints upon energy production. On the other hand, the proposed limitations opened up the use of renewable energy. The "soft path energy option" called attention to the environmental consequences of energy generation, and provoked a deeper inquiry into the relationship between ecology and energy.[93] In the mid 1970s, the split between technology-based enforcement of environmental law and ecology-oriented environmental law was continuing.

The seventh stage – the "Greening of Natural Resources Law" – witnessed a host of ecologically-oriented changes in laws governing the use of our nation's public lands, the protection of endangered species, and the management of national forests. Despite this ecological turn, at about the same time, toxic substances and solid waste were "rediscovered" and in the urge to regulate them, a national emphasis was placed upon technological solutions to their storage and cleanup (the eighth stage).

The ninth stage of the 1980s was the "Season of Spoils,"[94] a period of counterattack upon environmental regulations from the 1970s by the Reagan administration. However, this period also stimulated the rethinking of the environmental law regime – a rethinking which was to lead to new initiatives in the 1990s. In the tenth stage, during the 1980s and 1990s, a globalization of environmental law has taken place. In the eleventh stage, during the 1990s, we have witnessed efforts to return to an ecological paradigm for the guidance of environmental law and policy and the creative use of economic tools to create a public economy for environmental protection. Finally we project a new phase, the subject of this book, the creation of a comprehensive ecosystemic environmental law regime.[95]

The Kinds of Environmental Laws

Environmental laws may be organized in accordance with different principles, including medium (air, land, water), place of pollution (e.g., workplace laws), remedy oriented (e.g., restoration laws), pollutant defined (e.g., toxic legislation), ecosystem oriented (e.g., coastal management laws), threatened organism laws (e.g., endangered species laws), decision-informing laws (e.g.,

National Environmental Policy Act), cause of environmental problem laws (e.g., population control laws), districting laws (i.e zoning laws which geographically allocate activities recycling (e.g., state solid waste laws).[96] The following are brief summaries of selected examples of the major laws:

A Medium Oriented Law:
THE FEDERAL WATER POLLUTION CONTROL ACT

This act pledges to restore and maintain the chemical, physical and biological integrity of the nation's waters. To do so, the law provides for grants for public waste treatment facilities. The federal government (through EPA) develops water quality criteria on the effects of water pollutants and guidelines for states to develop their effluent limitation guidelines. EPA promulgates water quality standards and effluent limitation for point sources. EPA also publishes effluent limitations for a selected set of new sources of industries. Public treatment facilities must be constructed consistent with federal standards for such facilities. States must develop implementation plans approved by EPA, and which contain state water quality standards and state effluent limitations. These water quality standards and effluent limitations are set to assure the protection of public health, public water supplies, agricultural and industrial uses, and the protection and propagation of a balanced population of shellfish, fish and wildlife, and allow recreational activities in and on the water. A cost benefit balance may be used in establishing these limitations. Special standards, however, are established for toxic and a separate program is established for non-point sources, runoffs, such as agricultural runoffs. A national discharge permit system is established for each pollution source, and is customarily administered by the state. Permits are also required by dredge and fill operations and for ocean dumping.

A Law Focused Upon Causes of Environmental Problems:
POPULATION LAW

Family planning policy and legislation is ordinarily not considered to be part of the corpus of environmental law. The family planning regime of the United States is a complex mixture of constitutional freedoms (contraception and abortion), constraints upon involuntary sterilization and federal health and welfare funding for family planning services and information. Common law tort actions (for allegedly defective birth control devices) and regulation by the Food and Drug Administration affects the domestic availability of some contraceptive and abortifacient pills. In addition to U.S. federal laws for family planning abroad, there are a variety of international human rights and population conference reports supporting family planning throughout the world.

A Spatial Allocation Law:
STATE AND LOCAL LAND USE LAWS

State and Local Land Use laws enable planning and zoning agencies at the state and local levels to district the lands and allocate uses to different districts, such as residential, conservation, manufacturing. The underlying theory is that the spatial allocation process can limit or neutralize undesirable environmental impacts. Some states, such as Hawaii, Florida and Oregon, have identified districts on a statewide level and have adopted different regulations to apply to the different districts. Customarily, state laws enable localities to adopt comprehensive plans and land use control ordinances which allocate land uses on a district by district basis.

Place of Pollution:
THE OCCUPATIONAL SAFETY AND HEALTH ACT

The Occupational Safety and Health Act is a comprehensive attempt to protect the safety and health of workers in the workplace. The Act covers all companies employing one or more workers, but not self-employed persons, nor family-owned and operated farms. A general duty clause states that each employer shall furnish to each of his employees employment and a place of employment which are free from recognized hazards that are causing or are liable to cause death or serious physical harm to his employees. The Occupational Health and Safety Administration has adopted standards and enforced them, although recent relaxations during the 1980s became controversial.

Recycling and Material Balance:
STATE RECYCLING LAWS AND THE RESOURCES, CONSERVATION AND RECOVERY ACT

In 1976, Congress passed the Resource Conservation and Recovery Act (RCRA) to completely replace the Resource Recovery Act. The new law continued provisions on solid waste and resource recovery, closing most open dumps. It redefined solid waste to include hazardous waste, and ordered EPA to track and control hazardous waste. The Act required the setting of standards for treatment, storage, and disposal facilities for hazardous waste. The regulation and cleanup of hazardous waste has become one of the EPA's most important priorities. In 1978, the hazardous waste site at Love Canal in Niagara Falls, New York, heightened the controversy over the thousands of other abandoned dump sites, alarming the public and mobilizing the Carter Administration and Congress.

Decision Informing:
NATIONAL ENVIRONMENTAL POLICY ACT

This law has spawned twenty years of law suits by environmentalists seeking to delay or stop projects they believed harmful to the environment. Most federal agencies have incorporated the law's procedural requirements into their own regulations. The law requires Federal departments and agencies to prepare an environmental impact assessment of their actions and if these actions have a significant impact upon the environment, a detailed environmental impact statement must be prepared. This statement must be considered before the federal government takes action. The Council on Environmental Quality prepares the regulations for agencies having to adopt such statements and receives copies of the statements. The purpose of this law is to encourage federal agencies to consider environmental values and resources in their every day decision making. Another information based law was the Technology Assessment Act, which establishes a Congressional Office of Technology Assessment under a Congressional board for the purpose of assessing the impacts of new technology. The O.T.A. identifies the impacts of technology and alternative technologies, assesses the costs and benefits of these technologies and presents findings to Congress. O.T.A. has completed numerous assessments of all forms of new technology, including evaluations of their environmental impacts. Unfortunately, Congress has recently chosen to de-fund this valuable law.

Ecosystem Oriented:
THE COASTAL ZONE MANAGEMENT ACT

Most of the coastal states have adopted coastal management programs which contain an array of regulations and permitting programs for coastal uses. A unique feature of the law is a "reverse consistency" requirement by which federal actions must conform to state coastal management plans. The Coastal Zone Management Act's policy is to encourage states to preserve, protect, develop and restore or enhance the resources of the nation's coastal zone.

The coastal zone is described as the coastal waters and the adjacent shoreland strongly influenced by each other and in proximity to the shorelines of the coastal states, extending to the Great Lakes. Coastal states must develop programs which will meet certain very broad federal requirements administered by the National Oceanographic and Atmospheric Administration. These state programs are made up of state laws and regulations which guide activities on the coast. Major federal projects, activities and permits on the coast must be consistent with these state programs. The Act provides grants to the states to prepare and administer these plans as well as grants to states enduring energy development impact from offshore oil.

These laws illustrate different approaches of environmental law; as a consequence, they overlap extensively. For instance, dumping in the water may violate the Clean Water Act but also the Coastal Management Act (since the dumping occurs within a coastal ecosystem), and the Toxic Substance Control Act (since the dumping may involve a toxic substance); in addition, the dumping may threaten endangered species and may also require an environmental impact statement under federal or state laws. Whereas many environmentalists may believe a multiplicity of regulations is good, an industry subject to such regulations has a very different view, because of the cost and difficulty of complying with multiple regulations. Indeed, some have suggested the need for an impact statement measuring the cumulative impacts of all the regulations. But it is important for environmentalists and citizens to see individual laws in the context of other overlapping laws applying to industrial measures and protecting different aspects of the environment.

The Search for Unity in Environmental Law

This variety of kinds of environment laws reveals the fundamental pluralism in the principles of environmental law. Such a list of kinds of laws suggests several fundamental questions: which approach to environmental protection makes most sense or are they all appropriate in different contexts? Are they compatible with the ecosystem management approach or the application of conservation biology outlined above? Are they compatible, one with another? Our history of the relations between ecology and environmental law in Chapters 2 through 10 will highlight these issues. Given the myriad of environmental laws, all enacted at different times and for different purposes, courts, legislators and legal scholars have had difficulty achieving any integrated coherent statement of this relatively new legal field. Environmental legal texts and treatises, with few exceptions, such as Celia Campbell-Mohn, et al's *Environmental Law: From Resources to Recovery*, are collations of laws and court opinions, revealing the disorganized state of the law.

Four recent legal approaches have been taken seeking to comprehend in a coherent manner the entire environmental law field: (1) the traditional reliance upon substantive or process legal principles;[97] (2) the viewing of environmental law through the eyes of advocacy on behalf of one or another group or as part of nature affected by environmental laws;[98] (3) a "dominant formal paradigm" of environmental law;[99] (4) the viewing of environmental law as part of a larger natural and social system. (It is this fourth view which animates our approach to environmental law in this book.)

The ecosystem view advanced in this book contrasts with the dominant paradigm that has emerged in cross cultural studies of environment laws. This paradigm seeks to describe the general form of environmental law, whether in Japan, Europe or the United States. U.S. laws such as the Clean Air Act or Clean Water Act exemplify this paradigm. This paradigm is typically based upon the instrumental regulation of specific media or public resources, primarily for health protection or efficient natural resources use. The following is a listing of the components of the paradigm.

Table 1.6 TRADITIONAL PARADIGM OF ENVIRONMENTAL LAW

1. Statement of Findings and Purposes	5. Impact Assessment of Specific Projects
2. Substantive Criteria for Protection	6. Permitting and Enforcement
3. Standards	7. Citizen Participation in process
4. Instruments of Implementation	8. Judicial Review

Source: R.O. Brooks adaptation from Gerd Winter, ed., *European Environmental Law* (1996)

By contrast, our approach to environmental law begins with a larger natural or social system and views law as part of that system, in effect, regulating the interactions within that system. This approach relies upon recent strides made in the study of natural and social systems.[100] Insofar as we seek to explore the historical relationship between ecology and law within a broader context of public culture and social regimes, we are relying upon this fourth approach to environmental law.[101]

The Ecological Dimension of Environmental Law

Within an ecosystem regime, environmental laws and regulations seek to control human interrelations with the ecosystem. Let us illustrate this truth by exploring the relationship between ecology, its study of an ecosystem, and its legal protection through an ecosystemic regime. The following is a systems chart for carbon flows in a salt marsh:

Figure 1.2 SIMULATION MODEL OF A SALT MARSH

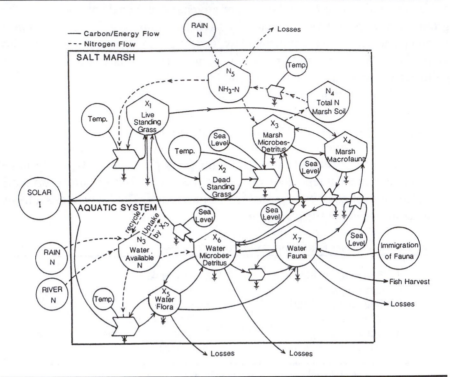

Source: Simulation model of salt marsh for Louisiana, "A Model of the
Barataria Bay Salt Marsh Ecosystem" in *Ecosystem Modeling: In Theory
and Practice*, C.A.J. Hall and J.W. Day, Jr. (1977) p. 248

Ecologists have studied this ecosystem, which through its interaction of
flora and fauna, supplies fish, which is a human food. Environmental law may
control fish supply through statutes regulating the production and harvesting of
fish. Other laws or regulations may control dredge and spill activities or
building activities, pollution activities, or the flow of water – all of which
directly affect water flow or marsh flora and fauna and hence, indirectly, affect
fish. Thus, regulations with apparently different subject matters, e.g., fish
harvesting, dredge and fill, wetland laws, may be viewed as intervening at
different points in the marsh ecosystem to affect the viability of the community
of fish.

Effective regulation of interventions in such an ecosystem is difficult
because of the multiple interactions within the ecosystem. For example,
dredging and dredge dumping may have a synergistic effect since it may affect
several direct and indirect food sources for the fish. Moreover, since we are
dealing with sets of organisms, there may be cumulative effects of actions, in
which the ecosystem stores the consequences of some action, which is then

added to another action at a later time. There may be threshold effects in which a part of the ecosystem is initially not affected by any activity at all, until a certain level of impact is reached and then severe effects may take place. Moreover, because of the web-like nature of the ecosystem, predicting what might happen as a result of any one intervention may be difficult.

There are three ways of viewing the present state of environmental law in relationship to ecology and its ecosystems. First, certain environmental laws – as part of coordinated ecosystem regimes – pay explicit attention to ecosystems as a whole, seeking to authorize ecosystem plans and management approaches. Second, laws not defined in ecosystemic terms may nevertheless be retrofit to create such regimes. Third, a variety of environmental laws may not explicitly direct their attention to ecosystems, but nevertheless, some specific provisions within the law may be directed at one or another aspect of ecosystemic regulation.

When a law establishes an ecosystem regime, some of the legal tasks of ecosystem regulation and problems encountered in each task may be reformulated in ecosystemic terms, as Table 1.7 indicates.

In this list, each stage is separated to highlight the extent to which the coastal regime in question must attend some aspect of the coastal ecosystem; i.e., its boundary, its functions, its stocks, its flows, and the intervention process, those functions, stocks, and flows across those boundaries. The order is important as a logical order, but the later stages of intervention and feedback may lead to revisions in the earlier stages of boundaries and objectives.

Table 1.7 ASPECTS OF ECOSYSTEMS, PROBLEMS AND LEGAL TASKS

THE STAGES	THE PROBLEM	RELEVANT EXAMPLE FROM COASTAL MANAGEMENT
1. Establishing boundaries of law and management	Multiple system sizes multiple jurisdictions	Setting boundaries for coastal zone management or coastal wetlands
2. Identifying relations & priority among multiple functions of ecosystem & objectives of regulation	The multiple objectives problem	Ranking priorities in wetland management
3. Determining proper ranges and distribution of biotic stock	The biodiversity problem	Biodiversity management in coastal wetlands
4. Determining proper ranges and distribution of abiotic stock	The biogeochemistry problem	Determining level of dissolved oxygen or salinity for coastal management

5. Determining the appropriate flow rate variables and means of control	The flow control problem	Determine oxygenization rates in estuarine management
6. Deciding whether to prohibit interventions into the ecosystem	The problem of prohibitory regulation	Dredge and fill management
7. Determining the mechanism for access	The gatekeeping problem	Governing access to dune
8. Establishing amount/kind of intervention permitted	The limit setting and tech-fix problem	Limiting amount & place of development in relation to coastal wetlands
9. The allocation of interventions	The allocation problem	Priority water related uses in coastal management
10. Feedback from interventions	The monitoring problem	Monitoring of coastal uses
11. Changing the amounts & kinds of intervention	The moving target problem	Limiting dredge & fill permits or conditioning
12. Remediation of impacts of interventions	The "how clean is clean?" problem	Wetlands mitigation or restoration

Source: Brooks, Jones and Virginia

Conclusion: Dimensions of the Relationship Between Law and Ecology

Forging Relations Between Ecology and Environmental Law

Our review of the history of ecology and law, their relations and the history of interdisciplinary frameworks in Chapters 2 through 10 has led to a variety of conclusions. These essentially optimistic conclusions suggest that both ecology and environmental law are undergoing transformations to better adapt to each other and to the environmental problems they are seeking to resolve. Moreover, the history of ecology and law has also revealed that a series of connections has been built between the two fields. Bridges such as interdisciplinary persons, migrating concepts, and bridge instruments operate to link the two fields. Most important, however, is the rise of place based, species based and earth systems regimes which further the joinder of law and ecology. We shall explore the emergence of these three kinds of ecosystemic regimes in the following chapters.

Notes

1. JOHN HART, STORM OVER MONO: THE MONO LAKE BATTLE AND THE CALIFORNIA WATER FUTURE (1996).

2. National Audubon Society, et al., Petitioners v. The Superior Court of Alpine County, Respondent, Department of Water and Power of the City of Los Angeles, et al., Real Parties in Interest, 658 P.2d 709 (1983).

3. NATIONAL RESEARCH COUNCIL, ET AL, THE MONO BASIN ECOSYSTEM: EFFECTS OF CHANGING LAKE LEVELS (1987).

4. Earlier ecological studies offered information for a steady stream of lawsuits and legislative proposals also seeking vainly to stop the water withdrawals. Finally, in 1983, the California Supreme Court found the Mono Lake to be held in "public trust" not only for selected human uses but for environmental protection and conservation as well. National Audubon Society, et al., Petitioners v. The Superior Court of Alpine county, Respondent, Department of Water and Power of the city of Los Angeles, et al., Real Parties in Interest, 658 P.2d 709 (1983). Ultimately, new state and federal legislation and the action of federal and state agencies led to the cessation of water withdrawals, the continuous monitoring of lake levels and the gradual restoration of the lake itself. Among the laws and regulations was the designation of the Mono Basin as a National Forest Scenic Area (*see* Hart, *supra* at note 1) – one of a variety of recent ecosystemic laws we will examine below.

5. Contemporary political scientists such as Oran Young and Elinor Ostrom have argued that resource regimes or common pool resources are often used or needed to protect ecological and natural resources.

6. The science of ecology, its concepts and conclusions are employed in different way within an ecosystem regime. We shall indicate those different ways later in the book.

7. We are fully aware that an ecosystemic legal regime is an "ideal type" to be realized more or less in actual practice. The rise of ecosystemic regimes is part of a more comprehensive historical process of growing regional, national and global interdependence, which has found expression in economic markets, global communication, international movement of peoples and new global and international institutions of governance. A heightened awareness of the interdependence of nature is part of this historical process. This recognition extends to global systems. These global systems are both valued and feared. We value the prosperity brought to some by global markets, while we feel the threat of global atmospheric pollution and a declining global biodiversity.

    The rise of the recognition of systematic interdependencies has led to the emergence of new disciplines devoted to the study of systems. (The history of systems thought as the background of ecology is set forth in FRITJOF CAPRA, THE WEB OF LIFE: A NEW SCIENTIFIC UNDERSTANDING OF LIVING SYSTEMS (1996).) One of those disciplines is ecology which seeks to study the interdependencies of nature.

8. Although the discipline of ecology began to emerge in the late nineteenth century, its development was then largely ignored by the public culture. Only a few "nature visionaries" such as George Perkins Marsh, John Muir, Aldo Leopold and Henry Thoreau grasped the implications of the recognition of the interdependency of nature. [These figures will be discussed in more detail in the next chapter.] Meanwhile, the nineteenth and twentieth century was a period of massive exploitation of nature in the pursuit of wealth. This exploitation was based upon an emerging legal system which emphasized the rights of private property and the private corporation. It was only in the beginning of the twentieth century and especially in the mid-twentieth century that an administrative law system was put into place which provided the eventual support for an environmental law regime.

9.   On the other hand, as we shall document below, ecology has had less effect upon media-based laws such as air and water pollution, as well as and waste disposal laws; in these laws, environmental science [we distinguish between environmental science – the myriad of disciplines which are employed within environmental policy making – and ecology, which seeks to organize those disciplines within the notion of an ecosystem and which promotes a series of concepts and methods unique to the study of ecosystems engineering, and economics prevail].

10.   The prospect of an emerging regime of ecosystemic law has produced high hopes and profound doubts. On the one hand, an entire new set of disciplines of ecological management has been built upon the linkages between ecology and the implementation of environmental laws. For example, John Clark's *Coastal Ecosystems* is an early influential example of the effort to apply systemically the insights of coastal ecology in the management of coastal zones, and numerous more recent books on ecological management have been published. [JOHN CLARK, COASTAL ECOSYSTEMS: ECOLOGICAL CONSIDERATIONS FOR MANAGEMENT OF THE COASTAL ZONE (1974).] On the other hand, skepticism with the recent flowering of ecological management is illustrated in Allan Fitzsimmons' recent book, *Defending Illusions*. [ALLAN FITZSIMMONS, DEFENDING ILLUSIONS: FEDERAL PROTECTION OF ECOSYSTEMS (1999).] Fitzsimmons believes the recent federal efforts to promote ecosystem management are based upon an erroneous philosophy of nature, and a basically defective science of ecology. He criticizes what he believes to be the unauthorized extension of federal power through its proposed ecosystemic laws – laws which he believes cannot resolve the environmental problems at which they are aimed or cannot do so while protecting individual rights and private property.

        This recent dispute over ecological management is not the important reason for studying in the relations of law and ecology. Rather, the current state of our national and global environment and the present state of our efforts to protect this environment demand such an inquiry because these problems have not been resolved. The environmental problems we faced in the mid twentieth century contributed to the rise of environmental law in the 1960s and 1970s. But this environmental law was formulated before ecology entered into the public consciousness. Without ecology, environmental law initially experienced fundamental difficulties in fully resolving environmental problems. These difficulties have led to reformulation based upon the insights of ecology of some environmental laws.

        Environmental law is part of a more complex set of institutions – local, state, federal, and integration of governmental and non-governmental organizations – which both shape and are shaped by law and legal practices. These institutions, insofar as they pertain to governance of ecosystems, are entitled "ecosystem regimes," "resource regimes," and/or "common pool resource" organizations. A new and exciting economic and political science study of the origin, history and activities of these regimes is now underway. [For one of many recent bibliographies of these studies, *see* JOHN VOGLER, THE GLOBAL COMMONS: A REGIME ANALYSIS (1995) pp. 215-224.] Although it is beyond the scope of this study of the interactions of ecology and environmental law, we return to a discussion of ecosystem regimes in the final chapters of this book because we believe an understanding of such regimes is essential to facilitating effective ecosystematic laws of the future.

11.   PETER M. HAAS, ROBERT O. KEOHANE, MARC A. LEVY, INSTITUTIONS OF THE EARTH: SOURCES OF EFFECTIVE INTERNATIONAL ENVIRONMENTAL PROTECTION (1993).

12.   In Chapters 2–10, we explore the complex history of their relations. The emerging ecosystemic legal regime may be useful understood in light of the following chart:

COMPONENTS OF ECOSYSTEMIC LAW

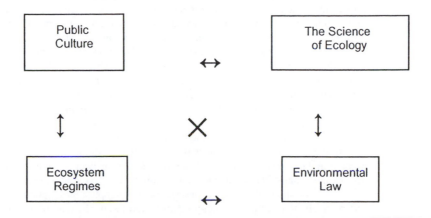

In Chapter 2, we discuss briefly the background public culture of the nineteenth and first part of the twentieth century leading to the rise of the science of ecology and environmental law. But the history within this book focuses upon ecology and environmental law in the latter part of the century.

13. A selection of representative studies includes: A. MYRICK FREEMAN, THE MEASUREMENT OF ENVIRONMENTAL AND RESOURCE VALUES: THEORY AND METHODS (1993); HERBERT MCCLOSKY, THE AMERICAN ETHOS; PUBLIC ATTITUDES TOWARD CAPITALISM AND DEMOCRACY (1984); RONALD INGLEHART, CULTURE SHIFT IN ADVANCED INDUSTRIAL SOCIETY (1990); AND DENNIS GILBERT, COMPENDIUM OF AMERICAN PUBLIC OPINION (1988).

14. *See* ROBERT C. BARRISTER, SOCIAL DARWINISM: SCIENCE AND MYTH IN ANGLO-AMERICAN SOCIAL THOUGHT (1979).

15. *See* RONALD INGLEHART, THE SILENT REVOLUTION: CHANGING VALUES AND POLITICAL STYLES AMONG WESTERN PUBLICS (1977).

16. RODERICK NASH, WILDERNESS AND THE AMERICAN MIND (1967, 1982).

17. We employ the term "ethos" to refer to the ethical principles implicit in our public culture.

18. *See* LAWRENCE BUELL, THE ENVIRONMENTAL IMAGINATION; THOREAU, NATURE WRITING AND THE FORMATION OF AMERICAN CULTURE (1995).

19. *See* Inglehart, *supra* at note 15.

20. Ordinarily, within law schools and many modern theories of law, ethics, the study of the nature of the good for individuals, and normative political theory, the evaluative study of politics, are not welcome subjects. With its inheritance of legal positivism, which seeks to sharply separate law from morals, and its background assumptions of liberalism, which seeks to promote a neutrality toward competing groups and interests within the modern state, law schools and legal theory feel uncomfortable with both the expressions of ethical commitments and inquiries into the nature of the good and just.

Environmental law and the science of ecology share this wariness with ethical inquiry. Most environmental law texts, after an obligatory chapter on environmental ethics, turn to a descriptive approach to statutes and legal opinions. Most law schools know that they are educating lawyers who may be asked to take either side in disputes over environmental protection, and hence, books prepared for such students tend to adapt to such a role. The separation of ethics and political theory from law is buttressed by theories of common law legal reasoning which not only do not find a place for these disciplines within the reasoning process, but also often argue for a positive excluding of ethics from the reasoning process. On the other hand, some of the scholarly writings within environmental law do adopt an explicit ethical position, or at least explore the implication of environmental ethics for law.

Similarly, most ecology texts are careful to segregate their chapters on ethics from the "real science" which they are seeking to teach. And within most environmental studies programs, environmental ethics is a separate course, segregated from the social and biological science courses. A positivistic approach to environmental science rules. This assumed separation of environmental law and science from environmental ethics complicates the task of demonstrating how environmental law and ecology are and should be joined within an ecosystemic regime. To be sure, a descriptive account of such linkages might be offered without moving from such an account to the normative account of the joinder. But such an account may involve a dishonest masking of the real agenda of the authors, which is to promote such linkages.

A position between strict description and complete prescription, might be to interpretively describe how ecology diffuses into the public culture, i.e., the ethos, while avoiding any full blown normative evaluation of that process of diffusion. (The notion of interpretation as a source of critical description bridges the gap between the descriptive and evaluative.) This is the position we shall take in this book. Our starting point for understanding the relationship of ecology, environ-mental law and ethics is to posit environmental law as facilitating the process of ethical inquiry and reflection. The process of enacting environmental laws, implementing them and subjecting them to judicial review, all with reference to ecology, is the starting point of an inquiry into what it means to be environmentally just within the specific contexts with which these laws and opinions deal.

21. *See* J.B. SCHNEEWIND, THE INVENTION OF AUTONOMY: A HISTORY OF MODERN MORAL PHILOSOPHY (1998).

22. The recognition of such interdependence has not only reflected in a new environmental ethic, but also in the new (or renewed) philosophy of the interdependence of reality underlying such an ethic. That philosophy is called process philosophy. [NICHOLAS RESCHER, PROCESS METAPHYSICS: AN INTRODUCTION TO PROCESS PHILOSOPHY (1996).] Thus the science of ecology, the metaphysics of process philosophy, an ecologically oriented ethic and common sense practical implication are all part of a package of fundamental reform in environmental thought.

23. Three more specific ethical positions emerge from the adjustment of traditional ethics to the discovery of the environment and its problems on the one hand, and the recognition of fundamental interdependency with or in nature on the other. [Each of these three ethical positions have unique tasks of inquiry suited to their own position. The natural humanist inquires into how the recognition of interdependence shapes her own decisions, deliberations and virtues. The proponent of the natural community seeks to inquire must seek to identify the elements of intrinsic value shared by herself and her natural community, and the practical implications of recognizing those intrinsic values. A cosmological ethicist seeks to identify how and what way the global processes by which we are shaped embody values which can guide our actions.] The first is a form of *natural humanism* in which human decisions, calculations, and virtues are shaped by an awareness that these decisions, calculations and virtues both are influenced by and influenced the interdependence of nature. Thus some theorists have even suggested that we can only understand human health by viewing it as the fitness of functioning within an ecosystem. The second form of ethics is one in which by recognizing our interdependence with nature, we can come to value not only ourselves

but also these processes and components of nature which we identify with other parts of the natural community. Aldo Leopold's recognition of the natural ecosystems as part of our human community illustrates this position. This is the *ethics of natural community*. The third form of ethics seeks to recognize the value of nature, not in ourselves nor in the broader natural community of which we are part, but in the larger processes of nature or the whole of nature. This is the form of *cosmological ethics* advanced by such modern thinkers as Alfred North Whitehead.

Environmental law may be regarded as part of the social process which facilitates the three ethical inquiries. Many environmental laws are preoccupied with the definition of the way in which our human welfare is included within a recognition of human interdependence. For example, the articulation of the proper nature and level of health to be secured in light of the system of nature in which we are located is a central inquiry in the setting of National Ambient Air Quality Standards (NAAQS) and more specifically, the lead ambient standards in the Clean Air Act. Other environmental laws are preoccupied with legal recognition of the intrinsic values of nature in, for example, the Wilderness Act and the Endangered Species legislation. Setting the appropriate levels of protection for such areas and species promotes an inquiry into the nature of the intrinsic values of nature and the obligation of humans to protect these values. Finally, environmental law has recently recognized certain global bio-geochemical processes, e.g., changes in atmospheric temperature, which may have to be protected from human interference. Yet, controlling human actions within the context of global processes may require controls on the large scale pursuit of human welfare. Such global processes and the placing of controls on the interference with such processes may precipitate tragic cosmic conflicts between human welfare and the values of a larger more encompassing nature.

24. Ecology encompasses many sub-disciplines defined either by the level of biological organization, the particular biological process that is the object of study, or whether the sub-discipline is concerned with the discovery of basic ecological principles or the application of these principles to environmental problems. Ecology includes, among other things, the study of the affect of the environment on 1) an individual organism's physiology, morphology or behavior (e.g., physiological ecology); 2) a single population of a species (population ecology); a community of two or more different species (community ecology); a distinct set of co-dependent and interacting communities (ecosystem ecology); or the entire planet (global ecology). *See* Louis J. Gross, *Ecology: An Idiosyncratic Overview* in MATHEMATICAL ECOLOGY: AN INTRODUCTION 3, 4 (Thomas G. Hallam & Simon A. Levin, eds. 1986).

25. Only some examples of concepts that ecology has borrowed from the social sciences include game theory, cost/benefit analysis, energy budgets, competition, and mutualism.

26. However, through the study of "systems" that include several ecological components, many ecologists have studied several ecological relationships at a time. As we will discuss in Chapters 2 and 3, there is still considerable debate over how well systems ecology deals with ecological relationships at the level of individuals, populations, and communities.

27. As with all of the divisions that we describe there has been considerable overlap between applied and basic ecology – particularly since in many cases an individual ecologist will do both. One example is the early study of population interactions driven to a large degree by the study of insect-plant interactions in agriculture.

28. Raymond L. Lindeman, *The Trophic-Dynamic Aspects of Ecology*, 23 ECOLOGY 399 (1942).

29.   *See infra* Chapter 3 for a discussion of ecosystem ecology in the 1960s and 1970s.
30.   *See* SUCCESS, LIMITATIONS, AND FRONTIERS IN ECOSYSTEM SCIENCE 287 (Michael L.
        Pace & Peter M. Groffman eds., 1998).
31.   During the 1960s ecosystem ecology would be the beneficiary of a federal government
        interested in what this new science could tell us about the effects of nuclear testing and
        war.
32.   *See* FRANK B. GOLLEY, A HISTORY OF THE ECOSYSTEM CONCEPT IN ECOLOGY: MORE
        THAN THE SUM OF ITS PARTS (1993).
33.   *See* ROBERT H. MACARTHUR, GEOGRAPHICAL ECOLOGY (1972).
34.   *See e.g.*, Daniel S. Simberloff, *Experimental zoogeography of islands: Effects of island
        size*, 57 ECOLOGY 629 (1976).
35.   The realization of most modern ecologists is that no one level of organization, whether
        it is an ecosystem or a single population, is the sole source of answers to any ecological
        problem. Still, ecologists know that some specific problems are best studied at one
        level of organization. Therefore, it is an understanding of the energy cycles of an
        ecosystem that is critical to the understanding of the function of whole ecosystems.
        However, it is population ecology's emphasis on growth rates and population
        interactions that usually provides the most accurate answers to questions about the
        short term health of a specific species.
36.   The descriptions of the hierarchical levels making up ecology come from; G. Tyler
        Miller, Jr., Living in the Environment (12th ed. 2002), CHARLES J. KREBS, ECOLOGY:
        THE EXPERIMENTAL ANALYSIS OF DISTRIBUTION AND ABUNDANCE (4th ed. 1994); PAUL
        R. EHRLICH & JONATHAN ROUGHGARDEN, THE SCIENCE OF ECOLOGY (1987); EUGENE
        P. ODUM, FUNDAMENTAL OF ECOLOGY (3rd ed. 1971).
37.   The study of life from DNA to organ system, while influencing ecological interactions,
        is the province of molecular, cellular, and physiological biologists. We hope that when
        we update this book at the beginning of the twenty-second century we will be able to
        discuss the ecology of other planets and how new environmental laws were developed
        to manage the creation of earth-like ecosystems on Mars (assuming it proves to be a
        "dead" planet).
38.   *See infra* Chapter 9 – a key ecological discovery related was that the spotted owls
        nesting behavior required old growth forest.
39.   H.G. ANDERWARTHA & L.C. BIRCH, THE DISTRIBUTION AND ABUNDANCE OF ANIMALS
        (1954); CHARLES J. KREBS, ECOLOGY (4th ed. 1994).
40.   *See* SHARON E. KINGSLAND, MODELING NATURE: EPISODES IN THE HISTORY OF
        POPULATION ECOLOGY (1985).
41.   *See infra* Chapter 9 and our discussion the use of ecology in the management of
        national forests in the U.S.
42.   EHRLICH AND ROUGHGARDEN, *supra* note 36 at 521. This general definition is
        essentially identical to more recent definitions. For example, the Encyclopedia
        Britannica defines ecosystem as "the complex of living organisms, their physical
        environment, and all their interrelationships in a particular unit of space." While most
        ecologists would agree with some form of the above definition, there have been, and
        still are advocates of the idea that the Earth, itself, is a single ecosystem.
43.   Physics, atmospheric sciences, and earth sciences (among others) are used in
        ecosystem, and higher levels of ecology studies.
44.   This is particularly necessary when most ecological research is relatively short term
        (two or three years), the average duration of most research grants and the normal length
        of time for a graduate student's dissertation research. These institutional limitations to
        ecological research are important topics of discussion among ecologists and
        environmental policy makers. *See* Stephen R. Carpenter, *The Need for Large-Scale*

Experiments to Assess and Predict the Response of Ecosystems to Perturbation, in SUCCESS, LIMITATIONS, AND FRONTIERS IN ECOSYSTEM SCIENCE 287 (Michael L. Pace & Peter M. Groffman eds., 1998). The result has been an increased emphasis on long term ecological studies (i.e., the funding of LTER – long term ecological research – is a relatively new initiative of the National Science Foundation, the federal agency most responsible for the funding of ecological research).

45. *See* GOLLEY, *supra* note 35.

46. *See infra* Chapter 8 for a discussion of the current use of landscape ecology in the management of the Florida Everglades.

47. *See* T.S. Sillett et al., *Impacts of a global climate cycle on population dynamics of a migratory songbird*, 288 SCIENCE 2040 (2000).

48. Until recently most ecological research has focused on a small part of one level of organization. *See* infra Chapter 3 for more detailed examples of early ecological research. Population and community levels studies would usually focus on estimating the demographic parameters (e.g., birth and death ratios) for one population or, at most, the interaction between two or three populations. Further, most population ecologists would limit their research to a specific population interaction (e.g., competition or predation) either by observing natural systems, performing experiments on relatively simple natural or laboratory systems of population interactions, or through the use of simple mathematical models. These approaches are not exclusive and many ecologists, now and in the past, have used a combination of all these methods. *See* FOUNDATIONS OF ECOLOGY (Leslie A. Real & James H. Brown eds., 1991) both for a review of the history of ecology and for its collection of classic ecological research papers. Meanwhile, ecosystem ecologists concentrated on measuring the input and output of one or two nutrients through relatively small, (spatially explicit) and for ease of study, simple ecosystems. During the 1960s and 1970s systems ecologists defied this trend by attempting to provide a more complete description of the energy flows and nutrient cycles through larger ecosystems. However, systems ecologists were no more able to measure these parameters in large systems than were the empirical ecosystem ecologists and instead attempted to understand large, complex ecosystems through the creation of a mathematical simulation of the system.

49. Institutionally this is best seen in the rapid increase in the number of environmental science or environmental studies programs at universities and in the growing acceptance of funding agencies (e.g., National Science Foundation) to provide support for ecological research that spans two or more traditional ecological subdisciplines.

50. *See* W.J. Bond, *Keystone species*, in BIODIVERSITY AND ECOSYSTEM FUNCTION 237 (E.D. Schulze & H. A. Mooney, eds., 1993).

51. *See* D.A. Wardle et al., *Biodiversity and ecosystem function: an issue in ecology*, 81 BULL. ECOLOGICAL SOC'Y AM. 235 (2000).

52. *See* D. Tilman et al., *Productivity and sustainability influenced by biodiversity in grassland ecosystems*, 379 NATURE 718 (1996).

53. *See* Donald R. Zak & Kurt S. Pregitzer, *Integration of Ecophysiological and Biogeochemical Approaches to Ecosystem Dynamics*, in PACE & GROFFMAN, *supra* note 30 at 372-403.

54. *See* Gary A. Polis et al., *Towards an Integration of Landscape and Food Web Ecology: The Dynamics of Spatially Subsidized Food Webs*, in 28 ANNU. REV. ECOL. SYST. 289-316 (1997).

55. Figure adapted from Zack & Pregitzer, *supra* note 53 at 374. This is a simplified diagram; a truly accurate figure would show connections, of various strength, among all levels and processes.

56.   *See* Ingrid C. Burke et al., *Progress in Understanding Biogeochemical Cycles at Regional to Global Scales*, in SUCCESS, LIMITATIONS, AND FRONTIERS IN ECOSYSTEM SCIENCE, *supra* note 33 at 171-172. While a detailed description of the mathematics behind ecology, either historical or present, is beyond the scope of this Chapter it is enough for now to realize that most mathematical methods used by any ecologists can be divided into two broad categories; linear and non-linear. Linear methods are the traditional tools of ecologists and were sufficient when it was believed that both populations and ecosystems behaved in a linear or equilibrium state. However, with the realization that most ecological systems are in a state of non-equilibrium it became necessary to use mathematical methods that could be applied to the unpredictable and non-linear state in which most ecologists now believe natural systems exist.

57.   *See* CHARLES J. KREBS, ECOLOGICAL METHODOLOGY (1989) for a description of different types of ecological methods. While somewhat dated this book still is useful, particularly since much of the current advance in ecological methodology comes from improvements in methods (improved computing power and ability to detect radioisotopes) and not in the creation of new ones. *See also* the Encyclopedia Britannica articles on *ecology* and related topics for good overviews of ecological methodology and other aspects of ecology.

58.   *See* S.R. Carpenter, *The Need for Large-Scale Experiments*, in SUCCESS, LIMITATIONS, AND FRONTIERS IN ECOSYSTEM SCIENCE, *supra* note 30, at 287. This growing awareness among ecologists is beginning to be matched by those who control funding for ecological research with the increase in the number and funding of Long Term Ecological Research (LTER) programs scattered throughout the U.S.

59.   *See* GENE E. LIKENS AND F. HERBERT BORMANN, BIOGEOCHEMISTRY OF A FORESTED ECOSYSTEM (2d ed. 1995).

60.   Physiological ecology has also been important in studying and managing species like the salmon that are faced with variable environmental conditions (much of it caused by human interference with streams and rivers).

61.   While there are several different estimates of a within species (or population) genetic variation, heterozygosity is particularly useful for purposes of conservation biology. [*See* Fred W. Allendorf & Robb F. Leary, *Heterozygosity and Fitness in Natural Populations of Animals*, in CONSERVATION BIOLOGY: THE SCIENCE OF SCARCITY AND DIVERSITY 57-76 (Michael E. Soulé ed. 1986).] Heterozygosity is a measure of the amount of different types of genes found within a population. [*See* DANIEL L. HARTL & ANDREW G. CLARK, PRINCIPLES OF POPULATION GENETICS (2nd. ed. 1989).] Low levels of heterozygosity are correlated to extensive inbreeding, which can be caused by population fragmentation through the loss of critical habitat. [*See* NATIONAL RESEARCH COUNCIL, SCIENCE AND THE ENDANGERED SPECIES ACT 136 (1995) [hereinafter SCIENCE AND THE ESA].] It is population fragmentation that is the most critical factor in a species being listed as threatened or endangered within the ESA. [*See id.* at 35.] Therefore, heterozgosity is a measure of biodiversity that is more closely related to the extinction process than those most often used in listing decisions. [The ESA requires five factors to be used in determining whether a species is listed as endangered or threatened. Of these factors only the first "the present or threatened destruction, modification, or curtailment of its habitat or range" is related to a biological concept (i.e., habitat fragmentation) and this only indirectly. 16 U.S.C. § 1533(a)(1)(A-E).]

62.   Recent implementing regulations of the Endangered Species Act have defined ESUs as functionally equivalent to a "species," as defined by the statute, and open to the same levels of protection as other threatened or endangered species. *See* Robin S.

Waples, *Evolutionary Significant Units, Distinct Population Segments, and the Endangered Species Act: Reply to Pennock and Dimmick*, 12 CONSERVATION BIOLOGY 718 (1998). Evolutionary Significant Units are distinct units of a species whose genetic isolation, due to habitat fragmentation or geographic isolation, make it necessary to design specific conservation plans for them. *See id.*

63. Endangered Species Act (ESA), 16 U.S.C. § 1532(16) (1988).

64. *See* Waples, *supra* note 62 at 718; SCIENCE AND THE ESA, *supra* note 61 at 56-8.

65. *See* MARK B. BUSH, ECOLOGY OF A CHANGING PLANET (2d ed., 2000) for a current treatment of applied ecology.

66. *See* P.M. Vitousek et al., *Human alteration of the global nitrogen cycle: Sources and consequences*, 7 ECOLOGICAL APPLICATIONS 737 (1997).

67. For a more detailed introduction to ecosystem functioning and services, *See* Diana H. Wall & Ross A. Virginia, *The world beneath our feet: Soil biodiversity and ecosystem functioning*, in NATURE AND HUMAN SOCIETY: THE QUEST FOR A SUSTAINABLE WORLD 225 (P. Raven & T.A. Williams eds., 2000).

68. *See, e.g.*, our discussion in Chapter 8 of the current attempts to restore the Florida Everglades and the Chesapeake Bay, as well as our discussion of newer "ecosystem" approaches to the management of the marine Fishery.

69. *See* RESTORATION ECOLOGY: A SYNTHETIC APPROACH TO ECOLOGICAL RESEARCH (Willian R. Jordan III et al. eds., 1987).

70. Ecosystem services are the conditions and processes by which ecosystems and their species sustain and fulfill human life. These services include the production of ecosystem goods such as timber, forage, medicinal plants, seafood, etc. For a full treatment of ecosystem services, *see* GRETCHEN C. DAILY, NATURE'S SERVICES. SOCIETAL DEPENDENCE ON NATURAL ECOSYSTEMS (Gretchen C. Daily ed., 1997). YVONNE BASKIN, THE WORK OF NATURE: HOW THE DIVERSITY OF LIFE SUSTAINS US (1997). Gretchen C. Daily et al., *Ecosystem services: Benefits supplied to human societies by natural ecosystems*, 3 ISSUES IN ECOLOGY 2 (1997).

71. *See* N.L. Christensen et al., *The Report of the Ecological Society of America Committee on the Scientific Basis for Ecosystem Management*, 6 ECOLOGICAL APPLICATIONS 665 (1996).

72. *See* GARY K. MEFFE et al., PRINCIPLES OF CONSERVATION BIOLOGY 20 (2d ed. 1997).

73. We will review the history of conservation biology from its formal development in the early 1980s to its present state as the applied science of biodiversity protection in Chapters 7 and 9.

74. DANIEL BOTKIN, DISCORDANT HARMONIES: A NEW ECOLOGY FOR THE TWENTY-FIRST CENTURY (1990).

75. *See, e.g.*, A. Dan Tarlock, *Environmental Law: Ethics or Science?* 7 DUKE ENVTL. L. & POL'Y F. 193 (1996); Jonathan Baert Wiener, *Law and the New Ecology: Evolution, Categories, and Consequences*, 22 ECOLOGY L.Q. 325 (1995); Judy L. Meyer, *The Dance of Nature: New Concepts in Ecology*, 69 CHI.-KENT L. REV. 875 (1994).

76. ORAN YOUNG introduced the notion of a "resource regime" in his book RESOURCE REGIMES: NATURAL RESOURCES AND SOCIAL INSTITUTIONS (1982).

77. *See, e.g.*, ROBERT B. KEITER, RECLAIMING THE NATIVE HOME OF HOPE: COMMUNITY ECOLOGY AND THE AMERICAN WEST (1998).

78. While this book takes an historical approach to the relations of ecology and law, the view that law is part of the social practices which make up a regime – i.e., a cluster of rules and roles with governance responsibility – is an important underlying assumption

of our approach. Since we see history as resulting in the emergence of ecosystemic regimes, the theory of regimes is important to understanding our account.

79.   It is worth mentioning that the resource regime approach depends very heavily upon the starting point of Garrett Hardin, who famously regarded environmental problems as problems of the commons. Hardin, however, is more willing to explore the use of private property devices to protect the commons.

80.   Private property can be reintroduced into the system in consideration of a number of the criteria including allocative efficiency, feasiblity, equity.

81.   Oran Young et al., *Institutional Dimensions of Global Environmental Change*, SCIENCE PLAN (1999) at 57.

82.   The legal system and its study are the product of two millennia of western civilization. Law is the body of promulgated rules of the centralized national governments and their subsidiaries. In the eighteenth and nineteenth century in Western Europe and the United States, this law became the instrument of democratic protection of individual freedom through the separation of powers, the election of legislatures, and the protection of human rights. [It is not our purpose here to place the emergence of environmental law into the complex of history of western democratic law; however, the reader should be aware that such a history lies behind our more recent account and that history provides a broad shape to more recent developments.] That history of western jurisprudence recounts a complex effort to relate law to nature, by means of natural law in ancient and medieval periods, and in our modern era, natural rights. When the scientific study of nature separated from other disciplines during the enlightenment period, the systematic study of nature was divorced from the legal sphere. [For a systematic history of the relations of "nature" to law, *see* LLOYD L. WEINREB, NATURAL LAW AND JUSTICE (1989).] In the nineteenth century, this divorce was buttressed by the growth of legal positivism which viewed law as a separate discipline. [For a history of legal positivism, *see* ANTHONY J. SEYOK, LEGAL POSITIVISM IN AMERICAN JUSRIPRUDENCE (1998).] The legal realist movement of the twentieth century [the history of legal realism is traced in WILLIAM TWINING, KARL LLEWELYN AND THE REALIST MOVEMENT (1985)] attempted to reintroduce science into the law. The recent effort to reestablish links between biology and law [*see* Chapter 11, *infra*] and between ecology and law is part of an effort to cure the diremption between law and nature. [For two of many recent efforts to bridge the gap between a descriptive view of nature and the norms of politics and law, *see* JOSEPH GRANGE, NATURE: AN ENVIRONMENTAL COSMOLOGY (1997) and RICHARD LEVINS AND RICHARD LEWONTIN, THE DIALECTICAL BIOLOGIST (1985).]

        The outlines of the American legal system were well established before the science of ecology emerged. The common law system, with its method of case by case decisionmaking, gradually established a system of private property which underlies our present legal regime. The Founding Fathers laid the U.S. Constitution on top of this common law system. Unlike many other countries, our federal constitution contains no explicit environmental clause, although several states have constitutional provisions establishing some form of environmental rights. [Richard Brooks, "A Constitutional Right to a Healthful Environment," 16 VT. L. REV. 1063 (1992).] This constitution embodied the separation of powers and established the federal system of national and state government. The result is a hierarchy of federal, state and local legislatures adopting laws to be administered by an executive bureaucracy empowered by statutes to adopt its own regulations. A system of federal and state courts engage in judicial review of specific cases arising out of the administration of these laws.

83.   For an excellent overview, *see* Celia Campbell-Mohn, Barry Breen, J. William Futrell, ENVIRONMENTAL LAW FROM RESOURCES TO RECOVERY (1993).

84.   J. WILLIAM FUTRELL, *The History of Environmental Law* in Campbell-Mohn, et al., *Id.* at 132.

85.   For a discussion and examples of coevolution, *see* STEPHEN SCHNEIDER & RANDI LODER, THE COEVOLUTION OF CLIMATE AND LIFE (1984).

86.   For one thoughtful account of this process, *see* BRUCE ACKERMAN, WE THE PEOPLE 35-37 (1991). Several authors have sought to put some pattern on events. At the level of world histories of the environment, CLIVE PONTING in A GREEN HISTORY OF THE WORLD: THE ENVIRONMENT AND THE COLLAPSE OF GREAT CIVILIZATIONS (1991) adopts a cyclical theory of history in which our present civilization fails to respond to modern industrialism and urbanization. [For an excellent typology of different approaches to history, *see* CHARLES VAN DOREN, THE IDEA OF PROGRESS (1967).] With the coming of the millennium, there have been numerous histories of the modern age, e.g., JOHN LUKACS, THE END OF THE TWENTIETH CENTURY AND THE END OF THE MODERN AGE (1993). These histories envisage the last part of this century as presaging massive changes including decline of American preeminence, the decline of the American state, the increase of social democracies, a profound ambivalence toward science and technology. These changes may give a radical new meaning to our more modest history.

        At a more specific level, there have numerous histories of environmental law and policy written in the past twenty years. RICHARD N.L. ANDREWS, MANAGING THE ENVIRONMENT, MANAGING OURSELVES: A HISTORY OF AMERICAN ENVIRONMENTAL POLICY (1999) contains an excellent bibliography of historical sources, pp. 433-451; SAMUEL P. HAYS, BEAUTY, HEALTH AND PERMANENCE: ENVIRONMENTAL POLITICS IN THE UNITED STATES, 1955-1986 (1987). Both histories fail to offer a clear description of a discernible pattern of history, but both, for different reasons, are only partly optimistic about environmental policies for the future. (Andrews sees a lack of coherent vision; Hays seeks a conflict between the middle class demands and the elites who see scarcity limiting environmental aspirations.)

87.   These steps of the history of environmental law in the United States (and their dates) do not necessarily correspond with the pace of similar developments abroad. For one excellent comparative treatment, *see* EUROPEAN ENVIRONMENTAL LAW: A COMPARATIVE PERSPECTIVE (Gerd Winter ed.,1996). The passage of significant environmental laws in other nations has tended to lag behind the United States. Certainly the environmental histories of the Pacific Rim and Eastern European countries exemplify this lag. The order of developments also differs from country to country. Thus Australia began with criminal penalties and moved to the "civilization" of environmental law at a later stage. Unlike the United States, many nations have adopted bold constitutional provisions for the protection of the environment, often prior to adopting a statutory regime. The modes of regulation adopted in other countries may also differ; for example, Japan began its environmental law regime with the adoption of an environmental compensation statute designed to respond to the horrible impacts resulting from mercury poisoning at Minamata. Unlike the United States, external regional environmental controls in Europe played an important role; the European Community's adoption of the Maestricht Treaty creating the European Union and its environmental provisions in 1986 were mandated in member nations. All of these worldwide variations in law and policy mean that the role of ecology's contribution to shaping the law may significantly differ from country to country.

88.   Curiously, recent U.S. political interests are calling for a grater emphasis on natural resource extraction (energy, forest products) to maintain a strong domestic economy in the face of a global recession.

89.   These statutes have preserved the rights of citizens to seek common law remedies such as damage remedies which may not be available under the new environmental statutes. A particularly important common law area is the field of toxic torts. Toxic torts require the complainant to prove that the defendant's dispersal of toxic pollutants proximately caused harm to the plaintiff. This requirement of cause-in-fact requires the plaintiff to introduce evidence regarding the pathways of the pollutant within the environment. At this point the insights of ecology and ecological studies become relevant.

90.   For both a historical and analytic treatment of modern administrative law, *see* Richard Stewart, *The Reformation of American Administrative Law*, 88 HARV. L. REV. 1669 (1975).

91.   Perhaps the prototype legal decision for environmental standing remains Sierra Club v. Morton, 405 U.S. 727 (1972).

92.   In Chapter 2 we shall address briefly the way in which the administrative law system treats ecology in our discussion of law and science.

93.   *See* AMORY B. LOVINS, SOFT ENERGY PATHS: TOWARD A DURABLE PEACE (1977).

94.   *See* JONATHAN LASH, KATHERINE GELMAN AND DAVID SHERIDEN, THE SEASON OF SPOILS: THE STORY OF THE REAGAN ADMINISTRATION'S ATTACK ON THE ENVIRONMENT (1984).

95.   The complexity of environmental law is further compounded by the complex structure of the U.S. government. Laws are adopted by the legislature, their implementing regulations are issued by the executive, and the application of both laws and regulations are contested in the courts. [Our historical discussion of this interplay is set forth in Chapters 3 to 9.] Our federal structure allows or enables the states and their local governments to promulgate environmental statutes and regulations within certain limits and they do so. In addition, there is both a system of federal and state courts. This organizational structure has significant implications for the relations of environmental law to ecology. The separation of federal and state governments and the multiple state governments with their politically established geographical boundaries makes any unified management of ecosystems in accordance with ecological principles difficult. For example, the individual states have had great difficulty regulating the national air shed and the flow of air pollutants across their boundaries. The management of multi-state rivers and watersheds is similarly difficult. Similarly, the separation of powers and tensions between legislatures, executives and courts make the management of ecosystems even more difficult.

96.   For a more comprehensive discussion of the interaction of the kinds of environmental laws within an ecosystem approach, *see* Richard Brooks, *U.S. Environmental Law: Ecosystems, the Commons, and Environmental Rights* (1993) [published in Portuguese by the Institu Nacional de Administracao, Lisbon, Portugal].

97.   *See* ZYGMUNT PLATER, ENVIRONMENTAL LAW AND POLICY: A COURSEBOOK ON NATURE, LAW AND SOCIETY (1992).

98.   Many of the environmental articles presently published in specialized environmental journals are, in fact, advocacy for the increased protection of the environment.

99.   *See* EUROPEAN ENVIRONMENTAL LAW (Gerd Winter ed., 1996) for one presentation of that paradigm.

100.   For one effort to link social and ecological systems discussion, *see* LINKING SOCIAL AND ECOLOGICAL SYSTEMS: MANAGEMENT PRACTICES AND SOCIAL MECHANISMS FOR BUILDING RESILIENCE (Fikret Berkes & Carl Folke eds.,1998).

101.   *See* WILLETT KEMPTON, ENVIRONMENTAL VALUES IN AMERICAN CULTURE (1995).

2 The Early History of Ecology and Environmental Law

... The state has an interest independent of and behind the titles of its citizens, in all the earth and air within its domain ... Let us give Nature a chance; she knows her business better than we do.
– Michel de Montagne [1]

At the beginning of the twentieth century, the state of Georgia brought a common law nuisance action against the Tennessee Copper Company in the Supreme Court of the United States.[2] In order to purify its copper ore, the Tennessee Copper Company had built large open air "roast piles" which were ignited to produce a "sulphurous smoke." That smoke not only carried onto neighboring lands, but drifted to the neighboring state of Georgia, laying waste to a swath of forest land. There was very little scientific evidence as to the amount and kind of damage, although the impact was reported to be devastating. All evidence of the pollution and its impacts was submitted to the Court in affidavits, but science did not speak to the decision. Despite this lack of science, Justice Holmes boldly enjoined the company. In the words of the court: *"... the state has an interest independent of and behind the titles of its citizens, in all the earth and air within its domain ..."*[3]

Introduction

What could be more inspiring than a U.S. Supreme Court decision stopping pollution and vindicating the rights of the polluted public and stopping the pollution of private economic interests? What could be more promising than the court's recognition of a global commons? Without science and modern regulatory environmental statutes to help, the pollution was stopped – at least for the moment – by the court. The Tennessee Copper Company v. Georgia opinion offered hope for the success of pollution control without *ecology or environmental law*. Unfortunately, the early history of common law efforts to control pollution did not follow this example. Thus, the common law was littered with legal opinions offering very little protection for the environment.[4] Clearly, something more was needed. It is the argument of this book that what was needed and remains lacking is an ecosystemic legal regime. We will trace the rise of this regime during the past half century, describe its present workings, and anticipate its future directions.

The failure of the early common law to protect the environment is evidenced in the cities and countrysides left scarred by the industrial revolution throughout the common law world. Charles Dickens painted a vivid portrait of such pollution in London as "smoke lowering down from chimney pots, making a soft black drizzle, with flakes of soot in it as big as full grown snowflakes – gone into mourning, one might imagine, for the death of the sun."[5] These environmental scars of the nineteenth century were deepened by the technology of the twentieth. It remained for the science of ecology and the slowly developing ecosystemic legal regime of the second half of the twentieth century to initiate measures to protect and restore that environment. It is the story of the emergence of ecology and ecosystemic legal regime which we begin to narrate in this chapter, to be followed by eight more chapters which bring the story up to the present time.

A reminder regarding preliminary definitions. Ecology is the science of nature, viewed in holistic terms; nature is made up of interdependent evolving components. That interdependence constitutes an ecosystem. An *ecosystemic* legal regime is one whose laws seek to establish mechanisms for the protection and restoration of ecosystems. An ecosystemic *legal regime* is that set of constitutional provisions, statutes, regulations, common law rules, related plans, and corresponding legal roles that deal with ecosystems. It is our contention that the understanding of nature as ecosystem, and of environmental law as part of an ecosystemic regime is central to understanding the history we are about to recount and the future direction of both ecology and environmental law.

The Public Political Culture of Ecology and Environmental Law

In order to understand how the emergence of an ecologically based environmental law regime is possible at the end of the twentieth century, one must understand not only the specific histories of ecology and environmental law set forth below, but also the history of the public political culture which makes such science and law publically acceptable and legitimate. By "public political culture," we mean the political theory implicit in our societal and governmental practice, the assumptions about citizenship, freedom, property and nature that inform our public life, (i.e., the unreflective background of our political discourse and pursuits).[6] Thus, the public political culture must evolve to support the notion that the duty of citizens and government is to protect ecosystems, and to regulate property, industry and technology in order to do so.

The Colonial and Revolutionary Period

All public culture is the product of history (i.e., the social process over time of both forgetting and remembering). The forgetting has clouded memories of the callous treatment by European settlers of the native peoples and their ecosystems at the time of American settlement. This callous treatment pre-vented the settlers from benefitting from those indigenous native perspectives of nature – perspectives which might have contributed to a more holistic and ecologically oriented approach to nature during settlement. In one sense, the task of our modern environmental regime is to recover that lost heritage and make it relevant today. This recovery is an underappreciated one.[7] The omission of native perspectives is only one piece of evidence showing that the usual histories of environmentalism are not complete.[8] Not only is the "ecological Indian" and his traditional knowledge of the environment forgotten (at least until recently), but so too is the rich colonial community tradition of regulating the use and produce of land. This tradition included an early history of municipal land conservation which has only been recently rediscovered as part of a recovery of our environmental heritage.

The customary starting point of our history of the environmental legal regime is the inheritance of the common law private property system from England. This private property system laid the foundation for the future unchecked development of U.S. lands and the exploitation of other natural resources during the eighteenth and nineteenth centuries.[9] Under this private property regime, given an apparent unlimited supply, the settlers soon treated land as a disposable commodity, often abusing its natural condition.[10]

Coexisting with private property, there was publically owned land as well, for which the U.S. Constitution assigned the federal government the powers of control and disposition.[11] Most public land, like its private counterpart, was initially regarded as disposable, and indeed was granted to the states and citizens for farming, grazing, mining, and other developments. Some of this public land – especially tidelands, navigable waters, and a variety of land types mainly in the West – was treated as commons land and subject to a law that recognized the interaction among its private and public uses and its public nature.[12] Unfortunately, this early recognition of these commons lands in our history was soon eclipsed by a commitment to private or public ownership, but the notion of *lex communis* has been recovered both in practice and as an object of study two centuries later.[13] The importance of the resurgent interest in commons land in the late twentieth century lay in the perceived need for a system of environmental management of the commons,[14] both at the national and more recently the international level (e.g., international regimes for ozone control, biodiversity, ocean protection and global warming).

Considerable attention has been given to the philosophy of private property which animated our Founders' thoughts and shaped our Constitution. According to one view of the political and constitutional thought immediately preceding the constitution, property was viewed as capital; a resource for wealth, and hence subject to political disputes over wealth and inequality. The Founders were primarily concerned about private property's role in protecting the political ideals of freedom, rather than as a protection for the abuse of nature by its owners.[15] The Founders' political views of property are part of a U.S. Constitution, with its checks and balances, its provisions for carefully enumerated powers of the legislature, and with the later amendment the protection of private property, all designed to protect the freedom of citizens. Ironically, in recent times these very Constitutional provisions have operated to limit the power of government to carry out vigorous environmental protection and comprehensive ecological management.

There was, however, another contemporary view of property, identified with civic republicanism, a theory of government which was influential at the time of our nation's founding.[16] The proper role of government was to promote the common good, not merely to secure individual rights and interests. It was expected that citizens, by participation in the government, would acquire and exercise civic "virtues." Property and its proper use was consequently seen as a shared resource for facilitating the exercise of "civic virtue" for the common good.[17] It is this civic republican view of property that is most compatible with a law of ecological management, which was only to emerge two centuries later. Unfortunately, this tradition of civic republicanism, like the early use of the commons, was largely eclipsed by the early 1800s.

As the village commons disappeared, and the interdependent aspects of private property faded from view, the greater shared landscape remained. That landscape mosaic, largely agricultural, with small compact villages, established a pastoral ideal in the minds of American settlers.[18] This ideal was to vest a perennial belief in the values of a cultivated pastoral nature, in which the workings of agriculture supported an environmentally benign way of life. In addition, the pastoral ideal fostered belief in the close connection between farming and democracy, a belief which strengthened the continued influence of the agricultural community (now agribusiness) on environmental policy.[19]

One final contribution of the colonial and revolutionary era to the progress towards a law informed by the science of ecology was the early respect for science itself. The Founding Fathers were not only deeply interested in matters scientific, but they couched their political rhetoric in scientific metaphors and injected their respect for science into the very provisions of the constitution.[20] The Founders' love for science was recognized throughout our political history and thus science itself, despite the recent concerns about the "two cultures" of science and the humanities has always been part of our public culture. The Founders' love for science was tinged with a pragmatism which viewed science as the means for developing new technology in the furtherance of progress.[21] This focus upon science as a vehicle for technological progress is part of an American tradition which has mixed implications for the environment. On the one hand, American technology, has been one of the principal factors in modern pollution problems.[22] On the other hand, this technology may offer at least one part of the solution for controlling the effects of pollution.

The Public Culture of the Nineteenth Century

From the viewpoint of the modern environmentalist, the history of the United States in the nineteenth century represents a challenge to everything the modern environmental movement stands for. As we shall see below, the public policy and law of this age fostered this challenge. The details are not important here, but the magnitude of the economic effort of nineteenth- century America has created in our modern age an economic and social momentum of controlled economic growth, which has catastrophic implications for any effective ecologically informed environmental law seeking to protect nature. As one author summarized that century: "The land of hyperbole, optimism and expansion – American culture has often been represented as obsessed with manifest destiny and the righteousness of its republic."[23] The nineteenth century was a period of history committed to an expanded population, economic markets, new technology, the industrial revolution, and the consequent abuses of nature which still scar the landscape of America, all to serve, in de Toqueville's words "the least wants of the body and ... the little conveniences of life."[24] This was an age of new inventions, the arrival of factory life and consumerism, the commodification of land, the gradual processes of urbanization, the expansion of markets and the use of nature as a resource for all of these activities.[25]

William Cronon describes these events in his monumental environmental history of the rise of Chicago, a history in which the fabric of the natural ecosystems which supplied the resources for Chicago's growth were destroyed.[26] For example, after documenting the development of the Chicago lumber industry, Cronon concludes:

> Chicago's relationship to the white pines had been exceedingly intricate emerging from the ecological and economic forces that for a brief time had come together into a single market, a single geography. The tensions in that market and that geography had finally destroyed the distant ecosystem which had helped create them – but by then it no longer mattered.[27]

Joel Tarr has offered a parallel historical account of the "search of the ultimate sink" for the disposal of pollution of cities in the nineteenth century.[28] Tarr demonstrates how Pittsburgh city engineers sought to cope with the complexity of urban pollution by transferring land pollution to water pollution through sanitary sewers at the expense of downstream cities, and how smoke pollution was controlled at the expense of low income groups.

The economic and social momentum of the nineteenth century's manifest destiny was accompanied by a fundamental change in ways of thought during this period. The economic spirit was captured in the literary works of Dickens (*Hard Times*), and the economic writings of Adam Smith (*The Wealth of Nations*). Smith's seminal economic writings not only described, but offered a reluctant justification of, the market which became part of the economic policy of economic liberals in the 1800s.[29] This economic paradigm transformed our nation's relationship to nature, resulting in the establishment of a basic public culture inimical to respect for the environment. Public culture quickly accepted the primacy of the market, with its consequent commodification of property, an exaggerated respect for wealth, and the accordance to it of political power. The "successful" individual responded with vigor, seeking a goal of "prosperity" at the expense of our natural world. In the words of one commentator on the century,

> Many narratives of health written during this period provide, however only a thin veneer of optimism for the age. One finds in these writings enormous cracks in the bravado of democracy ... Not merely an agrarian world, rushing to industrialize and offer up its wilderness to railroad magnates and real estate speculators, the nineteenth century appears curiously unhinged.[30]

But not everyone was estranged from the environment. For example, Vermont manufacturer Stephen Hinsdill of the mid-1800s advocated what is best described as "Christian capitalism." In his view, capitalism was a creative force, in harmony with social progress.[31] Unfortunately, this unique joinder of religion and economics[32] resulted in the transformation of the Christian notion of stewardship from the care of a cultivated environment to the careful tending of economic growth, and the generation of individual wealth. As a consequence, the earlier Christian notion of the continuous sharing and nurturing of a sustainable environment was eclipsed to become an afterthought, in which the law is left as the only resource to prevent and repair the ravages of uncontrolled economic growth.[33] To this very day, most environmental law is built upon the acceptance of economic growth, and the consequent need to mitigate its pollutant effects, rather than limit growth itself.[34]

The widespread exploitation of the environment of the 1800s, supported by a distorted legal system and corresponding political beliefs, resulted in a curious and perverse joining of natural science and political doctrine in "Social Darwinism." The first U.S. edition of Darwin's *Origin of the Species* was widely reviewed in America in 1860.[35] What followed was William Graham Sumner and Herbert Spencer's "learned" application of Darwin's principles of natural selection to the social and political world. The deepest intellectual harm that resulted from social Darwinism was the pitting of man not only against other men, but also indirectly against nature. Nature became the source of resources for competition, much as the countryside and its inhabitants become the object of rape and pillage during a war.

If economic growth was the broad theme of history for the nineteenth century, the slavery issue and the ensuing U.S. Civil War were the formative events of this period. Touching every aspect of our society, the war was indirectly important to any future environmental policy. As Roderick Nash has so eloquently pointed out, when slavery was overturned, a process of recognition of rights was underway which would eventually extend to women, the disabled, animals and perhaps in the future, all of nature.[36] The question we shall have to explore below is, what is the relationship between the rights of nature and the law of ecological management?

The Twentieth Century

The twentieth century began with waves of immigration, attracted by the country's economic growth and resulting significant urbanization. (Driven by concern for economic well being, these immigrants did not bring the environmental ethic so badly needed at this stage or any stage of American history.) In the early twentieth century, an early progressive political movement arose. This movement sought to curb the power of larger corporations on behalf of a national public good, but the movement never challenged the desirability of economic growth, and it soon made its peace with the necessity of "ordinary" corporations. Nevertheless, the progressive movement planted the notion that federal power and law could be employed for a federal common good. The movement also called the nation's attention to the alleged threat of exhaustion of our natural resources, thus originating a conservation movement which was to meld into the broader environmental movement of the late twentieth century. In light of the remorseless economic growth fueled by new labor and the exploitation of nature (which threatened that common good), the public political culture adopted several approaches that were to affect the environmental movement and environmental law in the late twentieth century. These approaches blended the romantic movement, an appeal to efficiency, and a rediscovered concern for environmental health into the early twentieth- century environmental movement.

It had become apparent that the rate of exploitation of pristine systems was unsustainable. A strategy was adopted to carve out parts of the environment (i.e., parks, national forests, and certain species), to save them from the economic onslaught. The strategy sprang from a romantic view of nature as a place to escape from the burdens of industrial life. The public policy of reservation of forest land was also part of a larger utilitarian conservation of renewable resources, including lumber and other allegedly threatened natural resources. Thus, the national forests could be justified by the "gospel of efficiency" of Gifford Pinchot and others.[37]

This strategy separated resources from the ecosystem that sustained them. It ripped away the tree from the land, viewed the tree as potential lumber, independent of its role in the habitat, and hence fragmented any holistic view of nature.[38] Nevertheless, the early conservationist's concern for efficiency and renewability took into account the future crops of trees to be harvested, and hence added a longer-term time dimension to resource management, which would later come to be a central element in ecologically oriented environmental law. In addition, a pragmatic concern for health and a romantic yearning for beauty among the urban populations led to both an urban sanitation movement and the "city beautiful" movement, as well as a body of associated land use and pollution control laws. These sanitation and public health laws were the early forerunners of modern environmental laws and remain important in their own right.

From this account above, it is seen that many of the early values of conservation, recreation, aesthetics and health began to infuse the objectives of an array of early environmental laws. These objectives became the underpinning principles of the environmentalism of the second half of the century. Environmental law at this juncture was not "holistic" in its perceptions of nature or in the statement of its objectives, nor did it value nature for itself. Such holistic views were the province of a few "nature visionaries" described below. Despite the limits of this early progressive movement, the saving of public forests and national parks was a turning point since it express the nation's commitment to a national public good, and laid the basis for a broader federal statutory approach to environmental protection, which was to characterize environmental laws of the mid-century. [These earlier programs were also the precursors for the later comprehensive planning of forest and national park ecosystems.]

The final stage in the evolution of a supportive political culture for the melding of ecology and environmental law was the advent of the "New Deal"[39] of the 1930s. Efforts to restructure the federal government to cope with the economic depression and the ensuing war of the era resulted in fundamental political and constitutional changes of importance to the field of environmental law. These New World changes, however, had mixed implications for any future ecologically oriented environmental policy. The acceptance of an activist federal government was primarily aimed at providing federal government support for continued economic growth and full employment. The primary objective was to guarantee economic security for the poor, the old, the disabled, and unemployed. Little attention was paid to the cost to the environment of such economic growth.

Nevertheless, it was in response to economic crises that the administrative branches of the federal government assumed the active powers later employed to plan and deal with the nation's natural resource and environmental problems.[40] This assumption of power, ratified by the Supreme Court, led to "framework laws" such as the Administrative Procedures Act, which sought to allocate a new arrangement of powers within the federal government and which would assume central importance in the later environmental law era.

The New Deal and its administrative law laid the basis for environmental law in several ways. First, it established an "affirmation of expertise" which was later to lead to demands for agency planning. This planning, as we shall see below, is an important part of an ecosystem regime. Second, the New Deal enshrined the notion of agency independence from central political control. Such independence, although sacrificed to some extent by later environmental laws establishing executive agencies, nevertheless established the tradition of independent ecosystem regimes. Third, the New Deal – at least until the 1970s – insured limited judicial review of agency decisionmaking, hence permitting flexibility of agency decisions.[41]

The consequence of the history of America's political culture is a profoundly divided heritage for the framing of future ecologically oriented environmental law. On one hand, the early revolutionary commitment to a limited and fragmented government, the social momentum of the economic growth of the nineteenth century, the acceptance of economic liberalism, the weak early twentieth century progressivism, and the New Deal reliance upon federally sponsored economic growth make any environmental law which seeks to protect sustainable natural ecosystems difficult. On the other hand, the recognition of decentralized government in the early Republic, the valuing of nature sufficient to seek preservation of selected areas in the nineteenth century, the assertion of a national public good by the progressives of the early twentieth century, and the acceptance of an activist national government at the mid-twentieth century, offered hope that with the recognition of new environmental crises toward the end of the twentieth century, an ecologically oriented ecosystemic legal regime might indeed be fashioned.

Environmental Culture and Nature's Visionaries

The early history of public culture has helped to shape the present field of environmental law, but another important influence is the work of the "nature's visionaries," figures who, by their bold formulations of nature and man's relationship to it, now shape the thoughts of generations of environmental leaders as well as scientists and the public. Environmental visionaries are holists who see the world in all its complexity.[42] Their view of nature is best interpreted as the result of theory and close observation.[43] The biographies of the major environmental visionaries of the nineteenth and twentieth centuries illustrate this conclusion. Most were possessed with a love of nature from their early childhood, viewed nature as under siege by human actions, and in their concern for environmental protection, often looked to the law for help.[44]

Almost invariably these nature writers, scientists and public servants engaged in efforts to protect nature. The modern history of environmental culture[45] in the century preceding the 1960s[46] confirms this generalization. Each of the lives of a selection of major figures – Henry Thoreau, Charles Darwin, George Perkins Marsh, Ernst Haéckel, John Muir, Aldo Leopold, Rene Dubos – embraced nature, viewed it whole, sought to protect it, and ultimately turned to law for assistance in its protection.[47] *At the most basic and personal level as represented in the lives of these visionaries, law and ecology are linked in a love of and respect for nature and its creatures.* Thus the environmental visionaries articulated the underlying values of a regime for the support of an ecologically oriented environmental law.[48]

It is useful to lay out in bold and simplistic fashion these underlying premises:

Table 2.1 BASIC CONTRIBUTIONS OF NATURE VISIONARIES

1.	Treating nature as an object of respect;
2.	Understanding nature in holistic terms;
3.	Believing nature to be under threat from human activities;
4.	Recognizing the complexity of nature;
5.	Accepting science as a principle means of understanding nature;
6.	Accepting humanity as part of nature;
7.	Tracing indirect harms to humans from harms to and through nature;
8.	Believing that humans can control and limit harms within their relationship to nature;
9.	Regarding law as a principal means of control of human activities in nature.

Source: Brooks, Jones and Virginia

By all accounts, Charles Darwin epitomizes the visionary who most influenced the development of the science behind our environmental laws, but a variety of major figures of early ecology influenced its development, each expressing a different kind of love of or respect for nature.[49] The Thoreauvian mellow contemplation of Walden Pond, Darwin's recognition of nature as cruel, Rene Dubos' finding of a "god within" a human-controlled nature, Aldo Leopold's finding himself as a member of a community of interactions between man and nature, and John Muir's pragmatic recommendations for cropping nature's excesses illustrate the range of attitudes towards the environment and its change over time. A century later, their influences would lead to many different rationales for human intervention into nature and a need to protect it. These different attitudes are reflected in contemporary thought, where the term "ecology" has come to mean different things to different people, as seen by the proliferation of fields and approaches, including ecophilosophy, ecosystem science (ecology), human ecology, political ecology, deep ecology, sustainability, conservation ecology, ecosystem management and global ecology.[50]

Each of these early ecologists advanced somewhat different views of the central message of ecology. For Darwin, the Malthusian[51] scarcity of resources in nature results in a natural selection of both human and non-human forms of life and leads to the evolution of both, offering a dynamic but perhaps bleak view of nature. Whether nature is, in the words of Tennyson, "red in tooth and claw," Darwin is credited with exposing its complex cruelty requiring the need for a watchful scientific study. Contrary to Darwin, Thoreau embraced the romantic tradition. "Every creature," wrote Thoreau, "is better alive than dead" – a most un-Darwinian viewpoint! This romance with nature continues in much current nature writing and, based upon the Walden experience, this romance with nature continues with the promotion of "the simple life" to protect nature.[52]

Donald Worster's *Nature's Economy,* an elegant history of ecology, points out that the forerunners of ecology also defined this science in different ways. Two principal approaches to ecology are the natural history of place-based nature and the abstract energy-based natural economy described in systems terms. The former, based upon the qualitative observations, include the works of Darwin, Marsh, Muir and Leopold. The latter includes the more quantitative work of Clements, Tansley and Odum. As we shall see below, the natural history-based ecology is reflected in the largely qualitative natural observations of modern nature writing with its popular appeal, while the more quantitative approaches of the scientific ecologists are taken in the use of quantitative environmental indicators in environmental law.

GEORGE PERKINS MARSH
George Perkins Marsh is the first major figure who established the connection between an ecological vision and "environmental regulation." At a time when neither ecology nor environmental law existed in 1864, Marsh published *Man and Nature*, a pioneering environmental study which perceived the interrelationships in nature and the ways in which man's developments, including clear-cutting and its consequent erosion, affected stream quality and aquatic life. He based his observations both on observation of his native Vermont and countries around the world, where he had traveled as a United States Ambassador. As a country lawyer in another stage of his career, Marsh acted as Fish Commissioner for Vermont and helped to pass laws protecting Vermont's streams. He was a strong proponent for a regulatory approach which was to flower almost a century later. George Perkins Marsh was the first major figure to establish the connection between an ecological vision and "environmental regulation."

In many ways, it was Vermonter George Perkins Marsh who first recognized that the interrelationships of nature magnified the damage to that nature by human action. Marsh, willing to weigh the costs and benefits of human impact on nature for the benefit of human civilization, promoted the public regulation of environmentally harmful actions.[53] Certainly, Vermonter Marsh best anticipates the rise of ecosystemic regulation and the emergence of ecosystem management.

Ernst Haeckel, inventor of the term "oekologie," the science of relations between organisms and their environment, put forth a set of "ecological beliefs," including the belief in a universe as a unified and balanced organism in which man and animals had the same moral and natural status. For Haeckel, nature was the source of truth, to be recognized and guided by the scientific observation of the natural world.[54] All of Haeckel's tenets have found recent expression in the "Gaia Hypothesis" and "deep ecology" beliefs,[55] as well as in the broad treatments of global ecosystems. On a more local level, John Muir was among the first to emphasize the participation of man within specific places of nature rather than as outside aesthetic or scientific observers.[56] Many of the current popular writings about nature follow in Muir's footsteps by recounting the writer's thoughts and emotions about his personal encounter with specific places in nature.[57]

In the face of insufficient scientific knowledge to guide our interactions with the natural world, these nature's visionaries appealed to a natural ethic to offer the basis for environmental protection. Aldo Leopold's vision of ecology was the most explicit early ecological effort to articulate such a natural ethic, built not upon Darwinian competition, but rather upon the cooperative duties of humans to nature derived from the reciprocal relations among all life. Recognizing such ethical relations justified Leopold in supporting the extermination of predators based upon an obligation to protect the entire natural community, thus providing a basis for the newly-emergent profession of game management.[58]

Another ethical point of view appealed to the values of health. The microbiologist Rene Dubos introduced the notion that human health and illness may be the result of adaption to a constantly changing nature.[59] Nature, its evolution and its pollution create stresses for the human organism resulting in ill health. Recent concepts of ecosystem health and environmental health embody and develop his insights.[60]

In summary, despite these different views of nature and the ways to protect it, the early major naturalists/ecologists share the view of nature as a whole, complex system of interrelated and interdependent elements to be respected and protected from thoughtless human action.[61] This view of nature is (or should be) central to the science of ecology and the field of environmental law, and it is the view that we will adhere to in this volume and later volumes.

The Dawn of Protection

The love of nature expressed through various ecological visions often led the early ecologists to seek to protect nature through legal means. However, this urge to protect nature was not universal. Darwin, for example, shrank from drawing political conclusions from his discoveries. The "social Darwinians" did not hesitate.[62] If Darwin was reluctant to step to the barricades of the battle to protect nature, the rest of the early ecologists were not. Thoreau's studies of seed dispersion and forest succession led to his recommendations for restoring the New England forests.[63] George Perkins Marsh's recommen-dations as Vermont Fisheries Commissioner included control of erosion to protect Vermont's "fishing streams." Muir's hikes across the Sierras and his unique experience with wilderness prompted his fight to establish and protect the western national parks.[64] Leopold's wilderness ethic led to his estab-lishment of the game management profession and laws governing it.[65] Haeckel, minter of the term "oecologie," founded the "Monist League," whose members were prominent reformers and political agitators.[66] Rene Dubos,[67] the micro-biologist and early global ecologist, became a major spokesman for the environmental health movement beginning in the 1960s.[68]

Despite the grand underlying themes pertaining to the environment as framed by the early visionaries, their vision was peripheral to the onrush of development in the nineteenth and early twentieth centuries. The momentum of development has led to the contrasting of the legal, political and ethical themes of the nature visionaries. For example, the degree to which respect should be accorded non-human nature is now much debated.[69] This debate, in turn, is often part of another debate about the extent to which humanity should be viewed as part of nature.[70] There also is little agreement on the scope and seriousness of the threats to our environment.[71] Environmentalists and others are still seeking to determine the appropriate role of science in general, and ecology in particular, in the understanding and appreciation of nature and its complexity.[72] To be sure, all have come to realize the harms to humans from our abuses of nature, and our need and ability to control those abuses. Yet the appropriate role for law and ecology remains a subject of intense discussion.[73] Nevertheless, the nature visionaries have bequeathed to us the questions we must answer, but we still have to articulate satisfactory answers about the role of science and law in protecting their new vision of nature.

Legal History Before the Advent of Ecology and Environmental Law

Early legal history, preceding the modern era of ecology and environmental law, is the story of the gradual and grudging adjustment of law to accommodate the use of ecology and science for environmental protection. This adjustment would require centralized planning and management for the protection and sustainable use of ecosystems as complex integrated systems.[74] For example, the centralized ecological management of a wildlife refuge or national forest of today is the product of a long legal evolution. The growth of law leading to such planning and regulation is a story of the emergence of regulatory administrative law.

This modern history of environmental law as a discipline stands in marked contrast to the history of ecology,[75] which in its earliest development contained the seeds of a holistic view of nature.[76] No central vision of a holistic interdependent nature entered the legal world until the 1960s. After a flurry of attention in the early 1970s, an ecological perspective did not emerge again until the 1980s, with a new set of issues including biodiversity and global change. Instead, lawyers and legal scholars responded to the need to promote the careful development and protection of specific natural resources on a case by case basis.

In the nineteenth century, environmental issues were treated either as aspects of property, tort common law doctrines or specialized statutes.[77] These statutes included a myriad of local public nuisance laws,[78] as well as the 1891 Forest Reserve Act,[79] the 1899 Refuse Act,[80] the Esch-Hughes Act of 1912,[81] the Federal Water Pollution Control Act of 1948,[82] the 1955 Clean Air legis-lation,[83] as well as national park legislation extending back to the late 1800s.[84]

In response to the increasing awareness of the environment during the first half of the twentieth century law, books and articles were written on wildlife and game laws, agricultural law, water resources, flood protection, and forest management. Yet not one was written about environmental law, let alone the law of ecosystems!

The consequence of this early piecemeal legal approach to nature and environment lingered to the end of the twentieth century. Even in 2001, separate sets of laws operate within the realms of federal and state common law and statutes. Most environmental law is statutory and bodies of statutes are now established for resource development or protective approaches to specific resources within the environment. These statutes and their underlying regulations are administered by different sets of "experts," and a loose collection of departments and agencies are established at the federal and state levels of government to execute "environmental policy."[85] (Recent efforts to "reorganize" these subjects according to ecosystemic or other principles within state and federal governments will be described later in this volume.)

Despite this persistent fragmentation of environmental law, in the century preceding the environmental law era, the building blocks for modern environmental law were being laid by scholars in legal subjects which on the surface seem far removed from environmental law; i.e., constitutional and administrative property, evidence, and other traditional areas of law. *They established a foundation for environmental law which included (1) the adoption of an instrumental view, i.e., law was viewed as a tool for public policy in general (and later for the protection of the environment); (2) the recognition of the importance of science in legal decisionmaking, and in the legislative, administrative and adjudicative processes; (3) the adoption of a system of administrative regulation and adjudication, which has become one of the principal mechanisms for environmental regulation; (4) the recognition of the full gambit of the constitutional powers to regulate interstate commerce and spending, as well as the state police power, both of which constitutionally undergird environmental protection law; and (5) the articulation of a law and policy approach that enabled a legal system to structure land use and environmental planning and regulation.* With these building blocks, these early major legal scholars laid the basis for the emergence of a modern environmental law regime.[86]

The Instrumental View of Law

Roscoe Pound, Dean of Harvard Law School, was a principal modern figure advocating the instrumental approach to law in the early twentieth century.[87] As a former botanist, Pound was deeply interested in the early ecology movement before entering the law. He urged the adoption of legislation as an instrument of public reform based upon social inquiry rather than reliance only upon the common law. Among the several public interests he believed should be pursued by law was a limitation on the consumption of allegedly scarce natural resources. To Pound, the instrumental approach to law required "more science and more research."[88]   Pound also held onto his early botanical education, adopting an "organic view of society" and the growth of law, keeping alive – at least in metaphor – the relationship between law and nature. From this point of view, his work may be seen as an early part of a tradition of viewing law in evolutionary terms: a tradition which continues today!

The Introduction of Science into Law

Ecological information, as one of the many materials of science, is used within the legislative, administrative, and judicial processes of environmental law. The workings of courts may offer the best window into understanding the relation of law and science. In the 1800s, scientific evidence in one form or another was initially admitted into courts as the evidence of experts. Such evidence was quickly made subservient to the adversary process, in which the contending parties submitted the evidence. Beginning with Jeremy Bentham and later through John Henry Wigmore, Edmond Morgan and others,[89] scholars established a rationalist tradition for guiding the admission of evidence. This rationalist tradition sought to find ways in which to admit scientific evidence in the search for a truth that would support "rectitude of decision." This rationalist, pro-scientific tradition was part of a growing faith in science, which was seized by the influential Oliver Wendell Holmes and also gave birth to the movement of legal realism.

In *Principles of Judicial Proof*, Wigmore sought to provide a coherent framework of general principles of proof and he welcomed those recent developments of science within the courts. In 1923, he endorsed the Supreme Court decision permitting the admission of scientific evidence under the so-called *"Frye* rule."[90]   His successor, Edmund Morgan, urged even freer admission of evidence as set forth in the 1942 American Law Institute Model Code of Evidence.[91] Although the code was not adopted, in 1961 the Federal Rules of Evidence[92] was adopted, setting the stage for the battles over the environmental evidence submitted in the courts of the 1960s and the environmental era to follow. Most science, however, was to enter the law through a different door, viz., administrative agencies.

The Growth of a System of Administrative Law

Regulation and protection of the environment are pursued through the intricacies of federal and state administrative law, in which administrative agencies issue regulations and permits that govern potential offenders. Although many judges, lawyers, legal scholars and economists helped to fashion our regulatory system within the environmental law regime, James Landis, a member of three regulatory commissions during the New Deal (a period of immense growth of the regulatory system), Dean of Harvard Law School, and author of a landmark study of the administrative process,[93] played an especially important role. Landis championed the necessity of independent regulatory commissions, with the power and expertise to govern a complex economy and set of human activities. Similar, albeit non-independent, federal and state regulatory agencies now seek to resolve our complex environmental problems.

Another key legal figure in the history of administrative law was Louis Jaffee, whose law journal articles of the 1950s led to the classic work *Judicial Control of Administrative Action*.[94] This work articulated the ways in which the judiciary could control the administrative agencies at the behest of citizens, hence providing a beginning legal basis for the challenges by environmental citizen groups in the 1960s and beyond.

An Expanded Constitutional Power to Regulate the Environment

Unlike the constitutions of many other nations,[95] the United States Constitution lacks an explicit affirmative power to regulate the environment. Such a power, however, is implied in the federal interstate commerce and spending clauses, as well as the police power of the federal and state governments.

The legal scholar who laid the intellectual foundations for the environmental law regime fifty years prior to its development was University of Chicago scholar, Ernst Freund. In his monumental 1904 book, *The Police Power: Public Policy and Constitutional Rights*,[96] Freund laid out the extensive federal and state police powers that could be evoked on behalf of the environment (i.e., government power to promote public welfare by restricting the use of liberty and property; for Freund, "public welfare," extended to a wide range of social and economic interests, including health and safety). Freund argued that such powers were primarily subject to the carefully defined limits set by constitutional rights of equality, freedom and vested property. Freund was quite clear that such vested property rights did not prohibit the regulation of property for health and safety, a controversial aspect of environmental law today.

In the mid-twentieth century, the central figure responsible for the expanded constitutional vision of the powers of the federal government to regulate commerce was Felix Frankfurter, a Harvard law professor, an advisor to President Roosevelt, and a Supreme Court Justice during the expansion of the New Deal.[97] In his Supreme Court opinions, Frankfurter limited access for challenges to federal power, set forth a permissive standard of review of federal agency action, and accepted the agency's interpretations of their own authorizing statutes and findings of fact.[98] These decisions were to greatly strengthen the hand of the federal government in future environmental regulation.

The Advent of Law and Policy

In the 1930s, several major figures advanced the importance of planning our nation's economy and natural resources. During the second World War, such planning was a necessity, but after the war, the ideology and motivation for public planning declined. During this period of inattention in the 1940s and 1950s, Harold Lasswell and Myres MacDougal nonetheless articulated the role of the lawyer as a public planner.[99] MacDougal advanced a law and policy approach in his property law text, *Property, Wealth and Land*,[100] arguing, among other things, the importance of regional planning and natural resources protection. A student of MacDougal, Vermont Law School's Norman Williams urged the importance of legally enabled public land use and environmental planning as early as the 1960s.[101]

Not only did the law of land use planning gradually lead to one kind of environmental planning, as revealed in McHarg's *Design With Nature,* but the law which enabled such land use planning to take place was gradually extended to other kinds of plans for water use, river basins, air quality, and natural parks,[102] and stimulated a more sustainable use of land and materials. The emergence of "green design" and "cradle to grave" management practices have their roots in the work of McHarg.[103]

The Evolution of Ecology as a Scientific Discipline[104]

By the beginning of the 1950s, the development of ecology and its interaction with law to form an ecosystemic regime was most closely associated with two major sub-disciplines: ecosystem and population ecology.[105] Until the 1950s, these two areas had separate defining histories and, more importantly for our purposes, were to have distinct influences in both the development of ecology and environmental law.

Some historians and ecologists date the origins of ecology to Aristotle.[106] Others date the beginning of the modern discipline of ecology, as a field separate from natural history, philosophy, or ethics "with the application of experimental and mathematical methods to the analysis of organism-environment relations, community structure and succession," in the late nineteenth and early twentieth centuries.[107] However, this starting point ignores the mostly descriptive and non-mathematical studies of Charles Darwin and other early visionaries which many historians of ecology and working ecologists, believe built the pillars of modern ecology.[108] We agree, and will assume that the modern science of ecology began with the publication of Charles Darwin's *On the Origin of the Species* in 1859.[109] Darwin's theory of natural selection, in which he explained the origin and evolution of species as a process arising out of the competition of individuals of the same species for scarce environmental resources, is explicitly based upon the core principle of ecology – the interaction of organisms and environment. It was Darwin's idea which transformed all of the life sciences and inspired the development of the science of ecology.[110]

The term "oecology" was created in 1866 by the German biologist Ernst Haeckel to describe a new branch of physiology,[111] designed for the study of the environmentally mediated natural selection outlined by Darwin.[112] "Ecology" was first used in America in the 1890s by a few botanists who had become dissatisfied with traditional descriptive natural history and wanted an experimental approach to adaptation, population interactions, and community organization.[113] The lead taken by botanists in ecology lasted until the 1920s, when animal ecologists started to make significant advances in the study of populations and the creation of population ecology.[114]

However, while early ecology was largely divided among botanists and zoologists, the first American ecologist, Stephen Forbes, was a natural historian whose concern with the relationships between organisms, regardless of whether they were plants or animals, would foreshadow much of the later developments in community and ecosystem ecology.[115] In his 1887 essay, *The Lake as a Microcosm*, Forbes used his knowledge of Darwin's theory to describe how a lake community achieved, through competition and predation among organisms, the "balance of nature" that Forbes and others believed was the normal state of any natural system.[116] The "balance of nature" concept is possibly the earliest ecological concept and assumes that diversity of plants and animals is required to maintain balance within ecosystems.[117] The concept and its companion concept of equilibrium, flourished within the history of social and economic thought as well as the non-scientific environmental movement of the 1960s and 1970s. Through this environmental movement, the concept was embodied within many of the environmental statutes and regulations of this period. As ecologists have learned more about the dynamic, non-equilibrium, nature of ecological systems, the "balance of nature" has been replaced with the idea that ecosystem diversity is necessary to maintain a dynamic, rather than a stable, ecosystem. However, the "balance of nature" concept still maintains a hold upon many non-ecologist environmentalists and the general public.

Forbes, like many early ecologists, partially justified his work because of its potentially practical benefit. In his case it was his belief that an understanding of food webs would provide a scientific basis for agriculture.[118] However, the other purpose of his research was to test the new science of evolutionary biology.[119] Unfortunately, while most of the other early American ecologists used important concepts from Darwinian theory (e.g., competition) they were not Darwinists, since they did not accept that natural selection among individuals was the guiding force behind evolution. This rejection of the critical concept of Darwinism would result in the loss of the early connection between ecology and evolutionary biology that Forbes had begun.[120] It was only decades later that ecology and evolutionary biology were rejoined.

The use of ecology in the U.S. university system took hold among botanists at the University of Nebraska and the University of Chicago at the turn of the century.[121] At Nebraska, Frederic Clements became the leading American ecologist of these times through his study of ecological succession in the grassland communities of the Midwest.[122] The seemingly stable species composition of grasslands led Clements to a view that most, if not all, plant communities were at or moving to a stable end point or "climax," at which they would remain unchanged unless disturbed by humans.[123] Clements formalized "climax communities" as one of the first "big ideas" in ecology. The concept that stability is the "normal" endpoint of all natural systems has had a major effect on ecology, the environmental movement, and environmental law. Early environmentalists and ecologically inclined environmental lawyers sought to protect natural systems by maintaining or establishing stability within the system.[124] Ecological stability, either separately or as part of the "balance of nature" and equilibrium concepts, would dominate ecology into the 1970s.[125] Stability, like balance of nature, has only recently been questioned by the newer scientific view that most, if not all, natural systems are in a constant state of change, a disequilibrium.[126]

Clements also envisioned the plant community as a "complex supra-organism" in which the life cycle of a plant community is analogous to those of individual organisms.[127] While Clements' use of the "community as organism" as a metaphor was hotly debated, it did provide the early inspiration for research and speculation on the nature of communities that would lead to the development of the "ecosystem concept."[128]

The other major figure at the beginning of American ecology, also a botanist, was Henry Cowles of the University of Chicago. Cowles also studied plant community succession. However, unlike the stable grassland communities that were Clements' early research focus, Cowles concentrated on the unstable (physical and temporal) sand dune communities of Lake Michigan.[129] While Cowles believed that the succession of plant communities was moving toward a stable equilibrium, he did not believe, as did Clements, that the equilibrium point climax was ever reached.[130] Cowles viewed communities as a constantly changing interaction of living and non-living components. This spatially and temporally "dynamic ecology" stressed the overall processes involved in the formation of communities over the success and failure of individual populations. Such processes include the cycling of nutrients through the living and non-living parts of an ecosystem as well as the movement of energy starting with the Sun's solar energy through its conversion by photosynthetic plants and its eventual incorporation into herbivores and carnivores.

With Clements and Cowles leading the way, American ecology, by the 1920s, had become the detailed, empirical study of dynamic systems of interaction between the living components and environmental factors making up a local community. However, the 1920s would witness the rise of a new animal ecology that believed an understanding of the formation of communities was best achieved by studying the processes that controlled the distribution and abundance of individual populations.[131] This juncture continued with the formation of distinct approaches to the study of the environment, one centered on populations, the other on something bigger; termed variously as biomes, communities, and eventually ecosystems.[132]

The Beginnings of Ecosystem Ecology. Ecosystem ecology developed for the purposes of understanding both the function of specific pieces of nature (e.g., a single lake) and the general rules that governed the function of all ecosystems.[133] As discussed above, ecosystem research has predominantly used a holistic approach in which the ecosystem is studied as a functional and structural whole, and each plant and animal population within an ecosystem, along with each abiotic factor (e.g., hydrologic cycle) is treated as one component of a complex system.[134] It was ecosystem ecology, mostly as interpreted by the popular environmental movement of the 1960s, that was one major influence in the development of the environmental statutes of the 1960s and 1970s.[135]

Many early ecologists were in agreement that ecology should focus on the study of the function (i.e., the physiology) of some unit of nature. However, there was disagreement about which unit of nature should be studied; the individual, population, community or something even bigger, such as Clements' amorphous biome concept.[136]

Clements' complex organism concept of biological communities was attacked, almost immediately, as being not just impractical, but wrong. Tansley criticized the concept as a metaphor that did not accurately capture the interactions between physical and biological components.[137] Tansley's ecosystem concept, articulated in 1935, corrected this deficiency by including both physical and biological concepts in its definition. Thus the ecosystem concept permitted ecologists to continue to approach the study of nature holistically without resorting to unproven metaphors of superorganisms.[138] The ecosystem concept drew upon a rich tradition of thought about systems in general, but without explicitly articulating its connections to systems theory or to the work of physicists and philosophers who were then writing about systems.[139]

The major advance in ecosystem ecology for the first half of the twentieth century occurred in 1942 with the publication of Raymond Lindeman's article, *The Trophic-Dynamic Aspect of Ecology*.[140] His "trophic dynamic" approach provided an experimental methodology and a new conceptual emphasis for ecosystem studies.[141] On the small Cedar Bog Lake in Minnesota, Lindeman and his wife intensively sampled organisms from the sediment and different levels of the lake during all seasons.[142] Lindeman explicitly used Tansley's ecosystem as the basic unit of nature, which he then divided into different trophic (feeding) levels determined by the movement of energy (food) from producers (e.g., photosynthetic plants) to consumers (e.g., carnivores) . He showed that these different trophic levels were linked by the transfer of biomass and energy from one level to another to form a food web. In a lake or pond, this could mean the flow of energy from photosynthetic water plants and algae to small crustaceans and insects and, finally to the fish that eat them.

Lindeman was the first to make energy transfer the prime focus of ecosystem study and to provide a methodology for its study.[143] Future ecosystem ecologists would make "energy transfer" a means of comparing the function of diverse types of ecosystems. Finally, and most importantly, Lindeman introduced a new level of abstraction and mathematical analysis into ecology that would become a hallmark of ecosystem study. Lindeman's approach of grouping ecosystem components that performed similar functions together, and then studying the dynamic process of energy flow between groups, would eventually become the dominant methodology of ecosystem ecology for the next 40 years.[144]

After the publication of Lindeman's article, there was only a slow awareness and acceptance of ecosystem and trophic dynamic concepts, even by plant ecologists who had been the early leaders in "holistic" ecology. However, this lack of appreciation of Lindeman's work ended in 1953 with the publication of Eugene Odum's influential textbook, *Fundamentals of Ecology*, in which the ecosystem, energy flow, and trophic dynamics were used as the fundamental organizing principles of ecology.[145] We shall discuss Odum's work in the next chapter.

The Birth of Population Ecology. In contrast to the holistic approach of ecosystem ecology, traditional population ecologists would focus on one or a few interacting populations and attempt to discover what factors control the "distribution and abundance" of these populations.[146] While these factors can include non-living components of the environment, most population ecologists concentrated on the study of the interactions among populations.[147] Recently, population ecology has become an important part of the ecosystemic regime as one of the components of the new conservation biology. Through conservation biology, population ecology theories and data have even found their way into the judicial opinions of many judges.[148]

A true population ecology began in the 1920s with the development of two important concepts that were to define this field; the ecological niche and competitive exclusion.[149] The niche has been defined in various ways, but one simple and useful one, developed by Elton in 1927, is the place in a food web occupied by each population within a habitat.[150] Competitive exclusion is the result of competition among population for these various niches.[151] The methodology developed by early population ecologists was the mathematical analysis of population demographics and interactions.[152]

The Russian ecologist Georgii Gause stressed, through both his experimental and mathematical work, the central importance that competitive exclusion had in population ecology.[153] Gause was the first to test population models in a laboratory and, in the 1930s, he developed the idea that competition among species would force species into separate niches.[154] This competition resulted in the stable regulated community structure that appeared to be the normal (i.e., equilibrium) state of nature. Competition became the means to relate populations with community structure and succession. Gause's work on competitive exclusion helped to make competition a central organizing concept of ecology in the 1950s and 1960s.

The development of mathematical population ecology began in 1920 with the work of Raymond Pearl, a statistician studying the growth of the human population. Pearl discovered that human population growth over time appeared as a "S-shaped" curve that he called the "logistic curve."[155] This discovery was vital to human (and non-human) demographics because it provided a simple graphical and mathematical principle to a common feature of all populations; that population growth is self-limiting and will cease to grow upon reaching its "carrying capacity" (the population size that can be supported by the environment). The differential equation that describes the logistic curve, $dN/dt = rN (K-N)/K$, is arguably the fundamental concept of population ecology, since most later mathematical work (and experimental work that tests the models) on predation, competition, and other forms of population interaction are elaborations of this simple model.[156]

Concurrently with Pearl, the Italian physicist Vito Volterra also developed the logistic equation to develop models of competition between two species.[157] Volterra also developed, concurrently with the American mathematical ecologist Alfred Lotka,[158] the two species competition and predation models which are now known collectively to ecologists as the Lotka-Volterra equations.[159] This model, like Volterra's competition model was an elaboration of the basic logistic function with added parameters representing the effects of a second population on the primary population's growth over time.

None of the early mathematical ecologists had as much wide-ranging influence as the American Alfred Lotka.[160] Lotka's interest in population growth and interaction arose out of his desire to make ecology more mathematical and predictive. Lotka carried out analyses of stable populations and, as mentioned above, of predator-prey interactions. Further, Lotka used systems of simultaneous differential equations to analyze population interactions, a method similar to the "general system theory" developed by Bertalanffy in the 1950s, which was a basis of system ecology.[161] Unfortunately, Bertalanffy did not credit Lotka for his prior work, and one early possibility to connect ecosystem and population ecology through system theory may have been lost. Lotka would influence ecosystem ecology, both through the application of his "energy" flow concepts by Lindeman[162] and by the later recognition and use of his work by Eugene and Thomas Odum.[163]

While mathematical population ecology would continue to develop during the first half of the twentieth century,[164] the work of Alfred Lotka is a fitting place to end our early history of ecology. Lotka's interest spanned more than just ecology or biology, to encompass the human realms of politics, economics, and the effects of technology on society. He worked diligently to apply his research to these human problems, a trait not particularly common for the other ecologists of his day, but one more apparent among some of today's ecologists. Therefore, Lotka provides an excellent early example of the ways in which ecological insights have always been applicable to human concerns. Further, Lotka also shares with many ecologists, past and present, the trait of having his work largely ignored by the non-ecologist policy makers of his day. However, Lotka's contributions to both population and ecosystem ecology, and his interest in various other scientific and non-scientific fields, does provide an early twentieth century example of both the integration and application of ecology.

Conclusion

The century preceding the emergence of ecology in the mid-twentieth century confronted the United States with a dilemma. On the one hand, there emerged a nation deeply committed to economic growth, often at the expense of the environment. On the other hand, this brutal process of industrialization produced a reaction reflected both in the works of the nature visionaries of the nineteenth century and the New Deal of the twentieth century. Environmental law was to build its legal edifice on the foundation of the administrative law shaped by the New Deal. Ecology, while borrowing some of its fundamental concepts of "an economy of nature,"[165] also was animated by a deep love of natural non-human species and the places in which they lived.

Ecosystem and population ecologists have traditionally been separated by the philosophical and methodological division between "reductionism" and "holism."[166] The "reductionist" approach in biology depends upon isolating and studying single components of natural systems. Classical physiology and molecular biology are examples of reductionist science in which a single element of an organism (e.g., the heart or a single gene) is studied in isolation of the entire individual. The "holistic" approach depends upon the identification and study of functional units and processes involving multiple components (e.g., energy flow through a food chain of a lake ecosystem). Believers in the holistic approach argue that for most natural systems, important information concerning the interaction of the system's components is lost when they are studied in isolation.[167] While the appropriateness of relying on a holistic or reductionist approach in ecology has been the source of debate, both approaches have informed the science adopted in modern ecosystemic laws.

The traditional division between ecological subdisciplines, particularly ecosystem and population ecology, has been and continues to be an important element in the histories of ecology and environmental law. Each of these two fields was separately introduced into environmental law in the late twentieth century. Population biology was transmitted via conservation biology into the forest and wildlife law. Ecosystem ecology made its debut in laws such as the Coastal Zone Management Act and the National Environmental Policy Act. However, as we described in Chapter 1, there is a relatively new attempt to integrate these once separate areas of ecology. This has resulted in a growing concern, by ecosystem ecologists, for the biology of the organisms within an ecosystem and, by population ecologists, the realization that the non-living components of an environment, and the flows of energy within an ecosystem, must be understood.[168] However, to fully appreciate this current trend towards a more integrated ecology it is necessary to understand the divisions that historically separated ecology and ecologists. A more important separation in the late nineteenth and early twentieth century was the diremption between our public culture, largely committed to growth and largely impervious to the abuses to nature which such growth created. It was this nature whose interconnections were being slowly uncovered by the new sciences of biology and ecology. But even those who lamented the impacts of the industrial revolution were largely unaware of the birth of sciences which were to transform their lives at the end of the twentieth century.

This history leaves the ecology and environmental law of the present day with two kinds of questions. There remains a potential chasm between a society and economy deeply committed to economic growth and the new ecosystemic regime composed, in part, of an ecology and environmental law historically shaped in reaction to this growth. One must ask a series of questions about the power of an ecosystemic regime and whether its science and laws are strong enough to contain our economy by means of administrative regulation.[169]

A second series of questions may be addressed to the bifurcated tradition of ecology with its population biology and ecosystem ecology. Is an integrated ecology possible? Is it possible to join the reductive nature of population biology and the holistic perspective of ecosystem biology?

Notes

1.   MICHEL DE MONTAGNE, *Of Experience*, ESSAYS, III, 13.
2.   In a previous suit, residents secured damages. *See* Madison v. Ducktown Sulphur, Copper and Iron Co., 113 Tenn. 331, 83 S.W. 658 (1904). The first quotation above is from Georgia v. Tennessee Copper Co., 206 U.S. 230 (1907). For a history of the litigation, *see* ROBERT PERCIVAL ET AL., ENVIRONMENTAL REGULATION: LAW, SCIENCE AND POLICY at 75-84, 97-102 (1992).
3.   *Id.*
4.   For a different point of view regarding the effectiveness of common law protection of the environment, *see* BRUCE YANDLE, COMMON SENSE AND COMMON LAW FOR THE ENVIRONMENT: CREATING WEALTH IN HUMMINGBIRD ECONOMICS (1997).
5.   CHARLES DICKENS, BLEAK HOUSE (1853).
6.   This definition of public culture is an adjustment of "public philosophy" as used in MICHAEL SANDEL, DEMOCRACIES DISCONTENT: AMERICA IN SEARCH OF A PUBLIC PHILOSOPHY 4 (1996). *See also* JOHN RAWLS, POLITICAL LIBERALISM 13 (1993) (adopting a similar notion of "public political culture" as a shared fund of basic ideas and principles).
7.   *See* SHEPARD KREICH, THE ECOLOGICAL INDIAN: MYTH AND HISTORY (1999).
8.   More inclusive histories have been written. *See generally* JOSEPH M. PETULLA, AMERICAN ENVIRONMENTAL HISTORY: THE EXPLOITATION AND CONSERVATION OF NATURAL RESOURCES (1977); RICHARD N.L. ANDREWS, MANAGING THE ENVIRONMENT, MANAGING OURSELVES: A HISTORY OF AMERICAN ENVIRONMENTAL POLICY (1999).
9.   For one of several accounts of this system, *see* ANDREWS, *supra* note 8 at 28-51. Behind the notion of private property is the division of its geography in accordance with human uses and the market place, the private control of its possession, use and disposal (although there were early limits upon "waste"), and the corresponding absence of community control.
10.   This cavalier attitude towards land was documented and criticized by J. HECTOR ST. JOHN DE CREVE COEUR, in his LETTERS FROM AN AMERICAN FARMER 354 (1782).
11.   *See* U.S. CONSTITUTION, ARTICLE IV, SECTION 2.
12.   Although the reference here is to lands which are treated as commons lands at law, a non-legal common landscape emerged as well, described in JOHN R. STILGOE, COMMON LANDSCAPE OF AMERICA, 1580 TO 1845 (1982).
13.   We shall discuss the concept of the public trust below.

14.   The notion of the governance of the commons is set forth in ELINOR OSTROM, GOVERNING THE COMMONS: THE EVOLUTION OF INSTITUTIONS FOR COLLECTIVE ACTION (1990).

15.   *See* JENNIFER NEDELSKY, PRIVATE PROPERTY AND THE LIMITS OF AMERICAN CONSTITUTIONALISM: THE MADISONIAN FRAMEWORK AND ITS LEGACY (1990).

16.   *See* G. WOOD, THE CREATION OF THE AMERICAN REPUBLIC, 1776-1787 (1978). *See also* J.G.A. POCOCK, THE MACHIAVELLIAN MOMENT: FLORENTINE POLITICAL THOUGHT AND THE ATLANTIC REPUBLICAN TRADITION (1975).

17.   For a comprehensive discussion of property as applied within the civic republican tradition, *see* Gregory S. Alexander, *Time and Property in the American Republican Legal Culture*, 66 N.Y.U. L. REV. 273 (1991).

18.   *See* LEO MARX, THE MACHINE IN THE GARDEN: TECHNOLOGY AND THE PASTORAL IDEAL IN AMERICA (1964).

19.   For an idealistic view of the relationship between farming and democracy, *see* WENDELL BERRY, THE UNSETTLING OF AMERICA: CULTURE AND AGRICULTURE 143 (1977); WHITNEY GRISWOLD, FARMING AND DEMOCRACY (1948) offers a more skeptical look at the relationship.

20.   *See* I. BERNARD COHEN, SCIENCE AND THE FOUNDING FATHERS, SCIENCE IN THE POLITICAL THOUGHT OF THOMAS JEFFERSON, BENJAMIN FRANKLIN, JOHN ADAMS AND JAMES MADISON (1995).

21.   This technological focus is reflected in the U.S. Constitution, which mentions science in the context of protecting patent rights. *See* U.S. CONSTITUTION, ARTICLE 8 (8).

22.   For a discussion of this issue, *see* ENCYCLOPEDIA BRITANNICA, INC., THE ANNALS OF AMERICA: GREAT ISSUES IN AMERICAN LIFE: A CONSPECTUS, VOLUME II, 500 (1968).

23.   JOAN BURBICK, HEALING THE REPUBLIC: THE LANGUAGE OF HEALTH AND CULTURE OF NATIONALISM IN NINETEENTH-CENTURY AMERICA 1 (1994).

24.   ALEXIS DETOQUEVILLE, DEMOCRACY IN AMERICA (Henry Reeve, trans., 1947).

25.   *See* PETULLA, *supra* note 8.

26.   *See* WILLIAM CRONON, NATURE'S METROPOLIS: CHICAGO AND THE GREAT WEST (1991).

27.   *Id.* at 206.

28.   JOSEPH TARR, THE SEARCH FOR THE ULTIMATE SINK, URBAN POLLUTION IN HISTORICAL PERSPECTIVE (1996).

29.   For an English perspective, *see* KARL POLYANI, THE GREAT TRANSFORMATION 135-162 (1944).

30.   BURBICK, *supra* note 23.

31.   *See* ROBERT SHALHOPE, BENNINGTON AND THE GREEN MOUNTAIN BOYS: THE EMERGENCE OF LIBERAL DEMOCRACY IN VERMONT 1760-1850, at 258 (1996).

32.   *See* MAX WEBER, THE PROTESTANT ETHIC AND THE SPIRIT OF CAPITALISM (1930).

33.   *See* ECOLOGICAL STEWARDSHIP: A COMMON REFERENCE FOR ECOSYSTEM MANAGEMENT (W.T. Sexton et al. eds., 1999).

34.   Few theorists have proposed no economic growth policies, and those who have are clearly marginalized, both in society and in academia. For one effort, *see* TOWARD A STEADY-STATE ECONOMY (Herman E. Daly ed., 1973).

35.   *See* CHARLES DARWIN, ORIGIN OF THE SPECIES BY MEANS OF NATURAL SELECTION OR THE PRESERVATION OF FAVORED RACES IN THE STRUGGLE FOR LIFE (E. Mayr ed., 1964).

36.   *See* RODERICK FRAZIER NASH, THE RIGHTS OF NATURE: A HISTORY OF ENVIRONMENTAL ETHICS (1989).

37.   GIFFORD PINCHOT, BREAKING NEW GROUND (1947). For a general history on the conservation movement, *see* STEPHEN FOX, THE AMERICAN CONSERVATION MOVEMENT: JOHN MUIR AND HIS LEGACY (1985).

38.   It remained for an ecologically informed conservation movement of the late twentieth century to restore the tree to its habitat.

39.   *See* BRUCE A. ACKERMAN, WE THE PEOPLE: FOUNDATIONS I, 105-131 (1991).

40.   *See* JAMES K. McCRAW, THE PROPHETS OF REGULATION (1984).

41.   *See* BRUCE A. ACKERMAN & WILLIAM T. HASSLER, CLEAN COAL, DIRTY AIR (1981) at 4-6; for an account of later planning, *see* Charles Reich, *The Law of the Planned Society*, 75 Yale L.J. 1227 (1966).

42.   There are numerous histories and surveys of ecology and environmental sciences. *See generally*, STEPHEN BOCKING, ECOLOGISTS AND ENVIRONMENTAL POLITICS (1997); PETER BOWKER, THE ENVIRONMENTAL SCIENCES (1992); ANNA BRAMWELL, ECOLOGY IN THE 20TH CENTURY: A HISTORY (1989); PETER COATES, NATURE: WESTERN ATTITUDES SINCE ANCIENT TIMES (1998); CLARENCE GLACKEN, TRACES OF THE RHODIAN SHORE (1967); FRANK BENJAMIN GOLLEY, A HISTORY OF THE ECOSYSTEM CONCEPT IN ECOLOGY: MORE THAN THE SUM OF ITS PARTS (1993); PETER MARSHALL, NATURE'S WEB: AN EXPLORATION OF ECOLOGICAL THINKING (1992); PETER MARSHALL, NATURE'S WEB: RETHINKING OUR PLACE ON EARTH (1993); CAROLYN MERCHANT, THE DEATH OF NATURE: WOMEN, ECOLOGY AND THE SCIENTIFIC REVOLUTION (1980); DONALD WORSTER, NATURE'S ECONOMY: THE ROOTS OF ECOLOGY (1977). For related histories of wilderness *see*, e.g., RODERICK NASH, WILDERNESS AND THE AMERICAN MIND (3d. ed. 1982). *See also* MAX OELSHLAGER, THE IDEA OF WILDERNESS (1991). There have been few treatments of ecology as an outgrowth of systems studies and its relationship to complexity. *But see* FRITJOF CAPRA, THE WEB OF LIFE (1996). *See also* NICHOLAS RESCHER, COMPLEXITY: A PHILOSOPHICAL OVERVIEW (1998); BIODIVERSITY (E.O. Wilson, Ed., 1988, 1989).

43.   The myriad of nature writings best capture this love of nature. For two excellent overviews of this literature, *see generally*, LAWRENCE BUELL, THE ENVIRONMENTAL IMAGINATION: THOREAU'S NATURE WRITING AND THE FORMATION OF AMERICAN CULTURE (1995); SIMON SCHAMA, LANDSCAPE AND MEMORY (1995).

44.   Most of the major figures in ecology were relatively naive about the role of law in environmental protection. They turned to law as an instrument to be freely employed, seldom realizing the subtle biases and conceptual underpinnings which make it difficult to adopt law for environmental protection.

45.   The selection of these figures is somewhat arbitrary. Since there are a myriad of different histories of "ecology," *see supra* note 42, there are a myriad of different "major" figures. A literary history finds the roots of our current environmentalism in the pastoral tradition, the literary themes of the simple life, the Transcendentalists' romanticism and much more. *See*, e.g., BUELL, *supra* note 43. Anna Bramwell finds a darker history in the German authors leading to the rise of the German fascist movement. *See* BRAMWELL, *supra* note 42. Frank Golley, a scientific ecologist in his own right, finds the major figures to include little-known biologists and systems theorists. *See* GOLLEY, *supra* note 42. Consequently, the above list is a somewhat arbitrary selection among the lists of major figures.

46.   Several of the books cited in note 42 cover the history back to Greek thought. For a recent in-depth treatment of Greek environmental thought, *see* THE GREEKS AND THE ENVIRONMENT (Laura Westra & Thomas Robinson eds., 1997).

47.   *See generally* CHARLES DARWIN, THE ORIGIN OF SPECIES, THE DESCENT OF MAN (1952). *See also* FREDERIC CLEMENTS, RESEARCH METHODS IN ECOLOGY (1905); RENE DUBOS, MAN ADAPTING (1965); ERNST HAEKEL, OECOLOGIE (1866); ALDO LEOPOLD, A SAND COUNTY ALMANAC (1948); GEORGE PERKINS MARSH, MAN AND NATURE (1864); JOHN MUIR, OUR NATIONAL PARKS (1901); EUGENE ODUM, FUNDAMENTALS OF

ECOLOGY (1953); ARTHUR TINSLEY, ELEMENTS OF PLANT BIOLOGY (1922); HENRY THOREAU, WALDEN (J. Lyndon Shanley ed., 1971).

48. Each of these premises is debatable, and a vast literature discusses these debates. Without citing all the literature here, the notion of nature as an object of respect is a central topic for the field of environmental ethics. This field is best understood initially in the context of the history of ideas; *see* PETER COATES, NATURE: WESTERN ATTITUDES SINCE ANCIENT TIMES (1998). Viewing nature in holistic terms is partly the result of a lengthy intellectual history of the concept of the web of nature; *see* FRITJOF CAPRA, THE WEB OF LIFE: A NEW SCIENTIFIC UNDERSTANDING OF LIVING SYSTEMS (1996). The view of nature under threat from the activities of humans is well described recently in THE EARTH TRANSFORMED BY HUMAN ACTIONS (B.L. Turner II et al., eds 1990). The notion of complexity in nature is explored in T.F.H. ALLEN & THOMAS B. STARR, HIERARCHY: PERSPECTIVES FOR ECOLOGICAL COMPLEXITY (1982). The argument that science is the appropriate discipline for understanding nature is set forth in ANDREW BRENNAN, THINKING ABOUT NATURE: AN INVESTIGATION OF NATURE, VALUES AND ECOLOGY (1988). Accepting humans as part of a larger nature is part of an intellectual tradition going back to Aristotle and St. Thomas Aquinas as well as a myriad of religions. *See* COSMOGONY AND ETHICAL ORDER, NEW STUDIES IN COMPARATIVE ETHICS (Robin W. Lovin & Frank E. Reynolds eds., 1985).

49. In some cases, the insights of the nature visionaries were widely communicated to the reading public. Thus, Thoreau, Muir and Dubos spoke directly to the public through their works. Others, such as Marsh and Haeckel, were less widely read, and their ideas (or ideas similar to theirs) were to be found in a rich literature which portrayed many of the themes listed above. Fortunately, with the recent rise of study in environmental literature, those themes are available to us. *See*, e.g., LAWRENCE BUELL, THE ENVIRONMENTAL IMAGINATION: THOREAU, NATURE WRITING AND THE FORMATION OF AMERICAN CULTURE (1995). For example, Lawrence Buell recently reviews not only the work of Thoreau, but that of Mary Austin, John Burroughs, James Fenimore Cooper, Edgar Allen Poe, Wallace Stevens, Joseph Wood Krutch, Rachel Carson, Herman Melville and Mark Twain, to name but a few. These poets, essayists, fiction and non-fiction writers pursued the themes of pastoral ideology, new world dreams, the aesthetics of relinquishment of the self to nature, nature's personhood, the importance of natural places and times (seasons), and the metaphor of apocalypse. Perhaps the most frequent theme was the pastoral idea of "the machine in the garden" described by Leo Marx in the book of this title. *See* Leo Marx, MACHINE IN THE GARDEN: TECHNOLOGY AND THE PASTORAL IDEAL IN AMERICA (1964). As Simon Schama has sought to show, the cultural images of literature both expressed and indeed shaped our view of the environment and in turn, our environmental science, policy and law respond to these images [SIMON SCHAMA, LANDSCAPE AND MEMORY (1995)].

50. *See* George Francis, *Ecosystem Management*, 33 NAT. RESOURCES J. 315 (1993).

51. Darwin read Malthus and was deeply influenced by his writings in formulating the principle of natural selection.

52. DAVID SHI, THE SIMPLE LIFE: PLAIN LIVING AND HIGH THINKING IN AMERICAN CULTURE (1985).

53. *See* DONALD WORSTER, NATURE'S ECONOMY 94 (1977).

54. *See* JANE AND WILL CURTIS & FRANK LIEBERMAN, THE WORLD OF GEORGE PERKINS MARSH 104, 105 (1982).

55. JAMES LOVELOCK, THE AGES OF GAIA: A BIOGRAPHY OF OUR LIVING EARTH (1988).

56. For such a collection, *see* EDWIN WAY TEALE, THE WILDERNESS WORLD OF JOHN MUIR (1954).

57.   *See, e.g.*, ERAZIN KOHÁK, THE EMBERS AND THE STARS: A PHILOSOPHICAL INQUIRY INTO THE MORAL SENSE OF NATURE (1984).

58.   ALDO LEOPOLD, SAND COUNTY ALMANAC (1949).

59.   *See* DUBOS, *supra* note 47.

60.   *See* ECOSYSTEM HEALTH: NEW GOALS FOR ENVIRONMENTAL MANAGEMENT (Robert Costanza et al., eds. 1992).

61.   It is important to emphasize that the intellectual developments in biology and related fields can be organized in different ways. For an alternative view to the one presented here, *see* ERNST MAYR, THE GROWTH OF BIOLOGICAL THOUGHT: DIVERSITY, EVOLUTION AND INHERITANCE (1982). In addition, each of the subsidiary concepts within the now standard descriptions of ecology has its own intellectual history, some of which we will trace below.

62.   *See* JANET BROWNE, CHARLES DARWIN VOYAGING (1995).

63.   *See* WORSTER, *supra* note 53, at 98-111. *See also* HENRY D. THOREAU, FAITH IN A SEED, xi-xviii, 3-17 (1993).

64.   *See* TEALE, *supra* note 56, at xix, xx. *See also* Peter Manus, *One Hundred Years of Green: A Legal Perspective on Three Twentieth Century Nature Philosophers*, 59 U. PITT. L. REV. 557, 588-616 (1998).

65.   *See* SUSAN FLADER, THINKING LIKE A MOUNTAIN: ALDO LEOPOLD AND THE EVOLUTION OF ECOLOGICAL ATTITUDE TOWARD DEER, WOLVES AND FOREST 206-260 (1974).

66.   BRAMWELL, *supra* note 42, at 39-63.

67.   James Hirsch and Carol Moberg, *Rene Jules Dubos*, in 58 BIOGRAPHICAL MEMOIRS 133-150 (National Academy of Sciences 1989).

68.   *Id.* note 47.

69.   For one extensive argument on behalf of the respect for nature, *see* PAUL TAYLOR, RESPECT FOR NATURE: A THEORY OF ENVIRONMENTAL ETHICS (1986).

70.   For the most rigorous discussion of this topic, *see* MORTIMER ADLER, THE DIFFERENCE OF MAN AND THE DIFFERENCE IT MAKES (1967).

71.   For a recent well argued optimistic view, *see* GREG EASTERBROOK, A MOMENT ON THE EARTH: THE COMING AGE OF ENVIRONMENTAL OPTIMISM (1995).

72.   *See* Chapter 1, *supra*.

73.   *See id.*

74.   By centralized planning, we do not necessarily refer to national centralized planning or management, but centralization relative to the ecosystem in question. In the final section of the book, we shall reexamine the assumption of centralized ecosystem management, and introduce and evaluate critiques of such an approach.

75.   The history of environmental law and policy in the United States has been set forth in several books, including SAMUEL P. HAYS, BEAUTY, HEALTH AND PERMANENCE: ENVIRONMENTAL POLITICS IN THE UNITED STATES 1955-1985 (1987). For a brief legal account, *see* Robert Percival, *Environmental Federalism: Historical Roots and Contemporary Models*, 54 MD. L. REV. 1141 (1995); *see also* ANDREWS, *supra* note 8.

76.   For the early philosophical origins of ecology in Europe. *see* ANNA BRAMWELL, ECOLOGY IN THE TWENTIETH CENTURY: A HISTORY (1989).

77.   We are not aware of an adequate history of the emergence of environmental law out of property law that has been written. William Rodgers, in his comprehensive discussion of nuisance law, almost provides a history of tort law as leading to environmental law.

78.   For a general account of nuisance law in the environment, *see* WILLIAM ROGERS, 1 ENVTL. L. 1-126 (1986).

79.   *See* Act of May 20, 1862, Ch. 75, 12 Stat. 392.

80.   *See* Act of March 3, 1899, Ch. 425, 30 Stat. 1151 (repealed 1972).

81.   *See* Pub. L. No. 62-112, 37 Stat. 81 (1912).

82.   *See* Act of June 30, 1948, Ch. 758, 62 Stat. 1155 (completely revised by Pub. L. No. 92–500, 52, 86 Stat 816 (1972) (codified as amended at 33 U.S.C. §§ 1251-1376 (1988 & Sup. V, 1993)).

83.   *See* Air Pollution Control Act of 1955, Pub. L. 84-145, 69 Stat. 322.

84.   *See* (Yosemite) Act of June 3, 1864, Ch. 184, 13 Stat. 325.

85.   *See* U.S. National Performance Review (Environmental Protection Agency 1993).

86.   This selection of major legal scholars is somewhat arbitrary, but serves to illustrate the mode of thought.

87.   *See generally* DAVID WIGDOR, ROSCOE POUND: PHILOSOPHER OF LAW (1974); N.E.H. HULL ET AL., SEARCHING FOR AN AMERICAN JURISPRUDENCE (1997); EDWARD B. MCLEAN, LAW AND CIVILIZATION: THE LEGAL THOUGHT OF ROSCOE POUND (1992).

88.   *Id.*

89.   These paragraphs rely primarily on WILLIAM TWINING, THEORIES OF EVIDENCE: BENTHAM AND WIGMORE (1985).

90.   *See* Frye v. U.S., 293 F. 1013 (D.C. Cir. 1923); overruled by Daubet v. Merrell Dow 509 U.S. 579 113 S.Ct. 2786, 125 L.Ed. 2d 469 (1993).

91.   *See* MODEL CODE OF EVIDENCE (American Law Institute 1942).

92.   *See* FEDERAL RULES OF EVIDENCE, 28 U.S.C.A.

93.   *See* THOMAS K. MCGRAW, PROPHETS OF REGULATION: CHARLES FRANCIS ADAMS, LOUIS BRANDEIS, JAMES LANDIS, ALFRED KOHN (1984). *See also* DONALD RITCHIE, JAMES M. LANDIS: DEAN OF THE REGULATORS (1980). *See also* JAMES LANDIS: THE ADMINISTRATIVE PROCESS (1938).

94.   *See* LOIUS JAFFEE, JUDICIAL CONTROL OF ADMINISTRATIVE ACTION (1965).

95.   HUMAN RIGHTS APPROACHES TO ENVIRONMENTAL PROTECTION (Alan Boyle & Michael Anderson eds., 1996).

96.   ERNST FREUND, THE POLICE POWER: PUBLIC POLICY AND CONSTITUTIONAL RIGHTS (1904).

97.   For a discussion of Frankfurter's contribution, *see* JEFFREY HOCKETT, NEW DEAL JUSTICE: THE CONSTITUTIONAL JURISPRUDENCE OF HUGO BLACK, FELIX FRANK-FURTER, AND ROBERT JACKSON (1996). *See also* NELSON DAWSON, LOUIS BRANDEIS, FELIX FRANKFURTER AND THE NEW DEAL (1980).

98.   Of course, these "New Deal" approaches were modified by the newer doctrines of the environmental era. *See* BRUCE ACKERMAN & WILLIAM HASSLER, CLEAN COAL/DIRTY AIR 4-13 (1981).

99.   This approach is reformulated in HAROLD LASSWELL & MRYES MACDOUGAL, JURISPRUDENCE FOR A FREE SOCIETY: STUDIES IN LAW, SCIENCE AND POLICY (1992).

100.   *See* MYRES MACDOUGAL & LUTHER MACDOUGAL, PROPERTY, WEALTH AND LAND: ALLOCATION, PLANNING AND DEVELOPMENT (1981).

101.   *See* NORMAN WILLIAMS, AMERICAN PLANNING LAW (1974).

102.   *See* IAN MCHARG, DESIGN WITH NATURE (1961).

103.   *See* WILLIAM MCDONOUGH, ET AL., CRADLE TO CRADLE: REMAKING THE WAY WE MAKE THINGS (2001).

104.   *See supra* Chapter 1. The breadth of ecology has led to different definitions of ecology, dependent on the viewpoint (or bias) of the author. For a general treatment of the science of ecology, it is best to use one of the most general definitions; the study of the interrelationship of organisms and their environment. *See* Louis J. Gross, *Ecology: An Idiosyncratic Overview,* in MATHEMATICAL ECOLOGY: AN INTRODUCTION pp. 3, 4 (Thomas G. Hallam & Simon A. Levin eds.,1986); CHARLES J. KREBS, ECOLOGY 3 (4th ed. 1994). While the generality of this definition makes it unusable as a research guide,

it does serve to emphasize that ecology is mainly concerned with the relationship between components of the environment, and not with the components themselves.

Several histories have been written which trace the development of specific ecological sub-disciplines, and we cannot hope to duplicate their detail in this limited space. However, no history has been written which relates how ecology has developed in parallel, and in some cases in interaction, with environmental law. This brief history will concentrate on the two disciplines of ecology which arguably have had the most impact on environmental law; ecosystem and population ecology. Any account of the history of ecology will suffer from generalizations, and many important exceptions exist for most every statement that follows. However, in this limited space we can only hope for a general overview of major trends. Further, while many ecologists have carried out their careers oblivious to the applied uses of their work, it is also true that much of the incentive for early ecological research arose from real world problems of resource management, pest control, and pollution abatement. As environmental law developed to deal with these problems, it interacted, most often indirectly through principles of resource management, conservation, or environmental ethics with ecology. These points of interaction will also be discussed. Finally, since we will mainly deal with U.S. environmental law, this introduction will concentrate on the history of ecology as it has developed in the U.S.

105.   A case can certainly be made for a primary importance of applied ecology in the development of an ecosystemic law. The various applied branches of ecology, such as ecotoxicology and restoration ecology, have the most day to day interaction with environmental laws and their implementation, whether by the setting of water quality standards or the restoration of an entire ecosystem. Also, ecologists have often used the results of applied ecology to test, refine, and even develop fundamental concepts of ecology (e.g., much of our knowledge of populations interactions came from agriculturally inspired work on plant-insect interactions). However, applied ecology by definition relies on concepts and approaches developed through the attempt to understand basic and fundamental ecological processes. SHARON E. KINGSLAND, MODELING NATURE: EPISODES IN THE HISTORY OF POPULATION ECOLOGY (1995).

106.   *See* W.M. Wheeler, *Natural History: "Oecology" or "Ethology?* 15 SCIENCE 971-76 (1902); *see* ROBERT P. MCINTOSH, THE BACKGROUND OF ECOLOGY, 9 (1985).

107.   Sharon E. Kingsland, *Defining Ecology as a Science*, FOUNDATIONS OF ECOLOGY 1 (Leslie A. Real & James H. Brown eds., 1991).

108.   *See, e.g., id.* at 1-2.

109.   *See* CHARLES DARWIN, ON THE ORIGIN OF THE SPECIES (1859). *But see* DONALD WORSTER, NATURE'S ECONOMY: THE ROOTS OF ECOLOGY (1977) for a treatment of the history of ecology that traces the roots of ecology to the eighteenth century.

110.   Competition and the interrelationship between the non-living environment and populations are the two components of Darwin's theory of natural selection that early ecologists most frequently used. However, while Darwin dealt with competition within a species, early ecologists were also interested in how competition among species affected population abundance and distribution. The third important component of Darwin's theory, that adaptations arising in a population can be inherited by the next generation, was not a part of early ecology (genetics and ecology would not merge until at least the 1970s). Given that many of the concepts used by environmental law were later to be borrowed from ecology (see below) it may only be slightly far-fetched to describe Darwin as one of the intellectual pillars of environmental law.

111.   While a layperson may believe that "physiology" is simply the study of the function of human organ systems (e.g., respiratory, nervous, and endocrine), it has always encompassed much more, including the functional responses of individual and groups

of plants and animals to environmental change. As we discussed in Chapter 1, ecological physiology, possibly the earliest branch of ecology, is still an active ecological sub-discipline. For a discussion of Haeckel's work from a cultural viewpoint, *see* ANNA BRAMWELL, ECOLOGY IN THE 20ᵀᴴ CENTURY: A HISTORY (1989). Bramwell finds uncomfortable connections between the work of Haeckel and other continental thinkers and the later National Socialist Movement.

112.   *See* MCINTOSH, *supra* note 106, at 7-8. Much of Darwin's thinking about natural selection and the competition among individuals within a species (which would later become a keystone of population ecology) developed through his study of Thomas Malthus' *Essay on Population* which first developed the idea that unchecked population growth led to within population competition for resources. *See* KINGSLAND, *supra* note 107, at 1.

113.   *See id.* at 2.

114.   *See generally Id.* at 6; MCINTOSH, *supra* note 103, at 85-93. *See also* infra notes 105-107 and accompanying discussion.

115.   *See* MCINTOSH, *supra* note 106, at 64. Forbes never finished college and completed much of his most important work before joining the faculty of the University of Illinois. His largely self-taught approach to ecology and natural history, while relatively common in the nineteenth century, would become rare to non-existent in the twentieth century as ecology became a more university based discipline.

116.   *See* Forbes, *The Lake as a Microcosm*, BULLETIN OF THE PEORIA SCIENTIFIC ASSOCIATION 77, reprinted in FOUNDATIONS OF ECOLOGY 14 (Leslie A. Real & James H. Brown Eds., 1991). Forbes and other early ecologists found their theoretical justification for the "balance of nature" concept in the work of Herbert Spencer who, along with Darwin, can justifiably be said to be one of the two sources "shaping the growth of budding science of ecology." MODELING NATURE, *supra* note 105, at 13 (describing the influence of both Darwin and Spencer on early American ecology). Through his writings, beginning with the 1862 publication of *First Principles*, Spencer promoted the view that all processes (biological and non-biological) were the result of the balance of differing forces. *See id.* at 14.

117.   *See* MCINTOSH, *supra* note 106, at 13; GOLLEY, *supra* note 42, at 100.

118.   *See* KINGSLAND, *supra* note 107, at 3; *see* Stephen A. Forbes, *On Some Interactions of Organisms*, 1 BULL. ILL. ST. LAB. NAT. HIST.1-17 (1880).

119.   *See* Kingsland, *supra* note 107, at 3. Forbes wanted to discover how Darwin's concept of natural selection led to the seemingly well regulated natural world (i.e., natural selection created the "balance of nature").

120.   Behind the separation of evolutionary biology and ecology was a cultural divide between neo Darwinian thought and those social theorists who emphasized cooperation.

121.   Both universities were founded in the late 1800s Nebraska, as a land-grant college had a vested interest in agricultural research which helps explain their ecologists' focus on the formation of grassland communities. The University of Chicago is a private university which was founded for the pursuit of scholarly activities and their ecologists have likewise concentrated on the more academic, theoretical, and mathematical branches of ecology. *See* MCINTOSH, *supra* note 106, at 34, 36. *See generally*, STEPHEN BOCKING, ECOLOGISTS AND ENVIRONMENTAL POLITICS (1997) for an in-depth study of the influence of political, social, and cultural factors on the early development of ecology.

122.   In one the most personal of interactions between ecology and law, Clements began his research as a graduate student at Nebraska working with Rosco Pound, a future Dean of the Harvard Law School, and one of the founders of sociological jurisprudence. *See*

supra note 87 and accompanying text. Together they wrote PHYTOGEOGRAPHY OF NEBRASKA (1898), in which they showed the advantage of an empirical approach to ecology over the traditional descriptive approach (they counted the number and distribution of individual plants in 5 meters square quadrants). *See* MCINTOSH, *supra* note 106, at 131-32. Clements also published the first American textbook of ecology, RESEARCH METHOD IN ECOLOGY, in 1905. It emphasized the statistical methods of analysis that he and Roscoe Pound had used in their Nebraska study. This textbook was the first in a long series of ecology texts that, because of their influence on future ecologists, would help shape the science of ecology. In 1940, Clements would co-write a second ecology textbook, this time in association with an animal ecologist, Victor Shelford. *See* FREDERIC E. CLEMENTS & VICTOR E. SHELFORD, BIO-ECOLOGY (1940).

123.   KINGSLAND, *supra* note 107, at 5.

124.   *See* Fred P. Bosselman & A. Dan Tarlock, *The Influence of Ecological Science on American Law: An Introduction*, 69 CHI.-KENT L. REV. 847, 857 (1994).

125.   *See id.* at 869.

126.   *See id. at 848.* While dominant concepts in ecology until recently, neither the "balance of nature" nor stability were universally accepted, especially among some population ecologists who studied, in nature or in equations, the very unstable oscillations that could affect natural populations. Interestingly, Thomas Malthus, in an earlier age, found oscillations in the human population as a consequence of growth and its constraint.

127.   *See* FREDERIC CLEMENTS, PLANT SUCCESSION (1916). While Clements may have come to believe that he developed this concept several other earlier and contemporary ecologists shared the view that some defined set of nature (e.g., community) could be treated as an individual organism. *See* MCINTOSH, *supra* note 106, at 77.

128.   The British ecologist, Arthur Tansley, coined the term "ecosystem" in his 1935 article as an answer to Clements' community as an organism concept. Arthur G. Tansley, *The Use and Abuse of Vegetational Concepts and Terms*, 16 ECOLOGY 284 (1935).

129.   *See* KINGSLAND, *supra* note 107, at 4. The sand dunes at Indiana Dunes State Park, the site of Cowles research, is still used for undergraduate field trips for University of Chicago students.

130.   *See* MCINTOSH, *supra note* 106, at 83.

131.   Practitioners of the "reductionist," or bottom-up, approach still believed the community was a critical aspect of ecology, but thought it was best understood by studying its individual components. *See* Jonathan Roughgarden & Jared Diamond, *Overview: The Role of Species Interactions in Community Ecology, in* COMMUNITY ECOLOGY 333 (Jared Diamond & Ted J. Case eds., 1986).

132.   Animal ecology before the 1920s was divided among aquatic and terrestrial ecologists. *See* MCINTOSH, *supra* note 106, at 57-61. Aquatic ecologists, taking the lead of Forbes, dominated the study of aquatic systems and, like terrestrial plant ecologists, adopted a holistic approach to their studies, which would eventually lead to a concept similar to that of Clements' complex organism; the lake as a super-organism. *See id.* at 59. Because of their well-defined boundaries, much like a patch of vegetation, lakes were the main research focus of early aquatic ecologists. Like Forbes' studies of lakes in Illinois, other aquatic ecologists concentrated their work on the explanation of how different levels of the food web (i.e., the trophic structure) interacted with each other and with the physical elements of the aquatic system. *See id.* at 60.

133. The term ecosystem is commonly credited to Arthur Tansley, one of the developers of the science of ecology in the early part of the twentieth century. *See* GOLLEY, *infra* note 42, at 8.
134. *See id.*
135. *See infra* Chapter 3. We will leave to the next three chapters the question of how many concrete effects, and not simply motivation, ecology has had on the development of specific environmental laws.
136. Therefore, while there was much agreement (among many) over what type of questions to ask, there was little agreement on what unit of nature would be the object of these questions.
137. *See* Arthur G. Tansley, *The Use And Abuse of Vegetational Concepts and Terms*, 16 ECOLOGY 284 (1935), reprinted in FOUNDATIONS OF ECOLOGY 318 (Leslie A. Real & James H. Brown eds., 1991).
138. While the ecosystem concept is the basis for much of modern ecological research, Tansley did not use the concept in his own research. Neither Tansley nor others who attacked Clements' concept meant that a community or ecosystem cannot be more than its biological components, only that at the time there was no scientific evidence to support these early metaphors. Ecosystems were not complex organisms but were, at most, "quasi-organisms" that, while not living, could be treated as a single entity for some research purposes. *See id.* at 306.
139. *See* Golley, *supra* note 42 at 31-34.
140. *See* Raymond L. Lindeman, *The Trophic-Dynamic Aspect of Ecology*, 23 ECOLOGY 399 (1942), reprinted in FOUNDATIONS OF ECOLOGY 157 (Leslie A. Real & James H. Brown eds., 1991).
141. *See supra* Chapter 1 for an explanation of trophic dynamics.
142. That fact that two people could carry out the necessary field work to characterize an ecosystem, even a small one like Cedar Bog Lake, would prove instructive to future ecosystem ecologists, particularly those not involved in the "Big Science" ecosystem ecology of the 1960s and 1970s. *See infra* Chapter 3.
143. Energy flow was most often observed as the transfer of biomass between trophic levels (e.g., predation of herbivores by carnivores). Biomass (kg/unit) can be transformed into energy units (kcal/unit).
144. *See* KINGSLAND, *supra* note 107, at 10; MCINTOSH, *supra* note 106, at 197. Lindeman also emphasized ecological succession and, in a manner similar to Clement's, stressed that the endpoint of succession in a lake was a "climax" community. *See* Lindeman, *supra* note 140 at 170-71.
145. *See* EUGENE ODUM, FOUNDATIONS OF ECOLOGY (1953).
146. H.G. ANDERWARTHA & L.C. BIRCH, THE DISTRIBUTION AND ABUNDANCE OF ANIMALS (1954). Community ecology, the study of how populations are ordered into interacting groups, has been dominated by population ecologists who have seen it as a natural progression from the study of two interacting populations.
147. *See* MODELING NATURE, *supra* note 105.
148. *See infra* discussion of the *Sierra Club v. Marita* cases of the 1990s.
149. *See* KREBS, *supra* note 104, at 243-45: KINGSLAND, *supra* note 107, at 6-7.
150. *See generally* CHARLES ELTON, ANIMAL ECOLOGY (1927) for a complete introduction to the ecological niche concept.
151. *See id.*; KREBS, *supra* note 104, at 243.
152. While originally used to model human population growth these same methods were soon used to model the increase in population size under different assumptions of, among other variables, birth and death rates.

153.   Gause's work would begin a decades long debate among ecologists on how important
         competition between populations was in the structure and function of populations.
         Unlike Elton, Gause used the mathematical methods being developed at the time and
         made many ecologists familiar with the use of mathematics in ecology. Gause based
         his contention of the importance of competitive exclusion on his experimental work
         on competition and predation among laboratory populations of yeast and protozoa. *See*
         GEORGII F. GAUSE, *Experimental Populations of Microscopic Organisms*, 18 ECOLOGY
         173-79 (1937). These experiments began the use, by population ecologists, of
         controlled laboratory experiments in order to reduce the complexity of nature to a few
         relatively simple parameters is an example of the reductionist approach in biology.

154.   *See* Georgii F. Gause, *The Principles of Biocoenology*, 11 Q. REV. BIOLOGY 320-36
         (1936); MODELING NATURE, *supra* note 105, at 155-59.

155.   N represents the number of individuals, t is time, r is maximum rate of population
         increase, and K is the upper limit of population growth (i.e., carrying capacity). Pearl
         also rediscovered the work of the Belgian mathematician Pierre-François Verhulst who
         had discovered the same function and named it the logistic curve. *See* KINGSLAND,
         supra note 107 at 7; Raymond Pearl & L.J. Reed, *On the Rate of Growth of the
         Population of the United States Since 1790 and its Mathematical Representation*, 6
         PROC. NAT. ACAD. SCI. U.S.A. 275-88 (1920). The logistic curve was adapted by
         human population demographers and would become an important tool in the effort to
         predict human population growth.

156.   The use of the logistic curve in ecology generated much controversy among those who
         disagreed with Pearl's contention that it represented a law of growth and not simply
         a workable description of growth. This is a fundamental distinction since if the logistic
         equation merely described particular sets of data, there would be no reason to assume
         that all population growth would be based on the logistic equation. However, even
         most of Pearl's opponents agree that the ease by which this equation could be
         translated into biological terms made it a useful tool, and, by the 1930s, it was widely
         used by ecologists who wanted to study variations in population growth. *See*
         BACKGROUND OF ECOLOGY, *supra* note 106. Besides becoming a part of basic
         population ecology research, the logistic equation soon became the basis for fisheries
         ecology and fisheries management. *See* D.H. CUSHING, MARINE ECOLOGY AND
         FISHERIES (1975).

157.   His highly mathematical work was beyond the abilities of most contemporary
         ecologists, and even now it is only his simple models and not his highly technical work
         that is known to most ecologists. *See* KINGSLAND, supra note 107, at 11.

158.   *See infra* notes 105-107 and accompanying text.

159.   *See id.*

160.   His attempt to create a new science, a "Physical Biology," was based on his application
         of thermodynamic principles to biology by focusing on how energy was transformed
         as it move through the biosphere. *See* ALFRED J. LOTKA, ELEMENTS OF PHYSICAL
         BIOLOGY (1925). This application led him to a focus on the transformation and flow of
         energy through the biosphere as the basic problem of biology. Lotka's focus on energy
         transformation attempted to analyze the earth as a single energy transformer in which
         the concepts of carbon cycles, nutrient cycles, and energy flows were all interrelated.
         Lotka's work on energy transformation was used by Lindeman in his conceptualization
         of trophic dynamics (see above) and was critical to the development of an ecological
         energetics approach in ecosystem ecology. However, while Lotka's work was
         important to the development of ecosystem ecology, it was his contributions to
         population ecology for which he is best known.

161. System theory would be the key conceptual framework of a major branch of modern ecosystem ecology; systems ecology. *See infra* Chapter 1.

162. *See* MODELING NATURE, *supra* note 105.

163. *See infra* Chapter 3.

164. The modeling of competition and predation through continuous-time differential equation models was not the only approach used to develop a mathematical population ecology. Alexander Nicholson and Victor Bailey approached the analysis of populations through different methods; realistic discrete-time models of host-parasite interactions. Nicholson and Bailey also introduced new concepts into the analysis of populations, including intra-specific competition, the effects of age distribution on population change, and most importantly, the concept of density-dependent population regulation. For Nicholson and Bailey, it was the competition among individuals (either of the same or different species) that occurred during the search for essential resources that was the major regulator of populations. By the 1950s and 1960s the question of density-dependant population growth had become a controversy, with the idea attacked by those who believed that density independent factors were most important and by those who did not accept the mathematical approaches (e.g., logistic equations) being used. *See* Alexander J. Nicholson & Victor A. Bailey, *The Balance of Animal Populations, Part I*, 3 PROCEEDINGS OF THE ZOOLOGICAL SOCIETY, LONDON 551-98 (1935).

165. DONALD WORSTER, NATURE'S ECONOMY: THE ROOTS OF ECOLOGY (1977).

166. *See* Eugene P. Odum, *The New Ecology*, 14 BIOSCIENCE 14-16 (1964). As we discussed in Chapter I, population and ecosystem ecologists have been divided in other ways as well, including the differing motivations of ecologists whose main interests are the study of natural places (e.g., ecosystems) and those whose main interests are single populations or groups of interacting populations (i.e., communities).

167. *See generally* RICHARD LEVINS & RICHARD LEWONTIN, THE DIALECTICAL BIOLOGIST (1985); NOVARTIS FOUNDATION SYMPOSIUM, THE LIMITS OF REDUCTIONISM IN BIOLOGY (1998) for the anti-reductionist prospective to the practice of biology in general. *See also* Odum reference for the advantages of a holistic treatment to ecology. *But see* John L. Harper, *After Description*, in THE PLANT COMMUNITY AS A WORKING MECHANISM 11-26 (E.I. Newman ed., 1982) for a defense of reductionism in ecology; "the complex is no more than sum of the activities of the parts plus their interactions." *Id.*

168. It is also one of our theses that the growing trend to integrate environmental laws to face complex environmental problems is good but that this will only be truly successful if this new, integrated environmental law uses all of ecology and not just those specific concepts, methods, or disciplines which seem most useful to the solving of specific environmental problems. An example of this trend is the newly proposed U.S. Forest Service regulations that recognize that a multi-hierarchical approach to biodiversity protection is needed; one that does not just look at populations, habitats, and ecosystems, but also considers genetics and landscapes and the interaction between all of these levels.

169. There are those theorists who urge a stationary economy or no growth society. *See* HERMAN E. DALY, STEADY STATE ECONOMICS: THE ECONOMICS OF BIOPHYSICAL EQUILIBRIUM AND MORAL GROWTH (1977).

3 Before the Dawn – Ecology and Environmental Law at Mid-Century

No one person can concentrate sufficiently in any one field to begin to grasp the complexity of this system ...[1]
Dr. Wurster – Wisconsin DDT Hearings

Introduction: The Wisconsin DDT Hearings

On December 2, 1968, the Citizen Natural Resources Association Inc. filed a petition with the Wisconsin Department of the Natural Resources requesting a declaratory ruling that the widely used and oft praised DDT was indeed a pollutant under the law. Thus began one of the first efforts to use the science of ecology in a legal forum to promote environmental protection. The hearings attracted not only environmental protest crowds to their front doors, but national media attention as well. Like the Storm King law suit, and the Santa Barbara Oil Spill, the humble petition in Wisconsin become one of the key environmental events leading to Earth Day and the birth of the environmental movement. But unlike these other two famous early environmental disputes, the Wisconsin petition rode on the fame of Rachael Carson's *Silent Spring* written in 1962 and presented to a lay audience, a view of pollution as an unwelcome intruder in the "house of nature," a complex ecosystem which magnified the effects of the pollutant.

The hearings which were to follow were to presage the drama of an environmental age born from the landmark environmental laws of the 1970s. The new heroes were the passionate and brilliant environmental lawyer, Victor Yannacone, and the non-profit environmental groups, the soon to be formed Environmental Defense Fund and the Izaak Walton League. Equally important were the environmental scientists Orie Loucks, Charles Wurster, Hugh Iltis, Joseph Hickey, and Robert Risebrough, all of whom presented the hearing board and the public with one of its first portraits of pollution within an ecosystem. The legal setting was an administrative hearing. Examiner Van Susteren was a careful bright and impartial hearing officer who was to write an analytic opinion which found DDT to be a pollutant and which carefully described its chemical composition, its pathway in the environment, its bio accumulation and its toxic impact on plant, animal and human species.

In some ways, the Madison hearings were a new paradigm for a legal approach to environmental problems based upon ecological knowledge. Orie Loucks appeared early in the hearing to define ecology, ecosystems and the role of water and weather on the Wisconsin ecosystem. He was followed by Charles Wurster who began by setting down the interdisciplinary ecological approach to environmental problem solving and then methodically traced the way in which DDT moved through the watershed (i.e., ecosystem) itself. He then provided an accounting of bio-accumulation and information on the DDT residues found in the water and in each level of the food chain. Dr. Risebough then testified about DDT in Lake Michigan and the food chain of organisms in Lake Michigan. He traced the impact of DDT on eggshell thickness and the consequent impact upon reproduction of individual birds, providing elegant detail to the issue that Rachel Carson framed for the public. Dr. Hickey then testified about the impact of DDT not merely upon individual birds, but upon the community as a whole. Both through cross examination and the testimony of Goran Lofroth, petitioners were able to establish the accumulation of DDT in milk and its harmful impacts upon fauna. Finally, petitioner's agricultural experts testified that they no longer advise farmers to use DDT because of its impact. To conclude the testimony for the petitioners, Yannacone brought back Orie Loucks who presented a systems analysis model which explained the total impact of DDT on the Wisconsin regional aquatic ecosystem. This was reputed to be the first use of systems analysis in a legal setting.

The details of this coordinated testimony are less important than the intellectual framework which guided its presentation and the historical time of the hearing. Yannacone understood the central message of ecology and its compelling relevance to his case and he was able to present witnesses who could give both a view of the entire ecosystem and the specific operation of DDT within it. The presentation, however, was not a fortuitous creation of a few brilliant lawyers and scientists. It was the result of more than a century's history which slowly had produced a public culture receptive to the challenge of a hitherto much valued and economically profitable technology. It was also the result of an changing environmental culture, informed by such visionaries as Rachael Carson and Aldo Leopold. And it was based upon a solid legal foundation of administrative law which could permit the flexible administration of justice. We will briefly recapitulate that history in the next section.

Equally important as the ecological content of the testimony and its presentation for the first time in a legal setting was the historical moment of the presentation. The University of Wisconsin had been the setting for radical student protests just prior to the hearings. During the hearings, student protesters, dressed in commando uniforms and carrying placards reading "Ban the Bug Bomb" squirted water pistols, claiming them to be filled with DDT. It was the 1960s, and whatever the deeper intellectual significance of the DDT hearings were, the political significance was undeniable, at least at the moment.

Despite the actions in the streets and the great accomplishments of Yannacone and his colleagues in Wisconsin, it would be a serious mistake to think that these hearings represented the achievement of the environmental millennium. Quite the contrary. The problems encountered in the hearings were to plague the next thirty years of the development of ecology and environmental law. These problems, include, but are not limited to:

1. The difficulty of introducing a systems perspective into a legal decision-making context;
2. The related problem of focusing upon the complex and diffuse ways in which pollutants find their way into and through the environment;
3. The difficulty of weighing the relative values of subtle environmental harms and balancing against the costs of control or the benefits of the pollutant in question;
4. The assessment and evaluation of risks of action and inaction, given uncertain information;
5. Determining the appropriate role for citizen groups within the legal process;
6. Securing the necessary scientific understanding by lay people assigned to play an important role in the decision-making process and the necessary legal understanding on the part of scientists.

The Wisconsin DDT hearings were early warning signs of these problems. After the systems perspective was introduced with the announcement that it was the first time such a perspective had been offered in a legal setting, one bewildered person at the hearing said: "I hope it's the last." The hearing examiner and the lawyers and non-scientific witnesses for DDT had a genuinely difficult time understanding the scientific implications of DDT and its use. Although the general story of the movement of DDT through the environment was persuasively offered, its precise impacts at each stage were still unknown. Moreover, honest legitimate "transcience" questions were raised about the relevance of information derived from the study of one ecosystem being transferred to estimate impacts in another ecosystem. All of these unanswered questions raised the further question of how in the face of uncertainty, decisions might be made about risky substances in the environment. This was before the development of risk assessment as a rigorous, yet controversial technique for dealing with decisionmaking in an uncertain world. These difficult questions naturally raised the issue of who could best answer them. These issues about who could best answer these questions arose in the hearing when expert qualifications were offered and challenged. Underlying the challenges of the experts and their qualifications were legitimate questions about the proper extent of scientific expertise, when scientists from traditional disciplines appeared to be conducting studies or reaching conclusions outside the traditional boundaries of their disciplines. In addition, ecologists, with their admittedly broad discipline, were challenged both as to whether their discipline equipped them to reach the conclusions they asserted and whether more traditional scientists could offer better evidence.

Finally, however, the biggest questions of all lay in weighing the values affected by the pollution and determining the nature of the appropriate controls in light of evident costs of abandoning the pesticide. (Ironically, some of the substitutes for DDT were organophosphates which themselves can cause biological damage.) Despite the longings of economists, there is no fully satisfactory science for assessing the costs and benefits in such a decision. Since the Wisconsin Hearing simply was deciding to label DDT a pollutant, it did not have to reach this difficult question about the degree and kind of control required. This question was left for another day and another forum. But such a question takes us ahead of us to the story of pesticide regulation after Earth Day, a story which we will summarize in later chapters of this book. First, we must return to the history which leads to the Wisconsin hearings in order to better understand how and why they were able to take place.

The DDT hearings were the culmination of broad historical changes in American public culture – a change beginning after the Second World War. Driven by the post-World War II prosperity, the resulting movement to the suburbs was stimulated by a new social demand for outdoor recreation and its attendant needs for pristine environments – wilderness, national parks, and clean waterways. In "fleeing" the cities people were in effect acting to protect their health. Severe (and fatal) air pollution incidents in the cities of Donora, Pennsylvania (1948), London (1952), New York City (1953), and Los Angeles (1954) dramatized the cities' problems and triggered a demand for more effective air pollution control. Major public health issues also erupted in the 1950s including public debates over fluoride in public water supplies, new concern over fallout from nuclear testing, and the "cranberry scare" over aminotriagole (3-AT) pesticide residues on cranberries.[2]

Despite the growing seriousness of the environmental problems facing society, the United States' politics of the 1960s was dominated by the climax of the civil rights movement, the urban riots, the Vietnam war, the assassinations of President Kennedy, Robert Kennedy and Martin Luther King, Lyndon Johnson's Great Society, and the emergence of a counter-culture movement. These public problems produced a new recognition of the limits of this nation's headlong pursuit of economic prosperity.[3] These dramatic political events and social movements in the 1960s both obscured and reflected the fact that the public was beginning to become aware of an environment requiring protection. New environmental literature, major new scholarship in law and ecology, as well as new statutes and legal decisions began to slowly reshape the environmental law regime.

The Rise of Scientific Ecology in the 1960s

The Wisconsin DDT hearings rested upon a scientific ecological vision which had been synthesized a decade earlier by Eugene Odum.

In the 1950s and 1960s, studies of whole ecosystems began to flourish, partly funded by the U.S. Atomic Energy Commission.[4] George Woodwell's study of an irradiated forest at Brookhaven not only showed the devastation of radiation on forest life and ecosystem processes, but provided a framework for the experimental manipulation of entire ecosystems. These studies embraced (1) study of ecosystem structure, (2) the dynamics of ecosystems, both their energy flow and productivity; (3) the interactions between components; and (4) the behavior of the entire system. Also during this period, scholars began the intensive study of specific ecological topics such as selection, adaptation, stability and succession, i.e., the response of biotic components of ecosystems over time. As we shall see later, many of these topics play a role within environmental law and policy.[5]

EUGENE P. ODUM ~THE FATHER OF MODERN ECOSYSTEM ECOLOGY – WHY?

No one scientist has shaped the discipline of ecosystem science more than Eugene P. Odum. How did Odum exert this influence? His contribution was a conceptualization of a model or world view that placed the ecosystem at the center of the study of nature. His clear statements about ecosystems and their function inspired a cadre of students to enter the emerging field of ecosystem science. Many of these scientists became the early leaders in promoting ecosystem science as the logical knowledge base for an ecologically informed environmental management. Perhaps this is, and continues to be, Odum's greatest legacy.

Eugene Odum's youthful interest in bird watching led him to graduate work in zoology and a position on the faculty of the University of Georgia. In response to what some say was an internal debate within his department about the identity of ecology as a discipline, Odum began in the late 1940s to organize his ideas about the position of ecology in science and its potential importance for solving human problems. The eventual result was the publication of his classic text in 1953, *Fundamentals of Ecology*. This compact book of 384 pages charted the path for the formalization of ecosystem science as a discipline with a set of principles, experimental approaches, and a rationale for its relevance to policy makers.

Odum's textbook was a seminal event in the history of ecology. In the preface of the first edition he defines the problem and his motivation for the book: "because of its wide scope, few attempts have been made to present ecology as a whole and to place it in logical perspective in relation to other divisions of biology and to other fields of learning." Odum's answer was the elaboration of the "ecosystem concept." He had found a holistic theme for integrating the disparate branches of ecology in a fresh and clear way.

Odum defined the term as "Ecosystem: any unit that includes all the organisms in a given area interacting with the physical environment so that a flow of energy leads to clearly defined trophic structure, biotic diversity, and material cycles within the system."

Table 3.1 EUGENE ODUM'S ECOSYSTEM

Eugene Odum created a framework for describing the ecosystem and identified the processes central to understanding ecosystem functioning. To describe an ecosystem he recognized these components:

- Inorganic substances involved in cycling
- Organic compounds that link abiotic and biotic
- Climate regime
- Producers
- Macroconsumers (animals)
- Microconsumers (bacteria and fungi)

To understand the function of ecosystems he identified these attributes for study:

- Energy circuits
- Food chains
- Diversity patterns (time and space)
- Nutrient cycles (biogeochemical)
- Development and evolution
- Control (cybernetics)

From this simple model emerged a perspective that the ecosystem was the basic unit of ecology and that energy flow and nutrient cycling were the critical and integrating processes governing the function of natural systems. Odum had framed the ecosystem concept in a way that it could apply to understanding units of various sizes. The ecosystem could range from the scale of a pond on up in size to extend to the entire earth. In this way, Odum had set the stage for the dawning of global ecology and earth systems science. Another significant contribution of his early model was the use of energy flow as a currency for measuring ecosystem function and as a tool for organizing biological interactions between plants (producers), animals (consumers) and microorganisms (decomposers). Odum also recognized the significance of organism interactions with the abiotic environment (the domain of ecology) in shaping ecosystem level processes.

Odum was profoundly aware of the impacts of man on ecosystems. That he chose to include humans as part of the ecosystem is shown in the last chapter of *Fundamentals of Ecology*, "Applications: Human Society." In this chapter Odum identified much of the agenda for the environmental movement that was to take shape around Earth Day. By the 3ʳᵈ edition of his book (now more than twice the size of the 1ˢᵗ edition) published in 1973, the last chapter had become "Toward an Applied Human Ecology." In it he points the way for the application of ecosystem science to ecosystem management. "Ecosystem management and applied human ecology thus become new ventures that require the merging of a host of disciplines and missions which up to now have been promoted independently of one another." Odum sums up his vision in the last sentence of the book where he calls for a greater emphasis in education on "the principle of the totality of man and environment, that is, ecosystem ecology."

Table 3.2 TOTAL ECOSYSTEM MANAGEMENT

Odum's analysis of ecosystems in the context of human activities led him to put forth a number of reforms and procedures that would have to be realized to implement "total ecosystem management."

- Population control and family planning
- Regional land-use planning (zoning) which is made analogous to territorial control in natural populations
- Greater emphasis in law and medicine on environmental and consumer protection
- Cost internalization and preservation of "capital stock" and human resources rather than an emphasis on rates of production
- "Stringent" conservation of biological resources
- Emphasis on waste disposal and recycling
- Political concern for the urban-rural complex as one system
- A shift to consideration of the whole from preoccupation with the parts, adoption of a systems perspective.

Following the publication of *Fundamentals of Ecology*, there was a sharp increase in the number of ecosystem studies focused on measuring energy flow, and the cycling of nutrients. Odum had presented the foundations for the ecosystem concept. It remained for the ecological community to adopt many of its concepts, and in the process a new discipline was recognized.

The emergence of ecosystem study is thus best traced by understanding the leadership of key scientists able to inspire the teams of researchers required to execute holistic study of organisms and environment.

"Big Ecology" – The Emergence of Systems Ecology

Ecosystem studies first expanded in the 1950s and 1960s once the Atomic Energy Commission became interested in the effects of radiation on the environment. This progression of increasing scale, complexity and expense of ecosystem study reached a peak in the late 1960s with the first wave of "Big Biology" projects – the International Biological Programme (IBP).[6] By 1965 several distinct programs were being planned with Eugene Odum in charge of the terrestrial productivity group whose explicit motive was to develop "new thinking at the ecosystem level."[7] The terrestrial group decided on a grassland site near Fort Collins, Colorado, to build a simulation model of a terrestrial ecosystem because grasslands were simpler and better understood than forests.[8] George Van Dyne was appointed director of the project. He was one of the leading proponents of the systems approach to ecosystem studies and a pioneer in the application of computer simulation models to study ecological systems.

System ecology, an outgrowth of information science, control engineering, and computer simulation, was moving to the front as a distinct branch of ecosystem ecology. The premise was the complex dynamics of entire ecosystems could be captured by mathematical expressions. For these ecologists the ecosystem needed to be studied as one mathematical integrated system and "systems theory," pioneered by Ludwig von Bertalanffy in the early 1950s, became the method of choice.[9]

Even though a system model is a simplification and abstraction of the real ecosystem, it still must capture the complexity of the natural world to generate predictive results. It became evident that the systems approach required intensive measurement of many biological parameters (e.g., energy at different trophic levels and number of animals per population) in order to build models of the total dynamics of the system (e.g., energy flux).

The large number of calculations required to solve the many simultaneous differential equations in even "simple" models required considerable computing power. Therefore, systems ecology co-evolved with computer technology. Many of the early failures of systems models to successfully mimic natural ecosystems were in part due to limitations of computer hardware and by today's standard, primitive software.

Figure 3.1 ECOSYSTEM BOUNDARY NUTRIENT RELATIONSHIPS

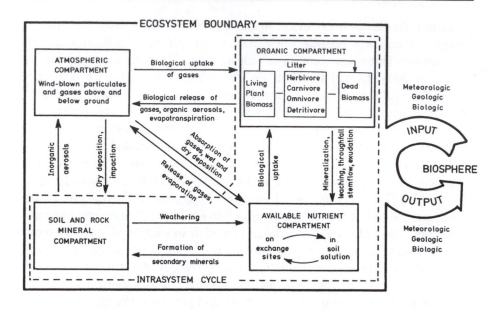

A model depicting nutrient relationships in a terrestrial ecosystem. Inputs and outputs to the ecosystem are moved by meteorologic, geologic, and biologic vectors. Major sites of accumulation and major exchange pathways within the ecosystem are shown.
Source: Biogeochemistry of a Forested Ecosystem, by Likens, et al. (1997)

A major rationale for the large investment in systems modeling in the IBP era was the promise that the models could generate predictions on ecosystem management strategies.[10] Agencies found it easier to justify research with applications to management, and not simply for the sake of understanding ecosystems.[11] In an era of unrealistic expectations of the state of ecosystem science, many thought that once ecosystem models were built, we could lessen expenditures on new research; the models would guide our actions.

How would the mass of data required to set up these models be obtained? The emergence of interdisciplinary teams of scientists focused on data-rich ecosystem-level study required a new science leader able to guide a diverse team, provide intellectual leadership, and manage the financial and political complexities of a big project. Van Dyne was an early example of this "new breed." He organized and led a large team of ecologists on one of the truly first large-scale ecology programs. While the project generated many successful results concerning the components and processes within the ecosystem, the grassland IBP project did not achieve the desired integration of the whole system.[12] Van Dyne blamed this failure on a lack of funding; however, some critics saw the problem as the methodology.[13] While the purpose of the grassland project had been to model the entire grassland ecosystem remained incomplete, its legacy was the building of rigorous models for specific ecosystem compartments and processes (e.g., phosphorus cycling).[14]

Hubbard Brook and the Non-Systems Ecosystem Ecology

In parallel with the grassland Biome Study, an alternative conceptual approach was evolving in the forests of New England. Beginning in 1963, a team of ecologists and geochemists began a long-term study of forest ecosystems in the White Mountains of New Hampshire: the Hubbard Brook study of "big biology." It had relatively large funding, a large multi-disciplinary team of researchers, and a long-term outlook (e.g., the study is still ongoing more than 35 years after it began). However, it did not rely on system based simulation models as the integrating focus for the field investigations.[15] In contrast to the IBP grassland project, the Hubbard Brook approach was to focus on small, well-defined ecosystem units (watersheds), to intensively measure important ecological parameters, and most importantly, to experimentally manipulate the system.[16] The Hubbard Brook project also set itself apart by focusing on nutrient cycling and its relationships with forest production, rather than energy flow, and in so doing advanced the theory and methodology for estimating nutrient losses from disturbed ecosystems.

Like the grassland study, strong leadership was essential to the start and continuance of the Hubbard Book study. Ecosystem research at Hubbard Brook was started in 1963 by three Dartmouth College scientists, E. Herbert Borman (a plant ecologist), Gene E. Likens (a limnologist), and Noye Johnson (a geochemist) with the help of Robert Pierce, a forest hydrologist with the U.S. Forest Service. Experimentation began at Hubbard Brook in 1965 when one 15.6 hectare watershed was clear-cut.[17] The experiment showed that an ecosystem's vegetation was important in regulating nutrient cycling and losses.[18] The effectiveness of this experimental approach at Hubbard Brook demonstrated that entire ecosystems could be treated as experimental units. The paradigm of large-scale manipulations of ecosystems to understand complex whole-system behavior would prove critical to the development of ecosystem ecology from the 1970s to today. One legacy of Hubbard Brook is that it documented long-term decline in stream pH and accelerated losses of nitrate and calcium from soils. These observations were convincing evidence of the effects of acid rain on forests and this site and Likens and Associates became centrally involved in acid rain policy and regulation.

The International Dimension

Our emphasis on the development of ecosystem science in the U.S. does not permit a rich discussion of the contributions from the international community. Close ties between U.S. and British universities were influential. In England during the 1950s and 1960s the British ecologists set The Nature Conservancy's research and conservation agenda. At Merlewood Station in the English Highlands, J. Derek Ovington pursued a woodlands research program that epitomized the ecosystem approach by focusing upon plant-soil relations, productivity, cooperation among ecologists and field experiments. By the 1960s, Ovington had identified organic matter production, energy flow, circulation of water, and circulation of chemical elements as aspects of "the fundamental unity of ecosystem physiology."[19]

Beginning in 1921, Canadian studies were conducted in the Great Lakes in an effort to maintain fish populations. Facing a declining fishery, conflicts over remaining stocks and an array of possible causes for the decline, a new generation of aquatic ecologists began their research in the 1960s and by the 1970s Henry Regier and others were linking the study of lake ecology with a strategic approach to fish management.[20] Their work in limnology con-tributed to the notion of a lake as a microcosm.[21] Culminating in the whole lake manipulations of Schindler and colleagues to study the effect of acid rain on lakes and their food webs.

Another international dimension was the contrasting of ecosystems found in different regions of the world, but functioning under similar climate. The comparative study of Mediterranean-type ecosystems of southern California, Chile, and South Africa led to insights on limiting factors for production and decomposition in dry ecosystems.[22]

The Mid-Century Environmental Legislation

Despite the dominant legal view of the environment at mid-century as a set of laws organized according to specific natural resource categories (agriculture, water, forests, wildlife), some laws were passed starting in the 1930s which began the alliance between law and ecology. These laws framed the practices of environmental assessment and restoration, as well as recognizing the need to define the boundaries and functional attributes of ecological features such as the continental shelves, river basins and watersheds.

In 1934, the Fish and Wildlife Coordination Act required the assessment of fish and wildlife diversity following impounding and controlling (or polluting) waters.[23] In 1956, the Fish and Wildlife Act was passed which had as one of its purposes "... the assistance for resource management to assure maximum sustainable production for fisheries ...".[24] These laws which introduced both the concepts of diversity and sustainability to the corpus of environmental law, were in many ways ahead of the science that was needed to assess impacts of management and development actions which would produce the sustained productivity and diversity of natural resources. One of the early alignments of law and ecology came when environmental laws began to recognize the importance of ecosystem boundaries over political boundaries. The outer continental shelf was recognized and defined in the Outer Continental Shelf Lands Act of 1953.[25] Watersheds were recognized as a unit of management in the Watershed Protection and Flood Protection Act of 1954.[26] Perhaps the best early statute to exemplify law and the use of ecology, was the Water Resource Planning Act of 1965.[27] This act established river basin emission standards to protect the water supply. This legal adoption of an ecosystem term, "river basin," the authorization of flexible planning, and the recognition of the multiple services supplied by the river basins anticipated later ecologically-based multi-purpose planning.

It is important, however, not to overstate the "ecological" orientation of the 1960s legislation. Scientists most often were consultants on specific issues and lacked resources to investigate specific problems uncovered during the case or planning process.[28] The emphasis on an economic rather than ecological perspective of the problem was particularly frustrating to the scientific community, and remains so today. The development of ecological economics in the 1990s can be seen as a response to this tension.

There were encouraging exceptions, to the ignoring of the ecology of river basins. In one program, "the Brandywine experience,"[29] the scientists played a more important role. With receipt of Ford Foundation and government funds, an interdisciplinary planning team[30] recommended appropriate land use controls to protect the water quality of the area. However, as would be seen many times again when such ecologically based plans were undertaken, the efforts to implement the scientific consensus produced a vigorous public debate. In the Brandywine project, the resulting plan was ultimately rejected by a virulent active minority of citizens in the region who feared land use controls and eminent domain.[31]

The Wilderness Act of 1963 was passed to "reserve" selected federal land as "untouched" wilderness areas, areas affected only by the forces of nature and with the import of man's work substantially unnoticeable. They were set aside to offer opportunities for solitude or primitive and unconfined recreation, and be of sufficient size to make practicable their preservation (at least 5,000 acres). They were to contain ecological, geological, scientific, educational, scenic or historical features of value.[32] This law established a connection between ecosystems and their preservation – a connection which still produces heated debate about how much wilderness do we need or can we afford, and how we can protect these lands from encroachment and human impacts on adjacent lands. Although ecosystems and preservation are often linked in the public mind, we shall see below that such a linkage is not a necessary one.

The Wild and Scenic Rivers Act in 1968 sought to preserve "outstanding remarkable scenic, recreational, geologic, fish and wildlife, historic, cultural or other similar values" in "free flowing condition" for the benefit of present and future generations.[33] Wild, scenic and recreational river areas were eligible for designation as part of the national wild and scenic river system and the Secretaries of Interior and Agriculture are authorized to acquire lands within the boundaries of such a system. The initiation of water resources projects such as dams were restricted on such rivers.

Although the Wilderness and Wild and Scenic Rivers legislation did not embody the specific application of ecological principles *per se*, the under-lying assumption of the presence of natural processes apart from human control[34] laid a foundation for later ecological study of these processes as part of legal regulation.[35] Since the Wilderness Act as well as other legislation such as the National Trails Systems Act in 1968[36] and wildlife refuge law[37] sought to preserve an allegedly pristine nature, rather than "conserve" this nature for future human exploitation, these laws also encouraged ecological study of these pristine areas.

The Advent of "Major" Environmental Litigation

A shift in public political culture toward environmentalism could be seen in the efforts of the Environmental Defense Fund and others in the years before Earth Day. However, it was the emergence of highly visible and dramatic cases (i.e., catastrophes) at the end of the 1960s which launched the environmental law era at Earth Day. A brief review of these cases highlights the role of ecology in the legal process, and shows the conflicts that arose in applying science to complex social and environmental issues. Three of these major cases were the Wisconsin DDT hearings (already described), the Scenic Hudson litigation, and the Santa Barbara oil spill.

Rachel Carson's Silent Spring

Like many, we recognize Rachel Carson as the most significant contributor to raising the United States public's awareness of ecology and its implications for public policy. Carson's holistic [i.e., systems] perspectives on nature were revealed in her first book, the prizewinning *The Sea Around Us*,[38] but *Silent Spring* offered the public their first view of the delightful complexity of ecosystems. In *Silent Spring*, Carson made an eloquent plea for the control of the use of insecticides. No better introduction to ecology had been given to the American public prior to her work.

Silent Spring was more than an ecology primer; it was a discussion of the need for an ecosystem regime. It linked human intervention into the ecosystem through pesticides, the indirect results of human and animal harms, and documented the failure of existing laws to prevent these harms and the need for new laws enabling a better pesticide regulatory regime. For our purposes, Carson's contributions were to demonstrate to the public how pesticides distributed themselves throughout all parts of the environment, moved through the food chain and bioaccumulated in individual organisms, thus affecting health and reproductive effects. Although the ecologists of the 1950s and 1960s often linked their work with conservation and environmental protection, it was not very accessible to the public; Carson's readable account changed this and in so doing, riveted the nation's attention on a specific abuse of the ecosystem. She launched an effort to control pesticides which continues to this day.[39]

Although Carson offered a broad framework for understanding pesticides in the context of the ecosystem, much remained to be clarified. Ecological reviewers criticized her assumptions about a "balance of nature," and her preferences for birds and animals over insects.[40] Later hearings were to struggle with whether broadly speaking, the benefits of pesticides would outweigh the harms Carson documented.

Legal responses to *Silent Spring* are inevitable. The Citizen Natural Resources Association Inc. and the Izaak Walton League of America, Inc., filed petitions in 1968 with the Department of Natural Resources in Wisconsin requesting a declaratory ruling on whether DDT was an "environmental pollutant" within Wisconsin statutes. Adjudicatory hearings were held, selected transcripts were published in book form.[41] This chapter opens with an account of the drama of these events.

The DDT hearings were a seminal event in ecology's legal history. The environmentalists sought to produce a full presentation of the role of DDT within the ecosystem. A tangle of legal issues arose. The effort to present an overview of the ecology of insecticides led to objections and cross examination to the witnesses' expertise and qualifications, the citation of scientific studies, the import of studies from other countries and ecosystems, and the relevance of the studies to determining whether DDT was or was not a "pollutant." Most of the hearing, however, was centered upon difficult and highly technical scientific issues pertaining to the physical properties of DDT, and its physiological consequences for organisms and the food chain, tracing its persistence, solubility in lipids, broad biological activity and mobility; documenting the storage of DDT in body fat, not only in pests but other creatures; measuring the biological accumulation of DDT through the food web; assessing the impact of DDT on the liver, the nervous system and certain hormones; and predicting the impact on reproductive activity and consequent population declines. Based upon this hotly-contested and at times incomplete evidence, DDT was found to be a "pollutant" under Wisconsin statutes.[42] It would be two decades before federal regulation of pesticides would achieve a similar ecological conclusion. Like Wisconsin, time and again it was left to municipal and state governments to identify key environmental issues and develop "solutions" that would later inform a national policy on the issue.

Scenic Hudson Preservation Conference v. Federal Power Commission

The *Scenic Hudson* decision was the first opinion in a long series of related litigation over the location of an electrical generating plant that had ecological consequences for the Hudson River and could create a visual blight decreasing the quality of life for some in an adjacent community. A traditional land-use conflict shaped up seven years before Earth Day, when an application was made to the Federal Power Commission to build the Storm King generating plant on the Hudson River north of New York. Consolidated Edison claimed that the electrical demands of New York City must be met. The residents of nearby Cornwall saw the plant as a tax bonanza, but were opposed by weekend residents of Cornwall and a handful of opponents across the Hudson who had no desire to admire Storm King mountain gouged out and "decorated" with transmission lines. The local conflict eventually escalated to a full-scale environmental battle with national interest fought by a coalition of local hiking, garden, conservation, and sporting clubs as well as by some of the country's leading environmental public interest groups.

The first opinion was rendered in 1965, and in a related 1970 decision (concerning the Hudson River Expressway) sustained the right of any responsible representative to sue in federal courts to protect the public interest in the environment. In 1971, the Federal Power Commission reopened its hearings and found to reissue a construction license. The *Scenic Hudson* citizen groups again appealed but lost this time. However, construction of the plant was then halted by an injunction, so the court (with science) could settle the issues raised by the entraining of fish eggs and larvae by the pumps in the proposed plant. Late in 1981, eighteen years after the start, the parties reached a working compromise by which Consolidated Edison agreed to halt construction of the pumped storage plant and donate the 500 acre site for a park. On the other side, the environmental groups agreed not to require closed-cycle cooling systems in three other plants. The utilities agreed to spend nearly $18 million on projects to reduce fish kills, stock the river, and study the plant's impact on the fish.

   This give-and-take approach to conflict resolution is a common strategy
to "balance" competition between economic and environmental interests. The
major issues that confronted the court in the *Scenic Hudson* case were:

   1. Who should be allowed to intervene in an administrative hearing
      and when can they intervene?
   2. What obligation does an independent regulatory agency, the
      Federal Power Commission, have to seek out facts other than
      those presented by a party requesting a license and are they
      compelled to consider alternative courses of action?
   3. To what extent must regulatory agencies weigh the impacts of
      their decisions upon preservation and natural beauty.

These issues were to be perennial topics of court discussion for the next thirty
years. Although these questions are simplified and their answers depend in part
upon the specific statutes and court cases of the time, they remain important to
environmental law today and will always remain difficult to answer.

   Scenic Hudson forced the articulation of these three questions which
helped define the next stage in the rise of the environmental law regime, opening
it up to more fully consider ecological evidence. In *Scenic Hudson*, the particular
ecological evidence was about the impact of the entrainment of fish eggs and
larvae by Storm King pumps on the river's fish populations. Based upon
evidence originally excluded by the Federal Power Commission, but which
recreational fishing groups presented, the court remanded to the Federal Power
Commission to "take the whole fisheries question into consideration." As a
consequence, the "Hudson River Policy" committee undertook the "Hudson
River Fisheries Investigations, 1965-1968.[43] This study opened up the complete
review of the fish ecology of the Hudson, a review which was to continue for
more than twenty years.[44]

   How did the 1965 *Scenic Hudson* case change the landscape of
environmental law? The court recognized the standing of citizen groups to
contest the Federal Power Commission's actions. Importantly, the court placed
the responsibility upon the Commission to affirmatively seek the facts related to
the environmental impacts of its action. In so doing, they expanded the
responsibility of the Commission to weigh environmental and natural beauty
values in their decisions.

   Charles Reich[45] recognized the significance of Storm King in his path-
breaking article "The Law of the Planned Society."[46] Based on principles
presented and sharpened during the long *Scenic Hudson* debate, Reich urged
recognition of the reality and necessity of public planning, the need for law to

foster democratic participation, consideration of broad values, and equality and public service as part of the planning process.[47]

The Santa Barbara Oil Spill[48]

In January of 1969, at offshore platforms belonging to Union Oil Company and just five miles off California's Santa Barbara coast, the world's then second largest oil spill began and continued throughout the year. From a half a million to two million gallons were spilled in the first two days and the slick dispersed 90 miles north to Pismo Beach and 65 south miles to Malibu. The large-scale killing of oil soaked birds, barnacle populations and surf grasses, and the aggravated impacts of cleanup efforts were mitigated only by the large near shorekelp beds which operated as a barrier to the oil's spread.[49]

The Santa Barbara oil spill was major environmental bad news, but not news since it was preceded by at least five other major spills in the world within the previous three years.[50] Dramatic images of oil-soaked birds and seals, and despoiled beaches filled the evening TV news reports. The nation identified with this perceived ecological disaster in an emotional way not shared by the DDT and *Scenic Hudson* cases. The previous spills, along with the highly visible Santa Barbara spill, sent marine biologists and oceanographers scurrying to labs and ocean and coastal sites seeking to determine the precise impacts of such spills and to consider how to clean up their damage. Oceanography – the study of the physical aspects of the ocean, and marine biology – the study of ocean and coastal biota, had been combined by Odum and others into marine and estuarine ecology.[51] Based upon this ecology, the post-spill studies documented the diffusion and persistence of the oil on the ocean bottom and its recurrent impacts upon marine and coastal organisms. These studies were to become a regular part of the history of the ecological study of damage from continuing oil spills during the next two decades.[52] Despite the knowledge gained from the Santa Barbara incident, ecological science remained ill prepared to prescribe exact clean-up plans and ecologists were often at odds about the best strategies for restoration. This uncertainty in the science has played a role in oil litigation cases.

The Emergence of Early Ecosystem Regimes[53]

> A disturbingly common environmental problem occurs when a lake, formerly in satisfactory condition, begins to produce dense populations of algae. One of the most remarkable things about the problem of the pollution of Lake Washington is that it was solved by

> public action and public vote. Further, the solution did not involve
> simply transferring the same problem somewhere else.
>
> – Edmondson, 1991, pp. 3, 20

The 1960s witnessed the first beginnings of ecosystem regimes – river and river basin planning, and laws for the protection of lakes,[54] mountains,[55] forests,[56] and coastal ecosystems.[57] In addition to statutes and court cases, the new ecological knowledge also informed and motivated the creation of new legislation as illustrated in the Lake Washington case study.

The pollution of one of America's most beautiful lakes was driven by the rapid growth of the City of Seattle and it presented a major environmental test for both the municipal and state governments. The Lake Washington case is significant because the actions taken by the citizens of Seattle and the State of Washington came in advance of federal leadership and legislation meant to ensure clean waters.[58] The actions to restore and protect Lake Washington were heavily influenced by the research and public participation by a University of Washington professor, W.T. Edmondson, and his colleagues. In his story of the Lake Washington struggle,[59] Edmondson recounts, "our study ... supplied new data that helped us understand the response of lakes to eutrophication, that provided novel and unusual examples of established ecological principles that were helpful to the public in making decisions about remedial action."[60] Lake Washington is an early and successful example of a process where the science of ecology became a full partner in the management regime that eventually reclaimed the lake from a path to near certain ecological disaster.

Formed at the end of the last Ice Age from the Vashon ice sheet, the pristine waters of Lake Washington's basin are deep and the lake, narrow with steep sides, stretching over twenty-one kilometers bordered by Seattle and its suburbs. The lake has a complex hydrology defined by inflows from the Cedar River at the south and Lake Sammamish to the north. The waters of Lake Washington flow into Puget Sound through a ship canal created in 1916.[61] The lake also receives natural runoff (minor hydrologic input, but important sources of pollutants) from seven other tributary streams.[62] The lake provides multiple uses and is important as a water supply for recreation and scenic beauty, and as a fishery.

Lake Washington did not always boast the clean water and natural beauty that it does today. In 1958, an assessment by the engineering firm of Brown and Caldwell described the situation gravely:

> Biological and chemical conditions indicate that the lake is in the
> first stage of degradation due to nutrient enrichment, resulting in part
> from the discharge of sewage effluents and overflows. If this situation
> is not remedied, the inestimable value of Lake Washington as a

recreational and scenic asset is likely to be greatly reduced, or
perhaps even lost completely.[63]

The Environmental pressures from a rapid post-World War II population
expansion began to affect the chemistry and biology of Lake Washington's
sensitive ecosystem. The problems created by people were many and included
contamination of water from sewage and the disposal of grease and oil, and
other industrial wastes. The most notable nuisance created was the excessive
growth of algae from the "inadvertent" fertilization of waters (i.e.,
eutrophication).[64] The inflow of both treated and untreated sewage dispensed
large amounts of phosphorus and nitrogen which contributed to the "over-
abundance" of algae that characterizes a eutrophic lake. At the height of public
controversy, ten sewage treatment plants were releasing nutrient-rich effluent
directly into the lake.[65]

The history of Seattle's growth is one of forest clearing, increasing
population, and the problem of sewage disposal.[66] As early as 1883, Seattle
faced the problem of sewage by constructing a primitive pipe system to avoid
direct dumping into the lake, as the lake also served as the early residents' water
supply.[67] This pipe system carried municipal sewage to approximately fifty
outfalls located around Puget Sound. Lake Washington soon became the
recipient of waste and by 1922, thirty outfalls from Seattle were in place. A
typhoid outbreak in 1907 prompted reevaluation of Seattle's drinking water
supply. In response, by 1936, the city had diverted all of its sewage from Lake
Washington to Puget Sound and the ocean.[68] This remedy helped, but continued
development in the area brought back sewage problems for the lake. Records
from 1898 discuss the invasion of the lake by the blue-green algae, *Oscillatoria
rubescens*.[69] The nutrient-rich water fertilized by the sewage inflow encouraged
blue-green algal growth that cause foul odors and turbid water.[70] In 1956, the
Pollution Control Commission recognized the detrimental effects of the sewage
effluent flowing into Lake Washington: "All sewage shall be treated and all
treatment plant effluents must eventually be diverted from Lake Washington and
Lake Sammamish to some point or points on Puget Sound."[71] After much public
education and debate regarding the deterioration of the lake's health, the local
public voted in 1958 to divert the sewage. Their plan took ten years to fully
implement. With the final diversion of sewage from the lake in February of
1968, the clarity and health of the lake improved, surpassing the expectations of
most experts.[72] After 1976, a large increase in transparency as well a shift in the
community composition and abundance of zooplankton indicate that the lake
had entered a new equilibria.[73]

The ecological visionary whose knowledge of and passion for the lake
ensured public attention to its problems was W.T. Edmondson. Sparked by the
analysis of a student's water sample that demonstrated the potential for

eutrophication of Lake Washington, Edmondson's many studies came to serve as a "whole-lake experiment," addressing the ecological and chemical complications of the entire lake ecosystem, arising as a result of rapid population growth. By demonstrating the link between phosphorus from sewage effluent and the resultant algal blooms in the lake, Edmondson provided the cause and effect guidance for management policy makers. His body of published research, though centering on Lake Washington, acted to inform others about lakes experiencing similar conditions.[74]

Edmondson's ecological evidence was compelling. A series of administrative actions and public appropriations created the regime to manage the lake. The 1981 Wastewater Management Plan prepared by the Municipality of Metropolitan Seattle (Metro) responded to the need for an increase in operating capacity for the sewage treatment facilities to meet demand of the growing population of the greater Lake Washington area.[75] While Metro prepared the actual plan, their efforts were meshed with federal government policy. The U.S. Environmental Protection Agency prepared the corresponding Environmental Impact Statement in accordance with National Environmental Policy Act (NEPA) requirements. The latter document proposes that federal funding be provided for long-term wastewater management facilities in the Lake Washington and Green River Basins.[76]

In constructing an ecosystemic regime for the management of the lake, a goal of restoring and protecting the ecosystem functions associated with healthy lakes is of utmost importance.[77] The effect from the sewage effluent impacted all levels of the ecosystem, and recovery is unpredictable. The excess phosphorus loading produces an "unnatural" nitrogen to phosphorus ratio[78] which alters the productivity of the lake and changed species composition. Phosphorus serves as a limiting element for the growth of algae, meaning that eutrophication (algal bloom) is best controlled by limiting the inputs of phosphorus into the lake.[79] Having confirmed the connection between phosphorus-loading of the lake via sewage effluent and eutrophication, Edmondson raised concern about the composition and disposal of phosphorous containing soaps and detergents.[80] It was found that the effects of sewage were amplified by the use of phosphorus-based detergents.[81] Thus, an integrated management attempt to control this excess of algal growth had to include curbing the release of domestic soaps and detergents.

The evolution of the ecologically-informed regime to manage Lake Washington was enabled by the early creation of a state agency system to protect its natural resources (the Department of Ecology) and a regional agreement (Metropolitan Enabling Act) that provided for public participation in lake management decisions for all the communities connected to the Lake Washington ecosystem. The legal regime in Washington is unique; the Metropolitan Enabling Act of 1958 established a metropolitan agency to address regulation and conflict in environmental matters. This new structure was designed to minimize interagency competition and conflict over jurisdiction. The Metro Enabling Act provided a system by which the public could vote to grant different groups of communities (minority interest protection) the opportunity to cooperate and influence local policy. It established a voting unit for the city of Seattle and a second for the smaller cities and towns in the surrounding area. A proposal would pass when both voting units produced a majority vote.[82]

In 1945, the state created the Water Pollution Control Agency which would become a part of the Washington State Department of Ecology in 1970. The Department of Ecology, now the state's overseer of environmental quality concerns also administers the Washington Water Quality Program which aims to " ... protect, preserve, and enhance Washington's surface and ground water quality, and to promote the wise management of water to benefit current and future generations."[83]

The Lake Washington "crisis" spurred the residents of the Seattle region to action in advance of federal mandates and oversight. Since the debates and policy changes concerning Lake Washington in the 1950s and 1960s, the role of the federal government regarding water quality has significantly developed. The Clean Water Act of 1972 provided the first comprehensive federal clean water legislation in response to concerns over the widespread water pollution in the nation's water supplies.[84] Thus, today the Lake Washington ecosystem is protected by a regime of both state and federal legislation.[85]

The water quality standards set for Lake Washington assure that the problems of previous decades should be prevented. The public is served by a monitoring program and more research on the basic ecological functioning of the lake that will inform lake managers about the effectiveness of their plans and the need for further intervention. The success in cleaning up Lake Washington came from the synergy created by a concerned public, a municipal and state government with an agency structure and local laws that were responsive in a timely way to citizen concerns, a body of sound ecological knowledge about the lake, and an involved scientist who persisted in educating the "players" about the need for and benefits of restoring Lake Washington.

Bridge Document 3.1 ENVIRONMENTAL IMPACT STATEMENT AND WASTEWATER
MANAGEMENT PLAN

The key bridge documents involved in the Lake Washington case are the Environmental Impact Statements (EIS) and Wastewater Management Plans for the Lake Washington/Green River Basins generated by the U.S. Environmental Protection Agency. The EIS documents describe possible environmental impacts related to the proposed management of the Lake Washington/Green River Basin region. By involving itself with Metro's management projects, the EPA aims to assist in the plans, provide financial support and ensure coordination with the federal Clean Water Act.[86] The plans detail the proposed diversions and facilities for waste-water treatment, including the secondary treatment plants and new Puget Sound outfalls.[87] Primarily, the 1981 management plan concentrates on the Renton treatment plant and the demand for augmentation of the facilities in order to accommodate the expanding population that it serves. Metro's plan also addresses the concern raised about effluent flow into the Duwamish River which reflects similar water quality problems as those seen in Lake Washington prior to diversion to Puget Sound. The plan proposes diversion of this effluent to Puget Sound as well.[88] The accompanying document put forth by the U.S. EPA in its Final Environ-mental Impact Statement considers the plan's cost-effectiveness and environmental viability in approval and support of the proposed actions. By aiding the local policy makers and environmental agencies, the EPA states its hope of achieving the goals of the federal Clean Water Act.[89] Recently, King County has completed a new multi-volume comprehensive plan (Regional Wastewater Services Plan) to readdress the management of Lake Washington and the surrounding areas. The approved RWSP passed in the King County Council in December, 1999. It's primary features include a new third treatment plant to be located somewhere in north King or south Snohomish County. Allowing for a greater wastewater treatment capacity, this plant will help to accommodate the area's growing population. King County is considering the possibility of recycling wastewater treatment byproducts including biosolids, methane and reclaimed water. Ultimately, it is their hope that highly treated wastewater could indirectly supplement the water supply.

The Early Parallel (but Unrelated) Development of Population Policy

Although most observers of the environmental scene would conclude that population growth contributes to our environmental problems, and some argue that it is the central contributing cause of those problems, population issues have not been a central part of the tradition of environmental law in the United States.[90] When a population policy is an important part of the laws of a nation, as in China, the motivation for such laws is not primarily environmental protection, but rather the prevention of famine and exhaustion of natural resources.[91] Similarly, the present population control measures in the United

States have been detached from environmental policy, and are tied to individual choice and control of fertility, and only recently have environmental groups begun to identify the environmental costs of population growth.[92]

This curious detachment of population growth control from environmental policy and law is the consequence of the way in which population policies have developed. Although concerns about population growth extend back to Plato and Aristotle[93] and have a deep and extensive tradition in political thought, ordinarily, the beginning of the history of population studies is marked by the writings of Thomas Malthus. In response to Condorcet's optimism[94] Malthus argued that the tendency for geometric increase in human population would outrun the predicted arithmetic increase in food resources, resulting in famine, poverty, and disease.[95] Although Condorcet was correct in his short term predictions, Malthus was prescient in predicting future population problems in the developing nations, and in providing a framework for later evolutionary and ecological treatments of animal populations. Both Darwin's view of evolution and later developments in population biology echoed the insights of Malthus.[96]

Ecologists like Odum in the 1960s recognized that human populations were an important part of understanding an ecosystem. Ecology, drawing on the earlier works of the population biologists, was able to describe alternative models of growth based upon dispersal, population structure and most centrally, the constraints upon that population imposed by natural resources and the environment.[97] It was the work of population biologists, Anne and Paul Ehrlich, which first made the major linkage in the public's mind between the insights of ecology and the need to control human population in their 1970 popular work: *The Population Bomb*.[98] In their more technical work, the Ehrlich's recognized the limited carrying capacity of the environment for the growth of animal populations. As applied to human population, the Ehrlich's presented a simple model, $I = PxAxT$, where environmental impact was a function of population size (and growth), affluence, and the technology available to people either exploit or in some cases ease human impact on the environment.

Despite this popular and provocative work, the public concern over population control took place outside of the environmental movement. The demographers captured the field and with the developing social science of demography,[99] focused upon the social correlates to human population growth and decline. Based upon demographic studies and responding to public concerns about the exhaustion of natural resources and famine at home and abroad, an international population policy developed.[100] The U.S. continued to avoid articulating a national population debate and policy. The 1966 "Food For Freedom" program was the first U.S. program to recognize "the population explosion" and provide funding for family planning assistance in the third world. In 1969, President Nixon created a separate Office of Population in the U.S. Agency of International Development and the U.N. Fund for Population Activities was created the same year.[101] On the domestic front, the first grant to support family planning services was made in 1965 under the Economic Opportunity Act and in 1967, Congress amended social security legislation to provide family planning services to welfare recipients, while the Secretary of the Health, Education and Welfare Department allowed family planning as part of medicaid. In 1970, the Family Planning services and Population Research Act was passed extending services to all persons.[102] Other legislation was passed in the early 1970s.[103]

These historical developments witnessed the gap between population control and an ecologically oriented environmental law. The focus of population policy was upon the provision of services for voluntary fertility control. On the other hand, the instrument of public policy adopted in environmental law is regulation. Therefore, it is not surprising that these two approaches, service provision and regulation, have been kept separate. The provision of services to be accepted or rejected on a voluntary basis corresponds with the deep values of privacy accorded to intimate sexual matters.[104] On the other hand, environmental law can and often does coercively regulate the public actions of polluters whether these polluters agree with the regulation or not. Hence, unlike fertility control, voluntary compliance is not central to environmental regulation. Thus, the respective values involved in the two areas of public policy, i.e., fertility control and environmental regulation, have historically been radically different.

This separation acts to perpetuate a distancing of the population problem from an ecological perspective within the realm of public policy. However, voluntary fertility control is not the only mechanism for controlling population growth. An ecological view of population growth suggests that not only self-regulation, but also manipulation of the carrying capacity for that population may influence the ways in which a population reproduces itself and the consequences of that reproduction. Hence, in more recent ecological thought about the population problem, the focus has centered upon the notion of carrying capacity and its implication for human population increases.[105]

Conclusion

During the 1960s, despite the excitements of the decade, no dawning of a new environmental consciousness successfully challenged American materialism. By the end of the 1960s, many of the fundamental concepts and methods of ecology were in place. The work of Odum and others permeated both large and small scale ecological studies. Some practical, environmentally-protective conclusions were being drawn from these studies. The broad language of selected new environmental laws permitted more specific ecological considerations to begin to enter the planning and regulation of the environment. Highly visible environmental cases raised the demand for more ecological research and increased the public's expectations of ecology to improve their quality of life.

The DDT problems and the efforts to protect the wilderness in the 1960s illustrated two distinct dimensions of our relationship with nature and the role of the science of ecology. Rachel Carson, in her study of DDT coursing through the pathways of the ecosystem, brought forcefully home to us the fact that we are part of ecosystems and our health is implicated by the way in which chemicals find their way through the systems.

The increased awareness of the wilderness as a relatively untouched ecosystem suggested to us that in some way, the workings of that system might produce intrinsic emergent values. The discovery of the ecosystem as a complex pathway of chemicals is a view compatible with the science of ecology. The notion of an ecosystem as a source of intrinsic emergent value seems a more troubling prospect for the science of ecology. The "reenchantment of nature" may hint at a world which the science of ecology cannot and should not grasp.

Yet the dramatic development of the 1960s raised as many questions about the relations between ecology and law as were answered. Some of these questions were:

1. To what extent do large-scale and well-funded programs of ecology provide information for environmental policy?
2. How useful is it to include explicitly ecological categories in legislation?
3. To what extent can ecological categories within legislation create administrative and political problems?
4. To what extent does wilderness-related legislation and its goals conform to ecological insights and does preservation facilitate an ecological approach to ecosystem management?
5. What level of qualification is and should be required for general ecologists to testify in court and administrative hearings, and on what matters may they testify?
6. How can administrative hearings be best structured to facilitate communication and understanding of ecological methods and conclusions and their limits?
7. How can one tailor administrative and legal proceedings to permit access or "standing" of a spectrum of citizens affected by interventions in ecosystems?
8. What objections should administrative agents have to undertake ecological studies?

9. What kind of government mandated planning should be required for ecological research?
10. What are the appropriate jurisdictions (federal, state, local) for considering ecological effects?
11. What is the relationship between ecosystems and their boundaries and public and private property?
12. Does the ecological concept of "limited carrying capacity" provide a useful benchmark for measuring the desirability of population growth?
13. How do the new localized ecosystem regimes fit into the pre-existing federal structure?

These were just a few of the myriad of questions to be addressed in the next thirty years.

Notes

1. *See* HARMAN HENKIN, ET AL., THE ENVIRONMENT, THE ESTABLISHMENT AND THE LAW (1971).
2. For a full historical account of the 1950s, *see* DAVID HALBERSTRAM, THE FIFTIES (1993). Two historical accounts of environmental policy and law may be found in RICHARD N.L. ANDREWS, MANAGING THE ENVIRONMENT, MANAGING OURSELVES: A HISTORY OF AMERICAN ENVIRONMENTAL POLICY (1999) [for the 1950s and 1960s, *see* pp. 201-255]; and SAMUEL P. HAYS, BEAUTY, HEALTH AND PERMANENCE: ENVIRONMENTAL POLITICS IN THE UNITED STATES 1955-1985 (1987).
3. *See especially* JOHN KENNETH GALBRAITH, THE AFFLUENT SOCIETY (1958, 1960).
4. For a detailed account of research at Oak Ridge, *see* BOCKING, *infra* note 5, at 63-115.
5. For accounts of the development of ecology in the 1960s, *see* GOLLEY, *infra* note 7; JOCK HAGEN, AN ENTANGLED BANK: THE ORIGINS OF ECOSYSTEM ECOLOGY (1992); STEPHEN BOCKING, ECOLOGISTS AND ENVIRONMENTAL POLITICS: A HISTORY OF CONTEMPORARY ECOLOGY (1997); and ROBERT P. MCINTOSH, THE BACKGROUND OF ECOLOGY: CONCEPT AND THEORY (1985).
6. *See* MCINTOSH, *supra* note 5, at 213.
7. *See* FRANK B. GOLLEY, A HISTORY OF THE ECOSYSTEM CONCEPT IN ECOLOGY: MORE THAN THE SUM OF THE PARTS (1993).
8. The recognition of the grasslands' relative simplicity goes back to Clements' early studies in the 1890s.
9. Besides applying systems theory to physiology he also provided a history of system theory that dates the origin of the theory to the Classical Greeks. *See* L. VON BERTALANFFY, GENERAL SYSTEMS THEORY: FOUNDATIONS, DEVELOPMENT, APPLICATIONS (1968). Other authors have provided different histories but most agree that the formation of the theory is obscure. *See* MCINTOSH, *supra* note 5, at 232.
10. *See* PAUL R. EHRLICH & JONATHAN ROUGHGARDEN, THE SCIENCE OF ECOLOGY 552 (1987).
11. *See* GOLLEY, *supra* note 7.
12. *See* GOLLEY, *supra* note 7, at 134-35.

13.   Part of the problem may have been the rapid evolution of model evolution and computer programming; the models and programs designed for the whole system grassland model were outdated before the project was even finished. *See id.*

14.   Some critics of the system approach argue that any system model is developed from the arbitrary combination of components and is therefore just another form of reductionism. *See* R. Levins & R. Lewontin, *Dialectics and reductionism in ecology*, 43 SYNTHESE 47-78 (1980).

15.   *See* MCINTOSH, *supra* note 5, at 206-7. However, while not a system ecology study, the Hubbard Brook researchers would use system models if useful, such as the use of the so-called JABOWA model to test their biomass accumulation theories.

16.   *See* MCINTOSH, *supra* note 5, at 205. This approach made Hubbard Brook and much more traditional scientific study. Unlike the grassland project, the data gathered at Hubbard Brook was collected for the main purpose of understanding the actual ecosystem, not to build a virtual (model) ecosystem.

17.   *See* Gene E. Likens et al., *Effects of Forest Cutting and Herbicide Treatment on Nutrient Budgets in the Hubbard Brook Watershed-Ecosystems*, 40 ECOLOGICAL MONOGRAPHS 23, 25 (1970).

18.   Many ecosystem ecologists had long believed that abiotic factors were critical to regulating plant and animal populations, but until Hubbard Brook the reverse relationship had not been considered as important.

19.   *See Woodland Ecosystems and Nature Reserves*, pp. 38-60 in BOCKING *supra* note 5.

20.   *See Ecology and the Ontario Fisheries*, pp. 151-178 in BOCKING, note 5.

21.   *See The Lake as a Microcosm*, pp. 35-60 in GOLLEY, *supra* note 7.

22.   *See* Philip C. Miller et al., *MEDECS: A Simulation for Mediterranean Ecosystems*, 30 SIMULATION 173-190 (1978).

23.   16 U.S.C.S. 661 et seq.; 662, 665. This remarkable early law identified the need for wildlife and habitat conservation, requiring public agencies, including public and private agencies under federal permits, to coordinate their action in order to minimize the impacts upon fish and wildlife and their habitat (16 U.S.C.661-666c).

24.   16 U.S.C.S. 741, 742(a)(3)(c).

25.   P.L. 212. This law is primarily concerned with facilitating the leasing process without affecting navigation and fishing [*Section 3*] and provides protection of aquatic life only in the process of exploration. [*See Section II.*]

26.   16 U.S.C.S. 1001 et seq.

27.   P.L. 89-80; 79 Stat. 244. The Water Resources Planning Act [P.L. 89-80; 79 Stat. 244] authorized the establishment of river basin commissions to plan the "optimum use" of water for multiple purposes, including agriculture, urban, energy, industrial, recreational, fish and wildlife and other resources. Despite concerns about population and conservation, the legislative history reveals little awareness of ecology and water ecosystems. [*See* the Legislative History of the Water Resources Planning Act in U.S. CODE AND CONGRESSIONAL NEWS (89th Congress, First Session 1965: Vol. 1) at 1921.]

28.   *Id.* at 54-56.

29.   *See* ANN STRONG, PRIVATE PROPERTY AND THE PUBLIC INTEREST: THE BRANDYWINE EXPERIENCE (1975). This program was a Ford Foundation-funded effort directed primarily at land use controls to protect watershed values.

30.   Although the teams consisted of lawyers, planners, social scientists, and hydrologists, it did not include the full range of ecosystem scientists.

31.   The reasons were many and are set forth in Strong's book (*Id.* p. 7, 9-12). In one ominous evaluation, Strong concludes "... we give too much weight to the quality of the natural environment and paid too little attention to the necessity for strong local leadership supporting the plan ..." (p. 11).

32.   Section 2(C) P.L. 88-577, 58 Stat. 890.

33.   16 U.S.C.S. 1271 et seq.

34.   The assumption of the possibility of any part of nature being independent of human regulation is a much debated topic. *See* MAX OELSHLAEGER, THE IDEA OF WILDERNESS FROM PRE-HISTORY TO THE AGE OF ECOLOGY (1991); RODERICK NASH, WILDERNESS AND THE AMERICAN MIND (1967, 1982); BILL MCKIBBEN, THE END OF NATURE (1989); WILLIAM LEISS, THE DOMINATION OF NATURE (1972).

35.   The regulation of wilderness areas evidences the entry of ecological concepts. 36 CFR 2932. Objectives of Primitive Areas, "... (a) Natural ecological *succession* will be allowed to operate freely to the extent possible ...".

36.   16 U.S.C. 1241 et seq.

37.   Refuge Recreation Act of 1996 (16 U.S.C. 668dd-668ee); Refuge Recreation Act of 1962 (16 U.S.C. 460K-460K-4). These acts were amended by the National Wildlife System Improvement Act of 1997. A review of more recent refuge comprehensive conservation plans (e.g., Comprehensive Conservation Plan, Lostwood, North Dakota (U.S.F. and W. Service, Dec. 1998) reveals broad use of ecological terms (p. 53), a description of the refuge in ecosystem terms, a statement of objectives in ecological language, and ecological analyses. The federal management of wilderness areas has specifically adopted ecosystem concepts, at least by 1977. It was, however, recognized that both the designation and management of such areas in accordance with ecosystems created an apparent intellectual contradiction, since "wildness" seemed to exclude public designation and management. [*See* U.S. Department of Agriculture, JOHN C. HENDEE, GEORGE H. STANKEY, ROBERT LUCAS, WILDERNESS MANAGEMENT [P.L. No. 1365 Oct. 1978] at 1-25, 169-281.]

38.   *See* RACHEL CARSON, THE SEA AROUND US (1950).

39.   *See* H. PATRICIA HYNES, THE RECURRING SILENT SPRING (1989); FRANK GRAHAM, SINCE SILENT SPRING (1970); DUNLOP, DDT: SCIENTISTS, CITIZENS AND PUBLIC POLICY (1981); JOHN WARGO, OUR CHILDREN'S TOXIC LEGACY: HOW SCIENCE AND LAW FAILS TO PROTECT US FROM PESTICIDES (1996).

40.   *See* L. C. Cole, *Book Review of Silent Spring*, SCIENTIFIC AMERICAN, December 173-180 [1950].

41.   *See* HENKIN, et al., *supra* note 1.

42.   *Id.* at 191-206.

43.   The study is cited in Scenic Hudson Preservation Conference v. Federal Power Commission, 453 F2d 463, ERC 1232, 1241 (1971).

44.   *See* LAWRENCE BARTHOUSE, RONALD KLAUDA, DOUGLAS VAUGHAN, ROBERT KENDALL, SCIENCE, LAW AND THE HUDSON RIVER POWER PLANTS: A CASE STUDY IN ENVIRONMENTAL ASSESSMENT (1988).

45.   CHARLES REICH was later to gain fame for his book THE GREENING OF AMERICA (1970). This book offered a cultural interpretation of American history in which the 1960s represented the dawning of a new consciousness. In light of the materialism of the 1980s and 1990s, it is easy to discount the valid insights Reich offered, including his insightful discussion of American culture.

46.   *See* Charles Reich, *The Law of the Planned Society* 75 YALE L.J. (1966) 1227-1270.

47.   *See id.* at 1258-1270.

48.   *See* A.K. KEIR NASH, DEAN MANN, PHIL G. OLSON, OIL POLLUTION AND THE PUBLIC INTEREST: A STUDY OF THE SANTA BARBARA OIL SPILL (1972).

49.   *Id.* at 26.

50.   *Id.* at 24.

51.   *See* PETER BOOKER, THE ENVIRONMENTAL SCIENCES p. 542; EUGENE ODUM, THE
        FUNDAMENTALS OF ECOLOGY (1959, 1971) pp. 324-362.

52.   For an overview of such studies, *see* JOANNA BURGER, OIL SPILLS (1997). For an
        ecological study of a later spill, see U.S. Dept. of Commerce (NOAA) and Centre Pour
        l'Exploration des Oceans Joint Scientific Commission, ECOLOGICAL STUDY OF THE
        AMOCO CADIZ OIL SPILL (1982).

53.   This section relies heavily on the work of Kathleen Stewart, Dartmouth Class of 2001.
        For an overview of the Lake Washington Regime, *see* W.T. EDMONDSON, THE USES OF
        ECOLOGY: LAKE WASHINGTON AND BEYOND (1991).

54.   *See* DOUGLAS H. STRONG, TAHOE: AN ENVIRONMENTAL HISTORY (1984).

55.   *See* TIMOTHY P. DUANE, SHAPING THE SIERRA: NATURE, CULTURE AND CONFLICT IN THE
        CHANGING WEST (1998).

56.   *See* PROTECTING THE NEW JERSEY PINELANDS (Beryl Robichand Collins & Emily W.B.
        Russell eds.1988).

57.   *See* RICE ODELL, THE SAVING OF SAN FRANCISCO BAY (1972); Gerald Swanson, *Coastal
        Zone Management From an Administrative Perspective*, 2 COASTAL ZONE
        MANAGEMENT JOU. 81 (1975).

58.   *See* Chapter 1, The Federal Water Pollution Control Act.

59.   *See* EDMONDSON, *supra* note 53.

60.   *See id.* at 3.

61.   *See* W.T. EDMONDSON, *Trophic Equilibrium of Lake Washington*, Environmental
        Research Laboratory – U.S. EPA. Corvallis, OR: 1977, p.5.

62.   *See* Brown & Caldwell, *Metropolitan Seattle Sewerage and Drainage Survey: A report
        for the City of Seattle, King County and the State of Washington* (1958) p. 226 on the
        collection, treatment and disposal of sewage and the collection and disposal of storm
        water in the metropolitan Seattle area.

63.   *See id.* Brown and Caldwell, note 62.

64.   Eutrophication refers to the nutrient enrichment of lakes, either from natural processes
        or from human activities. The productivity of most lakes is limited by the availability
        of phosphorous and then nitrogen. Sudden increases in the inputs of these elements can
        stimulate production leading to algal blooms and the attendant problems of decreased
        clarity, odors, fish die-offs, and loss of recreational value. For a general introduction
        to this issue and lake ecosystems, *see* JACOB KALFF, LIMNOLOGY: INLAND WATER
        ECOSYSTEMS (2002).

65.   *See* Brown and Caldwell, *supra* note 62, at 228.

66.   *See* EDMONDSON, *supra* note 53, at 5.

67.   *See* EDMONDSON, *supra* note 53, at 8.

68.   *See* EDMONDSON, *supra* note 53, at 9.

69.   *See* EDMONDSON, *supra* note 53, at 12.

70.   *See* Brown & Caldwell, *supra* note 62, at 237.

71.   *See* Brown & Caldwell, *supra* note 62, at 225.

72.   *See* EDMONDSON, *supra* note 53, at 33. Measuring transparency with a Secchi disc (a
        standard white disc that is used to measure transparency of water by the differential
        depth at which the disc can be seen), W.T. Edmondson (the primary expert on Lake
        Washington and its condition), along with students of his from the University of
        Washington, confirmed the hypothesis that the lake's lucidity would demonstrate a
        great difference from before the sewage effluent diversions to the recovery period.
        Thus, the beauty of the lake began to return. Described as a "clear" lake by the first
        settlers, Lake Washington began to recover to its pre-settlement state. Measurements
        by Edmondson indicate that transparency exceeded the 1950 value when measured
        again in 1971 and phosphorus values were nearly equivalent. *See supra* note 61, at 9.

73. *See* Edmondson, *supra* note 61, at iv.
74. Among others, the most prominent of Edmondson's publications include *Trophic Equilibrium of Lake Washington* (1977), *Daphnia in Lake Washington* (1982), and THE USES OF ECOLOGY (1991). A 1958 report by a local Seattle engineering firm, Brown and Caldwell, summarized the state of the lake with regard to sewage disposal at that time in an almost 600-page document. [Brown & Caldwell. *Metropolitan Seattle Sewerage and Drainage Survey.* Seattle: 1958.] Since this time, Edmondson's and the EPA's documents describing management of the ecosystem are the most adequate descriptions of the regime. [Municipality of Metropolitan Seattle. *Final Supplemental EIS on the Renton Effluent Transfer System Alternatives for the Wastewater Management Plan.* Seattle: 1984. U.S. Environmental Protection Agency. *Final Environmental Impact Statement of the Wastewater Management Plan for the Lake Washington/Green River Basins.* Seattle: 1981. United States Environmental Protection Agency. *Record of Decision and Responsiveness Summary for the Final EIS on the Wastewater Management Plan for the Lake Washington/Green River Basins.* Seattle: 1982.] These include management plans and environmental impact statements that describe the problems and the course of action prescribed to alleviate them with the greatest efficiency. Although available information lacks more complete histories of populations and their changes as well as more recent histories of the overall ecosystem, the documents offer insight into the methods used to address the environmental concerns.
75. *See* Municipality of Metropolitan Seattle. *Wastewater Management Plan, Lake Washington/Green River Basins.* Metro: Seattle, 1981.
76. *See* EPA, *Environmental Impact Statement: Wastewater Management Plan for the Lake Washington/Green River Basins.* U.S. EPA Region 10: Seattle, WA, 1981.
77. "Ecosystem function" refers to the interaction of all organisms naturally occurring in the given ecosystem and how they are affected by one another and by outside disturbances (in this case, particularly algal and fish populations, water clarity and nitrogen and phosphorous content). This may be heavily emphasized in the Edmondson reports because this seems to be *his* primary concern.
78. The N:P ratio of effluents and of lake waters allows prediction of algal growth responses. In general, temperate lakes that are not polluted have high N:P ratios. As P increases relative to N, the potential for algal blooms increases. These relationships were established in the whole-lake nutrient enrichment experiments carried out by David W. Schindler, et al., in the Lakes Area, Ontario, Canada. They found that neither N or carbon additions alone or together increased algal production significantly in non-polluted lakes, but that P additions increase algal biomass. D.W. Schindler, H. Kling, R.V. Schmidt, J. Prokopowich, V.E. Frost, R.A. Reed & M. Chapel, *Eutro-phication of Lake 227 by addition of phosphate and nitrate: The second, third, and fourth years of enrichment, 1970, 1971, and 1972.* CAN. J. FISH. RES. BD. 30:1415-1440 (1973).
79. *See* EDMONDSON, *supra* note 53, at 91.
80. *See* Brown & Caldwell, *supra* note 62, at 229. In the 1958 report, Brown and Caldwell relate that the content of inorganic phosphorus in domestic sewage had been on the rise as a result of the use of phosphorus-rich detergents in replacing basic soap.
81. *See* EDMONDSON, *supra* note 61, at 12.
82. *See* EDMONDSON, *supra* note 53, at 22.
83. Several additional state statutes address the complications of sewage effluent and water quality. Specifically, the Revised Code of Washington §35.88.080 (2000) states: "Inland cities over 100,000 – Discharge of sewage and other discharges prohibited – nuisance". This encompasses the Seattle region and thus, Lake Washington. In addition, Chapter 173-208 of WAC addresses the "Grant of Authority Sewerage

Systems" while Chapter 173-221A WAC concerns the "Wastewater Discharge Standards and Effluent Limitations" for Washington state. These grant to the Department of Ecology the authority to control the distribution of permits for sewage discharge. This is designated according to the level most acceptable and appropriate to maintain water quality pursuant both to the public interest and to the Water Pollution Control Act [WAC 173-208-010]. The latter asserts that the state's water be of "highest quality" with all effluents having been treated with all " ... known, available and reasonable methods ... " prior to discharge into the state's waters. This code, however, also introduces an exception for " ... those situations where it is clear that overriding considerations of the public interest will be served." [WAC 173-221A-020.] Such a caveat could introduce opportunity for abuses and uncertainties in defining where such a line might be drawn.

84.   "The Clean Water Act is a 1977 amendment to the Federal Water Pollution Control Act of 1972, which set the basic structure for regulating discharges of pollutants to U.S. waters. The law gave EPA the authority to set effluent standards on an industry basis and continued the requirements to set water quality standards for all contaminants in surface waters. The CWA makes it unlawful for any person to discharge any pollutant from a point source into navigable waters unless a permit (NPDES) is obtained under the Act. The 1977 amendments focused on toxic pollutants."
        <http://www.epa.gov/region5/defs/html/cwa.htm>

85.   As a governing body, Metro is currently subsumed by King County and continues to monitor the lake to ensure the maintenance of high water quality. Simultaneously, Edmondson and his University of Washington colleagues have continued for four decades to study and interpret the causes and effects of eutrophication in Lake Washington. ["Resolution", 181.] King County, currently exploring the option of water reuse and release into the lake, sees this as a favorable alternative as it could restore greater flow to the lake and provide for more efficient functioning of the locks of the ship canal to Puget Sound by encouraging constant water movement.
        <http://dnr.metrokc.gov/wtd/rwsp/tutorial/solution.htm.> A state act, passed in 1995, addresses the reuse of water and " ... requires Ecology (the state department) to develop standards, procedures, and guidelines for direct aquifer recharge using reclaimed water." This code (Chapter 90.46 RCW, Reclaimed Water Use) concerns both the Washington Departments of Ecology and Health for appropriate implementation. Thus, they have rescinded the old restriction on effluents. This is now a safe alternative because with federal legislation in place to protect the lake from excessive nutrient input (Federal Clean Water Act) there is less risk of local abuses exceeding levels at which harmful algal blooms could take place. This possibility is still being explored and a decision to allow such effluent will not be made for at least another ten years when proper assessment and study of the need for and results of such an action have taken place [John Glynn].

86.   *See* <http://www4.law.cornell.edu/uscode/33/ch26.html.>

87.   *See* EPA EIS, *supra* note 76.

88.   *See* Metro, *supra* note 75, at 41.

89.   *See* EPA EIS, *supra* note 76, at i.

90.   The principal writing on population law appears to concentrate upon its linkage to health law. (*See for example*, STEPHEN ISAACS, POPULATION LAW AND POLICY: SOURCE MATERIALS AND ISSUES (1981).)

91.   Both motivations (along with eugenics), played an important part in animating the birth control movement. *See* BETSY HARTMANN, REPRODUCTIVE RIGHTS AND WRONGS: THE GLOBAL POLITICS OF POPULATION CONTROL (1995) pp. 3-93.

92.   These groups have been especially incensed by the United State immigration policy, since approximately one-third of the U.S. population growth is due to immigration.

93.   For a collection of ancient and later sources, *see* GARRETT HARDIN, POPULATION, EVOLUTION, AND BIRTH CONTROL: A COLLAGE OF CONTROVERSIAL IDEAS (1964, 1969).

94.   *See* THOMAS ROBERT MALTHUS, AN ESSAY ON THE PRINCIPLE OF POPULATION (1978).

95.   *See* ANTOINE-NICOLAS DE CONDORCET, SKETCH FOR A HISTORICAL PICTURE OF THE PROGRESS OF THE HUMAN MIND (1795).

96.   The later development of demography, rather than focusing upon the natural selection of human population, sought to describe social correlates with rates of population increase.

97.   *See* EUGENE ODUM, ECOLOGY 162-234 (1970).

98.   *See* ANN AND PAUL EHRLICH, THE POPULATION BOMB (1968).

99.   Standard works on demography include COLIN NEWELL, METHODS AND MODELS OF DEMOGRAPHY (1988); J. MARJORIE STYROS, DEMOGRAPHY AS AN INTERDISCIPLINE (1989); PAUL NEUWIRTH, FROM MALTHUS TO THE CLUB OF ROME AND BACK: PROBLEMS OF LIMITS TO GROWTH, POPULATION CONTROL AND MIGRATIONS (1994); AND HOLLIE KITNER, DEMOGRAPHIES (1997). For a historical review of U.S. population policy, *see* DONALD T. CRITCHLOW, INTENDED CONSEQUENCES; BIRTH CONTROL, ABORTION AND THE FEDERAL GOVERNMENT IN MODERN AMERICA (1999).

100.   With the exception of ecological treatments, early demography was largely descriptive and replete with projections. Sophistication in projection of population grew with the advent of systems analysis and the computer. DONELLA MEADOWS and others were the first to bring the fruits of such projects to the general public's awareness in THE LIMITS TO GROWTH (1972).

101.   *See* CRITCHLOW *supra* note 99 at 93-113.

102.   It is revealing that early legislation focused upon the poor. The law began to broaden the group eligible for services.

103.   *See* ISAACS *supra* note 90, at 220-30.

104.   Hence, the legal issues involving contraception led to the constitutional formulation of the right to privacy in the United States. See Griswold v. Connecticut 381 U.S. 479 (1965).

105.   *See* MIGUEL SANTOS, MANAGING PLANET EARTH: PERSPECTIVES ON POPULATION, ECOLOGY AND THE LAW (1990); JOEL COHEN, HOW MANY PEOPLE CAN THE EARTH SUPPORT? (1995).

4 The Lovers' Quarrel Between Law and Ecology

The great question of the seventies is, shall we surrender to our surroundings or shall we make peace with nature and begin to make legislation for the damage we have done to our air, our land and our water.

– U.S. President Richard Nixon's 1970
State of the Union message

The *Boomer* Case. In 1970, a large cement plant (one court claimed it was one of the largest in the world when built) opened operations in upper New York State. The plant cost over $45 million to build and employed over 300 nearby residents. Owners of neighboring property, including Mr. and Mrs. Boomer, brought suit against the company, claiming that the dust and vibrations caused by the plant operations created a nuisance. As is appropriate for ongoing harms under the tort of nuisance, they requested an injunction – a court order requiring the plant to stop emitting dust and causing vibrations. The crucial problem in *Boomer* was simply that with the technology of 1970, a cement plant could not operate without producing dust and vibrations. The only way for the company to comply with an injunction would be to close the plant down.[1] The *Boomer* case reached the highest New York court as Earth Day was dawning. The court was acutely aware that a new Clean Air Act was on the horizon. Despite the dissent, which believed that the case should be decided with attention to this new national environmental policy, the court awarded environmental damages, yet it studiously ignored the new environmental law regime about to be enacted. Judge Bergen stated: "Effective control of air pollution is a problem presently far from solution, even with the full public and financial powers of government." The *Boomer* case was, however, prophetic in an important way. The court avoided consideration of the ecological impact of the pollutants, as well as the ecological impact of treating the pollutants; rather, it based the decision on economic considerations, balancing the industry's needs with the complainants' damages. In later years, environmentalists would seek to sue cement plants under the Clean Air Act and NEPA to force government administrators to attend to the massive pollution resulting from efforts to clean up air pollution from cement plants. The court refused to enforce such a multi-media approach, and it was years before the pollution resulting from such cement plants would be treated.

A new and startling view of our blue-green earth from space confronted the public and challenged the political rhetoric of our nation's leaders. Never before were we so aware of the unique wonder of the planet and connectedness of the land, oceans, and atmosphere. The "Spaceship Earth" view of our world began to influence our thinking about the environment, and eventually our laws and policies, too. This vivid picture of the earth was intellectually applied in James Lovelock's 1969 Princeton Seminar: "the Gaia hypothesis."[2]

> Gaia [is] a complex entity involving the Earth's biosphere, atmosphere, oceans and soil; the totality constituting a feedback or cybernetic system which seeks an optimal physical and chemical environment for life on this planet. The maintenance of relatively constant conditions by active control may be conventionally described by the term "homeostasis."

Table 4.1 CENTRAL ORGANIZING PRINCIPLES FOR UNDERSTANDING THE ENVIRONMENTAL CRISIS

PRINCIPAL AUTHOR AND WORK	PRINCIPLE AND THEORY	POLICY AND/OR LEGAL INSTRUMENT
Lovelock, *GAIA*	Cybernetics	Global pollution controls
Meadows, THE LIMITS TO GROWTH	Systems analysis	Modeling pollutants and ecosystems
Ehrlich, THE POPULATION BOMB	National carrying capacity	Growth controls
Commoner, THE CLOSING CIRCLE	Biogeochemical cycle	Pollutant pathway analysis

Lovelock's controversial Gaia vision, which attributed many of the behaviors of a living organism to the Earth system, was accompanied by three other popular ecological books. Anne and Paul Ehrlich's *The Population Bomb*[3] offered the possibility of an eco-catastrophe, arguing that unchecked population growth would irreparably harm the environment and human welfare. Barry Commoner's *The Closing Circle* sought to demonstrate that our "environmental problem" is the result of the production of synthetic pollutants,[4] created by the work of the reductive sciences (especially chemistry), driven by the profit-oriented economy. These long-lived synthetic pollutants interfered with the basic cycles of nature described by the science of ecology. For Commoner, who sought the U.S. Presidency to plead his case, only large-scale changes in our economic system and the reductive sciences' "submission" to the guiding principles of ecology could save the earth. Donella and Dennis Meadows' *The Limits to Growth*[5] offered a similarly grand visionary approach to the environmental problems of the 1970s. The Meadows were among the first to employ computer models to study and forecast the interdependence between population, food production, industrialization, consumption of non-renewable natural resources and pollution rates. Based upon the consequences of exponential human population growth, they projected a potential collapse in the earth's functioning if we continued on the present path.

All four of these visions were based upon theories that extended one or another aspect of the tenets, methods and concepts of ecology. Cybernetics (Lovelock), systems analysis (Meadows), population and natural carrying capacity (Ehrlich) and biogeochemical cycling (Commoner) were chosen as central organizing principles for understanding the environmental crisis. The same concepts and methodologies survive as the foundations for today's fields of Earth system science and global ecology.[6]

These visions, broad in concept, but limited by our fledgling understanding of complex system dynamics, were initially unable to shape the future directions of environmental law and policy. Instead, the immediate legal response to the package of environmental problems behind Earth Day took two different paths. One path was the pragmatic approach of organizing the new Environmental Protection Agency (EPA), and seeking to strengthen the already established national and state air, water and land use laws through technology-based effluent or emission standards. Unfortunately, these laws would offer a distorted view of the ecosystem by segmenting it into arbitrary, discrete categories such as air or water pollution, rather than beginning with a vision of an interdependent nature. The other path, the one less traveled, understood the spaceship analogy to the Earth Day vision and sought to shape the law to fit that ecological vision. To realize that vision, new laws were needed.

These two different approaches to the environmental crisis resulted from divergent views of pollution. For the public and their representatives (as well as many lawyers and engineers), pollutants were unwelcome intruders into the air they breathed and the water they drank. In the words of one statute, they invaded the environment's "integrity."[7] As a consequence, they needed to be cleaned up (i.e., removed from the medium of air or water).[8]

An ecologist looks at matters differently.[9] Pollutants are the residues of animal and human activities, not unknown in the natural environment. Ordinarily, these residues are degraded and recycled within the ecosystem.[10] "Pollution," from this point of view, is residue that may, over time, be recycled. If such pollutants are not naturally recycled, it is due to their amount, location or unique nature (i.e., non-biodegradable synthetics).[11]

Such an ecological view of pollution opens up different avenues to its treatment. Ecologists may encourage the natural recycling of pollutants.[12] They may seek to limit the rate, amount, or location of pollutants to facilitate natural degradation. They may seek to increase nature's capacity to absorb pollutants without loss to the ecosystem. They may seek to ban those synthetics that cannot be metabolized by soil and water. In order to accomplish any or all of these tasks, she will have to carefully determine the nature of pollutants and trace the pathways of pollutants within the environment.[13]

Figure 4.1 THE TWO INITIAL PATHWAYS IN ENVIRONMENTAL LAW

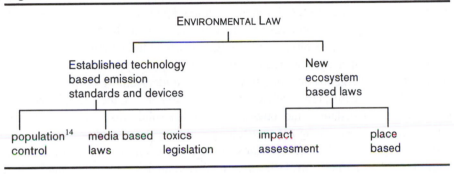

In short, two pathways were pursued: one based on controlling emissions, the other on managing the integrity of the ecosystem. For the most part, these two different paths were to be traveled under the aegis of the U.S. Environmental Protection Agency (EPA) and related departments. The path of resistance to ecology through the adoption of technology based standards will be explored in this chapter. The tentative embrace of ecology by means of new ecosystem based laws will be recounted in the next chapter.

The early history of the EPA illustrates both the possibilities and obstacles of pursuing an ecologically-oriented environmental law. The Environmental Protection Agency was organized in 1970 by executive order.[15] In an effort to encompass the entire environment, the agency brought together the regulatory and research programs scattered through many departments, including air pollution control, solid waste, water, radiological hygiene and pesticide research from the Department of Health, Education and Welfare; water quality administration and pesticide research, pesticide regulation from the Department of Agriculture; and radiation regulation from the Atomic Energy Commission. Despite this "unification" under the environmental banner, these programs remained authorized by existing statutes, and administered by pre-existing staff. Even with a gallant effort to encompass many environmental problems, other related programs were left within the Departments of Interior (e.g., national parks, endangered species), Agriculture (e.g., forestry), Commerce (e.g., coastal and marine management), and Defense (the Army Corps of Engineers).

The resulting "super" agency and a myriad of other departments were an uneasy collection of units representing different environmental media (air, water, land), pollutants (pesticides and radiation), disciplines (engineering, biology, planning, etc.), organizational cultures, ideologies, and functions (enforcement, research, policy analysis and administration).[16] Similar mixtures were conjoined in state environmental agencies. This "bureaucratic trail-mix" made a coherent ecological approach to environmental protection impossible. To quickly establish itself as the nation's protector, the agency's initial approach was to seek aggressive formulation of specific standards and their enforcement at the expense of careful preliminary systematic ecological planning.[17] It would not be until the 1990s that both federal and state agencies realized that an ecological approach required a total administrative reorganization and new scientific understanding of the ecosystem.

In some cases, laws such as with the Clean Air Act, the Clean Water Act, land planning legislation and laws pertaining to solid waste and toxics were established and functioning before ecology had fully developed as a science and had reached the public consciousness in a form available for environmental regulation. Furthermore, these laws were formulated in ways that made them inflexible to new ecological concepts. Since the Clean Air Act and the Clean Water Act were based upon the notion of a medium (i.e., air or water) whose integrity was violated by a pollutant, while solid waste and toxic laws focused upon the harmful nature of the pollutant itself, none of these major environmental laws began with a deeper view of pollution as a disturbance within an ecosystem. When Eugene Odum and others offered such an ecosystem view of pollution, and Barry Commoner popularized it in *The Closing Circle* at the time of Earth Day, the structures of the Clean Air Act and Clean Water Act were already established and even the approach to solid and hazardous waste had been determined.

This crystallization of the major environmental laws in terms of media and pollutants would create significant problems for the future efforts to require ecological knowledge to be used in the administration of these important environmental laws. By concentrating upon media and pollutants, these laws focused only upon parts of the ecosystem, i.e., air or water, or on a specific element being introduced into the ecosystem and ignored secondary effects on interlocking components within the ecosystem. Since these laws were hardened into the language of media and pollutants, they have continued to resist reformulation in ecosystemic terms. As a consequence, even in the new millennium there is a continuing tension; a "lover's quarrel" between ecology and these major areas of environmental law. Whether this early breach between ecology and these environmental laws can or should be healed will be explored in later chapters. This chapter will document the resistance of these laws to ecological influences.

The Clean Air Act[18]

The Clean Air Act of 1970 offers an excellent example of the pragmatic legal response to the environmental crisis preceding Earth Day. The Act authorized the promulgation of primary national ambient air quality standards (NAAQS). These were not new standards. Instead, they were health-based standards previously formulated by the Department of Health, Education and Welfare, an agency with little interest or competency in ecology. These standards were to be implemented chiefly by states, and included new source performance standards (technology-based), hazardous air pollution risk-based requirements and required automobile tailpipe emission controls. With the exception of brief mention of airshed districts, the early Act was not infused with ecological insight. Other than the exception of the NAAQS, the Clean Air Act authorized many technology based standards and focused only upon emissions (i.e., how pollution came out of the pipe). These emission standards were considered to be the best way to insure the enforceability of the law.

Despite the narrow focus, there were some lost opportunities for applying ecological insights. The opportunity for an ecological approach was offered in the authorization of criteria documents. These documents sought to set the ambient standards based upon tracing pathways of pollutants and their impacts upon human health and the environment. This ecological analysis was embodied in the National Ambient Air Quality Criteria (NAAQS). The air quality criteria were to include:

> ... to the extent practicable ... information on:
> (A) those variable factors (including atmospheric conditions) which of themselves or in combination with other factors may alter the effects of public health or welfare of such air pollutant;
> (B) the types of air pollutants which, when present in the atmosphere, may interact with such pollutant to produce an adverse effect on public health or welfare; and (C) any known or anticipated adverse effects on welfare.

In 1970, the Department of Health, Education and Welfare issued air quality criteria for particulate matter, carbon monoxide, sulphur oxides, nitrogen oxides. Some of the criteria documents offered general ecological portraits of the pollutants, tracing their natural and anthropogenic sources, interactions in the atmosphere, their pathways through the environment, and their impacts on some target organisms (plants and animals) and humans. The portrait did not attempt to treat the ecosystem as a whole. Later criteria documents, which are required to be updated on a periodic basis, began to give more attention to the air pollutant as part of the greater ecosystem.

Bridge Document 4.1 Summary of the Air Quality Criteria

Issued under the Clean Air Act, to provide a basis for the national ambient air quality standards, the criteria set forth the following as exemplified by the "Air Quality for Oxides of Nitrogen:"[19]

- The chemical and physical properties of NO_x and NO_x derived pollutants
- The nitrogen cycle
- Sources and emissions
- Environmental transport and transformation
- [Methods of] sampling and analysis of ambient NO_x (in air, water, soil, and plant and animal tissues)
- Observed concentrations of NO_x and other nitrogenous compounds
- Perturbations of stratospheric ozone layer
- Effects of nitrogen oxides on natural ecosystems
- Effects of nitrogen oxides on materials
- Effects of nitrogen compounds on animals
- Effects of exposures to oxides of nitrogen on humans

Despite the ecological "appearance given" by such charts and analysis of the nitrogen cycle and its impact upon the ecosystem, the criteria documents did not offer a rationale for the actual ambient standards. Although loosely "based upon" criteria which contained ecological information, the primary ambient air quality standards were and are most concerned with human health, and not the health of the ecosystem per se.[20]

Within the Clean Air Act of 1970, the more specific link between ecological information and the national ambient standards was to be triggered by the secondary ambient air quality standards which " ... specify a level of air quality the attainment and maintenance of which in the judgement of the Administration, *based upon such criteria*, is required to *protect the public welfare* from any known or adverse effects associated with the presence of such air pollutant in the ambient air." [*Emphasis added.*] "Public welfare" was to include environmental effects. The documentation of ecological harm proved too difficult for the EPA. This difficulty was exemplified by the history of efforts to establish sulphur dioxide standards. When EPA sought to set a secondary standard for sulphur oxide, it was contested, resulting in the 1972 *Kennecott Copper Co. v. EPA* case.

In the *Kennecott* decision, the court remanded for further information to support the annual mean 60/ug/m³ copper standard proposed by EPA since the only scientific support cited in the criterion document found "adverse effects on vegetation at an annual mean of 85 ug/m³ (.03 ppm)." Not only did the scientific information fail to support the standard set, but the criterion document merely recited studies which examined the impact of ambient pollution upon specific vegetation species – not upon the ecosystem supporting these species. The document also failed to trace the pathways of the pollutant within the system. After *Kennecott*, when the EPA avoided adopting secondary standards different from the primary standard, the Agency turned to the adoption of federal and state emission controls for both stationary sources and trucks and cars based upon health impacts. As a consequence, the focus shifted away from the ambient airshed and its ecology and towards the pollutants coming out of pipes and being breathed. Twenty years elapsed in the regulation of air pollutants before attention was again given to pollution as a component of ecosystems.

One area in which the Clean Air Act initially took a more ecosystemic approach to air pollution was in the regulation of lead. Unlike gaseous pollutants such as SO_2, lead was less reactive and in many ways easier to trace and quantify. Its potential effects on human health were also better known than the health effects of other elements. The air quality criteria describe trace natural and manmade sources of lead, its transformation and transport, the environmental concentrations and potential exposures, effects on the ecosystem and the evaluation of health effects.[21] The National Academy of Sciences traced the pathways of lead to, but not through the ecosystem. Even the court carefully traced the pathway of lead in order to uphold the EPA's promulgation of the National Ambient Air Quality Standards.[22]

In 1977, the Clean Air Act received a needed mid-course correction. In particular, the adoption of one section, the Prevention of Significant Deterioration,[23] allowed some opportunities for a more ecological approach to air pollution. This opportunity came in the provisions authorizing federal land managers to evaluate the impact of air pollutants upon "air quality related values."[24] These values inherent in the Class I areas include the structure and functioning of the ecosystem and the quality of the visitor experience.[25] Under this provision, the managers of national parks employed ecological analyses to evaluate the effect of air pollution on park flora and fauna.

The 1990 Clean Air Act was a massive overhaul of the previous Clean Air Acts. In addition to amending the Act to better cope with acid rain and ozone depletion,[26] Congress completely revised the hazardous air pollutant, non-attainment, permitting, enforcement and mobile sources sections of the law. With few exceptions,[27] these revisions moved away from ecological risk-based approaches and instead adopted a technology-based approach. The abandonment of risk-based approaches in the Clean Air Act was due to the inability to enforce those risk-based approaches in the adversarial climate in which opponents to proposed measures to control pollution would often litigate the accuracy of risk assessments.

One notable exception to the Clean Air Act's lack of attention to the ecosystem is the provision for assessment and consequent regulation of airborne toxic pollutants affecting coastal waters and the Great Lakes and Lake Champlain.[28] Under this provision, reports have been issued which track the ecosystemic impacts of air pollutant deposition upon the Great Lakes and Lake Champlain ecosystems. These provisions, along with the act's regulation of acid rain, represent some of the first specific efforts to regulate air pollutants based upon ecosystemic impacts. They were evidence of a growing recognition that air pollution was as serious as water and land pollution.

With the exception of the ozone depletion and acid rain provisions and the coastal areas/Great Lakes deposition program, the history and present operation of the Clean Air Act reveals a failure to enact an ecosystemic approach to environmental regulation. The technology-based approach to human health protection has obvious benefits, but a careful examination of the law reveals the costs of ignoring ecosystems. First, the act has had to develop entire new sections to deal with the ecosystemic damages threatened by acid rain and ozone depletion. Direct economic and recreational losses to forests and lakes can no longer be ignored. Second, by limiting the focus of regulation to air pollution within the political boundaries of states, the law has struggled to cope with cross-state and cross-national boundary pollution. New airshed districts crossing these political boundaries needed to be created to cope with long-distance pollution problems. Third, the focus of the law upon the immediate health impacts of ambient and hazardous pollutants ignored the long-term dangers of air pollutants that may bioaccumulate in the environment and have long acting, yet difficult to detect, impacts on ecosystems.

The Clean Water Act and Wetlands Protection:
Swamping Ecosystem Protection

In the mid 1800s, the drainage and filling of wetlands was part of our nations reclamation policy. The Rivers and Harbors Act of 1899 authorized the Corps of Engineers to permit or prohibit obstructions in navigable waters. Through court interpretation, this was extended to the permitting or prohibiting of polluting those waters. The Fish and Wildlife Coordination Act in the 1960s, provided that the impact of this pollution of fish and wildlife was to be considered. In 1970, in *Zabel v Tabb*, the Court upheld the Corps' authority to issue or deny permits for development in the wetlands.[29] In 1972, the Federal Water Pollution Control Act was adopted incorporating the Corps permitting of dredge and fill of wetlands in Section 404 of the Act.[30] The jurisdiction of the Corps control over the wetlands was extended to the high water mark as defined in the 1970s, although exemptions were secured for certain farming, forestry and ranching activities. Under the law, EPA was authorized to issue regulations for evaluating Section 404 permits, and in 1980, it issued those regulations.[31] The regulations were upheld by the Supreme Court in 1985.[32] In 1988, the Corps issued a comprehensive set of its own regulations, along with regulations pertaining to the application of NEPA to its permitting activity.[33] Among other developments important for our discussion, the Corps and EPA signed a memorandum of agreement on mitigation policy in 1990.[34]

The Clean Water Act of 1972, like its big brother Clean Air Act of 1970, was the continuation of laws adopted years earlier. Like the Clean Air Act, it sought to secure better enforcement against rampant water pollution, probably because the impacts of this pollution were not readily realized by the public. In search of its long-term goal of zero discharge, the law authorized the enforcement by means of technology based effluent standards as well as subsidies for water treatment facilities. In its quest for protection or restoration of the integrity of the waters, with a secondary goal of keeping them fishable and swimmable, the law also adopted water quality standards that sought to specify the criteria for measuring such waters.

The law was initially preoccupied with building treatment works and issuing permits for each point source of pollution based upon best available technology. However, it was gradually realized that this technology-based approach would not secure clean water and that a more ecosystem-based approach that took into account the cumulative impacts of multiple kinds of pollution from many sources (including non-point source runoff and air pollution) was needed. Over time, a more sophisticated view of rivers and lakes has evolved, recognizing that rather than being simply isolated channels or bodies of water, complex river and lake systems are interconnected within a landscape of terrestrial ecosystems, which together form watershed areas. This new sophistication has resulted in more adequate water quality models, a reformulation of aquatic criteria, the study of and planning for pollution within watersheds and/or ecosystems and new attention to urban and agricultural runoff. These models, criteria, watershed plans, and runoff analyses are bridges between an ecological understanding of rivers, lakes and marine environments and the regulation of these aquatic environments, primarily through permitting systems.

Of course, sophisticated planning and arcane models did not always work. In the early 1970s, an interdisciplinary team of ecologists, planners and land use lawyers sought to establish a plan for the Brandywine River Valley. In a post mortem of the failed plan, one of the project staff found the failure to rest not in the inadequacies of the ecology of the day, but in the private property system and local politics of the valley, neither of which were adapted to broad watershed planning.

Bridge Document 4.2 QUANTITATIVE MODELS

Ecology, its theory, methods and conclusions can migrate into legislation, regulation, and even the courtroom through the bridge document of quantitative modeling. An approach whereby ecologists set forth a quantitative description (and often a simulation) of the relationships within part or all of an ecosystem or an entire global system. Such models were initially developed to describe lakes and other natural systems. In the 1950s and 1960s, ecology, or at least its ecosystem part, merged with the developing field of systems analysis.[35] At the time of Earth Day, systems analysis was preoccupied with building grand, but simplistic models of the entire "world system." More immediate success has been seen in the years since 1970, where models have been employed at a specific practical level to predict the amount of pollution in a given context, resulting from one or more sources of pollution or the impact of other interventions into the environment upon natural populations in that environment. The Clean Air Act, the Clean Water Act, forestry management legislation, and many other laws have authorized the use of models, and have passed regulations or guidelines to determine their appropriate use. EPA and other federal agencies have fostered the development of more accurate models.[36] New uses for models have arisen, including sophisticated groundwater models, air emissions trading models, and even composite models for landfills.[37] Given both scientific and legal interest in models, they have proliferated[38] not only in ecosystem ecology, but in population ecology (endangered species) as well. These models either adopt regulatory assumptions, or have implications for regulation. As a consequence, they are "bridge documents," which should be viewed both from a legal and an ecological point of view. They are constantly contested in courts, both for their ecological and their tacit legal assumptions.[39] Perhaps the most recently celebrated of these bridges between ecology and law is the total maximum daily load (TMDL), and the waste load allocation (WLA), which take into account all sources of pollution into a given receiving water. In doing so, the TMDL and its allocation among dischargers seeks to link the issuance of any permit for water pollution to the impact of that pollution upon the water quality, taking into account other polluters.[40]

In 1975, an interdisciplinary team led by Bruce Ackerman anticipated the problems of ecosystem based environmental planning in an in-depth prize-winning study of the effort to model the pollution of the Delaware River Basin, *The Uncertain Search for Environmental Quality*.[41] The study also evaluated the economic cost-benefit analysis and the political decision-making of the Delaware River Basin Commission, as well as reviewing alternative plans to implement its studies. The study was particularly critical of the simplistic dissolved oxygen modeling by the Commission staff, a modeling that among other things, ignored the rich ecosystem complexity of the river.

The wetlands regulation program is perhaps the most extensive and continuous effort to ecologically regulate an aquatic environment. Wetlands have a rich cultural history, as the following quote from Dante indicates:

> Thus, we pursued our path round a wide arc of that ghast pool,
> Between the soggy marsh and arid shore,
> Still eyeing those who gulp the marish (marsh) foul.[42]

The sinister image is also captured in the movies such as "Swamp Thing" and "Key Largo." For a more benign image, one can turn to the U.S. Postal Service's commemorative "duck stamps." Nevertheless, as with wilderness and forests, there has been a long evolution in our attitudes towards wetlands, seeing them initially as swamps to fill and cover, while only gradually recognizing them as valuable ecosystems.

A variety of scientists described the wetlands in great detail beginning in the late nineteenth century and increasingly in the 1940s and 1950s.[43] It was in the later 1950s and 1960s that wetlands began to be described in ecosystemic terms by such scientists as Teal, Pomeroy and the Odums. A variety of definitions of wetlands have been offered. These wetland definitions often include three main components: (1) the presence of water; (2) unique soils that differ from adjacent uplands; and (3) vegetation adapted to the wet conditions (*hydrophytes*) and conversely, an absence of flooding-intolerant vegetation.

In addition to the presence of shallow water, unique wetland soils, and vegetation, wetlands have a number of other characteristics that distinguish them from other ecosystems yet make them less easily defined for legal and regulatory purposes. For example, the depth and duration of flooding varies considerably from wetland to wetland. Wetlands are often at the margins between deep water and terrestrial uplands and are influenced by both systems. Wetland location can vary greatly, from inland to coastal wetlands, and from rural to urban regions. And wetland condition, or the degree to which the wetland is influenced by humans, varies greatly from region to region and from wetland to wetland.[44]

Definitions of wetlands delineation criteria have percolated into legal regulations, key government documents and in several court opinions.[45] The court cases are not as focused on scientific issues underlying the definitions, as with regulatory issues. Several cases have dealt with and upheld the notion that wetlands are part of the "waters of the United States" as described in the Clean Water Act.[46] Popular types of wetlands have included swamp, marsh, bog, fen, peatland, mire, moor, muskeg, bottomland, wet prairie, reed swamp, wet meadow, slough, pothole, and playa. They have been classified by vegetation, hydrology, soil, pH, trophic state, salinity, and relations to riverine and coastal ecosystems.

Wetlands have been described in terms of their individual biotic and abiotic components, but also by their hydrology, biogeochemistry, the biological adaptations of plants and animals, and the wetland system development[47] set forth in models and schema.

Other models and schema include energy flow models, zonal classifications of species, and geomorphic features. A more recent part of the evaluation of wetlands has been the identification of their "ecosystem values," or the services they provide (e.g., water purification, flood mitigation, recreation, or wildlife habitat).

Historical Evolution of Wetlands Regulation

The federal wetlands program raised specific issues pertaining to the relationship between ecology and environmental law. These issues are raised in: (1) the delineation of the wetlands; (2) the permitting of developments in the wetlands; (3) the adoption of wetland mitigation; and (4) the enforced restoration of wetlands.

The Delineation of Wetlands

The delineation of wetlands determines whether the wetland is protected through federal law, by state law, or not at all. Part of the delineation is spacial; a matter of the acreage of the wetland. However, another part requires a more complex determination of the wetland's definition and the relation of the wetland to broader ecosystemic considerations. Generally speaking, the technical criteria adopted for wetland determination merely describe the abiotic and biotic features of the wetlands (presence of water, soil type and vegetation) rather than the morphological structure of the wetland and/or the relation of the wetland to other riverine, watershed or habitat systems. Mandatory criteria set forth in the 1989 Manual included only hydrophytic vegetation, hydric soils and wetland hydrology.[48] However, the method recommended to applicants included attention to "off site" determinations.

The Permitting Process

The strong ecologically oriented regulations governing wetlands have most applicability in the permitting process. These regulations identify the chemical and biological characteristics of the aquatic ecosystem, different kinds of "special aquatic sites," and the human values attached to the workings of the wetlands' ecosystems. The regulations require assessing the impact of any development upon these sites and their characteristics, and set forth a testing regime.[49]

The following is an excerpt from the regulations that captures the ecological detail of the testing regime:

> **§230.61 Chemical, biological, and physical evaluation and testing**
>
>   (b) *Chemical-biological interactive effects.* The principal concerns of discharge of dredged or fill material that contain contaminants are the potential effects on the water column and on communities of aquatic organisms. (1) *Evaluation of chemical-biological interactive effects* ... The Regional Administrator may require, on a case-by-case basis, testing approaches and procedures by stating what additional information is needed through further analyses and how the results of the analyses will be of value in evaluating potential environmental effects. If the General Evaluation indicates the presence of a sufficiently large number of chemicals to render impractical the identification of all contaminants by chemical testing, information may be obtained from bioassays in lieu of chemical tests. (2) *Water column effects.* (i) Sediments normally contain constituents that exist in various chemical forms and in various concentrations in several locations within the sediment. An elutriate test may be used to predict the effect on water quality due to release of contaminants from the sediment to the water column. However, in the case of fill material originating on land which may be a carrier of contaminants, a water leachate test is appropriate. (ii) Major constituents to be analyzed in the elutriate are those deemed critical by the permitting authority, after evaluating and considering any comments received from the Regional Administrator, and considering results of the evaluation in §230.60. Elutriate concentrations should be compared to con-centrations of the same constituents in water from the disposal site. Results should be evaluated in light of the volume and rate of the intended discharge, the type of discharge, the hydrodynamic regime at the disposal site, and other information relevant to the impact on water quality. The permitting authority should consider the mixing zone in evaluating water column effects. The permitting authority may specify bioassays when such procedures will be of value. (3) *Effects on benthos.* The permitting authority may use an appropriate benthic bioassay (including bio-accumulation tests) when such procedures will be of value in assessing ecological effects and in establishing discharge conditions.
>
>   (c) *Procedure for comparison of sites.* (1) When an inventory of the total concentration of contaminants would be of value in comparing sediment at the dredging site with sediment at the disposal site, the permitting authority may require a sediment chemical analysis. Markedly different concentrations of contaminants between the excavation and disposal sites may aid in making an environmental assessment of the proposed disposal operation. Such differences should be interpreted in terms of the potential for harm as supported by any pertinent scientific literature. (2) When an analysis of biological community structure will be of value to assess the potential for adverse environmental impact at the proposed disposal site, a comparison of the biological characteristics between the excavation and disposal sites may be required by the permitting

authority. Biological indicator species may be useful in evaluating the existing degree of stress at both sites. Sensitive species representing community components colonizing various substrate types within the sites should be identified as possible bioassay organisms if tests for toxicity are required. Community structure studies should be performed only when they will be of value in determining discharge conditions. This is particularly applicable to large quantities of dredged material known to contain adverse quantities of toxic materials. Community studies should include benthic organisms such as microbiota and harvestable shellfish and finfish. Abundance, diversity, and distribution should be documented and correlated with substrate type and other appropriate physical and chemical environmental characteristics.

(d) *Physical tests and evaluation.* The effect of a discharge of dredged or fill material on physical substrate characteristics at the disposal site, as well as on the water circulation, fluctuation, salinity, and suspended particulates content there, is important in making factual determinations in §230.11. Where information on such effects is not otherwise available to make these factual determinations, the permitting authority shall require appropriate physical tests and evaluations as are justified and deemed necessary. Such tests may include sieve tests, settleability tests, compaction tests, mixing one and suspended particulate plume determinations, and site assessments of water flow, circulation, and salinity characteristics.

Source: 40 CFR 230 (2001)

The Adoption of Wetlands Mitigation

Mitigation includes both the replacement of ecological resources lost in a permitted development and the lessening of the impact of the development itself. The concept of mitigation emerged out of the effort to restore or enhance other environments for fish disturbed by dam building. This concept was extended to the more general dredge and fill program. In 1989, the Corps and EPA signed a memorandum of agreement on mitigation. Included in the provision of the mitigation agreement is the following statement:

> In achieving the goals of the CWA, the Corps will strive to avoid adverse impacts and offset unavoidable adverse impacts to existing aquatic resources. Measures which can accomplish this can be identified only through resource assessments tailored to the site performed by qualified professionals because ecological characteristics of each aquatic site are unique. Functional values should be assessed by applying aquatic site assessment techniques generally recognized by experts in the field and/or the best professional judgment of federal and state agency representatives, provided such assessments fully consider ecological functions included in the Guidelines.[50]

This provision and others in the memorandum make clear the dependence on ecological knowledge in assessing the impact of any development, the success of any restoration at the development site, and the feasibility of off-site mitigation.

> Restoration is an important, but often ignored, aspect of environmental law. Environmental lawyers are often so preoccupied with preventing any disturbance of the environment that they ignore the need for restoration from legal and illegal developments and pollution activities. Restoration has become an important part of the wetlands enforcement process. The courts have set forth three criteria for restoration: (1) it must confer maximum environmental benefits; (2) it must be tempered with equity; and (3) it must take into account the degree of wrong and the practicability of the remedy.[51] To insure the meeting of the first and third criterion, ecological knowledge of wetlands is required. Restorations have been ordered and denied based upon these criteria.[52] Despite our best efforts, we have limited ability to predict the pathway of recovery and the final outcome of restoration projects.[53]

Land Use Planning and Ecology

Although much of ecology is focused on terrestrial ecosystems, the general system of state and local land use management and regulation does not embody the systematic application of ecological science.[54] There are many reasons for the failure of this regulation.[55] First and foremost, planning and zoning laws were developed and applied long before the full fruition of the science of ecology. These planning and zoning laws began in the early 1900s and were applied primarily in more developed areas to settle conflicts between different human uses of urban land.[56] Concerns about urban pollution were addressed, if at all, by more general public health laws. Even in post World War II America, when urban renewal and planning flourished with the help of federal funding, the focus of such planning and renewal was far from the preservation, protection or restoration of natural lands, concentrating instead upon economic growth.

In the 1970s, with the advent of Earth Day, a new concern for environmental protection as an objective of land use law arose. New state laws in Florida, Hawaii, Maine and Vermont sought to employ land use controls to protect "critical lands"[57] and new municipal laws[58] sought to rein in residential and commercial growth by means of "growth control" ordinances. On a national level, several western European nations and the United States adopted new towns programs seeking to guide national population growth patterns. The American Law Institute proposed a tentative Model Land Development Code, and Congress proposed national land planning legislation. Neither of these proposals was adopted.

In the late 1960s and early 1970s, drawing upon a unique planning tradition which extended back to Patrick Geddes[59] and Lewis Mumford,[60] Ian McHarg began to promote the application of ecological insights to land use planning in his classic book *Design With Nature*[61] (discussed above). This book carefully inventoried the kinds of ecological information necessary to determine where and how development should be located within selected ecosystems.

Based upon the work of McHarg, numerous efforts at land use oriented environmental planning and regulation flowered in the 1970s and 1980s. The application of environmental impact planning and assessment, site design and planing, as well as new environmentally oriented comprehensive land use plans were launched. Despite McHarg's clear grasp of the principles of ecology and their application in planning, most of this environmental planning and regulation did not embrace an ecosystem perspective.

There were several reasons for the failure to fully employ ecology within land use planning and regulation. First, such planning – at least as envisaged by McHarg – was to be comprehensive planning. Unfortunately, comprehensive planning was not in full fashion by the 1970s.[62] Second, planners themselves had not been carefully trained or educated in ecology and the environmental sciences. Third, planning emerged out of an urban setting and was necessarily preoccupied with the full gamut of urban problems, of which pollution was merely one. Fourth, to the extent that environmental planning did take place, it was predominated by the early preparation of environmental impact statements that, as we shall see below, were not ecologically oriented.

Despite the failure of McHarg's ecological design insights to lead to an ecologically oriented land use regulation, several unique regional land use planning and regulation programs, designed around such ecosystems as bays, unique forest areas, and watersheds, were undertaken in the 1970s. Thus the Pine Barrens and Lake Tahoe programs.[63]

The New Jersey Pinelands, or Pine Barrens, is a one million acre, relatively undeveloped expanse of central New Jersey. As part of the Atlantic Coastal Plain, the Pinelands have a low relief with the highest point being a mere 200 feet above sea level. As a consequence, the region has a high water table and a frequent mixing of surface and ground water. Beneath the Pinelands (of the state of New Jersey) lies one of the largest unpolluted aquifers on the East Coast, with an estimated storage capacity of approximately 17 trillion gallons of water.[64] Pitch pine (*Pinus banksiana*) dominates, primarily due to the area's nutrient-poor sandy soils and the ability of the pines to tolerate a wide range of moisture. The infertile soils also contribute to the formation of the 12,400 acres of low stature, pygmy pine forest, consisting of pitch pines which are only four to six feet high, but mature. The Pinelands are highly dependent on and adapted to recurrent fire that removes competing plant species and restores soil fertility. Fifteen to twenty percent of the Pinelands is considered wetlands, where white-cedar forests and red maples dominate. The mammals in the area are characteristic of the northeast: white-tailed deer, beaver, mink, fox, coyote, and river otter. Larger predators such as bobcat and black bear are not present. The Pinelands are also rich in fish, reptiles, amphibians, and birds. The region is an ecotone where ranges of many plants and animal species are at their respective geographic limits.[65]

The area is not pristine. Since European settlement, the forests of the Pine Barrens have been harvested several times.[66] The population of the Pinelands is increasing[67] and is surrounded by bedroom communities of New York and Philadelphia along the northern and western edges. Only one-third of the Pinelands is government owned. State parks and forests comprise over 300,000 acres, while the federal government maintains three military installations and a national wildlife refuge.[68]

Public interest in the Pinelands developed in the late 1950s and early 1960s, primarily as a response to a proposal by Burlington county (in the heart of the Pinelands) to develop a 32,500 acre Jetport. The Jetport was the heart of a grand plan that included a ring of commercial and industrial enterprises around the Jetport, creating a "New City" for 250,000 people, becoming the third largest city in the state. This development would have devastated unique ecosystems and the rural nature of the Pinelands. Conservation groups, both national and local, quickly formed to fight the project.[69]

By 1965, there was pressure for the federal government to step in and declare the Pinelands a National Monument. In response, the National Park Service initiated new ecological studies of the area and determined that portions of the Pinelands wetlands had "scientific value of national significance."[70] The National Park Service determined that designation of the Pinelands as a National Monument or Park was not economically feasible, but the Service did suggest some form of protection for areas of the Pinelands.[71] Development pressure waned somewhat when by 1969, the FAA and the airlines had decided to expand current regional airports rather than develop any new ones.

The national focus on the protection of the Pine Barrens[72] motivated the state legislature to establish the Pinelands Environmental Council (PEC) in 1972. The PEC was charged with developing a "coordinated, comprehensive plan" for protecting the pinelands and was given the authority to review development to ensure compliance.[73] This council had very little power, however. The PEC merely reported its findings to whichever governmental body was responsible for permitting and the findings could be rejected or poorly addressed. Furthermore, the PEC was dominated by developers and the plan that they had developed was criticized by environmentalists as a "land speculator's dream."[74] The polarization of conservationists and developers, along with improper financial dealings by members of PEC, made the PEC largely ineffective and it was dissolved in 1979.

In 1976, the federal government issued a report entitled *The Pine Barrens: Concepts for Preservation.* The report was a landmark in that it stated important concepts of preservation; that the "integrity of this total ecosystem must be protected in order to preserve each of the system's individual components; moreover, not only are the individual attributes of the ecosystem nationally significant, but also the very proximity of the resource to large urban centers must be considered significant."[75] This report also signaled the desire of the federal government that the state take control of the protection process by initiating and showing a commitment.

In 1977, the Pinelands Review Committee (PRC) was formed to coordinate state actions directed towards the protection of the Pinelands. The PRC was charged with delineating the boundaries of the Pine Barrens and preparing a plan to guide state decision making in the preservation of unique resources, promotion of agriculture, forestry, recreation, and the discouragement of scattered/piecemeal development.[76] The PRC was dominated by conservationists who helped develop the concept of the Pinelands Preservation Area, consisting of 1.1 million acres with a core Preservation Area and an outer Protection Area ringing the core.

Federal action soon followed. In 1978, President Carter signed into law a bill creating the Pinelands National Reserve. The National Reserve fell under the jurisdiction of the Department of the Interior and was modeled along the lines of the New York State Adirondack Park, rather than a traditional National Park such as Yellowstone. "Unlike traditional national parkland, greenline parkland need not be entirely owned by the federal government. Instead, the government would set standards and impose restrictions on use of private land within the boundaries of the 'park' to achieve the goals for which the park was established."[77] In the case of the Pinelands, the goals of the greenline parkland were to preserve open space, the rural nature of the area, and the driving force behind the process to protect the aquifer that lies beneath.

In 1979, the Governor of New Jersey created the Pinelands Planning Commission by executive order. This action was soon followed by the state legislature's passage of the New Jersey Pinelands Protection Act.[78] This Act was designed to implement the federal action.

The Pinelands Commission also conducts a number of environmental monitoring programs that focus primarily on the impact of development. The Commission's research focuses on three indicators: landscape-level (percentage of altered land and the effect on ecological integrity); watershed-level (the effect that altered land has on water quality and the related biological communities); and community-level (which species are affected by altered land).[79] The goal of these studies "is to provide scientific information that may be used to develop and evaluate the Commission's environmental policies and programs."[80]

The state and federal law establishing the protection of the Pinelands are laws that on their face do not reflect an ecological orientation, but are the product of ecosystemic inquiry. The Pinelands Protection Act directed that the Pinelands Commission must develop a comprehensive management plan (CMP). The CMP is the key bridge document that brings together ecology and the law.

Bridge Document 4.3 PINELANDS COMPREHENSIVE MANAGEMENT PLAN

The Pinelands are divided into two general areas, a Preservation Area and a Protection Area. The Preservation Area is the most stringently protected area of the Pinelands; "[i]n general, only new land uses compatible with the ecology of the central Pines are allowed." [New Jersey Pinelands Commission, *A Summary of the New Jersey Pinelands Comprehensive Management Plan.*][81]

The Protection Area, designed to minimize adverse environmental impacts of development, is further subdivided into four land use areas: Forest Areas, Agricultural Production Areas, Regional Growth Areas, and Rural Development Areas. Forest Areas are lands which "met the Commission's criteria for essential character." "The Plan allows one new house for each 15.8 acres of privately owned, undeveloped upland." *Id.*

"Blocks of more than 1,000 acres of active farmland and adjacent farm soil are grouped into Agricultural Production Areas where farming and related activities will remain the dominant land use." Regional Growth Areas are those which lie in the path of one of the three primary development fronts – Philadelphia-Camden metropolitan area, the retirement communities of Ocean County, and Atlantic City. The Plan determines overall base densities for each area. Rural Development Areas are transition areas between the Forest Areas and Regional Growth Areas. "The Plan attempts to protect the characteristic Pinelands features that can be found there while allowing modest development to proceed."

The CMP provides a standard for protection of the Pinelands. "Municipalities need not incorporate all Plan standards verbatim into their local land use regulations as long as the Plan's intent is met. ... However, until a municipality brings its master plan and zoning code into conformance with the Plan, the literal standards of the Plan's management programs are administered by the Commission when it reviews proposed development." [Id.] Ecosystemic considerations are reflected in the Plan to the extent which ecological considerations overlap environmental protection concerns such as preservation of wetlands, wildlife habitats, etc.

The CMP provides for a Technical Advisory Committee, which advises the Commission on scientific matters relating to the Pinelands. This advisory committee brings together scientists with diverse backgrounds, including ecologists.

Specific ecological concepts that are important in the management of the Pinelands are ecosystem boundaries' natural disturbance/ecological adaptation (with respect to the role of fire in the Pinelands), and ecosystem consideration, e.g., wetlands protection within the plan. The boundaries of the Pinelands were first delineated, based upon a floristic study, in 1911. In 1916, a plant geographer "published a map and comprehensive description of the types of plant communities found in the Barrens."[82] By the 1940s research was underway to study the importance of fire in maintaining plant communities in the reserve.[83] The establishment of an ecology program at Rutgers University in the 1940s helped to expand the amount of ecological research performed in the Pinelands. The Pinelands provided a readily accessible area for graduate students, including a project that delineated the Pine Barrens in 1957, and is still considered an authoritative guide.[84] Rutgers maintains an active research presence in the Pinelands through the Pinelands Biosphere Reserve Research Station. Researchers are studying forest fragmentation and biodiversity loss, acidic deposition and nutrient dynamics and the role of fire in pine barren ecosystem function.[85]

As mentioned above, there is a difference in size between the National Reserve and the state Pinelands Area, which is due to New Jersey's reliance on coastal protection laws to manage a portion of the National Reserve. The boundaries of the National Reserve follow roughly the ecological delineation of the Pine Barrens. However, there are approximately 50,000 acres within the ecological Pinelands that were excluded from the Reserve due to heavy development pressures in these areas.[86] Along the coast, development is "subject to the state's Coastal Management Program which is required to carry out the purposes of the state and federal Pinelands acts."[87]

The management of the Greater Pinelands is a complex task. Although the Pinelands is a National Reserve established under federal law, the area is administered by the state of New Jersey through the Pinelands Commission.[88] Federal representation exists through the commission, with one of the fifteen members appointed by the U.S. Secretary of the Interior. Development within the Pinelands must be consistent with the CMP and with the particular land use pattern allowed in the area (Forest Area, Rural Development Area, etc.). An application for development must be approved by municipal authorities as well as by the Commission. The Pinelands Development Credit System allows a greater flexibility than it appears. The program is based on allocation and resale of development credits to landowners in the Preservation Area District, Agricultural Production Areas, and Special Agricultural Production Areas.

These credits can be sold to developers owning land in Regional Growth Areas and used to increase the densities at which they can build. A credit seller still retains title to the land and may use the land for non-residential uses as authorized by the Plan. This landowner is required to enter into a deed restriction that would bind future owners to those same uses.[89]

The major problems with the protection regime for the Pinelands come from conflict over the restrictions on development. It is this aspect which has led to the most legal challenges and provoked the most public resistance against the plan. This problem can be indirectly attributed to the fact that protection is oriented towards preserving the general ecosystem of the Pinelands, rather than a particular wildlife habitat or specific wetland area. The Pinelands Commission is attempting to further understand the role of development in the environmental degradation of the area.[90]

A second ecologically-oriented land use program is the *Lake Tahoe Basin* program. The Tahoe Basin, occupying an area of approximately 500 square miles, straddles the Nevada-California border. The basin is ringed by 10,000 foot snow-capped peaks and the lake, covering about 38 percent of the basin, lies at an elevation of 6,000 feet.[91] The terrain of the basin is consequently very steep, with a high potential for erosion, forcing most development to occur along the shore.[92] The topography creates air inversions at all times of the year, allowing "[e]ven relatively weak local pollution sources [to] build-up to serious levels." The summer also brings air pollution from the Sacramento Valley in the form of ozone and particulates.[93]

Lake Tahoe is an oligotrophic alpine lake. Sixty-three streams drain into Lake Tahoe, providing almost all of the inflow into the Lake with groundwater flow providing 10 percent or less of the inflow.[94] The lake itself is 22 miles long and 12 miles wide.[95] At a depth of 1,646 feet, it is the second deepest lake in the United States and the tenth deepest in the world. The single outlet to the lake, the Truckee River, has been dammed since 1874, forming a reservoir consisting of the upper six feet, or about 0.6 percent of the lake.[96] "The average residence time of a drop of water in Lake Tahoe is about 700 years. This long residence time has ecological importance in the development of control plans because, for practical purposes, one must think of Lake Tahoe as a nutrient sink not subject to flushing action."[97]

Since the early 1970s, the EPA and other federal agencies have continued to study the area, both as an ecosystem and as individual components.[98] These research efforts continue today, albeit with reduced funding, in order to add to the ecological knowledge of the area.[99] The Tahoe Regional Planning Agency (TRPA) establishes environmental thresholds and carrying capacities, as mandated by the 1980 agreement, and then devised a plan to achieve these goals. Further development was partially limited until a new regional plan was adopted.[100] For the 1984 revised plan, the TRPA prepared

An Environmental Impact Statement For Adoption Of A Regional Plan For The Lake Tahoe Basin, published in February of 1983.[101] The State of California, however, sued TRPA to block the implementation of the plan, stating that it failed to establish land-use controls that would adequately protect the Tahoe Basin. An injunction was issued by the United States District Court for the Eastern District of California and "remained in force until a completely revised land-use plan – the 1987 Regional Plan – was adopted."[102] The 1987 Plan, with some modifications, has been in place since.

The Tahoe Basin is exceptional in that ecological information has been important in shaping the management of the lake. This information primarily examines the lake as a closed ecosystem, with an emphasis on nutrient cycling and protection of water resources. The Lake Tahoe Environmental Assessment[103] "influenced the amendment of the Tahoe Regional Planning Compact and helped establish ecological threshold-based planning in the Basin."[104] It is these ecological thresholds which "establish the environmental standards for the Region and, as such, indirectly define the capacity of the Region to accommodate additional development."[105]

The Tahoe Regional Planning Agency was created by three identical laws; one federal, one in California, and one in Nevada.[106] Article I of the Tahoe Regional Planning Compact discusses the "unique environmental and ecological values" of the Basin and the need to preserve and protect these values; as well as "scenic, recreational, educational, scientific, natural and public health values."[107] The jurisdiction of TRPA is established in Article II(a) of the TRPC. The boundaries roughly delineate the watershed of the Basin. In this sense, the legal boundaries are concurrent with a hyrdo-geological delineation of the watershed. The plan that the TRPA created pursuant to the TRPC consists of two parts; Goals and Policies and a Code of Ordinances. The Goals and Policies "sets forth standards for water quality, air quality, soils, wildlife, fisheries, vegetation, scenic quality, and recreation. One of the major purposes of the regional plan package ... is to establish regulations and programs to achieve and maintain these thresholds."[108] The Code of Ordinances outlines the specific ordinances that must be followed in order to achieve compliance with the established environmental thresholds.

The most contentious section of the TRPA regards land use. The plan states that the "primary function of the region shall be as a mountain recreation area with outstanding scenic and natural values."[109] "No new divisions of land shall be permitted within the region which would create new development potential inconsistent with the goals and policies of this plan."[110] To that end, TRPA has adopted an Individual Parcel Evaluation System (IPES), which takes into account erosion hazard and runoff potential in order to determine if development is allowed on a particular parcel.[111]

Bridge Document 4.4 LAKE TAHOE INDIVIDUAL PARCEL EVALUATION SYSTEM

1. Evaluation of each individual parcel for erosion hazard and runoff potential
2. Assignment of score
3. Rank of lot in comparison to counterpart lots
4. Establishment of a minimum score for development
5. Lots below minimum cannot develop
6. Lots above minimum can develop with conditions

IPES requires that "a team of experts shall evaluate each vacant residential parcel."[112] Scientific knowledge is thus essential to the implementation of the plan. Additionally, a Science Advisory Panel is established to "review periodically the technical assumptions, techniques, and procedures associated with monitoring and analysis efforts."[113]

Human activity is regulated via the Code of Ordinances, in the form of a standard. Ecosystemic considerations are reflected in the *Goals and Policies*, rather than in the *Code of Ordinances*. California, Nevada, and the Federal government all have identical laws establishing the TRPA. Under the Compact, legal actions may be filed in the appropriate courts of California, Nevada, and of the United States. The basin is divided into planning areas. TRPA has developed five land use designations: conservation, recreation, residential, commercial and public service, and tourist. Conservation areas are non-urban areas with value as primitive or natural areas, and carry strict environmental limitations on their use, hence deserving of preservation for dispersed recreation. Although these areas include public areas, some private land is also designated as conservation areas. Residential development is directed toward those areas that are already primarily urban and have pre-existing infrastructures.[114]

Management categories are identified for each planning area. The three categories are: (1) the maximum regulation designation applies primarily to conservation areas, which are strictly regulated to ensure preservation and enhancement of the existing environment, with little or no additional development; (2) the development with mitigation category is the most common management regime. These areas can accommodate development if the impacts are fully mitigated (on-site and off-site) and the land is capable of withstanding the use; (3) the redirection of development category is assigned to lands where the goal is to improve environmental quality and community character by changing either the direction of development or its density through relocation of facilities, rehabilitation or restoration of existing structures and uses, and by limiting new development. The objective of this designation is to reduce impervious coverage (decrease runoff to the lake), restore natural environments, improve the efficiency of transportation systems and decrease air pollution, improve scenic quality, and provide high quality facilities for residents and visitors alike.[115]

The Lake Tahoe Basin represents a complicated political and ecological system that has benefited from detailed ecological study and an iterative process of regulatory agreement between federal, state, and private interests. The result is a protective regime that works at the basin level. The more difficult task may be to protect this unique and highly sensitive ecosystem from damages caused by the long-distance transport of pollutants. The atmospheric transport of pesticides from the California Central Valley is affecting the lake waters[116] and organochlorine contamination has been detected in the tissues of lake trout.[117] The boundaries of the Tahoe Basin, unfortunately, reach far beyond the ridges of the mountains that define its topography.

Bridge Document 4.5 WATERSHEDS AND TDML

The wetlands and regional ecosystem management programs described in this chapter are parts of a more comprehensive effort to introduce ecology into environmental policy in the period from 1970 to 1990. After the eclipse of the river basin program of the 1960s, it was not until the late 1980s and early 1990s that environmental policy began once more to "enter the watershed."[118] New proposals for the objectives for watersheds to be "ecologically healthy" defined as *"the capability of supporting and maintaining a balanced, integrated adaptive biological system doing the full range of elements and processes expected in the natural habitat of the region."*[119] It was environmental laws and especially Oliver Houck, environmental lawyer and scholar,[120] who reanimated the demand that the Clean Water Act and its obligations to clean up water pollution, especially the non-point sources under Section 303(d),[121] of the CWA. Such a cleanup was to take place under ambient standards for each pollutant; standards which set maximum daily total loading of the pollutant. Courts have upheld environmental lawsuits requiring such TDMLs.[122] The determination of the TDML requires ecological science to determine degrees of water impairment, the pathway of pollutants, their interaction with the ecosystem and ultimate pollutant level. Numerous TDMLs have been promulgated and now implementation is being undertaken.[123]

Hazardous Pollutants and the Mirage of Recycling

When Rachel Carson traced the pathways of DDT within the environment, she not only introduced the public to pollution in its ecosystem context, but she also undertook an early exploration in a field not yet developed, "ecotoxicology." Ecotoxicology aims at characterizing, understanding and predicting deleterious effects of chemical substances on all biological systems. Not until the late 1980s and 1990s has there been a systematic formulation of the discipline of ecotoxicology as distinct from toxicology and environmental health.[124] In the interim period, the legal concern over toxics focused upon the direct human health impact of toxic pollutants in soil, air, and water. The major environmental laws of the early 1970s focused upon the media of pollution; the water and air in which pollutants are placed. With "land pollution," the public concern shifted to "hazardous waste." "Toxicity" was a possible permanent characteristic of the pollution and the waste itself. Once the public developed a focus on a toxic pollutant coursing through the environment, knowledge of the pathway of the pollutant became important, whether that pathway involved land, water, air or more likely, all three. Hence, regulatory agencies saw that the public concern about the pathways of hazardous pollutants increased, which in turn led back to a greater awareness of the multimedia of land, air and water, and then to the entire ecosystem.

Joel Tarr has traced the history of pollution control in the United States from the industrial revolution to the mid-twentieth century.[125] He describes that history as one of searching for the "ultimate sink" in which cities sought to transfer the land pollution to the waters of lakes and rivers, and then sought to avoid water pollution through incineration, which led to air pollution. Efforts to control air pollution has led to the problem of controlling residuals – at all times seeking to send pollution someplace else.[126] The early problem of environmental justice, in which the poor bore the cost of pollution, is documented in Tarr's study and brought to the public in the writings of Bullard.[127]

The more recent history of our treatment of waste shows the adoption of the landfill as "the proper place" in which to dispose of the "by-products" or "residuals" of our nation. Until the mid-1960s, the disposal of waste was largely a local matter, viewed as an offshoot of planning and zoning in which the "trick" was to allocate the locating of landfills to the proper district. This approach is exemplified by the Solid Waste Disposal Act of 1965, which authorized research and grant programs for the planning of appropriate land use disposal.[128] It was Barry Commoner's *Closing Circle* that offered the first popular ecological perspective on waste as material unsuitable either in composition, amount, or location for reprocessing by the cycles of nature. Specifically, Commoner was deeply concerned with new synthetic chemicals that would not be cycled within the ordinary decomposition processes of nature. Commoner argued for the use of biodegradable products and for their recovery and recycling.

In 1970, the Resource Recovery Act was adopted.[129] The very title of this law captured a new view of waste as something to be "recovered" as well as disposed. The Act was intended to "promote the demonstration, construction and application of solid waste management and resource recovery systems which preserve and enhance the quality of air, water, and land resources" and to "promote a national research and development program for improved management techniques, more effective organizational arrangements, and new and improved methods of collection, separation, recovery, and recycling of solid wastes and the environmentally safe disposal of nonrecoverable residues." Among other actions, the legislation promoted "sanitary landfills" as opposed to "open dumps." The economic view of recycling was set forth in Title II of the Act, which authorized a National Commission on Materials Policy to study the relationship between materials, population and environmental quality. The notion of a materials policy had first been advanced by Resources for the Future, which viewed the movement of goods through a process of extraction, production and consumption.[130]

Recycling is conceived as the return of a product to the consumption or production. Ecosystem recycling is referred to as "transformation in the environment." The role of a materials flow policy is to promote economic recycling and/or disposal. Little or no attention is paid to the "transformation" of residuals in the environment (nor, for that matter, the population growth and consumer habits which feed the demand for materials).[131]

In 1976, the Resource, Conservation and Recovery Act (RCRA) was adopted. The law, along with the Toxic Substances Control Act (TSCA) and the Comprehensive Environmental Response, Compensation and Liability Act (CERCLA or "Superfund"), was one of the principal laws focusing upon hazardous waste.[132] This law best embodies the beginnings of an economic recycling philosophy with its prohibition of open dumping of solid and hazardous waste and its "cradle to grave" approach to tracing the transport of hazardous waste.[133] RCRA sought to encourage recycling of hazardous waste materials.[134] The act established methods for listing and identifying hazardous wastes; a tracking system of the transport of those wastes; standards which generators, transporters, treaters and disposers of hazardous waste must meet; and a detailed permitting system to enforce the program. Despite the adoption of detailed regulations in 1980 and amending legislation in 1984, the law has been subject to vigorous criticisms in its operation[135] and continues to fail as a truly ecological approach to the waste problem.

Principles of ecotoxicology suggest an ecological approach to waste disposal. This ecological approach to hazardous waste begins with a detailed description of the structure, components and processes of the ecosystem. Then it seeks to trace the distribution and biogeochemistry of chemicals placed in the environment. Abiotic transformation reactions are described. Environmental processes of volatilization, sorpative processes, biotic and abiotic degradation and bioconcentration are studied. Effects of toxicity are measured not only upon individual flora and fauna but also at the population level. Finally, there is an effort to assess the risk of toxicity on the biodiversity and functioning of entire ecosystems.

These general processes can be better grouped at the more specific level by examining a common ecological problem of the disposal of hazardous materials (i.e., groundwater contamination). Groundwater is sub-surface water found in zones where the spaces (pores) between soil and rock particles are fully saturated. Such waters are important sources of drinking water, agricultural irrigation, and the general health of the ecosystem. Groundwater is ultimately replenished by precipitation that percolates through the soils of an aquifer recharge area. Soil and terrestrial microorganisms, by the process of assimilation and decomposition, remove certain impurities from the precipitation as it percolates through the soil to recharge the groundwater. When a contaminant enters the ground through a point-source (such as a toxic spill), and neither the soil nor the micro-organisms transform the contaminant into a harmless substance, it will percolate through the soil and, once in the groundwater, spread into a plume. This movement will depend upon its solubility in water, as well as many other facts. The plume may move slowly and the pollution may remain for an indefinite period.[136] A variety of plants and animals may be exposed to the pollution. Determining how the ecosystem then processes and reacts to the pollutant plume is the province of ecotoxicology.

Ecological considerations enter into various aspects of the Resource Conservation and Recovery Act, but clearly as afterthoughts to the basic approach of materials recycling and disposal. First, ecological considerations enter into (and conflict with) the definitions of hazardous waste and the exemptions established under the law.[137] Second, the listing and de-listing of hazardous materials embody implicit ecological judgements.[138] Third, the permitting of sites and their requirements involve ecologically based judgements.[139] And fourth, the recovery and bioremediation of selected sites rest upon ecological knowledge.[140]

Conclusion

The story of the lover's quarrel between ecology and the major pollution laws begins to capture the difficulty of establishing relationships between these two disciplines. These relationships were forged during the two decades between 1970 and 1990. The history of these two disciplines over this period reveals the following insights. First, an incredible variety of kinds of relationships occurred over this period. These relationships included not only those of tension and conflict between the two disciplines, but as we shall see in future chapters, more cordial relationships. Second, despite all the different permutations of ecology and law, the movement is increasingly toward adopting an ecological perspective, *even within the pollution laws themselves*. Laws like the Clean Air Act, which initially rejected an ecosystem approach, have in recent years sought to more adequately assess the ecological impacts of the pollutants they regulate, and to consider ecological impacts within the administration of these laws. Third, the history of ecology and law during this period reveals the co-evolution of the two fields. The laws have stimulated new developments in ecology and earth sciences; conversely, environmental law has increasingly drawn upon the results of ecology. Despite the lack of complete progress in the absorption of ecological insights in the fields of pollution law, we shall see below that the experiences of coastal and forest management, the acid rain experience, and global regulation in the fields of ozone depletion and global warming are leading to a new ecological paradigm of environmental law, in which extensive ecological research precedes the adoption of a plan or target that is implemented through regulations and the creation of public markets. This experience may, in turn, operate to reform the less ecologically inclined pollution laws reviewed in this chapter.

These optimistic conclusions may be accompanied by some less rosy concerns about the future prospects of the further rapprochement between ecology and environmental law. In parts of several environmental laws, such as hazardous waste and air pollution control, there has been a movement towards increased reliance upon technology-based controls rather than ecologically oriented, risk-based approaches, which invite litigation. As a consequence, important parts of these environmental laws have led policy in a direction away from ecosystemic laws. The reason for this movement away from ecosystemic law lies in the difficulty that arises when seeking to enforce ecosystemic laws. A detailed study of the relationship between ecosystem laws and their enforcement is needed.

Notes

1. *See* THOMAS M. HOBAN & RICHARD O. BROOKS, GREEN JUSTICE (1996).
2. *See* LAURENCE E. JOSEPH, GAIA: THE GROWTH OF AN IDEA (1990). The Gaia concept has been vigorously criticized by scientists, but has recently been scientifically reborn in the emergence of earth system science described in Chapter 10 below.
3. *See* ANNE & PAUL EHRLICH, THE POPULATION BOMB (1968).
4. *See* BARRY COMMONER, THE CLOSING CIRCLE (1971).
5. *See* DONELLA & DENNIS MEADOWS, THE LIMITS TO GROWTH (1972).
6. MATERIALS BALANCE: Another interesting theoretical offshoot of system ecology (combined with economics) was the origin of materials balance theory originated in 1970. [*See* ALLEN KNEESE & ROBERT AYRES, ECONOMICS AND THE ENVIRONMENT: A MATERIALS BALANCE APPROACH (1970).] Its source was the ecological study of

nutrient interchange among plants and animals. [*See id.* at 7-8, note 11.] Materials balance theory sought to trace the path of chemicals both in the environment and the economy. The materials balance approach was later made part of legal requirements for materials balance audits. In the 1990s, the materials balance approach reemerged as part of the "newly discovered" field of industrial ecology. [ROBERT C. AYRES, INDUSTRIAL ECOLOGY (1998).]

7.   The reference is to the Clean Water Act, 33 U.S.C. 1251(a).

8.   The history of western thought reveals a tradition of "pollution" as unwanted defilement. *See* MARY DOUGLAS, PURITY AND DANGER; AN ANALYSIS OF THE CONCEPTS OF POLLUTION AND TABOO (1966).

9.   *See* EUGENE ODUM, FUNDAMENTALS OF ECOLOGY 432-451 (1971).

10.   *See id.* at 83-106.

11.   In THE CLOSING CIRCLE, Barry Commoner based his view of pollution upon such a view of the cycling of nature. For Commoner, it was the advent of synthetics that created the environmental crisis. *See* BARRY COMMONER, THE CLOSING CIRCLE (1971).

12.   Since 1970, a new awareness has developed of the extent to which nature itself processes pollutants.

13.   As we shall illustrate below, describing the pattern of pathways and the possibility of recycling is indeed a complex business.

14.   The reference here is to the best recommended fertility control devices, although no enforceable standard were established.

15.   As a consequence, EPA is an "agency" rather than a department, and its administrator is not a department secretary.

16.   *See* RICHARD N.L. ANDREWS, MANAGING THE ENVIRONMENT; MANAGING OURSELVES 229-232 (1999).

17.   The tradeoff between ecological planning and rule based enforcement will be explained below, but deserves a specific later volume in this series.

18.   The Clean Air Act of 1970 was the result of previous regulation as well as a history of common law, illustrated by the *Boomer* case. Boomer v. Atlantic Cement, 26 NY2d 22; 309 N.Y.S. 2d 312 (1970).

19.   Environmental protection Agency, "Air Quality Criteria for Oxides of Nitrogen" (September 1982).

20.   For one of many accounts of the standard setting process, *see* THOMAS O. MCGARITY, REINVENTING RATIONALITY: THE ROLE OF REGULATING ANALYSIS IN THE FEDERAL BUREAUCRACY 45-62 (1991). Many of these studies document that ecology and ecosystem terms may be employed in the criteria documents, but do not guide the adoption of standards.

21.   *See* OFFICE OF RESEARCH AND DEVELOPMENT, U.S. ENVIRONMENTAL PROTECTION AGENCY, AIR QUALITY CRITERIA FOR LEAD (1977).

22.   *See* Lead Industries v. EPA, 647 F2d 1130 (D.C. Cir. 1980), cert denied 449 U.S. 1042 (1980).

23.   *See* 42 U.S.C. 7470-7492.

24.   *See* 42 U.S.C. 7475(d).

25.   *See* R.L. Glicksman, *Pollution on the Federal Lands I: Air Pollution Law*, 12 UCLA J. ENVT'L L. & POL'Y 160 (1993).

26.   Discussed in Chapter 7 below.

27.   In addition to those discussed in the text, exceptions include the mention of ecosystem effects in research (42 U.S.C. 7403 (e)); further acid deposition research, assessment of risks to ecosystems from criteria pollutants (42 U.S.C. 7409 (g)); new studies of the role of secondary standards, identification of hazardous pollutants to include

ecosystem effects (42 U.S.C. 7412 (a)-(c)); residual risk standards for hazardous air pollutants (42 U.S.C. 7412 (f)); site considerations under solid waste combustion (42 U.S.C. 7429); the adoption of a variety of interstate transport regions and commissions, the provision for assessment of air pollution on the interstate borders, and recognition of ecological damage as part of emergency enforcement (42 U.S.C. 7603).

28.   *See* 42 U.S.C. 7412 (m).

29.   *See* 430 F 2d 199 (5th Cir. 1970).

30.   *See* 33 U.S.C. 1344.

31.   *See* 45 Fed Reg. 85, 336-57 (Dec. 24, 1980).

32.   *See* U.S. v. Riverside Bayview Homes, Inc., 474 U.S. 121 (1985).

33.   *See* 51 Fed Reg. 41,206 (Nov. 13, 1986); 53 Fed. Reg. 3120 (Feb. 3, 1988).

34.   *See* MEMORANDUM OF AGREEMENT BETWEEN THE ENVIRONMENTAL PROTECTION AGENCY AND THE DEPARTMENT OF THE ARMY CONCERNING THE DETERMINATION OF MITIGATION UNDER THE CLEAN WATER ACT SECTION 404 (B) (1) GUIDELINES (issued Nov. 15, 1989, but revised and made effective Feb. 7, 1990).

35.   For one of several descriptions of this history, *see* ROBERT P. MCINTOSH, THE BACKGROUND OF ECOLOGY: CONCEPT AND THEORY 221-34 (1985).

36.   The criticism of models, both small and large scale, has been unremitting, although the critics usually do not have suggestions for their replacement. For one such criticism, set forth elsewhere in this book, *see* BRUCE A. ACKERMAN ET. AL., UNCERTAIN SEARCH FOR ENVIRONMENTAL QUALITY 9-81 (1974).

37.   *See* Mark Eliot Shere, *The Myth of Meaningful Environmental Risk Assessment*, 19 HARVARD ENVTL. L. REV. 409 (1995); Camille V. Otero-Philips *What's in the Forecast? A Look at the EPA's Use of Computer Models in Emissions Trading*, 24 RUTGERS COMPUTER & TECH. L. J. 187 (1998); Michael Sklash et. al., *Groundwater Models: Can You Believe What they are Saying?* 130 NAT. RESOURCES & ENV'T 542 (1999).

38.   *See, e.g.*, ECOLOGICAL MODELING IN A RESOURCE MANAGEMENT FRAMEWORK (Clifford Russell ed., 1975); CHARLES A.S. HALL & JOHN W. DAY, JR., ECOSYSTEM MODELING IN THEORY AND PRACTICE: AN INTRODUCTION WITH CASE HISTORIES (1977); INDIVIDUAL-BASED MODELS AND APPROACHES IN ECOLOGY: POPULATIONS, COMMUNITIES, AND ECOSYSTEMS (Donald L. DeAngelis & Louis J Gross, eds. 1992).

39.   *See* Charles D. Case, *Problems in Judicial Review Arising from the Use of Computer Models and Other Quantitative Methodologies in Environmental Decision-making*, 10 B.C. ENVTL. AFF. L. REV. 251 (1982).

40.   *See* Sarah Birkeland, *EPA's TDML Program*, 28 ECOLOGY L. Q. 297 (2001); OLIVER HOUCK, THE CLEAN WATER ACT TMDL PROGRAM: LAW, POLICY AND IMPLEMENTATION (1999).

41.   BRUCE ACKERMAN ET AL., THE UNCERTAIN SEARCH FOR ENVIRONMENTAL QUALITY (1974).

42.   DANTE ALIGHIERI, THE DIVINE COMEDY, CANTE VII at lines 126-129. This version is set forth in WILLIAM J. MITSCH & JAMES G. GOSSELINK, WETLANDS 12 (1986).

43.   For a thumbnail sketch, *see* WILLIAM MITSCH & JAMES G. GOSSELINK, WETLANDS 12 (1986).

44.   *See id.* at 15, 16.

45.   *See id.* at 15-20.

46.   *See* Zabel v. Tabb, 401 U.S. 910 (1971); Natural Resources Defense Council v. Callaway, 524 F.2d 79 (2d Cir. 1975).

47.   These are described in MITSCH, *supra* note 42.

48.　Considerable debate and legal issues have surrounded the FWS, Dept of Army, EPA, SCS "Federal Manual for Identifying and Delineating Jurisdictional Wetlands" in 1989. For a discussion of the history, *see* WILLIAM L. WANT, THE LAW OF WETLANDS REGULATION 4.2-4.33 (1989).

49.　*See* 40 CFR 230 1-61.

50.　Want, *supra* note 48, at 6.27-28.

51.　*See* U.S. v. Sexton Cover Estates 526 F 2d 1293, 1301 (5ᵗʰ Cir. 1976).

52.　*See* Want, *supra* note 48, at n. 16.

53.　*See* Joy B. Zedler, *Progress in Wetland Restoration Ecology*, 15 TRENDS IN ECOLOGY AND EVOLUTION 402-407 (2000). Despite the strong presence of ecology in the law governing the delineation, the permitting, the mitigation and the restoration of wetlands, it remains that wetlands are being lost to development at an alarming rate. This is not surprising. Wetlands are often in or next to economically valuable sites for development. The cultural history of wetlands suggests an inherited bias towards their development. The early legal history placed a development-oriented agency in charge of their permitting. But a careful study of the regulatory system itself reveals loopholes in the protection of wetlands. First, not all wetlands are protected, either by federal or state laws. Second, the criteria for designation may fail to capture lands near wetlands or in transition to becoming wetlands. Third, although a permit may be required, development is not prohibited. On the contrary, if no adverse impacts are found or no practicable alternative is available, wetlands may be developed. Lying behind the decision to deny a permit is the ever present threat of lawsuits based upon a constitutional claim of "taking" without just compensation. Many of the major taking cases are in fact wetlands cases. [*See* Want, *supra* note 50, at 10.1-10.15.] In addition, as mentioned above, there are a variety of exemptions in the wetlands laws. Finally, there may be a failure to detect wetland abuse and/or a failure to enforce the wetlands laws. The current status of wetlands indicates that even if there is careful attention paid to the application of ecology within environmental regulation, it need not follow that the environmental resource in question will be protected. What one must ask at this point is what else is needed to insure environmental protection and what, if anything, ecology can contribute to this problem with our environmental laws.

54.　For an overview of land use law, *see* DANIEL MANDELKER ET. AL., PLANNING AND CONTROL OF LAND DEVELOPMENT (1995).

55.　We will discuss these areas of "land use law" *infra* Chapters 5 & 6.

56.　For the early history, *see* DONALD HAUGMAN & JULIAN CONRAD JUERGENSMEYER, URBAN PLANNING AND LAND DEVELOPMENT CONTROL LAW 38-71 (1986).

57.　*See* AMERICAN LAND INSTITUTE, MODEL LAND DEVELOPMENT CODE (1975).

58.　*See* RICHARD BROOKS, MUNICIPAL ENVIRONMENTAL ORDINANCES (1972).

59.　*See* PATRICK GEDDES, CITIES IN EVOLUTION: AN INTRODUCTION TO THE TOWN PLANNING MOVEMENT AND TO THE STUDY OF CITIES (1968).

60.　*See* LEWIS MUMFORD, THE CULTURE OF CITIES (1970).

61.　*See* IAN MCHARG, DESIGN WITH NATURE (1971).

62.　For an account of comprehensive planning, *see* JOHN FRIEDMAN, PLANNING IN THE PUBLIC DOMAIN: FROM KNOWLEDGE TO ACTION (1987) (124 et seq).

63.　The following accounts are based upon memoranda prepared by Edward McNamara.

64.　*See* PROTECTING THE NEW JERSEY PINELANDS 5, 8. (Beryl Collins et al. eds., 1988). The following description is based upon a "New Jersey Pinelands" memoranda prepared by Edward McNamara. *See* NEW JERSEY PINELANDS COMMISSION, THE PINELANDS NATIONAL RESERVE <http://www.state.nj.us/pinelands/science/scintro.htm> (visited May 3, 2000). In 1983, the Pinelands was designated a Biosphere Reserve by the U.S. Man and the Biosphere Program and the United Nations Educational, Scientific and

Cultural Organization (UNESCO). This designation means, simply, that the Pinelands
is an example of the world's major ecosystem types. *See id.*

65.   *Id.*
66.   *Id.* at 28.
67.   *See id.* at 47; telephone conversation with Michael Broek, Public Information Officer,
         Pinelands Commission (August 3, 2000).
68.   *See* New Jersey Pinelands Commission, *supra* note 64.
69.   *See* Collins, *supra* note 64, at 37-41.
70.   *See id.* at 42.
71.   NPS suggested three options for designation: "a national scientific reserve of 175,000
         to 245,000 acres; a state forest or national recreation area of 267,000 acres, and a state
         Pinelands region of 373,000 acres." Collins, *supra* note 64, at 43.
72.   *See id.* at 44.
73.   *Id.* at 42.
74.   *See id.*
75.   *Id.* at 51.
76.   *See id.* at 54.
77.   *Id.* at 64.
78.   The federal legislation which created the National Reserve is 16 U.S.C.A. § 471. The
         New Jersey legislation that enables the National Reserve found at N.J.S.A. 13:18(A)
         et seq., the Pinelands Protection Act. The primary purpose of the act is to preserve the
         character of the Pinelands. State law which protects the coast is also important in
         managing the National Reserve. State law failed to include approximately 150,000
         acres along the coast, which were included in the National Reserve, as this area was
         already protected by the Coastal Area Facility Review Act. *See id.* at 79.
79.   *See* New Jersey Pinelands Commission, Environmental Research and Monitoring
         Activities of the Science Office. <www.state.nj.us/pinelands/science /scintro.htm>
         (visited July 16, 2000).
80.   *Id.*
81.   <http://www.state.nj.us/pinelands/cmp.htm> (visited 5/30/00).
82.   *Id.,* at 35.
83.   *See id.*
84.   *See id.*
85.   *See* Pinelands Biosphere Reserve Research Station website, (visited July 16, 2000)
         <http://www.obfs.org/ OBFS_Stations/NJ_Pinelands_Biol_Res.Stat.html>.
86.   *See* Collins, *supra* note 64, at 78.
87.   *Id.* at 79.
88.   The Science Office of the Commission conducts a long-term environmental monitoring
         program within the region; however, there is no institutional mechanism which dictates
         how the results of this program are to be incorporated into the CMP.
89.   *See* Collins, *supra* note 64, at 79.
90.   Legal challenges to the Pinelands protection have been in the form of unconstitutional
         takings claims. The case of *Gardner v. New Jersey Pinelands Commission* [*See* 125 N.J.
         193 (1991)] is illustrative. In this case, the plaintiff claimed that the restriction of
         her property to agricultural production was an illegal taking under the state constitution.
         The New Jersey supreme court declared that "[t]he preservation of agriculture
         and farmland constitutes a valid governmental goal." [Gardner, *supra* note 97, at 206.]
         The court went on to cite *Usdin v. Environmental Protection Dep't*, holding that
         "a property owner 'has no absolute and unlimited right to change the essential natural

character of his land so as to use it for a purpose for which it was unsuited in its natural state and which injures the rights of others'." [173 N.J. Super. 311, 327 (1980).]

91.   *See* Elliot-Fisk et al., *Lake Tahoe Case Study* in SIERRA NEVADA ECOSYSTEM PROJECT: FINAL REPORT TO CONGRESS, ADDENDUM. DAVIS: UNIVERSITY OF CALIFORNIA, CENTERS FOR WATER AND WILDLAND RESOURCES (1996).

92.   *See* DOUGLAS H. STRONG, TAHOE: FROM TIMBER BARONS TO ECOLOGISTS 2 (1999).

93.   *See* Elliot-Fisk, *supra* note 91, at 228.

94.   *See id.* at 225.

95.   *See id.*, at 3.

96.   *See id.*

97.   Elliot-Fisk, *supra* note 91, at 228.

98.   *See* Elliot-Fisk, *supra* note 91, 243-245.

99.   *See* S.G. Wells et. al., *Cooperative Efforts Around Lake Tahoe*, 402 NATURE 348 (1999).

100.   *Id.* at 240.

101.   *See* TRPA, *Regional Plan for the Lake Tahoe Basin: Goals and Policies*, Adopted by the Governing Board Sept. 17, 1986, printed April 1999. I-3.

102.   Tahoe Sierra Preservation Council v. TRPA, 2000 WL 770512 3.

103.   Prepared by the Western Federal Regional Council Interagency Task Force in 1979.

104.   Elliot-Fisk, *supra* note 91, at 245.

105.   TRPA, *supra* note 101, at I-2.

106.   94 Stat. 3233; Pub. L. 96-551; Cal. Gov't Code *66800; Nev. Rev. Stat. 277.200*.

107.   Cal. Gov't. Code *66800 Article I.*

108.   TRPA, *supra* note 101, at I-4.

109.   *Id.* at II-2.

110.   *Id.* at II-9.

111.   *See id.*, at II-13.

112.   TRPA, *supra* note 101, at VII-4.

113.   *See id.*, at VII-26.

114.   *See id.*, at II-3.

115.   *See id.*, at II-4. The major problem encountered in the development and utilization of the TRPAs regional plan has been resistance to what is seen as a taking of private lands. Development of private land has been at the heart of much of the controversy over TRPA. TRPA has "worked to resolve the on-going conflict through a consensus workshop process" involving key stakeholders, which has proved to be successful, for the most part. [Elliot-Fisk, *supra* note 100, at 245-46; Pryor, *supra* note 11, at 18.] "In a significant case, a Nevada court validated the scientific and legal underpinnings of TRPA's 1987 regional plan with regard to its water quality provisions." [*See* Kelly v. Tahoe Regional Planning Authority, 855 P.2d 1027 (Nev. 1993); *Elliot-Fisk, supra* note 100, at 241.] The case involved a developer who was unable to use some of his plots as he had hoped due to TRPA regulations, and subsequently sued TRPA claiming an illegal taking. The court utilized *Keystone Bituminous Coal Assn. v. DeBenedictis* [480 U.S. 470 (1987)] to determine if 1) TRPA regulations were in the government interest and 2) whether that common interest outweighed Kelly's private interest in developing the hilltop lots. [*See* Kelly, at 1034.] The court concluded that "TRPA regulations substantially advanced a legitimate government interest: the protection of Lake Tahoe Basin – a national treasure," and further that TRPA regulations "did not deprive Mr. Kelly of his interest in property in a manner requiring compensation."[*Id.* at 1035.]

116.   *See* L.L. McConnell et. al., *Wet Deposition of Current-use Pesticides in the Sierra Nevada Mountain Range, California, U.S.A.*, 17 ENVIRONMENTAL TOXICOLOGY 1908-16 (1998).

117. *See* S. Datta et.al., *Evidence of Organochlorine Contamination in Tissues of Salmonoids in Lake Tahoe*, 42 ECOTOXICOLOGY & ENVIRONMENTAL SAFETY 94-101 (1999).

118. *See* BOB DOPPELT, MARY SCURLOCK, CHRIS FRISSELL, JAMES KARR, ENTERING THE WATERSHED: A NEW APPROACH TO SAVE AMERICA'S RIVER ECOSYSTEMS (1993).

119. *See* P. ANGERMEIER & J.R.KARN, BIOLOGICAL INTEGRITY VERSUS BIOLOGICAL DIVERSITY AS POLICY DIRECTIVES IN WATER RESOURCE PROTECTION. For a discussion of some of the scientific issues in watershed planning, *see* ELOISE KENDY, SCIENCE INTO POLICY: WATER IN THE PUBLIC REALM (1999).

120. *See* OLIVER HOUCK, THE CLEAN WATER ACT TMDL PROGRAM: LAW POLICY AND IMPLEMENTATIONS (1999).

121. Clean Water Act, §303(d), 33 U.S.C. §1313(d).

122. *See* James Boyd, *The New Face of the Clean Water Act: A Critical Review of the EPA's New TMDL Rules* in 11 DUKE ENVT'L L & POLICY F 39 (2000).

123. *Id.*

124. *See* GERRIT SCHURMANN & BERND MARKERT, ECOTOXICOLOGY: ECOLOGICAL FUNDAMENTALS, CHEMICAL EXPOSURE AND BIOLOGICAL EFFECTS (1998).

125. *See* JOEL TARR, THE SEARCH FOR THE ULTIMATE SINK: URBAN POLLUTION IN HISTORICAL PERSPECTIVE (1996).

126. *See* L. Guruswamy, *Integrating Thoughtways: Reopening of the Environmental Mind*, 1989 WIS. L. REV. 463 (1989).

127. *See* R.D. Bullard, DUMPING IN DIXIE: RACE, CLASS, AND ENVIRONMENTAL QUALITY (2nd Ed. 1994).

128. *See* Pub.L. No. 89-272, 79 Stat. 992 (Oct. 20, 1965); William H. Rodgers, Jr., in his monumental four volume ENVIRONMENTAL LAW, offers a brief history. *See* 3 ENVIRONMENTAL LAW: PESTICIDES AND TOXIC SUBSTANCES (1988) Section 7. 2.

129. *See* Pub.L. No. 91-512, 84 Stat. 1227 (Oct. 26, 1970).

130. ALLEN KNEESE & ROBERT AYRES, ECONOMICS AND THE ENVIRONMENT: A MATERIAL BALANCE APPROACH (1970).

131. For a more sophisticated and less mechanistic discussion of "throughput" of materials in the environment, *see* KIMON VALASKAKIS ET. AL., THE SELECTIVE CONSERVER SOCIETY (1977).

132. We have seen above that the Clean Air Act, the Clean Water Act and Pesticide legislation also deal with toxic and hazardous pollutants.

133. This Act was amended in 1980 and 1984.

134. For an excellent succinct overview of the Act, and its problems, *see* Barry Needleman, *Hazardous Waste Recycling Under the Resource, Conservation and Recovery Act: Problems and Potential Solutions*, 24 ENVT'L. 971 (1994).

135. *See id.* at 1013-25.

136. This summary of ground water pollution is from George Bilicic, Jr., *Note: An Analysis of the Land Disposal Ban in the 1984 Amendments to the Resource, Conservation and Recovery Act*, 76 GEO L. J. 1563 (1988).

137. *Definitions of solid and hazardous waste:* "Hazardous waste treated as a subset of solid waste which is defined as "any garbage, refuse, sludge from a waste treatment plant, water supply treatment plant or air pollution control facility and other discarded material ..." Such a definition focuses upon material which is "waste" and hence defined in terms of its relationship to the economic process. Because EPA was reluctant to intervene in production processes, it initially excluded by regulation certain primary materials (i.e., "process-specific materials," which might be reused in the production process, and "facility specific materials," including, under some circumstances, accumulated materials for later recycling). [These

exclusions were qualified as applied to "discarded" solid wastes, resulting in a complex series of coverages and exemptions of materials in the production process. The regulatory exclusions and their qualifications were subject to various lawsuits.] In American Mining Congress v. EPA [824 F. 2d 1177 (D.C. Cir. 1987)], the court reviewed EPA's regulatory definitions of solid waste as applied to secondary materials which were not yet discarded but were still part of the production process. These materials were reprocessed ore, the metals removed from it, and the metal-bearing dusts, al of which were to be recycled. The court held that the materials which were to be reused were not "discarded" and that, by the language of the statute and its legislative history, such secondary materials are not covered by the Act.

This case and others [*See, e.g.,* American Petroleum Institute v. EPA, 906 F2d 729 (D.C. Cir. 1990); American Mining Congress v EPA, 907 F.2d. 1179 (D.C. Cir 1990); Shell Oil Co. v. EPA, 950 F 2d 741 (D.C. Cir. 1991)] demonstrate the ambiguity of solid and "hazardous waste." If one analyzes materials to be reused at some time in the production process, the materials may not be "waste," in some ultimate sense, since they are still in the economic process. On the other hand, the materials – whether to be used or not – also remain within the ecosystem and may cause it harm. If they are parked on the back lot, they may well be subject to wind, rain and other ecological processes that in turn may affect their fate in the environment. If one wishes to "ease" the economic process of recycling, one may not wish to regulate them; if one wishes to guard against their harm to the environment, one may wish to regulate them. (Another way of looking at the issue is that the court, legislature, and administrative agency are weighing the relative environmental damage of unregulated lower cost recycling vs. regulated higher cost – and perhaps less – recycling.) *An important observation about these cases is that they reveal that economic recycling and the prevention of environmental harm are not synonymous.*

138.   *Listing and de-listing hazardous materials:* Hazardous waste is defined as " ... solid wastes ... which ... may cause or significantly contribute to an increase in mortality, or an increase in serious irreversible or incapacitating reversible illness; or b) pose a substantial present or potential hazard to human health or the environment when improperly treated, stored, transported, or disposed of or otherwise managed." [42 U.S.C. Sec. 6903 (5).] Despite references to the environment, the first lists of materials were a compilation of known chemical dangerous to human health. Case specific determinations of materials are based upon the materials ignitability, corrosivity, reactivity, and toxicity. Only the last "toxicity" would have the most direct relationship to the natural environment. Unfortunately, in the original regulations, EPA declined to extend its analysis to organic toxicity, carcinogenicity, mutagenicity, teratogenicity, bioaccumulation, and phytotoxicity. [45 Fed. Reg. At 33095-96.] Spurred by the 1984 Act, EPA finally adopted toxicity measures based upon "health-based" concentration thresholds and a "dilution/attenuation" factor that was developed using a subsurface fate and transport model in 1990. [*See* 55 Fed Reg. 11798, 11855 (March 29, 1990). For a discussion of these levels, *see* Marcia Williams and Jonathan Cannon, *Rethinking the Resource, Conservation and Recovery Act of the 1990s*, 21 ENVTL. L. REP 10063 (1991).]

139.   *The Permitting of Treatment, Storage and Disposal Facilities ("TSDF"):* Most of the requirements for the location of TSDFs are technology rather than risk based requirements. However, among the federal requirements for the establishment and conduct of TSDFs are certain general siting requirements (e.g., location near faults and in flood plains), and groundwater monitoring. Groundwater monitoring assumed an ecological knowledge of soils, topography, geology, vegetation, and hydrology, a knowledge that may or may not be implemented in the monitoring process. In addition

to groundwater monitoring, a variety of federal and state siting requirements may apply to specific kinds of TDSFs. In addition, in order to secure permit for land disposal, a modified "no-migration" requirement must be met, which again requires some form of groundwater monitoring. [For a discussion of the origins of the no migration standard, *see* Bilicic, *supra* note 156.]

140.   *Bioremediation*: Bioremediation refers to the destruction of contaminants through the use of natural biological processes. Either environmental conditions are manipulated to stimulate microbial communities to degrade the compounds, or in some instances, specific microbes that have been selected or genetically altered to degrade the target toxic compounds, are introduced to the contaminated site. [*See* M. Alexander, BIODEGRADATION AND BIOREMEDIATION, (1994).] It may take place either within or outside of the area of contamination. Under RCRA, it may take place at the closure or post-closure of a regulated unit, under a corrective action or applied to non-permitted units such as pre-RCRA units or spill sites. It is particularly effective in cleaning up petroleum hydrocarbons. (Part of such bioremediation is the cleaning of groundwater.) An additional specifically regulated area is hazardous waste farming.

Aside from the regulatory provisions governing each situation in which bioremediation might apply [for a review of these regulations, *see* Teresa B. Salamone, *Bioremediation Under the Resource Conservation and Recovery Act*, 9 WTR NAT. RESOURCES & ENV'T 58 (1995)], the major question (also found within Superfund) is how clean is clean (i.e., what level of removal, elimination, transformation or containment is required on-site)? Without review of the complexity of legal issues here, the more general issue, which pertains both to all rehabilitation and restoration efforts, may involve not only human health standards, but ecological judgements as well. [This raises the more general question of ecology and restoration within environmental law. For a general discussion of restoration and the law, *see* Alyson C. Flournoy, *Restoration, Rx: An Evaluation and Prescription*, 42 ARIZ. LAW REV. 187 (2000). For one of many specific studies of the law of restoration, *see* Ludwig A. Teclaff & Eileen Teclaff, *Restoring River and Lake Basin Ecosystems*, 34 NAT. RESOURCES J. 905 (1994).]

Under the Resource, Conservation and Recovery Act, states may implement solid and hazardous waste regulation. The State of Vermont, for example, has adopted legislation enabling the adoption of a state solid waste plan and a hazardous waste management plan. Permitting or certification of a solid waste management facility and a hazardous waste facility must not only comply with the plan, but also a variety of laws and environmental regulations. For example, the solid waste facility must not create an unreasonable risk to the public health or be unreasonably destructive to the environment. In addition, the facility must comply with Vermont's "Act 250" and its environmental criteria. The application of these criteria requires careful examination of the possible pathways of pollutants through the environment. [For a description of Vermont's solid and hazardous waste program and Act 250, *see* RICHARD BROOKS ET. AL., TOWARD COMMUNITY SUSTAINABILITY (1996).] The Resource, Conservation and Recovery Act is only one of many laws seeking to control toxics. Many of these other laws, e.g., the Clean Water Act's toxic pollutants provisions, are increasingly becoming ecologically sophisticated, adopting wildlife criteria, biocriteria and sediment quality criteria. [*See* JEFFREY A. FORAN & LARRY E. FINK, REGULATING TOXIC SUBSTANCES IN SURFACE WATER (1993).] These efforts to develop a new ecologically sophisticated approach to waste disposal will be explored in a future volume in this series.

5   The Shy Embrace of Law and Ecology

Contemporary public concern for protecting nature's ecological equilibrium should lead to the conferral of standing upon environmental objects to sue for their own preservation.
— Justice Douglas in Sierra Club v. Morton

In 1972, the Supreme Court of the United States handed down a decision in *Sierra Club v Morton*[1] denying the Sierra Club access to contest the Disney Enterprises development of Mineral King Valley in the Sierra Nevada Mountains.

The court recognized environmental damage as a basis for injury in fact sufficient to secure standing for the Club's members, and Justice Douglas issued a unique opinion in which he argued for the legal standing of ecosystems. In his concurrence, Justice Douglas argued that the "valleys, alpine meadows, rivers, lakes, estuaries, beaches, ridges, groves of trees, swampland and even air feels the destructive pressures of modern technology and modern life." He went on to suggest that the federal agencies established to protect these areas are frequently co-opted by economic interests for development. As a consequence, the voices of these inanimate objects and those who visit them and know their values and wonders should have standing to challenge the legality of actions taken by federal agencies which might harm these natural areas. Although Justice Douglas's desire for the "standing" of inanimate natural objects was not endorsed by his colleagues (neither past nor future[2]), the Disney project was stopped and the recognition of the inherent value of nature, to be protected by the law, became a matter of serious and widespread public concern.[3]

As the court noted, Mineral King is an area of great natural beauty, and the U.S. Forest Service was planning to lease out lands to Walt Disney Enterprises to create a complex of hotels, restaurants, swimming pools, and parking lots designed to accommodate 14,000 visitors daily. Concerned about the traffic, noise and air pollution, and the stripping of the forest, the Sierra Club brought suit.

Introduction

The *Sierra Club v. Morton* case began wending its way through the courts just before Earth Day in April 1970. Earth Day is a symbol of the national launching of the modern U.S. environmental movement. In the late 1960s, nature preservation, sportsmen and civic citizen groups, city governments, neighborhoods threatened by large scale developments, college faculty and students found a common cause in the demand for federal action to protect the environment.[4] Unlike the traditional environmental laws dealing with air and water pollution and toxics – laws which resisted the new science of ecology – other new laws such as NEPA, Coastal Zone Management and the Great Lakes Compact, embraced ecology with fervor ... at least initially, and newly recovered common law doctrines such as the public trust doctrine helped to lay the basis for a more holistic view of the environment.

JUSTICE WILLIAM DOUGLAS

Justice Douglas was an outstanding environmental law judge on the U.S. Supreme Court from 1939 to 1975. He was a liberal on social and economic questions, an internationalist and a champion on civil rights. He authored several pathbreaking opinions protecting urban and land planning, as well as extending the reach of environmental pollution laws. Douglas was an avid hiker and walker, and a conservationist who promoted several important nature conservation causes. He authored *A Wilderness Bill of Rights.* His opinion, which rested upon Christopher Stone's classic, *Do Trees Have Standing?*, captured the depth of his commitment to the preservation of the environment and his vivid sense of the economic forces that support environmental abuses.

NEPA – The National Environmental Policy Act: An Ecologist's Dream?

In the 1960s, the *Scenic Hudson* cases, the Santa Barbara Oil Spill, and the Wisconsin DDT hearings focused upon the environmental impacts of power plants, oil blowouts, and DDT applications. In each of these cases, courts and administrative agencies strained to find and interpret the law authorizing the legal review of these environmental impacts. In 1970, the National Environmental Policy Act (NEPA) was adopted, requiring federal agencies to assess the impacts of their major decisions that could significantly affect the environment. For the first time, the range of environmental impacts from federally funded or permitted highways, power plants, and many other projects were the proper subject of government concern and court review. It was no longer federal government business as usual.

The principal architect of NEPA was ecologist Lynton Caldwell, who has carefully evaluated NEPA's workings since its inception. Among NEPA's purposes is to "prevent or eliminate damage to the environment and the biosphere," and "enrich the understanding of the ecological systems ..." Among the environmental policies of the law is to preserve "... an environment which supports diversity ..." The act states that "Congress recognizes that each person should enjoy a healthful environment and that each person has a responsibility to contribute to the preservation and enhancement of the environment ..."[5] Federal agencies are required to "utilize a systematic, interdisciplinary approach which will insure the integrated use of the natural and social sciences and the environmental design arts in planning and in decision making ..."[6] The most visible manifestation of NEPA was the requirement that an environmental impact statement (EIS) be created for legislation and other federal actions significantly affecting the environment. A President's Council on Environmental Quality, intended to rival the Council of Economic Advisors, was to be established to annually review the state of the environment and to recommend programs for remedying the deficiencies in environmental protection programs, based among other things on "investigations, studies, surveys, research, and analyses relating to ecological systems ..." This language made it clear that NEPA was intended to invoke an ecological perspective in efforts to protect the environment.

LYNTON CALDWELL

Lynton Caldwell is the Arthur F. Bentley Professor Emeritus of Political Science at Indiana University. Since the early 1960s, his interests have been concentrated on public policy for science and the environment. He has combined academic activities with extensive involvement in public affairs at national and international levels. He was one of the principal drafters of the National Environmental Policy Act of 1969 (NEPA). He has authored 12 books, some 250 articles in refereed journals and numerous reports for public and international agencies. Recent books include *International Environmental Policy: Emergence and Dimensions* (1996); *Between Two Worlds: Science, the Environmental Movement and Policy Choice* (1992); *Policy for Land: Law and Ethics* (with Kristin Shrader-Frechette) (1993); and *Environment As a Focus for Public Policy* (1995).

The novelty (and controversy) of NEPA lay in its bold commitment to an interdisciplinary scientific effort. As such, it represented a new stage in federal science policy. In Caldwell's words, "What was sought through NEPA was a joining of sciences in relationships that would fill the informational or conceptual interspace between the various sciences."[7] The philosophy of NEPA went beyond dreams for unified sciences, promising a novel reform in administrative law as well. The National Environmental Policy Act's broad policy mandates cut across the customary administrative jurisdictions of government, requiring agencies as distinct as the old Atomic Energy Commission and the Federal Highway Department to consider the environmental consequences of their actions. In this sense, NEPA was an environmental heir to the broad policy approaches of the New Deal, and an update/addendum to the federal Administrative Procedures Act (APA).[8] NEPA injected some environmental substance into the APA's formal constraint on the arbitrary and capricious actions of government agencies.[9]

The best ecological rationale for NEPA and its consequent history was provided by John Dryzek, who argued that pertinent features of the ecosystem *(emergence, interpenetration, self-regulation, and dynamism)* create certain unique problems, requiring social choices that are appropriate to resolve these problems.[10] For Dryzek, an ecological awareness requires social systems that can provide negative feedback, coordination, robustness, flexibility and resilience. Dryzek found the traditional forms of social choice – markets, traditional rules of law, governmental "polyarchy," force and moral persuasion – are not adequate to address the unique problems of the environment as they were ecologically understood.

Table 5.1 DERIVING CRITERIA FOR SOCIAL CHOICE

Pertinent eco-system features (General) →	Circumstance of ecological problems +	Normative judgment =	Criteria for Social choice	Social choice mechanism structures
Interpretation Emergent properties Self-regulation Dynamism	Complexity Non-reducibility Variability: spatial and temporal Uncertainty Collectiveness Spontaneity	Maintenance of capability of human and natural systems in-conjunction to cope with actual or potential shortfall in life support	Negative feed-back Coordination: across choices within choices Robustness Flexibility Resilience (contingent upon severe disequilibrium)	Markets Administered systems Law Politics-polygandy Moral persuasion Negotiation Force Conditional cooperation (decentralization) Discussion

Source: John Dryzek, *Rational Ecology* (1987)

The NEPA environmental impact statement, with its case-by-case coordination among federal agencies,[11] promised to provide the negative feedback and flexibility needed to cope with environmental problems. This case-by-case incremental approach dominated the administration of NEPA. The benefits and limits of NEPA both derive from this flexible and incremental approach.[12]

The National Environmental Policy Act, although explicit with respect to the agency and environment, was ambiguous about the role of the courts in the NEPA process. The *Calvert Cliffs* decision changed all that.[13] Judge Skelly Wright held that NEPA's requirement of the Environmental Impact

Statement was "action-forcing," requiring the agency not merely to prepare the report for the Council on Environmental Quality, but "to consider environmental issues just as they consider other matters within their mandate." Implicitly, the court made the agency fulfillment of this requirement subject to judicial review.

This decision established some linkage, however fragile, between the specific decisions which government officials had to make and the environmental views set forth in the environmental impact statement. With the court's door open to consider environmental matters, citizen groups now had a powerful tool for bringing legal actions, securing court review of agency actions in light of the environmental impact statement. Thus the prospect emerged for a legally mandated linkage between ecology as reflected in the environmental impact statement, and government action. Ecology and law could meet in the Environmental Impact Statement. Three decades later, with a history of thousands of environmental impact statements, hundreds of court decisions, and many studies of NEPA, the linking of ecology to law through NEPA mandates has been assessed. First, an outline of a typical environ-mental impact statement is set forth.

Bridge Document 5.1 SAMPLE ENVIRONMENTAL STATEMENT

[on Management of Habitat for Late Successional
and Old Growth Forest-Related Species (1994)]

I.   Purpose and Need: Protect forest habitat, produce forest products
II. Proposed Federal Action: Coordinate federal management of old-
                                    growth forest in the Pacific Northwest
III. Alternatives (10):
   - No action
   - Action alternatives example:
        Alternative 1: [24,455,300 acres of federal land]
        Congressionally reserved area   7,320,000
        Late successional reserve   11,402,400
        Riparian reserve   1,879,700
        Administratively withdrawn   1,079,900
        Matrix   2,772,700
        Maximum achievement of five biological criteria
        Standards and guidelines for each area
IV. Impacts
   - On ecosystems and species
   - On the economy and communities [timber harvest levels]
   - Other environmental consequences

Source: U.S.D.A., et al., *Final Supplemental Environmental Impact Statement* [1994]

1. The Environmental Impact Statement and Ecology

Under NEPA, each federal agency considering an action that could affect the environment must include a statement of the project's environmental impact that includes: adverse unavoidable environmental effects; alternatives to the proposed action; the relationship between short term uses and maintenance and enhancement of long-term productivity; and any irreversible and irretrievable commitments of resources in major federal actions significantly affecting the quality of the human environment. With the exception of the passing reference to "productivity," the statutory language in the impact approach does not set forth a systems approach to preparing the statement, but rather a more traditional comprehensive planning approach.[14] In short, the NEPA "embrace" of ecology through the EIS is "lukewarm."

Without ecological language and instruction to guide impact statements, the federal agencies were initially responsible for interpreting and carrying out the NEPA mandates. As Richard Liroff has documented, the early response revealed most agencies were unwilling or unable to seriously undertake the implementation of the Act, let alone in an ecologically focused way.[15] The Council on Environmental Quality faced the task of spelling out any ecological content in the law. It wasn't until 1978 that the Council on Environmental Quality finally issued a detailed set of regulations, designed to guide agencies to implement the Act.

COUNCIL ON ENVIRONMENTAL QUALITY (CEQ) REGULATIONS

The CEQ Regulations[16] specify that this assessment must include discussions of: (a) direct effects and their significance; (b) indirect effects and their significance; (c) possible conflicts between the proposed action and the objectives of Federal, regional, state and local (and in the case of a reservation, Indian tribe) land use plans, policies, and controls for the area concerned; (d) the environmental effects of alternatives, including the proposed action; (e) energy requirements and conservation potential of various alternatives and mitigation measures; (f) natural or depletable resource requirements and conservation potential of various alternative and mitigation measures; (g) urban quality, historic and cultural resources, and the design of the built environment, including the reuse and conservation potential of various alternatives and mitigation measures; and (h) means to mitigate adverse environmental impacts.[17]

Unfortunately, these regulations, like NEPA itself, do not embody a full grasp of ecological thought. Instead, intent upon reducing paper and delay, these regulations dictated the choice of a lead agency to prepare the statement, limited the range of actions and effects through up front "scoping," "tiering" of the reports from general to specific, and breaking down of the report into actions, alternatives and impacts with little attention to the ecosystem.[18] Instead of a comprehensive planning document or a complete examination of the ecosystem affected by the proposed action, the statements were reduced to "a variety of checklists, matrices of activities, and environmental components and other devices for identifying, organizing and displaying the numerous effects of a complex project."[19] With the focus placed upon the workability and usefulness of the environmental impact statement, the actual science in the statements suffered. A 1976 review of impact statements found them to be scientifically inadequate. This inadequacy was due in part to the lack of money and trained staff for preparation of such statements, but the report went on to indicate lack of ecological conceptualization of the statement itself.

The report, which evaluated the inadequacies of the environmental impact statements, nevertheless managed to lay out a taxonomy of ecological descriptors and suggested how those descriptors might enter in methods of effective ecological assessment.[20] The following tables set forth those descriptions and methods.

Table 5.2 ECOSYSTEM DESCRIPTORS

BIOTIC		ABIOTIC	
STRUCTURE		*STRUCTURE*	
Taxonomic	BS1	Geometric configuration	AS1
Population/abundance	BS2	Substrate composition	AS2
Trophic groups	BS3	Chemical composition	AS3
Indicator organism	BS4	Solar radiation	AS4
Similarity, biotic, niche,		Thermal stratification	AS5
and diversity indices	BS5	Function	
Function		Hydronamics	AF1
Energy transfer	BF1	Deposition-erosion rates	AF2
Material transfer	BF2	Chemical transformations	
Primary production		and exchanges	AF3
and respiration	BF3	Energy transfer (incl.heat flux)	AF4
Growth kinetics	BF4		
Tolerance limits	BF5		

Source: Committee on Ecological Research, Council on Environmental Quality

Table 5.3 ECOLOGICAL ASSESSMENT AND ECOSYSTEM STRUCTURE AND FUNCTION

Methods for ecological assessment	Ecosystem structure description(s) needed (from previous table)	Ecosystem function description(s) needed (from previous table)
Comparison of calculated water quality needed for ecosystem maintenance in similar areas	AS1, AS3	AF1
Comparison of calculated water quality levels to environmental requirements and/or limits or organisms present with judgment of stability	BS1, AS1, AS3, AS5	BF5, F1, AF4, AF3
Comparison of calculated water quality levels to individuals, assemblages, trophic levels, or communities with known responses to specific water quality constituents followed by judgmental evaluation of change	BS1, BS2, BS3, AS1, AS3, AS5, AS4	BF5, BF4, AF1, AF4, AF3, AFG2
Comparison of calculated mass flows of water quality constituents to ecosystem utilization of these inorganic and organic substances with judgemental evaluation of changes of energy and material flows in the ecosystem and consequently of its biological integrity	BS1, BS3, BS2, BS4, BS5, AS1, AS3, AS5, AS4, AS2	BF5, BF4, BF3, BF2, BF1, AF1, AF4, AF3, AF2

Note: Ecosystem structure and formation descriptor numbers given in decreasing importance (in current practice). Source: Committee on Ecological Research, Council on Environmental Quality

2. *Science, Law and Hudson River Power Plants*[21]

Although the Environmental Impact Statements did not embrace a complete ecological approach to assessing the impacts of projects, the regulations governing the impact statements often fostered careful ecological studies of impacts, including cumulative effects or the interconnection of one or another project's effects.[22] More important, the funding of impact statements led to the collection and undertaking of specific ecological research. This research often highlighted problems inherent in NEPA and the EIR process. One example of this was the research done for the impact of the proposed Hudson River power plants, described in the previous chapter.

During the 1970s, as a consequence of the *Scenic Hudson* litigation and concern over the permitting of Indian Point nuclear units, the Hudson River estuary was the focus of an intense environmental impact analysis. The studies embraced an ecosystem overview of the Hudson River Estuary. The studies focused on fish species composition and distribution; the dynamics of fish populations; the stock characteristics and distribution of striped bass, white perch, and Atlantic tomcod; a detailed study of the entrainment and impingement impacts of the fish; and finally, a study of the negotiated settlement, which was concluded in 1980.

Despite all the research, in 1988, the following conclusion was reached:

> Many of the major objectives of utility – and agency-sponsored Hudson River research programs were not achieved. Among these were identification and quantification of regulatory mechanisms and discovery of factors controlling year-class strength in striped bass and other important fish populations. *Questions about community-and ecosystem-level effects were not seriously addressed.* [*Emphasis added.*] Because of these limitations, an unambiguous assessment of the effects of power plants in the long-term production and persistence of Hudson River fish populations was not possible. In this paper we argue that the failure to reach a scientifically defensible "bottom line" was largely due to (1) institutional constraints on the design and conduct of assessment studies; (2) the complexity and spatiotemporal variability of estuarine ecosystems; and (3) the inadequacy of existing population and ecosystem theory. We conclude that, for the foreseeable future, estimates of short-term impacts on populations will continue to be the most useful indices of power plant effects. *Long-term monitoring and basic research on ecological processes in estuaries, funded and managed independently of the regulatory process, are essential to improving future environmental impact assessments.*[23] [*Emphasis added.*]

3. The Court Response to the Environmental Impact Statement

Law books are filled with citations to NEPA court opinions that profess to review the adequacy of the environmental impact statement. Yet few, if any, courts fault the impact statements for their inadequate treatment of ecological principles. In most cases, there is little indication that the court performs (or has the capacity to conduct) a careful assessment of the studies themselves. According to some courts, the adequacy of an EIS rests upon scientific support for the ultimate conclusions reached in the reports, but the Supreme Court has deferred to agency expertise in their use of the latest scientific information.[24] Given the fact that most ecological research is infected with considerable uncertainty, the history of the legal treatment of such uncertainty is an important part of any impact analysis. In the early 1980s, courts ordered that "worst case" analyses[25] be part of risk analysis. Worst case analysis explores low probability risks with severe consequences resulting from a proposed development. The Council on Environmental Quality responded by revising its earlier regulation to prevent "pure conjecture," but required scientifically supportable low probability catastrophes as part of the uncertainty analysis.[26]

RESERVE MINING AND UNCERTAINTY IN ENVIRONMENTAL LAW
Although risk and uncertainty were recognized in tort law before the environmental era, risk became a central issue within environmental law. In the 1978, *Reserve Mining*[27] decision, the court sought to weigh the probability and severity of harm from taconite tailings in the air and water of Minnesota citizens living near the mining operations. The opinion stimulated a path-breaking standard for evaluating environmental endangerment as the product of the probability and severity of risk. It also stimulated a classic law review article, "The Uses of Scientific Information in Environmental Decisionmaking," that described eco-systems, the uncertainty inherent in their functioning, and the costs of information collection, and the need to adopt burdens of proof in light of such uncertainty, written by A. Don Tarlock and Marcia Gelpe.[28] The authors offered powerful arguments for shifting the burdens of proof in environmental cases like *Reserve Mining* and other environmental cases.

---

4. The Legal Reactions to the Present State of NEPA

Legal scholars' present concerns regarding NEPA do not center upon the admitted lack of ecological content in many of the environmental impact statements. Instead, the major legal concern stems from the Supreme Court's transformation of NEPA into what many contend is merely a procedural requirement, rather than a substantive mandate for environmental protection.[29] In response, environmental law scholars now seek to find ways of strengthening NEPAs substantive mandate in ways comparable to some state mini-NEPAs.[30] Will substantive strengthening of NEPA result in a more ecological approach? If the substantive amendments do not specifically require an ecosystems-oriented EIS, but only focus upon the traditional non-ecological categories, the original ecological mandate of NEPA will not be achieved.[31] A second legal issue arises from a series of evaluations of the workings of NEPA. Several careful studies sought to evaluate the impact of the requirements for agency preparation, environmental assessments and impact statements. In 1979, Daniel Mazmanian and Jeanne Nienaber completed a detailed history of the environmental protection efforts of the Corps of Engineers.[32] They found that the Corps formally adopted environmental protection as a primary objective, and made a serious attempt to hire "qualified environmentalists" and reorganize the structure of the agency. Although few

Corps projects were halted as a result of its new goals or new environmentally oriented personnel, a number of controversial projects were eliminated and a considerable number were delayed or modified. Some of these modifications clearly reflected a new ecological awareness on the part of the Corps. In a limited number of projects, an open planning process was undertaken. In the 1980s, another more comprehensive study of NEPA was completed. Its authors found that when projects were contested by outside groups, some of the projects with "the greatest environmental costs and least political support" were eliminated, and even if there were no controversies, a full ranging EIS often led to mitigation of the project's impact.[33]

Assuming that an effective and substantive ecologically oriented NEPA requirement could be crafted and there was the demand for more ecologically-oriented environmental impact statements, would such a NEPA and its ecological impact statements be possible, and would they be effective? The answer to this question has to await our account of the 1990s, when two approaches were taken to reintroduce a more ecological content into NEPA. One approach was to introduce specific ecological concepts, such as the importance of biological diversity to ecosystems into the functions of NEPA. The other approach was a proposal to completely overhaul the NEPA statement to create an ecosystem impact approach. Each approach has advantages and disadvantages and will be discussed below.

The Coastal Zone Management Act

> The coast, that bright thin edge of the continent where you can sit with your back to the crowds and gaze into the seemingly infinite space, is now a theatre of discovery.
> Anne Simon, *The Thin Edge: Coast and Man in Crisis*

When Eugene Odum completed his third edition of *Fundamentals of Ecology*, he did not describe "coastal ecosystems." Rather, he identified freshwater, marine and estuary ecosystems (although he noted that others had identified various kinds of coastal ecosystems).[34] Estuary areas had received considerable attention from ecologists in the 1960s, leading to the publication of many coastal ecology studies and books in the 1970s.[35] Coastal areas were said to include the coastal water basin and adjacent shorelands to the extent that they had significant impact upon coastal waters. These areas were to include estuaries, tidelands, coastal wetlands and flood plains, and their accompanying biota. Vital areas of the coastal zone included coral reefs, kelp beds, shellfish beds, grass beds, drainage ways, wetlands, vegetated tidelands, tideflats, dunes and beach fronts, barrier islands, breeding areas, nursery areas, wintering areas, feeding areas, and migration pathways. A variety of specific uses and human impacts including residences, marinas, agricultural runoff, septic tanks, dredging, urban runoff, municipal sewage, and others affected the coastal areas; degrading water quality, eroding dunes and barrier beaches, and affecting the habitat of a variety of coastal birds and fish.

The Coastal Zone Management Act of 1972 (CZMA) was adopted after California and Rhode Island had taken steps to begin regulating their coastal areas on their own. Marine scientists who had been studying the coastal waters shaped these early state coastal management laws. The results were unique ecosystemic laws upon which the CZMA was modeled. These laws and the federal laws explicitly recognized complex natural interdependencies in coastal areas. In recognition of the dynamic quality of coastal ecosystems, the Coastal Zone Management Act does not set sharp coastal boundaries. The Federal Coastal Zone Management Act describes the coastal zone as "the coastal waters including the land therein and there under and the adjacent shorelands ... strongly influenced by each other."[36] In its findings, the law explicitly recognizes the "ecological fragility" and vulnerability of coastal natural resources, and the need to protect "important ecological, cultural, historic, and aesthetic values in the coastal zone."[37]

The Act required planning and data collection prior to the adoption of a regulatory system for the coast, and accepted the notion of adaptive planning to make changes as new information became available and the coastal ecosystem evolved. Within broad guidelines, the law left open to states the appropriate method of planning and regulation. States could establish criteria and standards for local implementation, adopt direct state and local land and water use regulations or provide for state administrative review of all development plans. The Act identified those natural resources, such as beaches and wetlands which require special protection, while at the same time recognizing the need to support coastal related and water related human uses of the coast. The purpose of the Act was to "balance" human activities and environmental health, promoting environmental protection, appropriate coastal development, and recreation.

The principal mechanism for implementing coastal management was the state coastal management "program," drafted according to federal guidelines and approved by the Federal Office of Coastal Zone Management.[38] This plan, in turn, regulated not only private activities on the coast, but also federal activities which were required to be "consistent" with the state coastal zone program. The specifics of the state coastal management program and the determination of consistency of federal projects with the program required the lesser or greater application of ecological knowledge to the coastal area.

IAN MCHARG and JOHN CLARK

In 1969, the planner Ian McHarg had published his classic *Design with Nature*. McHarg sought to show how planners had to carefully design the land and water uses of projects based upon a detailed ecological understanding of nature. Among natural areas he turned his attention to was the coast, where he began with a careful environmental profile of the coastal zone. McHarg and his students went on to develop environmentally-based planning throughout the world, and he shaped the thoughts of generations of planners after him.

Perhaps no other person better grasped the unique challenge of putting together a coastal management program than John Clark, a marine ecologist and author of numerous works on coastal management. In an elegant little book prepared for the Conservation Foundation, Clark distilled the ecologic principles and management rules of coastal management.[39] The rules were applied to both the descriptive components of the coastal system, e.g. biota, physical settings, and the processes (water circulation, succession, productivity and the movement of energy through the food web). He identified the environmental disturbances in the coastal area, the product of specific uses in this area. He identified the resources to be protected, e.g., coral reefs, kelp and shellfish beds, feeding areas and so forth, and indicated the kinds of constraints on uses needed to limit environmental disturbance and protect the resources.

Each of the coastal states adopted a coastal management program approved at the federal level and administered by the state. The program was to identify coastal boundaries, define permissible land and waters uses, inventory areas of particular concern, and establish the institutional mechanisms for regulating uses on the coast, prioritizing uses and protecting areas of special aesthetic, historical, cultural, recreational and ecological value and fighting against coastal erosion. Perhaps the best way to capture the flavor of a coastal program is to offer a thumb nail sketch of one. (See Bridge Document on the following page.)

The Coastal Zone Management Act, with its state coastal management programs, offers an interesting case study of the relationship between the ecology of the program and its legal aspects. The relationships of plans, programs, and legal implementation to the effectiveness of the regime is important in coastal management, as well as other areas. Ecological plans have been adopted under many federal, state and local environmental programs, and issues have arisen regarding enforcement of such plans.

Bridge Document 5.2 COASTAL MANAGEMENT PROGRAM STATEMENT

> The Florida Coastal Management Program has focused on many coastal ecosystems within the state. One especially important example is the Florida beach system, including the sandy coasts, the beach dune system and the barrier island system and coastal wetlands. These parts of the coastal system are undergoing change. The beach system is especially important and is continually under change due to natural erosion processes as well as a variety of human uses, including development, introduction of exotic species, and the recreation activity itself. As part of its coastal management program, the state has undertaken construction controls, coastal stabilizing, acquisition of beaches and shores, comprehensive planning, and beach renourishment. There are a variety of constraints on the stabilization and renourishment projects. The central ecological issues facing the plan are whether the measures taken can protect the beach system and whether the interventions taking place presently are compatible with or harmful to the ecosystem.[40]

Three kinds of relationship have been established between law and planning.[41] First, with comprehensive plans and programs, systems have been established to assure that regulations "conform" with each plan or program. Second, impact planning has been adopted, in which plans function to help measure the impacts of a proposed action. Third, implementation plans are adopted in which the implementing legal regulations are part of the plan itself. The coastal management program embodies all three approaches. First, in certain cases, federal government actions are evaluated to determine whether they are consistent with the plan. "Consistency determinations" under the Coastal Zone Management Act will be discussed below. Second, many of the coastal management plans adopt impact assessment procedures. Third, the regulations for the coastal area are adopted as part of the coastal management plan, and hence, the plan may be viewed as an "implementation plan." It is beyond the scope of this brief discussion to go into depth on each aspect of coastal management plans, but "consistency determinations" will be discussed below.

North Carolina's Southern Coastal Wetlands: A Case Study[42]

The North Carolina Coastal Management Act defines a coastal wetland as any marsh subject to regular or occasional flooding by wind or lunar tides. Coastal wetlands are among the world's most productive and diverse ecosystems. Wetlands provide wildlife habitat (often for endangered species), spawning grounds, and also supply flood and erosion controls, as they help absorb the shock of storm driven waves before they rush inland and cause destruction to property and human life. Wetlands are natural pollution-filtering systems. By cleansing industrial and domestic sewage water – just 5.6 hectares of wetlands – has the same pollution-reducing ability as a $1 million waste treatment plant.[43]

Ninety-five percent of North Carolina's wetlands are located within the coastal zone.[44] These coastal wetlands include lands in which there is the presence of water at the surface or within the root zone, as well as adjacent uplands with hydric soils or vegetation adapted to wet conditions. There are eight types of wetlands found in North Carolina's southern coast: salt marsh, pine savannah, pocosin, swamp forest, ponds, bottomland hardwood, pine plantation and wet pine flatwood.[45] The greatest threats to North Carolina's southern coastal wetlands are: draining and filling for agriculture, road construction, and urban and recreational development. Nonpoint pollution is another degrading element on coastal wetlands. An inevitable problem for coastal wetlands in the future is sea level rise caused by global warming. Commercial, industrial and residential development of coastal wetlands place the wildlife and fisheries dependent on these ecosystems at tremendous risk. The ditching and draining of wetlands during development fouls other coastal waters with sediment, silt and other pollutants. The destruction of coastal wetlands has polluted coastal habitats that are essential to North Carolina's fisheries.[46]

The destruction of coastal wetlands in southern North Carolina is devastating to many aspects of the coastal ecosystem. These wetlands provide critical habitat for neotropical songbirds such as the Black Throated Green Warbler, the Swainson's Warbler, and the Prothonotary Warbler.[47] Forested coastal wetlands in southern North Carolina provide habitat for scarce populations of black bears and endangered red wolves.[48]

For at least the past two decades, the human population of North Carolina's coastal zone has been increasing at a rate roughly twice that of the rest of the state.[49] The permanent and seasonal populations have invested heavily in coastal real estate. The new residents of the coastal zone are using the land much differently and more intensively than did earlier residents. Golf courses and gated communities of luxury homes are replacing ecosystems, fields and forests in the region, while marinas and condominiums are replacing fishing grounds and intertidal marshes.[50]

Bridge Document 5.3 WETLANDS DELINEATION MANUAL

In 1987, the Army Corps of Engineers issued a wetland delineation manual. The delineation manual contained technical criteria to be used to determine whether a wetland was subject to the jurisdiction of Section 404 of the Clean Water Act.[51] The manual was jointly prepared by the Corps, EPA, FWS and the National Marine Fisheries Service, and these federal agencies now use the manual to determine their responsibilities under Section 404.[52] Most determinations of what qualifies as a "jurisdictional" wetland are based on soils and vegetation, not hydrology.[53] Determining the boundaries of a wetland is as controversial as determining the definition of a wetland. The Clean Water Act defines wetlands as "those areas that are inundated or saturated by surface and ground water at a frequency and duration sufficient to support, and that under normal circumstances do support a prevalence of vegetation typically adapted for life in saturated soil conditions. Wetlands generally include swamps, marshes, bogs, and similar areas."[54]

The jurisdictional boundaries of a wetland are based on the Corps' delineation manuals. The delineation manuals that determine the legal jurisdictional boundaries of a wetland can change from time to time to reflect political, scientific or public opinion. A small change in the delineation manual can have a tremendous effect on the amount of area considered to be part of a wetland. An example is the Clean Water Act's wetland definition or the phrase "frequency and duration," has varied over time. As the meaning of the phrase "frequency and duration" fluctuates, the size of the wetland changes. The shorter the saturation period, the more land that will be considered wetlands. Conversely, the longer the saturation period, the less land that will be considered wetlands.[55]

It is equally difficult to determine wetland boundaries from a ecosystemic perspective. Some of the most widespread plant indicators are commonly found outside of wetlands. Also, most wetlands are dry at some point, possibly for years at a time.[56] Often, hydric soils do not appear hydric in important parts of their profile. Wetland vegetation can change by only an inch. Past disturbances of wetlands can make determining the boundaries difficult as well. Hydric soils could have been drained, or if a wetland has been invaded by an exotic species, the soil may be dried out by increased evapotranspiration. Both the ecosystemic and the legal jurisdictional boundaries rely heavily on the determination of hydric soils.

The fate of North Carolina's southern coastal wetlands is controlled largely by Section 404 of the Clean Water Act and the North Carolina Coastal Area Management Act (CAMA). Section 404 of the Clean Water Act provides a basis for a comprehensive, nationwide scheme for permitting alteration of wetlands. CAMA controls the development of land use plans for the coastal area of North Carolina.[57] These two laws are mostly concerned with management, but conservation issues are also involved. Section 404 of the

CWA and CAMA are considered, along with local land use laws for individual counties.

In 1974, the North Carolina General Assembly enacted the North Carolina Coastal Area Management Act (CAMA) in an attempt to enter the federal Coastal Zone Management program.[58] CAMA provides a guide for devising land use plans for the twenty-county coastal area, listing criteria for identifying critical areas in need of protection ("areas of environmental concern") and installing a permitting system for land development in those critical areas.[59]

Although there are numerous bridge documents in North Carolina's coastal wetlands regime, the permit itself is one such document. CAMA requires permits for development in "areas of environmental concern." For these purposes, development includes filling or dredging wetlands or waters, construction of piers, bulkheads, marinas, roads and oceanfront surfaces.[60]

Bridge Document 5.4   STATE COASTAL ADMINISTRATIVE PERMIT RULINGS ON CUMULATIVE IMPACTS OF DREDGE AND FILL PROJECTS

One of the many ecological concepts employed in coastal management is that of cumulative impact. Florida courts have adopted its formulation as set forth in the Department of Environmental Rulings:[61]

"In order to [show] entitlement to a dredge and fill permit, an applicant must show that he has provided reasonable assurance that water quality standards will not be violated and that the project is not contrary to the public interest, and both of those tests must take into consideration the cumulative impacts of similar projects which are existing, under construction, or reasonably expected in the future.

* * * The applicant's burden of proof includes the burden of giving reasonable assurance that cumulative impacts do not cause a project to be contrary to the public interest or to violate water quality standards."

* * * The purpose of cumulative impact analysis is to distribute equitably that amount of dredging and filling activity which may be done without resulting in violations of water quality standards and without being contrary to the public interest. In order to determine whether the allocation to a particular applicant is equitable, the determination of the cumulative impact is based in part on the assumption that reasonably expected similar future applications will also be granted.

"Specifically in the context of permitting access roads and bridges, it has been the policy of the Department to consider what will be at the end of the bridge or road."

* * * Of course, if the activities or impacts proposed at the end of the bridge or road are remote in distance or conceptual relationship from the dredge and fill activity, those activities or impacts should be weighted accordingly in applying the statutory balancing test.

As these excerpts illustrate, a holistic approach to water quality leads also to a recognition of the equitable interdependence of several projects – past, present, and future – and their effects upon the coastal system in question.

North Carolina wetlands have been a legal focal point on a federal level. In 1993, the North Carolina Wildlife Federation and other environmental agencies challenged the Corps' determination that developers did not need a Section 404 permit because their ditching activities consisted of only minimal incidental releases of soil and other dredged material in the wetlands being drained.[62] In response, the Corps and the Environmental Protection Agency adopted an environmentally demanding standard, the "Tulloch Rule." The Tulloch Rule stated that any redeposit of dredged material in a wetland constituted a discharge that required a permit if the deposit acted to degrade or destroy the wetland.[63] The permit requirement became an effective disincentive for developers considering dredging and draining wetlands.

In 1998, the National Mining Association challenged the Tulloch Rule in a lawsuit against the Corps, and the D.C. Circuit Court invalidated the Rule. The Court determined that "incidental fallback" of soil was not pollution under the Clean Water Act and the Corps had exceeded its authority.[64] The environmental impacts of this court case were tremendous. Immediately after the Tulloch Rule was overturned, developers took advantage of the less stringent environmental laws. According to the Southern Environmental Law Center, by May of 1999, over 14,000 acres of wetlands had been drained and ditched without permits in southeastern North Carolina alone.

We have identified three problems which are closely related to the ecosystemic approach of the Coastal Zone Management Act: the problem of "fixing" ecosystemic boundaries, the problem of intergovernmental relations which embrace different jurisdictions over the same ecosystem, and the problem of regulation of private property.

The boundary problem arises when the implied flexibility of an ecosystemic definition of the spatial dimensions of the ecosystem conflicts with the need to have more specific boundaries for regulation and enforcement purposes. The inland boundary illustrates the problem. The Coastal Zone Management Act requires that the location of the inland boundary be drawn "to the extent necessary to control shorelands, the uses of which have a direct and significant impact on the coastal waters."[65] In theory, such a boundary is defined by jurisdictional claims that inland uses distant from the shore have coastal impacts. Such an approach is consistent not with a customary geographically limited ecological definition of coastal ecosystems, but rather encompasses a broad definition which includes human impacts on the coastal system originating from distant places. Practically and politically speaking, however, the boundary adopted by coastal zone management programs is usually more in line with the standard ecological definition of the coastal zone based on biophysical properties than the broad statutory definition.

Unfortunately, setting this more limited inland boundary for the coastal ecosystem means that the coastal management program lacks control over major forces affecting the coast, like inland agricultural and urban runoff. Nor do the programs offer control for pre-treated sewage from inland industrial plants entering the coast, or of air pollution originating outside the immediate coastal zone. Hence, an ironic conclusion appears to result in which the more ecologically accepted boundary of coastal zone is less effective in protecting the ecosystem than a boundary based on a regional planning model. This irony may be resolved by adopting a hierarchical approach to ecosystems and then linking it to a similar hierarchy of regulation.

Intergovernmental coordination is a large problem that arises with the ecosystemic approach to coastal zone management. The coastal ecosystem contains possible areas of jurisdiction for several federal, state and local government agencies, the coordination of whose activity becomes a logistically difficult political problem. One such provision which requires coordination has received considerable attention: the "consistency provision."[66] It states that federal activities, permits and funding must be "consistent" with the policies of the state's coastal management program. The CZMA establishes a mechanism for a review for determining consistency. These reviews raise interesting questions about what actions are "consistent" with an "ecologically oriented" management plan, and to what extent the agencies involved share a common vision for the management or protection of the coastal ecosystem. These difficult questions have been explored in considerable detail both in court cases and legal literature.

A third problem encountered in the administration of the coastal zone management program is that of regulating private development actions. Although the uneasy relationship between environmental law and private property is not unique to coastal management law, this relationship is particularly troubled on the coast, where real estate values are among the very highest. This is reflected in the many high profile court cases rising out of coastal regulatory actions. These cases involve constitutional challenges to coastal regulations based upon appeals to the Fifth and Fourteenth Amendments of the U.S. Constitution and comparable state constitutions.

A fundamental conflict lies beneath constitutional cases involving private property ownership challenges to coastal regulation. This conflict is between our inherited concept of private property (with its rights of use, sale and freedom to develop, gift), and an ecosystemic view which values the nature of the land, air, and water, subject to property rights, as part of a larger a web of nature extending far beyond the immediate boundaries of the property. Courts and scholars will probably always struggle with this issue.

> An early lake coastal management case arose in Wisconsin in the case of *Just v Marinette County*[67] A developer, ignoring the state and county's Shoreland Zoning Ordinance, proceeded to fill in his shoreland property without the required permit. Upon notification of fine for violation, he contested the ordinance as an unconstitutional taking of his property. In a remarkable opinion, the Wisconsin Supreme Court upheld the fine, finding that the regulation in question did not "take his property," since he did not own development rights. If he had filled the area, he would harm the lake ecosystem. The court found that the lake was held in trust under the laws of Wisconsin.

In 1990, under pressure from environmental groups and others, the Coastal Zone Management Act was revised. A new Coastal Zone Enhancement Grant Program was created to encourage states to improve their plans in one or more of eight areas of coastal concern, including: coastal wetlands protection, management of development in high hazard areas, public access, control of marine debris, studying cumulative and secondary impact of coastal development, special area management planning, ocean resources planning and siting of coastal energy and governmental facilities. Part of the motivation for these changes was the desire to make more specific protective efforts than those that had hitherto been employed as part of the ecosystem management effort.[68]

The coastal zone management legislation, perhaps more than any other piece of land use legislation, embodies the hopes and dreams of the new regime of ecologically based environmental law. The coast is an area treasured by most as a source of nature-based aesthetic and recreational enjoyment. The coastal area has received the attention of scientists, who have articulated an ecosystem view of its structure and functions. The law has recognized its natural value and offered a flexible tool to the state (working with the federal government) for its planning and regulation. Significant federal funds have been offered to the states for planning and management. A back-up system of continuous management research has been established, some of it performed by "sea-grant" universities. As a result, an excellent management literature has gradually been prepared and ecosystem models have been built. Continuous sophisticated evaluation has been mandated and funded. Yet all would agree that the quarter-century experience with coastal zone law has led to mixed results at best.

Environmentally oriented mid-course corrections were made to the law in the 1990s, but the coast remains under siege from development, pollution, and now more diffuse human influences such as global warming. The limited success of the coastal management law raises profound questions about the possibility of turning to ecosystemic laws to protect and rescue the rest of our environment.

The Great Lakes Ecosystem Agreement and Nature's Metropolis

> *The smoke of Chicago has a peculiar and aggressive individuality due, I imagine, to the natural clearness of the atmosphere ... It does not overhang the streets in a uniform canopy, but sweeps across and about them in gusts and swirls, now dropping now lifting again its grimy curtain.*
>
> William Archer, *America Today (1990)* quoted in William Cronon's *Nature's Metropolis*

If any bit of nature might be thought of in ecosystemic terms, lakes are a good candidate. Aquatic ecosystems were high on Eugene Odum's early list of such systems, and ecological modeling of lakes was an early enterprise. Efforts were made by the 1960s to control the pollution in lakes through ecosystemic planning and implementation.[69] It is little wonder that some of the major efforts at describing pollution control within ecosystems focused upon lakes.[70]

Similarly, lakes may be the best candidates for discussing ecosystemic regimes, since some of the best legal writing on such regimes has applied them to freshwater lakes. Specifically, Jutta Brunnée and Stephen Toope have applied the regime concept to the Great Lakes.[71]

The grandest of all U.S. lakes are the Great Lakes, and no other set of lakes has received more attention in ecosystemic theory, planning and law. Since the 1978 Great Lakes Water Quality Agreement between Canada and the United States, there has been a concerted effort to think about this area in ecosystemic terms. This rapid embrace of an ecosystem approach in defining a management agenda was doomed to initial disappointment when regulation of lake pollution proceeded under already established laws and regulations, which lacked an ecosystemic framework. Only in the 1990s has the consideration of the Great Lakes in ecosystemic terms been coupled with new ecosystemic plans and proposals.

Unlike many ecosystems, lakes were principal objects of ecological enquiry. In 1942, Raymond Lindeman published a scientific paper entitled "The Trophic-Dynamic Aspect of Ecology."[72] This paper applied to the Cedar Bog Lake the full range of ecosystem concepts, energy flows through trophic levels and plant successional stages with the consequent productivity of each level and stage.[73] Other works also permitted the early understanding of lakes as ecosystems. This understanding of lakes was not merely a theoretical understanding, but led to practical environmental measures in lake protection.

W.T. Edmundson has recounted the research and efforts to protect Lake Washington beginning in the 1930s and extending into the 1970s in his history.[74] The initial focus of the Washington Lake study and protection efforts was the eutrophication process in the lake; a natural process aggravated by sewage outfalls, resulting in nutrient enrichment which in turn may, depending upon the abiotic condition of the lake (including temperature), produce the rapid multiplication of organic matter, principally in the form of the algae blooms. (These blooms were later to provide food for the aquatic organism Daphnia,which grazed on the increased algae). In short, the problem illustrated the interrelated workings of the food chain, predator-prey relationships, and the abiotic conditions, all of which comprise the lake ecosystem. The legally-mandated recovery of the lake was based upon this knowledge.[75] It was not until the late 1960s and early 1970s that deteriorating water quality in the Great Lakes forced governments to consider an ecosystem approach to regulation.[76]

The difficulties encountered by an ecosystemic approach to Great Lakes management are not due to the failures of ecosystemic theory. The fundamental problems are laid bare in William Cronon's history of the Great Lakes environment in *Nature's Metropolis: Chicago and the Great West.*[77] What Cronon revealed is how the water and railroads of Chicago became the conduit for grain, lumber, and meat in the city – Chicago – which Sandberg called "the hog butcher of the world."[78] Turning prairie to farm, detaching lumber from forest, annihilating a progression of animals from bison to pigs for meat, and overcoming the seasons of the year through refrigeration, Chicago's history is the story of a profound transformation of nature in the city and its hinterlands. Describing such an area as "an ecosystem" is possible only if one understands the history and the reality of our modern urban life in the national context of the Great Lakes watershed. The challenge of viewing the Great Lakes as an ecosystem to be planned for and regulated is that of knowing how to apply an approach originally designed to study a more pristine nature, to Cronon's less pristine "nature's metropolis." It is no accident that most ecological theory does not begin with the city as its object of study. Yet, we are a civilization of cities. And hence, to be of any use, ecology itself must come to the city and make sense of "nature's metropolis."

Due the international nature of the problem, however, the management story of the Great Lakes begins earlier in the century. The Boundaries Waters Treaty of 1909, signed between the United States and the United Kingdom (then responsible for Canadian foreign affairs), was designed to solve an immediate dispute over jurisdiction and international boundaries.[79] Article VII of the treaty also provided a mechanism for resolving future difficulties between the two countries concerning the use of waters along the boundary:

"the Parties agree to establish and maintain an International Joint Commission ... composed of six Commissioners, three from the United States, three from Canada."[80] Over the years, Article VII has been read to confirm the independence of the Commission from either country's jurisdiction, an important characteristic when considering the tasks the Commission would later be assigned.[81] The signing of the treaty is a good starting point for the discussion of the ecosystem management of the Great Lakes, as the International Joint Commission (IJC) remains an important force in deciding all international problems confronting this system.

The potential of using an ecosystem approach for regulatory management of the lake basin sprang not from the IJC or either government, but from the faculty of Canadian and American universities.[82] Faculty from both countries had been engaging in bringing about acceptance of a Great Lakes Basin Ecosystem management strategy by the both governments.[83] Recommendations for "a comprehensive examination of the problems associated with multiple purpose management of the Great Lakes" had been offered by the first Canada/United States Inter-university seminar in 1971–1972.[84] These seminars lead the countries to sign the bilateral Great Lakes Water Quality Agreement in 1972.[85] The Agreement expressed the commitment of each country to restore and maintain the chemical, physical, and biological integrity of the Great Lakes Basin Ecosystem, and included a number of objectives and guidelines for achieving this goal.[86] The IJC and the two advisory boards under its authority, the Research Advisory Board (RAB) and the Science Advisory Board (SAB), were involved in implementing the 1972 agreement.[87] In 1977, the RAB urged the IJC to adopt the broader concept of "ecosystem quality," rather than that of "water quality," in evaluating Great Lakes degradation – a fundamentally important distinction.[88] In 1978, the RAB pushed fervently on IJC to "explicitly recognize as policy the need for an ecosystem approach to problem identification, research, and management in the Great Lakes Basin."[89] The IJC supported the recommendation, and that same year, the Canadian and American governments followed suit by signing the second Great Lakes Water Quality Agreement, which explicitly recognized the ecosystem concept.[90]

In the agreement, the Great Lakes Basin Ecosystem was defined as "the interacting components of air, land, water and living organisms including man within the drainage basin of the St. Lawrence river ..."[91] In language reminiscent of the Federal Water Pollution Control Act of 1972, the agreement pledged "to restore and maintain the chemical, physical and biological integrity of the waters of the Great Lakes Basin Ecosystems."[92] Unfortunately, aside from specifying more specific objectives in pollution control language and identifying the sources of water pollution, the IJC was only given powers to gather information and advice from the respective domestic government agencies.

Later that year (1972), the second Canada/United States Inter-university seminar convened and put forth two recommendations.[93] First, it called for a strengthening of the role of the IJC, so it could better handle proposed solutions.[94] Second, it urged the two governments to form a science policy for the Great Lakes Basin, which would require more expansive scientific knowledge of the lake ecosystem.[95] The SAB was also actively recommend that IJC implement Article VII of the 1978 Agreement to insure "that all facets and concerns of the Great Lakes Ecosystem area adequately considered."[96] To this end, the SAB began submitting annual reports on areas of scientific and environmental concern to the IJC on the Basin.[97] The use of workshops to serve the purposes of education, analysis of short-term and long-term problems, and proposing solutions, has been a favorite tool of both the IJC and the governments.[98] The Ecosystem Study Board (ESB), which was established by the IJC, has proven particularly fruitful.[99] These workshops and simulations have been used as instruments to gather readily known data about the interrelationships between different parts of the ecosystem.[100]

The IJC view of ecosystem management matured with experience, and in a 1995 report in collaboration with the EPA and Environment Canada, it defined an ecosystem approach as "a process framework to account for the interrelationships among land, air, water, and all living things, including humans, and to involve them all user groups [sic] in comprehensive management."[101] The Great Lakes Basin is an excellent test case to examine the efficacy of integrated environmental management because like all large ecosystems, it faces threats from cross-media pollution, and its current environmental regulatory system is badly fragmented along medium and intergovernmental lines.[102] The IJC report said that for regulatory and resource management agencies, adopting an ecosystem approach has initiated a shift from a narrow perspective of managing a single environmental medium or resource to a broader perspective that focuses on managing human uses and abuses of watersheds and bioregions.[103] A key aspect to this broader perspective is the need for comprehensive management of all media, due to the fact that the ecosystem concept dictates that any change in system status at one point will impact a continuum of other points in space or time.[104]

The Great Lakes ecosystem approach was deemed attractive because of the focus it places on "holistic management." In the past, government efforts at regulating pollution have been specifically focused on point-source pollution, e.g., factories and businesses; the advent of the ecosystem management changes this dynamic.[105] As the cost of further reductions in point source loadings increase, the relative importance of non-point source loadings increase, and with it the need for multimedia, comprehensive environmental management.[106] This type of management places a greater emphasis on a cooperative approach, which stresses the use of incentives and education.[107] The IJC has consistently recognized the need for public education on the ecosystem approach:

> Ecosystem-based education will be critical to the success of the ecosystem-based management processes. No one has all the answers. Everyone will be learning their way out. The process of cooperative learning must ensure respect for different perspectives, while striving for agreement on common goals and actions.[108]

Despite adopting an ecosystem model for lake management, there are still impediments to making it work. The split between U.S. and Canadian state and provincial sovereignty over their own environmental regulations, which impact nearly every facet of life for the resident of a particular state or province, is one such impediment. Importantly, while there is a general consensus that an ecosystem approach should be implemented, there is no general consensus on how that approach should be defined. A third identifiable obstacle to implementing an ecosystem approach is the plethora of traditional regulatory methods that are not useful to ecosystem-level management, yet remain entrenched at all levels of government.[109] For example, political and fiscal incentives remain heavily concentrated within medium-based programs.[110] Unless highly fragmented, medium-specific legislation is changed to take into account cross media pollution, it may be difficult for agency officials to substantially redirect policy to take into account cross-media pollution.[111] There remains a great reluctance of many agency officials from Environment Canada and the EPA to let go of the tried and true medium-specific methods, such as the Clean Water Act and the Clean Air Act.[112] Congress is even more reluctant to change a national environmental policy that has been in place for over twenty years. Finally, the judiciary is unlikely to offer any shelter for an approach not specifically codified in law and not universally accepted by lawmakers.

Assuming that policy makers can be convinced to attempt a more integrated approach, there remains the practical issue of whether there is a sufficient understanding of ecosystems to institute a large-scale comprehensive regulatory system.[113] An ecosystem approach demands a high level of scientific knowledge about the interrelation between all organisms and the media in which they exist.[114] No one is quite sure whether this knowledge exists, and if it does, whether it can be disseminated effectively to policy makers and the public.[115] This is a real concern to the IJC, which is constantly trying to involve the public in the regulatory process. Another obstacle for the implementation of more integrated regional approach in the Great Lakes Basin is the limitations placed on the regulatory authorities of existing regional institutions.[116] Neither the IJC, nor any of the other regional entities in the Basin possess cross-cutting regulatory authority.[117] Most of these regular groups serve in an advisory capacity to local, state, and national governments.[118] The reluctance of the states and provinces to abdicate their authority over Great Lakes' management suggests that the role of these institutions will remain advisory for some time.

The movement towards a consensus-based ecosystem approach had also been hampered by the existence of adversarial relationships among some of the groups and institutions within and outside the ecosystem.[119] Government departments operate within particular statutes, which makes them the regulators of and advocates for particular constituencies.[120] Thus, various non-governmental groups are formed not with the idea of cooperating in the regulation of resources, but to guarantee that they receive their share of influence through sufficient, aggregate political pressure.[121] The most fundamental and impairing adversarial situation that exists is the "environment versus economy" dispute.[122] The idea that the operation of an ecosystem approach will necessarily hurt business interests has been proven incorrect again and again, yet it remains a prevalent view in society.[123] Another impediment to integrated environmental policy is "the lack of concrete proposals for considering cross-media transfers in devising regulatory policy." Much of the analysis of integrated environmental management has taken place at a very high level of abstraction.[124]

Finally, and perhaps most fundamental in the implementation of an ecosystem approach to management of the Basin, is the issue of societal resolve.[125] While there is general public support for environmental programs that go well beyond current government efforts to deal with problems in the area, no one is exactly sure how far public concern reaches, and how much reform the public will accept. There is a general lack of any sense of crisis in the region, and unless policy makers are receiving the message that transformation to an ecosystem approach is a "hot issue" politically, change will be slow, at best.[126]

Despite these obstacles, most governments and institutions in the Great Lakes Ecosystem Basin have adopted an ecosystem approach at the conceptual level, and considerable efforts have also been made to make an ecosystem approach a reality at the practical working level. These steps have manifested themselves in the form of Remedial Action Plans, the emergence of regional entities, the refinement of ecosystem techniques and concepts, and the more important emergence of policy professionals dedicated to implementing an integrated environmental approach.[127]

The 1987 Amendments to the Great Lakes Water Quality Agreement led to the creation of forty-two Areas of Concern (AOC) in various areas around the Basin.[128] The most seriously contaminated of these AOCs have suffered from major cross-media transfers and highly fragmented environ-mental management in the past.[129] In each AOC, a broad participatory process is initiated to examine the problems facing the area and to suggest remedial action involving local, state, and regional officials, as well as industry leaders, environmental group representatives, and citizens is.[130] These recommendations are finalized in documents known as remedial action plans (RAP), which are to outline both short and long-term goals, and offer strategies for attaining them.[131] RAPs provide tangible examples of how ecosystem management is supposed to operate on a small scale. They are based on a careful review of environmental data from all media, with the purpose of fostering strategies and coalitions that can transcend the fragmented medium-based approaches of prior federal, state, and local regulatory efforts.[132] Although the overall progress of the program and the implementation of the RAPs has been uneven,[133] the forty-two AOCs are still in the early stages of development, and several sites have given indications of progress toward integrated management.[134] For every site where there has been some progress toward integrated management; another indication of progress toward the implementation of an ecosystem approach in the Basin is the emergence of new, regional entities (consortia) representing a wide range of Great Lakes constituencies.[135] These stakeholder groups include environmental advocacy groups, industry, and non-profit policy institutes.[136] At first glance, it may appear that these groups have sprung up to protect their respective interests, but their regional nature encourages adoption of a more ecosystemic approach.[137]

Two important, interrelated goals must be met if the Basin is to further progress towards the implementation of an ecosystem approach. First, as Dr. Michael J. Donahue remarked in testimony before Congress in 1994, the Great Lakes Water Quality Agreement of 1972 (as amended in 1978 and 1987) must be amended to correct certain critical flaws in the Agreement.[138] Second, many of these flaws are tied to the lack of account-ability in implementation of the Agreement and the emasculation of the IJC by the 1987 amendments.[139]

As matters stand now, the IJC is merely a policy advisory commission on the federal, state and provincial level[140] to the two nations. The region may be in need of an enforcement body that has the international jurisdiction to accomplish the goals of implementing an ecosystem approach. The IJC's charter provides it with "enormous potential" to protect water quality on a regional basis, more than any other regional organizations. No other organization is better equipped or has more knowledge on how to accomplish this goal.[141] However, water is only one part of the ecosystem. The agreement grants little or no control over land uses and air pollution sources.

There is a deeper problem underlying the mixed success in the effort to carry out an ecosystem approach for the Great Lakes. One way of understanding this limit is to note that the Great Lakes Water Quality Agreement included "man" in its definition of the basin ecosystem. This approach appears to accept the reality that humans are very much part of ecosystems, and not merely their managers or visitors. In the case of the Great Lakes, this means that William Cronon's "nature's metropolis" of Chicago, along with Detroit, Toronto and Buffalo, are very much part of the Great Lakes Ecosystem. Past and present patterns of the uses of nature make up the lives of these cities and create myriad of complex relationships above and beyond those of any complex uninhabited ecosystem. It is that complexity with which any full ecological planning effort must cope. The Great Lakes agreement fails to go this far.

The Public Trust Doctrine

Not all the law embracing ecology's new view of nature has been statutory. One principal common law legal doctrine was rediscovered at about the time of Earth Day-the public trust doctrine.[142] Recovered from the mists of Roman law, English history, and early opinions of the U.S. Supreme Court, the doctrine was discovered by Joseph Sax, then a professor of law at Michigan Law School. Sax not only recovered the doctrine from legal history, but also demonstrated how it might operate as a potent tool in the beginning legal warfare over protecting the environment.

Joseph Sax has left an indelible imprint upon the field of environmental law. As a professor of law, first at Michigan Law School then at California/Berkeley, he completed meticulous research, not only in the field of Public Trust Law, but in the broader reaches of Water Law and Environmental Law. He has also written several more popular books, including *Defending the Environment*,[143] *Mountains Without Handrails*,[144] and *Playing Darts With a Rembrandt*.[145] Each offers unique insights and deep rationales for our environmental law, our conservation policy and our historic preservation programs. Joseph Sax has also played a major role in government, both as member of the legal advisory committee to the first Council on Environmental Quality, and later, as advisor to the Secretary of the Interior.

The public trust, in a nutshell, means that the environment is held in trust for the people. The doctrine was originally applied to navigable waters, but it has since been extended to many other legal problems. Originally intended to protect the people's navigational, water-related commerce and fisheries, the doctrine was extended to embrace access to recreation and conservation as well. The doctrine operates to grant standing to citizens who wish to contest government decisions that may be harmful to the environment, hence, in effect, breaching the public trust. Joseph Sax argued that granting citizens such access to government decisions was essential to counter the environmentally harmful forces in the depths of the government bureaucracies.

Since Joseph Sax proposed the public trust concept, courts have invoked it in many cases. The doctrine has been incorporated into some statutes, initially at the instigation of Sax. Public trust language has also found its way into state constitutions.[146] But the importance of the doctrine extends far beyond its admittedly important legal dimensions. The moral resonance[147] of the doctrine carries with it several assumptions: that humans owe a duty of stewardship or care for the environment, the assumption that we should protect nature for future generations (since trusts are often designed for just such a purpose), the assumption that the natural resources and fruits of nature should be accessible to all citizens, and the common law (as well as statutory and constitutional in some cases), duty that the government should adopt environmental protection measures, or at least to weigh carefully the impact of its decisions upon the environment. These assumptions, or "resonances" of the public trust doctrine, are probably as important as the doctrine's legal implications, since such assumptions mirror the tenets held by many in the environmental movement.

Although not designed deliberately to provide a legal structure for the application of the science of ecology, the public trust operated to provide such a structure in several cases, including the Mono Lake case (summarized above, see Chapter 1). With the lowering of the water level in Mono Lake, and the litigation seeking to halt water withdrawals, it was important to determine what the impact of further withdrawals would be. As a consequence, the National Research Council and others undertook an ecological study of the law and the water basin. The study, entitled "The Mono Basin Ecosystem: Effects of a Changing Lake Level,"[148] not only traced the ecological history of the lake and its upland system and their morphology, but also the hydrology of the lake, its physical and chemical characteristics, and most important, the biological system of the lake itself. The report centered upon the ecology of the brine shrimp, and was able to predict the impact of increasing salinity of the lake upon the shrimp and upon its predators. The report was able to determine the appropriate lake level for the sustainability of the shrimp, as well as the impact upon other life in the lake. The following chart, for example, documents the impact of lake levels upon the snowy plover.

Table 5.4 PREDICTED RESPONSE OF SNOWY PLOVERS TO CHANGES IN LAKE ELEVATION

Lake Elevation (ft)	Response of Snowy Plovers
6430-6410	Nesting population reduced from current level to a few pair located in elevated dunes
6410-6380	Nesting population decreased from current level in proportion to area of exposed playa
6380	Nesting population of approximately 350 pair
6370-6360	Nesting population increased in proportion to area of exposed lake bed
6360	Nesting population probably approaches maximum level
6360-6330	No further increases in nesting population, possible decreases

Source: National Research Council, et al., *Mono Basin Ecosystem* (1987) p. 199

The Mono Lake Report was only indirectly related to the public trust doctrine invoked in ongoing litigation to stop the withdrawals. In fact, the report was authorized by a separate Congressional directive.[149] However, the report functioned as a way of giving scientific content to the otherwise vague appeals of the public trust doctrine. To hold nature in trust is commendable, but what nature, how described, and how is it to be held "in trust?" The Mono Basin Ecosystem Report sought to answer those questions, at least in part, by describing both the ecosystem and the impacts of water withdrawal upon it.

Conclusion

NEPA, the Coastal Zone Management Act, and the Great Lakes Agreement all adopted ecological language. The public trust doctrine is a powerful tool which facilitates such an ecological approach. We have characterized the laws above as adopting a "shy embrace" of ecology. In NEPA, this embrace was joined to the comprehensive planning outline of the required environmental impact statement. The Coastal Zone Management Act was even more explicit with its ecological approach to the coastal zone, identifying key coastal features and encouraging coastal management plans. The Great Lakes Agreement, despite its breadth and scope, most explicitly claimed to mandate an ecosystem approach, and despite obstacles, continues to try to implement such an approach.

The statute, the agreement, and the trust doctrine, continue to experience very real difficulty within the implementation of an ecosystemic approach. NEPA, with all its requirements of impact statements on proposed actions, is not structured to conduct the required baseline and evaluative research necessary for a full-blown ecological approach. The principal concern of its administration has been to make practical its mandate for prompt and specific statements to inform the decisionmaker. The Coastal Zone Management Act enabled a more extensive ecological planning process, but that planning process had to be limited to the immediate coastal area, at the expense of ignoring some of the most important influences on the environment of the coastal zone. The Great Lakes Agreement lacked the resources for any thoroughgoing ecosystem planning of the Great Lakes area, failing to establish a strong linkage between the ecosystem-oriented planning and administration of environmental regulation. The public trust doctrine is simply not specific enough to guide an ecological approach.

The staff and scholars interested in these laws recognize their shortfalls. For NEPA, the major shortfall lies in a routine conventional planning approach to the environmental impact statement which often lacks a serious underlying research effort. Only in selected and exceptional situations, such as the Hudson River controversy, did extensive ecological research take place to support the environmental impact statement. In the late 1980s, as biodiversity and endangered species considerations became a high priority, ecological perspectives were "reintroduced" into the preparation of some environmental impact statements. The coastal zone management program returned to ecological concerns through the identification of some specific natural coastal features to be protected, such as beaches, barrier islands, coastal wetlands and estuaries. The Great Lakes program has sought to reassert its ecosystem planning and administration in the late 1980s, at least on paper.

These programs and their difficulties have also stirred theoretical interest in new questions. How can an ecosystem-oriented impact statement be formulated? Can a coastal zone program be structured encompassing all of the major influences on the coastal areas? How does one formulate an ecosystem approach in a large and complex basin that include myriad of already established activities? We will return to these questions in later sections of this book and the series of books to follow.

Notes

1.   *See* Sierra Club v. Morton, 405 U.S. 727 (1972).
2.   The law of standing has steadily been restricted by the court since Sierra Club v.
          Morton. *See* Karin P. Sheldon, *Lujan v. Defenders of Wildlife: The Supreme Court's
          Slash and Burn Approach to Environmental Standing*, 239 ENV. LAW REP. 10031
          (1993).
3.   The basis for the Douglas dissent was CHRISTOPHER STONE, SHOULD TREES HAVE
          STANDING? (1972). Although the book had little impact upon the law, it opened up a
          rich debate and discussion in environmental circles, which continues to the present.
4.   One of the co-authors of this book, seized by the spirit of Earth Day, litigated to stop
          the construction of a nuclear power plant. *See* Richard Brooks, *Millstone Two and the
          Rainbow: Planning Law and Environmental Protection*, U. CT. L. REV.(1971).
5.   *See* LYNTON K. CALDWELL, SCIENCE AND THE NATIONAL ENVIRONMENTAL POLICY ACT:
          REDIRECTING POLICY THROUGH PROCEDURAL REFORM (1982).
6.   42 U.S.C. §4332(A) (1969).
7.   CALDWELL, *supra* note 5, at 16. This dream, eloquently seconded in the words of
          BARRY COMMONER'S THE CLOSING CIRCLE, was reasserted thirty years later in Edward
          Wilson's restatement of the dream for a unity of knowledge in his book CONSILIENCE.
          See EDWARD O. WILSON, CONSILIENCE: THE UNITY OF KNOWLEDGE (1999). The dream
          of the unity of science is a hardy perennial; *see, e.g.*, SCOTT BUCHANAN, TRUTH IN THE
          SCIENCES (1972).
8.   For an excellent discussion of this New Deal approach, *see* BRUCE ACKERMAN &
          WILLIAM HASSLER, CLEAN COAL, DIRTY AIR (1981). For mention of the Administrative
          Procedures Act, *see* Chapter 2.
9.   In another sense, NEPA was heir to the renewed interest in government planning, an
          interest which emerged out of the New Deal and Great Society. In this tradition, NEPA
          urged both old agencies and its new Council of Environmental Quality to
          environmentally plan by means of the environmental impact statement and the CEQ
          annual report.
10.   *See* JOHN DRYZEK, RATIONAL ECOLOGY (1987).
11.   Both the Council on Environmental Quality and the required cooperation between
          agencies during the impact statement process were intended to secure that
          coordination.
12.   For an account of the incremental approach, *see* DAVID BRAYBROOK & CHARLES
          LINDBLOM, A STRATEGY OF DECISION (1963) 81-111.
13.   *See* Calvert Cliffs Coordinating Committee, Inc. vs U.S. Atomic Energy Commission,
          449 F2d 1109 (1971).
14.   *See* Richard Brooks, *The Law of Municipal Comprehensive Planning*, in ZONING AND
          LAND USE CONTROLS (Patrick Rohan, ed., 1990).
15.   *See* RICHARD LIROFF, A NATIONAL POLICY FOR THE ENVIRONMENT (1976).
16.   *See* 40 C.F.R. §1502.16 (1978).
17.   43 Fed. Reg. §55,996 (1978); 44 Fed. Reg. 873 (1979).
18.   40 CFR §1500 et seq. (43 F.R. 55990, November 28th 1978).
19.   *See* GLENN SUTER, ECOLOGICAL RISK ASSESSMENT, p. 10 (1993).
20.   *See* COMMITTEE ON ECOLOGICAL RESEARCH, COUNCIL ON ENVIRONMENTAL QUALITY,
          AND FEDERAL COUNCIL FOR SCIENCE AND TECHNOLOGY, THE ROLE OF ECOLOGY IN THE
          FEDERAL GOVERNMENT (1974), NATIONAL RESEARCH COUNCIL/THE INSTITUTE OF
          ECOLOGY, JOINT REPORT: ON ECOSYSTEM ANALYSIS, METHODS FOR AQUATIC
          ECOSYSTEMS ANALYSIS: A REPORT TO THE NATIONAL COMMISSION ON WATER QUALITY

(1975) (summarized in Richard Carpenter, *The Scientific Basis of NEPA - Is it Adequate?* 6 ENVTL. L. REP. 500014 (1976)).

21. The account of the Hudson River environmental impact assessment relies heavily upon SCIENCE, LAW AND THE HUDSON RIVER POWER PLANTS: A CASE STUDY IN ENVIRONMENTAL IMPACT ASSESSMENT (Lawrence Barnthouse et al., eds.,1988).

22. Under 40 CFR 1500, 1508.25, attention was to be paid to cumulative and connected actions as well as cumulative and indirect effects.

23. *See supra* note 21. To be fair, other essays in the monograph emphasized the important information about fish population which was gathered.

24. *See* Sierra Club v. U.S. Army Corps of Engineers, 701 F2d 1011 (2nd Cir. 1983); Marsh v. Oregon Natural Resources Council, 490 U.S. 360 (1989).

25. *See* Sierra Club v. Sigler, 695 F2d 957 (5th Cir. 1983); Save Our Ecosystems v. Clark, 747 F2nd 1240 (9th Cir. 1984).

26. *See* 40 CFR 1502.22.

27. *See* Reserve Mining Co. v. EPA, 514 F2d 492 (1975).

28. *See* Marcia Gelpe & A.Dan Tarlock, *The Uses of Scientific Information in Environmental Decisionmaking,* 48 S. CAL. L. REV. 371 (1974).

29. *See* Stryker's Bay Neighborhood Council, Inc. v. Karlen, 444 U.S. 223 (1980).

30. For one comprehensive analysis of a substantive mini NEPA state program, *see* RICHARD BROOKS & KATHY LEONARD ET AL., TOWARD COMMUNITY SUSTAINABILITY: VERMONT'S ACT 250 (1995).

31. *See* Philip Michael Ferester, *Revitalizing the National Environmental Policy Act: Substantive Law Adaptations from NEPA's Progeny,* 16 HARV. ENVTL. REV. 207 (1992). For one of many recent recommendations for reform, see Paul S. Weiland, *Amending the National Environmental Policy Act: Federal Environmental Protection in the Twenty-First Century,* 12 J. LAND USE AND ENV'TL L. 275 (1997).

32. *See* DANIEL MAZMANIAN & JEANNE NIENABER, CAN ORGANIZATIONS CHANGE? ENVIRONMENTAL PROTECTION, CITIZEN PARTICIPATION AND THE CORPS OF ENGINEERS (1979) pp. 180-194.

33. *See* SERGE TAYLOR, NEPA: MAKING BUREAUCRACIES THINK: THE ENVIRONMENTAL IMPACT STATEMENT STRATEGY OF REFORM (1984).

34. *See* EUGENE ODUM, FUNDAMENTALS OF ECOLOGY 254-256 (1971). Odum referred to H.T. ODUM, B.J. COPELAND, AND E.A. McMAHAN COASTAL ECOSYSTEMS OF THE UNITED STATES (1969).

35. There is very little doubt that this work was stimulated by the grants available under the Coastal Zone Management Act of 1972. *See e.g.,* JOHN CLARK, COASTAL ECOSYSTEMS: ECOLOGICAL CONSIDERATIONS FOR MANAGEMENT OF THE COASTAL ZONE (1974).

36. 16 U.S.C. § 1453 (1972).

37. 16 § 1451(d)(e) (1972).

38. *See* THE COASTAL MANAGEMENT PROGRAM. In 1972, The Coastal Zone Management Act was passed in lieu of a national planning legislation which was lingering in Congress at the time. This legislation was the result of a dawning recognition of the importance of an environmentally oriented land use planning, which had received the imprimatur of the American Law Institute and the American Planning Associations. Several states had adopted statewide environmentally oriented planning and land use laws. Scholars were interested in national planning to direct and control growth. At the same time, there was a growing sophistication about the reasons for frequent lack of success in planning. The comprehensive planning process had been evaluated and found wanting. Since the 1960s, various efforts had been made to better articulate the policies of planning, secure consensus among conflicting groups, and better implement

the planning results. One important characteristic of the coast is its natural dynamism and consequent change. Barrier beaches, coastal wetlands, and dunes do not stay put. Consequently, the coastal management program envisaged an adaptive management process adjusting to both natural changes and new man made pressures. The management approach can refer not only to flexible changes, but also reliance upon more general standards, guidelines, and policies. The federal court upheld such an approach in American Petroleum Institute v. Knecht, 456 F. Supp. 889 (C.D. Cal. 1978) (affirmed 609 F2d 1306 (9th Circuit. 1979)). Such a planning process also had to adapt itself to the multiple uses to which the coast is put and these often conflicting uses needed to be "allocated," "balanced" or "prioritized."

39.   *See* JOHN CLARK, COASTAL ECOSYSTEMS: ECOLOGICAL CONSIDERATIONS FOR MANAGEMENT OF THE COASTAL AREA (1974).

40.   *See* Joy R. Brockman, *Coastal Ecosystem Protection in Florida*, 20 NOVA L. REV. 859 (1996).

41.   *See* Richard Brooks, *The Law of Plan Implementation in the United States*, 16 URB. LAW. ANNUAL 225 (1979).

42.   The following is based upon a memorandum prepared by Erin Flynn.

43.   *See* GARY A. KLEE, THE COASTAL ENVIRONMENT 25-27 (1999).

44.   *See* SEGIP, *Natural Resources Wetlands*, 1
        <http://www.fcpm.fsu.edu/segip/states/NC/over12.html> (visited 7/17/00).

45.   *See* SEGIP, *Designated Use Support of Wetlands*, 1
        <http://www.fcpm.fsu.edu/segip/states/NC/desig.html> (visited 7/17/00).

46.   *See* Southern Environmental Law Center, *Wetland Protection, Regional*
        <http://www.southernenvironment.org/act_wetland_protect.shtml> (visited7/17/00).

47.   *See* SELC, *supra* note 46, at 1.

48.   *See* SELC, *supra* note 46, at 1.

49.   *See* DIRK FRANKENBERG, THE NATURE OF NORTH CAROLINA'S SOUTHERN COAST: BARRIER ISLANDS, COASTAL WATERS AND WETLANDS 219-220 (1997).

50.   The Division of Environmental Management estimates that 34 percent of North Carolina's original coastal wetlands have been impaired by development. Of that total, 52 percent have been affected by agricultural development, 10 percent by urban development and 38 percent by forestry. In the 1970s, concern about the rapid disappearance of coastal wetlands began to grow on North Carolina's state and a federal level, which led to the two present controlling legal regimes: Section 404 of the Clean Water Act and CAMA.

51.   *See* National Council for Science and the Environment, IB97014: *Wetland Issues*, 4
        <http://www.cnie.org/nle/wet-5.html> (visited 7/13/00).

52.   *See id* at 4.

53.   *See* Sierra Club, North Carolina Chapter, *Wetlands*, 3
        < http://www.sierraclub-nc.org/chapter/conservation/welands.html > (visited 7/06/00). North Carolina uses hydric soils as the basis for wetland evaluations. [*See* SEGIP, *supra* note 44, at 1.] In 1993, the Division of Environmental Management conducted a wetland study. The study used aerial photographs to provide random samples of wetlands in the coastal plain, using hydric soils as an indicator. [*See* SEGIP, *supra* note 44, at 1.]

54.   *See* Sierra Club, *supra* note 45, at 2.

55.   *See Id.*

56.   *See Id* at 6.

57.   *See* Milton S. Heath, Jr. and David W. Owens, *Coastal Management Law in North Carolina*, 72 NCLR 1413, 1 (1994).

58.   *See Id.*

59. *See Id.*

60. *See* DCM, *Developing Under CAMA: Permits*, 1
<http://dcm2.enr.state.nc.us/Rules&Permits/develop2.htm> (visited 7/12/00). There are three types of CAMA development permits: minor permits, general permits and major permits. An exemption certificate authorizes some development. Minor permits are required for projects that do not require a general or major permit, such as a single family home. Minor permits are reviewed, issued and administered to Coastal Resource Commission (CRC) standards by local governments under the supervision of the Division of Coastal Management. Major permits are necessary for projects that cover more than 20 acres or for construction covering more than 60,000 square feet. Major permit applications are review by four federal and ten state agencies before a decision is made. General permits are used for routine projects that usually pose little or no threat to the environment, and the permit is basically an expedited version of the major permit. In 1999, 88 percent of CAMA general and major permits were processed in less than seven days. Another bridge document is the Nationwide Permit 26. This federal wetlands program has recently been reformed. On June 5, 2000, the NWP 26 was cancelled and replaced by five new NWPs and modifications to the six existing NWPs. NWP 26 authorized the discharges of dredged or fill material into headwaters and isolated waters of the United States. The modified and new NWPs authorize some of the same activities that NWP 26 was responsible for, but the new NWPs are activity-specific. The new NWPs contain conditions and terms that guarantee that activities result in minimal adverse effects on the aquatic environment. *See* US Army Corps of Engineers, *Corps Facts*, 3 (visited 7/15/00)
<http://www.usace.army.mil/inet/functions/cw/cecwo/reg/>.

61. Peebles v. State of Florida, Dept. of Environmental Regulation, 12 FALR 1961 (1990).

62. *See* SELC, *supra* note 46, at 1.

63. *See* SELC, *supra* note 46, at 1.

64. *See* NCSE, *supra* note 8, at 6.

65. 16 U.S.C. 1453(1).

66. 16 U.S.C. 1456(c).

67. *See* 201 N.W.2d 761 (Wis. 1972).

68. These new laws represent a tacit admission that the original embrace of an ecosystem management program was not sufficient either to protect key coastal resources or give assurance for needed coastal developments.

69. *See* EUGENE ODUM, FUNDAMENTALS OF ECOLOGY 295-334 (1971).

70. *See* W.T. EDMONDSON, THE USES OF ECOLOGY: LAKE WASHINGTON AND BEYOND (1991).

71. *See* Jutta Brunnée & Stephen J. Toope, *Environmental Security and Freshwater Resources: Ecosystem Regime Building*, 91 AM. J. INT'L L. 26 (1997).

72. *See* Raymond Lindeman, *The Trophic-Dynamic Aspect of Ecology*, 23 ECOLOGY 399 (1942).

73. *See* a brief summary of Lindeman's work and its significance in the history of ecology; *see* DONALD WORSTER, NATURE'S ECONOMY 306-311 (1987). *See also*, FRANK BENJAMIN GOLLEY, A HISTORY OF THE ECOSYSTEM CONCEPT IN ECOLOGY: MORE THAN THE SUM OF THE PARTS 50-54 (1993).

74. *See* W.T. EDMONDSON, THE USES OF ECOLOGY: LAKE WASHINGTON AND BEYOND (1991).

75. The background of the Great Lakes approach embraced not only the lake ecosystem approach, but watershed and coastal ecosystem views which were then current. The

Great Lakes were the only freshwater lakes initially included in the Coastal Zone Management Program of 1972.

76.   *See* W.J. Christie, *The Ecosystem Approach To Managing The Great Lakes*, 26 U. TOL. L. REV. 279, 280 (1995). *See also* THE CONSERVATION FOUNDATION'S INSTITUTE FOR RESEARCH ON PUBLIC POLICY, GREAT LAKES; GREAT LEGACY (1990).

77.   *See* WILLIAM CRONON, NATURE'S METROPOLIS: CHICAGO AND THE GREAT WEST (1991).

78.   *See* CARL SANDBERG, CHICAGO POEMS (1916).

79.   *See* Chandler, James & Vechsler, *The Great Lakes-St. Lawrence River Basin From An IJC Perspective*, 18 CAN.-U.S. L.J. 261, 261 (1992).

80.   *See id.*

81.   *See id.*

82.   *See* Leonard B. Dworsky, *Ecosystem Management: Great Lakes Perspectives*, 33 NAT. RESOURCES J. 347, 348 (1993).

83.   *See id.*

84.   *See id.* at 349.

85.   *See id.*

86.   *See* International Joint Commission, *Ninth Biennial Report On Great Lakes Water Quality – Executive Summary* <www.ijc.org/comm/9br/exsume.html> (visited August 1, 1999).

87.   *See* Dworsky, *supra* note 82.

88.   *See id.*

89.   *See id.*

90.   *See id.*

91.   1978 Agreement Between the United States and Canada on Great Lakes Water Quality, TIA S9257 Article I: Definitions (g).

92.   *See id.* Article II: Purpose.

93.   *See id.*

94.   *See id.*

95.   *See id.*

96.   *See id.*

97.   *See id.*

98.   *See id.* at 353.

99.   *See id.* at 354.

100.   *See id.* at 349. In 1987, a Protocol was signed amending the 1978 Agreement. International Joint Commission, *Ninth Biennial Report On Great Lakes Water Quality – Executive Summary* <http://www.ijc.org/comm/9br/exsume.html> (visited August 1, 1999). The amendment's aim was to strengthen the programs, practices, and technology described in the 1978 Agreement. To increase accountability for the implementation of certain programs, timetables were set. During the 1980s and 1990s, the IJC issued biennial reports to document the progress of Great Lakes restoration and to make recommendations for future action. These biennial reports have sometimes had the impact of shifting the focus of the IJC and the two respective governments at all levels of administration. Such was the case with the *Fifth Biennial Report*, issued in 1990, which recognized the need to address persistence toxic substances that remained in the Lakes ecosystem. The most recent report, the *Ninth Biennial Report*, which included nineteen targeted recommendations that, when implemented, will allow the Commission to measure progress toward the Agreement's purpose and help society move in the desired direction.

101.   International Joint Commission & Wayne State University, *Practical Steps to Implement an Ecosystem Approach in Great Lakes Management* <http://www.ijc.org/boards/wqb/toc.hmtl> (visited July 24, 1999).

102.   *See* Barry Rabe & Janet B. Zimmerman, *Cross-Media Environmental Integration in The Great Lakes Basin*, 22 ENVTL. L. 253, 257 (1992).
103.   *See supra* note 101.
104.   *See* Christe, *supra* note 76.
105.   *See supra* note 101.
106.   *See id.*
107.   *See id.*
108.   *See id.*
109.   *See id.*
110.   *See id.*
111.   *See id.*
112.   *See id.*
113.   *See id.*
114.   *See id.*
115.   *See id.*
116.   *See id.*
117.   *See id.*
118.   *See id.*
119.   *See id.*
120.   *See id.*
121.   *See id.*
122.   *See id.*
123.   *See id.*
124.   *See id.*
125.   *See supra* note 76, at 279, 286.
126.   Barry Rabe & Janet B. Zimmerman, *Cross-Media Environmental Integration in the Great Lakes Basin*, 22 ENVTL. L. 253, 278 (1992).
127.   *Id.* at 262.
128.   *Id.*
129.   *Id.* at 263.
130.   *Id.*
131.   *Id.*
132.   *See id.*
133.   *See id.*
134.   *See id.*
135.   *See* Rabe, *supra* note 126 at 264.
136.   *See id.*
137.   *See id.* at 265. Rabe notes that the proliferation of Great Lakes regional organizations is the result of three factors. The growth of these groups may be the result of several forces at work. First, the environmental movement has matured in recent decades, moving from a position of being highly adversarial with government and industry, to a position that stresses greater cooperation and development of strategies with mutually beneficially results. Second, the business and industry throughout the Basin have increasingly recognized the extent to which their own economic well being depends on the protection and promotion of the economic and environmental integrity of the Great Lakes. A third factor is the decentralization of environmental regulation. Increasingly, both federal governments are delegating regulation to the states, and as the states are often less than dependable with funding, private and regional organizations have moved in to fill the gaps left by governmental entities. The bottom line in ecosystem management terms is that more regional organizations, which have

synthesized their respective views, may mean easier, less complicated, and more effective integrated management.

Conceptual advances and the refinement of old techniques have also proven instrumental in the implementation of an ecosystem approach to the Basin. [*Id.* at 268.] An example of a conceptual advance in the Basin is the shift in environmental policy in both nations from pollution control to pollution prevention. The growing knowledge of the way in which pollution transfers from one media to another is leading to a more preventative approach towards pollution, a "don't put it in the environment in the first place" approach. Far more than an abstract goal, pollution prevention is emerging as a major vehicle within the EPA and state agencies, to reduce overall pollution increases and cross-media transfers. New York, Minnesota and both national governments have taken the lead in focusing on pollution prevention.

Although traditional environmental regulatory tools and methods, such as environmental impact statements, formal efforts to coordinate permit issuance, and agency reorganization, have not fulfilled their expected potential for fostering more integrated, in Basin-wide management there have been examples of progress using these tools. [*Id.* at 272.] Individual states have led the way. New York, in enacting the State Environmental Quality Act, opened the door towards more integrated management. [*Id.* at 273.] In Illinois, the Coordinated Review Of Permits (CROP) program was established to oversee major projects that would require the issuance of multiple permits. Under the program permit managers from each of the major permit programs are expected to jointly track these projects making integrated management more of a reality. Wisconsin provides a concrete example of agency reorganization with the purpose of accomplishing more integrated management. The Department of Natural Resources has adopted practices, such as the rotation of administrative assignments for environmental managers, to broaden the perspectives on the range of cross-media problems and their potential solutions.

138.   *See Joint Hearing on the EPA Great Lakes Program. Before the Subcomm. on Environment and Natural Resources*, 104th Congr. 1-2 (Statement of Dr. Michael Donahue, Executive Director Great Lakes Commission).

139.   *See id.*

140.   *See* International Joint Commission & Wayne State University, *supra* note 101.

141.   *See id.*

142.   For a good detailed account of the public trust doctrine, its history and present application, *see* DAVID SLADE, ET AL., PUTTING THE PUBLIC TRUST DOCTRINE TO WORK: THE APPLICATION OF THE PUBLIC TRUST DOCTRINE TO THE MANAGEMENT OF LANDS, WATERS, AND LINING RESOURCES OF THE COASTAL STATES (1990).

143.   JOSEPH SAX, DEFENDING THE ENVIRONMENT: A STRATEGY FOR CITIZEN ACTION (1971).

144.   JOSEPH SAX, MOUNTAINS WITHOUT HANDRAILS: REFLECTIONS ON THE NATIONAL PARKS (1980).

145.   JOSEPH SAX, PLAYING DARTS WITH A REMBRANDT: PUBLIC AND PRIVATE RIGHTS IN CULTURAL TREASURES (1999).

146.   *See e.g.*, the constitutions of Virginia, Pennsylvania, and Michigan.

147.   For a discussion of the concept of trust from the point of view of political theory, *see* ADAM B. SELIGMAN, THE PROBLEM OF TRUST (1997).

148.   *See* NATIONAL RESEARCH COUNCIL, ET AL., THE MONO BASIN ECOSYSTEM: EFFECTS OF CHANGING LAKE LEVEL (1987).

149.   *See* Public Law 98-425 and House Report 98-291.

6 The Courtship of Law and Ecology

The forest community, then, consists of an assemblage of plants and animals living in an environment of air, soil and water. Each of these organisms is interrelated either directly or indirectly with virtually every other organism in the community. The health and welfare of the organisms are dependent upon the factors of the environment surrounding them; and the environment surrounding them itself is conditioned to a considerable degree by the biotic community itself. In other words, the plants, the animals, and the environment – including the air, the soil, and the water – constitute a complex ecological system in which each factor and each individual is conditioned by, and in itself conditions, the other factors comprising the complex.[1] Thus it is doubtful whether the timber and watershed that the Court prizes so highly could flourish without a complement of wildlife. The recognition by modern science of this vital interdependence is by no means a new discovery.
                                                              – U.S. v. Mexico[2]

Introduction

Forestry regulation, the Endangered Species Act and National Park legislation did not initially view their environmental missions in ecological terms.[3] But over a two decade period, the administrators of these laws gradually but grudgingly realized the relevance of ecology to their missions. The Endangered Species Act gradually incorporated a new understanding of habitat modification. The National Park legislation and its implementation in Yellowstone began to adopt an ecosystem approach. The National Forest Management Act gradually adopted serious planning for biodiversity. Pesticide legislation slowly migrated toward the prevention of bio-accumulation.[4]

Each of these laws shares a common historical development. In the first stage, each law and its traditional purposes was challenged by environmentalists who saw the law as causing harm to the environment. The laws ignored habitat modification in protecting species, or they permitted clearcutting in national forests without attention to forest species, or allowed people to overrun the national parks, or ignored the diffusion of pesticides and their cumulative impact in the environment. Environmentalists' challenges, with the help of the academic community, forced changes, new interpretations of statutes, and new regulations. These changes allowed for gradual infiltration of an ecological perspective in the administration of the transformed law. These challenges to the traditional natural resource laws were assisted by the development of a new subdiscipline of ecology: conservation biology.[5] This subdiscipline, along with ecosystem ecology, was to provide both the methods and conclusions needed for the scientific support of a new ecological approach to these laws.

The courtship between ecology and environmental law took place over three decades. The older purposes of the laws continue to linger, some like vestigial remains in the process of evolution. "Bambi" is still protected for his own sake under the Endangered Species Act, the sound of saws still rings in the national forests, people still crowd the national parks, and many pesticides are still sprayed. The central question then focuses on the extent to which the old practices are still necessary and whether the new ecologically-oriented insights can transform these practices.[6] In short, can these laws be ecologically retrofitted?

The Endangered Species Act: From Species to Habitat Protection

Environmental law has evolved from concern for policies to protect species threatened with extinction to policies designed to protect their niches and habitat. In the early stages of this evolution, even the protection of individual species was not taken for granted. With Darwin, the extinction of species was accepted as a necessary part of the workings of evolution. Darwin viewed the fossil records of extinct species as evidence of an inevitable natural selection at work. Early legal efforts to protect wildlife were less concerned with extinction, and more concerned with insuring a supply of game. The primary focus of wildlife laws during the first half of the twentieth century was the protection of populations deemed to be threatened by human activity. Nevertheless, the passage of these wildlife laws over time gradually culminated in the Endangered Species Act of 1973,[7] which sought to protect the species themselves. Protecting species from extinction became the early focus of modern environmental law and policy. The threat of extinction became a kind of symbol for the degradation of nature. Hence the public culture of species protection was wrapped up in the environmental myths and a growing biocentrism that swept America in the early 1970s.

The Endangered Species Act also mentioned ecosystems and required the identification and protection of the "critical habitat" of the species.[8] The Act also provided for protection from "jeopardizing" the habitat through ill-advised government actions.[9] A simple but useful definition of "habitat," for these early arguments, is "the place where a species lives." The Act provided for the regulation and recovery plans for habitats.[10] This mention of "habitat" in the law, however, was not accompanied by early systematic attention to the identification, protection, or recovery of disturbed habitats. Although this early failure of attention to habitats was partly due to the law's enforcement concentration on protection of the species themselves, the failure may also have rested in the limited development of the concept of habitat within ecology itself. As we shall see below, law and environmental management did as much as ecology in developing the concept of habitat.

During the late 1970s and 1980s, concern for the protection of the underlying habitat of endangered species increased. This concern took the form of political and legal pressure to list habitats and adopt adequate recovery plans. Perhaps most significant, however, was the effort to transform the language of the Endangered Species Act through legal interpretation to include the modification of the species habitat as a "taking" of the species.

While the Fish and Wildlife Service was increasing its attention to habitats under the Endangered Species Act, other laws were passed that began to focus upon habitats as well: these laws included the Forest and Rangelands Renewable Resources Planning Act, the Marine Mammal Protection Act and the Fishery Conservation and Management Act. All of these laws struggled with the appropriate definition of habitat in their efforts to protect endangered species within the forest, oceans, and other fisheries.

To the extent that the Endangered Species Act and the other laws embrace habitats as important to the protection of populations and species, they call upon the science of ecology and its applications in defining habitats and how they are important. The key ecological concepts of species, extinction, niche and habitat came to be incorporated into the laws. These concepts are applied within various "bridge documents," which reflect both legal objectives and the methods and conclusions of ecology. One such "bridge document" that struggles with defining "habitats" for protected plant and animal species and populations is the "biological assessment"/"biological opinion" required under the Endangered Species Act. This "bridge document" lays bare the promise and problem of linking law and ecology to protect endangered species and their habitats.

The environmental law issues regarding species extinction are anything but dull. Take the case of *Tennessee Valley Authority v. Hill.*[11] In 1966, the Tennessee Valley Authority (TVA) proposed building a dam on the Little Tennessee River. The Tellico Dam would turn 30 miles of the shallow turbulent Little Tennessee River into a deep reservoir with over 16,000 surface acres of water. This rural development project was intended to benefit a poor economic "backwater" of Tennessee. According to the proceedings of a congressional hearing, the area was characterized by "underutilization of human resources and outmigration of young people." The reservoir was intended to provide stimuli to tourism and industrial development, as well as to contribute to increased electrical generating capacity. All these side effects were expected, in addition to the more obvious benefits of flood control and an economic jolt to a depressed area.

One person's cornucopia is another's pork barrel. From the start, the Tellico Dam was opposed by a coalition of local property owners, conservationists, and other people who felt – for differing reasons – that the dam had to be stopped. Although these groups won some initial skirmishes, in 1973 a federal court in Tennessee decided that construction could continue. Soon, however, the dam's opponents had discovered a formidable tactic, one utilizing a new environmental statute and enlisting the aid of a most unlikely soldier, a 3-inch long tannish-colored fish.

On August 12,1973, Dr. David Etnier, an ichthyologist from the University of Tennessee, had discovered this new species of perch, *Pircina (Imostoma) tanasi*, about 7 miles from the mouth of the Little Tennessee. For all practical purposes, the snail darter, as it became known, lived only in the Little Tennessee and could reproduce only in the clear, flowing waters that characterized the river. In a still water reservoir environment, the fish would be doomed. Darters are not an extraordinary fish. There are almost a hundred identified species in Tennessee alone, and a new species is added to the list at a rate of about one per year. However, this snail darter's limited range, its even more limited spawning area, and thus its extreme vulnerability to habitat deprivation, made it unique. Searches in the area failed to turn up any additional colonies, even though TVA employees eventually looked in more than sixty rivers in Alabama and Tennessee, trying to turn up another self-sustaining population. Even in the Little Tennessee, the snail darter seemed to exist solely in the very stretch the Tellico Dam would flood.

Waving the new banner of the Endangered Species Act, the pro-snail darter, anti-Tellico Dam partisans lost no time enlisting the forces of the Interior Department in their battle against the TVA. In January 1975, they petitioned the Secretary of the Interior, under the citizen petition provision of the Act, to declare the snail darter an endangered species. On November 10, 1975, the snail darter made the list, and the following April, the crucial 17-mile stretch of the Little Tennessee was declared a critical habitat.[12]

Only two months after the additional Tellico funding was approved, and a mere three months after the snail darter had been declared an endangered species, a group of environmentalists brought suit claiming that TVA was violating the Endangered Species Act, and demanding a halt to further work on the dam. By then the work was about 80 percent completed, and the only major action remaining to complete the dam was to impound the water and turn the Little Tennessee into a lake. What proved decisive in the district court was the tremendous economic waste that would result if the environmentalists were granted their remedy, allowing the river to continue to flow through an unclosed dam.

The district court agreed with TVA. Although it recognized that its decision was the snail darter's death warrant, the court was forced to examine, among other factors, the irreversible and irretrievable commitment of resources. The environmentalists appealed the judge's decision on the grounds that he had concluded that TVA could ignore the law. In legal terms, they claimed that the court had abused its discretion. The appellate court agreed with the environmentalists and reversed the district court's decision on the basis of separation of powers. By this, the court meant that the Secretary of Interior is responsible for listing endangered species, and that once a species is put on the list, a violation of the Endangered Species Act requires an automatic injunction.[13] The appeals court thought that the district court had in effect allowed TVA to choose an alternative action, when none was available. Congress had stated what it wanted, and the court could not usurp congressional authority.

The effect of the appeals court decision was to halt all further work on the dam – to keep the gates open until TVA decided what to do. Not surprisingly, TVA petitioned the Supreme Court to overturn the appeals court's decision and reinstate the district court's. The Supreme Court affirmed the Appeals Court decision. Accepting the endangered species listing and the designation of the critical habitat as given, the Court interpreted Section 7 of the Endangered Species Act to permit no exceptions to the mandate that federal agencies insure that their actions not jeopardize the continued existence of endangered species, and that appropriations for the continued building of the Tellico Dam after the adoption of the Endangered Species Act did not amend the provisions of the Act.[14]

In an ironic footnote to the entire controversy, another colony of snail darters was discovered 80 miles away the following year, and the year after that, enough other colonies had been discovered to render frivolous the threat of immediate extinction.

To implement the Endangered Species Act, biologists began to articulate the concept of habitat in the 1980s.[15] As stated above, under the Endangered Species Act a "critical habitat" of the species was to be listed, federal actions "jeopardizing habitats" as well as species were prohibited, recovery plans involving habitats were to be developed, and habitat conservation plans (HCPs) were to be developed as part of the "incidental taking" procedures.

The procedures that require the Secretary to determine habitat jeopardy best reveal how the "ecology of habitats" is translated into legal language. To guide such determinations, the Endangered Species Act offers the definition of critical habitat as "a portion of the area occupied by a listed species, the entirety of the species' occupied area, or even areas outside the currently occupied area, including areas into which the future expansion of a listed species is essential to assure its survival and recovery." In 1976, regulations under the Endangered Species Act provision prohibiting "the distribution or modification of habitat of such species which is determined ... to be critical," defined modification as "a deleterious effect upon any of the constituent elements of critical habitat which are necessary to the survival or recovery of such species and such effect is likely to result in a decline in the numbers of the species."[16] In 1986, the Fish and Wildlife Service offered new regulations that reaffirmed with slight change the existing regulations. The sequence of litigation involving an effort to protect the Palila bird during the 1980s, illustrates the convoluted move away from the protection of an individual member of a species to the protection of a generic species as part of a functioning habitat.

SPECIES AND THEIR EXTINCTION

Underlying the concern for the extinction of species are very difficult notions of species habitat and modification. In the Snail Darter litigation, the fish was one of many subspecies of snail darters. Such a fact raises questions about how important the subject was in the grand scheme of things, and whether its elimination was so significant. Although the Tellico Dam threatened to inundate the entire local habitat of the snail darter, most federal government actions that threaten to affect the habitat of a species are less catastrophic, requiring a subtle evaluation of the impact of the actions upon the habitats, as well as difficult-to-answer questions about how habitat modification results in species extinction. Extinction can refer not only to species, but also populations, higher taxa, or other biological entities (such as alleles, gene lineages, or cell lines). Within environmental law, the common reference is to species. Species are classes, sets, or kinds of similar organisms; similar because of their morphology, or their apparent ability to reproduce only among them-selves, or some mixture of the two.

A complex intellectual history precedes the present debates over species, and there is presently neither agreement about the criteria for determining species nor the resulting taxonomy. There is also disagreement about the nature of subspecies classification, such as races, families, genera, etc. This disagreement has surfaced in the administration of the Endangered Species Act, but has not impeded its administration. Extinction of species can refer to the massive evolutionary extinction, or the "biological extermination" due to human activities, or both. This extinction may refer to the elimination of taxa, or whole lineages of species, the global extinction of a species, or the local extinction of a species. Ecologists attribute such human-related extinctions to habitat disturbance, hunting, introduction of competing or predatory species, pest or predatory controls, collecting of specimens, and pollution. The purposes for seeking to prevent further human-related extinctions include valuing the species for its own sake or for its human-related aesthetic, recreations and economic value, protecting the "gene pool" held by such species, primarily for future medical uses, and the protection of ecosystems in which such species function. Habitat protection is only one of several means of securing protection of species. These means include constraints on hunting, pollution, introduction of new non-indigenous species, and collection of species. Habitat protection is viewed as one of the most important approaches, and protection is a major focus of conservation biology.

The Palila Litigation

In March of 1967, the native Hawaiian bird species, *Loxioides bailleui,* commonly known as the Palila, was listed as "endangered" under the Endangered Species Preservation Act. By definition, the Palila is a "species which is in danger of extinction throughout all or significant portions of its range."[17] The Palila, the largest member of the Hawaiian Honeycreeper family, is one of 28 bird species endemic to Hawaii. The Palila is currently protected by the Endangered Species Act.[18] Historically located in the abundant mamane – naio forests on the mountain slopes of Mauna Kea, Hawaii, the Palila is now forced to reside within only a small fragment of this diminishing forest area (between elevations 6,400 and 9,500 feet). The causes of the disappearance of Hawaii's native wildlife include the introduction of new species (i.e., mongoose, a predator), competition for diminishing resources, prior lack of concern or legal protection by the government and public, and most instrumental, habitat loss or degradation due to human intervention.[19]

The Palila's survival is dependent upon the mamane trees, both for food and nesting behaviors. The birds use the crowns of the mamane trees, specifically the older, taller trees, for nesting and rearing their young. The taller trees give the Palila an advantage in protecting their young from ground-dwelling predators. Due to the overgrazing of the forest by feral (non-domesticated) sheep and goats, and more recently mouflon sheep – introduced by the State of Hawaii for sport hunting – the mamane trees have been devoured and unable to regenerate. Only small areas of the older trees (10 percent of the original Palila range) are still intact with an advanced ecosystem to provide for its habitants.[20]

In 1979, the Palila flew into the U.S. District Court and into the news. The District Court ruled that the presence of mouflon sheep within the mamane forest constituted a "taking" under the Endangered Species Act. "Taking" an endangered species is prohibited under the Act. This decision, affirmed by the

Court of Appeals, provided protection for the ecosystem of the mamane forests, and indirectly provided protection for the Palila.[21]

The court found that the state sustained a population of feral sheep and goats for recreational sport hunting that caused significant harm within the critical habitat of the native Palila. The state was held to have violated §9(1)(B) of the ESA, which asserts that "it is unlawful for any person subject to the jurisdiction of the United States to take any species within the United States or the territorial sea of the United States."[22]

To "take," within the ESA, means to harass, harm, pursue, hunt, shoot, wound, kill, trap, capture, or collect or to attempt to engage in any such conduct. The court focused on "harm," specifically, and determined whether the activities of the feral sheep and goats (consumption of the mamane leaves, stems, seedlings and sprouts) fell within the definition. At the time of this lawsuit, "harm" had been defined by the Secretary of Interior to include significant environmental modification or degradation that actually injures or kills wildlife. The state of Hawaii argued that because there was no actual harm to any individual members, such as the sheep or goats killing a Palila bird, a "taking" had not occurred, and offered to institute the Mauna Kea Plan; fencing off 25 percent of the existing bird habitat for hunting, based on the belief that the bird, sheep and goats could coexist. The court disagreed and ordered the state to remove the feral animals from the critical habitat at the state's expense. On appeal brought by the state of Hawaii in 1981, the state supreme court affirmed the finding that a "taking" had occurred, in direct violation of the ESA. The court also affirmed that because the species could not coexist, the state would have to remove the grazing animals.[23]

In 1986, the same players brought another suit against the Hawaii Department of Land and Natural Resources (referred to as "Palila III"). The state was once again charged with violating the ESA,[24] yet the focus shifted from the maintenance of feral sheep and goats to mouflon sheep.[25] At the time of Palila I, the studies on the effect of mouflon sheep (in comparison to the feral sheep and goats) were not included, due to insufficient data. However, by 1986, it was proven that the activities of these sheep were as destructive and devastating to the mamane forests as the feral animals. The mouflon sheep were introduced into the mamane forests by the State Division of Fish and Game during the 1960s. The state hoped to eliminate certain undesirable traits of the existing sheep population by interbreeding the two types of sheep. These populations of grazing ungulates were maintained within the Mauna Kea Game Management Area, located within the critical Palila habitat.

Based on the activities of the sheep in comparison to the activities of the feral species, the court determined that the state had violated the ESA and ordered the removal the mouflon sheep in conjunction with the continuing removal efforts of the feral sheep and goats.[26] The grazing activities of the mouflon sheep on the mamane trees constituted "harm" within the new definition of the amended ESA. The District Court emphasized that one of the primary purposes of the ESA was the "preservation and conservation" of the critical *ecosystems* that endangered species depend upon for survival.[27] Emphasis was placed on the fact that while the sheep still exist within the forest, and continue to graze upon the mamane trees, seedling, leaves, etc., the forest, as well as the population of the Palila, would not be able to regenerate. The court had determined that the mouflon sheep and the Palila were incompatible and they rejected the state's premise that the two can coexist. The Palila was a federally protected species, within the ESA, and the sheep were not. The sheep, consequently, had to be removed.

In 1988, the Court of Appeals affirmed the District Court's decision, stating that activities of the mouflon sheep fell within the definition of "harm" and had to be removed accordingly.[28] The court of appeals decision defined "take" in a broad manner, and proclaimed that "harm" could be interpreted to include both actual and potential results. The activities of the mouflon sheep "harmed" the Palila within the amended meaning in two ways: (1) the presence of the sheep and their grazing habits, if continued, could lead to the extinction of the Palila due to lack of food and nesting site availability; and (2) if the mouflon continued to eat away at the forest, and maintain a significant population level, the forest would not be able to regenerate – the Palila would also be hindered from increasing their population, and would remain on the "endangered species" list. As stated in Palila II, the purpose of the Endangered Species Act is to conserve and preserve the ecosystems that endangered species rely upon. "Conserve," within the Act, is defined as "to use or the uses of all methods and procedures which are necessary to bring any endangered species or threatened species to the point at which the measures provided pursuant to this Act are no longer necessary," (i.e., scientific resources management – research, transplantation).[29] If the mouflon sheep remained, even within a small area, the state would be in direct violation of the ESA because harm will be constantly occurring.[30]

As the *Snail Darter* and the *Palila* opinions illustrate, litigation centers upon determining the point at which a species is either "jeopardized" by federal government actions or "taken" by public or private actions. Such a determination rests upon a biological opinion.

If the *Palila* opinions reflect a new awareness of habitat modification as part of the "taking" of a species, then the biological opinions represent a crystallization of law and ecology in an effort to protect the species and its habitat. However, the legal notion of habitat itself was not new to environmental law, nor was it limited to the narrow confines of the Endangered Species Act. Other laws were to develop and extend the habitat concept in the 1990s.

Bridge Document 6.1 THE BIOLOGICAL OPINION

Under §7(a)(2) of the Endangered Species Act, every federal agency must "insure that any action authorized, funded, or carried out by such agency ... is not likely to jeopardize the continued existence of any endangered species or result in the destruction or adverse modification of [critical] habitat of such species."[31] Under § 7(c) of the Act, "a biological assessment" must be conducted if a listed or to-be-listed species occurs in the area of the proposed action.[32] If a listed species is found likely to be jeopardized, the federal agency must "consult" with the Secretary of the Interior[33] and a "biological opinion," based upon a "biological assessment," is to determine how the action will affect the species and suggest reasonable and prudent alternatives to avoid these effects.[34] Under the broad statutory language, more detailed regulations set forth the steps to be taken within the assessment.[35] The U.S. Fish and Wildlife Service has issued a detailed hand-book for the conduct of such assessments and the issuance of opinions.[36] In regard to the species themselves, this hand-book requires the designation of the way in which the federal action relates to the range of the species and the status of the critical habitat (taking into account the species, its life history, its population dynamics, status and distribution). This description of the habitat is an environmental "baseline" of the current human and natural factors affecting the species, and the direct, indirect and cumulative effects of the proposed federal action upon the species. The analysis of the critical habitat requires identification of those physical and biological features essential to conservation of the species within the habitat, including space, nutritional or physiological requirements, cover or shelter, breeding sites and protected habitats.[37] As stated above, the Endangered Species *Consultation Handbook* includes within "the action area" the area including all direct and indirect effects, which may be lesser or greater than the range of the species and may include effects not at the project site.[38] According to the *Handbook,* the habitat includes physical and biological features essential to the conservation of listed species, including space for individual and population growth and normal behavior, food, water, air, light, minerals and other physiological requirements, cover or shelter, sites for breeding, reproducing, recovery of offspring, germination or seed dispersal, and "habitats protected from disturbance or representative of the historic, geographic and ecological distributions of a species."[39] "Adverse modification" of the habitat occurs when the action will affect the critical habitat's constituent elements or their management in a manner likely to "appreciably diminish or preclude the role of that habitat in both the survival and recovery of the species."[40]

National Parks: From "Pleasuring Grounds" to Ecosystem Management to Wilderness

National Park management offers another example of the linkage of ecology and law. With preservation of natural treasures as a principal purpose, management of national parks invites attention to the workings of ecosystems. However, the national parks were defined long before the science of ecology had been developed, and their original purpose as "pleasuring grounds" did not insure that their primary recreation role would be compatible with sensitivity to the ecosystem. The history of the parks is, in fact, a history of cycles of scientific attention to parks, balanced with the agenda of management for other purposes.[41] National parks have offered the setting for serious exploration of applying the concepts and methods of ecology to their management. Yellowstone Park offers the best example of efforts by lawyers, park managers, ecologists and others to "retrofit" the management of our parks in ecological terms.

The history of Yellowstone has been recounted many times.[42] The early days established the park itself, its infrastructure and the management of its natural resources. A "conservation period" followed, in which the effort focused upon the control of predators to "protect" a variety of park fauna and to lessen predation of livestock at the park's margins. It was not until the "Leopold Report" and the National Academy of Sciences report in 1963 that the entire park was viewed in ecosystemic terms and, in 1975, attention was first paid to the "greater Yellowstone" complex of forests, other national parks, and wildlife refuges.

The legal structure (or regime) of Yellowstone is a complex one, since the laws that apply are, in fact, a complex matrix of legislation including, but not limited to, the Yellowstone National Park Act,[43] the National Park Service Organic Act,[44] the General Authorities Act of 1970,[45] the Antiquities Act of 1906,[46] the Historic Sites, Buildings and Antiquities Act,[47] the Resources Protection Act of 1979,[48] the Land and Water Conservation Act of 1965,[49] National Environmental Policy Act of 1969,[50] The Clean Air Act,[51] the Clean Water Act,[52] the Endangered Species Act,[53] and the Wilderness Act of 1964.[54]

Many of the lawsuits about Yellowstone arise out of problems requiring an understanding of basic ecological processes. The culling of the elk herd on the basis of the limited carrying capacity of its range, coping with bison, their diseases and the impact of those diseases upon private herds, predator management of wolves and grizzly bears and their restoration and management as endangered species, management of goats and bighorn sheep, adoption of appropriate water policies, control of exotic species, regulation of bioprospecting, and management of the natural processes of fire are simply a few of the major tasks that have created much public controversy, litigation and scholarship.[55] These present conflicts arise in the context of the National Park Service's adoption of (or a defaulting to) a strong non-interventionist policy.

YELLOWSTONE PARK AND THE
GREATER YELLOWSTONE ECOSYSTEM

Yellowstone Park was designated a national park in 1872. The Park itself was placed under the management of the National Park Service in 1916. Yellowstone National Park lies at the heart of what is now recognized as the Greater Yellowstone Ecosystem (GYE), an area encompassing approximately 18 million acres in the northern Rocky Mountains. The life zones of the GYE range from the sagebrush-grass zone, through the montane (elevation 6,000-8,000 ft.), and the subalpine region (elevation 8,000-10,000 ft.), to the alpine region (elevation over 10,000 ft.).[56] There are three major river systems and watersheds in the GYE: the Snake, Yellowstone and Green. The biological diversity of the GYE can be attributed to the range of climates and habitat types in the region. The GYE is home to about 60 species of mammals, 303 bird species, 17 fish species, 10 species of reptiles and amphibians, 12,000 insect species (including 128 types of butterfly species), and 1,700 species of vascular plants.[57]

    Within the indefinite and flexible boundary of the GYE exist a number of political boundaries. The GYE includes the states of Wyoming, Montana and Idaho; Yellowstone and Grant Teton National Parks; seven National Forests managed by the U.S.D.A. Forest Service; three National Wildlife Refuges managed by U.S. Fish and Wildlife Service; and an Indian Reservation. The Bureau of Land Management owns or manages different areas throughout the GYE, and nearly a million acres of land are privately owned. In areas of such ecological and political diversity, management and protection of the ecosystem can be difficult due to the different interests at stake. Some issues currently associated with the GYE include encroaching development outside of the park and its affect on the recovery of the grizzly bear and on biodiversity in general, pollution caused by winter use of the park (e.g., snowmobiles), invasions of exotic species, wolf reintroduction, bison management, effects of elk population size, diseases such as brucellosis and whirling disease, fire, and bioprospecting.

In 1963, the "Leopold Report" recommended the maintenance of "biotic associations" to preserve or restore a natural biotic ecosystem. The report was buttressed by the National Academy of Sciences, which concluded that the national parks should be managed to perpetuate natural features and processes. Interior Secretary Stuart Udall instructed the Park Service to implement the reports and in 1968, the Park Service issued a policy document stating that the national parks should be managed as ecological entities, which would require application of ecological management techniques to neutralize the unnatural influence of man, thus permitting the natural environment to be maintained essentially by nature. The Park Service has reaffirmed this approach in its 1988 Management Policies document, stating that it would try to "maintain all the components and processes of naturally evolving park ecosystems including the natural abundance, diversity, and ecological integrity of the plants and animals" in accordance with the best science.[58] This approach has been ratified by the National Parks Omnibus Management Act of 1998, which mandated that the national parks use only the highest quality science from inventory, monitoring and research, to understand trends in the condition of park resources and to aid managers in making decisions.[59]

Without delving into the specific controversies that have animated park policy, what would an ecological approach to national park management be? Stephen Woodley has sought to outline such an approach which identifies five ecological goals: (1) maintain once viable populations of native species *in situ*, (2) representation of all native ecosystem types across their natural range of variation, (3) maintenance of evolutionary and ecological processes, (4) management over periods of time long enough for the evolutionary potential of species and ecosystems to be expressed, and (5) accommodation of human uses and occupancy within these constraints. Taking into account the greater ecosystem area and recognizing issues of uncertainty and value, Woodley sketches a detailed program for protected areas within the ecosystem, which among other things recommends the employment of ecological indicators of ecosystem structure, functions and stressors.[60]

The identification of indicators of ecosystem function and the stressors that alter the structure of ecosystems and the services they provide was also a major focus of the U.S. EPA during this same time, under the auspices of Environmental Monitoring and Assessment Program (EMAP). EMAP's goals were to develop new tools to monitor and assess the status and trends in national ecological resources, with an eye toward predicting future risks to the sustainability of our natural resources. EMAP was to provide an approach for building a national inventory of ecosystems and their dynamics. EMAP is currently relying on work by the President's Committee on the Environment and Natural Resources (CENR) and the National Park Service (NPA) to identify research sites for testing intensive, multi-media, long-term monitoring programs to gain the knowledge necessary for ecosystem management of National Parks and other federal lands.[61]

Despite a rich history of varying attention to the ecosystem and to the ecological processes that have taken place within and outside of the park, there remain a variety of serious problems specific to the management of national parks in general and Yellowstone in particular. Some of these problems are legal problems, created by the limited jurisdiction of the National Park Service over the greater Yellowstone area and the presence of private land holdings in and around the Park.[62]

Table 6.1 INDICATORS OF ECOLOGICAL INTEGRITY IN NATIONAL PARKS

ECOSYSTEM STRUCTURE	ECOSYSTEM FUNCTIONS	STRESSORS
Species richness: Changes in species diversity Number and extent of exotic species	Succession retrogression: Disturbance, frequencies and size (fire, insect, flooding) Vegetation age class distribution	Land-use patterns (human) Land-use maps, roads, building, development areas
Population Dynamics: Reproduction, mortality, emigration and immigration rates of indicator species Population viability of indicator species	Productivity: Remote sensing – large-scale Site specific monitoring program	Habitat fragmentation: Patch size, inter-patch distance, forest interior remaining
Trophic structure: Size and distribution of all taxa predation levels	Decomposition: Site specific monitoring program	Pollutants: Sewage, petrochemicals long range transport of toxics
	Nutrient retention: Sitespecific monitoring program for Ca, N	Other: Park specific issues

Source: A suite of ecological indicators chosen to assess ecological integrity by Parks Canada for their State of Parks Report [63]

One particularly important problem has been the difficulty of defining the appropriate ecosystem boundaries in Yellowstone. In recent years, there has been a vigorous attempt to expand the boundaries of Yellowstone to include, in various ways, the "Greater Yellowstone Ecosystem." Still underway, it probably represents the most systematic effort to define, both ecologically and legally, the boundaries of an ecosystem.[64] A second set of problems comes from the uncertainties arising out of any effort to apply ecology carefully to the management of a large and complex ecosystem. Uncertainties abound in estimating the carrying capacity of an area both for humans and fauna (e.g., elk), and in predicting the consequences of a non-intervention policy for fire management and the control of predators. A third set of problems arises from the philosophical issues that have arisen in determining the relationship of ecological management to preservation. The questions revolve around determining what level of nonintervention, i.e., "naturalness" the park should have in light of both its past evolution and the history of human interventions in its past life. To what extent is the park "natural" if there has been a long history of human intervention? In addition, the inevitable present interventions of park management, along with human activities outside the park, continue to affect the park and its ecosystem, creating an "end of (pristine) nature," a state where the alleged or idealized pristine nature of the park is stained by subtle, but real human activities. This last set of issues is not resolvable by an appeal to the science of ecology, but rather requires a careful exploration of the ethical implications of ecology in general and national park management in particular (i.e., to what extent are humans part of nature).

Perhaps unique to environmental law has been the amount of attention paid to the appropriate role of science in the management of Yellowstone in particular, and the national the parks in general. The history of the contributions of wildlife biology, ecology, conservation biology and island biogeography to the efforts to manage the parks is unique, as was the controversial non-intervention policy of the Park Service. It is perhaps to be expected that even Congress would get into the act and review the use of science in park management.[65]

Forest Management: From a Natural Resource to Biodiversity

Forests have a rich cultural history.[66] As Roderick Nash revealed in his definitive history, *Wilderness and the American Mind*, this history subtly affects how we regard the forest today.[67] This story of forests extends to ancient Rome and beyond and provides a primitivist standard of "the natural," contrasted with civilization. Robert Pogue Harrison in his *Forests: The Shadow of Civilization* finds the forests to be a curious contradiction, a lawless place and a haven for the unjustly treated, a place of profanity, yet sacred ground, a world of darkness and obscurity, yet a stage for revelation.[68] Whether one talks about the Greek myths, the Christian bible, the vision of Dante, the Knights' Adventure, Rousseau and Conrad, Wordsworth or the Brothers Grimm and Thoreau's *Walden*, the woods have entered our consciousness in one way or another. Not only literature, but a rich tradition of painting portrays the woods as fearsome or gentle, wild or civilized.[69]

When we turn to the history of this nation, the first human inhabitants of the forest were the Native Americans and they lay claim to these forests even today.[70] Their occupancy of the forest was relatively benign, perhaps in part because they viewed the trees and animals as animated by spirits, and fire was used with moderation.[71] In the early stages of colonial life, the forests were local resources contributing not only wood resources, but public welfare and education, recreation, and conservation. The stewardship of these resources is a little studied part of American history.[72]

Modern views of forests are less romantic, and include the forest as an economic machine (i.e., a source of natural resources); an ecosystem or a place of biodiversity; a wilderness for solitude and recreation. These visions of the forest still compete for the attention in our public culture. Thus, after the arrival of the first settlers, and for the next two centuries, our nation's forests became resources for wood, water, recreation and game.[73] At the end of a century of uncontrolled economic growth, the Forest Service Organic Administration Act of 1897 was passed limiting the purposes of our federal forests to "the protection of the forest," securing favorable water flows and furnishing a supply of lumber.[74] Later laws protected the fish stocks in forest rivers. For the most part, comparable state laws managed lumbering and fishing.[75] Thus, the primary focus of public policy on the forests for more than a century has been the "gospel of efficiency," according to which forests were protected for a long-term timber supply.[76]

Charles Wilkinson and H. Michael Anderson have described the history of forestry law in the United States:[77]

> ... the Forest Service has a long tradition of land and resource planning. Early plans focused on developing the timber resource and protecting rangelands. Recreation and wilderness planning became important elements in national forest management soon after World War I. As timber demand increased following World War II the Forest Service attempted to resolve multiple-use conflicts through a land zoning system. Following enactment of NEPA in 1969, planners sought better inventory data and public involvement. Finally, during the 1970s congress established elaborate national and local planning structures for the national forests. The NFMA and its implementing regulations required the Forest Service to follow a range of legal standards in developing local forest plans and to manage the national forests in accordance with the plans ...

Closely allied to the growth of forest management was the development of the "applied science" of silviculture (see below).

Despite Earth Day and the advent of an environmental consciousness, the Supreme Court reaffirmed the nineteenth century resource-oriented approach to national forest lands as late as 1978 in *U.S. v. New Mexico*.[78] In that case, the federal government was diverting some waters for wildlife use and retaining waters for instream uses of fish preservation in its Gila National Forest. The United States claimed that it was entitled to minimum instream flow for aesthetic, environmental, recreational and 'fish' purposes. The court held that under the Organic Act, forests were reserved for the economic use of water flows and timber supply. Although the court recognized the expanded purposes of the Multiple-Use-Sustained Yield Act of 1960,[79] it held these purposes did not apply to previously reserved forests.

SILVICULTURE AND POPULATIONS

Silviculture is the theory and practice of controlling forest establishment, competition, structure, and growth. The purpose of this field is primarily the production of trees, "silvies" deals with the growth and development of the single tree and the forest as a biological unit. Specific topics include site preparation, choice of species and genetic improvement, tree nutrition and soil fertility, seeding, production of planting stock, plantation tending and intermediate cutting, clearcutting, shelter woods methods, selection systems, and uneven aged management and vegetative regeneration.

Although silviculture draws upon ecological insights, it focuses upon the tree population and is primarily concerned with the way in which the ecosystem may affect the continuous production of trees.[80] Hence it may be regarded as based upon the field of population ecology; i.e., the study of the factors that effect the number of individuals of a particular population over time.

Although the Multiple Use and Sustained Yield Act (MUSYA) broadened the narrow economically-oriented purposes of forest management, the language of MUSYA continued to treat the forest as an aggregate of products and services requiring that a vague "due consideration" be given to the values of the various resources.[81] This aggregate approach to forest planning and management was fortified by a long tradition of breaking down the geography of the forests into smaller units for planning purposes.

It remained for the Wilderness Act, passed almost fifteen years earlier in 1964, to lay the basis for a more ecological approach to our nation's forests – not that wilderness presumes an explicit ecological understanding. Rather, the wilderness includes the lands "where the earth and its community of life are untrammeled by man, where man himself is a visitor who does not remain,"[82] leaving an allegedly pristine nature. The purpose of this law was to preserve federal wilderness land in its natural state for present and future generations to use, study and enjoy with "the imprint of man's work substantially unnoticeable," and where the land "retains its primeval character and influence."[83] Although the statute's definition of wilderness includes a reference to its "ecological features" of "scientific value," such a definition does not suggest a scientific ecological approach to nature, but rather a romantic primitivism. To be sure, at the end of his life Aldo Leopold appeared to believe in identity between wilderness and the paradigmatic ecosystem. Underlying a belief in such an identity might be the tacit assumption of some form of ecosystems climax in which the processes of nature are self-regulating. But such a belief is more an article of faith than the result of scientific inquiry.[84]

The tension between the assumptions of ecology and wilderness philosophy were well illustrated in *Sierra Club, et al., v. Lyng*, in which environmentalists sought to stop the Secretary of Agriculture from spot cutting the woods in wilderness areas of Arkansas, Louisiana and Mississippi in an effort to control infestations of the Southern Pine Beetle, which was affecting the surrounding private farm lands, and to protect the endangered red cockaded woodpecker.[85] The pesky pine beetles, as part of a working ecosystem, were challenging the basic assumptions of the Wilderness Act, a pristine and untouched wilderness to be safely set aside within an encompassing human economy which included nearby farms. Although the courts ultimately upheld the cutting program, after several suits the Forest Service limited the tree cutting to preserve the woodpecker habitat from beetle infestations.[86]

The Wilderness Act, with its recognition that federal agencies may have to control fire, insects and diseases within the wilderness, reveals the paradox of the requirement for human intervention into the wilderness in order to "preserve" the wilderness. In fact, the wilderness has not and cannot fully escape human influence. Similar problems arise when one seeks to think about the wilderness in ecosystem terms. The wilderness is often erroneously regarded as exemplifying a pristine ecosystem, but in fact, given the past and present human interactions affecting wilderness areas (not excluding air pollution), the wilderness is not pristine. Today it is more often defined by limited access and its remoteness. Moreover, the somewhat "accidental" selection of the borders of the wilderness often make it part of a larger ecosystem.[87]

Despite these bumps along the road, the Wilderness Act stimulated more careful attention to the workings of ecosystems and, perhaps more importantly, pried loose the American psyche from its customary utilitarian orientation when contemplating forest lands. The Wilderness Act and its administration were steps on the historical road to a broader vision of the values of our national forests.[88] The wilderness legislation and its full implication for ecological management is outside the scope of this book, but it deserves mention that those planning for wilderness areas, as well as their regulation and ensuing litigation, have struggled with ecological planning issues.[89]

The wilderness legislation represented a movement away from component populations of the forest to a more holistic perspective of nature. In 1976, after a century of numerous forest laws, congress adopted the National Forest Management Act.[90] This law amended the Forest and Rangeland Renewable Resources Planning Act, which had been designed to promote long-range planning for the renewable resources of the forest.[91] This planning was to use "a systematic interdisciplinary approach to achieve integrated consideration of physical, biological, economic and other sciences."[92]   The

National Forest Management Act supplied some of the content for such a planning approach. As part of the National Forest Management Act, "the regulations" were to provide for "diversity of plant and animal communities based upon the sustainability and capability of the specific land area."[93]

Bridge Document 6.2 THE FOREST MANAGEMENT PLAN

> This plan includes description of the forest and its problems, the human activities within it, the specific objectives and policies for the forest, and a series of regulations and specific projects for the forest as well as maps. The Green Mountain Land and Resource Management Plan for the Green Mountain National Forest describes the location of the Green Mountain forests and documents the demands for recreation lumber. It identifies the camping sites, downhill ski areas, windmill and electronic sites, the public access points and the relationship to state forest management areas. The problems identified include a concern over amount and types of timber management, the need for wildlife habitats primarily through vegetation management, the need to protect special areas to be preserved (bogs, ridges, ponds etc.), the designation of appropriate mineral extraction areas, and the management of grazing lands. A variety of research needs were identified: acid rain, regenerating oak, succession in old growth communities, the assessment of the genetic quality of tree species, and the impacts of development upon remote habitat. Many of these concerns bear upon promoting diversity. The plan then sets forth a series of regulations for wilderness, primitive, semi-primitive, roaded natural, highly developed and unclassified areas. The standards then apply to mineral exploration or extraction, road construction, ski lifts and trail construction, and timber sales, seeking to protect soil and waters, air quality, wildlife and fish, and visual sites. Detailed "management prescriptions and standards and guidelines" are set forth. Although the picture of an interdependent forest ecosystem does not emerge from this plan, references are made to ecological processes throughout the plan.[94]

The plan, and more specifically its prescriptions, follows a series of statutorily authorized federal regulations and the Forest Service Handbook. These regulations play a major role in litigation described below. They are the product of advocacy groups active in seeking conservation of biological diversity in national forests. This joinder between ecological insights and environmental legal regulation is well illustrated in the 1986 booklet, authored by both lawyers and ecologists, on "Conserving Biological Diversity in Our National Forests," issued by the Wilderness Society. This booklet set forth the arguments for the importance of biodiversity in the national forests, and argued that conclusions drawn from the ecological study of changes in ecosystems, the genetics of population and the results from island biogeography support the need for an ecosystem approach to planning within the national forests. That planning must take into account the detrimental consequences of habitat fragmentation for maintaining viable populations. Insufficient area and population sizes, ecological imbalances, and negative edge effects on population size suggest the need for appropriate ecological management. Such management, in addition to preventing harmful fragmentation, also manages harvest, regeneration and vegetation to secure diversity. The pamphlet identified the legal requirements for biodiversity and reviewed the elements for reviewing a forest plan to secure diversity. It then described how biological diversity can be obtained in specific large wildlands, i.e., the Greater Yellow-stone Ecosystem.

BACKGROUND THEORY OF DIVERSITY

Diversity and extinction have been constant concerns of ecology since Darwin and before. Darwin himself was deeply affected by the diversity of nature he observed on his trip aboard the H.M.S. Beagle. He also recognized the importance of extinction, not as a result of man's actions, but rather in the operation of natural selection itself. His work was followed by the work of the animal ecologist, Charles Elton, and population biologists, A.J. Lotka and V. Voltera. By the 1950s, Odum and his colleagues were seeking to demonstrate how species and populations fit within the functioning and evolution of the ecosystem. In the 1960s, E.O. Wilson and R.H. MacArthur advanced their theory of island biogeography, and in the early 1970s, MacArthur advanced his influential model of diversity.

Today, the standard approach to diversity begins by distinguishing among genetic variations within species, community types within regions, landscapes within larger areas, and the number and abundance of species, (including distribution of abundance, biomass, productivity and prevalence of species) within an area. Factors contributing to such diversity may be geographical, climactic variability, input of energy, productivity of the environment, evolutionary age, harshness of the environment, as well as the biological functioning of the ecosystem (predation, competition, spatial and architectural hetero-geneity, and successional status). In a simple model, species can be related to the range of resources, degree of species specialization, amount of overlap and the degree of saturation.

Threats to diversity may be viewed either as threats to an individual species (i.e., extinction), threats to the viability of the population, or threats to an entire ecosystem. These threats may be natural or manmade (or both), and if manmade, may be due to habitat loss, overexploitation, species modification, or predators. Threats to individual species may depend upon the geographical range and span of the habitat and the size of the population. In assessing the threat to populations, it may be necessary to assess a minimum viable population, look to models of population persistence, view simulation models based upon survivorship rates or perform decision tree analysis. To look at the impacts of species or community loss, it may be necessary to identify the role that the species plays within the ecosystem, with an awareness of chains of extinction, food web consequences, the functional integrity of habitats and ecological redundancy.

Scientists and society became enamored with the concept of biodiversity of the 1980s. The term "biodiversity" was offered by Walter Rosen in 1985 for the first planning meeting of the "National Forum on Biodiversity." At the 1986 National Forum, a group of scientists brought the "biodiversity crisis" to the attention of the global society.

EDWARD O. WILSON

Edward O. Wilson is the Frank B. Baird, Jr. Professor of Science and Curator in Entomology, Museum of Comparative Zoology, Harvard University. He is the author of the best-selling *Sociobiology* and two Pulitzer Prize-winning works, *On Human Nature*, and *The Ants*. More recently, he has published *The Diversity of Life* and *Consilience* and with Steven Kellert, edited *The Biophilia Hypothesis*.

With the public recognition of biodiversity, the field of conservation biology acquired a focus on the preservation of biodiversity.[95] Before the notion of biodiversity flowered, the NFMA required the Forest Service to promulgate regulations controlling how their management plans will affect plant and animal diversity.[96] One regulation[97] establishes the purpose of maintaining viable populations of existing species.[98] It also mandates the selection of management indicator species (MIS)[99] with both the *amount* and *quality* of habitat and of *animal population trends* of the management indicator species.[100] "*Population trends* of the management indicator species [are to] be *monitored* and relationships to habitat changes determined."[101] Further, the regulations provide, in part, that:

> Forest planning shall provide for diversity of plant and animal communities and tree species consistent with the overall multiple-use objectives of the planning area. Such diversity shall be considered throughout the planning process. Inventories shall include *quantitative data making possible the evaluation of diversity in terms of its prior and present condition.*[102]

While mandating a consideration of biodiversity, the NMFA and its regulations do not require the use of any specific scientific methodology. Agencies therefore have been given wide discretion to choose their own methods. Litigation concerning diversity will be described in the chapter below.

A Very Brief History of Conservation Biology[103]

The concept of a science of "conservation biology" is relatively old, dating back to at least the mid-1930s, and was first used to describe those aspects of basic (e.g., ecology, zoology and botany) and applied biology (e.g., forestry, fishery science, and range management) that were used in natural resource management.[104]

The modern discipline of conservation biology, while owing a debt to these earlier traditions, arose mainly from the awakening of ecologists in the 1960s and 1970s to the loss of natural habitats to human actions. Among the earliest attempts by ecologists to discuss how to use their science for the conservation of natural spaces and species were Raymond Dasmann's *Environmental Conservation*, and David Ehrenfield's *Biological Conservation*.[105] These books began the combination of traditional conservation science and ethics with the newer developments in population and evolutionary ecology that were being led by David Lack, G. Evelyn Hutchinson, and Robert MacArthur.[106] Conservation biology, as a scientific discipline distinct from ecology or resource science, did not arise until the late 1970s.[107] As a result of two factors,[108] the growing desire among many ecologists to use their science to solve environmental problems, particularly the loss of biodiversity, Robert MacArthur and E.O. Wilson promoted the theory of island biogeography in the 1960s and 1970s. Island biogeography, with its focus on the effect of habitat or refuge size on the number of species, would prove to be a powerful, if often controversial concept among both ecologists and conservation biologists and would be one of the first points of interaction between conservation biology and environmental law.[109] The formalization of conservation biology started in 1980 with the publication of Michael Soulé and Bruce Wilcox's book, *Conservation Biology: An Evolutionary-Ecological Perspective*, which argued that modern concepts in evolutionary biology and ecology (mostly population ecology) should be the building blocks of a new conservation science.[110]

The history of Conservation Biology since 1987 parallels that of the science of ecology: an increased integration of different disciplines into a broader science dealing not only with the conservation of single populations or species, but of communities, ecosystems, and landscapes.[111]

Pesticide Regulation: From Pesticide Residues to Bio-accumulation

The twentieth century opened with a new awareness of dangers to public health created by lead based pesticide residues on food. Initially these residues were to be controlled by better techniques of pesticide application as well as the screening of pesticides. In the second half of the century, beginning with Rachel Carson, a broader recognition of bio-accumulation of pesticides in the environment had emerged. This century-long history of pesticides and their control is a history of increasing recognition of the role that these chemicals play in disrupting the workings of ecosystems. The mechanism of bio-accumulation and more specifically, bio-magnification, rests upon a background and understanding of the ecological concepts of trophic levels, predator-prey relations, and food webs of ecosystems. More recently, the scientists have discovered subtle biological effects of pesticides and ecotoxins, including compounds that act as endocrine disruptors in both humans and animals, with possible negative effects on reproduction.[112] With the discovery of the increasing resistance of pests to pesticides, a search for more ecologically sophisticated ways of controlling plant and animal pests through ecosystem management and genetic manipulation is now underway.

As the pesticide industry has grown, so has the impact of their products throughout the world. A "circle of poison" exists in which the developed countries, in response to pesticide controls, "dump" their unwanted pesticides on other nations, only to have them be returned in the form of residues in imported foods and diffused throughout the global environment. Thus the domestic environmental law is rendered less effective, and the need for an international environmental legal regime increases.[113]

BARRY COMMONER

Aside from Rachel Carson, it was perhaps Barry Commoner who best captured the role of pesticides in the environment in his ecological classic, *The Closing Circle*. In this treatise, Barry Commoner sought to demonstrate how radioactivity, photochemical smog, nitrates, DDT and substances creating biological oxygen demands invaded the air, water, and earth of ecosystems, interfering with the process of natural cycling within nature. These pollutants, he argued, were the synthetic products of the reductive sciences such as chemistry and biology, which ignored the ecological connections in nature. These reductive sciences, he argued, were driven by the demand for economic growth and profits of the capitalist systems. *(Soon after Commoner wrote his book, others were to lay bare pollution in the communist and socialist economies of the world.)*

The ultimate irony of the "persistent pesticides" is that unlike many other pollutants, it is their very harmful qualities, i.e., health and environmental harms, which produce the benefits, i.e., the elimination of pests. The recognition of the subtle harms of pesticides in the environment forced the public to carefully weigh the control of unwelcome pesticide residue, the costs of banning the use of these poisons and the desirability of eradicating organisms causing economic or cosmetic damage to crops in the ecosystem.

Just after the turn of the twentieth century, public concern rose over the residues of lead and arsenic on food products. These residues posed a threat to the health of their applicators. In 1910, the first Pesticide Act was passed, which recognized the alleged benefits of pesticides with a consequent unwillingness to seriously interfere with their use. The Act focused upon food residues and potential harm to the applicator alone, placing weak controls administered by the Department of Agriculture, whose primary interest was food production and farm income. The first measurement of tolerance levels for exposure to pesticides was made in the 1930s, but the legal registration of pesticides was left until 1950 under the Federal Food, Drug and Cosmetic Act.

At mid-century, there was an explosive growth of new chemicals, partly the product of German and Japanese research, leading to 25,000 products registered by 1945. The 1947 Federal Insecticide, Fungicide, and Rodenticide Act (FIFRA) focused upon displaying labels for users of the pesticides. In 1954, the Food and Drug Administration was handed the task of registering pesticides if such pesticides resulted in the residues on the food that did not pose a danger to the public. The level of control was to be established to reflect the recognition of the need for an adequate, wholesome and economical food supply. In short, at mid-century, the flood of pesticides was met with a halfhearted and ambivalent effort at environmental control.

Change was on the way, however. In 1958, with worries about increasing rates of cancer running high, the Delaney Amendment was passed, providing that the Secretary of the Food and Drug Administration "... shall not approve for use in food any chemical additive found to induce cancer in man or, after tests, found to induce cancer in animals."[114] With the arrival of *Silent Spring* on the scene in the 1960s, the science and politics changed, and distrust of the U.S. Department of Agriculture grew. In 1970, EPA was established, and it took over the pesticide control responsibilities of the Department of Agriculture and the Health, Education and Welfare Departments. In 1972, two years after Earth Day, the Federal Environmental Pesticides Control Act was passed, turning over to the EPA the task of registering, canceling or re-registering pesticides by determining their "unreasonable effects on the environment." In the Spring of 1972, the EPA canceled the uses of DDT for crop production, basing its decision in part upon the detailed tracing of the pesticide through the environment and its bio-accumulation.[115] Despite this early attention to bio-accumulation, it played a limited role in the cancellation of other pesticides over the next two decades.

Although the FIFRA amendments of 1972 did not include bio-accumulation in their text, EPA did adopt regulations that established six separate risk criteria for determining pesticide risk to humans and the environment: (1) acute toxicity, (2) chronic or delayed acute toxicity including carcinogenic, mutagenic, fetotoxic and teratogenic potentials, (3) the potential for residues to induce toxic changes in non-toxic organisms, (4) the possible effects on threatened or endangered species, (5) the possible effects on the habitats of threatened or endangered species; and (6) whether the compound might pose other types of risk to humans or the environment. These risk criteria laid the basis for future attention to bio-accumulation.

The first major court decision involving pesticides was a DDT case argued shortly after Earth Day and decided by Judge Bazelon, famous for his environmental and other administrative law decisions of the 1960s and 1970s. In *Environmental Defense Fund, Inc. v. Ruckelshaus*,[116] Judge Bazelon required the Secretary of Agriculture to consider whether DDT should be suspended as an approved pesticide, and to formulate risk related criteria along with weighing the benefits of the pesticide for evaluating suspension decisions. In the course of this decision, Bazelon articulated his approach to health and environmental risks, i.e., measuring both the relative probability and the severity of harm.[117]

     In this early decision, Bazelon also appeared to endorse recognition of the delayed threats of pesticides and the acceptance that public health includes the "public" of fish and wildlife.[118] Although the DDT decisions were based upon tracking the persistent pesticide through the pathways of the environment, and hence relying upon an ecological understanding of the workings of that environment, not all pesticide decisions are based upon such ecological information. For example, in the 1979 case of *Dow Chemical v. Blum*,[119] the court upheld a suspension of 2,4,5-T and Silvex herbicides for forest clearance and other uses when the court found the application of such herbicides on forest areas to be correlated with spontaneous abortions for women living near such areas. Similarly, in cases of direct exposure to pesticide residues in food, ecological concepts are not needed to establish the determination of the seriousness, immediacy and probability of the threatened harm (although such knowledge may be relevant to determining the benefit of such pesticides).[120]

     In 1985, the Environmental Protection Agency amended its regulations to establish "Special Reviews" of pesticides to determine whether they posed an unreasonable adverse effect to humans and the environment.[121] The rules expanded the six risk criteria used to assess adverse effects. Part of this expansion included requirements for expanded exposure information on both targeted and non-targeted effects. Under the rules, the Agency may seek to trace the route of exposure by employing information about the "environmental fate," persistence and mobility, absorption, presence in the food chain, and presence in human tissue.[122] "Environmental fate" in the regulations referred, among other things, to the presence of widely distributed persistent pesticides in the environment. The regulations also provided for specific study of the accumulation of pesticides in ground water.

     The cancellation of diazinon by EPA in 1988 illustrates the special review process at work.[123] Marketed under several brand names, this pesticide was used on golf courses and sod farms. Despite the fact that the pesticide was found to be the most economical pesticide, its use was canceled based upon its acute toxicity, residue levels, exposure evidence, the estimated doses consumed by birds, the reported bird kills, and the effects upon endangered species. As part of an assessment of the costs of the pesticide, the agency traced its route of exposure through the feeding habits of the birds and the route of diazanon through seeds, invertebrates, and drinking water, which were food sources. This exposure route became part of a risk assessment model accepted by the agency.[124] The agency also estimated that bird kill data meant that the pesticide posed an ultimate risk, not only to individual birds, but to the bird population.

     The special review of pesticides must be examined against the background of EPA's struggle to cope with the avalanche of pesticides, both new and old. FIFRA required re-registration of a large number of pesticides.[125] The problem of registration of new pesticides and re-registration of old pesticides was created in part by the sheer number of pesticides and the complex task of evaluating their impacts.[126] This problem precluded the adoption of complex studies of bio-accumulation as part of the pesticide evaluation process. Instead, a sophisticated ecological approach to pesticides began to emerge under the aegis of other laws and programs. At the same time, the special process that, in the 1980s began to review the impact of pesticides on the environment, was the beginning of a new concern for bio-accumulation of pesticides.[127]

Bridge Document 6.3 A PESTICIDE SPECIAL REVIEW

Before initiating special review, EPA must notify the applicant of its intentions and give the applicant at least 30 days to respond. EPA then reassesses its preliminary decision after analyzing the comments. If after reviewing the comments EPA concludes that special review is not needed, a proposed decision not to undertake special review must be published in the *Federal Register* and 30 days given for any interested party to respond. EPA's final decision whether to proceed with special review must be published in the *Federal Register* along with a statement of the reasons. EPA establishes a public docket for the review and invites comments from any interested party. Any party may provide information or argument pertinent to whether the product satisfies any of the risk criteria. Moreover, persons wishing to comment may submit relevant information to aid in the determination of whether the economic, social and economic benefits of the pesticide outweigh the risks of use. After reviewing the comments received and other relevant material obtained during the special review process, EPA makes a decision on the future status of registration of the pesticide.

The special review process may be concluded in various ways depending on the outcome of EPA's risk/benefit assessment. If EPA concludes that all of its risk concerns have been adequately rebutted, the application for registration will be granted. If all risk concerns are not rebutted, EPA proceeds with a full risk/benefit assessment. In determining whether the use of a pesticide poses risks that are greater than its benefits, EPA considers possible terms and conditions of registration that can reduce risks and the impacts of such modifications on the benefits of use. If EPA determines that appropriate restrictions will reduce risks to the level where the benefits outweigh the risks, it will condition registration and may require that such changes be made in the terms and conditions of the registration. Alternatively, EPA may determine that restrictions cannot adequately assure that the use of the pesticide will not pose any unreasonably adverse effects. In that case, EPA publishes a "notice of intent to deny" the registration.

Source: K. Jack Hagru, in Celia Campbell-Mohn, et al., *Environmental Law: From Resources to Recovery* (1993)

Since the late 1960s there has been growing concern about pesticides in water. Transport of chlorinated compounds was found in public water supplies, estuaries, surface waters, groundwater, and even rainwater was documented in the 1960s through the 1980s.[128] Although the Safe Drinking Water Act applied to the protection of drinking water supplies affected by pesticides and other pollutants, it was the Clean Water Act which specifically addressed the problem of bio-accumulation. Under the Clean Water Act, in the late 1980s, the Environmental Protection Agency developed a bio-accumulation guidance document.[129] This document, relying upon log-P data, proposed the identification of bio-concentratable and bio-accumulative compounds present in effluents, non-point source runoff, receiving waters, bedded sediments, dredged materials, and tissues of aquatic organisms as part of the water quality permitting process in states.[130] During the 1970s and 1980s, the administration of broad spectrum pesticides led to the discovery that pests were developing resistance to pesticides, as well as an increased awareness of the health impacts of pesticides. One of the major results of these developments was the discontinuance of major broad spectrum pesticides. Integrated Pest Management originated as a consequence of these developments.

INTEGRATED PEST MANAGEMENT

Integrated pest management (IPM) was intended to put pesticide use on a more sound ecological footing. The term *integrated control* was introduced and defined it as "applied pest control which combines and integrates biological and chemical control. Chemical control is used as necessary and in a manner which is least disruptive to biological control." The founding principles of IPM are that natural processes can be manipulated to increase their effectiveness, and chemical controls should be used only when and where natural processes of control fail to keep pests below economic-injury levels.

Source: Marcos Kagan, *Ecological Theory and Integrated Pest Management Practice* (1986)

Integrated Pest Management (IPM), however, was simply part of a larger range of efforts to control pests through biological controls. These controls included biological controls, as well as augmentation or preservation of natural enemies.[131]

These controls, in turn, were the product of, and stimulated the development of, ecological theory. That theory sought to apply a host of specific ecological theories, including island biographical and population theories, insect/plant interaction and host/plant resistance, plant/herbivore/parasite interactions and plant/plant pathogen/insect interactions.[132] Perhaps the final step in the development of an ecologically sound way to conduct agricultural activities requires rethinking the entire agricultural enterprise. Such a rethinking is underway with writings on "biodynamic," "integrated," "low input," "organic," "permaculture," "regenerative," and "sustainable" farming.[133]

Conclusion

The brief stories of the "ecologization" of the Endangered Species Act, the National Forest Management Act, national park planning, and the pesticide legislation reveals a twenty-year courtship between ecology and law, in which ecological concepts are gradually introduced in the language and administration of these laws. To change metaphors, these laws are being gradually retrofitted with ecological knowledge. Whether courtship or retrofit, the pattern is one in which the laws are already established, environmental advocacy groups push for the introduction of ecological concerns in the administration of these laws and their amendments. As a consequence, new laws and regulations may be adopted in which ecological language is inserted, or new ecologically sensitive administration of the laws takes place. In some situations, completely new programs such as the new approaches in handling pests within agriculture are suggested. And sometimes the very purpose of the law itself begins to shift as in the shift, from concern about endangered species to biodiversity.

It is difficult to determine why ecology's courtship with these laws has been more successful than her similar courtship with the clean air and clean water acts and toxics legislation. Perhaps these "older laws" were more established, or their administrators more intent upon securing immediate enforcement of their narrow media-oriented objectives. Perhaps the advocates in the fields of forestry, endangered species and pesticides are more open to ecological information and more willing to advocate its use. Probably a more careful inquiry is needed to determine the many factors that may contribute to the adoption of ecology within an existing law.

Another inquiry that is left unanswered in our brief history is whether this pattern of joining ecology and law makes sense. In other fields, retrofits often don't work, because originals are not well adapted to the retrofit. On the other hand, perhaps slow and the gradual introduction of applied ecological concepts makes good sense, because these concepts, even if established within the science of ecology, may not be tested in their application as tools of law and policy. Again, a more in-depth analysis of this history is needed to evaluate how effectively these concepts are employed.

Notes

1.   *See* S. Spurr, Forest Ecology 155 (1964). *See also* Gosz, Holmes, Likens & Bormann, *The Flow of Energy in a Forest Ecosystem*, 238 Scientific American No. 3, 92-102 (1978).

2.   U.S. v. Mexico, 438 U.S. 696 (1978).

3.   This assertion may seem questionable when applied to the Endangered Species Act, which did mention the ecosystem. Nevertheless, species were initially not perceived as part of ecosystems, but rather as freestanding "Bambis" to be preserved from "taking" in the sense of hunting, capture, and harassment. As we shall see, it was only over time that habitat became important and modification of habitat became a principal concern of the Act.

4.   This chapter will concentrate only upon four such areas of legislation: endangered species, national forests, national parks, and pesticides. Yet other laws relating to resource conservation, e.g., fishery management; and other preservation law, e.g., Wildlife Refuge and Wilderness legislation, follow similar patterns of development over the past two decades. *See, e.g.*, Ecosystem Management for Parks and Wilderness (James K. Agee & Daryll R. Johnson eds.,1988); *see* R.J. Fink, *The Theory, Practice and Prospect*, 18 Harv. Envtl. L. Rev. 1 (1994) for an account of conservation biology and its implications for refuge planning.

5.   *See* Michael E. Soule, *What is Conservation Biology?* 35 Bioscience 727 (1985).

6.   The courtship of environmental law and ecology over the past two decades is part of a larger historical transformation. This transformation is illustrated in the history of pesticides, which are part of a rapidly transforming, highly technocentric agricultural sector, both in the United States and increasingly abroad. The use of pesticides is a part of this transformation of the agricultural sector. For one account of this history, *see* John H. Perkins & Nordica C. Holochuck, *Pesticides: Historical Changes Demand Ethical Choices*, 390-417. The Pesticide Question: Environment, Economics and Ethics (David Pimental & Hugh Lehman, eds.,1993). Similar patterns of change may be found in the forestry and fishery industries. Recognition of these technological changes as part of a broader historical process of our public culture may help to put in perspective the more specific changes in law and ecology, which we will discuss here.

7.   *See* 16 U.S.C. 1531 et seq. (1973).

8.   *See* 16 U.S. C. 1533(b)(2).

9.   *See* 16 U.S.C. 1536(a)(2).

10.   *See* 16 U.S.C. 1533(f).

11.   This account is taken from the author's previously published discussion; *see* Richard Brooks & Thomas Hoban, Green Justice (1996).

12.   Throughout all of this, TVA viewed the discovery of the snail darter as an inconvenience or an annoyance that had to be dealt with but certainly not as a serious threat to the dam. The authority's initial reaction, naturally enough, was to try to prove that the snail darter was not an endangered species. When turning up other populations failed, it attempted a transplanting operation, but in the short time available for study, no real conclusions could be drawn about the likelihood of the darters' success in new streams.

        In hearings before both the House and Senate at which it requested continued funding for the Tellico project, TVA argued that the Tellico Dam project had simply gone too far toward completion to be stopped at this late date. Congress either agreed with TVA or was hoping the matter would somehow just go away – funding for the Tellico project was included in the Public Works for Water and Power

Development and Energy Appropriation Act of 1976, despite the language of the Endangered Species Act. The battle lines had been drawn.

13.   An injunction is a legal order that commands a person to stop immediately what he or she is doing.

14.   Both the appeals court and Supreme Court opinions assumed that if Congress wished to correct the snail darter-Tellico Dam problem, it could. Senator Howard Baker of Tennessee succeeded in exempting the Tellico Dam from the provisions of the Endangered Species Act, and on September 25, 1978, President Carter, "with regret," signed the legislation that approved the completion of the dam. One more attempt to block the project was undertaken by Cherokee Indians, who claimed that because the reservoir would flood ancient burial grounds, its completion would infringe upon their constitutional guarantees of freedom of religion and would violate a 1978 statute recognizing their right of access to sacred places. To no avail. Their suit was dismissed on November 2, 1978. Justice Potter Stewart denied an emergency injunction on November 9, the last residents were evicted on November 14, and the dam was closed on November 30, 1978.

15.   "Habitat" was an important concept in such early legislation as the Migratory Bird Treaty Act, 16 U.S.C. §703; however, habitat modification was not a "taking" under the law. Seattle Audubon Society v. Evans, 952 F2d 297 (9th Cir. 1991).

16.   *See* 51 Fed. Reg. 19926 (1986). These were followed up in 57 Fed. Reg. 1822 (1992). *See* also 59 Fed. Reg. 34271 (July 1, 1994).

17.   *See* Endangered Species Act §3, 16 USCA §1532 (1973).

18.   *See* Endangered Species Act.

19.   PAUL EHRLICH ET AL., BIRDS IN JEOPARDY: THE IMPERILED AND EXTINCT BIRDS OF THE UNITED STATES AND CANADA 63-78 (1992).

20.   See EHRLICH, ET AL., *supra* at 78.

21.   The legal battle for the Palila began in 1979 when numerous nonprofit organizations [Sierra Club (SC), National Audubon Society, Hawaiian Audubon Society (HAS) along with Alan C. Ziegler (a member of the SC and HAS, and head of Division of Vertebrate Zoology at Bishops Museum in Honolulu)] brought suit against the State of Hawaii in name of the Palila,. They were seeking declaratory and injunctive relief against the state Department of Land and Natural Resources for violating the ESA by maintaining a population of feral sheep and goats within the Palila's "critical habitat." [*See* Palila v. Hawaii Department of Land and Natural Resources, 471 F.Supp. 985 (HI, 1979) ("Palila I").] The ESA defines "critical habitat" as the "specific areas within a geographical area occupied by the species, at the time it is listed … on which are found those physical or biological features that are essential to the conservation of the species and which may require special management considerations or protection." [*See* Endangered Species Act §3, 16 USCA §1532 (1973).] To ecologists, "habitat" refers to the physical and social environment used by an individual, or a population, or a species or group of species. Unlike ecosystems, the term implies a relationship between the individual (or species …) and the place it inhabits. Habitat is a place concept unlike "niche" which refers to the organism's role in the environment. The habitat may include both the abiotic environment and other organisms. Types of habitats are loosely referred to as freshwater, marine, terrestrial, estuarine.

22.   *See* Endangered Species Act §9, 16 USCA §1538 (1973).

23.   *See* Palila v. Hawaii Department of Land and Natural Resources, 639 F.2d 495 (HI 1981) (Palila II). After the decisions in Palila I and II, the Secretary of Interior received continuous pressure to redefine "harm." In 1981, the ESA definition of "harm" was amended to include "significant habitat modification or degradation where it actually kills or injures wildlife by significantly impairing essential behavioral

patterns, including breeding, feeding or sheltering." [50 CFR §17.3.] The difference was a focus on habitat modification resulting in both potential and actual harm rather than solely on actual harm in the previous definition. "The finding of harm does not require death to individual members of the species, nor does it require a finding that habitat degradation is presently driving the species further toward extinction ... Habitat destruction that prevents the recovery of the species by affecting essential behavioral patterns causes actual injury to the species and effects a taking under §9 of the ESA." [Palila v. Hawaii Board of Land and Natural Resources, 649 F. Supp. 1070, 1075 (HI, 1986).]

24.   *See* §9(a)(1)(B).
25.   *See* Palila, 649 F. Supp. 1070 (HI, 1986).
26.   *See* Palila, 649 F. Supp. 1070 (HI, 1986).
27.   The court cited Tennessee Valley Authority v. Hill in stating that it was the intent of Congress to afford endangered species "the highest of priorities" and to avoid further habitat destruction. TVA v. Hill, 98 S.Ct. 2279, 57 (1978).
28.   *See* Palila v. Hawaii Department of Land and Natural Resources, 852 F.2d 1106 (1988) (Palila IV).
29.   *See* Endangered Species Act §3, 16 USCA §1532 (1973).
30.   The *Palila* case illustrates at one level the gradual process by which the important legal concept of habitat is defined. In *Palila*, habitat was defined as the place in which essential behavioral patterns of the species take place. These essential behaviors include breeding, feeding and sheltering. It remains for the Fish and Wildlife Service to spell out how such a habitat is to be described in detail. A key document for doing so, bringing ecology and law together, is the "biological opinion" under the Endangered Species Act. This document and its adequacy has been controversial and the subject of much litigation. Although the notion of species itself is much debated in biology, litigation regarding this issue has been limited. The Endangered Species Act as originally passed and then amended in 1978 adopted a broad view of species to include not only species, but subspecies and distinct populations. [*See* 16 U.S.C. §1532(16). In 1978, protection of populations was limited to vertebrate animals. By including subspecies and distinct populations, the law succeeds in legally avoiding some – if not all – of the issues arising from the failure of biological consensus about species.] Similarly, the legal dispute over endangerment of extinction has been limited, since endangerment includes "any species which is in danger of extinction throughout all or a significant portion of its range." [*See* 16 U.S.C.§ 1532(6). See R.R. Lackenmeier, *The Endangered Species Act of 1973: Preservation or Pandemonium*, 5 ENVTL L. 29 (1974).]
31.   *See* 16 U.S.C.§ 1536(a)(2).
32.   *See* 16 U.S.C. § 1536(c).
33.   *See* 16 U.S.C. § 1536(a)(2).
34.   *See* 16 U.S.C. § 1536(b)(3)(A).
35.   *See* 50 C.F.R. 402.12, 402.14; 51 FR 19957 (June 3, 1986); 54 FR 40350 (Sept. 29, 1989); 59 FR 166 34271-34275 (July 1, 1994).
36.   *See* U.S. Fish and Wildlife Service, National Marine Fisheries Service, Endangered Species Consultation Handbook, Procedures for Conducting Section 7 Consultations and Conferences (1998). F49.6/2:EN/2/4.
37.   *See id.* at Chapter 4-1 through 4-65.
38.   *See* CONSULTATION HANDBOOK 4-15 to 4-18. This approach reflects 50 CFR 424.02(d). The Handbook extends coverage to unoccupied habitat "when such areas are essential to the conservation (recovery) of listed species." (Handbook 4-33.)
39.   *See* CONSULTATION HANDBOOK 4-39.

40.   *See* CONSULTATION HANDBOOK, 4-39. Actual habitats are described in 50 CFR §17.94, 17.95, 17.96 et seq.

41.   For an excellent history of the relationship of the use of ecology and related sciences in the history of the national parks, *see* RICHARD WEST SELLARS, PRESERVING NATURE IN THE NATIONAL PARKS: A HISTORY (1997). For a discussion of the relationship of preservation to diversity and science, *see* JOHN PASSMORE, MAN'S RESPONSIBILITY FOR NATURE: ECOLOGICAL PROBLEMS AND WESTERN TRADITIONS (1974).

42.   In addition to Sellars, *supra* note 41, there are specific descriptions of the application of science in Yellowstone; *see* JAMES A. PRITCHARD, PRESERVING YELLOWSTONE'S NATURAL CONDITIONS: SCIENCE AND THE PERCEPTION OF NATURE (199).

43.   *See* 16 U.S.C. 21, et seq. (1988), March 1, 1872, ch. 24, 17 Stat. 32.

44.   *See* 16 U.S.C. 1, et seq. (1988), Aug. 25, 916, ch. 408, 39 Stat. 535.

45.   *See* 16 U.S.C. 1a-1-1a-8 (1988), 84 Stat. 825, Pub.L.91-383.

46.   *See* 16 U.S.C. 431-433 (1988), June 8, 1904, ch. 3060, 34 Stat. 225.

47.   *See* 16 U.S.C. 461, et seq. (1988), Aug. 21, 1935, ch. 593, 49 Stat. 666.

48.   *See* 16 U.S.C. 470aa (1988), 93 Stat. 721, Pub. L. 96-95.

49.   *See* 16 U.S.C. 4901-4, et seq. (1988); 78 Stat. 897, Pub. L 88-578.

50.   *See* 42 U.S.C. 4321, et seq. (1988), 83 Stat. 852, Pub. L. 91-190.

51.   *See* 42 U.S.C. 7401-7671q (as amended in 1990), 91 Stat. 685, Pub. L. 101-549.

52.   *See* 33 U.S.C. 1251-1376 (1988), June 30, 1948, ch. 758, 62 Stat. 1155.

53.   *See* 16 U.S.C. 1531, et seq. (1988), 87 Stat. 884, Pub. L. 93-205.

54.   *See* 16 U.S.C. 1131, et seq. (1988), 78 Stat. 890, Pub. L. 88-577.

55.   For a brief overview of these issues, *see* Robert B. Keiter, *Preserving Nature in the National Parks: Law: Policy and Science in a Dynamic Environment* in 74 DENV. U. L. REV. 649 (1997). There is copious literature on these issues. For one of many collections of discussions, *see* THE GREATER YELLOWSTONE ECOSYSTEM: REDEFINING AMERICA'S WILDERNESS HERITAGE (Robert B. Keiter & Mark S. Boyce eds., 1991).

        The difficulties of managing the Yellowstone are well illustrated in *Greater Yellowstone Coalition v. Babbitt.* [*See* 952 F. Supp. 1435 (1996).] The National Park Service adopted an interim management plan for bison infected with brucellosis. This plan proposed culling the herd (after years of progressive non-intervention in its growth and mobility). The plaintiffs claimed violation of the National Park Service Organic Act and the Yellowstone Act. The court upheld broad discretion of the Park Service to adopt such a plan under statutory language, which stated that the purpose of parks was "to conserve the scenery and the natural and historic objects and wildlife therein and to provide for their enjoyment and leave them unimpaired for future generations." [*See id.*] The court found the culling acceptable, in light of the neighborhood government's legal authority to shoot members of the herd if they crossed the boundary line.

56.   *See* Dr. Harry Corwin, Lecture at Yellowstone Field Course (7/97).

57.   NATIONAL PARK SERVICE, YELLOWSTONE RESOURCES AND ISSUES HANDBOOK (2000).

58.   *See* National Park Service, U.S. Dept of Interior, Management Policies (1988).

59.   *See* Nat. Parks Omnibus Management Act, 16 U.S.C.1a-5 (2001).

60.   *See* Stephen Woodley, *Science and Protected Areas Management: An Ecosystem Based Perspective* in NATIONAL PARKS AND PROTECTED AREAS, KEYSTONE TO CONSERVATION AND SUSTAINABLE DEVELOPMENT (James Nelson & Rafel Serafin, eds., 1997).

61.   *See* M.E. McDonald, *EMAP overview: Objectives, approaches, and achievements*, 64 *Environmental Monitoring and Assessment* 3-8 (2000).

62.   Robert B. Keiter is one of the few law scholars who has systematically studied the relationship between law and ecology. Professor of Law and Director of the Wallace Stegner Center for Land, Resources and the Environment at the University of Utah, PROFESSOR KEITER has completed groundbreaking studies of the greater Yellowstone ecosystem and co-edited a book entitled THE GREATER YELLOWSTONE ECOSYSTEM (1998). More recently he has edited *Reclaiming the Native Home of Hope: Community, Ecology and the American West* (1998), which seeks to explore the relations of a sense of place with modern ecology.

63.   Parks Canada, State of Parks Report (1997).

64.   *See* Duncan T. Patten, *Defining the Greater Yellowstone Ecosystem*, 19-27 in Keiter & Boyce, *supra* note 55.

65.   *See* Subcommittee on National Parks and Public Land of the House Committee on Resources, 105ᵗʰ Congress. SCIENCE AND RESOURCES MANAGEMENT IN THE NATIONAL PARK SERVICE (1997).

66.   *"This was the order of human institutions: first the forests, after that the huts, then the villages, next the cities, and finally the academies"* ~ GIAMBATTTISTA VICO, THE NEW SCIENCE 36 (Thomas Bergin & Max Fisch trans., 3d ed. 1970).

67.   *See* RODERICK NASH, WILDERNESS AND THE AMERICAN MIND (1967).

68.   *See* ROBERT POGUE HARRISON, FORESTS: THE SHADOW OF CIVILIZATION (1992). *See* J. MANWOOD, A TREATISE AND DISCOURSE OF THE LAWS OF THE FOREST 6 (1598).

69.   *See* SIMON SCHAMA, LANDSCAPE AND MEMORY (1995).

70.   *See* Hilda Robtoy, et al., *The Abenaki and the Northern Forest*, CHRISTOPHER MCGRORY KLYZA & STEPHEN C. TROMBULAK, THE FUTURE OF THE NORTHERN FOREST 11-27 (1994).

71.   *See* SHEPARD KRECH III, THE ECOLOGICAL INDIAN (1999).

72.   *See* ROBERT MCCOLLOUGH, THE LANDSCAPE OF COMMUNITY: A HISTORY OF COMMUNAL FORESTS IN NEW ENGLAND (1995).

73.   The first forest laws were state and local laws. For one account, *see* RICHARD BROOKS, ET AL., TOWARD COMMUNITY SUSTAINABILITY, Vol. II, Chapter 3, pp. 20-28 (1997).

74.   *See* 16 U.S.C. 475.

75.   For a discussion of federal and tribal regulation of wildlife, *see* MICHAEL BEAN & MELANIE ROWLAND, THE EVOLUTION OF NATIONAL WILDLIFE LAW (1997) pp. 7-107, 449-515.

76.   *See* SAMUEL HAYS, CONSERVATION AND THE GOSPEL OF EFFICIENCY 27-48 (1959).

77.   *See* CHARLES WILKINSON & H. MICHAEL ANDERSON, LAND AND RESOURCE PLANNING IN THE NATIONAL FORESTS 45 (1987).

78.   *See* 438 U.S. 696 (1978).

79.   *See id.* at 713.

80.   *See* DAVID SMITH, THE PRACTICE OF SILVICULTURE (1986).

81.   *See* 16 U.S.C. §529. Later cases under MUSYA did not demonstrate serious consideration of "other values."

82.   *See* 16 U.S.C. §1131(c).

83.   *See* 16 U.S.C. §1131(c)(1982); 16 U.S.C. §1131(a) (1982).

84.   Wilderness may be a symbol for a nature independent of human affect. If so, it is a misleading symbol, since all of earth's nature is now influenced by human action. *See* BILL MCKIBBEN, THE END OF NATURE (1989). The ideas of wilderness have been artfully tracked by RODERICK NASH, Wilderness and the American Mind (1982) and MAX OELSCHLAEGER, THE IDEA OF WILDERNESS (1991). Both conclude that the ideal of wilderness is shaped by our cultural and intellectual history. Oelschlaeger sees our current views of wilderness as shaped by the somewhat different premises of preservationism, ecocentrism, and deep ecology. Nash has more recently viewed

wilderness in the context of the expansion of mankind's vision of rights in THE RIGHTS OF NATURE (1989).

85. *See* Sierra Club v. Block, 614 F. Supp. 488 (D.D.C.1985); Sierra Club v. Block, 614 F. Supp. 134 (ED Texas, 1985); Sierra Club v. Lyng, 662 F. Supp. 40 (1987); 663 F. Supp. 560; 694 F. Supp. 1260 (Ed. Texas, 1988).

86. For a fuller account, *see* MICHAEL BEAN &MELANIE RAWLAND, THE EVOLUTION OF WILDLIFE LAW 323-7 (1997). For an analysis, *see* Daniel Rohlf & Douglas Honnold, *Managing the Balances of Nature: The Legal Framework of Wilderness Management*, 15 ECOLOGY L.Q. 249 (1988).

87. For an excellent discussion of these issues, *see* Daniel Rohlf & Douglas L Honnold, *Managing the Balances of Nature: The Legal Framework of Wilderness Management*, 15 ECOLOGY L.Q. 249 (1988).

88. The tradition of a broader vision of forests is recounted in ROBERT POGUE HARRISON, FORESTS: THE SHADOW OF CIVILIZATION (1992). *See also*, DAVID DOBBS & RICHARD OBER, THE NORTHERN FOREST (1995).

89. For an excellent text on wilderness planning, *see* WILDERNESS MANAGEMENT (John C. Hendee et al., eds., 1990). For details, *see* THE GREAT NEW WILDERNESS DEBATE (J. Baird Callicott & Michael P. Nelson eds., 1998). For example, the U.S. Forest Service regulations describe the objectives of the wilderness to include "(a) natural ecological succession will be allowed to operate as freely as the extent possible ..." 36 CFR 293.2(a). For a discussion of several court cases, *see* Daniel Rohef & Douglas Hamold, *Managing the Balances of Nature: The Legal Framework of Wilderness Management*, 15 ECOLOGY L.Q. 249 (1988).

90. *See* 16 U.S.C. §1601-1614.

91. *See* Pub. L. No. 93-378, 88 Stat. 476 (1974).

92. *See* 16 §1604(b).

93. *See* 16 §1604(9)(3)(B).

94. *See* NATIONAL FOREST SERVICE: LAND AND RESOURCE MANAGEMENT PLAN: GREEN MOUNTAIN NATIONAL FOREST (1986).

95. *See* Babbit, 839 F.Supp. at 752. For a history of the idea of biodiversity, *see* DAVID TAKOES, THE IDEA OF BIODIVERSITY: PHILOSOPHIES OF PARADISE (1996).

96. *See* NFMA §§ 1601-1614. *See also* Seattle Audubon Society v. Evans, 952 F.2d 297 (1991) (holding that Forest Service was required to account for diversity in its management plan).

97. *See* 36 C.F.R. § 219.19.

98. *See* 36 C.F.R. § 219.19 (1991).

99. *See id.*

100. *See* 36 C.F.R. § 219.19(a)(2) (emphasis added).

101. *See* 36 C.F.R. § 219.19(a)(6)(emphasis added).

102. *See* 36 C.F.R. §219.26 (emphasis added).

103. Much of the material for our history of conservation biology comes from the section A Brief History of Conservation Biology in Gary K. Meffe & C. Ronald Carroll, *What is Conservation Biology? in* GARY K. MEFFE, ET AL., PRINCIPLES OF CONSERVATION BIOLOGY 3, 7–16 (2d ed. 1997). Other histories of conservation biology that we used are found in Daniel Simberloff, *The Contribution of Population and Community Biology to Conservation Science*, 19 ANN. REV. ECOL. SYST. 473-511 (1988) and Peter F. Brussard, *The Current Status of Conservation Biology,* 66 Bull. Ecol. Soc. Amer. 9-11 (1985).

104. *See* P.L. Errington and F.N. Hamerstrom, Jr., *The evaluation of nesting losses and juvenile mortality of the ring-neck pheasant.* 1 J. WILDL. MGMT. 3-20 (1937). ("In the new field of conservation biology ...") *See id.* This conservation science is not the

same as the conservation ethics that was developed in the mid-eighteenth Century by, among others, Henry David Thoreau and George Perkins Marsh. [*See* Hal Salwasser, *Conservation Biology and the Management of Natural Resources*, in PRINCIPLES OF CONSERVATION BIOLOGY, *supra* note 103, at 9-10.] We will discuss the ethical foundations of the conservation movement in general, and conservation biology specifically, in a later chapter. *See infra* Chapter 10. For now, it is sufficient to point to Meffe and Carrolls' treatment of the ethical underpinning of the conservation movement in which they trace the American conservation movement to three philosophical movements: 1) the Romantic-Transcendental Conservation Ethic personified by Thoreau, Muir, and Ralph Waldo Emerson and their "quasi-religious" description of nature, 2) the Resource Conservation Ethic championed by Gifford Pinchot (the first director of the U.S. Forest Service) and based on the utilitarian philosophy of John Stuart Mill. For this school it was the usefulness of nature to human that was most important, and 3) the Evolutionary-Ecological Land Ethic, developed by Aldo Leopold in *A Sand County Almanac. See* Meffe & Carroll *supra* note 103, at 11-12. It is an updated version of the Evolutionary-Ecological Land Ethic that is the philosophical basis of modern Conservation Biology. Conservation ethics, as we will describe in later chapters, transcends science and mostly involves the question of why humans should care and protect the natural world, not with the methods of protecting the natural world.

105.   *See* R.F. DASMANN, ENVIRONMENTAL CONSERVATION (1959); D.W. EHRENFELD, BIOLOGICAL CONSERVATION (1970).

106.   *See supra* Chapters 2 and 3 for history of the population/evolutionary ecology. While the Conservation Biology of the 1990s and today attempts to integrate all sub-disciplines of ecology, earlier versions of Conservation Biology were focused on the protection of individual populations and, therefore, mainly used concepts and methods of population and evolutionary ecology. *See generally* MICHAEL E. SOULÉ & BRUCE A. WILCOX, CONSERVATION BIOLOGY: AN EVOLUTIONARY-ECOLOGICAL APPROACH (1980); CONSERVATION BIOLOGY: THE SCIENCE OF SCARCITY AND DIVERSITY (Michael E. Soulé ed., 1986) for conservation biology's initial focus on population and evolutionary ecology. *See also* O.H. FRANKEL & M.E. SOULÉ, CONSERVATION AND EVOLUTION (1981) for an early description of the importance of population genetics and evolutionary theory in conservation. *See generally* MEFFE & CARROLL, *supra* note 1 for the current integration of ecosystem, community, and population ecology into a modern conservation biology.

107.   When we discuss a separate discipline of Conservation Biology, we do not simply mean the integration of different sciences into a new "conservation science." That, as pointed out above, goes back at least to the 1930sBy the discipline of Conservation Biology we mean something more formal, where Conservation Biology, like ecology, has its own academic departments, journals, professional societies, and, most importantly, individual practitioners who call themselves conservation biologists, not simply biologists concerned with conservation. This formalization of Conservation Biology started in the late 1970s and continues through today.

108.   *See* Michael E. Soulé, *Conservation Biology and the "Real World"* in CONSERVATION BIOLOGY: THE SCIENCE OF SCARCITY AND DIVERSITY, *supra* note 106, at 4. *But see* Simberloff, *supra* note 1, at 474. Simberloff does not deny the importance of island biogeography, but discusses the important of community ecology and earlier studies of habitats by ecologists as important components to modern Conservation Biology.

109.   *See infra* Chapter 7 for a discussion of the Sierra Club v. Marita cases during the 1990s in which island biogeography would be the central issue litigated by lawyers representing conservation biologists and environmental groups, on one side, and

traditional forest scientists from the U.S. Forest Service on the other. Generally, island biogeography theory states that small islands (or island like habitats, e.g., patches of forest in a meadow or clearcut) will contain fewer species of plants and animals then larger islands. This had obvious importance those interested in the design of wildlife refugees. *See infra* Chapter 7 for a more detailed description of island biogeography.

110.   *See supra* note 4 for a partial list of influential books, in the early 1980s, that helped create modern Conservation Biology as a discipline based on evolutionary theory, population biology, and genetics. This and other books were followed in 1985 by the creation of the Society for Conservation Biology and the publication in 1987 of the first issue of that societies journal, *Conservation Biology*.

111.   *See infra* Chapter 7 for a discussion of the developments in Conservation Biology from the late 1980s to the year 2000.

112.   *See* T. COLBORN, ET AL., OUR STOLEN FUTURE (1996).

113.   *See* 786 SW 2d 674 (1990). Dow Chemical Co. v. Alfaro. In 1990, Domingo Castro Alfaro, a Costa Rican resident and employee of a Standard Fruit Company banana plantation, and eighty-one other Costa Rican employees and their wives brought suit against Dow Chemical Company and Shell Oil Company. They claimed that they suffered personal injuries from exposure to dibromocholopropane (DBCP), a pesticide manufactured by Dow and Shell which was furnished to Standard Fruit. They claimed to suffer from several medical problems, including sterility. The pesticide had been suspended in the U.S., but was "dumped" on the international market. Dow sought to avoid liability through invoking the legal doctrine of "forum non-conveniens." The court rejected Dow's efforts to escape responsibility in U.S. courts through innovation of this technical legal doctrine.

114.   Delaney Amendment [Food Additive Amendments of 1958, 21 U.S.C. 301].

115.   *See* In the Matter of Stevens Industries, et al., 1972 WL 31768. *"Bio-accumulation"* is the popular term for several different processes. In its narrowest meaning, it refers to the process by which a toxic substance is taken up from water or food by an organism. *"Bio-concentration"* is the process by which a toxic substance enters an aquatic organism through the gills of epithelial tissues and is concentrated in the body. *"Bio-available"* is the portion of a chemical substance found in the environment that can readily be ingested or otherwise absorbed by living organisms. *"Bio-magnification"* is the process by which a compound concentrates as it moves up the food chain. A *"Bio-concentration factor"* (BCF) is an experimentally derived expression of the bio-accumulation potential of a chemical substance, i.e., the concentration of a substance in a test organism divided by the exposure concentration over some defined time period. *"Log P Value"* is the measurement of substances that have a high propensity for bio-accumulation. [For an excellent discussion of *Log P* and its relevance in toxic determinations, *see* Richard Williams, et al., *Gathering Danger: The Urgent Need to Regulate Toxic Substances That Can Bioaccumulate*, 20 ECOLOGY L.Q. 605 (1999).]

116.   *See* EDF Inc. v. Ruckelshaus, 439 F2d 584 (1971).

117.   The recognition of the relative probability and severity of harm in environmental opinions was a transplant from the common law of torts and the famous decision of Judge Learned Hand in United States v. Carroll Towing Company. [*See* 159 F2 169 (2nd Cir. 1947).] Ironically, although Judge Hand later rejected the utilitarian balancing implied in such an approach, the cost-benefit balancing which was to become an important part of tort law, environmental law and specifically pesticide regulation. such risk benefit balances have been built into environmental statutes, as well as set forth in environmental opinions.

118.   *See id.* at 597.

119.   *See* Dow Chemical v. Blum, 469 F.Supp. 892 (1979).
120.   The importance of tracking the biological impact of pesticides in order to determine their benefit is illustrated in Nagel v. Thomas, 666 F.Supp. 1002 (1987) (upheld in part, reversed in part, and remanded in Love v. Thomas, 858 F 2d 1347 (1987)), where the court traced the impact of denesob upon week growth impeding the growth of various commercial crops.
121.   For a detailed account of the Special Review process, *see* William Rodgers, *Cancellation-Suspension-Special Review*, 3 ENVTL. L §5.18. (1988). The special review process involves in practice the review of a scientific advisory panel and in theory, the possibility of referrals to the National Academy of Sciences. A more detailed examination of the relation of ecology and law in this area would require a study of these reviews and referrals.
122.   *See* 50 FR 49003 (Nov. 27, 1985). The reference to the tracing of the environmental path of pesticides in the food chain in the 1985 regulations renewed Rachel Carson's ecological recognition of the ecosystem setting for pesticides. Carson's description of the pathway of DDT, and the more recent attention to exposure, mobility, bio-magnification, and environmental fates, reflects the tacit recognition of the trophic structure of organisms through which nutrients and energy cycles. The feeding relationships that are part of this structure is called the food chain. The variety of feeding relationships within a community is often referred to as a "food web." The kinds of "ecological efficiency" by which energy is passed through the web will affect or be affected by, among other things, bio-accumulation and bio-magnification. [*See also* K. Jack Haugrud, *Agriculture*, in CELIA CAMPBELL-MOHN, ET AL., ENVIRONMENTAL LAW FROM RESOURCES TO RECOVERY 296, 357-8 (1993). *See* ROBERT RICKLEFS, THE ECONOMY OF NATURE 142-68 (1973).]
123.   *See* In the Matter of Ciba-Geigy Corporation, et al., 1988 WL 525240 (EPA).
124.   Similarly, in measuring the benefits of the pesticide, the agency traced its pathway to grubs in the turf and sod farms.
125.   *See* Haugrud, *supra* note 122, at 359-67.
126.   For a description of the approach which was taken to overcome the flood of pesticides, *see* Haugrud, *supra* note 122, at 359-63.
127.   NATIONAL ACADEMY OF SCIENCES, REGULATING PESTICIDES IN FOOD: THE DELANEY PARADOX (1987) Table 3.9.
128.   *See* JOHN WARGO, OUR CHILDREN'S TOXIC LEGACY: HOW SCIENCE AND LAW FAIL TO PROTECT US FROM PESTICIDES 139-44 (1996).
129.   *See* EPA, *Assessment and Control of Bioconcentratable Contaminants in Surface Waters: Draft Guidance*, 56 FR 1150 (1991).
130.   The appendix to the guidance document reported several studies claiming to demonstrate the relationship between the log-P value of the chemical and the consequent tissue concentration down stream from its effluent.
131.   *See* ENHANCING BIOLOGICAL CONTROL (Charles H. Pickett & Robert L. Bugg eds., 1998).
132.   *See* MARCOS KOGAN, ECOLOGICAL THEORY AND INTEGRATED PEST MANAGEMENT PRACTICE (1986).
133.   *See* ENHANCING BIOLOGICAL CONTROL (Charles H. Pickett & Robert L. Bugg eds., 1998).

7 The Marriage: Ecological Planning for Environmental Law

We live in a closed chemical system and the persistence of life in that
system demands that we manage it well – for ourselves and for the
myriad of other species that help determine its stable condition.
 – William H. Schlesinger, *Biogeochemistry: An Analysis*
 of Global Change

Introduction

To join ecology and environmental law together, one need not seek to build
ecological concepts into law, filling the statutes books and regulations with
foreign sounding terms such as "carrying capacity," "succession," "biodiversity"
and so on. Nor need one introduce ecological language into the implementation
of environmental laws, adding ecological insights to government programs,
which didn't originally envisage an ecological approach. Another way of
proceeding is to employ the insights of ecology in the initial research of an
environmental problem, taking its conclusions of that research and building
environmental law based upon the conclusions, without including ecology either
in the language of the law or in its implementation. In this approach, ecology is
like the Cheshire Cat's smile, which disappears when the law steps in! Such a
relation of law and ecology is illustrated in the history of efforts to control acid
rain, ozone depletion, the pollution of the Mediterranean, and global warming.
In each of these examples, legal regulations are preceded by extensive research,
and the regulations themselves reflect in whole or in part the conclusions of the
research. But despite the fact that the environmental law is to based upon the
results of the research, the law itself does not explicitly reflect the ecological
vision of the research that preceded it, nor does it incorporate the language and
concepts of ecology *in the law itself.*[1]

Acid Rain and the Biogeochemistry of Nature

Acid rain, whether fog, dry particles or rain, has been called "nature going sour."[2] First uncovered as early as 1872 with Robert Angus Smith's book *Air and Rain: The Beginnings of a Chemical Climatology*,[3] the phenomenon was present at the birth of the industrial revolution. The abandonment of charcoal for coal in England, the invention of the steam engine, steam train and loom that needed the power produced by coal created an air pollution "celebrated" by Dickens and other Victorian writers. Coal that was removed from the earth, especially if it was originally formed in salt water bogs, was rich in sulphur content and when burned, released oxides of sulphur and nitrogen into the sky. In some cases, these gases were released high into the skies, courtesy of tall smoke stacks first perfected in the mid 1900s, ironically intended to disperse the pollution.[4]

England and Western Europe began to bestow their acid rain upon Scandinavia. The Midwestern United States gave its gift to the Northeast and Canada, and other countries began to receive the steady sour drizzle and fog. As atmospheric chemistry and weathering modeling improved over the past century, the notion that sulphur (and nitrogen) might be wafted over long distances was no longer unbelievable. It was a Scandinavian ecologist who demonstrated in 1969 that much acid rain originated as SO_2 emissions in England and Central Europe. At the United Nations Conference on the Human Environment in 1972, the Swedish government presented the report, "Air Pollution Across National Boundaries: The Impact of Sulphur in Air and Precipitation."[5]

In the 1950s, ecologist Eville Gorham wrote about the effects of acid precipitation on Canadian ecosystems. Eugene Odum and other ecologists had already conceptualized sulphur precipitation as part of a larger sulphur cycle in nature. That cycle was eventually published in Odum's 1971 ecology book.[6] We understood the basic reactions and their connections, but we lacked the critical specifics on the amounts of materials being cycled, and the physical and biological processes controlling the grand cycle. Viewing sulphur as part of a grand cycle was not enough. It was necessary to conduct the painstaking work of tracing its impact upon the ecosystem. Although many studies were completed in this period, it was the painstaking work by Gene Likens, F. Herbert Borman and their colleagues at Hubbard Brook who carefully documented the biogeochemistry of this element and others. During the 1960s, these ecologists traced the biogeochemistry of a northeastern forest,[7] including the development of an annual sulphur budget. In studying both the sulphur cycle and budget in the forested ecosystem, they discovered an accumulated excess of sulphur, but did not describe its negative impacts. What they offered was a conceptual model for the flowthrough of sulphur that looked like this:

Figure 7.1 ANNUAL SULPHUR BUDGET FOR AN AGGRADING FORESTED ECOSYSTEM AT HUBBARD BROOK

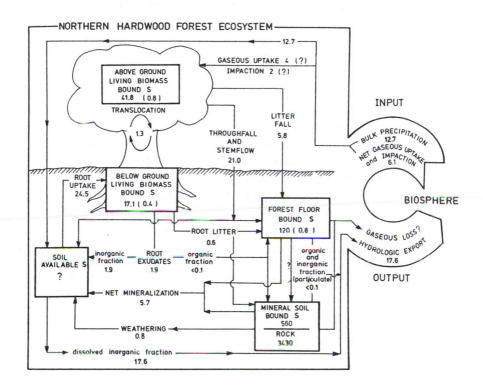

Standing crop values are in kg/ha and sulphur fluxes are in kg/ha'yr. Values in parentheses represent annual accretion rates. *Source:* G. Likens, et al., *Biogeochemistry of a Forested Ecosystem* (1977)

By 1980, a survey of 1,000 lakes in the Adirondacks of New York State showed that almost one quarter of the lakes had been acidified and no longer supported game fish populations. In 1981, the National Academy of Sciences and the National Research Council released two reports that found clear evidence of a serious risk to health and the biosphere and some evidence of atmospheric transport.[8] The first report summarized evidence of the pathways of acid deposition in the environment. The second explored the models of atmospheric processes that link emissions to deposition. Although the reports identified many unanswered questions about the linkage of specific sources to specific polluted sites, the entire analysis adopted an emissions to pollutant effect approach which, although not relying upon a nutrient modeling and budgeting approach, nevertheless exemplified an ecosystem approach.

Should Likens and others have been surprised by their results? Acid pollution was not unknown to the law. Several notorious nuisance cases, both in the United States and England, had involved acid pollution from some stage of the coal production. For example, in the 1954 case of *Washak v Moffat*,[9] plaintiffs sued for harm to their home from burning culm piles, coal refuse, that emitted hydrogen sulfide (HS) gases. In a 1969 decision, the Wisconsin court found liability for harm to farmlands from high sulphur coal burning by an electric generating plant.[10] Yet the common law was ill-equipped to handle these pollution cases.[11] The highest visibility cases involved not only air pollution but transboundary air pollution. In an earlier chapter, we introduced the turn of the century case of *Georgia v Tennessee*, in which a smelting operation resulted in serious sulphur related pollution drifting across state lines, it required the U.S. Supreme Court to settle the battle between these two states. In one of the first international environmental cases, *The Trail Smelter Arbitration* in 1941, a special arbritral tribunal held Canada responsible for pollution in the United States, enjoined the pollution and awarded damages.[12]

Although these early court cases received much public attention, it was not until 1970 and the new Clean Air Act that the serious prospect for the control of acid rain began. The 1970 Clean Air Act offered the promise – if not the reality – of regulation acid rain regulation. The act initially enabled the possible regulation of air sheds, which could embrace more than one state, encompassing the area in which sulphur related pollutants flowed. It enabled the adoption of national ambient air quality standards: primary standards aimed at protecting human health and therefore applicable to sulfates; secondary standard applicable to environmental damage and hence covering the environmental effects of acid rain. The act further required states to adopt implementation plans that would control pollutants significantly affecting other states and enable the Environmental Protection Agency to make appropriate findings of such interstate influences, upon request, requiring the polluting state to stop such pollution. The initial Clean Air Act also mandated the adoption of national performance standards for new stationary sources which could be applied to electric generating facilities to insure that the best pollution control technology will be used.

Unfortunately, the promise of the Clean Air Act during its first decade was not realized. Interstate air quality districts were not formed, sulfates were not controlled under the primary standards, the secondary standards were never fully implemented, EPA shrunk from the full enforcement of interstate pollution controls, and the national performance standards were not applied to the older, dirtier plants.

In 1972, the *Kennecott Copper Corporation v. EPA*[13] decision constituted a fateful turning point for the enforcement of the Clean Air Act. Judge Leventhal overturned EPA's secondary national ambient air quality standards which were designed to protect the visibility, vegetation and materials. Leventhal could not find a basis for the precise standard that EPA had chosen. EPA, fearing litigation over all of its secondary standards and holding better information on the health effects of pollutants, proceeded to set the secondary standards at the same level as the primary (health) standards. For the next twenty years, the Clean Air Act largely ignored environmental effects of air pollution. Although the health impacts of air pollution could also be approached from an ecosystem point of view, EPA largely relied upon dose-response risk studies, which abstracted from the complex pathway of pollutants through the environment. In 1990, this approach began to change.

However, the 1970s were a time of fruitful research on acid rain. Some of the research, relating to forestry impacts, was published in 1989 in James J. MacKenzie and Mohamed T. El-Ashry's *Air Pollution's Toll on Forests and Crops*.[14] Although complicated by other factors, air pollution – specifically, ozone and sulphur oxides – were found to have detrimental effects upon crop productivity and forests. The forest damage included impacts on the pines of the San Bernardino Mountains that ring the Los Angeles basin, the white pines of the Eastern United States, multi-species decline in central Europe, red spruce and fraser firs in the Eastern United States, yellow pines in the Southeast, and sugar maples in the Northeast. A complex of biotic and non-biotic factors, including both natural processes and air pollution contribute a series of stress factors that constitute a forest decline syndrome. This syndrome has to be understood in ecological terms.[15]

In 1980, Congress enacted the Acid Precipitation Act,[16] which found that acid rain could have a variety of adverse environmental effects, and proposed the "National Acid Precipitation Assessment Program (NAPAP)" to identify the causes and sources of acid rain, its detrimental consequences and "take action" within the limits of existing law. The Act established an inter-agency task force and a "research management" consortium to prepare a ten year comprehensive research plan which would among other things establish and carry out system studies with respect to plant physiology, aquatic ecosystems, soil chemistry systems, soil microbial systems, and forest ecosystems. The act illustrated a new approach to the relations of ecology and environmental law in which the planning and ecological studies were to precede the adoption of any new legislation and control.[17] During the next ten years, despite internal management problems, the Precipitation Assessment Program, pursuing an "integrated assessment process," completed an integrated assessment report in 1990, as well as a myriad of individual reports on all aspects of the acid precipitation process. In a nutshell, the integrated assessment process adopted alternative energy and pollution control scenarios, sought to measure actual and projected emissions and the control of costs of emissions, to determine the method of transport and transformation and the deposition, to trace the effects on aquatic, terrestrial, materials, visibility and health, and to measure the benefits from alternative control scenarios.[18]

Despite the impressive effort, both in individual state-of-science reports and in the conceptualization of the entire policy problem, the program itself was subject to vigorous criticism.[19] This criticism was based upon the fact that the Clean Air Act Amendments were adopted in 1990, setting emission limits of 10 million tons, without the benefit of the research, which was still being completed. In addition, even in 1990, the NAPAP study had not completed the requisite cost/benefit studies on which legislation might be based. The delay in the research was partly due to internal political difficulties, but was also due to a focus upon large scale modeling. Some criticisms of the research, however, were based upon the conclusions about the research drawn by its administrators. These conclusions were that the acid rain problem, was not as serious as the environmental community and some scientists were claiming. In addition, the study recommended conservation, low sulphur coal and coal washing as appropriate low cost mechanisms for resolving the problem while the environmental community had been pushing for smokestack scrubbing on old plants. In its own internal criticism of its efforts, the program focused upon the early lack of adequate research data, the difficulty of conducting adequate economic analyses, the uncertainty of projections and measurement of environmental effects, including the effects from "acidic episodes" and nitrogen deposition, and the problems of reaching conclusions about Canadian sites. Despite the external and internal criticisms of NAPAP, the program was re-authorized to evaluate the impacts of the 1990 Act.[20] As part of this evaluation, a series of ecosystem studies was proposed.[21]

While NAPAP's systematic planning and research effort to evaluate acid rain was being undertaken, three major developments were also taking place. First, the public culture, both in the United States and abroad, was slowly being shaped to understand the problem of acid rain, if not its precise significance. Second, a number of legal actions undertaken in the 1980s revealed the failure of the "command and control" Clean Air Act to regulate interstate pollution. At the same time, the idea of new economic instruments (i.e., tradable permits) for pollution control was being explored. Third, a Canadian/U.S. dialogue was proceeding, which would result in a treaty between the two nations. Although the election of Ronald Reagan to the U.S. Presidency represented a backlash against environmental controls, the Reagan administration almost immediately earned public disfavor for ignoring serious environmental problems. This dissatisfaction was to grow over the years, and with the end of the cold war and the apparent return of U.S. prosperity, the public once again turned to the unfinished environmental agenda.

The public awareness of acid rain gained legal expression in a myriad of lawsuits leveled in the 1970s and 1980s. Pennsylvania, New York, and Maine sought to force the EPA to find impairment of visibility due to SO_2 emissions from mid-western states. The states won the battle and the court ordered such a finding, but EPA won the war and denied the petitions. The states appealed, and in 1988 the court deferred to EPA modeling data allegedly showing no violation and refused to take the states' combined SO_2 impact into consideration under the Act.[22] Similarly frustrating developments took place internationally, as courts refused to enforce a reluctant EPA's "finding" of acid rain pollution in Canada and the requisite reciprocity of regulation, which Canada had undertaken of its own pollution in *Her Majesty The Queen in Right of Ontario v. EPA.*[23]

The early failures of the Clean Air Act to respond to the serious U.S. polluting of Canada with acid rain must be examined against a backdrop of continuous negotiations during the late 1970s and 1980s. In the early 1980s, bilateral research groups were established and completed reports on the long range transport of air pollutants.[24] The environmental community was uneasy, feeling that the U.S. response to the acid rain problem was to study it to death, buying time for polluting industries to profit from a less restrictive regulatory environment. Among the conclusions was the recognition of terrestrial ecosystem impacts. In addition, control options were identified, including liming. In 1991, Canada and the United States signed an Air Quality Agreement to address transboundary pollutants between the two countries. This agreement, while committing both nations to sulphur oxide and nitrogen oxide controls as part of their domestic legislation, also provided for emission, deposition, and ecosystem monitoring and the further exploration of emission trading regimes in both countries.[25]

In 1990, the United States adopted the new Clean Air Act.[26] Among other new provisions amending the 1970 and 1977 Clean Air Acts was Title IV, which established a trading regime for sulphur oxide emissions.[27] This regime established allowances of one ton of sulphur oxides and distributed an amount of allowances to secure a ten million ton reduction in sulphur oxide emissions over a period of time extending to 2010. Utilities can either use these allowances, save them for a limited period, or trade them. The ten million ton reduction was not based upon the NAPAP research, nor to our knowledge on any other solid research. Rather, it was a "golden number" adopted in the political process and employed for the purpose of adopting a cap in permitted emissions. More important, the cap and trade system, with its fixed number of allowances, makes difficult any short term changes based upon newly discovered ecological information about the relative impacts of acid precipitation due to acid rain.[28]

The history of acid rain and the efforts to regulate it reveals a pattern of interaction between ecology and environmental law. Early ecologists were aware of the broad contributions that fossil fuel burning might make as part of the sulphur cycle. Early legal cases identified the impact of sulphur oxides on the environment. In the 1970s, attempts to regulate those impacts failed, in part because of a lack of knowledge about the precise relationship between emissions, long distance transmitting, and pathways of deposition in the environment. During the 1970s and 1980s, such research was undertaken. Although the formal research of the Acid Precipitation Act failed to provide timely information for the Clean Air Act in 1990, other research offered strong circumstantial evidence of the need for substantial reductions in sulphur oxide emissions. The form of regulation was primarily a trading regime which would not require for its administration continued on site ecological research into the impacts of acid rain. But both the Canada/U.S. Agreements and the re-authorization of the Acid Precipitation Act provided for continued evaluation of the acid rain problem and the effectiveness of the controls.

The acid rain problem has recently been cojoined with a larger set of issues linking the atmosphere with ecosystems and the law. Coal burning is a major contributor to increasing levels of atmospheric carbon dioxide and the global problem of climate change. Ironically, the reduction of SO_2 from coal combustion is also contributing to global warming. Sulfate particles suspended in the atmosphere reflect incoming solar radiation and act to cool the earth. The scientific research community is engaged in an assessment of carbon and sulphur cycling effects on climate as part of the Intergovernmental Panel on Climate Change (IPCC) mandate.[29]

Mending the Ozone Hole[30]

Stratospheric ozone depletion is not acid rain. Unlike acid rain, ozone depletion affects the entire globe and threatens serious human health and ecosystem problems. Accordingly, the United States and the world community have taken serious steps to prohibit the release of most ozone depleting substances. Herein lies the paradox. Despite the world scope, the complexities, and the consequent uncertainties, the world has moved relatively quickly to prohibit ozone depleting substances, while acid rain, with its more specific regional effects remains less controlled, both domestically and internationally.

The relative success of controls for ozone depletion is especially amazing in light of the dubious track record of environmentalists' prediction of global catastrophes over the decades. In the early 1970s, some leading environmental scientists predicted environmental disaster and famine as a result of population increases.[31] The Meadows' models predicted collapse based upon the current assumptions about food production used in their computer models.[32] Even Barry Commoner anticipated significant and wide-spread health problems from our synthetic pollutants.[33] Without denying for a moment that serious environmental problems face the globe, it is also fair to say that the rash predictions of environmental catastrophe have not been confirmed and we continue on our way, lurching from one problem to another. With this history of failed prognostications, the success at achieving controls of ozone depleting chemicals offers a kind of "poster boy" model for viewing how science might inform successful environmental policy.

The early history of ozone depletion is important, since it helps us to understand the present success of ozone policy. The stratosphere and its relative warmth (caused by the absorption of biologically harmful incoming UV radiation) and ozone content were discovered in the 1800s. In 1881, W.N. Hartley submitted a paper offering the theory of atmospheric ozone. In 1931, with the help of others, Sidney Chapman fully described the workings of the ozone layer.[34] The manner of discovery was as important as the discovery itself. Both Hartley and Chapman were concerned about explaining the apparent cutoff of UV light. Chapman's description, which also explained the warming of the atmosphere, inspired the popular conception of the ozone layer as a vital atmospheric barrier protecting living organisms from ultraviolet light. In the early 1930s, science writers were already assigning this important role to the ozone layer. Ironically, while new scientific knowledge about the ozone layer was growing, some chemists were developing the very substances that could threaten the existence of that layer. In April of 1930, Thomas Midgely, the inventor of the ethyl addition to gasoline, gave a demonstration of chlorofluorocarbon as a safe refrigerant. The wonder gas, "freon" was born. Eleven years later, Lyle Goodhue bought five pounds of freon, and combining it with other ingredients, created the first "bug bomb," an aerosol pesticide. With the contemporaneous invention of DDT and the desire for such an insecticide in the pacific theatre of the Second World War, aerosol insecticides were launched.

The ozone layer faced its first major threat in the late 1960s. Inspired in part by the stratospheric exploits of the French scientist Picard, who flew on a balloon ten miles up into the atmosphere, people began to envisage a supersonic airplane that could transverse the globe at high speeds. Opponents to the notion were at first concerned about sonic booms carpeting the countryside. Their demand for a quiet countryside and their opposition to headlong technology was an early sign of the developing environmental movement. But the threat to the peace and quiet, although real enough, was not what ultimately defeated the SST (Super Sonic Transport).

Since Sidney Chapman had developed his chemical description of the workings of the ozone layer in 1931, scientists had been refining his work. In 1965, John Hampson, who was studying reentry problems of intercontinental missiles, suggested that hydrogen oxides produced in missile reentry might result in a reduction of the ozone layer. Arizona physicist John McDonald had concluded that the water vapor in the ozone layer would have a similar effect. Other scientists were soon able to show a relationship between nitrogen oxides and ozone depletion. In 1971, Congress rejected subsidies to develop the SST. In retrospect, the decision might have been wise for other reasons, since the more economical and large air bus, without sonic booms, was soon in production.

In 1970, with adoption of the Clean Air Act, there was no attention paid to stratospheric ozone. The prime concern was the lower atmosphere (troposphere) and preventing the formation of ozone pollution (smog) resulting from the interactions of hydrocarbon emissions and sunlight. However, in 1971, an international Climatic Impact Assessment Program was being undertaken, which was to stimulate interest in atmospheric chemistry, partly as a result of past concern about atomic testing. As part of this new interest in the atmosphere, Richard Stolarski and Ralph Cicerone published research in 1974 indicating that chlorine atoms released into the atmosphere might continue to destroy ozone over several decades. In the same year, Mario Molina and Sherwood Rowland demonstrated that CFCs can remain intact and migrate into the stratosphere and, when broken down by solar radiation, may release large quantities of chlorine. The results of this research sparked a major research campaign of the National Academy of Sciences, the National Oceanic and Atmospheric Administration, NASA, and several leading universities.[35] In 1976, the National Research Council published the first of several reports on the effects of CFCs on the atmosphere.[36] In 1995, Molina, Rowland and Paul Crutzen were awarded the Nobel prize in chemistry for their work on the formation and decomposition of ozone. This is the only Nobel Prize that has been awarded for work that is directly related to the environment.

In 1977, amendments to the Clean Air Act were passed to "provide for a better understanding of human interactions with stratospheric ozone," and information for further legislation.[37] Congressional findings included a recognition of the threat and the existing legal authority to control ozone depleting substances. Studies by EPA, the National Academy of Sciences and others were authorized, and NASA was mandated to monitor the stratosphere. The Administrator of EPA was explicitly authorized to adopt regulations based upon research and studies authorized. In 1978, as part of a popular movement in both the United States and Europe, the Toxic Substances Control Act banned the use of CFCs in non-essential applications.[38]

For the next ten years, a stream of national and international scientific reports on ozone depletion were published, more carefully identifying the emissions and emission sources, the stratospheric chemistry, the state of the ozone layer itself, and the impacts of ozone depletion upon human health, the environment, and agricultural productivity.[39] In 1986, a landmark report was published by NASA, which had coordinated a variety of research efforts. The report published the result of 150 scientists' work in a comprehensive study of the atmosphere.[40] It identified the doubling of selected CFCs in the atmosphere in the previous decade, despite a stagnation in production of chemicals. The reports also identified several new CFCs. In 1985, the "ozone hole" was discovered over the Antarctic, but the precise significance of this hole was not understood. Nonetheless, this startling observation was evidence that our planet was changing, with unknown consequences for its inhabitants. In 1986, a workshop reviewed the links between ultraviolet radiation and skin cancers, reduction of the immune system, and major damage to agriculture and the food chain.

By this time, pressure was mounting not only from the scientific community, but also from citizen groups and environmental lawyers. In 1985, the Natural Resources Defense Council brought an action under the Clean Air Act provisions of 1977, claiming that the Administrator of the Environmental Protection Agency should make a finding of endangerment of health and welfare, and should adopt regulations to control the release of ozone depleting substances. In a court settlement, EPA agreed to publish a decision on whether further controls were necessary by 1987.

During the mid 1980s, the ozone depletion issue increasingly became an issue of politics and negotiation, rather than science. In 1986, Dupont, a principal producer announced that it could find some substitutes for CFCs within time. This announcement in turn created pressure on the rest of the industry and on some of the European countries that were dragging their feet. In 1986, UNEP sponsored an informal conference in Vienna, and formal diplomatic negotiations began in 1987. Aside from the politics, the negotiations faced eight major issues, which were to resurface in contemplation of controlling global C-emissions: (1) which chemicals would be included; (2) whether production or consumption would be controlled; (3) the base year from which reductions would be calculated; (4) the timing and size of cutbacks; (5) how the treaty would be placed into force; (6) restrictions on trade; (7) treatment of developing countries, and (8) special provisions for the European Community. Several of these issues raised scientific questions, and meetings of scientists were included in the negotiating process.

In 1987, the landmark Montreal Protocol was signed.[41] The protocol contained an agreement to scale back the production and consumption of ozone depleting materials. A trading regime was established whereby parties could purchase rights to produce or consume from other countries. The agreement was to be enforced by a trading ban on non-complying countries. Special arrangements were made for developing nations. For our purposes, the important observation is that the face of the treaty itself contains no process of risk regulation requiring science to assess the impact of the substances controlled. The use of science to determine the nature and amount of sub-stances to be controlled and at what rate preceded the agreement itself. In this sense, the agreement is analogous to the trading regime for sulphur oxides to control acid rain in sub-chapter IV of the Clean Air Act.[42] The 1990 Clean Air Act embraced the Montreal Protocol, and with some modifications, included a similar schedule for phase out and trading in its provisions.[43]

Bridge Document 7.1 THE PROTOCOL AND PANEL REPORTS

The only "scientific provision" in the Montreal Protocol is Article 6: "Assessment and Review of Control Measures." This section provides:
        "Beginning in 1990, and at least every four years thereafter, the Parties shall assess the control measures provided for in Article 2 on the basis of available scientific, environmental, technical and economic information. At least one year before each assessment, the Parties shall convene appropriate panels of experts qualified in the fields mentioned and determine the composition and terms of reference of any such panels. Within one year of being convened, the panels will report their conclusions, through the secretariat, to the parties."[44]

This provision was to prove essential to the protocol, since new scientific information has arisen since 1987 regarding substances that can deplete the ozone layer, the rate of chlorine buildup in the atmosphere, and the rate, timing and location of the layer's depletion. Thus a major report of the Ozone Trends Panel in 1988 produced new evidence of depletion, large springtime decreases in the Antarctic, and depletion over populated areas. This led to more rapid phaseouts under amendments to the Treaty. In addition, in further Treaty revisions, the role of developing nations, the voting arrangements of all the countries and the uncovering of new substances have been addressed.

The Montreal Protocol, the research and negotiations leading up to the Protocol, and the revision of the Protocol have created a unique "experimental jurisprudence." According to this experimental jurisprudence (see also discussion in Chapter 10), the law and the controls it mandates may be treated as well grounded hypotheses, which are to be further tested by scientific evaluation after the law is passed. Such an approach, at least in theory if not in practice, provides both for the formulation of a law based upon significant scientific preparation, but also allows for the modification of the law on the basis of new information at a later time.

The success of the science and law partnership in the control of ozone depleting substances is not due solely to its relatively unique "experimental jurisprudence." A long history of concern about the ozone layer preceded the adoption of the Montreal Protocol. Deep concerns about cancer and environmental catastrophe undoubtedly motivated many of the individuals involved. The availability of replacement substances, favorable cost/benefit and risk analyses, and the willingness of the Dupont Company to give up producing the harmful substances undoubtedly contributed to the solution. The large scale investment in scientific research and the credibility of "hard scientists," i.e., physicists, chemists, and medical researchers, probably also contributed to the outcome. Out of the entire effort came a strengthened International Council of Scientific Union, which seeks to promote the new discipline of *Earth System Science* by integrating chemistry, physics, biology, geology, anthropology, meteorology, oceanography and other subjects to understand interrelated planetary forces.[45] A more detailed discussion of the history and contributions of earth systems sciences to global environmental regimes is found in Chapter 10.

The Mediterranean and Ecologically Epistemic Communities

By the 1970s, the Mediterranean Sea faced serious pollution problems.[46] Along the coasts of the multiple European Community and developing countries surrounding the sea, the industrial and tourism facilities, as well as inland facilities dumped into the rivers feeding into the sea. This contributed an intense load of sewage and industrial pollutants including metals, inorganic wastes, pesticides, bacteria, oil and organic wastes and nutrients.[47] Ironically, many of these major pollutant sources were only discovered after research attention was given to more visible oil spills and marine dumping. Humans had fouled a historic water body,[48] the "wading pool" of Europe,[49] and a beautiful and much valued marine resource.

Under French leadership, a cooperative regional regime[50] was formed in the early 1970s to tackle the marine pollution dumping problems, but it soon turned its attention to the pollution generated by onshore activities. In the mid 1970s, UNEP took over the promotion of the effort to control pollution of the sea, although France continued to finance a major share of the activities in the 1970s. In 1975, sixteen governments approved the Mediterranean Action Plan

(Med Plan) "to take all appropriate measures ... to prevent, abate, and combat pollution ... and to protect and enhance the marine environment."[51]

Bridge Document 7.2 THE MED PLAN

> The Med Plan consists of an interconnected set of four components: regional treaties; coordinated research and monitoring; integrated planning; and administrative and budgetary support. Beginning in 1976 with seven pilot monitoring and research projects, a protocol banning marine dumping, a protocol urging cooperation in case of oil spills, and a framework convention, the participating states have now developed a far more comprehensive program. They completed the first phase of studying pollution in the region, and established the monitoring program as continuing institution supported by governments rather than by international organizations. They established regional centers to co-ordinate oil spill management actions, the preservation of species, integrated development planning, and studies of development projects of specific interest to developing states. A coordinating headquarters unit was established in Athens, with a Mediterranean staff supported by annual contributions from all of the Mediterranean countries. Governments meet biannually to review the program. The parties adopted legal agreements that establish marine parks to preserve endangered marine species and to ban pollution from land-based sources.
>
> The Land-Based Sources Protocol, which was signed in 1980 and entered into force in 1983, is the most important part of the Med Plan, as it sets limits on industrial, municipal, and agricultural emissions into the Mediterranean, as well as controlling wastes transmitted via rivers and through the atmosphere. Politically, the adoption of this protocol was the capstone of the Med Plan, as it was the most contentious issue negotiated between the developing (LDCs) and developed states (DCs). Controlling land-based sources directly influences industrialization policies, about which the LDCs are extremely sensitive. The protocol's adoption without significant alteration, and its subsequent ratification by Algeria and Egypt, who initially opposed it, demonstrates a dramatic change from considering environmental protection and economic development to be incompatible goals to accepting an uneasy balance between them.

Source: Peter Haas, *Saving the Mediterranean* (1990)

An important stimulus in the development of the plan and its subsequent expansion was the marine pollution "epistemic community," a group of scientists and professionals, both public and private, who were committed to addressing the problems of the Mediterranean. Through international secretariats, especially UNEP, these scientists set an agenda for looking at the entire sea, identifying all major sources of pollution and their pathways, establishing a monitoring system for pollutants, and proposing specific standards. These scientists were the most constructive supporters of the Med Plan in their specific countries, and supported the domestic measures needed to implement the plan. The scientific community's sustained focus on the water quality problems of the Mediterranean was pivotal in keeping pressure on the political community to reach international agreement.

In the words of Thacher, the UNEP sponsorship envisioned a comprehensive interlinked program based upon an ecosystem perspective which was:

> ... to achieve efficient management of their coastal resources on a *sustainable* basis. They admit the need for truly comprehensive plans reflecting the idea that for the effective protection and development of a marine region, all factors, maritime and land based, affecting their ecoregion should be taken into account when formulating development strategies for their individual nations. In other words, rather than addressing only the problems which appear to be consequences of poor resource management and environmentally inappropriate development practices, the key to a successful protection of and development within an ecosystem lies in proper and sustainable resource management and careful application of development practices which are consistent with the health of the environment.[52]

This approach supplied a model for the resolution of other regional pollution problems around the world.[53]

The Med Action Plan was followed by an abstract conceptualized plan called the "Blue Plan," which envisaged twelve "consolidated diagonal" studies which extended from land-marine systems, a range of influences upon those systems, as well as a study of the impacts of non-Mediterranean influences on the Mediterranean Basin. This plan, which included extensive mathematical modeling, was completed in 1987. Its results were largely ignored, while countries focused upon six priority action programs embracing soil protection, water resource management, fisheries and aquaculture management, human settlements, tourism and soft energy technologies. In addition to the planning activities, several followup protocols, including one focusing upon land-based pollution sources and another on "special protection" areas were adopted, as well as implementing programs and various initiatives within each of the nations.[54]

Bridge Document 7.3 THE EPISTEMIC COMMUNITY

> A knowledge-based group is an epistemic community. "An epistemic community is a professional group that believes in the same cause-and-effect relationships, truth tests to assess them, and shares common values. As well as sharing an acceptance of a common body of facts, its members share a common interpretive framework, or consensual knowledge," from which they convert such facts, or observations, to policy-relevant conclusions. They identify problems in the same manner

and process information similarly. They also share a common vocabulary, common political objectives to which such policies should be addressed, and a common network in which findings are exchanged and shared concerns are formulated. Although members of an epistemic community may be drawn from different scientific disciplines, all will share some common world view and concern about the same subject matter. Although they concur on appropriate methods for validating their knowledge, they need not be positivist. Many of these conditions may be adduced from accepted exemplars, such as textbooks.

An epistemic community need not have a monopoly on relevant knowledge, but it must share a common approach to understanding. Scientists split on causal knowledge cannot be members of an epistemic community. Presented with incomplete or ambiguous evidence, members of an epistemic community would draw similar interpretations and make similar policy conclusions. If consulted or placed in a policymaking positions, they would offer similar advice. Individuals who were not members of the same epistemic community would be much more likely to disagree in their interpretations. Unlike an interest group, confronted with anomalous data, they would retract their advice or suspend judgment.

An epistemic community's power resource, domestically and internationally, is its authoritative claim to knowledge. Presented with observations, it may convert them into common policy by drawing common inferences. To the extent that its members can penetrate the walls of government and maintain their authority, new orders of behavior are possible. Insofar as members' policy proposals are accepted, they exercise unobtrusive control. By heeding an epistemic community's advice, governments may come to identify new policies or new policy objectives.

Source: Peter Haas, *Saving the Mediterranean* (1990)

Although not all of the language of the protocols reflect their origin in an ecological epistemic community, some language of the protocols contains ecological language. The discussion of the fourth protocol dealing with protected areas [Article 3] included the statement that " ... such areas shall be protected in order to safeguard in particular: a) sites of biological and ecological value – the genetic diversity, as well as satisfactory population levels, of species, and their breeding grounds and habitats – representative types of ecosystems, as well as ecological processes ..." [Article 7] included " ... the organization of a planning and management system ... " which in addition to adopting a variety of ecological oriented regulations would include "any other measure aimed at safeguarding ecological and biological processes in protected areas." Another purpose of the protocol was to prevent exemptions which would "endanger the maintenance of ecosystems ... or the biological processes contributing to the maintenance of those ecosystems ..."[55] Not only are some of the protocols replete with ecological references, but some of the more specific followup programs, water quality criteria, monitoring measures and other implementation programs incorporate a variety of ecological concepts.

On the other hand, many of the protocols and their implementing devices make little if any direct mention of the ecology of the sea, relying rather upon more general references to pollution or contamination and codes of practices and other technology based standards. Moreover, as Haas concluded in his pathbreaking study of the Mediterranean regime, even when governments followed the protocols and their ecological standards, there was little indication that the governments adopted the integrative ecological view which UNEP and its "epistemic community" hoped for. The nations' failure to follow the results of the "Blue Plan's" comprehensive planning illustrates their failure to grasp the integrative vision of UNEP.

Global Warming and the Cycles of Nature

Like acid rain, the historical roots of global warming rest in the industrial revolution. The mining of coal and oil, combined with the advent of the engines of power, the steam engine, the internal combustion engine, and the dynamo to power the looms, railroads, automobiles and smelters of our modern life were dominated by a Baconian vision of knowledge as power and applied knowledge as the route to unlimited progress. There was no recognition that this new organization of the manufacturing process was to be the beginning of fundamental disturbances in the fundamental cycle of life, the carbon cycle.

Western European and American writers of the nineteenth century recoiled in horror at the advent of the industrial revolution. One reviewer of American literature termed their response as picturing "a machine in the garden."[56] The aesthetic revulsion to industry and its production of crowded polluted cities was part of a deeper critique of the social organization (Marx) and the manner of thought (Dickens) spawned by the new industry.[57]

For the most part, the modern environmental movement has accepted the industrial revolution. Indeed, one might argue that the environmental movement is based upon the very prosperity that ensued from that revolution. But, as we see below, many nineteenth and twentieth century "nature visionaries" sought a more simple life,[58] and more recent radical critiques such as those of Lewis Mumford and Barry Commoner were to follow in the next century. These critiques were aimed not only at technology and its consequences, but at a kind of reductive knowledge that appeared to ignore the organic interdependent qualities of nature and community.

The phenomenon of global warming has stimulated the re-examination of the industrial revolution's costs and the applied science which produced it. Our recent encounter with the severe problems of nuclear power (a kind of second generation technology) already has shaken our confidence in man's unlimited Promethean powers. Global warming constitutes the next shock to our easy confidence. Industrial production is resulting in excess atmospheric carbon, unabsorbed by the sinks of nature (with which we have also tampered). This excess carbon is accumulating in the atmosphere at a rate of 3.2×10^{15} g/yr (~1.5 percent/yr) is producing a "greenhouse" effect, warming our atmosphere. The warmed atmosphere, in turn, has a variety of unknown, and in some cases unpleasant, consequences for our planet. The recognition of this process is slowly bringing us back to a recognition of the cycles of nature in general, and the cycle of carbon in particular.[59]

Figure 7.2 THE PRESENT DAY GLOBAL CARBON CYCLE

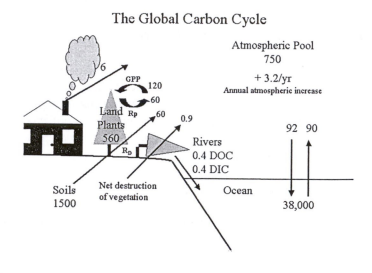

The pool sizes (e.g., ocean, soils) are expressed in units of 10^{15} g C and all fluxes shown by arrows are in units of 10^{15} g C per year. GPP=gross primary production, RP=plant respiration, DOC=dissolved organic carbon, DIC=dissolved inorganic carbon. *Source:* Modified from William H. Schlesinger, *Biogeochemistry: An Analysis of Global Change* (1997)

Recognition of these cycles and the way in which we are affecting them may begin to constrain our modern notions of unlimited progress.[60]

The uncovering of global warming was not due to the systematic application of full blown theories, but came out of a series of ad hoc discoveries over time. It began with French natural philosopher Jean-Baptiste-Joseph Fourier, who at the time of the French Revolution envisaged the earth as a giant greenhouse, analogous to a bell jar, whose atmosphere trapped the radiant heat from the sun, warming the planet and giving life to every plant and animal.

About the same time, James Hutton and Charles Lyell paved the way for modern geology which understood modern geological forces as operating in the same way, throughout time. This allowed for an understanding of how coal and oil could come to be formed as part of the earth's development.

Table 7.1 THE CARBON CYCLE

The biological cycling of carbon in the ecosystem is more direct than the cycling of oxygen. The carbon cycle involves only organic compounds and carbon dioxide (Figure 7.2). Photosynthesis and respiration fully complement each other. Photosynthesis assimilates carbon entirely into carbohydrate; respiration converts all the carbon in organic compounds to carbon dioxide. Large inorganic pools of carbon – atmospheric carbon dioxide, dissolved carbon dioxide, carbonic acid, and carbonate sediments – enter the carbon cycle to different degrees. The carbon in igneous rocks, calcium carbonate (limestone) sediments, coal, and oil is exchanged with other more active pools so slowly that these sources have little influence on the short-term functioning of the ecosystem.

Plants assimilate about 120×10^{15} g of carbon each year, of which about 60×10^{15} g are returned to the carbon dioxide pool by plant respiration. The remainder, 60×10^{15} g, supports the respiration and production of animals, bacteria, and fungi in herbivore-and detritus-based food chains. Anaerobic respiration (without oxygen) produces a small quantity of methane (CH_4) that is converted to carbon dioxide by a photochemical reaction in the atmosphere. Plants and animals annually cycle between 0.25 and 0.30 percent of the carbon present in carbon dioxide and carbonic acid in the atmosphere and oceans, hence the total active inorganic pool is recycled every 300 to 400 years (1â0.003 to 1â0.0025). Because the atmosphere and oceans exchange carbon dioxide slowly, they may be considered as separate pools over short periods. Terrestrial ecosystems annually cycle about 12 percent of the carbon dioxide in the atmosphere. The transit time of atmospheric carbon is, therefore, about eight years (1â0.12).

Source: William Schlesinger, *Biogeochemistry: An Analysis of Global Change* (1997)

In 1896, Swedish chemist Svante Arrhenius showed that CO_2 absorbed energy and conjectured that industrial pollutants, especially carbon dioxide, were accumulating in the Earth's atmosphere. It was George Callender who in the middle of the twentieth century claimed that humans could influence the wind and weather. Charles Keeling designed the instruments for the careful measurement of carbon dioxide and accidentally discovered that the levels of carbon dioxide were rising more rapidly than anyone had assumed. The Keeling curve (Figure 7.3) is arguably the piece of scientific data most widely recognized by the general public. It is an amazing record of a change in the metabolism of the earth, Gaia.

It was Joseph Farman who in discovered the ozone hole in the Antarctic. In the 1970s, the scientific community was alerted to the possibility of global warming. Careful measurements of growth rings in Amazon forests and ice cores in the Arctic were able to provide some scientific support for the warming hypothesis, and large scale models of climate change began to be build and tested.[61]

Figure 7.3 THE KEELING CURVE

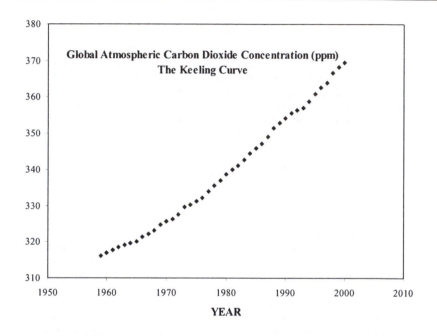

The plot beginning in 1958 showing the rise in atmospheric carbon dioxide measured in the remote Pacific (Mauna Loa, Hawaii) is commonly referred to as the Keeling Curve. It represents the longest continuous record of atmospheric carbon dioxide for any location in the world. Between 1958 and 2001, the annual mean carbon dioxide concentration has increased by 17 percent. *Source:* C.D. Keeling & T.P. Whorf, 2002. Atmospheric CO_2 records from sites in the SIO air sampling network. In Trends: A Compendium of Data on Global Change. Carbon Dioxide Information Analysis Center, Oak Ridge National Laboratory, U.S. Dept. of Energy, Oak Ridge, Tennessee, USA

The problem of global warming is, in fundamental ways, different from the problem of ozone depletion. Unlike ozone depletion, which is caused by a limited number of substances that have a direct link to their atmospheric consequences which in turn have fairly predictable health consequences, global warming is very complex. The substances giving rise to global warming are not limited to carbon dioxide, but also include methane, nitrous oxide, and chlorofluorocarbons. The sources of carbon dioxide are not limited to the use of fossil fuels by industrialized countries, but also include the burning of biomass during deforestation and C released from organic matter through decomposition. Although the rise of carbon dioxide is well documented, the rate at which that carbon dioxide is cycled to terrestrial and ocean sinks is less well known. The extent, timing and distribution of global warming both of the atmosphere and the oceans is becoming evident by observation and these data are consistent with predictions made by large-scale models. General circulation models, which seek to simulate and predict the climate's changes are presently being developed and tested. Thus, the long-term climatic consequences of human-caused global warming are not certain.

Then there are the consequences of the climate change on the bio-sphere itself. It is very difficult to determine the near term consequences of changes in precipitation, temperature, soil moisture and snow and ice coverage for specific locations with confidence. Thus, predictions about the migration of ecosystems, impacts upon agricultural productivity, pest and disease outbreaks and sea rise remain couched in terms of uncertainty. A different kind of uncertainty, normative uncertainty, also hangs over the global warming issue. There was very little doubt that depletion of the ozone layer would be harmful. There is more doubt among the scientific and public communities about the harms of global warming. Even the initial discoverer of the ozone hole, Svante Arrhenius, while predicting in 1908 in his *Worlds in the Making: The Evolution of the Universe*, welcomed the phenomenon as a "boon" to mankind. With the uncertainty about the extent and consequences of global warming, there is also uncertainty about the future nature of the problem and the range of solutions to be undertaken. Thus, the design of a program of solutions involves predicting the direction of technology, industrial activity and emissions, forestry and land use change. A new international science institution was required to met this mission, i.e., the IPCC.

The World Meteorological Organization (WMO) and the United Nations Environment Programme (UNEP) established the Intergovernmental Panel on Climate Change (IPCC) in 1988 in response to evidence of human influences on the composition of the atmosphere and the uncertainty surrounding subsequent effects on climate and the function of global scale systems. Membership is open to all nations who are members of the UNEP and WMO. The IPCC does not collect new data or conduct primary scientific studies and experiments. Rather, the responsibilities of the IPCC are to assess the existing peer-reviewed scientific, technical and socioeconomic information relevant for the understanding the nature and risks of climate change. The broad objective of the IPCC is to provide a "consensus" on global change science for the international community to use as the basis for possible global action through UN treaty system and other international frameworks affecting trade.

The IPCC has three working groups and a Task Force. Working Group I is charged with summarizing scientific understanding of the global climate system and climate change. Working Group II focuses on the sensitivity of ecosystems and socioeconomic systems to climate change and the consequences (both positive and negative) and also considers options for these systems to adapt to climate change. Working Group III assesses options for controlling (as in limiting) greenhouse gas emissions and assess strategies for mitigating climate change. The Task Force on National Greenhouse Gas Inventories oversees the National Greenhouse Gas Inventories Programme, information ultimately essential for assessing compliance to international agreements.

The Panel meets annually to consider and accept IPCC reports and to decide upon the charge for the working groups. The IPCC First Assessment Report was distributed in 1990. This report drew global political attention to the issue and was a foundation document used to constitute the Inter-governmental Negotiating Committee for a UN Framework Convention on Climate Change (UNFCCC) by the UN General Assembly. The UNFCCC reports were adopted in 1992 and came into force in 1994.

A consensus on the predictions of what is likely to happen is developing in the IPCC process, but determining what should be done to prevent, adapt and mitigate climate change is also difficult. Setting priorities among alternative solutions is difficult. For example, it is hard to choose between limiting deforestation and the promotion of reforestation, the movement away from a fossil fuel economy and the adoption of new constraints upon methane and chlorofluorocarbon emissions. The effort to control fossil fuel emissions will be exceedingly complex and politically difficult. Demand-oriented and supply-oriented approaches have been discussed, and within supply controls, options such as carbon taxes, tax incentives, marketable permits and regulatory standards are being explored.

One source of difficulty at the international scale is that choosing among such proposed solutions raises fundamental problems of environmental justice. The industrialized nations, and the U.S. in particular, are the major contributors to global change, yet a solution will require participation of lesser-developed nations. These nations question being required to make "sacrifices" in fossil fuel use at a time when they aspire to enlarge their economies and increase industrial activity. Although such "distributive justice" issues arose with ozone depletion, they were not as severe. In the case of global warming, both the geographical distribution of the present and future causes and proposed solutions to global warming among developing and developed nations accentuate the problems of *which* sources should be controlled and *who* should bear the cost of that control.[62]

Environmental law is not well equipped to cope with the serious problems of long term uncertainties regarding global warming and the overt problems of environmental justice. Environmental law has based its solutions to date upon an acceptance of the growth of industrial economy, which in turn provides the resources for a new "green technology" to control pollution. Most environmental law has avoided the problem of explicitly dealing with environmental justice issues, and has papered over such issues in order to reach agreement on the means for reducing pollution. If the carbon cycle does set limits upon industrial growth, requiring a cutback of that growth and the explicit distribution of the costs of such a cutback, it will be a unique and severe problem for environmental policy. The legal response to global warming to date suggests the problem is likely to arise in the future.

In 1980, a carbon dioxide study was funded along with the acid precipitation study.[63] An early U.S. legal response to the global warming problem was the Global Climate Protection Act, which sought to sponsor and coordinate research efforts on global warming.[64] In 1990, Congress passed the Global Change Research Act, which established a Global Change Research Office and promoted further research.[65] Unfortunately, the landmark Clean Air Act of 1990 failed to undertake any direct efforts to regulate carbon dioxide, although its regulations of some chlorofluorocarbons as part of its ozone depletion control provisions indirectly controlled some global warming sources.[66]

A major step in the ecological approach to controlling global warming was the 1992 Earth Summit in Rio de Janeiro. This conference was an especially important event, as it mapped a variety of ecological approaches to the resolution of global environmental problems, including the problem of biodiversity. During the summit, the United Nations Framework Convention on Climate Change[67] was adopted. This convention recognized "the role and importance to terrestrial and marine ecosystems of sinks and reservoirs of greenhouse gases" and expressed concern that global warming of the atmosphere may adversely affect natural ecosystems. Specifically, the convention recognized the threat to "low-lying and other small island countries, countries with low lying coastal, arid and semi-arid areas or areas liable to floods, drought, and desertification and developing countries with fragile mountainous ecosystems" as "particularly vulnerable." Among other agreements, the parties committed to sustainable management, adopting national policies to limit emissions of greenhouse gases and protecting greenhouse gas sinks and reservoirs. Parties to the convention also committed to international systematic research, and a subsidiary body was established for scientific and technological advice. Although the convention itself contained no specific control commitments by developed nations, and any commitments by developing countries depended on assistance from the developed nations, an annex to the convention provided for the developed countries to mitigate climate change by reducing emissions to 1990 levels by the year 2000.

After the convention, the Conference of Parties adopted a "Berlin mandate" to adopt a follow up protocol. In 1995, the UN Intergovernmental Panel on Climate Change (IPCC) issued a second assessment report, prepared and reviewed by some 2,000 scientists, concluding "the balance of evidence suggests that there is a discernible human influence on global climate." In 1996, the following report was issued:

Table 7.2   GLOBAL WARMING: DIFFICULTIES ASSESSING COUNTRIES'
PROGRESS STABILIZING EMISSIONS OF GREENHOUSE GASES

The United Nations Framework Convention on Climate Change entered into force on March 21, 1994. As of June 1996, 159 countries had ratified the Convention. The Convention's ultimate objective is the "stabilization of greenhouse gas concentrations in the atmosphere at a level that would prevent dangerous interference with the climate system from human activities." To achieve this goal, the Convention, all parties are to do the following:

- Prepare and communicate to the Conference of the Parties inventories of greenhouse gas emissions caused by human activity using comparable methodologies.
- Develop and communicate to the Conference of the Parties programs to mitigate the effects of greenhouse gases and measures the countries might take to adapt to climate change.
- Cooperate in the transfer of technology addressing greenhouse gas emissions in all relevant sectors of the economy.
- Promote sustainable management of greenhouse gas sinks and reservoirs.
- Cooperate in preparing for adaptation to the impacts of climate change.
- Integrate considerations of climate change with other policies.
- Conduct research to reduce the uncertainties about scientific knowledge of climate change, the effects of the phenomenon, and the effectiveness of responses to it.
- Exchange information on matters such as technology and the economic consequences of actions covered by the Convention.

In addition to the above commitments, the Convention required developed countries and other parties included in Annex I* of the Convention to do the following:

- Adopt national policies and take corresponding measures to mitigate climate change with the aim of returning human-induced emissions of greenhouse gases to 1990 levels by the year 2000 and by protecting and enhancing greenhouse gas sinks and reservoirs.

- Communicate, within 6 months of the Convention's entry into force and periodically thereafter, detailed information on policies and measures to limit greenhouse emissions, as well as on the resulting projections of greenhouse gas emissions and removals by sinks.
- Identify and periodically review policies and practices that encourage activities that lead to greater levels of human-induced emissions of greenhouse gases that would otherwise occur.

* *[Editor's note: There are 36 Annex I countries as follows: Australia, Austria, Belarus, Belgium, Bulgaria, Canada, Czech Republic, Denmark, Estonia, Finland, France, Germany, Greece, Hungary, Iceland, Ireland, Italy, Japan, Latvia, Lithuania, Luxembourg, Netherlands, New Zealand, Norway, Poland, Romania, Russian Federation, Slovak Republic, Spain, Sweden, Switzerland, Turkey, Ukraine, United Kingdom of Great Britain and Northern Ireland and the United States of America. Of these, Belarus, Turkey, and Ukraine have not yet ratified the Convention.]*

Source: GAO/RCED-96-188 (Sept. 1996)

The report concluded that as of 1996, information was not available to assess progress on the proposed controls, although projections offered by the countries themselves indicated that only 24 out of the 159 countries were likely to comply. It was projected that the United States, Canada and Europe would not comply.

In December 1997, the Kyoto Protocol was signed. We will discuss this protocol in more detail in Chapter 10, where its structure and effectiveness are compared with other international environmental regimes. This protocol set binding emissions targets at levels below the 1990 level for developed nations over a five year budget period from 2008 to 2012. The emissions targets cover all six major greenhouse gases (carbon dioxide, methane, nitrous oxide, as well as synthetic substitutes for ozone depleting substances). Offsets were offered for the expansion of sinks, such as tree planting programs. Emissions trading was provided for, as well as credit for "clean development" in developing countries. The developing countries have the option of joining the program. Unlike the ozone depletion program, there is no enforcement mechanism through trading sanctions.

In many ways, the global warming problem, both in science and in law, poses the ultimate challenge of successfully relating ecology (including earth systems science) and law. For ecology, the challenge lies in reaching credible scientific conclusions about an immensely complex and comprehensive system, which can only be ultimately simulated by comprehensive climate change models and models of the resulting temperature and precipitation changes of the biosphere. A similar challenge faces international environmental law. Aside from developing a suitable international institution for implementing a framework for control of global warming gases, each nation will have to craft an appropriate legal regime to enforce controls within its own nation. In turn, the effectiveness of that regime must be internationally transparent if its legitimacy is to be recognized.[68]

Conclusion

In this section, we have reviewed the role that ecology plays in documenting the problems of acid rain, ozone depletion and global warming. The regulations arrived at addressing these three problems all drew upon the research results of ecology. (Since all three of the problems involved the atmosphere and climate, earth system science was the fundamental science involved.) Unlike the previous areas of law, the resulting statutes did not begin by embracing an ecological viewpoint as NEPA had, nor was the pattern of development one of a gradual courtship of law and ecology. Rather a program of systematic ecological research was mandated by law, such as in the 1977 ozone depletion research amendments of the Clean Air Act, or the 1980 law mandating research of acid rain, and the 1987 law authorizing research of global warming.

Following the research efforts, key conclusions emerged in published reports and assessments. In the case of the National Acid Precipitation Assessment Program, reports were published throughout the 1980s and the final report was published in 1991. In the case of ozone depletion, a series of domestic reports began to be issued in the late 1970s and continued throughout the 1980s. In the case of global warming, a number of studies were issued in the late 1980s and a key international assessment was issued in 1995. All of the studies here included large scale modeling, involving large geographic areas, long time periods, and multiple variables.

The climatic and biosphere models include a significant degree of complexity, which can raise serious questions about their accuracy and reliability. Moreover, this complexity makes it difficult, if not impossible, for lay decisionmakers to evaluate the results of the models. Such a situation raised profound questions about the use of such models in and between democratic regimes. In the cases involving acid rain, ozone depletion, and global warming, the research effort was followed by legislation and/or international agreements. First, there was the Montreal Protocol covering acid rain. The acid rain and ozone depletion controls were included in the 1990 Clean Air Act. The global warming controls were contained in the 1992 Annex of the Rio Framework Agreement and the 1997 Kyoto Accords.

In each of these laws and conventions, ecology was not an important part of the face of the law or convention, nor was ecology part of the administration of the law. Ultimately, all three laws turned to establishing fixed amounts of emissions (acid rain) or fixed scheduled reductions of emissions, leading to prohibition in some cases (ozone depletion) or fixed reductions of emissions (global warming). In all three cases, the laws and conventions established trading regimes. In order to achieve a fixed reduction, each law or convention had to set the "golden number" of emissions permitted. For example, for acid rain, allowances were permitted that envisaged an eventual 10 million ton reduction in emissions. For control of ozone depletion, certain substances were phased out on a percentage basis over time. For control of global warming, reductions to a percentage below 1990 levels were mandated.

These "golden numbers"[69] of reduced emissions were not the specific results of research efforts. Indeed, in the acid rain situation, the extent of reduction was established prior to the research being completed. In the case of ozone depletion, the feasibility of finding and developing substitutes set the period for eliminating some substances. Other substances were added later, only when their ozone depleting potential was realized. In the case of global warming, the reductions were a matter of political compromise. This weak relationship between the research conducted and the "golden numbers" selected for control purposes requires more inquiry that can be provided here. In later chapters, we shall identify some of the questions raised by such a weak relationship.

The activity of research, however, does not end with the adoption of laws. In these three case studies, ongoing research was to be continued after the adoption of the laws in question. In all three cases, acid rain, ozone depletion, and global warming, government sponsored research is continuing. The purpose of such research is identified in its enabling statue, but it consists of continuing to study the problem, and to evaluate the controls already adopted. Thus, this research can provide corrections to the initial formulation of the problems that gave rise to the controls. For example, research in ozone depletion has uncovered other ozone depleting substances and a faster rate of depletion than originally thought. On the other hand, the research of NAPAP completed after the 1990 Clean Air Act suggested the possibility that the amount of control mandated by the Act was unnecessary. Presumably, other research can measure the effectiveness of the measures adopted to attain the objectives specified in the law. The question that is raised by this "after the fact" research is whether it can result in scientific conclusions that, if necessary, can be subjected to mid-course corrections with corresponding changes in the legislation. If those conclusions can be reached, how can the law be altered?

Notes

1.   It may incorporate the concepts of other disciplines, such as economics.
2.   *See* ROY GOULD, GOING SOUR: SCIENCE AND POLITICS OF ACID RAIN (1985).
3.   *See* ROBERT SMITH, AIR AND RAIN: THE BEGINNINGS OF A CHEMICAL CLIMATOLOGY (1872).
4.   *See* GALE E. CHRISTIANSON, GREENHOUSE: THE 200-YEAR STORY OF GLOBAL WARMING (1999).
5.   *See* ARNOLD W. REITZE, AIR POLLUTION LAW (3d ed. 1971).
6.   *See* EUGENE ODUM, FUNDAMENTALS OF ECOLOGY (1971).
7.   *See* GENE LIKENS, F. HERBERT BORMANN, ET AL., BIOGEOCHEMISTRY OF A FORESTED ECOSYSTEM (1977).
8.   *See* NATIONAL RESEARCH COUNCIL ET AL., ATMOSPHERE-BIOSPHERE INTERACTIONS: TOWARD A BETTER UNDERSTANDING OF FOSSIL FUEL COMBUSTION (1981); NATIONAL RESEARCH COUNCIL ET AL., ACID DEPOSITION, ATMOSPHERIC PROCESSES IN EASTERN NORTH AMERICA: A REVIEW OF CURRENT UNDERSTANDING (1983).
9.   *See* Waschak v. Moffatt, 379 Pa. 441, 109 A 2d 310 (1954).
10.   *See* Jost v. Dairyland Power Cooperative, 45 Wis. 2d 164, 172 N. W. 2d 647 (1969).
11.   In the *Waschak* case, there were many other plaintiffs waiting in the wings. The *Jost* court was uneasy about how to balance the benefit of electrical generating against harm to farms. *See supra* notes 9 and 10.
12.   *See* Trail Smelter Arbitration (U.S. v Can.) (1941), 3 U.N.R.I.A.A 1938 (1949).
13.   Kennecott Copper Corporation v, EPA, 462 F. 2d 846, 149 U.S. App.D.C.231 (1972).
14.   *See* JAMES J. MACKENZIE & MOHAMED T. EL-ASHRY, AIR POLLUTION'S TOLL ON FORESTS AND CROPS (1989).
15.   For a variety of analyses, *see* JAMES J. MACKENZIE & MOHAMED T. EL-ASHRY, AIR POLLUTION'S TOLL ON FORESTS AND CROPS (1989).
16.   *See* 94 Stat. 611, 704, Title IV "Acid Precipitation Program and Carbon Dioxide Study."
17.   Although, as the language of the Act implied, interim actions within the existing law might be undertaken.
18.   *See* NATIONAL ACID PRECIPITATION ASSESSMENT PROGRAM, NATIONAL ACID PRECIPITATION ASSESSMENT PROGRAM: 1990 INTEGRATED ASSESSMENT REPORT (November 1991).
19.   *See Learning from the Acid Rain Program*, News and Comment: 251 SCIENCE March 15, 1991.
20.   *See* 1990 Clean Air Act Amendments, Public Law 101-549, Title IX, Section 901, j.
21.   *See* U.S. NATIONAL ACID PRECIPITATION ASSESSMENT PROGRAM, MISSION, GOALS, AND PROGRAM PLAN POST 1990 (November 1991).
22.   *See* State of New York v. Ruckelshaus, 21 ERC 1721 (D.C. Cir., 1984); New York v. EPA, 852 F. 2d 574 (D.C. Cir. 1988).
23.   *See* 912 F2d 1525 (D.C. Cir. 1980).
24.   *See* A.P. ALTSCHULER & G.A. MCBEAN, THE LONG RANGE TRANSPORT OF AIR POLLUTANTS PROBLEM IN NORTH AMERICA: A PRELIMINARY OVERVIEW, (1979); SECOND REPORT ON THE LONG RANGE TRANSPORT OF AIR POLLUTANTS (1980).
25.   For a history and evaluation of the agreement, *see* INTERNATIONAL JOINT COMMISSION, UNITED STATES-CANADA AIR QUALITY AGREEMENT: PROGRESS REPORT (1996).
26.   *See* 42 U.S.C.7401-7671q (1990).
27.   *See* 42 U.S.C. 7651-7651o.

28.   There are many exceptions to this statement. States are still free to regulate utilities under their state implementation plans, and the federal Clean Air Act provides for other approaches to nitrogen oxide related acid rain and prevention of significant deterioration. These other approaches may involve further assessment of the ecological impact, although states are also moving toward market-based approaches.

29.   *See* W.H. SCHLESINGER, BIOGEOCHEMISTRY: AN ANALYSIS OF GLOBAL CHANGE (2nd ed., 1997).

30.   The title comes from ARJUN MAKHIJANI & KEVIN R. GURNEY'S MENDING THE OZONE HOLE: SCIENCE, TECHNOLOGY AND POLICY (1995).

31.   *See* PAUL AND ANNE EHRLICH, THE POPULATION BOMB (1968).

32.   *See* DENNIS & DONELLA MEADOWS; MODELS OF DOOM was the title of a book critiquing the Meadows book. *See* H.D.S. COLE, MODELS OF DOOM: A CRITIQUE OF THE LIMITS TO GROWTH (1973).

33.   BARRY COMMONER, THE CLOSING CIRCLE, NATURE: MAN AND TECHNOLOGY (1971).

34.   For a popular account, *see* SETH CAGIN & PHILIP DRAY, BETWEEN EARTH AND SKY: HOW CFCs CHANGED OUR WORLD AND ENDANGERED THE OZONE LAYER (1993).

35.   Here and throughout, we draw upon RICHARD ELLIOT BENEDICK, OZONE DIPLOMACY: NEW DIRECTIONS IN SAFEGUARDING THE PLANET (1998).

36.   NATIONAL RESEARCH COUNCIL, HALOCARBONS: EFFECTS ON STRATOSPHERIC OZONE, (1976).

37.   42 USC 7470-7479 (repealed 1990).

38.   *See* Toxic Substances Control Act, 15 U.S.C. 2605, Sec. 6; 43 Fed. Reg. 11301-19 (1978).

39.   For an excellent brief bibliography, *see* Benedick, *Ibid.* 434, 435.

40.   *See* WMO, ATMOSPHERIC OZONE 1985: ASSESSMENT OF OUR UNDERSTANDING OF THE PROCESS CONTROLLING ITS PRESENT DISTRIBUTION AND CHANGE (1986).

41.   Montreal Protocol on Substances That Deplete the Ozone Layer (with Annex A and as Adapted) (concluded at Montreal, 16 September, 1987. Entered into force, 1 January 1989. 26 I.L.M. 1550 (1987)).

42.   42 U.S.C. §7651-7651o.

43.   *See* 42 U.S.C. 7671-7671q.

44.   ARTICLE 6, MONTREAL PROTOCOL ON SUBSTANCES THAT DEPLETE THE OZONE LAYER, September, 1987.

45.   For an account of the International Council of Scientific Union, *see* FRANK GREENAWAY, SCIENCE INTERNATIONAL: A HISTORY OF THE INTERNATIONAL COUNCIL OF SCIENTIFIC UNIONS 172-83, 212-28 (1996).

46.   For the definitive account of the effort to control pollution in the Mediterranean, *see* PETER HAAS, SAVING THE MEDITERRANEAN: THE POLITICS OF INTERNATIONAL ENVIRONMENTAL COOPERATION (1990).

47.   *See id.* at 1-33.

48.   The classic study of the Mediterranean is FERNAND BRAUDEL, THE MEDITERRANEAN AND THE MEDITERRANEAN WORLD IN THE AGE OF PHILIP II (2 Volumes 1966).

49.   For a current description of the region, *see* ROBERT FOX, THE INNER SEA: THE MEDITERRANEAN AND ITS PEOPLE (1993).

50.   The concept of a natural resource regime was first advanced by Oran Young in his classic work, RESOURCE REGIMES: NATURAL RESOURCES AND SOCIAL INSTITUTIONS (1982). This concept was to apply to a cluster of rules and roles of public and private entities, organized to protect or manage or develop a given natural resource or ecosystem.

51.   *See* Haas, *supra* note 46, at 67.

52.   *See* Peter S. Thacher, *The Stockholm Process*, THE SIREN (May, #20) 1983:2.

53.   For one article questioning the general applicability, *see* SUH-YONG CHUNG, *Is the Mediterranean Regional Cooperation Model Applicable to Northeast Asia?* 11 GEO. INT'L ENVTL.L. REV. 363 (1999).

54.   *See* Haas, *supra* note 46, at 96-165.

55.   For a compilation of the Mediterranean Plan documents, *see* EVANGELOS RAFTOPOULOS, BARCELONA CONVENTION AND PROTOCOLS: THE MEDITERRANEAN ACTION PLAN REGIME (1993).

56.   LEO MARX, THE MACHINE IN THE GARDEN: TECHNOLOGY AND THE PASTORAL IDEAL IN AMERICA (1964).

57.   Although Karl Marx focused upon the internal working conditions, CHARLES DICKENS portrayed not only the pollution as in BLEAK HOUSE (1853) but also the change in mind set, as in HARD TIMES (1850).

58.   DAVID SHI, THE SIMPLE LIFE: PLAIN LIVING AND HIGH THINKING IN AMERICAN CULTURE (1985).

59.   *See e.g.,* ROBERT E. RICKLEFS, THE ECONOMY OF NATURE (1983).

60.   Although it is beyond the scope of this book, the fundamental notion of progress, built upon the application of science to nature through technology, may be a fundamental barrier to living peacefully with the planet. If so, a fundamental shift in popular culture will be required, a shift of perspective on the course of history and our part within it. For a review of alternative views of progress and historical change, *see* CHARLES VAN DOREN, THE IDEA OF PROGRESS (1967).

61.   This history is compellingly recounted by GALE E. CHRISTIANSON, GREENHOUSE: THE 200-YEAR STORY OF GLOBAL WARMING (1999).

62.   *See* ENVIRONMENTAL PROTECTION AND JUSTICE: READINGS AND COMMENTARY ON ENVIRONMENTAL LAW AND PRACTICE (Kenneth Manaster ed., 1995); PETER WENZ, ENVIRONMENTAL JUSTICE (1988).

63.   *See* 94 Stat. 611, 711.

64.   *See* 15 U.S. C. 2901, 101 Stat 1407.

65.   *See* 103 Stat. 3096.

66.   The Clean Air Act did require the continuous emissions monitoring to cover CO_2 as part of its acid rain controls.

67.   *See* United Nations Framework on Climate Change (Concluded at Rio de Janeiro, 29 May 1992, Entered in force 21 March 1994. 31 I.L.M. 849 (1992).

68.   For one collection of recent articles addressing this problem, *see* PETER M. HAAS, ROBERT O. KEOHANE, AND MARC A. LEVY, INSTITUTIONS OF THE EARTH: SOURCES OF EFFECTIVE INTERNATIONAL PROTECTION (1993).

69.   The concept of "golden numbers" was first discussed in the Tock's Island case study. *See* BOUNDARIES OF ANALYSIS: AN INQUIRY INTO THE TOCK'S ISLAND CONTROVERSY (Harold Feineson, et als., 1976).

8 Ecology and Law in the 1990s – The Law of Place-Based Ecosystem Regimes and Management

... because EPA has concentrated on issuing permits, establishing pollutant limits, and setting national standards, the Agency has not paid enough attention to the overall environmental health of specific ecosystems. In short, EPA has been 'program-driven' rather than 'place-driven.'

– EPA's Ecosystem Protection Workgroup, 1994

Ecologists and marine biologists knew for decades that nutrient enrichment of Chesapeake Bay (from industry and farms), along with the overexploitation of commercial fish species, was a threat to the health of this ecosystem. However, as is true of most cases of ecosystem management, attempts to reverse the deterioration of this ecosystem did not begin until both health risks and economic impacts increased to a critical level.[1]

The restoration of the Chesapeake Bay is one of the first large examples of federal and state agencies working with local industry, farmers, ecologists, and private citizens to manage an entire ecosystem. The beginning of this effort, in 1983, predates the common use of the term "ecosystem management."[2] However, most elements that characterize a complete legal regime that incorporates ecology into the management process can be found; interagency cooperation, creation of an ecosystem specific legal agreement, the use of current ecological data and methods, and the balancing of this ecological information with economic goals in a comprehensive adaptive plan.

Despite the long-term efforts of these various groups, the management of the Bay remains difficult and uncertain. This was made clear in 1997 when, despite the best efforts of the management partners, a dramatic increase in fish kills and human health problems began to surface. The effects were traced to a population explosion of the algae, *Pfiestra*, which was a result of the continued eutrophication of the shallow waters of the bay from industrial and farm-based pollution. The scientists and policy makers were able to work together to discover the source of the problem and the health effects of this contamination. However, despite nearly 20 years of management, nutrient loading into the bay had not dramatically decreased. This example unfortunately showed that increased efforts to restore or preserve ecosystem functions may also require control of population and economic growth.[3]

Introduction

By 1990 the role of ecology in environmental law was a topic of discussion and debate in congressional committees, policy think tanks, environmental groups, government agencies, academia, and, most dramatically, in the court room.[4] This discussion was accompanied by the growing integration of the ecological disciplines themselves. Ecology as a fragmented discipline composed of historical divisions between sub-disciplines began to give way to an ecology in which multiple hierarchical levels and the processes occurring at these levels are considered as an interconnected system.

Three kinds of ecosystemic regimes came to fruition in the 1990s: (1) regimes devoted to the preservation or restoration of unique natural places, (2) regimes devoted at least in part to the protection of biodiversity, and (3) regimes for the management of global systems. In this chapter we will focus on the proliferation of ecosystemic regimes dealing with unique places. We will trace the development of one of the three major paradigms which dominated the interaction of ecology and environmental law in the 1990s: ecosystem regimes management. In the next chapter we will discuss the changing interaction of ecology and law as they relate to biodiversity protection and will focus on the second paradigm which drove the ecosystemic regime in the 1990s: conservation biology. In Chapter 10, we shall turn to the law and ecology of earth systems science regimes.

A theme common to all three chapters is that the changes within the ecosystemic regime of the 1990s mirror the developments in ecology during this decade. Environmental managers, advocates, and policy makers began to realize that many environmental problems were complex and involved several different environmental concerns (e.g., toxic waste management, clean air, water use, and biodiversity) which traditionally were treated with separate laws and regulations. The result of this realization was that citizens and environmental managers began to create legal regimes to deal with inter-connected environmental problems by combining the relevant parts of multiple local, state, and federal laws and regulations. The combination of this legal approach with the newer, more integrated ecology of the 1990s was a major step in the development of the ecosystemic regimes in the 1990s.

In particular, since 1990, there has been a proliferation of place based ecosystemic regimes which include regimes focused upon different ecosystems – lakes, marine coastal areas, wetlands, watersheds, riverine systems, mountains, forests, and national parks. They embrace different goals, ranging from research and ecosystem restoration to education and land conservation. The regimes are scattered across the nation and embrace sub-state areas, multi-state areas, and international sites. They include laws authorizing federal, state, and local laws authorizing management efforts.

Table 8.1 PLACE-BASED ECOSYSTEM REGIMES

AGENCY SPONSORS	PROJECT GOALS	ECOSYSTEM STRESSES
Federal	Preserve ecosystem	Agricultural practices
State	Restore ecosystem	Disruption of fire regime
Non-profits	Obtain stakeholder	Exotic/invasive species
Private landowner	support	Grazing/range management
Local agency	Maintain economy	Hydrologic alteration
Industry	Develop guidelines for	Land conversion
Regional university	ecosystem management	Mining
Private citizen	Conduct research	Overuse of natural resources
Tribes	Promote aggregate land uses	Non-point source pollution
	Conduct education and	Point source pollution
	Outreach	Recreation
	Carry out legislative	Roads and infrastructure
	Mandate	Timber/forest management

Source: Steven L. Yaffee, et al., *Ecosystem Management in the United States: An Assessment of Current Experience* (1996)

Most of these regimes were initially strongly influenced by definitions of place supported by the public culture. The Chesapeake, the Pinelands, the Everglades, Lake Tahoe, Yellowstone Park, and many others were historically recognized as important places. But most are not nationally recognized and many remain in the initial planning stages.[5]

In recent years, as the public increasingly recognized the value of such nature-based places, geographers, philosophers, planners, and nature writers began to advance theories of place. At the same time, another group of theorists began to advance the notion of resource regimes and common pool resource institutions. These theories were designed to explain how non-market institutions might collectively manage environmental resources. The notion of "ecosystem regimes" emerged and appears particularly appropriate for discussing the legal structure of the management of ecosystemic places. Conclusions about these regimes, which are designed to accommodate common resources, e.g., fisheries, may be extended to the management of shared ecosystems.

The Rise of Ecosystem Management and its Scientific Foundations

While the term "ecosystem management" and its application to environmental protection is recent, proponents of the approach and the ecological concepts behind it have been around for decades.[6] Individuals scattered within government agencies realized that the best way to protect natural resources and human health was not to manage on a resource by resource or pollutant by pollutant basis, but to focus upon the spatial and temporal scale relevant to solving the problem.[7] The focus could include an entire watershed threatened by pollution or a forest threatened with over-logging. It was during the 1990s that the idea that environmental management should be based upon ecosystems entered environmental law, facilitating the application of ecology to that law.[8] In 1993 President Clinton, responding to Vice President Gore's recommendation, directed all federal agencies to establish ecosystem management as the method of choice for environmental management.[9]

In 1996 a committee of the Ecological Society of America produced a report on the scientific basis of ecosystem management, co-written by several leading ecologists in government and academics.[10] This report highlighted the scientific components of ecosystem management and provided a blueprint for how to apply them to achieve the goal of ecosystem sustainability.[11] The ESA report advanced the view that ecosystems should be managed for sustainability rather than adopting the more traditional view that a main goal of environmental management was "maximizing short-term yield and economic gain."[12]

Ecosystem management has its ecological roots in the ecosystem concept as first defined by Tansley and later given a modern form by Eugene Odum, Gene Likens, and others.[13] The main difficulty in applying the ecosystem concept to management is determining what is the ecosystem that needs to be managed. This difficulty arises because ecosystems, unlike populations, are not clearly delineated in nature.[14] The difficulty of classifying ecosystem boundaries has forced ecologists to sometimes define ecosystems operationally; based upon the particular process that they are interested in studying.[15] Therefore, as the ESA Report points out, an operational ecosystem can range from a dung pile, to a watershed, to an ocean, and, finally, to the entire globe. This approach has long worked for the modern ecosystem ecologist,[16] and it is starting to work for the environmental manager where defining an ecosystem operationally depends upon the scale of the management problem being addressed.

Watersheds (e.g., Hubbard Brook) are a convenient model for ecological study because they are relatively self-contained with identifiable inputs and outputs. This allows the ecosystem ecologist to manipulate the system and collect data in ways that would be impossible in a larger, more ill-defined ecosystem. This relative ease of measurement also allows the environmental manager to monitor environmental changes at the scale of the entire watershed, due to human causes, using the same methods as the ecologist. Therefore, it should not be surprising that some of the most successful examples of ecosystem management involve lakes or other watersheds (e.g., Mono Lake, Lake Washington, Chesapeake Bay, and the Florida Everglades). However, for both the ecologist and the manager of other areas, e.g., national parks or forests, the watershed would be too small a system for the study or management of widely dispersing vertebrate species such as the wolf.[17] Thus, in the management of the Yellowstone Park, the boundaries of planning were expanded beyond the park to include "the Greater Yellowstone Park" area.

Ecosystem ecology is of obvious importance in the development of ecosystem management. There are other ecological sub-disciplines which focus on other spatial and temporal scales that are of equal importance.[18] An understanding of the ecological processes at lower levels (e.g., population and communities) and higher levels (e.g., landscape and global) of organization than the ecosystem are necessary for two reasons. First, in many instances the focus of a particular ecosystem management strategy is not the ecosystem itself (as it is in the Florida Everglades), but a particular component of the ecosystem (e.g., one endangered species such as the Northern Spotted Owl in the Pacific Northwest). It is necessary to understand the ecology of that species as well as the structure and function of the ecosystem in which it exists.[19] The second reason is that even when the ecosystem is the primary focus of a management plan it is usually necessary to understand the function of the lower and higher levels of organization in order to fully explain the function of the ecosystem. It was this realization that more than one level in the ecological hierarchy must be studied that is the most important and lasting contribution of "systems ecology."[20] This integration of different aspects of ecology, all concerned with different levels of organization, in the formation of ecosystem management mirrors the parallel development that was occurring among academic ecology; the creation of a new ecology in which single research questions were studied at multiple levels of organization.[21]

The ESA report, which remains today the best review of ecosystem management from the ecologists' perspective ends with a call to ecologists to become more involved in the ecosystem management process by communicating new data to environmental managers and by developing new methods of monitoring ecosystem structure and function.[22] More generally, the increased presence of ecologists in the planning and operation of environmental management might be what is necessary for the ecosystemic regime to reach fruition.

Table 8.2   VARIATION IN ECOSYSTEM MANAGEMENT APPROACHES – LISTS OF GUIDING
                PRINCIPLES

ESA REPORT[23]	INTERAGENCY TASK FORCE[24]	GRUMBINE[25]
Sustainability	Shared vision of goals	Hierarchical context
Goals	Account for existing and	Ecological boundaries
Sound ecological models	future social and economic	Ecological integrity
and understanding	conditions/goals	Information base
Complexity and	Coordination and	Monitoring
Interconnectedness	collaboration among	Adaptive management
Recognition of the dynamic	federal agencies and local	Interagency cooperation
character of ecosystems	governments	Organizational change
Context and scale	Restore/maintain biodiversity	Humans are embedded
Humans as ecosystem	and sustainability	in nature values
Components	Respect private property	
Adaptability and	rights	
Accountability	Ecosystems are complex	
	and dynamic over space	
	and time	
	Use adaptive approach to	
	Management	
	Determine baseline	
	ecosystem conditions	
	and monitor changes	

Source: ITF, *The Ecosystem Approach* (1995); Grumbine (1994)

Ecology, along with the political science and planning/management theories are the three perspectives that combine to form the framework termed ecosystem regime management. The analysis of socioeconomic factors in the design of environmental management plans made EM a success among government agencies and politicians and a source of concern and controversy among many ecologists and environmental activists. The single most important socioeconomic assumption is that humans, like rivers, endangered species, and the climate, are part of the ecosystems.[26] From the ecosystem management perspective this means both that human effects on the ecosystem must be considered and that the effect of the management plan on human social and economic concerns must be factored into the design of a management plan.[27]

Unfortunately, we lack a single definition of ecosystem management and, as a result, agencies have struggled to define and implement ecosystem management to meet their mandates. Such a definition should embrace an integrated ecology, a theory of place, the emerging notion of ecosystem regimes, and an art of ecosystem management, the latter which has been articulated in a welter of books and papers on the subject.

We will review the development of the ecosystem management concept and the myriad forms of its application. Ecosystem management arose out of the Forest Service's need to manage national forests under the multiple use mandate of the National Forest Management Act (NFMA). This was particularly critical when balancing the use of ecology and the need to account for socioeconomic factors. From this start, ecosystem management quickly became a guiding principle of most federal and state agencies involved in environmental management. However, as we will see, the very ubiquitous nature of the concept resulted in a proliferation of definitions of what is ecosystem management.

Following this review of ecosystem management we will show how ecosystem management is being used in the 1990s. We will concentrate on the management of the Florida Everglades, since the current management of the Everglades demonstrates what can be done when federal, state, and regional governments work together to apply the "best science available" to environmental law and management. However, the history of the various management strategies used in the Everglades also provides the lesson of what happens when ecology is not integrated into environmental management.

Some Definitions of Ecosystem Management

DEFINITIONS BY ECOLOGISTS

"Management of natural resources using system-wide concepts to ensure that all plants and animals in ecosystems are maintained at viable levels in native habitats and that basic ecosystem processes are perpetuated indefinitely."[28]

"Integrating scientific knowledge of ecological relationships within a complex socio-political and values framework toward the general goal of protecting native ecosystem integrity over the long term."[29]

"Any land-management system that seeks to protect viable populations of all native species, perpetuates natural disturbance regimes on the regional scale, adopts a planning timeline of centuries, and allows human use at levels that do not result in long-term ecological degradation."[30]

"Ecosystem management is management driven by explicit goals, executed by policies, protocols, and practices, and made adaptable by monitoring and research based on our best understanding of the eco-logical interactions and processes necessary to sustain ecosystem composition, structure, and function."[31]

DEFINITIONS BY GOVERNMENT AGENCIES

"To restore and maintain the health, sustainability, and biological diversity of ecosystems while supporting sustainable economies and communities."[32]

"Protecting or restoring the function, and species composition of an ecosystem, recognizing that all components are interrelated."[33]

"Ecosystem management is the integration of ecological, economic, and social principles to mange biological systems in a manner that safeguards long-term ecological sustainability. The primary goal of ecosystem management is to develop management strategies that maintain and restore the ecological integrity, productivity, and biological diversity of public lands."[34]

"The ecosystem approach is a method for sustaining or restoring natural system and their functions and values. It is goal driven, and it is based on a collaboratively developed vision of desired future conditions that integrates ecological, economic, and social factors. It is applied within a geographic defined primarily by ecological boundaries."[35]

DEFINITIONS BY MULTI-STAKEHOLDER GROUPS

"A strategy or plan to manage ecosystems to provide for all associated organisms, as opposed to a strategy or plan for managing individual species."[36]

"A collaborative process that strives to reconcile the promotion of economic opportunities and livable communities with the conservation of ecological integrity and biodiversity."[37]

DEFINITION BY NATURAL RESOURCE USER GROUP

"The strategy by which, in aggregate, the full array of forest values and functions is maintained at the landscape level. Coordinated management at the landscape level, including across ownerships, is an essential component."[38]

The range of definitions above is reminiscent of the earlier debate about how to define "ecosystem,"[39] but there is a far greater variation in views about how ecosystem management should be defined and applied. This is expected because, while ecosystems are defined by scientific principles alone, ecosystem management involves the interaction of ecological principles with socio-economic and institutional factors.[40] Thus, ecosystem management is defined by the relative weight given to each of these factors by the environmental manager or agency. For example, while an ecologist would place great weight on preserving ecosystem function and biodiversity, a resource agency such as the U.S. Forest Service or the Bureau of Land Management who are required to follow their "multiple-use" mandate, should give relatively more weight to the economic value of the resources they manage.[41]

The newfound acceptance of ecosystem management arose in parallel with the acceptance among most environmentalists of a "new ecology" in which the non-equilibrium, dynamic view of ecosystems replaced the earlier equilibrium view of ecosystems.[42] This realization has affected ecosystem management in two important ways. First, has been the growing use of "adaptive management," in which ecosystem management plans are continuously modified as new ecological (and non-ecological) information is obtained.[43] The second result of the "new ecology" has been the growing controversy over what should be the endpoint of ecosystem management; the return of the ecosystem to "pristine" state identical to pre-European settlement or a healthy ecosystem able to change in a dynamic fashion in response to natural and anthropogenic forces. Ecosystem management also developed at the same time that more economists began to factor environmental variables into the traditional economic cost/benefit equations to create the new discipline of environmental economics. The ecosystem management of the 1990s would be affected by all of these changes.

The components of an idealized ecosystem regime management program are as follows:

Table 8.3 ELEMENTS OF A PLACE-BASED ECOSYSTEMIC MANAGEMENT REGIME

1. A history of social practices establishing a public culture of place.
2. A social movement of citizens advocating the management of the place.
3. An enabling law focusing upon the ecosystem and defining the objectives of its management.
4. The establishment of a collaborative ecosystem governing process.
5. The establishment of the collection of ecosystemic information.
6. The adoption of ecosystemic plans.
7. Adoption of ecosystem related criteria and standards.
8. Mechanism for coordinated ecosystem regulation.
9. A system of feedback evaluation and related citizen participation.

Source: Brooks, Jones and Virginia

Both law and ecology may play an important role in each stage of this management regime. In its beginnings, the social practices, which have either protected or threatened a given ecosystemic place, may be built into or supported by legal practices. These legal practices are part of a socially conditioned ecosystem. The laws undergirding the citizen participation and social movements which led to the formation of the regime may have facilitated demands for the establishment of the regime.

With the formation of an ecosystemic regime, its enabling laws and/or agreements and ecosystemic objectives, the relationship between law and ecology becomes more specific. With the formation of governance mechanisms and the adoption of specific ecosystemic plans and policies in accordance with law, the practical difficulties of implementing ecosystem regimes emerge. These difficulties include legal and political conflicts between the regime and more traditional federal, state and local jurisdictions. These conflicts often end up in the courts. The ecosystem related objectives of the regime (often stated in law) may be contradicted and compromised by economic and other non-ecological objectives. The regime boundaries may incorporate private lands protected by the constitution, as well as state statutes and local ordinances. The resources may or may not be readily available to implement the ecosystem plans and programs under separate regulation.

The construction of ecosystem regimes has required the invention of new "bridge documents" for each stage of the ecosystem management regime. Some of these bridge documents include the following:

Bridge Document 8.1 SELECTED BRIDGE DOCUMENTS WITHIN ECOSYSTEM REGIMES

1. Inter-jurisdiction authorizing agreements.
2. Ecologically-oriented legal objectives.
3. Enabling laws for ecological planning and information gathering.
4. Ecosystem plans and models.
5. Legally authorized coordinative management arrangements.
6. Ecosystem-focused regulations and permitting.
7. Legally mandated impact assessments.

Source: Brooks, Jones and Virginia

These measures are designed to cope with the bioregional relations among government agencies having jurisdictions over different parts of a place-based ecosystem. Case studies have been undertaken of each of these bridge documents, but no fully interpreted study has been completed.

One example of bridge documents is the memoranda of understanding agreements in place-based management programs. The federal Coastal Zone Management Program has promoted the employment of interagency agreements, or memoranda of understanding among different agencies in the implementation of the coastal management program. State laws and regulations adopted to implement the Coastal Zone Management Act may embody coastal ecosystem objectives and authorize the memoranda of understanding which will bind the different state agencies (which may have more narrow jurisdictions) to pursue coastal management objectives.[44] One recent example is the 1990 Coastal Zone Management Act which amended the law to provide for control of non-point source pollution in coastal areas.[45] To implement management measures, the agency requires the programs to include "mechanisms to improve coordination ..."[46] The coordination of different jurisdictions within the coastal management program is further advanced by the consistency requests of the Coastal Zone Management Act, which requires a variety of federal actions be consistent with the states' coastal zone management plan.[47]

The shortfall of the workings of these ecosystemic regimes has stimulated regime theorists to study the relative effectiveness of regimes. Effectiveness measures have included the following:

Table 8.4 REGIME EFFECTIVENESS

Problem solving	Solving the initial problem giving rise to the regime
Goal attainment	Attaining long-term goals
Behavioral effectiveness	Changing attitudes and actions of participants
Process effectiveness	Adoption of appropriate plans, regulations, etc.
Constitutional effectiveness	Investments and activities of governance personnel
Evaluative effectiveness	Regime related evaluative measures

Source: Adapted from Oran Young, *International Governance* (1994)

This framework also provides an interesting way of categorizing and assessing the ecosystem laws themselves.[48] Unfortunately, there has been little comparative study of the different kinds of effectiveness of the ecosystem regimes. Such an assessment is beyond the scope of this introductory book.

Ecosystem Management in Practice

The Chesapeake Bay Program

The Chesapeake Bay Program embraces an ecosystem which is a combination of forests, wetlands, and rivers located around a 200-mile long bay, fed in part by the Atlantic Ocean and encompassing parts of Delaware, Maryland, Pennsylvania, New York, Virginia, West Virginia, and Washington, D.C. The history, nature and culture of the Chesapeake is captured in James Mitchener's bestseller *Chesapeake*. Encountering problems of the over-harvesting of oysters and blue crab, loss of habitat land for bay species, as well as pollution (especially non-point source pollution), the program began in the 1960s under the private Chesapeake Bay Foundation, which initially promoted citizen action and education. In 1983, the Chesapeake Bay Agreement was signed. Among the principal partners were the U.S. Environmental Protection Agency, the Chesapeake Bay Commission (a tri-state legislative body), the District of Columbia, Virginia, Pennsylvania and Maryland, all hoping to restore fin fish, shellfish, and other aquatic life, wildlife, bay grasses, and other habitats. Because the area was an estuary, the advance and application of estuarine science to management was also encouraged by the agreement. In 1987, a second agreement was signed seeking the reduction of non-point pollution by nitrogen and phosphorous entering the Bay as runoff from agricultural and municipal watersheds. Federal legislation, including the Estuary Restoration Act and Chesapeake Bay Restoration Act, have provided funds for restoration projects.[49]

In order to guide its efforts, the Chesapeake Bay program has developed a watershed model, an estuary model and an airshed model.[50] These models seek to predict changes within the ecosystem due to management actions such as sewage treatment, fertilizer and manure applications, and urban sprawl resulting in phosphorous and nitrogen entering the bay. One of the unique aspects of the watershed model was the careful documentation of population growth, and the resulting changes of land and water use activity with the consequent growth in non-point source pollution. Another of the unique aspects of the Chesapeake Bay program is its use of an estuarine model to help guide the restoration of its estuary. For example, estaurine water quality improvements resulting from leaving riparian forest buffer strips along Chesapeake watersheds have been modeled and studied in the field.[51]

Estuarine models are applications of ecology within specific ecosystems. One such larger ecosystem is the coastal area, and within the coastal area is the estuary. An estuary is a semi-enclosed body of seawater measurably diluted by the freshwater that flows into it, resulting in high biotic diversity and primary production. In addition to the Coastal Zone Management Act, there are specific federal laws and a natural program directed at the protection and restoration of estuaries. The Chesapeake Bay program deals with the specific Chesapeake estuary.

As a consequence of these laws, an estuarine science has developed[52] – a synthetic approach that applies more general ecological concepts to the management and restoration of estuaries.[53]

A comprehensive management plan for estuarine areas includes a myriad of goals and measures. One of the most significant and contentious parts of such a plan is to assess and control the impacts of non-source pollution in general and storm water more specifically.[54] The following is the outline of an example that seeks to assess such impacts as part of such a plan for assessing the impact of stormwater runoff.

Table 8.5 EXPECTED EFFECTS OF STORMWATER CONTAMINANTS OR CONDITION ON INTEGRATIVE MEASURES OF ECOSYSTEM RESPONSE

INPUT	Suspended solids (organics).
EXPECTED ENVIRONMENTAL CONSEQUENCE	Dissolved oxygen (DO) depletion enrichment banking.
ENERGY DYNAMICS	1. Alter carbon flux. 2. Reduce complexity of energy pathways and control functions.
FOOD WEB STRUCTURE AND COMPLEXITY	1. Reduce complexity in food web. 2. Eliminate sensitive organisms. 3. Favor species tolerant to low DO and high organic enrichment. 4. Change connection between organisms and trophic levels.
BIODIVERSITY	1. Minimal effect if source areas of colonizing species exist. 2. Urbanization as a process reduces diversity so change must be viewed holistically.
CRITICAL SPECIES	1. Direct effect on species intolerant of low DO and high organic enrichment.
GENETIC DIVERSITY	1. Minimal short-term effect unless species permanently lost due to urbanization. 2. Continuous discharges and highly variable discharges may lead to local loss of gene pool.
DISPERSAL AND MIGRATION	1. Local effects on colonization in altered habitat. 2. Potential interference with movement by blocking zones of passage.
ECOSYSTEM DEVELOPMENT	1. Alteration of successional processes may re-set to community to an earlier successional state. 2. Enrichment leading to alternate stable state. 3. Transient effects associated with frequency and magnitude. 4. Continuous discharges block advanced successional states in zone of influence.

Source: Michael J. Kennish, ed., *Estuary Restoration and Maintenance: The National Estuary Program* (2000)

The Florida Everglades[55]

The ecosystem regime of the Florida Everglades provides an up to date example of large-scale ecosystem management. The Florida Everglades wetland is one part of a larger watershed that covers most of Southern Florida and is divided into three connected basins; the Kissimmee River Basin, Lake Okeechobee, and the Everglades.[56] Drainage starts in the Kissimmee River Basin, enters Lake Okeechobee, and then seeps south into the Everglades.[57] The entire watershed extends over more than 50,000 km².

The ecology of the Everglade ecosystem is dominated by the annual cycle of wet (summer thunderstorms) and dry seasons, which control the short-term (i.e., yearly) fluxes in hydrology and energy flow.[58] Other, longer and shorter scale climate cycles also affect the Everglades, including extensive periods of drought and floods. The proper implementation of an ecosystem management strategy requires an understanding of these processes at the different levels of organization across which they operate. In the Everglades, important processes occur at several scales including the local habitat, the landscape, and the regional scales.[59] One example of a local habitat is the "Alligator Hole," which consists of pools surrounded by emergent marsh plants. The pool itself is kept plant-free by the activity of alligators. At this relatively small scale the observed patterns (e.g., distribution and abundance of plant and animal species) are caused by population-level activities such as predation and competition for resources. Alligator holes are permanent home to many small aquatic animals and plant species and must be protected to ensure survival of these species. However, for the alligator, which requires a larger-scale habitat to survive, it is the ecosystem and landscape levels that are critical.

The Everglade landscape includes alligator holes embedded within several other habitats. Landscape scale processes include the hydrologic system of water cycling within and among the basins, as well as the fires and storms which affect the Everglades. While most critical processes within an alligator hole occur in hours or days, those of the large landscape can occur over decades. The mosaic pattern of a landscape is created and maintained by variation at the habitat level and the landscape processes that can both create or destroy new habitats. This complex interaction between different scales of an ecosystem is both the subject of much ecological research and a difficult but necessary variable to be considered by an ecosystem management plan.

At the regional scale, the Everglades is one part of a massive watershed where there is interaction between the habitat and landscape scale. The annual pattern of wet and dry seasons cause water levels to fluctuate throughout the Everglade landscape. There are also other climatic cycles, some caused by El Nino, that will function on a greater than yearly cycle, while others occur over a period of months.[60] Also, during times of drought (another region-scale process) the alligator holes will function as refuges for animals that would not normally use them.

During the twentieth century, human population growth and development, and the resulting need for water and farmland, has impacted on all spatial levels of organization in the Everglades.[61] What was once a subtropical wetland of over one million acres, and home to many bird, mammal, reptile, and plant species found nowhere else in the U.S., is now half of its original size (with only 1/5 of this being included within the Everglades National Park). The intensive management of the Everglades proceeded throughout the last century, but the particular management strategy has varied in response to large-scale and unpredictable regional changes in the weather. These changes have resulted in four clearly distinguishable eras in the management of the Everglades.[62]

During the first main era of the management of the Everglades, from the 1880s to the mid-1940s, the strategy was to drain as much of the Everglades as possible, both to produce more agricultural land and to control the natural flooding of the watershed.[63] To the early settler of south Florida, like the homesteader of the Great Plains, the goal was to "reclaim" land lost to nature and put it "to the plow." This was particularly tempting in the Everglades, because once water was drained, what was left was an extremely fertile soil usable for farming year round.[64] The end of this first management era came in 1947, the year that the Everglades National Park was established, when over twice the normal rain fell on South Florida and the canals, just like the earlier period of heavy rain, were unable to control the resulting flooding.[65]

The second management era involved a massive new federal management plan carried out by the Army Corps of Engineers called the Central and South Florida Project for Flood Control. This plan was designed to avoid future flooding and called for the establishment of land use areas (agriculture, water conservation, and national park), and the building of over 2200 km of canals and levees as well as pumping station with an almost 4 billion liter/day capacity.[66] One of the major problems that water managers during this period faced was how to maintain the Everglades National Park in as natural a state as possible while still managing the entire watershed for the dual purpose of flood control and increased agricultural productivity. This balancing of interests would prove to be an impossible task.[67] The end of the second era in 1971 would also be caused by a natural but unpredictable weather event; the worst drought in 40 years.[68] This drought, coupled with a recent demand for increased agriculture in the area, led to a heightened concern for the available water supply.[69]

This third era of environmental management witnessed the increase in the role that the state would play in the management of the Everglades.

Following the recommendation of state sponsored panel of experts (resource managers and policy makers but few, if any ecologists) the state passed a statute, the Water Resources Act, mandated the creation of a new state agency, the South Florida Water Management District (SFWMD), and the development of an new management plan. It resulted in; (1) the increased participation of the state in the management of the environment and (2) the growing awareness that the problem of water management in the Everglades may not be solvable by the traditional "command and control" methods of most contemporary environmental statutes. However, this awareness did not translate into a plan based upon anything but the traditional idea that increased technology could fix the water management problems.[70]

The final management era leading to an ecosystem management perspective began in the early 1980s, after yet another serious drought (in 1981) followed by another flood (in 1983). Florida's response to this latest series of climatic oscillations was the creation of the "Save Our Everglades" program, with the stated goal of restoring the Everglades to a near pristine condition by the year 2000.[71] It is during this period that we can witness one of the most extensive examples of the new applied discipline of ecology, restoration ecology, at work.

This era began with the stated purpose of restoring the Everglades, but ecosystem management was not yet a developed method. Instead, Florida collaborated with the Army Corps of Engineers to begin the restoration of the "ecological integrity" of the Everglades through the reduction of the extensive diversion of nutrient rich waters and an attempt to reduce the eutrophication of the watershed.[72] The movement towards an ecosystem management approach in the Everglades began in the late 1980s when ecologists from the SFWMD and the Everglades National Park began to apply modern ecological concepts and methods to the restoration of the Everglades. The process of deciding what ecological methods and concepts should be used, as well as what the proper goals should be, was itself a non-trivial exercise in consensus building among ecologists, resource managers, and policy makers.[73] After three years of workshops, a consensus among scientists and state politicians was reached concerning the problems, goals, and solutions for restoring the Everglades ecosystem. For the ecologists, this consensus provided the blueprint for the ecosystem management approach in the Everglades for the remainder of the 1990s. For the politicians, it provided the incentive to follow the Clinton administration embracement of ecosystem management with its own. In 1993, the Florida Legislature created a new Department of Environmental Protection with the mandate "[t]o protect the functions of entire ecological systems through enhanced coordination of public land acquisition, regulatory, and planning programs."[74]

In 1999, after years of work by several federal and state agencies (led by the U.S. Army Corp of Engineers and the South Florida Water Management District) a restoration plan for the Florida Everglades watershed was submitted to Congress and was adopted in 2000 as part of the Water Resource Development Act of 2000.[75] The Comprehensive Everglades Restoration Plan (CERP) is really a collection of several plans ranging from water management to endangered species protection (e.g., the Florida panther). As part of the implementation of the plan, the SFWMD is develop-ing a "Everglades Landscape Model" which, when completed, will be used to integrate all levels of ecological data in an attempt to make predictions of the long-term effects of various planning strategies.[76]

This resulting multi-scale ecosystem management plan, while complex in its details, is based upon a few accepted principles. First, there needs to be an increased flow of water through the watershed in order to counteract the effects of decades of drainage and to provide enough water for the aquatic and marsh organisms normally found in this type of environment. Second, for decades the Everglades watershed has been used as an endpoint for waste water from human development. Besides the toxic effects on plants and animals the input of polluted waters pushes the resiliency of the ecosystem to the breaking point. As we discussed in previous chapters, an ecosystem is defined as much as anything by its complex network of nutrient cycles and energy flows.[77] While most ecosystems can adapt to some human-made perturbations, there is a limit to how much pollutants can be processed through the system without causing a net loss in energy and nutrients and biodiversity. The third principle of the Everglades management strategy was that there is enough water currently available in the watershed to meet the restoration needs. However, as mentioned above, this water needs to be cleaner and this can only be done at significant social and economic cost; a clear example of the interaction between ecology and economics within ecosystem management. Our introduction to ecosystem management stressed that social and economic concerns must be accounted for when designing a plan. That is true, however it is also necessary to factor in the social and economic cost of implementing the ecological goals. This is where the third aspect of ecosystem management, the institutional organization, is most directly affected. Whether it comes from state or federal funding or from private interests, the money must be found and the people paying for it (usually the taxpayer) must be convinced of the need to divert it from traditional socioeconomic concerns to environmental ones.

The final principle is that the management of the Everglade ecosystem management must be adaptive. The implementation of each management technique is treated as an experiment that can be modified in face of the uncertainties inherent in any ecological system.[78] Adaptive management is a concept that predates and improves ecosystem management. It is the resource managers' answer to the uncertain and dynamic nature of natural ecosystems.[79] While adaptive management principles have been used in a wide variety of complex non-ecological systems they have only recently been applied to ecosystems.[80] Adaptive management requires an ability to accept a range of outcomes of each management decision, the ability to learn from present results, and to modify future plans. As the previous chapters of this book have shown, and later chapters will show, none of these are traits that have commonly been associated with environmental management, and they are not unique to environmental management within ecosystem regimes.

Adaptive management was previously applied to the Everglades ecosystems in various ways by both the state and federal government. First, the SFWMD designed the Everglades Nutrient Removal Project (ENR) for the purpose of reducing total phosphorous entering the watershed and to provide a test model for a larger proposed system, the Stormwater Treatment Areas (STA).[81] Therefore, besides actually being used to reduce phosphorous loads (something the project has been successful at) the ENR was designed as an experiment, the results of which would be used to implement future management strategies. However, this project also points out the problems faced with implementing an adaptive management approach. While adaptive management requires flexibility in the choice of management options, ecosystem management requires the balancing of ecological and socio-economic interests. The results of the ENR have convinced environmental managers to proceed with the larger STA project which would require permits from the Environmental Protection Agency in order to acquire the necessary lands. Much of this land is private and the owners, and the EPA, want assurances that the new project will actually result in water quality standards being met.[82] However, the results of the ENR, like any other experiment in ecosystem ecology, do not come with assurances but only with probabilities. Therefore, the final test for ecosystem management is a political one; how to convince people to give up certain economic value for possible (maybe even probable) environmental gain?

The federal government is also attempting to apply adaptive management, on a large scale, to the Everglades ecosystem. The U.S. Department of State's Man and the Biosphere Program is an holistic attempt to combine geographic information systems (GIS) and computer simulation models to develop a range of land and water use strategies. Each strategy would provide different levels of environmental protection and economic development. These different strategies can then be studied and debated by those with an interest in the Everglades ecosystem (the shareholders) with the intent of implementing the program that best balances all interests.[83]

The history of environmental management in the Florida Everglades shows the failure of previous methods that did not use ecological principles.

It also shows the promise of ecosystem management, the method of choice in the 1990s and the one that explicitly does use ecological principles and methods. However, ecosystem management is not without its severe critics. These include those who see it as an attack on private property rights[84] and those ecologists and environmentalist who see ecosystem management as simply another way to allow human economic concerns to overwhelm ecological knowledge, particularly when the trade-off is between economics and the biodiversity protection. We will return to this last criticism after a discussion of the second great paradigm of environmental management in the 1990s, conservation biology, in the next chapter, and the third paradigm, earth systems science, in the following chapter.

Conclusion

The Chesapeake Bay program and Comprehensive Everglades Restoration Plan and their implementation exemplify the place-based ecosystem regimes and management efforts which have flowered in the 1990s. The regimes are based upon a newly integrated science of ecology. The formation of the regimes themselves have been accompanied with a new understanding of regimes, yielded by the work of Oran Young, Elinor Ostrom and others. A new discipline of ecosystem management has been formulated to enable the adaptive planning and management of these systems. The study of the law of place-based regimes is in its infancy, consisting largely of case-based studies of the various bridge documents to be found within the management process. By identifying the steps in the ecosystem regime management process, describing the bridge documents which link ecology and law and listing the different criteria of effectiveness, we have sought to offer a framework for future legal research pertaining to place-based ecosystem regimes.

Notes

1.   *See* THE CHESAPEAKE BAY PROGRAM, THE STATE OF THE CHESAPEAKE BAY (1995) for a general review of restoration efforts. *See also, A Special Section of Pfesteria Outbreaks in the Chesapeake Bay*, 51 BIOSCIENCE 827 (2001) for a series of articles to the continuing threat to the Chesapeake Bay ecosystem and restoration efforts.

2.   The restoration effort, titled the Chesapeake Bay Program (CBP) was initiated in 1983 with the goal of restoring the biological resources to the bay through large scale management. *See* GARY K. MEFFE, C. RONALD CARROLL, ET. AL., PRINCIPLES OF CONSERVATION BIOLOGY 2nd Edition, 410-14 (1997).

3.   As a result of toxic outbreak of *Pfesteria*, Maryland, Virginia, and Delaware enacted the first laws in the country requiring the management of agricultural nutrient runoff.

4.   *See e.g.*, our discussion of the *Sierra Club v. Marita* cases in Chapter 9 in which the principles of conservation biology were debated in court, as well as the follow-up debate of what ecological concepts and methods should be used in public land management.

5.   For a list of 105 "ecosystem management projects" (which does not include the national parks), *see* STEVEN YAFFEE, ET AL., ECOSYSTEM MANAGEMENT IN THE UNITED STATES (1996). This book, financed by the Wilderness Society, catalogs various ecosystem management projects initiated in the first part of the 1990s and emphasizes that the best projects are those that explicitly manage an ecosystem for sustainability.

6.   *See* Chapter 2 for a history of ecosystem and population ecology.

7.   As mentioned above the ESA, in 1973, implied that ecosystem protection was necessary part of protecting endangered species. Other examples include the management of National Parks which we discussed in an earlier chapter.

8.   The acceptance of Ecosystem Management would reach its peak in 1995 with the report of the Interagency Ecosystem Management Task Force in 1995 which was endorsed by all federal agencies.

9.   *See* Thomas T. Ankersen & Richard Hamann, *Ecosystem Management and the Everglades: A Legal and Institutional Analysis*, 11 J. LAND USE & ENVTL. L. 473, 474 (1996).

10.   Norman L. Christensen et al., *The Report of the Ecological Society of America Committee on the Scientific Basis for Ecosystem Management*, 6 ECOL. APPL. 665 (1996) [hereinafter ESA Report].

11.   This was only one of many reports and studies outlining the features of ecosystem management. The ESA report represents an example of a relatively scientifically focused approach and is similar, at least as to the application of scientific principles, to those produced by most government agencies.

            According to the ESA report, sustainability of an ecosystem across generations should be the main purpose of environmental management. This view was accepted by most, if not all, of those in the environmental movement who accepted ecosystem management as the method of choice. *See generally*, ECOSYSTEM MANAGEMENT FOR SUSTAINABILITY (John D. Peine ed., 1999); YAFFEE, *supra* note 5.

12.   ESA Report, *supra* note 10, at 665. Commentators have noted several other differences between traditional management and EM. EM emphasizes the nonequilibrium view of nature (noted above) as well as the holistic view that has dominated the thinking of ecosystem ecologists since the time of Forbes (see Chapter 3). EM, at least as viewed by ecologists and environmentalists, also emphasizes the balance between economic, human, and ecological concerns with the proper balance being achieved through discussion and consensus building among stakeholders (i.e., those people with interests in the implementation and outcome of the management process). Traditional management, besides viewing ecosystems as being in equilibrium or moving towards a predictable "climax community," also emphasized an optimization approach both to achieving maximum economic gain and by trying to achieve, often through coercion of the stakeholders, a single "best" method of management. *See* PRINCIPLES OF CONSERVATION BIOLOGY, *supra* note 2, at 365.

13.   *See* Chapter 3 for a detailed discussion of the early development of the ecosystem concept. There were ecologists during the early decades of ecology who dismissed the very notion of ecosystems as artificial constructions and representative of real distinguishable aspect of nature. However, by the 1970s and certainly by 1990, all respected ecologists accepted the reality of ecosystems, even though many still believed it was difficult to actually delineate the boundaries of specific ecosystems. The ESA Report uses the following definition of ecosystem: "a spatially explicit unit

of the Earth that includes all of the organisms, along with all components of the abiotic environment within its boundaries." G. Likens, *An Ecosystem Approach: its Use and Abuse*, EXCELLENCE IN ECOLOGY, BOOK 3 (1992).

14. It is, of course, an overstatement to imply that all populations can be easily classified. However, this is a relatively small problem compared to that of classifying ecosystems. The problem of defining the boundaries exists within both ecology and environmental law. Traditionally, boundaries within environmental law are defined by property law; a publicly owned federal forest is managed not because it is a separate biological division but because of historical patterns of land sale. Only recently has there been an attempt to equate the boundary concept in ecology with that used in environmental law. *See* Chapter 9's discussion of the U.S. Forest Service's proposed regulations for one attempt to conform the boundaries that are managed by one environmental law, the NFMA, to ecological reality.

15. *See* ESA Report, *supra* note 10, at 670. An excellent example of this operational definition of ecosystems is the long-term Hubbard Brook study discussed in Chapter 3. The researchers defined this ecosystem based upon where inputs and outputs of nutrients (e.g., nitrogen and phosphorous) could be localized.

16. *See* Chapter 1 for a review of the modern research approach among ecosystem ecologists.

17. During the 1980s and 1990s the National Park Service recognized that even Yellowstone National Park was too small a system for the management of many species including the Grizzly bear, and created the Greater Yellowstone Ecosystem in which the park is only one part. THE GREATER YELLOWSTONE ECOSYSTEM: REFINING AMERICA'S WILDERNESS HERITAGE (Robert B. Keiter & Mark S. Boyce eds., 1991).

18. *See* ESA Report, *supra* note 10, at 671.

19. *See* MEFFE, ET AL., *supra* note 2; The importance of this elements is highlighted in Chapter 9 where we discuss the role of conservation biology in the management of national forests and endangered species.

20. Or, at least, the system ecology that developed during the 1980s and that stressed the hierarchical structure of natural systems. *See* O'NEIL, ET AL., A HIERARCHICAL CONCEPT OF ECOSYSTEMS (1986). This work was discussed in Chapter 1 and represents that part of system ecology most accepted and used by other ecologists during the early 1990s.

21. We use the term "new ecology" differently than most environmental law commentators who, when they discuss a new ecology, are referring to the relatively new awareness (especially among non-ecologists) that most ecosystems, populations, and communities exist in a state of disequilibrium. It is true that the extent of this disequilibrium has only recently been fully appreciated by many ecologists. However, the study of nonequilibrium systems (e.g., populations and ecosystems) has been a part of ecology for decades. *See* Chapter 3.

22. *See* ESA Report, *supra* note 10, at 684.

23. ESA Report, *supra* note 10, at 669-70.

24. INTERAGENCY ECOSYSTEM MANAGEMENT TASK FORCE, THE ECOSYSTEM APPROACH: HEALTHY ECOSYSTEMS AND SUSTAINABLE ECONOMIES VOL. 1 (1995).

25. R. E. Grumbine, *What is ecosystem management?*, 8 CONSERV. BIOL. 27 (1994).

26. *See e.g.,* ESA Report, *supra* note 10, at 676; MEFFE, ET AL, *supra* note 2.

27. As we shall see, particularly in connection with the Northern Spotted Owl controversy in the Northwest, it is the relative weight given to the human concerns that has caused the most concerns with specific ecosystem management plans.

28.   *See* T.W. Clark and D. Zaunbrecher, *The Greater Yellowstone Ecosystem: The Ecosystem Concept in Natural Resource Policy and Management*, 5 RENEW. RES. J. 8 (1987).

29.   *See* R.E. Grumbine, *What is Ecosystem Management?* 8 CONSERV. BIOL. 27 (1994).

30.   *See* R.F. NOSS & A. COOPERRIDER, SAVING NATURE'S LEGACY: PROTECTING AND RESTORING BIODIVERSITY (1994).

31.   ESA Report, *supra* note 10.

32.   *See* ENVIRONMENTAL PROTECTION AGENCY, INTEGRATED ECOSYSTEM PROTECTION RESEARCH PROGARM: A CONCEPTUAL PLAN. WORKING DRAFT (1994).

33.   *See* U.S. FISH AND WILDLIFE SERVICE, AN ECOSYSTEM APPROACH TO FISH AND WILDLIFE CONSERVATION. INTERNAL WORKING DRAFT (DECEMBER 1994).

34.   *See* U.S. DEPARTMENT OF INTERIOR. BUREAU OF LAND MANAGEMENT, ECOSYSTEM MANAGEMENT IN THE BLM: FROM CONCEPT TO COMMITMENT (1994).

35.   *See* INTERAGENCY ECOSYSTEM MANAGEMENT TASK FORCE, THE ECOSYSTEM APPROACH: HEALTHY ECOSYSTEMS AND SUSTAINABLE ECONOMIES, VOL.1 (1995).

36.   *See* FOREST ECOSYSTEM MANAGEMENT ASSESSMENT TEAM, FOREST ECOSYSTEM MANAGEMENT: AN ECOLOGICAL, ECONOMIC, AND SOCIAL ASSESSMENT (1993).

37.   *See* THE KEYSTONE NATIONAL POLICY DIALOGUE ON ECOSYSTEM MANAGEMENT (1996).

38.   *See* SOCIETY OF AMERICAN FORESTERS, SUSTAINING LONG-TERM FOREST HEALTH AND PRODUCTIVITY (1993).

39.   *See* Chapter 2.

40.   *See supra* note 2.

41.   As we discussed in earlier Chapters, this "multiple-use" mandate is of a statutory nature, with such statutes as the NFMA, FLPMA, and the aptly named Multiple-Use, Sustained-Yield Act of 1960 (MUSY) requiring public land managers to balance conservation with socioeconomic issues (e.g., industry and tourism).

42.   As we described in Chapter 1, most of this "new ecology" was new to the non-ecologist only. The idea that most, if not all ecosystems, are in a state of dynamic disequilibrium has only been given extensive coverage among legal scholars recently, but was an accepted part of ecology decades ago.

43.   *See* ADAPTIVE ENVIRONMENTAL ASSESSMENT AND MANAGEMENT (C.S. Holling ed., 1978) for an early explanation of the adaptive management concept. This book still represents one of the founding documents of adaptive management.

44.   Two examples were the initial Massachusetts and Connecticut Coastal Zone Management programs which depended heavily upon such interagency agreements.

45.   16 §1133 (1990).

46.   *Id.* §1133 (6). This provision fits with the federal laws request that state programs be coordinated with state and local water quality programs. 16 U.S.C.A. §1455b (1990). Note that the statute also provides for joint project agreements. *See also* Note, *Implementation and Enforcement of the 1990 Coastal Zone Amendments Reauthorization Act Section 6217, 75* B.U. L. REV. *889 (1995).*

47.   *See* 16 U.S.C. §1455. For an early overview of coordination with case studies, *see* Marc J. Hershman, *Achieving Federal-State Coordination in Coastal Resources Management*, 16 WM & MARY L. REV. 747-772 (1975). For a review of the recent developments re consistency, *see* Jack Archer, *Evolution of Major CZMA Amendments Restoring Federal Consistency and Protecting Coastal Water Quality*, 1 TERR. SEA. J. 1911 (1991). Other environmental programs have also relied upon such interagency agreements, including the Southern Oregon/Northern California Coast Evolutionary Significant Unit of Coho Salmon, 62 F.R. 24588.

48.   Yaffee *(see supra note 5 at,* 3-49) sought to evaluate the relative success of these efforts.

49.   For a more detailed history, *see* Robert Costanza & Jack Greer, *The Chesapeake Bay and its Watershed: A Model for Sustainable Ecosystem Management?* in BARRIERS AND BRIDGES OF ECOSYSTEMS AND INSTITUTIONS (Lance H. Gunderson, C.S. Holling & Stephen S. Light eds.,1995).

50.   For one of several descriptions of these models, *see* Carl F. Corio, *Chesapeake Bay Eutrophication Model,* ESTUARINE SCIENCE, A SYNTHETIC APPROACH TO RESEARCH AND PRACTICE, 363-405 (John E. Hobbbie ed., 2000).

51.   *See* R. Lowrence, et al., *Water Quality Functions of Riparian Forest Buffers in Chesapeake Bay Watersheds,* 21 ENV'TL MANAGEMENT 687-712 (1997).

52.   *See* Hobbie, *supra* note 50. *Note* Donald F. Boesch et. al., *Scientific Synthesis in Estuarine Management* at 507-526.

53.   The restoration of estuaries is part of a larger effort to apply ecology to the restoration of many environments. *See* ENVIRONMENTAL RESTORATION: SCIENCE AND STRATEGIES FOR RESTORING THE EARTH (John J. Berger ed., 1990).

54.   ESTUARY RESTORATION AND MAINTENANCE: THE NATIONAL ESTUARY PROGRAM (Michael J. Kemish ed., 2000).

55.   Much of the our discussion on the Florida Everglades is based on an article by a former Vermont Law School student, Warren T. Coleman. Warren T. Coleman, *Legal Barriers to the Restoration of Aquatic Systems and the Utilization of Adaptive Management,* 23 VT L. REV. 177 (1998).

56.   *See* MEFFE, ET AL., *supra* note 2, at 454.

57.   *See* Coleman, *supra* note 55, at 181; Stephen S. Light & J. Walter Dineen, *Water Control in the Everglades: Historical Perspective,* in EVERGLADES: THE ECOSYSTEM AND ITS RESTORATION 47, 51 (Steven M. Davis & John C. Ogden eds., 1994).

58.   *See* MEFFE, ET AL., *supra* note 2, at 454; Energy flow into, out, and within an ecosystem has been a dominate theme of research among ecosystem ecologists at least from the time Lindeman's research on trophic dynamics in a Minnesota lake and the work of Thomas Odum on a spring system in Florida. *See* Chapter 3.

59.   *See* MEFFE, ET AL., *supra* note 2, at 452.

60.   *See* L.H. Gunderson, *Vegetation of the Everglades: Composition and Determinants,* in EVERGLADES, THE ECOSYSTEM AND ITS RESTORATION (S.M. Davis & J.C. Ogden eds., 1992).

61.   *See generally,* DAVID MCCALLY, THE EVERGLADES: AN ENVIRONMENTAL HISTORY (1999). This book traces the history of the Everglades from its formation approximately five thousand years ago, through the early settlements of Native Americans to the present. As McCally points out the first concerted attempt to manage the Everglades was in the 1880s and consisted of an attempt to drain it for agriculture, and effort that would almost succeed in the early 1900s.

62.   *See* Stephen S. Light, et al., *Evolution of Management in a Turbulent Ecosystem,* in BARRIERS AND BRIDGES TO THE RENEWAL OF ECOSYSTEMS AND INSTITUTIONS 103, 117 (Lance H. Gunderson et al.. eds., 1995).

63.   *See* Coleman, *supra* note 55 at 181; Light, et. al., *supra* note 62, at 116-19.

64.   Early attempts at drainage, initiated by Governor Napoleon Bonaparte Broward concentrated on building canals. Besides producing farmland the second major purpose for drainage was the control of flooding. The canals were successful at this, at least during years with average rain. However, when the unpredictable periods of heavy rain came the canals could not cope and extensive flooding would occur as it did in 1903 due to heavy rains and in 1926 and 1928 as a result of hurricanes. *See* MEFFE, ET AL., *supra* note 2, at 455-56.

65.   This period of heavy rain was partially a result of another hurricane and came just two years after the most severe drought on record. *See* Coleman, *supra* note 55, at 182.

66.   *See* MEFFE, ET AL., *supra* note 2, at 456; Coleman, *supra* note 55, at 182; Light et al., *supra* note 62, at 125.

67.   *See* Coleman, *supra* note 55, at 182. As we showed in earlier chapters this attempt to balance socioeconomic goals with the mandate to preserve national parks in as pristine a state as possible has been a long battle for the National Park Service, and often lost.

68.   *See id.*

69.   While maybe not as unpredictable as hurricanes and droughts the increased demand for water for agriculture in the late 1960s and early 1970s was a result of increased sugar cane production following the U.S. ban on sugar imports from Cuba; an example of how political factors must also be balanced in the management of an ecosystem. *See* MEFFE, ET AL., *supra* note 2, at 456.

70.   *See* Coleman, *supra* note 55, at 183.

71.   *See id.*

72.   *See* LIGHT ET. AL., *supra* note 62, at 143; Coleman, *supra* note 55, at 184. This attempt at state-federal collaboration at solving an environmental problem is a positive sign. However, it was not without its setbacks. In 1988 the federal government sued Florida alleging that it had violated the water quality standards and water quality agreements made between the state and federal governments. *See id.*

73.   *See* EVERGLADES: THE ECOSYSTEM AND ITS RESTORATION (S.M. Davis & J.C. Ogden eds., 1994).

74.   1993, Fla. Laws ch. 93-213 (codified as amended at FLA. STAT. § 20.255 (1995)). This statutory acceptance of the need to protect ecological processes and functions, and not just components (e.g., single species), is not found in any federal statute. This is not the only example of a state government going further then the federal government in implementing ecological principles during the 1990s.

75.   Pub. L. No. 106-541, 2000. Section 601 of Title VI deals specifically with the Everglades Restoration Plan. The plan, and other related information is available at <www.everglades.org>.

76.   EVERGLADES LANDSCAPE MODEL (visited October 24, 2001) <http://www.sfwmd.gov>.

77.   *See* Chapters 1 and 3 for a discussion of the development and current state of ecosystem ecology.

78.   As we have already shown, the history of the Florida Everglades and of human attempts to manage it, are ripe with unpredictable and often catastrophic climatic events. Traditional management methods ignore these ecological uncertainties and impose a single management method that is meant to handle all possible events. However, most interpretations of ecosystem management include the need to be adaptive to change by adopting new methods and changing old ones in the light of new information or events (ecological or socioeconomic).

79.   *See* ADAPTIVE ENVIRONMENTAL ASSESSMENT AND MANAGEMENT, *supra* note 43; CARL WALTERS, ADAPTIVE MANAGEMENT OF RENEWABLE RESOURCES (1986).

80.   For an overview of complex systems, in and outside of science, and the need to apply an adaptive approach to their management *see* NICHOLAS RESCHER, COMPLEXITY (1998).

81.   *See* S. FLA. WATER MGMT. DISTRICT, THE EVERGLADE NUTRIENT REMOVAL PROJECT – YEAR TWO SYNOPSIS (1997); Coleman, *supra* note 55, at 188. Phosphorus is chief component of water pollution caused by human development and interferes with the proper function of aquatic ecosystems by interfering with normal nutrient cycles.

82.   *See* Ankersen & Hamann, *supra* note 9, at 497.

83.   The strategies ranged from land and water use patterns similar to pre-European settlement to a strategy that involved maximizing short term economic gain at the expense of environmental protection. The results of this program indicate that only minor changes in current water use in the Everglades would maintain the necessary water balance within the ecosystem and lead to agricultural sustainability. *See* MEFFE, ET AL., *supra* note 2, at 400-01; M.A. Harwell et al., *Ecosystem Management to Achieve Ecological Sustainability: The Case of South Florida*, 20 ENVIRON. MGMT. 497-521 (1996).

84.   *See e.g.*, ALTON CHASE, IN A DARK WOOD (1995).

9 The Ecosystemic Regime and Biodiversity Protection in the 1990s

Conservation biology is, by its own terms, an applied science. As such, the extent of its application will define its utility and function as much as the integrity and importance of its research results. Thus, the ultimate role this science will play in reforming land management will be determined in large part by the legal duties accepted by, or imposed upon, governmental agencies to respond to the merits of this science. We must not simply wait for new statutes to be debated by Congress, but must closely attend to the ongoing development of law and policy in Wisconsin, in the Northwest, and throughout the land, to establish a substantial legal duty to protect biodiversity in the terms being articulated by conservation biology.
                    – Walter Kuhlmann, lead attorney for the plaintiffs
in Sierra Club v. Marita[1]

During the 1990s, Conservation Biology would become the major tool for the protection of overall biodiversity, through changing practices of land management, and through the protection of individual species. *Sierra Club v. Marita* represents the former approach and the Northern Spotted Owl is the classic example of the new use of ecology to protect endangered and threatened species. In the 1988 case, *Northern Spotted Owl v. Hodel*,[2] a federal district court held that the 1987 U.S. Fish and Wildlife Service's (USF&WS) decision not to list the Northern Spotted Owl as endangered or threatened under the Endangered Species Act was "arbitrary and capricious." For a court to hold that any federal agency decision is "arbitrary and capricious" is unusual. However, what made this case even more startling was that the agency decision in question was a based upon its interpretation of data and ecological models, the USF&WS's area of agency expertise.

Within its area of expertise an agency would usually be required to show only that the decision was not unreasonable (i.e., that some biologists could agree with it). However, in *Northern Spotted Owl* the court found that, "The Service's documents also lack any expert analysis supporting its conclusion. Rather, the expert opinion is entirely to the contrary." Not only had independent ecologists called for the listing of the Northern Spotted Owl, but so had the agency's own biologists.[3]

The court would not totally disregard the usual deference to federal agencies. The court remanded the matter to the agency for it "to provide an analysis for its decision that listing the northern spotted owl as threatened or endangered is not currently warranted."[4] No such analysis was forthcoming and within a year the USF&WS had proposed to list the Northern Spotted Owl as a threatened species.

Introduction

The *Northern Spotted Owl* decision illustrates the advent of a new conservation biology in which population and ecosystem ecology are integrated. This change in conservation biology is just one example of the growing integration among ecological sub-disciplines that occurred in the 1990s. This new integrated ecology accompanied new legal regulations under the Endangered Species Act (ESA) and the National Forest Management Act (NFMA), and exemplifies the gradual application of integrated ecology not only as applied to forests and endangered species but also under several other laws, including those governing marine mammals and fisheries (as well as internationally endangered species described in the next chapter).

A fundamental distinction can be drawn between the Endangered Species Act and the other biodiversity laws. The ESA operates at least in part as a biocentric law which regards ecosystems as instruments to support an inherently valuable biodiversity. The other biodiversity laws presume bio-diversity within the constraints of seeking to maintain a sustainable ecosystem – a sustainability which includes a primary role for human purposes. The retrofitting of these latter laws with new ecology has not expunged them of their controlling utilitarian purposes.

The ecological background to the *Northern Spotted Owl* decision reveals the influence the science of ecology was beginning to have upon environmental law. In 1988 Russ Lande, a theoretical ecologist at the University of Chicago, published an article in the ecology journal *Oecologia* in which he critiqued the population ecology model used by the U.S. Forest Service as a basis for their management plan of the old growth forests of the Pacific Northwest, as well as its most famous resident, the Northern Spotted Owl. Lande also presented two of his own ecological models for the Northern Spotted Owl. One model was an estimate of the population's growth rate and the second was a prediction of how the future loss of habitat, resulting from the then current U.S. Forest Service management plan, would affect the population.[5] This article was written for ecologists, but was inspired by a 1986 request from Andy Stahl, a lawyer with the Portland office of the National Wildlife Federation. This report was to be used to convince the U.S. Fish and Wildlife Service both to list the owl as endangered or threatened and to set aside an ecologically justified amount of critical habitat (i.e., old growth forest).[6] While Lande's methodology, based upon differential calculus and stochastic (random) environmental variation, was foreign to most environ-mental lawyers, his conclusion was clear. The Northern Spotted Owl required a habitat containing approximately 21 percent old growth forest while the Forest Service's plan would, if followed, result in a habitat of only 7 to 16 percent old growth forest, a size insufficient to prevent extinction of the Spotted Owl. Ecologists in and out of government accepted Lande's model, but not the Forest Service nor the USFWS; not until they were forced by the 1988 *Northern Spotted Owl* decision.

The species listing decision, which was the issue in *Northern Spotted Owl*, is only the first step in the management of threatened and endangered species under the ESA (see Chapter 6 for a discussion of the various sections of the ESA). Once a species is listed the ESA, with exceptions, requires: (1) A determination of the species' critical habitat (i.e., the amount of habitat required for long-term survival);[7] (2) The development and implementation of a conservation plan for the listed species; (3) A determination that a federal project will not jeopardize the survival of the listed species; (4) The enforcement of the "no take" provision against listed animal species and occasionally listed plant species; and (5) The development of a Habitat Conservation Plan (HCP) to mitigate the effects of "incidental takes" of listed species. An integrated ecology may be relevant to each of these steps in the protection of endangered species.

In a previous chapter, we recounted that during the 1970s and 1980s the Forest Service's approach to biodiversity protection emphasized a habitat approach to biodiversity protection; one in which population size and the number of species were optimized through the maintenance of an adequate type and amount of habitat. During this period the ESA took an almost exclusively species-specific approach, in which species identified as threatened or endangered and their habitats were singled out for protection.[8] In this chapter we will continue our story of the changing application of ecology in the two most important environmental laws dealing with bio-diversity: the Endangered Species Act (ESA) and the National Forest Management Act (NFMA). The recent litigation over the application of these two statutes reveals some of the most interesting and contentious discussions of the proper role of ecology in environmental law.

MANAGEMENT OF THE NORTHERN SPOTTED OWL IN THE 1990S
The immediate impact of listing the Northern Spotted Owl was the convening of an Interagency Spotted Owl Scientific Committee (ISC) in 1989 to "develop a scientifically credible conservation strategy for the Northern Spotted Owl."

The Committee first used field data to test three hypotheses to determine if the Spotted Owl was threatened by old growth logging practices (the acceptance of any one hypothesis would indicate that the Spotted Owl was not threatened):

1. The finite rate of population change of owls is ≥ 1.0 (i.e., the population was growing).

2. Spotted Owls do not differentiate among habitats on the basis of forest age or structure.

3. No decline has occurred in the areal extent of habitat types selected by Spotted Owls for foraging, roosting, or nesting.

The Committee rejected all three hypothesis and instead proposed five principles of nature reserves that are derived from the theory of island biogeography and are a basic part of conservation biology (and similar to the proposals of the *Marita* plaintiffs): (1) Species that are well distributed across their ranges are less prone to extinction than species confined to small portions of their ranges; (2) Large blocks of habitat containing many individuals of a given species are more likely to sustain that species than are small blocks of habitat with only a few individuals; (3) Blocks of habitat in close proximity are preferable to widely dispersed blocks of habitat; (4) Contiguous, unfragmented blocks of habitat are superior to highly fragmented blocks of habitat; (5) Habitat between protected areas is more easily traversed by dispersing individuals the more closely it resembles suitable habitat for the species in question.

To address the scientific uncertainty related to how much habitat Spotted Owls need, the committee used computer simulation models based upon the 1987 population demographic modeling of Russ Lande. Based upon the ultimate goal of 95 percent certainty of persistence of Spotted Owls in their range for 100 years, the models suggested that the best habitat size and structure for locally stable populations would be a network of blocks, each capable of supporting at least 20 pairs of birds.

Source: Modified from Gary K. Meffe et. al., *Principles of Conservation Biology* 433-39 (2nd) 1997

In the remainder of this section, we will briefly outline some of the major developments in biodiversity laws in the 1990s. We will then describe the recent developments in conservation biology from its roots in population ecology to its current application as the science of biodiversity protection. Following this history, we discuss the effectiveness of the ESA, given its species-centric focus, in protecting various levels of biodiversity. We will then trace some of the tumultuous history of the second major American biodiversity law, the NFMA, and how recent applications of this law illustrate a growing trend to better integrate ecology into environmental law. Finally, we will outline the increasing use of ecosystem management, complete with its use of a multi-level integrated ecology.

Except for the law dealing with the management of the marine fishery, the language of the federal statutes dealing with biodiversity protection remained fundamentally unchanged during the 1990s.[9] The Endangered Species Act (ESA) continued to protect single endangered or threatened species (species-level biodiversity). Most importantly, the ESA would remain the only domestic federal statute designed to deal with biodiversity protection on private lands; Especially important was the requirement that Habitat Conservation Plans be developed and approved when "incidental takes" of listed species take place. For the protection of overall biodiversity[10] on public lands or common water, the National Forest Management Act for national forests, the Federal Land Policy and Management Act (FLPMA) and the Taylor Grazing Act for public range-lands, and fisheries legislation for marine fish resources all require the protection of biodiversity and their respective regulations provide guidelines, of various detail, on how to achieve this protection. Although other laws deal with biodiversity, we will concentrate on how biodiversity laws use ecology to protect single species (as with the ESA) or some more general measures of biodiversity such as number of species or diversity of habitats (e.g., the NFMA and Fishery Management Act).

Despite the relative lack of change in the statutory language of biodiversity laws during the 1990s, the application of these laws would change dramatically. During the 1990s the biodiversity laws would move away from the original "species only" focus of the Endangered Species Act and its habitat to one based upon the holistic view that populations could only be protected if their habitat and ecosystems were also protected.[11] A major result of this change was the development of a distinct type of "biodiversity" ecosystem management.[12] This form of ecosystem management focuses not upon the ecosystem itself, but upon the biodiversity (species, communities, and habitats) within the ecosystem.

The move towards a "biodiversity" ecosystem management policy by federal agencies resulted in dramatic changes in how ecology would be applied to biodiversity protection. In 1990, as exemplified by the Spotted Owl controversy, listing and critical habitat designations were the focus for the debate on how to apply ecology to the ESA. These continue to be important issues to both ecologists and environmental lawyers concerned about endangered and threatened species.

OTHER BIODIVERSITY LAWS

The emphasis on the Forest Service and the ESA should not be taken to mean that these laws are the only sources of interaction between ecology and biodiversity law. Other important laws include:

1) The Marine Mammal Protection Act which, with its emphasis on maximum sustainable yield and optimum sustainable populations on the one hand and marine ecosystem health and stability on the other, is a statute that explicitly combines concepts from both population and ecosystem ecology. A relatively new concept seen in marine mammal protection internationally, but one not seen in this Act, is the *precautionary principle* (see Chapter 10 for more discussion). The precautionary principle holds that when ecological information provides no certain answer to the levels of protection needed, we should err on the side of maximizing protection; even if that means a complete ban on all killing (i.e., "take") of individual members of protected species.[13]

2) The Fishery Conservation and Management Act which includes its own sections dealing with maximum sustainable yield and optimum yield (both modifications of population ecology models) as well as a requirement that "essential fish habitat" be identified and that any management plan developed should "[M]iminize to the extent practicable adverse effects on such habitat caused by fishing, and identify other actions to encourage the conservation and enhancement of such habitat."[14]

3) Other statutes designed for the specific purpose of preserving particularly fragile or "important" (in a biological or aesthetic sense) lands (e.g., the Wilderness Act of 1964, the National Marine Sanctuaries Act, The National Park Organic Act, and the National Wildlife Refuge System).

Source: Michael J. Bean & Melanie J. Rowland, *The Evolution of National Wildlife Law* (3rd ed. 1997)

As the decade wore on, habitat conservation plans (HCPs) would become the main area of ESA controversy and litigation with the chief question being: How well do HCPs integrate ecological concepts and methods?[15] Debates about these questions would be particularly heated because most HCPs involve the use of ecology to manage one of the most precious of American legal institutions: private property rights. On the other hand, for NFMA and the other biodiversity laws which apply to public resources, the most significant change would be the appreciation that a multi-level approach to biodiversity and ecological processes was necessary for the protection of biodiversity. These policy changes would also result in changes in how the science of biodiversity, i.e., conservation biology, was carried out in the 1990s.

THE BIODIVERSITY CRISIS

In the 1980s, the biodiversity concept was formulated and the increasing threat to biodiversity, and some of the human causes of biodiversity loss (e.g., overexploitation and habitat fragmentation) was recognized. During the 1990s there was a growing consensus among biologists that the earth was in the beginning stages of a human-made mass extinction of species.[16] The current mass extinction could reach the magnitude of the previous five mass extinction periods, that have occurred sporadically over the last 450 million years, and wiped out most existing species at the time.[17] The mass extinction of 245 million years ago was the largest, wiping out as many as ninety-six percent of all marine animal species as well as much of the terrestrial biodiversity. The recovery of biodiversity from those earlier mass extinctions took from between 10 and 100 million years.[18] Recovering from the present mass extinction could take just as long and would probably require returning large portions of the Earth to their natural state, so that the natural evolution of new species could take place.[19] In the new millennium, much of the disagreement among conservation biologists and government officials over how to integrate ecology into biodiversity laws stems from differing opinions on how acute is this biodiversity crisis and how much science is required to solve it.

Conservation Biology: From Scientific Theory to Management Policy

The main scientific framework used for biodiversity protection since 1990 has been the applied science of conservation biology.[20] In Chapter 6 we sketched the early history of conservation biology under the leadership of Michael Soulé and other ecologists.[21] The early 1980s' version of conservation biology was mostly a combination of population ecology, population genetics, and evolu-tionary theory.[22] The conservation biologists of the early and mid-1980s applied well-established ecological principles to evaluate the biological risks to populations, species, and habitats resulting from human actions.[23]

In these formative years, conservation biology focused on four issues. First was the use of the population ecology principles developed by MacArthur and his successors to estimate the minimum size at which any population could persist (i.e., Minimum Viable Population). Second, was the use of principles of population genetics and evolutionary biology to estimate the minimum amount of genetic variation required to insure survival of any population.[24] Third, was the renewed interest in the estimation of the patterns of distribution of known and newly discovered species.[25] Finally, a major new issue of interest to conservation biologists and environmental policy makers was the effect of habitat fragmentation on resident species. It was by becoming a theoretical framework for the effects of habitat fragmentation that MacArthur and Wilson's theory of island biogeography became a part of conservation biology.[26]

Since the mid-1980s conservation biology has developed by integrating its traditional emphasis on populations with the concepts and methods of ecosystem ecology, landscape ecology, and global ecology. Modern conservation biology is also more actively dealing with the effects of human in "both natural and degraded ecological systems."[27] For the land manager, this acceptance of the human element often means the balancing of human economic and social interests with ecological factors (see previous chapter). In turn, for the conservation biologist, it means the consideration of human activities, both within and outside conserved or protected areas. The conservation biologist in the 1990s has found it necessary to add knowledge of economic and social sciences to the practice of a discipline that once was largely an applied form of population ecology.

Biodiversity Protection in the ESA

The ESA does not explicitly require the measurement or consideration of any level of biodiversity (unlike the NFMA),[28] except for endangered or threatened species.[29] While the ESA does contain a stated purpose to conserve "eco-systems,"[30] neither the concepts nor methodologies of ecosystem ecology, landscape ecology, nor global ecology are mentioned again in either the statue or its regulations. The ESA does require the protection of "critical habitat" as a way to protect individual species and the "no take" provisions of section 9 has been interpreted as including some forms of habitat modification. However, both of these requirements were designed as methods to protect individual species, not as ways to protect higher level ecological structures or functions; the ESA is designed to protect ecosystem components (e.g., species), not ecosystems themselves. A major ESA mechanism for the protection of individual species is the requirement that no person, public or private, is allowed to "take" an endangered species, without obtaining an exemption.[31] This exemption requires the creation of a Habitat Conservation Plan (HCP), which along with the no taking requirement, is the main mechanism for protecting endangered species and biodiversity on private lands; the HCP and the associated "No Surprise Policy" were the most important and controversial developments in the ESA at the end of the 1990s.[32]

A thorough discussion of the various HCPs that were developed during the 1990s is beyond the scope of this chapter. However, in general HCPs can be thought of as analogous to the place-centered ecosystem management plans (e.g., the Everglades Restoration Plan) which we discussed in the previous chapter. Like those plans, the HCPs developed in the 1990s attempted to balance environmental protection, in his case the statutory requirement of protecting endangered or threatened species, with the economic and social drive for development. How ecology is used by the various HCPs has been criticized in a recent review by the National Center for Ecological Analysis and Synthesis. The study found that the two major problem areas in most HCPs was the estimation of impacts and the development of reliable methods for monitoring populations. The study further found that it was in their treatment of scientific uncertainty that most HCPs fail to properly implement ecological concepts and methods. This is seen in such basic elements of a HCP as the estimation of local population sizes; most HCPs fail to implement pre-cautionary measures to account for the high level of uncertainty inherent in these estimations. The lack of attention to this initial uncertainty leads to the development of mitigation methods that may grossly underestimate the impacts of planned developments on listed species.

A second potential problem with the ESA's approach is that the definitions of key terms in the ESA (e.g., harm and taking) are not generally defined in an ecologically meaningful way. An example of this problem is the often quoted language of Justice O'Connor's concurrence in *Babbitt v. Sweet Home*, "In my view, the regulation [concerning takings] is limited by its terms to actions that actually kill or injures individual animals."[33] Even more restrictively, Justice Scalia, in the *Sweet Home* dissent, would even eliminate impairment of breeding from the statutory definition of harm and restrict take to actions that directly kill or harm an individual.[34] It is language similar to that of Justice O'Connor which was codified into agency regulations.[35] Many commentators have applauded this language, and the Court's interpretation, as explicitly allowing some forms of adverse habitat modification to be included within the statutory definition of "take."[36] This is certainly an important development and is far more biologically meaningful then the restrictive definition that Justice Scalia would have adopted in *Sweet Home*.[37] However, any definition which limits harm to actions that directly kill or cause harm will eliminate many possible detrimental actions from possible judicial review. These and other ecological shortcomings of the ESA were addressed in the 1995 National Research Council (NRC) report, *Science and the Endangered Species Act*,[38] which was undertaken after a Congressional request to the NRC to review the following issues:[39]

- Definition of species. The committee was asked to review how the term species has been used to implement the ESA, and what units would best serve the purposes of the act.
- Conservation conflicts between species. The committee was asked how frequent or severe conflicting conservation needs are when more than one species in a geographic area are listed as endangered or

threatened under the ESA, and to make recommendations to resolve these conflicts.

- Role of habitat conservation. The committee was asked to evaluate the role of habitat protection in the conservation of species and to review the relationship between habitat-protection and other requirements of the act.
- Recovery planning. The committee was asked to review the role of recovery planning under the act and to consider how recovery planning could better contribute to the purposes of the act.
- Risk. The committee was asked to review the role of risk in decisions made under the ESA (such as what constitutes sufficient "endangerment" to require listing of a species, what constitutes jeopardy, adverse modifications, reasonable and prudent alternatives, taking, conservation, and recovery). It was also asked to review whether different degrees of risk ought to apply to different types of decisions (e.g., should an endangered species be at greater risk than a threatened species to justify listing?) and to identify practical methods for assessing risk to achieve the purposes of the act better while providing flexibility in appropriate circumstances to accommodate other objectives as well.
- Issues of timing. The committee was asked to review the timing of key decisions under the ESA and to consider ways of improving such timing under the act to serve its purposes better while minimizing unintended consequences.

For our purposes, three of the above issues are of particular importance; definition of species, role of habitat conservation, and the consideration of risk. These issues were raised in an important 1990s case, *Sierra Club v. Marita*, which focused on the application of the newly emerging science of conservation biology to the protection of biodiversity under the National Forest Management Act.

Sierra Club v. Marita: The Forest Service, Judicial Deference and Conservation Biology

In 1994 a Federal District Court in Wisconsin decided two related cases that brought conservation biology into the forefront of the debate on how government agencies should use ecology in the protection of biodiversity.[40] In the two *Sierra Club v. Marita* district court cases, and the appeal that followed, the courts considered whether a government agency was required to use principles and methodologies of conservation biology in the management of public lands. For the U.S. Forest Service, the issue was maintaining the discretion to choose among scientific methodologies and concepts in designing a plan that would protect biodiversity. To environmental groups, the question was whether the government should be required to accept and use the principles that had come out of the "new ecology" of the 1980s. These cases highlight issues that would become the prime focus of the relationship of ecology and environmental law in the 1990s. First, the protection of overall biodiversity and not just listed species became important in determining the development and implementation of some environmental laws.[41] Second was the growing reliance that environmental laws would place on an ecosystem level of management, the ecosystem management paradigm discussed in the previous chapter. Third was the influential role of judicial deference to the agency's practices in the decisions they reach on what scientific concepts and methods to apply to management.[42] Finally, these cases show that while the use of ecology in biodiversity protection increased during the decade, it was still balanced by the government's explicit desire to consider economic interests in the management of natural resources.[43] *This uneasy balance between ecological principles and economic interests is a major issue facing all of environmental law.*

The Nicolet and Chequamegon National Forests in northern Wisconsin contain 1.5 million acres of land managed by the U.S. Forest Service. They are second growth forests containing both pine and hardwoods along with hundreds of lakes and streams and have multiple uses (as mandated by the multiple use doctrine of the NFMA); recreation, logging, and scientific research.[44] Since 1976 the Forest Service has managed all national forests under the mandate of the National Forest Management Act (NFMA) and its implementing regulations.[45] NFMA was designed to provide a "comprehensive framework for the development and implementation of [forest] management plans"[46] that will protect plant and animal diversity.[47] These regulations do not mention conservation biology, but focus on the identification and monitoring of Management Indicator Species (MIS) as a means of assessing the effects of management on biodiversity.[48] As required by NFMA, in 1986 the Regional Forester for the Eastern Region presented final plans for the management of the commercial and recreational uses of these forests for at least the following ten years.[49] However, the development of these plans actually began in 1979, under the supervision of the respective supervisor for each forest, with the formal presentation of draft management plans and environmental impact statements (EIS) for public comment.[50]

NFMA and its regulations require three types of diversity considerations. First, the Forest Service is required to determine how diversity will be affected by various planning alternatives.[51] Second, the final management plan must maintain diversity of plant and animal communities at a level similar to a natural, nonmanaged forest.[52] While both of these considerations emphasize NFMA's general purpose of protecting diversity, neither provides the Forest Service with any guidance on selecting a methodology, ecological or otherwise, to use to measure, maintain, or enhance diversity.[53] However, the third diversity consideration, the protection of "Fish and Wildlife Resources," does set out specific guidelines for the Service. Further, while the first two diversity considerations are silent on what level of diversity (e.g., genetic diversity, species diversity, or habitat diversity) should be considered, this third consideration specifically requires the Service to identify, monitor, and protect individual species.[54]

Table 9.1 POPULATION VIABILITY ANALYSIS

Population Viability Analysis, or PVA is a heterogeneous group of analyses to evaluate the threats to a given species or population. PVAs are increasingly being used to allow better management of species and populations. The elements of a PVA may include:

Current population size and spatial distribution
· *Habitat* – what is it, how much is there, is it declining, what is likely to happen to habitat in the future?
· *Threats from human activities*
· *Community interactions* – What other species are important to the management of this species? Predators, competitors, parasites, mutualists?
Demography – What are the age-specific survival and fecundity rates for this species. Considers density dependence, spatial structure and the degree of variation in the demographic rates.
Genetics – What is known about the population genetics of the species. Is there any indication of a loss of variation? Of inbreeding depression?
Gaps in knowledge – What don't we know about this species' biology?
Extinction threat – some assessment, qualitative or quantitative of the risk of extinction to the population. This is often carried out with a computer population model. The analysis tries to estimate the probability of the species going extinct in some fixed period of time (e.g., 200 years). Sometimes average population size or growth rate are the parameters that are used to assess population performance instead of extinction risk.
Sensitivity analysis – Parameters of the model are varied to see which parameters are more important in affecting extinction risk.
Policy – What policies are relevant to the management of this species and how do they affect it?
Management recommendations – Based on all of the information reviewed and the preceding analyses, recommendations can be made as to the appropriate management practices to achieve conservation of this species.

Source: Douglas Bolger, Environmental Studies Program, Dartmouth College

To account for overall species diversity, the Forest Service used two similar measures of diversity, which were based upon the assumption that overall animal and plant diversity is a function of the diversity of habitats.[55] Therefore, as a first step in their biodiversity analysis, the Service estimated the overall amount of vegetative diversity that would result from each alternative forest plan.[56] For both forests this was done by first assigning relative values to each of the variables that the Service believed would maximize the amount of species-level animal and plant diversity (i.e., number of species). The Service then determined how close each alternative came to achieving a maximum level of biodiversity by summing the ecosystem variables.[57] For neither forest did the Service select the alternative that achieved optimum diversity, but rather other uses were also considered; in Nicolet a resource use based alternative was chosen while in Chequamegon a recreational use alternative was chosen.

Besides accounting for overall biodiversity, the NFMAs implementing regulations require an explicit Population Viability Analysis (PVA) based upon the use of Management Indicator Species (MIS) to estimate the affect of the alternative plans on target species.[58] To meet this requirement, the Service used two similar, but not identical, five-step analysis for each forest. They compiled lists, of all vertebrate species that were rare, uncommon, or "associated with habitats subject to significant change through planning alternatives"[59] and they also determined what habitats were associated with these species.[60] The Chequamegon management plan took one additional step; the 25 different habitats were divided into ten "indicator communities" (e.g., aquatic, wetland, permanent opening, etc.).[61]

Possibly the most important step in the PVA was the identification of Management Indicator Species (MIS) that would be used for the estimation of minimum viable populations (MVP), minimum habitat size, and the monitoring of the effects of the alternative plans and ultimately the final plan on the listed vertebrate species. In Nicolet, 14 habitats were identified for the 65 species that were determined to require a PVA.[62] One MIS was selected for each of the 14 habitats by selecting the species that required the largest territory.[63] To determine whether the alternative management plans would maintain a MVP for each indicator species, the Service multiplied the population density of each MIS by the amount of habitat that each plan would leave after 150 years. Finally, the Service compared the effects of each alternative management plan on the MIS by estimating the likelihood that a MIS would become extinct.[64] Alternative management plans were rejected if they resulted in the probable extinction of any MIS.[65]

In contrast, the Service chose a different and more complicated method of identifying the MISs in Chequamegon. First, the Service did not use a subset of species to identify habitats, but used all of the more than 300 identified vertebrate species found in the forest. Second, the Forest Service did not choose a MIS for each of the 25 identified habitats, but only for the ten "indicatory communities" that were made up of one or more of the habitats. Finally, instead of simply choosing the one species that required the largest territory in each habitat, they picked the MIS by using five criteria: (1) highly sensitive to habitat change, (2) was threatened or endangered, (3) a game species, or (4) was a non-game species of "special interest" or (5) was a "true indicator" of effects of management activities.[66] The PVA in Chequamegon also differed from that done in Nicolet. The minimum viable population for each of the MIS was calculated by first assuming that "short-term fitness" requires a minimum population of 50.[67] This minimum population size was then adjusted, for each MIS, based upon factors specific to each MIS.[68] Finally, the Service estimated the total population that would be supported by each alternative plan.[69]

While they used two distinct methods, the managers of both national forests provided a detailed methodology that explicitly focused on the diversity requirements of the NFMA and its regulations. They considered and "provided" for diversity, as required by NFMA and carried out a detailed population viability analysis using rationally selected Management Indicator Species. How could environmental groups challenge the Forest Service's management plans in court and claim that the Service had "failed to consider the plan's effect on biological diversity?"[70] To understand why, it is necessary to understand the scientific bases of the Forest Service's methodology as well as the evolution of conservation biology from the early 1980s to the present.

The Forest Service's plans incorporated much of the terminology of conservation biology, but they contained little of its substance. Several assumptions were made in the selection of MIS, as well as in their use as measures of diversity, which were are not supported by current ecological thought.

The plaintiffs in the *Marita* cases challenged the Forest Service plan because, they claimed it did not use "new" concepts from conservation biology[71] (e.g., island biogeography[72]). Despite the ecological shortcomings of the management plans, the courts deferred to the Forest Service view that there were enough disagreements among scientists over concepts in conservation biology in general, and the theory of island biogeography in particular, at the time, to defer to the Forest Service's opinion that these "new" scientific principles need not be followed.[73]

Given the "arbitrary and capricious" standard that courts use to evaluate agency decisions, it was unlikely that the *Marita* plaintiffs could have convinced the court that their position on what science should be used by the Forest Service was correct. However, we find that the differences in how conservation biology was interpreted by the Forest Service and the plaintiffs provides a marked contrast in how ecological principles are interpreted within the legal system. During pre-trial administrative proceedings the plaintiffs proposed a specific management plan, based upon conservation biology principles, for the national forest.[74] This plan called for creation of large, unfragmented areas of forest that would be off-limits to lumbering. The necessity of large reserves is a basic tenet of conservation biology because they are more likely to preserve biodiversity by maintaining adequate population size.[75]

The *Marita* plaintiffs diverged from the then current thinking in conservation biology by basing their definition of diversity on population level diversity only and not also on lower (genetic) or higher levels of diversity (e.g., ecosystem processes or landscapes).[76] Even the Forest Service *considered* the effect of their management strategies on genetic diversity, and rejected plans that would have led, in their opinion, to high inbreeding and a loss of genetic diversity.[77] However, the Forest Service's plan called for protecting diversity by maintaining many small blocks of forest. While the *Marita* plaintiff's did argue that this approach was directly opposed to the principles of conservation biology, they did not stress the deleterious effects of small blocks of habitat on genetic variation. Fragmented habitats usually result in loss of genetic variation and increased probability of extinction.[78] This omission is particularly important given the Service's explicit use of population genetic assumption in their selection of alternative plans.[79] As much as anything, the correlation between reduced habitat size and loss of genetic variation is a long-standing "fact." Courts tend to give more weight to scientific facts than to different theories or concepts. As shown above in discussing the Spotted Owl litigations, when the Forest Service tries to develop plans that contradict known scientific facts, the usually granted judicial deference disappears.[80]

Created during the late 1970s and early 1980s, the Forest Service's management plans for the two northern Wisconsin forests could not incorporate today's development's in conservation biology. Also, given that island biogeography had not been tested on deciduous forests by the early 1980s it is hardly "arbitrary and capricious" for the Forest Service not to have explicitly used that theory. However, by the early 1980s it was already well established that larger habitats could maintain larger populations than smaller habitats and that small populations are more likely to become extinct than larger ones. Instead of basing their case on the lack of island biogeography theory in the management plan, the plaintiffs could have emphasized this "fact," one well known to ecologists at the time the management plans were developed. Further, while the methods of Population Viability Analysis have advanced since the 1980s, the Forest Service's viability analysis did not adequately use the principles and methods available to them at the time.[81]

While the Forest Service was victorious in the challenges of its Management Plans in the *Marita* cases, the environmental groups and, more importantly, conservation biology were the long-term winner. In the Nicolet and Chequamegon National Forests the Forest Service, while not required by the *Marita* court, has voluntarily adopted some of the conservation biology principles earlier fought as untested.[82] Further, some recent court cases, while still granting the Forest Service much of the deference seen in *Marita*, have made it clear that the NFMA and its regulations require the Service to meet strict methodological requirements in determining the effects of any management plan on biodiversity.[83] The Forest Service has, both before and after the 1976 passage of the NFMA, attempted to maximize its discretion in determining how to manage the national forests. In *Marita*, and all other recent cases challenging management plans, the Forest Service has claimed that while they have a congressionally mandated duty to protect biodiversity, they should be granted the deference to determine the specific methodology used and the power to consider other constraints (e.g., recreation, timber harvesting) on management plans.[84]

Ecosystem Management comes to the National Forests

The Forest Service tried in 1995 to answer years of criticism and litigation over their management of the national forests by proposing sweeping changes to their original 1982 regulations.[85] The 1995 proposed regulations were the Forest Service's first major attempt to adopt ecosystem management as the paradigm of future National Forest plans; with all of the inherent problems of balancing ecology and biodiversity with economic and social factors.[86] These proposed regulations modified all aspects of the Forest Service's management of the national forests. However, it was in the treatment of plant and animal diversity, as well as in the regulation's goal of insuring sustainable ecosystems, that these proposed rules continue the trend of treating the biodiversity crisis as an ecosystem problem.[87]

The stated goal of these proposed regulations was the maintenance of sustainable ecosystems.[88] While this goal should result in a more modern, holistic approach for forest management, there are no proposed standards for what "sustainable" would mean; the defining of such standards would be left to the discretion of the Forest Service.[89] However, these proposed regulations did incorporate concepts and methods from recent developments in conservation biology, an action at least arguably a result of the litigation of the *Marita* plaintiffs.

One major concept adopted from conservation biology was that of the coarse filter/fine filter method of protecting biodiversity. Coarse filter methods assume that providing for suitable ecosystems or habitats will protect most species within those habitats.[90] This method was to be used for any plant/animal/fungi/lichen species which, although not listed under the ESA, the forest service believed required protection. In contrast, fine filter methods are population specific methods that, according to the 1995 proposed regulations, would only be used for vertebrates, principally those listed under the ESA.[91]

Related to the reliance on coarse filter methods to deal with vertebrate species management is the proposed regulation's adoption of a habitat approach (instead of a population approach) to biodiversity protection.[92] This habitat approach, implied in the management plans under attack in *Marita*, would have resulted in the almost complete lack of diversity assessment at any level below (genetic or population) or above (ecosystem, landscape, and biome) the habitat. This is interesting since many Forest Plans of the 1980s, including those challenged in *Marita*, included an assessment of genetic and population level diversity; something the proposed regulations would not require.[93] Another new result would have been the limitation, if not complete abandonment, of the Management Indicator Species (MIS) concept as the major tool of monitoring diversity.[94]

During the public comment period the 1995 proposed regulations were criticized by scientists and others, for their treatment of biodiversity. Plant/animal diversity was maintained through the preservation of habitats and not through the monitoring and management of individual populations, which the Forest Service explained was too expensive and time consuming to be practical.[95] Another problem was the seeming abandonment of population "viability" as the main standard to achieve diversity goals in national forests.[96] The Forest Service saw the extensive population viability analysis (the necessary method of monitoring individual populations) as being too expensive and time consuming to be carried out on a regular basis. They also argued that the concept of viability was open to many different interpretations and that it had no statutory basis in the NFMA.[97]

The 1999 Committee of Scientists' Report

In 1998, as a response to these mounting criticisms, the Forest Service empaneled a new Committee of Scientists to ensure a scientific background to future Forest Service regulations and planning.[98] Interestingly, this Committee was not formed to help develop the 1995 proposed regulations (unlike the original Committee in the late 1970s) but only in response to the scientific criticisms of the 1995 proposed regulations. The Forest Service has used this Committee's report, published in March 1999, as the basis of proposed regulations. The Committee provides examples of successful ecosystem management programs (e.g., interior Columbia Basin and Tongass National Forest), and, most importantly, makes several recommendations for how future Forest Service planning should be carried out.[99]

First, the Committee stressed the need for assessments, during and after the planning stage, of the effects of management plans across the multiple hierarchical levels (e.g., genes, populations, habitats) of an ecosystem. The Committee recognized that it is impossible to monitor all populations and all levels of diversity (from genetic to landscape). However, they believed that it was necessary to identify and continuously monitor the appropriate scale or scales (e.g., endangered population, watershed, or ecosystem) inherent to each management problem. This focus on monitoring and assessments is the most important factor distinguishing the Committee's proposals from current Forest Service planning.[100]

Next, the Committee implied that it would reject the 1995 proposed regulations use of habitat as the single most important measure of biodiversity.[101] The Committee recognized that the "presence of suitable habitat does not ensure that any particular species will be present or will reproduce."[102] The Committee recognized that not all populations in any given habitat or ecosystem could be monitored. Instead, they recommended the selection and monitoring of a relatively few "focal species" to provide information about the larger ecosystem.[103] The focal species method is based upon the ecological concept that some species (e.g., keystone species, umbrella species, and endangered species) provide important information of higher order (habitat or ecosystem) ecological processes and ecosystem health.

The Committee, as did the 1995 Rule, recognized "Ecological Sustainability" as a major purpose of any future Forest Service Plan. They also recognized the hierarchical nature of ecological systems and the importance of considering these different levels in the planning stage; an important difference between the Committee's recommendations and the proposed regulations. Further, the Committee explicitly recognized the newer non-equilibrium paradigm in ecology.[104] This paradigm requires even more extensive temporal monitoring of the effects of management plans, as well as the continuous modification of plans to account for changes in ecological systems; in other words, adaptive management.[105] Finally, the Committee discussed the importance that the boundaries of any management plan be determined by the ecological systems involved (e.g., extent of a watershed) and not by more convenient political or economic divisions. This requires inter-agency and inter-government cooperation in the development and implementation of management plans. It also requires the collaboration of government and non-government scientists in the development of all future forest plans; the Committee believed that this collaboration was important enough to write it into any future regulations.

The main differences between the Committee's 1999 report and the 1995 proposed Rule was its emphasis on the need to deal with management problems at the appropriate level of ecological organization. For biodiversity management, this means that, along with providing suitable habitat, individual populations (as limited by time and money) must be monitored during both the planning and implementation stages of future Management Plans. It also means that the planning process must account for ecosystem health and integrity, as well as landscape scale concerns. In summary, the Committee would challenge the Forest Service to apply the most modern methods and concepts of conservation biology, where the original regulations required no use of conservation biology at all; to the disappointment of the *Marita* plaintiffs.

1999 Forest Service Proposed Rule

On October 5, 1999, the Forest Service published a new proposed rule which, if adopted, would significantly amend the current Forest Service regulations regarding the use of ecology and the protection of biodiversity.[106] To a large extent this proposed rule adopts the framework suggested in the 1999 Committee of Scientists' report. The treatment of biodiversity is divided into three parts: the use of ecosystem management; an increased emphasis on the assessment of all aspects of population, habitat, ecosystem, and landscape health and integrity; and, the monitoring and maintenance of ecological sustainability as the primary goal of any future management plan.

Ecosystem Management

The proposed regulations would adopt ecosystem management to balance ecological, social, and economic sustainability.[107] The maintenance and restoration of ecological sustainability would be the first priority in any future management plan.[108] Future Forest Service plans would not "maximize the protection of plant and animal species to the exclusion of human values and uses,"[109] but rather the Forest Service would meet their "multiple use" mandate (e.g., timber and recreation) by maintaining ecological sustainability.[110]

Assessment

The proposed regulation §219.5 (Information development and interpretation) would provide for both broad-scale assessments and local analysis of current and future effects of management activities.[111] As with the original regulations, and as was done in the Wisconsin national forests litigated in the *Marita* cases, these new regulations grant the Forest Service considerable discretion in choosing what spatial scales should be studied and, more generally, what type of data should be collected. This section does formalize the need to continuously collect and analyze information to insure proper planning and explicitly recognizes the need to consider ecological realistic boundaries (e.g., including lands outside of national forests), and not political boundaries, when doing these large scale assessments.

Ecological Sustainability

The most important of the proposed regulations, at least regarding biodiversity, are those dealing with ecological sustainability and ecological monitoring. The proposed regulations provide a framework on how ecological information is to be collected in §219.11 (Monitoring and evaluation). Details on what type of information should be collected and how this information should be used to maintain or restore ecological sustainability is in §219.20 (Ecological sustainability).

The ecological sustainability section (219.20) provides most of the details on what ecological concepts and methods should be used to guide the collection of information at each particular geographic scale (e.g., population, ecosystem, and landscape). Specifically, §219.20(a)(1) would require, depending upon the particular geographic scale being analyzed, the measurement of the composition and structure of ecosystems and landscapes (e.g., types of species, soil condition, and stream channel) while §219.20(a)(2) would require the measurement of ecological processes.[112] Importantly, this section also requires the collection of data regarding the historical range of variability (HRV) of ecological systems, including the conditions prior to European settlement. This information is to be compared to current conditions and does not imply any requirement, by the Forest Service, to restore national forests to pre-European conditions.[113]

These proposed regulations reject the 1995 proposal with its emphasis on habitat analysis and protection as the main method of protecting biodiversity (see above). Instead, these regulations would adopt the Committee of Scientists' method of identifying focal species and species at risk (e.g., listed or considered to be listed under the ESA). Unlike the Management Indicator Species Concept, focal species are used as surrogate measures of ecological integrity (e.g., ecological structure, composition, and processes) and, only rarely, as surrogate measures of other populations.[114]

In theory this move away from the MIS and to a focal species concept has benefits. The MIS concept attempted to use one species to represent the effects of Forest Service plans on other species without attempting to isolate or measure the ecological factors that accounted for this assumed correlation between populations (i.e., it treated the ecological factors which made a specific species an "indicator species" as a black-box). The focal species concept eliminates this problem by requiring the Forest Service to focus on those previously unconsidered ecological factors (i.e., it attempts to determine how different populations function within their habitat and ecosystem). However, in practice, it is not clear that Forest Service planners will be able, or are willing, to gather the ecological information necessary to properly carry out this process.

An important improvement of the proposed regulations is the increased emphasis on obtaining actual estimates of populations size and trends, instead of simply using habitat size as a sufficient measure.[115] These actual population estimates would only be for populations at high levels of risk (as determined by the Service in consultation with scientists) or when there is high uncertainty about "the habitat conditions needed for species viability." Also, even for "at risk species," habitat monitoring may be used as one measure of population change if it is determined to be reliable. These limitations on the direct use of population estimation are a recognition of the difficulty, in time and money, to carry out individual population viability analyses.

Finally, proposed §§219.22-25 requires a much higher level of scientific involvement, including non-agency scientists, in the develop and implementation of the plan and, most specifically, with determining what and how to monitor species and other ecological factors. Given the previous lack of involvement of non-forest service scientists in the development of management plans, it is in these sections of the proposed regulations, and not those sections detailing with ecological methods, that most of the protection for a future forest plan's ecological sufficiency may be found.

As of Winter 2002, these proposed regulations have not yet been formally adopted, but are being used as guidelines for current forest management plans. However, even if accepted, the Forest Service will maintain it discretion to choose how to apply these ecological principles to the actual management of biodiversity. Given the deference granted to agencies (see discussion of *Marita* above) a skeptic may assume that it will not matter what ecological principles are written into a regulation, if the agency is allowed to interpret them as it sees fit. However, there is some reason to believe that the Forest Service and other federal agencies may, either voluntarily or through pressure from scientists and environmentalists, be moving to a more ecological based management for the sustainable use of our national forests.

BIODIVERSITY PLANNING IN THE BLM

The Bureau of Land Managment's use of ecological concepts and methods, as well as their treatment of diversity is simpler than for the Forest Service. This is because: (1) The BLM adopted new regulations in 1995 that, unlike the current Forest Service regulations, adopt an ecosystem perspective to range planning, and (2) the relevant BLM regulations are shorter and less detailed, in both their treatment of ecological concepts and application of ecological methods, than the Forest Service regulations. The most relevant BLM regulations are 43 C.F.R. 4180.1 (Fundamentals of rangeland health) and 4180.2 (Standards and guidelines for grazing administration).

Section 4180.1 (Fundamentals of rangeland health) has proved the most controversial of the regulations.[116] This regulation requires range-land mangers to modify existing grazing management needs to ensure: healthy watersheds, maintenance of ecological processes (e.g., nutrient cycles, energy flow), water quality, maintenance or restoration of habitats, and protection of species listed (or candidate species) under the the ESA.[117]

Section 4180.2 requires state and regional managers to implement these fundamentals as required standards to be met (4180.2(d)(1)-(5)) and guidelines (developed to achieve the standards) for the management of each rangeland.[118]

The regulations provide for the consideration of species, habitat and ecosystem level processes. In particular, their focus on ecosystem processes, habitats, and water quality shows a good grasp of current ecological thinking in relation to the problems facing grazing lands. However, as with the Forest Service regulations, individual managers are given wide discretion (but not as much guidance) on how to develop standards and guidelines. This is particularly important because the BLM regulations, unlike the proposed Forest Service regulations, do not require or suggest that scientists be involved in rangeland planning.[119]

Source: 43 C.F.R. 4180.1; 43 C.F.R. 4180.2

Ecosystem Management of the Marine Fisheries[120]

The management of the marine fisheries, as with the national forests, requires a balancing between the protection of biodiversity (species and habitats) and the maintenance of an important natural resource (commercial fish). This balancing act is seen in all fisheries, both domestic and international. For our example, we will look at the Northwest Atlantic fishery off New England and Eastern Canada. However, identical ecological and legal mechanisms can be seen working in other Atlantic as well as Pacific fisheries.

The Northwest Atlantic fishery consists of several marine shelf ecosystems that stretch from the Northeast United States to Southeast Canada in the Northwest Atlantic. The area is bounded by the Gulf Stream on the east and by the coast of North America on the west. The Grand Banks, the Scotian Shelf, Georges Bank and the Gulf of Maine are all found within this region and are the focus of concern for the "collapse" of the fishing industry in New England and Atlantic Canada. In a 1996 publication the Large Marine Ecosystems group examined the ecosystem boundaries of the fishery in detail.[121] There are also political boundaries for this region. In 1984 The Chamber of the International Court of Justice established a delimitation zone between the U.S. and Canada in the Gulf of Maine after the two countries could not resolve a dispute over the gulf.[122] The line drawn by the Chamber was considerably different from the lines claimed by the two countries and left only a small area of Georges Bank on the Canadian side. There is also an exclusive economic zone (EEZ) that is internationally recognized by all nations that stretches 200 miles out to sea from all the coastal nations in the world and are governed by the adjacent nation.

By the early 1990s, the Northwest Atlantic fisheries experienced catastrophic declines in the stocks of fish mostly do to overfishing by international fleets of "factory" ships. Total catches of cod and pollock were at the lowest on record. Total Canadian Atlantic coast commercial landings of groundfish fell from 625,707 metric tones (live weight) in 1991 to 152,502 metric tones (live weight) in 1994. Landings of Northern cod had fallen to record low levels as early as 1992.[123] The fisheries were forced to close down because of the depleted stocks and the Canadian government imposed a moratorium on groundfishing in the area. The majority of these fisheries are still closed today.

The current protection and restoration of the fishery is based on management plans, similar to forest management plans. These plans, developed under the Magnuson-Stevens Act (MSFCMA) of 1976,[124] attempt to integrate multiple levels of ecology (e.g., population, community, and ecosystem), other natural and physical sciences (e.g., climatology), and economic, political, and legal considerations.[125] The MSFCMA Act set up eight regional management councils that were to come up with their own Fishery Management Plans as related to their region. The New England Fishery Management Council's jurisdiction extends from Maine to southern New England. The Council develops management plans that are submitted to the National Marine Fisheries Service (NMFS) and the Secretary of Commerce for approval and implementation. Since its inception in 1986, there have been eight amendments to the NEFMC's Groundfish Fishery Management Plan (FMP).[126]

Each major actor (the U.S., Canada, and the International Community) has several specific laws that establish the regime of the Northwest Atlantic fisheries and ecosystem. These laws have evolved significantly within the last ten years to encompass a more significant ecological approach in order to restore depleted stocks and manage the ecosystem as a whole. The MSFCMA is administered by two major departments: the National Marine Fishery Service (NMFS), a division of the National Oceanic and Atmospheric Administration; and the New England Fishery Management Council (NEFMC), one of eight regional councils.

Exclusive federal management authority was vested in the National Marine Fisheries Service (NMFS) within the National Oceanic and Atmospheric Administration of the Department of Commerce by the MFMCA. On October 11, 1996, as part of the result of the collapse of the groundfishing industry in New England, President Clinton signed the Sustainable Fisheries Act into law. This Act changed the focus of fishery management from economic sustainability of the fisheries to an increasingly conservation-minded species sustainability approach. Ten major ecological, economic, and political considerations are addressed by the Sustainable Fisheries Act, all of which are important to an ecosystem management regime:

1. Individual fishing quota programs.
2. Bycatch, discards, and waste.
3. Overfishing and capacity reduction.
4. Fees.
5. Fishery management plans.
6. Fishing gear.
7. Council conflicts of interest.
8. Habitat protection.
9. Observers.
10. Council composition.

Since the passing of the Sustainable Fisheries Act, the NMFS policy has predominately focused on conservation. The NMFS carries out a wide range of specific research and regulatory activities. These activities are undertaken pursuant to the fisheries management responsibilities specified in the MSFCMA. The NMFS sponsors research on the marine and fishery resources and has its own regional science department called the Northeast Fishery Science Center.

The New England Fishery Management Council is the organization responsible for preparing the fishery management plans (FMPs) for the fisheries that it determines require active federal management. Its policies have also shifted with the mandates as set forth in the Sustainable Fisheries Act. The NEFMC's earlier focus on promoting the development of a domestic fleet has changed to setting limits on the fisheries in order to prevent overfishing, rebuild depleted stocks, reduce bycatch and minimize the mortality of unavoidable bycatch, and to conserve fish habitats.[127] As of 1997 the NEFMC was in the process of addressing the SFA mandates by amending its five fishery management plans by October 1998 and as of June 4, 1999 the Northeast Multispecies (Groundfish) Fishery Management Plan had eight Amendments with a ninth undergoing review by the NMFS.[128] At first these Amendments (1-4) were established in an effort to manage the efficiency of the fishing industry. By 1994 and afterward the Council established Amendments 5-8 which began to reflect the urgency of the fishery dilemma and the need for severe cutbacks in fishing capacity.

Table 9.2 FISHERIES MANAGEMENT RESEARCH

MAGNUSON FISHERY CONSERVATION AND
MANAGEMENT ACT (1976)
Established 200 mile exclusive fishery management zone
Responsibility for management of fisheries given to the National Marine
    Fisheries Service (NMFS) within Department of Commerce
Created 8 regional councils to create regulations for individual fisheries
Councils made up of government and industry representatives
· NFMS fishery scientists advise councils
· Councils create Fishery Management Plans

SUSTAINABLE FISHERIES ACT (1996)
– amendment to Magnuson
Preventing overfishing, and ending overfishing of currently depressed stocks
· Rebuilding depleted stocks
· Reducing bycatch and minimizing the mortality of unavoidable bycatch
· Designating and conserving essential fish habitat
· Reducing conflict of interest on Regional Councils
· Establish user fees
· Five year moratorium on Individual Transferable Quotas

Source: Brooks, Jones and Virginia

In its efforts to implement the SFA, the NMFS Office of Science and Technology finalized a five-year Strategic Plan for Fisheries Research (Plan) in 1997. This plan also fits the mandates set by the United Nation's Food and Agriculture Organization for the Code of Conduct for Responsible Fisheries. "The Plan covers fisheries, habitat, and protected species research to meet requirements of the Magnuson-Stevens Act. Fishery managers use this research to make scientifically sound decisions to achieve sustainable use of our Nation's living marine resources."[129] The Fisheries Strategic Plan is organized around three programmatic areas: sustainable fisheries; recovered protected species; and healthy living marine resource habitat.[130] Sustainable fisheries include applied fishery (e.g., setting of quotas and use of large mesh nets to allow for the survival of juvenile fish), economic, and cultural considerations. The other two areas are predominately ecological.

The SFA mandate on habitat protection is an integral part of the entire fisheries management process and is the area where ecosystem ecology could be most relevant. Through the Sustainable Fisheries Act, the Secretary of Commerce, on behalf of NMFS: "shall establish '... guidelines to assist the Councils in the description and identification of essential fish habitats in fishery management plans ...' and in response to actions by any other Federal or State agency that would adversely affect essential fish habitats, shall recommend to such agency measures to conserve such habitat."[131] Most of the mandates called for under the SFA are for the purpose of conservation, restoration and management. In order to ensure that these mandates are met, the NMFS established an Ecosystem Principles Advisory Panel which reviews the results of current management plans and provides advice on ways to improve upon existing management strategies. This Panel gave a report to Congress in 1999 urging more ecological emphasis in fisheries management. Therefore, while fishery managers do appear to be incorporating some ecology into management plans, there is a need for even more ecology in management plans and in the legal regime itself.[132]

Conclusion: Biodiversity Protection in the 1990s

To most people "biodiversity" means the number of species found in a particular area and the biodiversity crisis is their loss as a result of habitat destruction, fragmentation, and other factors. To a large extent, the ecosystemic regime dealing with biodiversity protection in 1990 mirrored this public culture by making species protection the primary purpose of the Endangered Species Act, the most important biodiversity law. As a result, the primary legal questions in the late 1980s and early 1990s were whether a species met the legal requirements to be listed as endangered or threatened. While this determination did rely to some degree on the habitat requirements of a species, it only did so if it could be shown that the decreasing size or fragmentation of habitat would cause the decline and eventual extinction of the species. Therefore, population ecology, either by itself or through early population centered conservation biology was the primary type of ecology to interact with the ESA at the start of the 1990s and population growth rates were the critical ecological data to be collected.

Despite several attempts to rewrite the ESA during the 1990s, this law remains relatively unchanged in substance. However, the application and relative importance of the various sections would change dramatically. The most important of these changes would be the rise of the habitat conservation plans (HCPs) and their use to manage larger systems (e.g., habitats or ecosystems) which contained one or more endangered or threatened species.

The creation and acceptance of an HCP by the agencies administering the ESA, (Fish and Wildlife Service and Dept. of Commerce), would exempt the landowner from the strict "no take" restriction of the ESA, permitting the land owner to develop their property and modify, even if this resulted in the "incidental" take of a species. Thus, the balancing of ecological and economic concerns. Overall, the trend in biodiversity law is to develop plans to manage listed species as part of a larger habitat or ecosystem, while at the same time accounting for human economic (land development) or cultural (land ownership) factors. This form of biodiversity management would parallel the ecosystem management of place-centered environmental protection and restoration that we discussed in the last chapter.

The growing use of this habitat or ecosystem based approach to the protection of endangered or threatened species developed at the same time as ecology was becoming more open to the integration of the previously divided disciplines. Many ecologists saw HCPs as a positive step in allowing for population, community, and ecosystem level methods and concepts to be used together in the design of management plans. However, as more and more HCPs were written and implemented, ecologists' enthusiasm for them would wane for the same reason as many ecologists are unsure about ecosystem management in general; ecosystem management requires ecology to be only one of many factors to be considered. Therefore, where once the protection of an endangered species was the sole purpose of the ESA, it is now a factor that, like the natural resource statutes (e.g., NFMA), allow for balancing by agencies and courts.

Another major federal law dealing with biodiversity protection, the National Forest Management Act, took a broader view of biodiversity in 1990 and was not solely concerned with species-level protection. However, NFMA was and still is limited both because it deals only with national forests and because, as a multiple-use statute, biodiversity protection is only one of many factors to be considered in management within national forests. Both NFMA, and its implementing regulations, allow regional foresters discretion in designing management plans. Ecologically, this discretion allows plans to be designed to meet the specific ecological issues of a forest. Plans could focus on the protection of specific species that are considered important to a particular national forest (i.e., a focal species) or on maintaining a relatively high degree of overall plant and animal diversity. However, in practice, early forest management plans would focus on habitat level measures of diversity (e.g., the Vegetative Index used in the Wisconsin forests), and not species, ecosystem, or landscape levels of biodiversity.

While the ESA was moving toward a biodiversity management reminiscent of early forest management plans, the U.S. Forest Service was considering an expansion of their approach in their use of ecology. With the

Committee of Scientists' Report and the proposed regulations of the late 1990s, the Forest Service would consider a multi-level approach to forest management in which genetic, population, habitat, community, ecosystem, and landscape levels and processes would be considered and monitored to ensure the proper management of a national forest. This approach, if adopted, would match the recent evolution of ecology in considering all relevant ecological levels. It would also stress the consideration of ecologically relevant factors (keystone species versus game species) and boundaries (ecosystem or landscape versus administratively drawn border). However, there are critics of these proposed regulations both within ecology and environmental law who say that while multiple ecological concepts are to be considered, no enforceable standards are provided.

The initial motivation for the ESA and the Forest Service's move towards ecosystem management was the continued litigation surrounding the Northern Spotted Owl after its listing in 1989 as an endangered species. However, the Forest Service's management of these forests and of the Northern Spotted Owl is a history of far more than just the Service's acceptance of ecosystem management or of the function of the ESA in protecting bio-diversity. It is also the story of federal agencies' continued attempt, as in the *Marita* cases, to maximize their discretion on how to implement environmental statutes. It is also a story of how different biodiversity laws have been integrated, usually as the result of multiple statutory claims brought in litigation, and of how the modern, more integrated ecology is being considered, if not always adopted by these laws.

These changes in the ESA and the NFMA have been mirrored in other biodiversity laws, most notably in those protecting the marine fishery. Changes in both the ESA and the NFMA are, to a large part, the result of an increasing biocentric and ecocentric view of the world, one in which biodiversity is valued as a "good" in and of itself. However, the new ecosystemic approach to fishery management has been motivated mostly by the economic and social pressures resulting from the collapse of several major fisheries. This loss of a major "ecosystem service" (i.e., commercial fish) makes the ecosystemic regime of the marine fishery a classic example of utilitarian purpose resulting in similar biocentric and ecocentric results.

Notes

1.   *See* Walter Kuhlmann, *Defining the Role of Conservation Biology in the Law of Protecting Ecosystems*, in Environmental Policy & Biodiversity 209, 218 (1994).
2.   Northern Spotted Owl v. Hodel, 716 F. Supp. 479 (W.D. Wash., 1988).
3.   *See* Northern Spotted Owl, 716 F. Supp. at 481.
4.   *Id*. at 483.

5.   *See* Russell Lande, *Demographic models of the northern spotted owl (Strix occidentalis caurina),* 75 OECOLOGIA 601-7 (1988). The Forest Service's model had used a "truncated" life table to model spotted owl population growth which assumed that there were no individuals older then 10 years, even though field workers knew that was false. Further, the Service's model did not include any analysis of individual dispersal among habitats, something that juvenile owls are known to do in order to find their own breeding grounds. Finally, in order for their model to fit the known 1 percent decline in owl population size per year, the Forest Service was required to give added weight to two variables in their model, juvenile survival and adult fecundity, as being the most important population parameters for spotted owls, an assumption which was not supported by any previous studies. In contrast, Lande's model included both juvenile dispersal and biologically reasonable estimates of juvenile survival and adult fecundity and, therefore, did not need to be "recalibrated" to match the known one percent decline in population per year. In his model it was adult survivorship that was the most important variable controlling spotted owl population growth, a variable given little weight by the Forest Service's management plan.

6.   *See* STEVEN LEWIS YAFFEE, THE WISDOM OF THE SPOTTED OWL 98 (1994).

7.   For the Spotted Owl, disagreements among environmental groups and the U.S. Forest Service over how much habitat is critical to the owl, fueled again by differences of opinion on the proper use of ecology, would immediately begin a new round of litigation and debate on how to use ecology to manage this species.

8.   As described in Chapter 6, the two main tools used by the ESA for species-specific protection are the "no jeopardy" and "no take" provisions of Sections 7 and 9, respectively. Section 7 generally requires federal agencies to carry out no actions that would put an endangered species at jeopardy of extinction, while section 9 generally prohibits actions, by public and private parties, that, among other things, would result in the harm or death of an individual of an endangered species. However, exceptions to both of these requirements are allowed and will be discussed later in this Chapter 8.

9.   State laws would also be an important element of biodiversity protection during the 1990s with several states, most notably California, providing more protection for biodiversity then the federal government through there own versions of the Endangered Species Act, as well as state laws protecting state forests and other, non-federal, public lands.

10.   As we explained in Chapter 1 as well as in this Chapter, in connection to the Forest Service's multi-level approach to biodiversity protection, there are may levels and measures of biodiversity depending upon the particular ecological level of interest; e.g., genetic variation within a population, number of individuals within a species, number of species in a habitat or community, and number of habitats in an ecosystem. The ESA has traditionally only been concerned with the number of individuals within a species, while the NFMA and other "land-use" biodiversity statutes have in practice dealt with some or all levels in its various management plans.

11.   The species by species approach relies on the listing, no jeopardy, and no take provisions of the ESA to protect individual species at high risk of extinction. *See supra* Chapter 6. The species by species approach has been criticized as not accounting for habitat or ecosystem level ecological factors. This criticism has led to an increasing emphasis in both the ESA and other biodiversity statutes on the protection of species' habitats. However, the species by species approach still exits and, in cases of many endangered or threatened species is still the necessary approach of assuring viability.

12.   In the last chapter we discussed how ecosystem management also became a dominant management paradigm for environmental law related to place-based protection and restoration.

13.   *See* The Marine Mammal Protection Act, 16 U.S.C. §§ 136–1421h.

14.   U.S.C. § 1801-1882.

15.   Much of our discussion about ecology and the ESA is based upon two recent surveys of the ESA done by committees of scientists. The first is NATIONAL RESEARCH COUNCIL, SCIENCE AND THE ENDANGERED SPECIES ACT (1995) [hereinafter SCIENCE AND THE ESA]. This study, commissioned by the National Research Council, looked at several aspects of how science (principally ecology and evolutionary biology) is used in the different ESA processes (e.g., listing, habitat determination, risk assessment, etc.). The second is a critique of the science within Habitat Conservation Plans (HCPs), which generally found a lack of good application of modern ecological concepts and methods in Habitat Conservation Planning. *See* PETER KAREIVA, ET. AL., USING SCIENCE IN HABITAT CONSERVATION PLANS (1998) [A joint project of the National Center of Ecological Analysis and Synthesis and the American Institute of Biological Sciences involving 13 ecologists from several universities along with 106 undergraduate and graduate students]; *see also* E.K. Harding et al., *A quantitative assessment of the use of science in habitat conservation plans*, 15 CONSERVATION BIOLOGY 488 (2001); Laura H. Watchman et al., *Science and Uncertainty in Habitat Conservation Planning*, JULY-AUGUST AMERICAN SCIENTIST 351 (2001) (providing relatively short summaries of the HCP report's methodology and results).

16.   *See* EDWARD O. WILSON, THE DIVERSITY OF LIFE 191 (1992).

17.   *See id.*

18.   *See id.* at 330.

19.   *See id.*

20.   *See supra* Chapter 6 for a discussion of the development of conservation biology primarily as a combination of ecology, population genetics, and evolutionary biology.

21.   Early efforts to create a conservation biology can be found in RAYMOND DASMANN, ENVIRONMENTAL CONSERVATION (1959) and DAVID EHRENFELD, BIOLOGICAL CONSERVATION (1970). While both works provide important foundation for conservation biology, neither directly led to the development of a separate scientific discipline.

22.   *See generally* GARY K. MEFFE ET AL., PRINCIPLES OF CONSERVATION BIOLOGY (2nd ed. 1997) (one of many current textbooks on Conservation Biology); Reed F. Noss, *Some Principles of Conservation Biology, as They Apply to Environmental Law*, 69 CHI.-KENT L. REV. 893 (1994) (a short introduction to conservation biology written for the non-scientist, this article was also cited by the court in the *Marita* cases). Today, these three scientific disciplines are still the core elements of conservation biology, but conservation biology has been expanded with the inclusion of elements from, among other areas, ecosystem ecology, economics, and sociology.

23.   Because many of the early conservation biologists came from the ranks of population ecology, there was greater use of the concepts and methods of population ecology and genetics than of ecosystem ecology. *See* CONSERVATION BIOLOGY: THE SCIENCE OF SCARCITY AND DIVERSITY 57-76 (Michael E. Soulé ed. 1986) for an excellent overview of the state of conservation biology after its first half decade of existence. This work is divided into chapters dealing with the scientific principles behind conservation biology and selected case studies of the application of these principles to particular management problems. The 1986 Conservation Biology book's treatment of case studies deals with "sensitive habitats" as the level within the ecological hierarchy needing protection, although the effects of some ecosystem processes (e.g., nutrient

flow) on these habitats are discussed. However, ecosystem ecology, as discussed earlier in this book would become, with the advent of ecosystem management, an important aspect of the conservation biology of the 1990s.

24.   The estimation of one population genetic parameter, inbreeding coefficients (the loss in genetic variation due to decreased population size) of endangered populations was an early goal of many conservation biologists. Also, as described above it was of explicit concern to the developers of the Nicolet forest management plan.

25.   It is this aspect of conservation biology that is most accurately called "biodiversity" studies. This growing awareness that the protection of populations and habitats required a detailed knowledge of the distribution and abundance of all species gave new life to the old biological discipline of systematic biology. *See* WILSON, *supra* note 16.

26.   *See* ROBERT H. MACARTHUR & EDWARD O. WILSON, THE THEORY OF ISLAND BIOGEOGRAPHY (1967). Originally developed to explain natural patterns of species diversity on different size islands, this theory would be used by conservation biologists as evidence that populations in small human-made fragments of habitat were more likely to go extinct than populations in larger "island" fragments ("island" could include any habitat type that was surrounded by a different habitat that was incompatible to its resident species).

27.   *See* MEFFE, ET AL., *supra* note 22, at 19.

28.   No mention of biological diversity or biodiversity is found in the statute. *See* 16 U.S.C. §§ 1531-1541. The only mention of biological diversity, related to the ESA, is found in the committee report. *See* H.R. Rep. No. 93-412 (1973).

29.   The ESA gives "species" a broad definition that includes, for vertebrates, "sub-species" and "Distinct Population Segments." 16 U.S.C. § 1532(16).

30.   16 U.S.C. § 1531(b).

31.   16 U.S.C. § 1538.

32.   *See* 16 U.S.C. § 1539. The "no surprise" policy, while not explicitly an example the interaction of ecology and the ESA was recently criticized by ecologists as an example of how the ESA permits economic concerns to increase the risk of extinction to endangered and threatened species. *See* KAREIVA, ET AL., *supra* note 15.

33.   Babbitt v. Sweet Home, 115 S.Ct. 2407, 2419 (1995).

34.   *See id.* at 2422.

35.   "[S]ignificant habitat modification or degradation where it actually kills or injuries wildlife by significantly impairing essential behavioral patterns, including breeding, feeding or sheltering." 50 CFR 17.3.

36.   *See e.g.,* Laurie M. Stone, *Harm Means Harm: Babbitt v. Sweet Home Chapter of Communities for a Great Oregon*, 24 PEPP. L. REV. 695 (1997).

37.   However, as described above harm is directly related to the biological concept of fitness. Significant reductions in fitness (i.e., the health or reproductive ability of an individual or population) can occur at any stage of the life-cycle and by both direct action on a species or its habitat, or by indirect action (e.g., acid rain will cause slow destruction of a habitat and a slow but, ultimately, complete reduction in fitness). *See* DOUGLAS J. FUTUYMA, EVOLUTIONARY BIOLOGY 370-71 (3d ed. 1997).

38.   SCIENCE AND THE ESA, *supra* note 15.

39.   *See id.*

40.   *See* Sierra Club v. Marita, 843 F.Supp. 1526 (E.D. Wis. 1994); Sierra Club v. Marita, 845 F.Supp. 1317 (E.D. Wis. 1994); Sierra Club v. Marita, 46 F.3d 606, 609 (7th Cir. 1995).

41. Biodiversity is a measure of biological variety at several levels of organization, such as the genetic variation present within a species, the number of species, and the variety of ecosystems. The protection and extension of biodiversity, usually defined as the presence of a large number of animal and plant species, is now a main objective of conservation biologists and others interested in preserving the natural world. *See* WILSON, *supra* note 16, at 393; Ruth Patrick, *Biodiversity: Why Is It Important?*, in BIODIVERSITY II 15, 15-24 (Marjorie L. Reaka-Kudla et. al., 1997); BIODIVERSITY (E. O. Wilson, ed., 1988).

42. A long line of cases, based upon *Chevron, Inc. v. Natural Resources Defense Council*, 467 U.S. 837 (1984), have held that when a statute does not specifically address an issue (such as what ecological concepts and methods to use in protecting biodiversity) an agency's interpretation should be followed unless it is found to be "arbitrary, capricious, or manifestly contrary to the statute." Agencies have used this judicial deference to fight several attacks on the science it has chosen to use, including the *Marita* cases and many of the Spotted Owl cases.

43. The main exception this general rule is the Endangered Species Act's "no take" provision, which does not allow balancing of economic interests with species extinction. *See supra* Chapter 6.

44. *See* Sierra Club v. Marita, 46 F.3d 606, 609 (7th Cir. 1995). The Forest Service and environmental groups both believe that the overall diversity of these forests (e.g., number of different tree species) is greater now than in the original old growth forest of the early 1800s.

45. *See supra* CHAPTER 5; NFMA §§ 1601-1614; 36 C.F.R. § 219.19 (1991).

46. S. Rep. No. 94-893, 94th Cong., 2d Sess. at 8, 10 (1976).

47. *See* MEFFE, *supra* note 22.

48. *See* id. at 69 (Management Indicator Species is a concept used by resource managers in which changes in population size of one or more species are assumed to indicate the overall health of a habitat or ecosystem). It certainly would not be fair to criticize the drafters of the NFMA or its early regulations for ignoring "conservation biology" since this discipline would not even be born until the early stages of the development of the forest management plans.

49. *See* U.S. Forest Service, U.S. Dep't of Agriculture, CHEQUAMEGON NATIONAL FOREST LAND RESOURCE MANAGEMENT PLAN, *Final Environmental Impact Statement and Record of Decision* (1986) [hereinafter CHEQUAMEGON PLAN]; *see* U.S. Forest Service, U.S. Dep't of Agriculture, NICOLET NATIONAL FOREST LAND RESOURCE MANAGEMENT PLAN, *Final Environmental Impact Statement and Record of Decision* (1986) [hereinafter NICOLET PLAN]. The plan established specific objectives for the commercial and recreational use of the forests as well as methods to achieve these objectives. *See* CHEQUAMEGON PLAN at 22. The commercial (i.e., timber) use objectives were defined as 97 million board feet a year in Nicolet and 70 million board feet a year in Chequamegon. Also, in both forests, recreational use objectives were defined by the number of visitors per year engaging in specific types of recreation (e.g, hunting, semi-primitive motorized recreation, and "developed" forms of recreation).

50. The EIS compared the effects of alternatives to the proposed management plan on plant and animal diversity as well as other NFMA mandated criteria. The most accessible source for a description of the forest management plans treatment of diversity are in the court opinions for the two district court cases arising from challenges to the final management plans of each forest. *See* Sierra Club v. Marita, 843 F.Supp. 1526 (E.D. Wis. 1994); Sierra Club v. Marita, 845 F.Supp. 1317 (E.D. Wis. 1994). The fact that the court analyzed the details of the Forest Service's ecological methodology is

interesting by itself and represents one of the most detailed, if not one first, descriptions and analysis of an ecological methodology by a court.

51.   *See* 16 U.S.C. § 1604(g)(3)(B). Diversity is defined as "the distribution and abundance of different plant and animal communities and species within the area covered by a land and resource management plan." 36 C.F.R. § 219.3.

52.   *See* 36 C.F.R. § 219.27(g). However, diversity can be reduced from this baseline level if required to meet the multiple-use mandate of the Forest Service.

53.   In the *Marita* cases this lack of any specific procedure, either in the statute or its regulations, would be used by the Forest Service as evidence that it had the discretion to use a methodology of its own choice. *See e.g.*, Sierra Club v. Marita, 46 F.3d 606, 620 (7th Cir. 1995).

54.   *See* 36 C.F.R. § 219.19.

55.   *See* Marita, 843 F. Supp. at 1533. In both management plans habitat diversity was assumed to be a function of "vegetative diversity." NICOLET PLAN, app D., *supra* note 49, at 3. FEIS, App. D at 3. This assumption corresponds to some of the early thinking of ecologists, particularly plant ecologists, who also defined a habitat by resident plant species only. *See supra* Chapter 2. Further, in Nicolet, the Forest Service determined that habitat diversity was dependent on three variables; distribution of tree types, variety of timber age-classes, and the amount of intensive management in any specific area. Similarly, in Chequamegon, the Service determined that variety of tree species and age classes, the acreage of "permanent upland openings," and the method of harvesting were the main variables of habitat diversity. *See Final Environmental Impact Statement*, in NICOLET PLAN, *supra* Note 49, ch. 3 at 26-7.

56.   *See id.*

57.   *See e.g.*, NICOLET PLAN FEIS, *supra* note 49, ch. 3 at 44-5. The end result of the Services "vegetative" or habitat diversity analysis was the determination of a "Wildlife Habitat Diversity Index" which measured the percentage that each alternative plan met the optimum diversity levels. Diversity Indices were calculated for each variable and a Total Diversity Index was calculated as an average of the three individual indices (which gives equal weight to the three variables). However, it is not clear from the management plan, the associated FIES or from the documents associated with the subsequent court cases what method the Forest Service use to calculate all the diversity indices.

58.   *See* 36 C.F.R. § 219.19.

59.   Sierra Club v. Marita, 843 F.Supp. 1526, 1536 (E.D. Wis. 1994); *see also* Sierra Club v. Marita, 845 F. Supp. 1317, 1323 (E.D. Wis. 1994).

60.   For Nicolet, 65 of the listed species were determined to require a population viability analysis and the associated habitats for only these species were determined. However, for Chequamegon the habitats of all of the more than 300 listed vertebrate species were identified. This resulted in the Service determining that there were 14 different habitat types in Nicolet and 25 different habitat types in Chequamegon. *See* Sierra Club v. Marita, 46 F.3d 606, 617 (7th Cir. 1995). As with the Forest Service's determination of habitat type, a community was defined by vegetative type only.

61.   *See* Marita, 845 F. Supp. at 1323.

62.   *See* Marita, 843 F. Supp. at 1536; *Final Environmental Impact Statement*, in NICOLET PLAN, *supra* Note 49. In Nicolet there was two broad types of habitats; forested and non-forested which, the Service determined, included 14 different sub-types of habitats in which one or more of the 65 critical species could be found. *See id.*

63.   *See id.* The Service assumed that if enough habitat was present for this species there would be enough for all other species in the same habitat.

64. For this estimate the Nicolet planners used, like the designers of the Chequamegon plans, principles from population genetics. Based upon the of population size for each MIS after 150 years, the Service estimated the "inbreeding coefficient" for each population. In breeding coefficient is a measure of how much the breeding pattern of a population differs from a hypothetical "out breed" population. Extensive inbreeding is associated with low fitness and increased likelihood of extinction due to the increased frequency of deleterious genes, an overall decrease in individual fitness (e.g., health) due to a lack genetic variation, and a decreased ability of a population to adapt to a changing environment. *See* FUTUYMA, *supra* note 37, at 312-16; DANIEL L. HARTL & ANDREW G. CLARK, PRINCIPLES OF POPULATION GENETICS 235-61 (2ND ED 1989).

65. The Forest Service used an inbreeding coefficient of greater than 0.5 as indicating that a MIS would go extinct. *See* NICOLET PLAN, *supra* note 49.

66. *See id.*

67. A population size of 50 has long been used by ecologists, population geneticists, and conservation biologists as a minimum populations size necessary to maintain sufficient genetic variation so as to limit the adverse affects of inbreeding. *See* HARTL & CLARK, *supra* note 64.

68. These factors included: variation in relative amount of contribution to breeding by each adult, male/female ratio, generational overlapping, and fluctuation in birth and death rates. *See id.*

69. The Service based their calculations on the determination of how much habitat each plan would leave and how much habitat was required by each breeding pair of MIS. *See Final Environmental Impact Statement*, in CHEQUAMEGON PLAN, *supra* Note 49, ch. 2 at 130, tbl II-45.

70. *See* Sierra Club v. Marita, 843 F.Supp. 1526, 1530 (E.D., Wis. 1994).

71. *See* Sierra Club v. Marita, 46 F.3d 606, 610 (7th cir. 1995).

72. *See* Noss, *supra* note 22 (provides an introduction to some, non-genetic, biological concepts in conservation biology, including island biogeography). *See also*, Walter Kuhlmann, *Making the Law More Ecocentric: Responding to Leopold and Conservation Biology*, 7 DUKE ENVTL. L. & POL'Y F. 133 (1996) (written by the lead lawyer for the plaintiffs in the *Marita* cases, this article provides one lawyer's perspective on conservation biology).

73. *See* Marita, 46 F.3d at 622. There were several key factors in the *Marita* case which could distinguish it from similar cases today and could lead to a decrease in the deference granted to federal agencies in choosing which scientific principles to employ. First, the court was required to judge the case by the level of scientific knowledge at the time of the creation of the Forest management plan (i.e., 1982), and not at the time of the cases, a decade later. The Forest Service correctly contended that many conservation biology principles had not been adequately tested, and, therefore, were not accepted by all biologists. By the time of the *Marita* decisions in the early and mid 1990s, the conservation biology principles in question were both tested and accepted by most conservation biologists. As we have seen in many other environmental cases, the discretion courts give agencies to ignore widely accepted scientific principles in their management plans is an issue of critical importance. *See* Marita II, 843 F.Supp. At 1526 n.11; Marita III, 46 F3d at 618; Noss, *supra* note 22, at 900; Patricia S. King, *Applying Daubert to the "Hard Look" Requirement of NEPA: Scientific Evidence Before the Forest Service in Sierra Club v. Marita*, 2 WIS. ENVTL. L. J. 147 (1995) (discussing both the proper application of the scientific method and data to conservation issues and how the Forest Service misapplied the scientific method in these national forests).

74. *See id.*

75.   *See* SCIENCE AND THE ESA, *supra* note 15 at 72-73.

76.   We mean conceptual mistake in this case; there is no indication that case presenting
        the need manage these national forests as ecosystems or landscapes would have had
        any more success with the court; not in the light of the deference given by the court to
        the Forest Service.

77.   However, the Forest Service's method of assuming populations of 50 would minimize
        the probability of inbreeding would be considered by most population geneticists, then
        and now, to be inadequate.

78.   *See* SCIENCE AND THE ESA, *supra* note 15, at 134.

79.   This omission is also important because both island biogeography and population
        genetic principles state that small habitat size leads to loss of genetic variation pre-
        dates the creation or acceptance of conservation biology. This principle is based upon
        theoretical and empirical studies dating back to the early century and are a foundation
        of population genetics and evolutionary biology. The inbreeding coefficient they use
        for selection of alternative plans was based upon general population genetic
        assumptions and not on any direct estimation of the genetic variation present in any
        MIS or needed to limit the probability of extinction for any MIS.

80.   However, the plaintiff's lack of discussion of genetic diversity may not be a critical
        defect. The plaintiff's chosen method of forest management, island biogeography,
        would have led to larger reserves with corresponding larger populations. Most models
        of population genetics would assume that larger populations would be more likely to
        maintain higher levels of genetic variation. *See* HARTL & CLARK, *supra* note 64.
        Further, the plaintiff's lack of consideration of higher levels of ecological organization
        (e.g., ecosystem health or processes) may be partly forgiven, since the initial challenges
        to the management plans had occurred during the 1980s, when populations were the
        primary focus of conservation biologists. However, given that the cases themselves
        were litigated during the 1990s, it would have been possible for the plaintiffs to present
        a case with a more up-to-date conservation biology, one more fully integrating
        population. However, as with the Forest Service's consideration of genetic variation,
        the plaintiffs rely on assumption instead of actually monitoring changes in genetic
        variation.

81.   *See* Mark L. Shaffer, *Minimum Population Sizes for Species Conservation*, 31
        BIOSCIENCE 131-34 (1981).

82.   In a 1996 Notice of Intent for an Environmental Impact Statement for a revision to the
        Management Plan, the Forest Service stated that it was necessary to consider larger
        spatial scales of landscape and to more fully consider biological diversity. *See* Notice
        of Revision of the Land and Resource Management Plan for the Chequamegon and
        Nicolet National Forests, 61 Fed. Reg. 33,084 (1996).

83.   *See* Sierra Club v. Glickman, 974 F.Supp. 905 (E.D. Tex. 1997) (holding that Forest
        Service had failed to carry out intensive population census, as required under the
        NFMA regulations). *See also* Sierra Club v. Martin, 992 F.Supp. 1448 (N.D. Ga.
        1998) (holding that Forest Service is required to carry out extensive population surveys
        of MIS meet NFMA requirements). *But see* Inland Empire Public Lands Council v.
        U.S. Forest Service, 88 F.3d 754 (9th Cir. 1996) (upholding the Forest Service's use
        of "habitat viability analysis" instead of population viability analysis as a discretionary
        action by the Service in choosing between different scientific methodologies). In
        Glickman, the court concluded that the NFMA regulations create a requirement that
        the Forest Service collect inventory data of all MIS "that permits evaluation of
        diversity in terms of its *prior* and present condition." Further, the collection of
        inventory data, on all MIS, must be carried out, not just after the establishment of the
        plan, but during the planning stage. It was this collection of data on specific

populations, during the planning state, that the Service had avoided in the Wisconsin forests. While these recent interpretations have refined some of the details of how the Forest Service determines biodiversity, they still allow the Service wide discretion on the choice of MIS. More importantly, the Forest Service is still allowed complete discretion on limiting their measures of biodiversity to a simple census of populations and, thereby, ignoring all other levels of biodiversity (e.g., no measures of genetic variation are required).

84.   *See generally* Greg D. Corbin, *The United States Forest Service's Response to Biodiversity Science*, 29 ENVTL. L. 377 (1999); Heidi J. Mcintosh, *National Forest Management: A New Approach Based On Biodiversity*, 16 J. ENERGY NAT. RESOURCES & ENVTL. L. 257 (1996).

85.   *See* 60 Fed. Reg. 18,886.

86.   *See infra* Chapter 9 for a more detailed discussion of the balancing of factors that commonly goes into ecosystem management.

87.   *See* Greg D. Corbin, *The United States Forest Service's Response to Biodiversity Science*, 29 ENVTL. L. 377 (1999); Julie A. Weis, *Eliminating the National Forest Management Act's Diversity Requirement as a Substantive Standard*, 27 ENVTL. L. 641 (1997) for recent treatments of the legal elements of these proposed regulations.

88.   *See* 60 Fed. Reg. 18,886.

89.   It is the discretion that the Forest Service has in developing and implementing their plans that was the source of much of the criticisms that led to the 1995 proposed regulations. *See* Corbin, *supra* note 84, at 406-407.

90.   *See* Noss, *supra* note 22. While the Forest Service never mentioned the coarse filter concept in *Marita* they used it was the basis of their management plan for diversity; assuming that maintaining significant diversity in vegetation would result in animal diversity.

91.   *See* 60 Fed. Reg. 18,886 (1995). *See also* Noss, *supra* note 22 for a discussion of the contrast between coarse and fine filter methods.

92.   *See* 60 Fed. Reg. 18,886 (1995). As was the case in *Marita*, a habitat approach assumes that animal diversity can be maintain by protecting an adequate amount of habitat that is used by those animals. A population based approach monitors the population growth that is assumed to be at risk by human habitat modifications.

93.   The results of these regulations would be to make explicit the assumption made by the planner in the two Wisconsin forests; that a diversity of habitat means a diversity of animal and plant life.

94.   *See e.g.*, Walter Kuhlman, *Making the Law More Ecocentric: Responding to Leopold and Conservation Biology*, 7 DUKE ENVTL. L. & POL'Y F. 133 (1996) for a criticism of the original Forest Service regulations by the plaintiff's lead attorney in the *Marita* cases.

95.   *See* 60 Fed. Reg. 18,886 (1995).

96.   *See* 60 Fed. Reg. 18,886, 18,895 (1995) (1995). ("[T]he term 'viability' has been subject to continuously evolving scientific interpretation and no longer meets the agency's expectations at the time the rule was written.")

97.   *See id.*

98.   As we discussed in Chapter 5, the original regulations were developed largely through the efforts of the original Committee of Scientists.

99.   *See* Committee of Scientists, U.S. Dep't of Agriculture, Sustaining the People's Lands: Recommendations for Stewardship of the National Forests and Grasslands into the Next Century (March 15, 1999).

100.   *See id.*

101.   *See id.* While never addressing the substance of the 1995 proposed regulations, the Committee report's stated purpose was to answer the criticisms of these proposed regulations, including the use of a habitat based approach to protecting biodiversity.
102.   *Id.*
103.   *Id.*
104.   *See id.* at 24. *See also supra* Chapter 1 for a discussion of the role of the non-equilibrium theory in modern ecology.
105.   In the next chapter we will discuss how adaptive management can be applied within the Ecosystem Management paradigm. The Committee of Scientists' report is an example of its specific use in relation to biodiversity management.
106.   *See* 64 Fed. Reg. 54074 (October 5, 1999).
107.   *See* proposed regulation §§219.19 through 219.21; 64 Fed. Reg. 54076 (1999).
108.   *See* Proposed §219.19 ("To achieve sustainability, the first priority for management is the maintenance and restoration of ecological sustainability to provide a sustainable flow of products, services, and other values from these lands consistent with the laws and regulations guiding their use and enjoyment by the American people.") 64 FR 54103 (1999).
109.   64 FR 54078 (1999).
110.   *See supra* Chapter 5 for a discussion of the congressional multiple-use mandate written into both the National Forest Management Act and the Multiple Use and Sustained Yield Act (MUSYA).
111.   *See* 64 Fed. Reg. 54099 (1999).
112.   "The principal ecological processes that influence the characteristic structure and composition of an area. This includes the intensity, frequency, and magnitude of natural disturbance regimes, occurring at the multiple geographic and temporal scales." Proposed Rule §219.20(a)(2). These proposed regulations implicitly recognizes three part division of ecosystems described in the 1995 proposed regulations and the 1999 Committee of Scientists' report: composition, structure, and processes. The recognition of the importance of monitoring and maintaining ecological processes, and not just the outward physical characteristics of an ecosystem, is an important advance in these proposed regulations over earlier federal agencies treatment of ecology.
113.   *See* 64 Fed. Reg. 54087 (1999).
114.   *See* 64 Fed. Reg. 54104 (1999).
115.   *See* Proposed 219.11, 64 Fed. Reg. 54102.
116.   *See* Oliver A. Houck on the law of biodiversity and ecosystem management, 81 MINN. L. REV. 869, 942 (1997). The guidelines provide details of the types of considerations that a management plan should consider when setting and meeting these standards. Further, if any state or regional manager does complete standards and guidelines, section 4180.2 contains its own set of fallback standards and guidelines which must be applied. For example, 4180.2(f)(1)(iv) would set, as one fallback standard that, "Healthy, productive and diverse populations of native species exist and are maintained." The fallback guidelines provide help on how to achieve this standard (e.g., "Conservation of Federal threatened or endangered, Proposed, Category 1 and 2 candidate, and other special status species is promoted by the restoration and maintenance of their habitats" – 4180.2(f)(2)(viii)).

   The fallback guidelines also attempt to deal with natural diversity, within a rangeland, by directing: (vi) Management practices maintain or promote the physical and biological conditions necessary to sustain native populations and communities; (vii) Desired species are being allowed to complete seed dissemination in 1 out of every 3 years (Management actions will promote the opportunity for seedling establishment when climatic conditions and space allow). 4180.2(f)(2)(vi)-(vii). As discussed by Houck, this seems analagous to the current Forest Service approach; animal and plant diversity is to be maintained through the maintenance and restoration of habitat not, as the proposed Forest Service regulations would, through an active monitoring and consideration of individual populations.

117.   43 C.F.R. 4180.1(a)-(d).

118.   4180.2(e)(1)-(12).

119.   Forest Service proposed sections §§219.22-25 would provide for a much higher level of scientific involvement (including non-agency scientists) in the develop and implementation of the plan and, most specifically, with determining what and how to monitor species and other ecological factors. It is in these sections of the proposed regulations, and not those sections detailing ecological methods, that most of the protection for a future forest plan's ecological sufficiency may be found. However, the degree of consultation is under the discretion of the relevant Forest Service official.

120.   Bryan Wasmer Dempsey, Vermont Law School Class of 2002, completed most of the research and the first draft for the section on the fishery. A "fishery" can refer to both the economic act of exploiting aquatic and marine species for food and profit and to the *place* where the fishing takes place. Most important commercial fisheries are found in identifiable geographic locations defined by a high concentration of commercial fish species. This increased population density is usually result of ideal biotic (e.g., food) and abiotic (e.g., temperature and currents) conditions – a healthy ecosystem.

121.   *See* K. SHERMAN, ET AL., THE NORTHEAST SHELF ECOSYSTEM: ASSESSMENT, SUSTAINABILITY, AND MANAGEMENT (1996). The ecological complexity of the fishery ecosystem can be seen from the following description, "Each subarea is characterized by distinct bathymetry and circulation. The region is influenced by winds, climate changes, river runoff, estuarine exchange, tides, and Gulf Stream meanders and rings, producing a complex circulation regime. Biota found in the region range from estuarine and coastal species to large pelagic predators, whose range includes the Slope Sea on the east. Strong temperature gradients from north to south influence species occurrences. The LME is a highly productive region and is facing pressures from overfishing, land-based inputs of nutrients and toxic materials, and mineral exploration" (citations omitted). This report is available on the internet at <www.edc.uri.edu/lme/text/lme7.htm>.

122.   *See* The Chamber of the Int'l Court of Justice in the Case Concerning Delimitation of the Maritime Boundary in the Gulf of Maine Area (Canada/United States of America), 1984 I.C.J. Rep. 246.

123.   *See* Canadian Landings Information, Summary Tables for 1989-1998, Landings section of the Department of Fisheries and Oceans website (visited 06/26/00) <http://www.ncr.dfo.ca/communic/statistics>

124.   Pub.L. 94-2656, and its 1996 Sustainable Fisheries Act amendment, Pub.L.104-297, which changed the Act name to Magnuson-Stevens (MSFCMA). *See* 16 U.S.C.A. § 1801 (1999).

125.   *See* MARK KURLANSKY, COD (1997). This book examines both the cultural history and the management history of the Northwest Atlantic fishery and the Cod fishery in particular.

126.   *See* Structure of the New England Fishery Management Council, from the NEFMC website (visited 07/22/00) <http://www.nefmc.org.>

127.   *See* Introduction to the Federal Fishery Management Process, New England Fishery Management Council website <http://www.nefmc.org/overview/into.htm> (visited 07/14/00). The Northeast Multispecies (Groundfish) Fishery Management Plan is the Council's most comprehensive management plan. It covers 13 species of fish with three more species to be added soon.

128.   *See* Introduction to the Federal Fishery Management Process, found on the New
        England Fishery Management Council website <http://www.nefmc.org>
        (visited 07/22/00)
129.   *See id.* at Five-Year Strategic Plan for Fisheries Research.
130.   *See* Implementation Plan for the Code of Conduct for Responsible Fisheries, 1997,
        found on National Marine Fisheries Service website (visited 07/22/00)
        <http://www.nmfs.noaa.gov.>
131.   *See id.*
132.   Currently, there is a bill in the House of Congress and one in the Senate to reauthorize
        the MSFCMA. On March 21, 2000, the first bill (H.R. 4046) proposing to reauthorize
        the MSFCMA in the 106th Congress was introduced and named the Fisheries Recovery
        Act of 2000. The Act proposes to amend the MSFCMA to recover depleted fish stocks
        and promote the long-term sustainability of marine fisheries, and for other purposes.
        One of these other purposes is section eight of the amendment, Conserving Marine
        Ecosystems. *See* H.R. 4046, 106th Cong. (2000). The other bill was introduced in
        Senate June 29, 2000 S. 2832 also to reauthorize the Magnuson-Stevens Fishery
        Conservation and Management Act, and for other purposes. Section 118 of the bill is
        titled: SCIENTIFIC AND STATISTICAL COMMITTEES REPORT ON ECOSYSTEM RESEARCH
        PRIORITIES: PILOT PROGRAM FOR FISHERY ECOSYSTEM PLANS. This plan calls for the
        development of a Fishery Ecosystem Plan (FEP), as suggested by the Ecosystem
        Principles Advisory Panel, for at least one fishery within one of the eight regional
        fishery councils. "After identifying the pilot Fishery Ecosystem Plan, the Secretary
        shall coordinate with the appropriate regional fishery management council to identify
        any information or conduct any research that may be needed to complete such a plan
        including a model of the food web, habitat needs of organisms identified in the food
        web, rates of mortality, identification of indicator species, and any other relevant data
        and monitoring needs."
                See S. 2832, 106th Cong. Sect. 2 (2000). These bills can be found in the
        Federal Register: April 24, 2000 (Volume 65, Number 79)] [Rules and Regulations]
        [Page 21658-21667], from the Federal Register Online via GPO Access (visited
        07/22/00) <http://www.wais.access.gpo.gov.>

10 International Environmental Law Regimes: Coming of Age in the 1990s

Perhaps the most poignant image of our time is that of Earth as seen by the space voyagers: a blue sphere, shimmering with life and light, alone and unique in the cold blackness of the cosmos. From this perspective, the maps of geopolitics vanish, and the underlying interconnectedness of all the components of this extraordinary living system – human, animal, plant, water, land, and atmosphere – become strikingly evident. This realization must determine the global diplomacy of the future.[1]

Introduction

The flowering of ecosystemic regimes and their law during the 1990s did not only take place in the United States, but was a global phenomenon as well. The emergence of multiple international regimes that addressed regional ecosystems to global scale environmental problems was stimulated by the maturation of the theory of regimes and common property systems as well as public awareness of the need for collective action on issues affecting public health and shared natural resources.[2] The 1985 National Research Council (NRC) conference on common property resource management[3] marked an important recognition that throughout the world, there was an alternative to either public property, private property, and "the commons" (*res nullius*) (the latter recognized by Garrett Hardin in his famous article on the "tragedy of the commons"). The NRC conference recognized the existence of common property resource management organizations such as common grazing lands, agricultural irrigation districts, watershed management units, and collective forests located throughout the world. The systems of governance of these regimes was described in 1990 by Elinor Ostrom in her path breaking book, *Governing the Commons*.[4] The notion of commons governance has also become important to ecosystem management, since both perspectives begin with the assumption of a common resource that requires collective management.

At the same time, Oran Young and Gail Osherenko of Dartmouth College were publishing a series of path-breaking works pertaining to resource regimes. These studies focused especially upon international environmental regime formation in the Arctic including the governance of polar bears, north pacific fur seals, and other shared natural resources.[5] Scholars soon extended the regime approach to the analysis of other resources and ecosystems, which in addition to the Mediterranean Sea and Great Lakes governance mechanisms described in previous chapters, included the oceans, the Arctic and Antarctic regions, outer space, and atmospheric regimes (ozone and global warming).[6] In a related set of efforts, theorists began to develop and implement the adoption of trading mechanisms (e.g., tradable permits for carbon emissions) for the governance of both domestic and international environmental resources.[7]

What makes an international agreement or regime effective and how can these instruments be designed to absorb changes in scientific knowledge and public culture?

> *In this chapter we suggest that any "mature" system of international environmental governance that has a foundation in ecosystemic law will include: a scientific basis in global ecology for understanding the problem; an institutional framework to support, conduct and then apply the science in an international context; appropriate incentives (political and financial) for international compliance; and, a flexible legal system of evaluation and feedback where new science can contribute to the solution of the international environmental issue, i.e., an "experimental jurisprudence."*

We have selected three international environmental regimes that have been introduced earlier in this book and which during the 1990s illustrate key developments in the evolution of ecosystemic law as applied to global problems. Important features of these regimes are summarized using a comparative framework in Table 10.1 (below) and are discussed in this chapter.

These international agreements and key distinguishing features that illustrate both current progress and problems facing international regime systems are: (1) the CITES (Convention on International Trade in Endangered Species) agreement which illustrates the variety of problems that arise with the application of ecological knowledge (mainly population ecology and systematics) to achieve species protection, and which also shows the importance of NGOs in developing and applying the science necessary for the operation of international regimes; (2) the Kyoto Protocol Climate Regime which promoted the development of a major new field (Earth System Science) drawing from ecosystem science and ecology and which is our best example of a highly developed international framework for the synthesis of current scientific information relevant to global environmental policy; and (3) the governance of the ozone depletion regime by means of the Montreal and other protocols; which illustrate the operation of a legally based feedback mechanism (an experimental jurisprudence) for modifying, with new scientific knowledge, the original ozone depletion agreements and the subsequent implementation of ecologically informed regulation through market mechanisms.

Table 10.1 A COMPARISON OF INTERNATIONAL ENVIRONMENTAL REGIMES

	MONTREAL PROTOCOL	CITES	KYOTO PROTOCOL
Global Issue	ozone depletion	species loss	climate change
Scientific basis of the problem	physical sciences	ecology	earth system science
Scientific tools	modeling, remote sensing	population census	modeling, ecosystem experiments (FACE)
Certainty of problem	very high	very high	high
Uncertainty of outcome with no-action	very low	low	medium
Amount of mandated science, data collection	high	medium	high
Updating of regime with current science	high	medium	high
Economic impact of the regime	moderate	low	very high
Participation by industry/private sector	high	low	low
Reliance on NGOs for data, enforcement	low	high	medium
International participation	very high	very high	high
U.S. Agreement	yes	yes	no

Source: Brooks, Jones and Virginia

CITES: International Species Protection

The international mandate to preserve species of value (aesthetic and economic) to humans is one of the most visible consequences of the "environmental movement". Ecologists played a critical role in drawing public attention to the alarming loss of global biodiversity resulting from habitat destruction, pollution, and over-exploitation.[8] Two of the most influential ecologists in species conservation science and policy at this time and today are

Edward O. Wilson and Thomas Lovejoy. Their contributions are focused on species, but always from a perspective that recognizes the centrality of the ecosystem concept in conservation and the need for science-based laws to protect species from human activities.

The culmination of conservation efforts inspired by ecologists like Wilson and Lovejoy and championed by the international wildlife NGO community was the Convention on International Trade in Endangered Species of Wild Fauna and Flora (CITES).[9] CITES acts to protect endangered species by prohibiting their international trade and regulating the trade of threatened species.[10] In this sense, CITES is not a full ecosystemic regime for the protection of a diversity of species and ecosystems, since it was crafted to regulate the trade of individual species. However, the administration of CITES has sought to adopt monitoring approaches and criteria for identifying endangered species that draw heavily upon ecology. To understand CITES as a regime, one must view it as part of a tradition of laws and practices controlling trade of species, preceded and followed by a number of international treaties.[11] In short, the administrative framework of CITES is a combination of public and private institutions coordinated to promote the protection of species.[12]

The CITES agreement was signed in March 1973, coming out of discussions held at the 1972 UN Conference on Human Environment held in Stockholm. Concern about the growing threat of international trade in rare species led the World Conservation Union (IUCN)[13] to draft the framework of an international agreement that was circulated to nations in 1967, 1969 and 1971. The final draft document was accepted by 21 of the 80 countries that attended a Plenipotentiary Conference in Washington and the Convention became enforceable in 1975.

Over 150 nations have joined the CITES regime and it is considered one of the most successful international environmental agreements. Approximately 30,000 species of plants and animals fall under CITES protection. Parties to the Convention are legally bound to follow CITES provisions, but adherence is voluntary. Countries must adopt their own domestic laws and policies authorizing a management authority and a scientific authority[14] to meet CITES expectations. In the U.S., CITES issues reach the office of the Secretary of the Interior, with the U.S. Fish and Wildlife Service and the U.S. Department of Agriculture Animal and Plant Health Inspection Service acting as lead agencies. A number of U.S. laws and policy statements provide the domestic framework for the enforcement of CITES.

Table 10.2   Some of the U.S. Laws and Protocols that Function to Support
the Regime Regulating Trade in Endangered Species (CITES)

African Elephant Conservation Act of 1989
Asian Elephant Conservation Act of 1997
Conservation of Arctic Flora and Fauna (CAFF)
U.S. Endangered Species Act
Great Apes Conservation Act of 2000
Nature Conservation Protocol with China
Neotropical Migratory Conservation Act of 2000
Rhinoceros and Tiger Conservation Act of 1994
The International Structure of CITES

Source: Brooks, Jones and Virginia

Species falling under CITES protections are assigned to one of three Appendices to the Convention that designate the level of protection required to ensure viability.

Appendix I	Threatened with extinction, trade is permitted only in exceptional circumstances.
Appendix II	Not necessarily threatened with extinction, but trade must be controlled for survival.
Appendix III	Species that are protected in at least one country that has asked CITES for help in controlling trade.

Once a species is listed on an Appendix, it is regulated through a permit requirement. Appendix I and II species require both export and import permits. Trade (import or export) of a CITES listed species requires the appropriate documents at the port of entry or exit. Documentation varies with the species and whether the specimen is captive bred or cultivated or has been taken from the wild. The allowable number of permits issued is based upon a determination that the trade in question "will not be detrimental to the survival of the species." In practice, most commercial trade of species in Appendix I is banned.

The determination of "not detrimental to the survival of a species" is made by the Scientific Authority of each party.[15] "Whenever a Scientific Authority determines that the export of specimens of any such species should be limited in order to maintain that species through its range at a level consistent *with its role in the ecosystem in which it occurs* [emphasis added] and well above the level which that species may become eligible for inclusion in Appendix I, the Scientific Authority shall advise the appropriate Management Authority of suitable measures to be taken to limit the grant of exports for specimens of that species."[16] The Management Authority then grants and regulates the permits.[17] CITES is administered through the office of the Secretariat, which is responsible for coordinating and managing the working of the Convention. It collects and distributes information to the Parties (the member States to CITES) and is responsible for holding a periodic Conference of the Parties every 2-3 years. At the Conference conservation status of species is reviewed, proposals to amend the list of species in Appendix I and II are considered along with measures to improve the operations of the convention, and a budget is adopted for the work of the Secretariat. Proposals to add, remove or delist are passed by a two-thirds majority of the parties present and voting. Non-members are allowed to attend and NGOs with a stake in conservation or trade may participate in discussions at the discretion of the Parties. This is an important dimension of the CITES regime, which seeks to include all relevant stakeholders in the process to protect biota.

Between Conferences, the three Standing Committees (Plants, Animals, Nomenclature) are responsible for the ongoing work of the Convention by providing policy guidance to the Secretariat. These committees have been heavily involved with follow up studies regarding the decision to reopen limited trade in elephant products and in developing monitoring programs to track illegal elephant hunting and trade. The Nomenclature Committee has the difficult task of ensuring standard names of plant and animals down to the level of subspecies or variety. This is an essential service since taxonomists and evolutionary biologists and ecologists are constantly revising the taxonomic "tree of life." Confusion caused by a change in the scientific name of an organism or a taxonomic group should not result in a change in the protection afforded by CITES.

There have been 11 Conference of the Parties meetings since CITES began. Important developments occurred at the 8th Conference in Kyoto in 1992, when the original criteria for listing a species (the Bern Criteria, 1976) were challenged as too general. This led to the adoption of the Lauderdale Criteria (1994), a more ecologically based system of criteria based on "sound science" to guide amendments to Appendices I and II.[18] The Lauderdale Criteria are the only aspects of CITES that appear to have any ecological influence on the listing and permitting mechanisms.

The Lauderdale Criteria provide more specific, quantifiable indications for the placement of a species on Appendix I. For example, a species will be listed on Appendix I if it has: a population of 5,000 or less; a limited geographic range; a projected decrease in population, or the possibility of one of these criteria being met in 5 years.[19] These criteria draw from population ecology, but they do not necessarily mandate the application of the best possible science to understand the fate of a population in a given habitat. In fact, CITES recognizes that the requisite data for state-of-the-art population projections are usually lacking for the species under its jurisdiction. As a result, prescribed criteria are applied across species with very different habitat requirements, life history traits, and abilities to recover from low numbers. The Lauderdale Criteria have also been criticized because final decisions about listing of species still include considerations of both policy and science, and not just science alone.[20] The final determination of status is made by secret vote, which allows politics to trump science without the provision of adequate rationales for such "trumping" and without a court remedy for the exploration of the relationship between the criteria and the decision.

Table 10.3 EXAMPLES OF SOME OF THE CRITERIA USED IN THE CITES APPENDIX LISTING PROCESS TO DEMONSTRATE THE TYPES OF ECOLOGICAL INFORMATION THAT ARE REQUIRED TO ADMINISTER THE CONVENTION

According to the new criteria [in Appendices I and II], "any species that is or may be affected by trade should be included in Appendix I if it meets at least one of the biological criteria listed in Annex 1." ... Annex 1 states that a species should be listed in Appendix I if it meets any one of the following criteria (A, B, C, or D):

A. The wild population is small and is characterized by at least one of the following: a decline (observed or projected) in numbers or the area and quality of habitat; or each sub-population being very small; or large short-term fluctuations in numbers; or a high vulnerability due to the species' biology or behavior (including migration).

B. The population has a restricted area of distribution and is characterized by at least one of the following: fragmentation or occurrence at very few locations; or large fluctuations in area of distribution or projected decrease in the area of distribution; or – the number of sub-populations; or – the number of individuals; or – the area or quality of habitat; or – reproductive potential.

C. A decline in the number of individuals in the wild, which has been either: observed as ongoing or as having occurred in the past; or a decrease in area or quality of habitat; or – levels or patterns of exploitation; or – threats from extrinsic factors such as the effects of pathogens, competitors, parasites, predators, hybridization, introduced species and the effects of toxins and pollutants; or – decreasing reproductive potential.

D. The status of the species is such that if the species is not included in Appendix I, it is likely to satisfy one or more of the above criteria within a period of five years.

Terms used in Annex 1 are defined in the following way: Decline: A decrease of 50 percent or more in total within five years or two generations, whichever is the longer, has been found to be an appropriate guideline. *Fragmentation:* An area of distribution of 500 km^2 or less for each sub-population has been found to be an appropriate guideline. *Large fluctuations:* A figure of two years or less has been found to be an appropriate guideline of what constitutes a short-term fluctuation. *Population:* A figure of less than 5,000 individuals has been found to be an appropriate guideline of what constitutes a small wild population. *Sub-populations:* A figure of less than 500 individuals has been found to be an appropriate guideline.

The CITES regime emerged out of a tradition of efforts to protect endangered species by regulating the trading in these species. Prior treaties had provided for such trade controls, which offers an effective means of enforcing international agreements.[21] Such a focus on trade, although partly relevant to the African elephant threatened by the ivory trade, is not applicable to most other species, (including the Asian elephant), which are threatened by other forces. Most evidence suggests that habitat loss, hunting, competition from introduced species and other external factors such as climate change are usually more important determinants of a species fate.[22] Clearly the control of trade alone is not likely to be a sufficient strategy for maintaining a viable population of a species. In addition, the species by species regulatory approach fails to take into account that species exist in communities and function in ecosystems. As a consequence, critics have urged the revision of CITES either to subsume it under the Convention of Biological Diversity[23] or provide for increased habitat protection, perhaps through a quota system.[24]

Two developments which may suggest a path for an increased role for ecology in CITES are the advent of the precautionary principle and a shift from only considering protection and preservation options to include objectives that are based on the concept of sustainability.[25] The precautionary principle, as applied in CITES, is embodied in the requirement that species be listed in the Appendices, even if it is uncertain that trade is affecting the species.[26] However, the form of the principle set forth in CITES resolutions is relatively weak since the principle is merely a "deliberation informing principle" and the structure of CITES makes it difficult to fully consider the range of uncertain factors which arise in setting wildlife policy.

Table 10.4 PRECAUTIONARY PRINCIPLE

The history of the precautionary principle is rooted in the conflict of protecting the environment and human health and maintaining our economic activities in the face of incomplete and uncertain scientific information regarding cause and effect relationships.[27] Few policies for risk management have been as controversial in their implementation. Given the complexity of global scale issues that require scientific information (e.g., climate change, biodiversity loss, use of genetically modified organisms in agriculture) and the fact that science does not have the "all the answers" for policy makers, some are calling for decisions based on precaution first, science second.[28]

The precautionary principle in the context of international agreements was articulated in the Rio Declaration (Agenda 21) from the 1992 UN Conference on Environment and Development and states: *"In order to protect the environment, the precautionary approach shall be widely applied by States according to their capabilities. Where there are threats of serious or irreversible damage, lack of full scientific certainty shall not be used as a reason for postponing cost effective measures to prevent environmental degradation."* The U.S. is bound by the principle under international treaties containing the provision. However, the United States and the European Union differ in their reliance on the precautionary principle in domestic environmental law.[29] The principle is the basis for European environmental law under the Treaty of the European Union 1992 and it provides explicit guidance for decision making by EU countries. In the U.S., environmental laws may contain precautionary elements and have precautionary management goals as seen in endangered species law, some ecosystem management plans and in pollution control standards. However, in most instances U.S. law seeks to balance precaution against other factors, usually economic, and the application of the principle is not explicit.

One of the more substantive changes in the CITES regime in the 1990s has been movement from a preservation oriented law to one aiming at sustainability.[30] Although the CITES agreement never uses the term "sustainable use" the regime does adhere to this guiding principle since the survival of a species is not the sole concern, but rather species are to be maintained at "a level consistent with its role in the ecosystem,"[31] a goal that implies sustainability of the species and its ecosystem. Paradoxically, this change is championed both by nations who are seeking to escape what they perceive to be the rigid externally placed preservation goals of CITES, as well as conservation-minded nations who recognize that wildlife resources, whether traded or used domestically, e.g., ecotourism, are an important source of revenue and should be sustained. In the context of CITES, sustainability requires that wildlife harvest and trade be kept within a species capacity for renewal. This is different from past game management that sought to achieve a maximum sustainable yield (MSY), indefinitely.[32]

Both sustainable use and MSY have an economic and socioeconomic dimension. CITES in seeking to regulate trade, is necessarily concerned with the direct economic value (or use) of species. However, many argue that the economic value of species must not be restricted to value from "use" (as in harvest), but must also capture non-market values that are derived from the ethical and spiritual uses associated with wildlife and nature. Stephen Kellert in an attempt to define the types of values of nature and living diversity offers a schema of nine values: utilitarian, naturalistic, ecologistic-scientific, aesthetic, symbolic, dominionistic, humanistic, moralistic, and negativistic.[33] Kellert's list captures the complexity in designing domestic and international laws that incorporate a multidimensional perspective on the value of species as part of sustainability.[34]

Table 10.5 SUSTAINABILITY

The IUCN proposed at its 1994 General Assembly in Buenos Aires, that the use of a species is "likely to be sustainable" if:

– It does not reduce the future use potential of the population or impair its long term viability;
– It is compatible with the maintenance of the long-term viability of both supporting and dependent *ecosystems* (emphasis added);
– It does not reduce the future use potential or impair the long-term viability of other species.

This perspective emphasizes the role of species in ecosystems, the importance of ecosystems and their functions in sustaining species, and the importance of interspecific interactions in managing species and populations. This statement clearly reflects an ecosystemic approach to biodiversity management.

Sustainability as a central theme in CITES gains importance in light of the needs of local self-managing commons organizations for wildlife management (community based conservation) and the economic and social benefits it brings. Marshall Murphee describes a successful example by the Mahenye, in Zimbabwe. This community has successfully launched meaningful conservation efforts that advance wildlife and economic sustainability through a combination of eco-tourism, wildlife trade and animal farming. He finds that such efforts remain partially in conflict with the operation of CITES[35] and this realization has led him to advance a challenge to CITES as follows:

> There is, however, an aspect of this linkage that can frustrate its potential for synergy. The chain links together two polarities, which march to different drummers and that, operate within different regulatory cultures. CITES is historically rooted in the industrialized and urbanized societies of the developed world, with its emphasis on the existence and recreational value of wild places and wild species. Its implementation is largely in the hands of an international epistemic community of scientists, bureaucrats, and agency professionals that place great faith in the predictive capacity of science and the efficacy of legal proscription. It tends therefore to be reductionist and compliance oriented in its thinking and in its approach to regulation.
>   Community management as exemplified by our Mahenye case study is faced with a different set of incentives and regulatory dynamics. It values wild flora and fauna instrumentally, as a means to human livelihoods and the incentive for conservation lies in the desire to maintain this natural

capital. It is inductive and experimental, accepting contingency and risk. It is adaptive and opportunistic, aligning itself with the opportunities of the market than the promises and demands of the state. It is efficiency oriented and regulation has its source in the need for communal compliance if the collective enterprise is to succeed.[36]

This conflict between local perceptions of nature and those held by a more global external community parallels accounts of conflicting views of nature by American Indians and government regulators.

The partnership of CITES with the wildlife and conservation NGO communities is a defining trait of this regime and offers an example for other international regimes that are seeking mechanisms to improve the scientific basis for their actions and to improve compliance.[37] NGOs are becoming more integral to other international environmental regimes by providing research, oversight, and in some cases enforcement services. The scientific resources of CITES are extended through alliances with conservation organizations with international reach and high fund-raising potential. Especially important is Trade Records Analysis of Flora and Fauna in Commerce (TRAFFIC),[38] the international wildlife-monitoring program of the World Wildlife Fund for Nature and IUCN – the World Conservation Union. TRAFFIC was created to gather and review information on wildlife trade and to move this data to the public and governments in the hope of improving regulation of wildlife trade. TRAFFIC participates at CITES COP meetings as an observer and in this capacity can help nations resolve conflicts "behind the scenes."

Table 10.6 TRAFFIC

TRAFFIC was founded in the mid-1970s with its main mission to assist with the implementation of CITES. More recently, TRAFFIC has taken an ecosystem management approach to the preservation of species and biodiversity through its Ecoregion Conservation Initiative. Just as the Endangered Species Act in the United States increasingly considers that ecosystems may be protected to ensure the survival of endangered species, TRAFFIC is grouping specific habitats and their wildlife along with the ecosystem dynamics that define their interactions, into biogeographic units termed ecoregions.[39] This approach ignores the artificial boundaries of political states and seeks to develop management approaches where populations, critical habitats, migration routes, and ecological processes are conserved as a whole.[40] Examples of TRAFFIC Ecoregions are the Chihuahuan Desert in North America, the Mekong River Basin, and the Bering Sea.

In a similar vein, the UNEP World Conservation Monitoring Centre (WCMC) was formed in 2000 to support CITES by conducting research on endangered species and biodiversity indicators to provide early warning signals for policy makers and managers. WCMC acts as a data clearing-house for organizations working to conserve species and their habitats.

CITES and the African Elephant

The application of CITES to the worldwide effort to protect the elephant offers a particularly revealing example of the difficulties of the use of scientific information within CITES.[41] Perhaps no species carries more emotional, political and ecological impact than the African elephant;[42] it is a most protected species under CITES. International trade in ivory was banned to reduce the intense poaching pressure that had dramatically reduced elephant populations in many areas of Africa, especially the eastern region. In response to the ban however, countries in southern Africa soon experienced a population explosion of elephants in protected areas and amassed large inventories of ivory that were kept from reaching the world market by the CITES agreements. In 1997 at the 10th meeting of the Conference of Parties in Harare, the nations of Zimbabwe, Botswana, and Namibia were granted a limited one-time sales permit to reduce their inventories of ivory. Elephant populations in these countries had reached levels allowing a transfer of the elephant from the most protected status under CITES to a lower level of protection. Permission was granted for these nations to sell to Japan more than 30 tons of ivory, with the proceeds of the sale to benefit elephant conservation. This decision created an outcry from conservation groups and some African nations fearing that opening ivory sales would create an incentive for poachers to move their illegal stocks into the marketplace and to poach new stocks.

This brief recent history captures the complexity and tension surrounding endangered wildlife issues, and points to the need for effective international legal regimes to manage threatened species and to resolve conflict between nations.[43] The task of protecting the African elephant may become even more complicated. Recent science on elephant taxonomy could stir new international debate on elephant trade and conservation. The controversy over trade in elephant ivory illustrates the growing complexity of international wildlife issues and managing the operations of CITES when both the number of nations joining the Conference of the Parties and the number of listed species are increasing.[44]

Table 10.7 THE AFRICAN ELEPHANT: TWO SPECIES OR ONE?

A study published in August 2001 by the leading journal *Science* provides evidence that elephants from the tropical forests of Africa are genetically distinct from savannah dwelling populations based on DNA sequence data collected from 21 populations.[45] The tropical forest elephants are smaller and their tusk and skull morphology are also distinct from the savanna populations. The authors of this study propose that there are now two distinct species of elephants in Africa, *Loxodonta africana* (the previous descriptor for all African elephants) and the new species of the forests, *Loxodonta cyclotis*.

The implications of this study to CITES are large. If the new species is accepted by the Nomenclature Committee, then instead of a total population of about 500,000 for the African elephant, there are now many fewer of each species, and therefore each species is much more threatened that previously held. This is especially true for the new forest species, which makes up about a third of the total elephant numbers in Africa. The regional conflicts between African states over elephant management and ivory sales that we describe can only be exacerbated if this new scientific information is accepted by CITES.

How then can we save the elephant with or without CITES? The options for preserving or sustaining the elephant and its habitat may be based on the application of modern ecological science or traditional commons management or a synthesis of both. Daniel Botkin, in his classic *Discordant Harmonies: A New Ecology for the Twenty-First Century*,[46] was stimulated to rethink the foundations of modern ecology by the experience (among others) of the elephants of Tsavo Park, Kenya.[47] The effort to both protect these elephants and build a game park (established in 1948), after initial success, failed; the population protected from poaching boomed and then crashed during a drought. Even with the tools of modern ecology, consultants and managers differed as to whether to simply let the herd alone or alternatively manage it (e.g., cull excess animals to limit vegetation damage) either locally or on a larger geographic scale. As Botkin relates, "the disagreement at Tsavo was among conservationists who shared basic goals and a fundamental love of wild nature: they wished to conserve in perpetuity fine examples of wild nature for their own sake and for people to view. But they disagreed on methods." This disagreement was not about the simple choice of one management tool vs. another, but rather was a manifestation of opposing worldviews about what Botkin calls "wild nature." Tsavo's first-warden and architect David Sheldrick rejected culling of the rapidly increasing elephant herd believing that left to its own, wild nature would find a balance (natural ecological climax) that would persist if humans did not disturb it. Botkin challenges this perspective as failing to recognize the uniqueness of individual settings, the inherent stochastic character of population abundance and the overall complexity of ecosystems. A very important task for the science of ecology is to help ecosystemic regimes reconcile (or understand) opposing views of wild nature, as each perspective will suggest different management recommendations.

The scientific, political, and cultural conflicts that we have described over ways to manage, utilize, and sustain the elephant encapsulate the considerable challenges facing the CITES regime. In our view, the long-term success of the CITES regime is dependent on its continued modification into the framework of an ecosystemic regime, with more emphasis on holistic solutions that link species protection to the fate of ecosystems while considering human needs for the sustainable utilization of plants and animals.

Ozone Depletion and the Rise of an Ecological Experimental Jurisprudence

The law of ozone depletion is probably our most successful international environmental regime and shows the benefits of a new "experimental jurisprudence" that builds upon the fruits of two millennia of legal thought and practice. Part of the history of law from Justinian in ancient Rome to the present has been preoccupied with the search for the proper way to create a "science of law." This quest spurred the creation of legal codes in Europe and elsewhere. In the early enlightenment, Francis Bacon promoted an experimental method, which with the help of Descartes and others was to revolutionize our pursuit of scientific knowledge. With the separation of the empirical sciences from law during the enlightenment, the search continued in common law countries, with the early case method searching for "scientific principles," while legal realism sought to employ social science to guide law. In the mid-twentieth century, there was a search for "an experimental jurisprudence," which borrowing from the scientific method would treat laws as hypotheses to be tested with follow-up evaluation and a restatement of the hypotheses based upon new knowledge. Despite the fact that some legislatures and regulatory agencies have established offices to evaluate the workings of laws, philosophers and legal scholars have not been entirely successful in formulating a viable experimental jurisprudence to guide law making or legal scholarship.

The joinder of ecology and environmental law, particularly in the regime to control ozone depletion, is demonstrating how such an experimental jurisprudence might look and function. An analysis of the ozone depletion regime finds a treaty based upon scientific research, a treaty which established the scientific bodies to implement and evaluate its law, and most importantly providing for a scientifically-guided amendment process that is based upon flexible international and domestic legal instruments. This case offers an example of how an experimental jurisprudence might be shaped to handle other global-scale problems with the atmosphere, such as greenhouse gases and climate change.

Table 10.8 EXPERIMENTAL JURISPRUDENCE

"Experimental jurisprudence" was the title given to one outgrowth of legal realism in the early and mid-twentieth century. Legal realism sought to go beyond formal legal language to measure empirically the effects of legal rules and doctrines. In latter versions, the effort was to evaluate the effects of the law in light of their policies. Influenced by the early pragmatism of O.W. Holmes, Jr. and John Dewey, refined by Roscoe Pound and Myres McDougal, law came to be regarded as hypotheses to be tested for its claimed real world effects.[48] The Conventions and Protocols pertaining to acid rain, ozone depletion and global warming exemplify such an experimental jurisprudence since the program of reduction they authorize may be regarded an hypotheses which, in turn are tested by followup scientific study to assess their effects. Such an experimental jurisprudence is feasible in situations in which there is a sustained consensus on relatively specific objectives of the laws, an absence of strong salient competing objectives, legitimacy of the agency pursuing the objectives and measurability of the results of the program, (i.e., a lack of con-founding variables). Other ecologically informed domestic laws may be tested for their alleged effects; however few have been systematically monitored and their effects are often confounded by other variables.

In Chapter 7, we traced the origin of ozone depletion regulation: both international and in the United States. In that chapter, we took our story up to 1989, when the Montreal Protocol was adopted. The Montreal Protocol was to implement the Vienna Convention of 1985. In the decade following the Vienna Convention, there was considerable scientific uncertainty about the nature and extent of the ozone depletion, its chemical basis, its human health and ecological effects, and the cost and effectiveness of controls. As a con-sequence, the Vienna Convention itself explicitly recognized the reality of changing and improving science and the need to evaluate the relative effectiveness of the measures adopted against this shifting science. The Convention in turn authorized further protocols that would implement controls based upon new science which might better define the problem and new information about the cost and effectiveness of controls which could guide problem resolution.

The feedback relationship between science, law, and assessment is an essential element of international agreements, but is also found in some domestic environmental law. For example, flexibility was built into domestic legislation that dealt with air quality issues, such as the original Clean Air Amendments of 1977 that called for research into the problem of acid rain and the 1990 provision which provided for a system of continuous updates based upon the changing protocols following the Meetings of the Parties to the Montreal Protocol. The effect of this science-based regulatory flexibility was to subordinate the domestic law to the international law of ozone depletion, essentially recognizing the necessity of a global solution to a global problem.

In order to carry out such a scientifically-guided program, while, at the same time, securing agreement of the parties to controls, the Montreal Protocol put together a collage of institutions which is consistent with our definition of "a regime." Figure 10.1, below, outlines the institutional framework of the ozone depletion regime and highlights the functional and structural complexity of the Protocol.

The 1990s was the decade of adjustments in the operation of the Protocol as changes were under consideration even before the agreement came into force on January 1, 1989. Some of the important events in the history of the ozone regime are chronicled in Table 10.9, below. There have been five major revisions of the Protocol at Meetings of the Parties beginning in 1990. The major work at these meetings is the revision of Article 2, which defines the phase-out schedules for ozone depleting substances (ODS). From this process most of the ODS listed in the original 1987 Protocol (e.g., CFCs) were phased out in developed nations by late 1995. There are now three major categories of ODS that are slated for phase-out in 2002 (bromochloromethane), 2005 (methyl bromide) and 2030 (HCFCs). This timeline is extended for developing countries, an example of the flexible enforcement provisions of the protocol.

Figure 10.1 MONTREAL PROTOCOL INSTITUTIONS

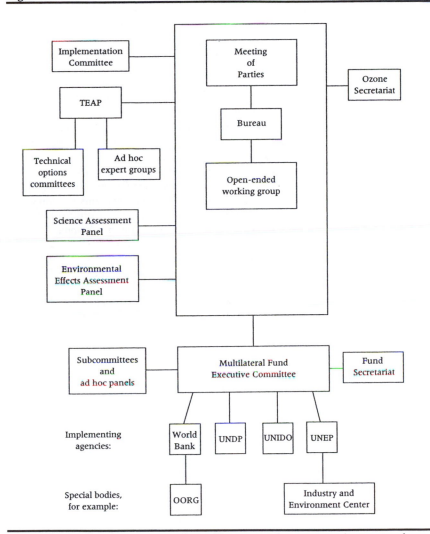

In actuality, there are many lines of interconnection among various protocol institutions. For example, the Implementation Committee interacts with the Executive Committee in addition to reporting to the Meeting of Parties. *Source:* Richard Eliot Benedick, *Ozone Diplomacy* (1998)

Table 10.9 A BRIEF CHRONOLOGY OF THE MONTREAL PROTOCOL MILESTONES AND
TARGETS WITH AN EMPHASIS ON DEVELOPMENTS SINCE 1990[49]

1989	Montreal Protocol enters into force
1990	Meeting in London, parties agree to provide financial and technical assistance to developing parties
1991	Interim Multilateral Fund is operational. UNEP launches the Ozone Action Programme and assessment panels agree that more stringent controls are needed
1992	Meeting Copenhagen where parties agree to speed up phase-out plans and control new substances for developed nations (HCFSs, HBFCs and methyl bromide)
1993	Parties agree to not allow exceptions for production of halons beyond the agreed upon deadlines in Copenhagen
1994	Total phase-out of halons in developed countries, consumption of halons and CFCs dropped by 50 percent between 1989–1992
1995	10th Anniversary of Vienna Convention celebrated in Vienna. Agree to more stringent phase-out schedules for HCFCs and methyl bromide for developed countries, agree schedules for all substances for developing countries, and consider non-compliance in some transitional economies
1996	Total phase-out in developed countries for carbon tetrachloride and methyl chloroform and HBFCs in all countries. Growing problem of illegal trade in CFCs is discussed
1997	10th Anniversary of Montreal Protocol celebrated in Montreal. Montreal Agreement adopted, which introduces a license system for trade in ozone depleting substances (ODS)
1998	Prominent issues are ways to decrease exemptions in ODS use and the time spent on non-compliance matters
1999	HCFCs in developed countries–Assessment reports show that rate of ozone depletion is slowing, nearly all developing nations meet first targets (freeze in production and consumption). Meeting of the Parties in Beijing sets phase out schedules for developing countries and adds new substance to control schedules
2002	Total phase-out of bromochloromethane
2005	Total phase-out of methylbromide in developed countries
2010	Total phase-out of CFCs, halons, and carbon tetra chloride in developed countries
2015	Total phase-out of methyl chloroform and methyl bromide in developing countries
2030	Total phase-out of HCFCs in developed countries
2040	Total phase-out of HCFCs in developing countries

Source: UNEP Ozone Secretariat, *Action on Ozone* (2000)

A primary lesson provided by the ozone depletion regime was that a reliance on science and the use of current research eventually led to a best-case outcome with acceptable economic cost. Science provided the basis for describing the ozone problem and is used for the continuous assessment of the issue. The mandated role of science led to new measurements of "chlorine loading" in the upper atmosphere, i.e., the amount of chlorine accumulating in the stratospheric ozone layer, data which were critical for modeling and predicting the potential for ozone depletion under different ODS emission scenarios.[50] These measurements revealed the nature and progress of the "ozone hole" over Antarctica and confirmed its later stabilization in response to the controls on ODS required by the Montreal Protocol. Early on with more study additional compounds were found to be ozone depleting, some of which were transitional substitutes for CFCs. It was later discovered that some of these (e.g., HCFC, bromochlormethane) were equally dangerous to the ozone layer and had to be replaced. The scientific assessment protocols of the regime provided the data to catch new problems created in the attempt to solve the original problem.

Not only was there the continuous scientific assessment, but also the individual parties, i.e., the nations, had to devise their own legal regimes for the governing of ozone depletion substances within their domestic borders. As mentioned above, in the United States, this meant the adoption of a major provision of the Clean Air Act which tied the Clean Air Act regulation of ozone depletion substances to the further international protocols which were to be adopted after the Montreal Protocol. For an international environmental regime to operate effectively it must have a mechanism to promote "compliance" by the parties. Some object to the term compliance since it tends to promote the framing of issues as disputes, and instead believe the notion of "implementation" better captures the dynamic process of a progressive development of norms necessary for a flexible and effective agreement.[51] The Montreal ozone regime uses an Ad hoc Working Group of Legal Experts on Non-Compliance that aims to encourage and facilitate compliance, rather than solely defining non-compliance for the purpose of identifying breaches of obligations by the parties.

A regime based on scientific jurisprudence must be able to measure its progress in abating the environmental problem and make needed adjustments to optimize its effectiveness as new information and understanding accumulate. The success of the ozone regime is easily seen at the global scale through studies made by atmospheric scientists.[52] In 1998 worldwide production of the CFCs controlled in the original protocol had declined by 95 percent from the base year, 1986. It appears that the total abundance of ozone depleting chemicals in the lower atmosphere peaked in 1994, which suggests that with an expected six-year lag for these substances to reach the upper atmosphere, that their peak concentrations in the stratosphere may have been seen in 2000. It is estimated that without the Protocol, ozone depletion would have reached

50-70 percent in the middle latitudes creating a 2-4 fold increase in levels of harmful UV-B radiation.

Why has this regime been judged to be so effective? The ability of industry to "sign-on" and cooperate in the ozone regime by finding chemicals that could replace ODSs and designing equipment that did not require these compounds was a major factor in controlling emissions of ODS to the atmosphere. The problems for science and policy are more difficult when alternatives are less apparent, as is the case for certain classes of ODS such as the agricultural fumigant, methyl bromide. Methyl bromide is now the single largest contributor of stratospheric bromine, a potent consumer of ozone.[53] This compound is widely used to fumigate field and greenhouse soils for parasitic nematodes and plant pathogens and to control pests in stored products and import/export commodities such as grains, coffee, fresh fruits and flowers. While methyl bromide use is decreasing in developed countries, its use in lesser-developed countries has increased in the 1990s because of its relatively low cost and high efficacy. Its scheduled withdrawal from routine use as an agricultural fumigant by 2015 is problematic, since phosphine, the only current alternative product worldwide is under regulatory review in the U.S.[54] In this case, science will need to foster alternative agricultural practices that move away from chemical inputs and emphasize biological control, the development and use of disease resistant cultivars, and improve crop storage systems. Whether the rate of anticipated advances in agricultural practices could compensate for the "loss" of methyl bromide remains a troubling question.

It became apparent during the 1980s and into the 1990s that the solution and mitigation of global scale environmental problems required a new science up to the job. In order for a continuous global scale scientific assessment to work, an ecological discipline of suitable scope was needed. This discipline had to be "invented" and emerged as Earth System Science. In the words of Richard Benedick, a participant and biographer of the ozone depletion treaty:

> The new environmental threats to national and planetary security –
> of which climate change appears to be the most far-reaching
> – challenge both traditional science and diplomacy. A new science
> has evolved in recent years, made possible by advances in
> computer modeling, satellites, and measurement technologies.
> Known as earth system science, this discipline attempts to integrate
> chemistry, physics, biology, geology, anthropology, meteorology,
> oceanography, and other subjects in order to understand more
> fully the interrelated forces that govern this planet. In 1986, the
> International Council of Scientific Unions (ICSU) launched a
> long-term inter-disciplinary initiative that has been described as the
> biggest inter-national scientific effort ever organized. Its purpose is

to develop new insights into planetary processes and the ways that they are being affected by human activities. Designated as the International Geosphere-Biosphere Programme (IGBP), it was adopted unanimously by the more than 70 national academies and 20 international scientific unions that form the membership of ICSU – the manifestation of universal concern about the seriousness of the problems.[55]

This new science was to be brought to bear upon an even more difficult global problem, i.e., the problem of global warming.

Earth System Science: A New Discipline in Support of International Environmental Regimes

Optical magnification instruments once brought about the Copernican revolution that put the Earth in its correct astrophysical context. Sophisticated information-compression techniques including simulation modeling are now ushering in a second 'Copernican' revolution. The latter strives to understand the 'Earth system' as a whole and to develop, on this cognitive basis, concepts for global environmental management.[56]

The emergence of Earth System Science (ESS) as multidisciplinary and interdisciplinary science framework for understanding global scale problems has been driven by the issue of global environmental change, which encompasses the environmental problems under the headings of climate change, ozone depletion, and land-use change and ecosystem degradation (e.g., desertification, fisheries decline). In this sense, Earth System Science has developed in close association with the international political community and agencies responsible for addressing international environmental problems. The IPCC (see discussion in Chapter 7) is probably the best current example of this relationship. Science has made rapid progress in developing new technologies and techniques for studying the linkages between humans, ecosystems and global-scale processes and these new tools (remote sensing, geographic information systems, computer simulation models, large-scale experimental systems for ecosystem manipulations) have had a large influence on the development of ESS.

The discipline of Earth System Science seeks to understand the coupling and functioning of global systems that include the land, oceans and the atmosphere. This requires an understanding of the component parts and their interactions, how they have evolved and currently function, and how the earth's systems will respond naturally and in response to human activities over short to long time scales. The early U.S. programs in ESS were funded by large agencies such as NASA and the NSF and had a number of common elements and goals, which collectively shaped the development of ESS into a recognized discipline.

Table 10.10 COMPONENTS OF AN ESS AND ITS APPROACH TO GLOBAL SCIENCE
AS IDENTIFIED BY NASA[57]

- Global observations using remote-sensing, near earth to space platforms with an emphasis on documentation of global change.
- Information systems to process the massive data sets generated from global observation networks.
- Numerical simulation models using global observation data to examine coupled reactions between the earth's physical, chemical, and biological systems with an emphasis on reaching predictive power to anticipate future global trends.
- Funding structures to support interdisciplinary science and interagency participation and cooperation.
- Fostering worldwide political awareness of the need for coordinated, international approaches to study earth systems and human influences.

The framework of Earth System Science owes much to the methodologies of ecosystem science and biogeochemistry and their studies of the cycling of carbon and nitrogen. It was the extrapolation of small-scale ecosystem studies to the larger spatial scales of the landscape and region that laid a foundation for the construction of global-scale nutrient budgets. In this respect the "tools" used to scale-up information from small studies to provide information relevant to large spatial areas (up to the globe) have had a major impact on the development of ESS. Schellnhuber describes three distinct ways that the tools have aided Earth System Science in reaching holistic perceptions of the "planetary inventory, including human civilization."[58]

First, the space race to the moon of the 1960s led to the eventual development of satellites, the space shuttle and space station, and aircraft mounted sensors that would gather information about atmospheric gases and climate, productivity (the greenness of the earth), ocean currents, and land use change (forest fragmentation in the tropics, advancing deserts). By leaving the earth and looking back, science could gain a panoramic view of our system and quantify its stocks and processes of ecosystems. The progression of remote sensing is intimately tied to our understanding of human influence on the global system. The U.S. National Space and Aeronautics Agency (NASA) plays the lead role in developing the hardware and software technologies for earth observation.

Table 10.11 A BRIEF HISTORY OF GLOBAL OBSERVATION FROM SPACE AND FUTURE OBJECTIVES OF THE NASA EARTH SCIENCES PROGRAMS[59]

- Early 1960s: First weather satellites allow tracking of global weather systems.
- Early 1970s: Initial development of remote sensing capabilities for land surface features and vegetation and the launch of Landsat, the first commercial satellite and still in use to monitor rainforest disappearance and to provide crop yield predictions.
- 1970s and 1980s: Total Ozone Mapping Spectrometer begins monitoring of annual fluctuations in ozone and mapping of the ozone-hole over Antarctica, information is critical to the implementation of the Montreal Protocol.
- 1980s: Earth Radiation Budget Experiment (satellite-based) allows first model of the Earth's energy budget.
- Early 1990s: The first remotely sensed global maps of ocean circulation to allow monitoring of El Nino formation and associated climate events and for the first time allow climate prediction for 12 to 18 months in advance.
- Late 1990s: SeaWiFS ocean color measuring instrument increases understanding of the role of oceans in removing CO_2 from the atmosphere as phytoplankton productivity.
- 1998-2002: First series of EOS (Earth Observing System) satellites. The mission objectives are to better characterize the earth system including terrestrial productivity; precise measurements of global temperature and humidity; global winds to drive global change models; and, three-dimensional maps of the entire inhabited surface of the earth.
- 2003-2010: NASA objectives are increased understanding of earth system function including: quantifying global carbon stocks in oceans and forests; assessing the impacts of climate change on ecosystems using coupled GCM and ecosystem models; incorporate ocean surface winds, sea surface temperatures and precipitation into climate and weather prediction models.
- 2010-2025: NASA objectives are to predict changes in the earth system and conduct research to predict regional-scale impacts of decadal climate change; assess sea level rise and effects.

A second large-scale approach that characterizes the ESS approach is simulation modeling or "digital-mimicry."[60] The current family of global scale models traces their lineage to the early ecosystem models of the IBP (for example, the grassland biome models of Van Dyne, see Chapter 3). Today, General Circulation Models (GCMs) that divide the globe into grids (often 250 x 250 km, by 1-km depth if the ocean) are used to predict mean climate, climate variability and climate cycles. These models are based on physical laws and the empirical data gathered by global networks monitoring ocean temperatures and currents, land temperatures and clouds. The current generations of GCMs are linked with other simulation models to examine interactions between the atmosphere and oceans and terrestrial vegetation. An example is the coupling of the EVE (the Equilibrium Vegetation Ecology) model to a GCM to study vegetation feedbacks on climate change at atmospheric CO_2 levels twice current levels.[61] In this model the biodiversity of the earth's vegetation is simplified into 110 plant life forms[62] which are expected to respond in predictable ways to climate change, including their migratory response (change in spatial distribution). The model is based on correlations between current climate and plant life form distributions. The coupled GCM model then provides information on the spatial distribution of new climate conditions under elevated CO_2, the effects of which alter plant distributions based on new combinations of temperature, precipitation and relative humidity. For example, this model predicts that the global desertification of subtropical grasslands that scientists attribute to complex biological and physical feedbacks between grazing regimes and climate[63] will be largely reversed due to enhanced monsoonal precipitation, which results in part from vegetation interactions with climate that emerge at elevated atmospheric CO_2. Modeling is a core activity in ESS and it has the definite advantage that many global scenarios can be explored without direct manipulation of the earth. The primary disadvantages relate to uncertainty and the problems common to all models in validating results.

Earth System Science is moving forward with new experimental approaches to examine large-scale system dynamics. The free air carbon exchange (FACE) experimental system to expose ecosystems to elevated CO_2 is one example (see Table 10.16). Some believe that the "incredible shrinking earth" model, as exemplified by the Biosphere 2 experiment, holds promise for studying the dynamics of earth systems.[64] Biosphere 2 started as a privately funded research project in Oracle, Arizona to test the feasibility of a self-sustaining space colony. It is a large (1.3 ha) nearly airtight environmentally controlled facility (similar in appearance to a glasshouse) in which five ecosystem types (desert, grassland, marsh, rainforest, ocean) were constructed. The original objective was to determine is a self-sustaining and completely enclosed system (including humans) could be created and maintained relying on feedback mechanisms between organisms and the atmosphere to maintain livable conditions in the enclosed space. Eight people lived isolated in the Biosphere from 1991-1993, but declining oxygen levels forced this gas to be pumped into the facility in 1993. A second human occupation experiment was started in 1994 and soon abandoned over financial and management problems. The Biosphere 2 program has since been taken over by Columbia University for environmental research and education. The Biosphere project, although unsuccessful in demonstrating the ability of humans to live in complete isolation from the earth's atmosphere and life systems, did provide a large-scale laboratory for studying the operational stability of living systems and the self-organizing behavior of linked biological and physical systems.

The trajectory of ESS as a discipline relies on the rapid development of new remote sensing technologies and high speed computers to provide the computational power and data that are required to simulate changing environmental conditions on the scale of the global system. Smaller-scale manipulations (such as FACE) will remain critical for understanding specific linkages between vegetation, soils, and the atmosphere.

Global Warming: Enforcing Earth System Science

In Chapter 7, we told the early history of the problem of global warming and ended with the Kyoto Protocol. Here we pick up the climate change story and interpret recent developments using background knowledge and lesson learned from the CITES agreement and the international and domestic programs to reduce and eliminate ozone depleting substances. The stories of these treaties (regimes) reveal that a significant internationalization of environmental law is underway, partly driven by the application of ecology and earth system science to problems operating at much greater scales than individual countries. Obscure international efforts to legally apply ecosystem concepts, which began in the early 1970s and 1980s, (such as the 1971 Ramsar Convention of Wetlands of International Importance and the 1980 Convention on the Conservation of Antarctic Marine Living Resources)[65] have flowered in the 1990s, with a myriad of international treaties.

Whereas the CITES agreements illustrate the problems of defining the role of ecology in developing nation's programs of preservation and sustainability, and the ozone depletion regime reveals the importance of a experimental jurisprudence which defines the scope and solution to the problem over time, the global warming issue poses the problem of how to structure and enforce an expensive program to control the emission of greenhouse gasses, a plan which many contend is based upon uncertain science, and which does not adequately face serious problems of inequity in time (between generations)[66] and in space (between the developed and less developed world).[67]

The difficulty of the effort to establish a global regime using an ecosystemic framework to approach the problem of climate change reveals much about the relationships of ecology to law, and in particular, international law. The science of global warming is complex and there is uncertainty. This is not unique, as we have seen from earlier chapters, ecosystem/human interactions are inherently complex and as a consequence society has limited predictive knowledge of system dynamics; human or ecological. The climate change issue is fraught with problems for science and the social sciences, especially economics.[68] For example, we know that greenhouse gases can alter the earth's radiation balance, but by how much? Might not poorly understood natural climate cycles be more important factors? What will be the precise impacts of global warming on ecosystems and society? The uncertainties in answering these questions make it difficult not only to reach agreement regarding the definition of the global warming problem, but also to allocate the burden of emission limits across the international community.

The scientific community recognizes a link between the emissions of greenhouse gases and the energy balance and climate of the earth. Arrenhius published on the basic physics of the relationship more than 100 years ago. However, determining the rate at which humans are changing climate, measuring the subsequent effects on natural and managed ecosystems, and designing ways by which we can adapt to or mitigate against these climate change effects, are much more complicated tasks. As the scientific evidence on climate change accumulated, the international community began to realize that a process was needed to gather this information and synthesize it into a form that could address the questions of concern. A new generation of computer models (integrated assessment models for economic and ecosystem effects;[69] general circulation models for climate responses[70]) would be needed to capture best available current knowledge and allow predictions of future composition of the atmosphere and climate under various policy options.

Relative to the CITES and the Montreal Protocol, the Climate regime is mature when it is measured by its development of a science institution (the IPCC) but, it is immature in using this science to achieve a broad international agreement on policy and enforceable actions. This lack of political action is at a time when scientists participating in the climate regime's mechanism for reaching consensus, the IPCC, are taking an increasingly "strong" position on the significance of humans in altering global climate.

The IPCC has continued to provide scientific and socioeconomic analysis and advice to the world community, and in particular to the more than 170 parties to the UNFCCC through its periodic assessment reports on the state of knowledge of the causes of climate change, its potential impact, and response strategies. The Second Assessment Report, Climate Change 1995, provided key input to the negotiations, which lead to the adoption of the Kyoto Protocol to the UNFCCC in 1997. The IPCC also prepares Special Reports and Technical Papers on topics where independent scientific information and advice is deemed necessary and it supports the UNFCCC through its work on methodologies for National Greenhouse Gas Inventories.

Table 10.12 PROBABILITY OF FUTURE CHANGE IN GLOBAL WARMING

CONFIDENCE IN *OBSERVED* CHANGES (LATTER HALF OF THE 20TH CENTURY)	CHANGES IN PHENOMENON	CONFIDENCE IN *PROJECTED* CHANGES (DURING 21ST CENTURY)
Likely	Higher maximum temperatures and more hot days over nearly all land areas	Very likely
Very likely	Higher minimum temperatures, fewer cold days and frost days over all land areas	Very likely
Very likely	Reduced diurnal temperature range over most land areas	Very likely
Likely, over many N. Hemisphere mid-to high-latitude land areas	More intense precipitation events	Very likely, over many areas
Likely, in a few areas	Increased summer continental drying and risk of drought	Likely, over most mid-latitude continental interiors
Not observed in the few analyses available	Increase in tropical cyclone peak wind intensities	Likely, over some areas

Source: Modified from the IPCC WGI Third Assessment Report. Shanghai Draft 21-01-2001

The Third Assessment Report is currently under production and will highlight new research since 1995, and provides more focus on regional scale impacts along with the global scale analysis. The IPCC Working Group I (science group) approved its contribution to IPCC Third Assessment Report, "Climate Change 2001: The Scientific Basis in January 2001." The Third Assessment Report is significant for the increased certainty in its assessment of the degree of climate change and its consequences. The Second Assessment Report concluded that "the balance of evidence suggests a discernible human influence on global climate." Since the SAR there has been progress in reducing uncertainty in assessing the magnitude of responses of the climate system to external influences. The latest report (TAR) concludes "an increasing body of observations gives a collective picture of a warming world and other changes in the climate system." The scientific community has concluded "confidence in the ability of models to project future climate change has increased." In particular the report finds that "*most*" (emphasis added) of the warming observed over the past 50 years is attributable to human activities" and that humans will continue to alter our atmosphere throughout the twenty-first century. The shift in the position of the scientific community from the Second to the Third Assessment Reports is easily seen in the language used in stating confidence in projected changes in climate for the twenty-first century and also from the larger spatial scale of some climate effects. In the case of the IPCC "process" the rate of accumulation of knowledge and the consensus reached by the scientific community on this issue has not been matched by international agreement or a consensus within the social and economic sciences about recommended options for action. The issue (dilemma) of global warming fully captures the complexity and tension between science, policy and the law.

Table 10.13 SELECTED OBSERVATIONS AND STATEMENTS FROM THE IPCC WORKING GROUP I THIRD ASSESSMENT REPORT, SUMMARY FOR POLICY MAKERS MEANT TO HIGHLIGHT THE DEGREE AND EXTENT OF THE GLOBAL WARMING PROBLEM

• The global average temperature has increased in the past century by about 0.6C, about 0.15C higher than estimated in the SAR.

• The global averaged surface temperature is projected to increase by 1.4 to 5.8C, much higher than the 1.0 to 3.5C range that was estimated in the SAR.

• Snow cover and ice extent have decreased (e.g., about a 40 percent decrease in Arctic sea-ice thickness during the summer months).

• Global average sea level has risen (as has heat content), between 0.1 and 0.2m during the twentieth century.

• Confidence in the ability of models to predict future climate has increased across a range of space and time scales. Attribution studies consistently find evidence of an anthropogenic signal in the climate records for the past 35-50 years.

• Anthropogenic climate change will persist for the long term (many 100s of years).

A synopsis of key events since 1990 for the climate regime is provided in Table 10.14 below. The 1992 Framework Convention on Climate Change (FCCC) stated as its objective the "stabilization of greenhouse gas concentration in the atmosphere at a level that would prevent dangerous anthropogenic interference with the climate system." The framework sets forth the norm of precautionary action: *"The parties should take precautionary measures to anticipate, prevent or minimize the causes of climate change and mitigate its adverse effects ... lack of full scientific certainty should not be used as a reason for postponing such measures."*

The original framework convention did not mandate a regulatory system, a carbon tax or a trading system, but merely required national inventories of greenhouse gas sources and sinks and policies related to their control. The nations are to make formal pledges to abate greenhouse emissions and, to some extent, these are to be enforced through publication and process of international peer review. Like the initial steps in the control of ozone depletion, heavy emphasis was placed upon continued research and systematic observation as well as continued negotiations.

Table 10.14 A BRIEF CHRONOLOGY OF THE KYOTO PROTOCOL AND THE GREENHOUSE GAS AND CLIMATE CHANGE ISSUE

1988	IPCC established.
1990	UN General Assembly agrees to negotiate a climate convention.
1991	Intergovernmental Negotiating Committee meetings begin.
1992	UN Conference on Environment and Development held at Rio de Janeiro and the FCCC created and signed.
1994	FCCC enters into force.
1995	First Conference of the Parties, Berlin. Berlin Mandate – urges legally binding targets and timetables.
1995	IPCC Second Assessment Report. "Balance of evidence suggests a discernable human influence on global climate."
1996	2nd Conference of the Parties, Geneva. Targets will not be met.
1997	U.S. Senate passes the Byrd-Hagel Resolution urging U.S. not to sign without reasonable participation by developing countries.
1997	3rd Conference of the Parties, Kyoto. Kyoto Protocol – Annex B countries target emissions at 5 percent below 1990 levels to be reached by 2008-2012.
1998	4th Conference of the Parties, Buenos Aires. Flexible mechanisms discussed.
1999	5th Conference of the Parties, Bonn.
2000	6th Conference of the Parties, the Hague. Disagreement among US and EU over limits on international trading and carbon sequestration.
2001	IPCC Third Assessment Report concludes that Earth climate is warming more quickly and more than previously predicted.
2001	Pres. Bush declares Kyoto Protocol dead (March).

Source: Brooks, Jones, and Virginia

A complex structure of research organizations linked by memoranda of understandings and funded research projects has emerged under the Convention which provides for "research and systematic observation."[71] The Inter-governmental Panel on Climate Change played a significant role in the initiation of the negotiations for the original convention. Its 1990 report is recognized as the transition between exploratory discussions on how to deal with greenhouse warming and formal negotiations towards an international convention. During the negotiations, the IPCC reported to the negotiators. Reorganized into several working groups (science, impacts, and policy), the IPCC will continue to operate during the development of the regime. The IPCC draws from a bewildering range of international research efforts such as the World Climate Research Programme and the International Geosphere-Biosphere Program. All of these organizations are part of the global regime pertaining to climate change, and their cluster illustrates well the process of experimental jurisprudence of a resource regime consisting of a "cluster of rules and roles" linked by a variety of bridge documents.

The Kyoto Accord[72] adopted to implement the framework in 1998 identified a number of alternative actions for nations to take to reduce global warming, including energy efficiency, protection of sinks, promotion of sustainable agriculture, adopting new carbon dioxide sequestration technologies, phasing out incentives for green house gas emitting sectors, limitation of methane production and other actions. The treaty allocated emissions 8 percent below 1990 levels for most European countries and a 7 percent reduction in similar levels for the United States, to be implemented between 2008 and 2012. Six greenhouse gases were covered: carbon dioxide, methane, nitrous oxide, hydrofluorocarbons, perfluorocarbons, and sulphur hexafluoride. Several transition countries can choose alternative base years, when their emissions were higher than 1990. Target levels could be met, in part, through afforestation, reforestation, and deforestation may also be taken into account. Market based mechanisms are authorized as well as joint fulfillment of commitments. The developed nations may adopt "clean development mechanisms" through funding of activities enabling developing countries to reduce emissions.[73]

The critique of the Kyoto accord has been fierce, both by scholars and the public. It is beyond the scope here to canvass all the criticisms of the protocol.[74] In the summer of 2001, the United States announced its dissatisfaction with the Treaty. At the same time, the other nations signed a follow up accord which authorized emission credits for carbon sinks, emission trading, credits of investment in emissions reducing projects in developing countries, financing to assist developing countries in adapting to climate change and non legally binding enforcement of failure to meet targets.[75]

Unlike the potential of an unchecked, rapid ozone depletion that would directly harm humans, global warming does not, in the near term, threaten an immediate large-scale global catastrophe. Hence, the scientific uncertainty around this issue is not likely to be overlooked in order to cope with the prospect of imminent disaster. The harms of global warming in the near term are likely to be greatest for those island nations with minimum political strength. The nations contributing most to global warming in the present (U.S.), and the future (Russia, India and China), are less likely to be motivated in the near term to resolve the problem. Moreover, the cost and complexity of the problem makes the allocation of permissible emissions controversial in the face of serious equity issues. Equity issues are central to the global warming problem because the developing countries are contributing relatively little to global warming emissions at the present time, but promise to be major contributors in the future. Moreover, unlike the ozone depletion problem, there are a myriad of contributors to global warming and a lack of fully developed inexpensive technological solutions.

Because the technological solutions to reducing carbon emissions are expensive, the search for less expensive mechanisms for reducing net carbon emissions has been at the center of the policy debate, especially in the U.S. Chief among these options is the use and enhancement of natural biological sinks that remove CO_2 from the atmosphere and store it as plant biomass. However, there is also great uncertainty about the relative effectiveness of carbon sinks. These carbon sinks are an important ecological aspect of the problem and are also considered a potential "ecosystemic solution" to the problem by enhancing their capacity to remove carbon from the atmosphere.

Managing the Carbon Budget by Manipulating Carbon Sinks

The global mean atmospheric concentration of CO_2 has increased from about 280 ppm in 1750 to 367 ppm in 1999. Today's atmosphere has the highest CO_2 concentration during the past 420,000 years and probably during the past 20 million years. This is predominantly due to the oxidation of organic carbon by fossil fuel combustion and deforestation. Most of the carbon emissions to the atmosphere since 1980 are from the burning of fossil fuel, the remaining 10-30 percent coming largely from land use change such as deforestation.[76]

These trends are seen beneath in the IPCC Global C budget (Table 10.15), which is perhaps the most important single product from the emerging discipline of earth system science.

This budget represents the synthesis of numerous studies from ecosystem science, atmospheric science, and marine science, the results from which have been extrapolated to global projections by using remote sensing and large-scale simulation modeling techniques. The quality of the policy debate on climate change is highly dependent on the ability of science to accurately quantify the global carbon cycle and in turn to identify possible sinks that can be managed to sequester carbon, preventing it from reaching the atmosphere. This task has been a central activity of the IPCC, which has published a consensus global carbon cycle showing where carbon resides (pool sizes), sources to the atmosphere (emissions, land use change, respiration), and the annual transfer of carbon to sinks (vegetation uptake, oceans).

Table 10.15 THE ANNUAL BUDGET OF CARBON DIOXIDE FOR THE PERIOD 1980 TO 1989[77]

CO_2 Sources

1. Emissions from fossil fuel combustion and cement production   5.5 (0.5)
2. Net emissions from changes in land use   1.6 (1.0)
3. Total anthropogenic emissions [1+2]   7.1 (1.1)

CO_2 Increase in the Atmosphere

4. Atmosphere increase (contributing to climate change)   3.2 (0.2)

CO_2Sinks

5. Oceanic uptake   2.0 (0.8)
6. Uptake by N. Hemisphere forest regrowth   0.5 (0.5)

7. Additional terrestrial sinks* calculated from above   1.4 (1.5)
     as [1+2] - [4+5+6]

---

*Missing sinks and carbon storage resulting from the CO_2 fertilization effect, nitrogen fertilization, and climatic effects on plant production (CO_2 uptake) and respiration (CO_2 release). Values are given in Gt C/yr (billion tons) and the error limits in parentheses are estimated 90 percent confidence intervals. Note the size of potential sinks and the relatively higher uncertainty in their magnitude. *Source:* R.J. Norbay et al., 150 *New Phytologist* 215 (2001)

The rate of change in atmospheric CO_2 is the difference between emissions (fossil fuel use) and uptake by physical sinks (CO_2 dissolution in oceans) and biological sinks (vegetation, soil). Measurements show that annual fluctuations in the rate of increase of atmospheric CO_2 are large. For example, during the 1990s, this rate of CO_2 increase varied from 0.9 to 2.8 ppm/yr.[78] This annual variation can be correlated with short-term climate variability, which influences the rate at which atmospheric CO_2 is taken up and released by the oceans and terrestrial sinks. This is one of the many sources of variability and uncertainty in projecting the behavior of the carbon cycle into the future.

The goal of stabilizing the concentrations of greenhouse gases in the atmosphere can be accomplished by reducing emissions to the atmosphere (largely fossil fuel combustion), increasing the storage or sequestration of carbon in terrestrial and marine sinks, or some combination of the two. The stakes in this debate for "getting the science right" are high. If natural ecosystems and human managed systems (agriculture, forests, grazing lands) can be manipulated to increase their stocks of carbon in biomass (vegetation) and soil organic matter, then relatively higher emissions of carbon dioxide to the atmosphere could be permitted. Thus, if the strength (absorptive capacity) of biological sinks can be increased, then more flexibility is created for reaching agreement on emissions standards. The U.S. argued strongly for the crediting of sinks in national plans for meeting carbon emissions. The European nations are less enthusiastic about sinks and favor more attention placed on emissions.

The IPCC Second Assessment published in 1994 contains an analysis of the sources and sinks of CO_2 (*see* Table 10. 15) and information in the IPCC Third Assessment is in close agreement. Of the approximately 7 gigatons C/yr reaching the atmosphere, just under half remains to act as greenhouse gas while the rest is sequestered in sinks. Identifying the geographic location of specific sinks and their magnitude is a difficult task, but one of importance to the Kyoto Protocol. The terrestrial sink (biota) gained carbon during the 1980s and 1990s. This means that the CO_2 released by tropical deforestation and other land use changes was more than compensated by uptake by other terrestrial sinks. We still face considerable uncertainty in estimating the CO_2 release due to land use change. This problem exacerbates the difficulty in estimating the size of the other terrestrial sinks, which are calculated as a residual after the size of the land use term (upon which their estimate is determined) has been set. On a global scale, terrestrial and ocean carbon process models indicate that enhanced plant growth due to higher CO_2 (CO_2 fertilization) and anthropogenic nitrogen deposition (acid rain) contribute to enhanced CO_2 uptake by biota. These factors contribute to the residual terrestrial sink described above.

Table 10.16 Ecosystem Response to Elevated CO_2: FACE Experiments

If the potential of specific sinks under the control of nations is to be part of the international regime to stabilize the greenhouse gas concentration of the atmosphere, then science must develop the technology, the experimental techniques and the synthesis necessary to inform decision makers. One of the major advances in "big science" at the ecosystem level of organization has been the development of technology to expose relatively large portions of natural systems to elevated atmospheric CO_2 concentrations using FACE (free air carbon exchange) techniques.[79] Exposing vegetation to CO_2 concentrations that are still decades away (in most cases about 500 ppm) provides us with a window to assess future effects of a CO_2 rich world on plants, soils, and the organisms that cycle energy and nutrients. Scientists have concluded from small-scale experiments exposing potted plants to twice the current ambient CO_2 concentrations, that vegetation growth (CO_2 uptake) will be strongly stimulated, thereby enhancing the terrestrial C-sink and helping to limit the full effect of CO_2 emissions to the atmosphere. However, FACE experiments that allow plants to experience water and soil nutrient limitations under field conditions show that plant response to elevated CO_2 is often much less than predicted, meaning this sink may be smaller than some have claimed.

Policy makers have hoped that planting forests might be a strategy that could substitute for reducing CO_2 emissions. Loblolly pine (*Pinus taeda*) trees exposed to 600 ppm CO_2 in a FACE study at the Duke University forest experienced enhanced growth for only three years, and thereafter the forest reverted to growth rates typical of today's CO_2.[80] Soil nitrogen availability was not high enough to sustain long-term increases in tree production caused by the CO_2 fertilization effect. In addition, nearly half of the carbon fixed by the trees ended up in leaf tissues. Unlike woody tissues, leaves decompose in a period of a few years and release their carbon back to the atmosphere.[81] For sinks to be effective in the context of the Kyoto Protocol they must sequester carbon for the long term. These studies show the complexity of predicting the magnitude and the duration of terrestrial sinks. Properties of the ecosystem such as soil fertility, soil moisture and the supply of other essential limiting resources act to regulate plant response to elevated CO_2 and the capacity of vegetation to act as a sink.

Conclusion: International Regimes and Global Science

The international environmental regimes we have described differ greatly in their histories, the scale and perceived urgency of the environmental problem, and the anticipated economic impact of implementing the regime. The variable nature of regimes (*as shown in Table 10.1*) has spurred a critique of their effectiveness and a search for common structural and behavioral characteristics that define successful approaches.[82] The difficulty lies in assigning the proportion of any favorable improvement in the problem to the function of the regime as opposed to other influences operating outside the legal and political boundaries of the regime. Oran Young points to the benefits of developing a database of regimes along with quantitative indices that capture regime effectiveness to provide guidance in dealing with issues of public policy. We might expand his call to consider how ecosystemic environmental laws might be scored for effectiveness.

The Montreal Protocol is perhaps our most effective international agreement. It has its foundation in compelling scientific evidence concerning the cause and the consequence of the problem, a problem that has direct effects on human health (increased risk of skin cancer). Parties agreed upon an equitable set of schedules for the phase out of ODS which depended on the type of chemical and the economic status of the Party. By limiting production of damaging substance on a set schedule, the development of cost-effective alternatives has been possible. The relatively limited scope of the ODS issue compared with the challenge of controlling carbon dioxide emissions, which are derived from near all our industrial and agricultural activities, has also contributed to the success of the ozone regime. The distinctive feature of this regime is its "flexibility" and an effective amendment process that relies on science for regulation and enforcement. The ozone regime best meets the operational definition of a legal agreement guided by the principles of an experimental jurisprudence.

The Climate Change regime is centered about a much more complicated set of scientific issues than the Montreal Protocol. As Benedict states "Against this background of complexity, uncertainty, and frustration, some observers have contended that the ozone experience has little relevance to the climate convention."[83] He recounts how the Climate Convention is now benefitting from the lessons learned during the ozone diplomacy, among them: the use of an independent and international science assessment (i.e., IPCC), periodic reviews of commitments and of national reporting, a differentiation of the expectations from developed and developing nations, and mechanisms for financing and technology transfer. A defining difference between the climate and ozone regimes is the lack of interest shown by industry (mainly transportation and energy producers) in stabilizing CO_2 levels in the atmosphere. This stance by the private sector stands out against a highly constructive (albeit after early opposition) behavior by the chemical industry and ODS users.

To the public, the issue of species decline and extinction is the easiest to "visualize" and understand. We have a long history of game management and a system of parks and reserves where wildlife is protected. The success of CITES comes in part from the financing and political actions of the NGO community which are motivated by a public awareness of the need for an effective species preservation policy. The continuing challenge to the CITES regime is finding the requisite knowledge on the myriad of species under threat so that an ecosystemic perspective can be applied to a regime originally designed to regulate trade and not ecosystems.

The ozone regime has produced a measurable effect on the problem, whereas greenhouse gas emissions and concentrations in the atmosphere continue to increase at alarming rates as does the number of species threatened with decline or extinction. Against this seemingly mixed record of success, how can we create more effective regimes that assure a sustainable future for humans and ecosystems? Increasingly, international environmental regimes, their formation and implementation are seen as linked to international diplomacy and global security.[84] Environmental security encompasses the maintenance or reestablishment of ecosystems (ecological balance), or from another perspective it refers to the prevention and management of conflict over scarce or degraded resources. In this effort to develop a global consensus for action, science and law intersect with diplomacy. From an analysis of the Ozone regime, Benedick collected the lessons and outlines the elements of a global diplomacy for addressing ecological threats such as climate change and biodiversity loss. They provide a departure point for considering the process to reach an effective environmental regime:

- Scientists must play a central role in negotiations.

- Governments may be required to act despite scientific uncertainty, balancing the risks and costs of delayed action.

- An informed public can influence politicians and industry to act responsibly on behalf of the environment.

- Multilateral, international negotiations are essential when the issues have global repercussions.

- Strong leadership by a major power can be a significant force in forging international consensus.

- Preemptive environmental protection by leading countries (or groups of countries) in advance of global agreement can legitimize action by others.

- NGOs and industry (civic sector) have a central role in the "new environmental diplomacy."

- A consideration of economic differences among countries must be equitably reflected in the regime.

- Market incentive that spur technological innovation enhance regime effectiveness.

- The signing of a treaty is not always the most significant event in the negotiation, the process leading up to and then after is critical to success.

- Balancing of firmness and pragmatism is required to achieve diplomatic success.

- Individuals and unanticipated events can make a difference.

In Benedick's cautionary words, "Real negotiations are, however, both richer and more treacherous than academic models."

Notes

1. *See* RICHARD ELIOT BENEDICK, OZONE DIPLOMACY: NEW DIRECTIONS IN SAFE- GUARDING THE PLANET 332 (1998).
2. *See* JOHN VOGLER, THE GLOBAL COMMONS: A REGIME ANALYSIS (1995).
3. *See* NATIONAL RESEARCH COUNCIL ET AL., COMMON PROPERTY RESOURCE MANAGEMENT (1986).
4. *See* ELINOR OSTROM, GOVERNING THE COMMONS (1990).
5. *See* ORAN YOUNG, INTERNATIONAL GOVERNANCE: PROTECTING THE ENVIRONMENT IN A STATELESS SOCIETY (1994); POLAR POLITICS: CREATING INTERNATIONAL ENVIRONMENTAL REGIMES (Oran Young & Gail Osherenko eds., 1993).
6. *See* JOHN VOGLER, THE GLOBAL COMMONS: A REGIME ANALYSIS (1995).
7. For a broad but brief overview of these approaches on a domestic level, *see* Robert Stavins & Bradley Whitehead *Market Based Environmental Policies*, in MARION R. CHERTOW & DANIEL C. ESTY, THINKING ECOLOGICALLY: THE NEXT GENERATION OF ENVIRONMENTAL POLICY 105 (1997).
8. *See* BIODIVERSITY (Edward O. Wilson ed., 1988); BIODIVERSITY II (Marjorie L. Reaka-Kudla et al., eds., 1997).
9. Convention on International Trade in Endangered Species in Wild Fauna and Flora, March 3, 1973, 27 U.S.T. 1087, 993 U.N.T.S. 243.
10. For a good overview of the treaty, *see* ENDANGERED SPECIES, THREATENED CON- VENTION: THE PAST, PRESENT AND FUTURE OF CITES (Jon Hutton & Barnabas Dickson eds., 2000) [hereinafter ENDANGERED SPECIES].
11. For an overview of these treaties, *see* R. VAN HEIJNSBERGEN, INTERNATIONAL LEGAL PROTECTION OF WILD FAUNA AND FLORA (1997).
12. For a detailed discussion of the law related nature of a regime, *see* Jutta Brunée & Stephen Toope, *Environmental Security and Freshwater Resources: Ecosystem Regime Building*, 91 AM. J. INT'L L. 26 (1997).
13. The World Conservation Union was previously the International Union for Conservatories of Nature and Natural Resources (IUCN), which played a major role in the formation of CITES. *See* SIMON LYSTER, INTERNATIONAL WILDLIFE LAW 239 (1985).
14. These authorities manage the permit program in the U.S., the Dept. of Interior, 16 U.S.C. §4221(a) (1997).
15. *See* CITES, *supra* note 9, at art. III, para. 2a, 3a, and art. IV, para 2a.
16. *Id.* at art IV, para. 3.
17 *See* CITES, *supra* note 9, at art. IV, para. 1a.
18. Shawn Dansky, *The CITES Objective Listing Criteria: Are They Objective Enough to Protect the African Elephant?*, 73 TUL. L. REV. 96 (1999); *Note: The CITES Fort Lauderdale Criteria: The Uses and Limits of Science in International Conservation Decisionmaking*, 14 HARV. L.R. 1769 (2001).
19. *See* Shawn M. Dansky, Comment, *"The CITES "Objective" Listing Criteria: Are They Objective Enough to Protect the African Elephant?*, 73 TUL. L.REV. 961, 965-966 (1999).
20. *See* Dansky, *supra* note 18.

21.   Such trade controls have been extended to tackle the problem of ozone depletion and are proposed to control carbon emissions.

22.   For a general discussion of the ecological determinants of biodiversity and population viability *see* BIODIVERSITY II. UNDERSTANDING AND PROTECTING OUR BIOLOGICAL RESOURCES (Marjorie L. Reaka-Kudla, Don E. Wilson & Edward O. Wilson eds., 1997).

23.   R.B. Martin, *CITES and the CBC*, in ENDANGERED SPECIES, *supra* note 10, at 125.

24.   Swamson *in* ENDANGERED SPECIES, *supra* note 10, at 138.

25.   The general relationship between sustainablity and ecology will be discussed below in our discussion of ecological economics.

26.   For a brief description of the precautionary principle in general and as applied to CITES, *see* Barnabas Dickson, *Precaution at the Heart of CITES, in* ENDANGERED SPECIES, *supra* note 10, at 38.

27.   *See* Kenneth R. Foster et al., *Risk Management – Science and the Precautionary Principle*, 288 SCIENCE 979 (2000); PROTECTING PUBLIC HEALTH AND THE ENVIRONMENT: IMPLEMENTING THE PRECAUTIONARY PRINCIPLE (CARLOYN RAFFENSPERGER & JOEL TIDSNER eds., 1999).

28.   *See* comment by David Appell, *The New Uncertainty Principle*, SCIENTIFIC AMERICAN, Jan. 2001.

29.   The following articles provide a good basis for comparing the U.S. and European perspectives on the precautionary principle. P.H. Sand, *The Precautionary Principle: A European Perspective*, 6 HUM. AND ECOLOGICAL RISK ASSESSMENT, 445 (2000); J.S. Applegate, *The Precautionary Preference: An American Perspective on the Precautionary Principle*, 6 HUM. & ECOLOGICAL RISK ASSESSMENT, 413 (2000).

30.   *See* John L. Garrison, *The Convention on International Trade in Endangered Species of Fauna and Flora (CITES) and the debate over sustainable use*. 12 PACE ENVTL. L. REV. 301 (1994).

31.   *See* CITES, article IV, para. 3.

32.   *See* John G. Robinson, *The Limits to Caring: Sustainable Living and the Loss of Biodiversity*, 7 CONSERVATION BIOLOGY 20 (1993).

33.   *See* STEPHEN R. KELLERT, THE VALUE OF LIFE. BIOLOGICAL DIVERSITY AND HUMAN SOCIETY 10 (1996).

34.   The reader is referred to Chapter 1, where some of the ethical frameworks for considering the value and standing of species and ecosystems are discussed.

35.   *See* MARSHALL W. MURPHEE, THE LESSON FROM MAHENYE: RURAL POVERTY, DEMOCRACY, AND WILDLIFE CONSERVATION (1995).

36.   *See* Marshall M. Murphee, *The Lesson from Mahenye*, in ENDANGERED SPECIES, *supra* note 10, at 194.

37.   *See* Daniel Vice, *Implementation of Biodiversity Treaties: Monitoring, Factfinding, and, Dispute Resolution*, 29 N.Y.U. J INT'L L AND POL. 577 (1997).

38.   Trade Records Analysis of Flora and Fauna in Commerce.

39.   For the problem of defining boundaries, *see* Kevin J. Madonna, *The Wolf in North America vs. Defining International Boundaries*, 10 J. LAND USE & ENV'TL L. 305 (1995).

40.   For a comparison of the Endangered Species Act and CITES, *see* David S. Faure, *The Risk of Extinction: A Risk Analysis of the Endangered Species Act as Compared to CITES*, 6 N.Y.U. ENV'TL L.J. 341 (1998).

41.   For a parallel inquiry pertaining to other species and treaties, *see* Daniel Vice, *Implementation of Biodiversity Treaties: Monitoring, Fact Finding, and Dispute Resolution*, 29 N.Y. U. J. INT'L & POL. 577 (1997).

42.   The elephant is a "charismatic species," creating problems of constituency within CITES. *See* Grahame J.W. Webb, *Are All Species Equal? A Comparative Assessment*, in ENDANGERED SPECIES, *supra* note 10, at 98.

43.   For an extensive history, *see* L. DALTON CASTO, THE DILEMMA OF AFRICANIZATION: CHOICES AND DANGERS FOR SUB-SAHARAN AFRICA (1998).

44.   For East and Southern Africa, *see* Joseph Berger, *The African Elephant, Human Economics and International Law: Bridging a Great Rift*, 13 GEO. INT'L ENVT'L L. REV. 417 (2001).

45.   *See* Alfred L. Roca et al., *Genetic evidence for two species of elephant in Africa.* 293 SCIENCE 1473 (2001).

46.   *See* DANIEL B. BOTKIN, DISCORDANT HARMONIES: A NEW ECOLOGY FOR THE TWENTY FIRST CENTURY (1990).

47.   *Id.* at 15; DAPHNE SHELDRICK, THE TSAVO STORY (1973).

48.   Experimental Jurisprudence was set forth in FREDERICK K. BEUTEL, SOME POTENTIALITY OF EXPERIMENTAL JURISPRUDENCE AS A NEW BRAND OF SOCIAL SCIENCE (1957). For a critique, *see Book Note*, 72 Harv. L. Rev. 207 (1958). For a recent more sophisticated version in the environmental law field, *see* BRUCE A. ACKERMAN & WILLIAM T. HASSLER, CLEAN COAL, DIRTY AIR (1981). *See also* BRUCE A. ACKERMAN, RECONSTRUCTING AMERICAN LAW (1983).

49.   Information in this table comes from ACTION ON OZONE, 2000 EDITION, UNEP Ozone Secretariat, United Nations Environment Programme (2000).

50.   *See* Susan Solomon, *Stratospheric Ozone Depletion: A Review of Concepts and History*, 37 REV. GEOPHYSICS 275 (1999).

51.   *See* Jutta Brunnée & Stephen J. Toope, *Environmental Security and Freshwater Resources: Ecosystem Regime Building*, 91 AM. J. INT'L L. 26 (1997).

52.   *See* J. Staehelin, et al., *Ozone Trends: A Review*, 39 REV. GEOPHYSICS 231 (2001).

53.   *See* D. Serca, et al., *Methyl Bromide Deposition to Soils*, 32 ATMOSPHERIC ENV'T 1581 (1998).

54.   *See* C. H. Bell, *Fumigation in the 21st Century*, 19 CROP PROTECTION 563 (2000).

55.   *See* RICHARD ELIOT BENEDICK, OZONE DIPLOMACY: NEW DIRECTIONS IN SAFE-GUARDING THE PLANET (1998).

56.   *See* H.-J. Schellnhuber, *Earth System Analysis and the Second Copernican Revolution*, 402 NATURE C19 (1999).

57.   *See* NATIONAL AIR AND SPACE ADMINISTRATION ADVISORY COUNCIL, EARTH SYSTEM SCIENCES COMMITTEE, EARTH SYSTEMS SCIENCE OVERVIEW: A PROGRAM FOR GLOBAL CHANGE (1986).

58.   *See supra* note 58.

59.   For a brief history of NASA earth sciences initiatives and a description of the Earth Sciences Enterprise program that outlines NASA priorities and vision to 2025, *see* NATIONAL AIR AND SPACE ADMINISTRATION, EXPLORING OUR HOME PLANET: EARTH SCIENCE ENTERPRISE STRATEGIC PLAN (2000).

60.   *Id.*

61.   *See* J.C. Bergengren et al., *Modeling Global-climate Interactions in a Doubled CO_2 World.* 31 CLIMATIC CHANGE 50 (2001).

62.   Plants with similar physiological and morphological traits are often grouped into life forms or functional types for the purposes of large-scale modeling. The set of species placed in a functional group or a life-form is expected to respond in a similar way to a specified perturbation such as climate change. For a detailed discussion of functional types and their use in global models, *see* PLANT FUNCTIONAL TYPE: THEIR RELEVANCE TO ECOSYSTEM PROPERTIES AND GLOBAL CHANGE, VOL. I. (T.M. Smith et. al., 1997).

63.   See the review by William H. Schlesinger et al., *Biological Feedbacks in Global Desertification*. 247 SCIENCE 1043 (1990).

64.   *See* BIOSPHERE 2 – THE SPECIAL ISSUE, ECOLOGICAL ENGINEERING VOL. 13 (1999). This issue offers a collection of papers describing the history of the Biosphere project and results of studies of ecological processes and systems dynamics in this virtually airtight environmental research facility.

65.   *See* GLOBAL ENVIRONMENTAL CHANGE (Stern, Young & Druckman, eds, 1992); SIMON LYSTER, INTERNATIONAL WILDLIFE LAW (1985).

66.   *See* Richard B. Howarth & Richard B Norgaard, *Intergenerational Resource Rights, Efficiency, and Social Optimality*, 66 LAND ECONOMICS 1 (1990).

67.   *See* J.B. Wiener, *Something Borrowed For Something Blue: Legal Transplants and the Evolution Of Global Environmental Law*, 27 ECOLOGY L.Q. 1295 (2001).

68.   *See* F.S. Rowland, *Atmospheric Changes Caused by Human Activities: From Science to Regulation*, 1261 ECOLOGY L.Q. 27 (2001).

69.   *See* Edward A. Parson & Karen Fisher-Vanden, *Integrated Assessment Models of Global Climate Change*, 22 ANN. REV. ENERGY & ENV'T (1997).

70.   *See* D.M.H. Sexton et al., *Detection of Anthropogenic Climate Change Using An Atmospheric GCM*, 71 CLIMATE DYNAMICS 669 (2001).

71.   *See* JOHN VOGLER, THE GLOBAL COMMONS: A REGIME ANALYSIS 144-6 (1995).

72.   KYOTO PROTOCOL TO THE UNITED NATIONS FRAMEWORK CONVENTION ON CLIMATE CHANGE.

73.   For a site with all relevant global warming documents, *see* <www.unfccc.de>.

74.   For a detailed account, *see* DAVID B. VICTOR, THE COLLAPSE OF THE KYOTO PROTOCOL AND THE STRUGGLE TO SLOW GLOBAL WARMING (2001).

75.   *N.Y. Times*, July 24, 2001 at A7.

76.   *See* WORKING GROUP I, THE IPCC THIRD ASSESSMENT REPORT, CLIMATE CHANGE 2001: THE SCIENTIFIC BASIS (2001). This report has been accepted by Working Group I, but has not been approved in detail. Available at <www.ipcc.ch/pub/wg1TARtechsum.pdf>.

77.   *See* review by R.J. Norby et al., *Rising CO_2 – Future Ecosystems – Commentary*, 150 NEW PHYTOLOGIST 215 (2001).

78.   *Id.*

79.   *Id.*

80.   *See* Ram Oren et al., *Soil fertility limits carbon sequestration by forest ecosystems in a CO_2 enriched atmosphere*, 411 NATURE 469 (2001).

81.   *See* H. William & J. Lichter, *Limited Carbon Storage in Soil and Litter of Experimental Forest Plots Under Increased Atmospheric CO_2*, 411 NATURE 466 (2001).

82.   *See* Oran R. Young, *Inferences and Indicies: Evaluating the Effectiveness of International Environmental Regimes*, 1 GLOBAL ENVTL. POLITICS 99 (2001).

83.   *See* RICHARD ELIOT BENEDICK, OZONE DIPLOMACY: NEW DIRECTIONS IN SAFEGUARDING THE PLANET 327 (1998).

84.   *See* LAWRENCE E. SUSSKIND, ENVIRONMENTAL DIPLOMACY. NEGOTIATING MORE EFFECTIVE GLOBAL AGREEMENTS (1994).

11 Conclusion: Lessons of History and Future Directions

Introduction

A paradox emerges from our description of ecology and environmental law and our history of their relations. Our description of ecology and environmental law reveals them to be two very different, internally complex disciplines. Ecology is a synoptic scientific discipline seeking a comprehensive account of the systematic interdependencies of nature based upon scientific investigation and experimentation. This comprehensive science has been internally divided into several subdisciplines, the most important of which have been population ecology and ecosystem ecology. Environmental law is a historically conditioned pragmatic discipline which in seeking to resolve concrete environmental problems, assumes its shape and definition through the gradual incremental decisionmaking processes of the Anglo-American legal institutions: the legislatures, courts, and administrative agencies. In many ways, environmental law is a syncretic field joining several other preexisting fields of law: administrative tort, land use and municipal law. *How can these two very different disciplines be joined within one ecosystemic regime?* If one relied only upon this formal description of these two disciplines – one synoptic and scientific, one incremental and pragmatic – we would be pessimistic about their rapprochement.

And yet our history recounts that slowly over the past half-century, ecology and environmental law have established many connections with each other, occasionally even co-evolving together. A myriad of ecosystemic regimes have flourished. To be sure, in this history we discovered some tensions in the relationships between ecology and environmental law, but we have also documented a surprising degree of cooperation and even some co-evolution between these two disciplines. How could this coordination happen? How could these very different disciplines manage to work together? What are the prospects of their working together in the future?

In this conclusion, after briefly expanding our discussion of the apparent radical differences between these two disciplines and then summarizing the impressive history of their working together, we will identify at least four principal reasons why these two disciplines have emerged as partners in an ecosystemic regime. First, both disciplines have partly transformed themselves internally to accommodate their relationship with one another. Second, bridges have been established which create unique linkages between the two disciplines. These linkages include "linkage persons," "bridge documents," "migrating concepts," and "interdisciplinary conceptual frameworks." Third, both disciplines have become part of more comprehensive institutions which we have called "ecosystem regimes,"[1] which employ science and undertake both planning and management as well as implementation through law. Finally, both disciplines have been enveloped in a public culture which increasingly values both natural places and species, and seeks to avoid recognized global ecosystemic catastrophes. We have tried to document that both place and species have become important foci for efforts to join these two disciplines in one common effort. In addition, we have documented how the seeking of protection from threatened global disasters is another stimulation to both ecological thought (as earth system science), and its application through international conventions and their protocols.

This chapter will simply extract from the history set forth above the major lessons of the growing linkages between ecology and environmental law. These lessons lay the groundwork for projecting in more detail the possible internal transformation of the disciplines, the building of bridges between ecology and law, the construction of ecosystemic regimes, and the importance of the preservation of places, species and the global environmental health in further promotion of the partnership of law and ecology.

The Synoptic and Incremental Disciplines of Ecology and Law

The effort to "apply ecology" should be approached from the point of view of relating two different disciplines. Although the science of ecology, at least in its most comprehensive formulation, is a synoptic discipline, Anglo-American law is an incremental discipline. Thus, ecology and law embody two radically different disciplines of thought. Ecology seeks to obtain an integrated view of nature and it views nature, whether as an ecosystem or an ecology of biodiversity, as a complex interdependent system.[2] Law as practiced in the Anglo-American common law tradition[3] is an incremental discipline which focuses upon the specific problems it encounters, statute by statute, case by case, resolving them seriatim within their specific context. Each discipline seeks to cope with its own problems. Environmental law is struggling with how to mesh with or alter the common law legal system out of which it has emerged and to fit within the generic administrative law system, which was constructed prior to its full flowering. The applications of ecology take place largely within this administrative system. At the same time, ecosystem science is continuing to struggle with demons of its own – the need to analyze simultaneously the multi-dimensional issues of time and space and the function of complex biophysical systems, and choose, manage, and relate the different scales of study which are presently being undertaken.[4] One way to understand the problems of relating systematic ecology to incremental legal decisionmaking is to examine a past effort to relate comprehensive science and law and policy making. In the 1950s and 1960s, there was an effort to develop a comprehensive approach to welfare economics which was then to be applied to practical economic planning and policy. This application proved to be difficult and in 1960, David Braybrooke and Charles Lindblom, in their classic work *A Strategy of Decision*,[5] examined carefully the difficulties of such an undertaking. Braybrooke and Lindblom identified two methods of thought which characterized welfare economics and practical economic policy making. They denominated these methods: "synoptic" and "incremental." The synoptic method of welfare economics assumed to set forth an agreed upon comprehensive set of values or parameters, sought a detailed inventory of the variables and interrelationships, and canvass all relevant economic policies.

This synoptic approach was to be implemented through comprehensive planning. Braybrooke and Lindblom found that the efforts to directly apply welfare economics through comprehensive plans failed. Braybrooke and Lindblom listed the reasons why the direct application of synoptic methods of policymaking failed: the comprehensive synoptic methods were not adapted to the limited problem solving capacities of the policy makers; these methods failed to take into consideration the inadequacy of information and the costliness of gathering and analyzing it; the method did not offer a means of evaluating the data nor was it adopted to the close relationships between facts and values in policymaking situations; the method was not adapted to the openness of systems in which variables "from outside" would affect the workings of the system; the method did not provide strategic sequences for resolving problems and was not adapted to the diverse forms in which policy problems arise.

All of these observations, originally applied in the context of seeking to apply comprehensive welfare economics to applied economic policy, held true of many early attempts to apply synoptic ecological methods to environmental problem solving. For example, the efforts of the 1960s to apply synoptic watershed land use planning in the Brandywine Valley failed when the planners could not cope with the town-by-town concerns about private property rights which appeared threatened by the proposed watershed plan and its controls. A study of the Brandywine project concluded that the effort at comprehensive watershed planning led the team to ignore crucial legal and political factors which ultimately defeated the entire plan.[6] The inadequacy of information for synoptic ecological plans is another problem, illustrated by the first large-scale model of the Meadows which by design omitted key economic variables as part of their predictive models.[7] The close interaction between fact and value was documented in Bruce Ackerman's discussion of the effort to use a dissolved oxygen model in the planning for cleanup of the Delaware River waters.[8] Ackerman revealed how a narrow and technocratic use of water quality indicators seriously interfered with a sensible planning approach. In the chapters above, we have documented other problems with the effort to join comprehensive ecology and incremental law. We have seen how value judgements hover about and stimulate disagreement over the criteria for identification of endangered and threatened species under the endangered species and forest management legislation.[9] We discovered important pollution sources outside the coastal "system" which have bedeviled a coastal management program which has sought to identify and manage a coastal zone.[10] We have witnessed how systematic planning has been unable to cope with change. After a comprehensive environmental plan or model is developed, issues arise which were unanticipated by the plan or model. Often the plan or model does not provide any resolution for these new issues without radical amendment of the plan or model.[11] Thus, the history of "failures" in seeking to adopt holistic disciplines and their comprehensive plans to the legal resolution of environmental problems indicate the need to carefully reexamine the appropriate relationship between holistic science, comprehensive planning and policy making, and legal implementation.[12]

This history demonstrates that it is relatively easy to identify the problems of establishing working relationships between ecology and law. One can "cherry pick" historical anecdotes to illustrate these problems, and despite the recent effort at compromise between comprehensive planning and incremental decisionmaking recently promoted in the name of "adaptive planning," these problems continue. *But despite these problems, our previous history of ecology and environmental law should caution anyone from drawing hasty and negative conclusions about their relationship. That history reveals many successful working relationships between the two disciplines.*

Patterns of the Relationship

We began this book by positing a "co-evolution" of the two disciplines, in which changes in one discipline produce changes in the other. Evolutionary perspectives both of the development of intellectual disciplines in general and environmental law and ecology in particular have been written.[13] But we assumed something more, viz., that the evolution of one discipline influenced the evolution of the other. The fact of the matter, however, is that we found that the environmental law regime was shaped over a hundred year period, and the science of ecology was slowly put together during the same period, but both developed quite independently of one another. Such a long period of independent evolution explains the very different shapes of the two disciplines.

It has only been since the mid to late 1960s till the end of the century that there have been significant points of interaction between the two disciplines. Four pivotal points of interaction may be listed: the adoption of an ecosystem view in Wisconsin DDT hearings in 1970, stimulated by Rachael Carson's adoption and publication of the description of DDT coursing through the ecosystem in Silent Spring; the adoption of NEPA (National Environmental Policy Act) as an outgrowth of ecologist Lynton Caldwell's ideas; the emergence of conservation biology in the 1980s as part of the evolution of endangered species and forestry management regulation; and the formulation of earth systems sciences as a response to the global pollution problems of acid rain, ozone depletion and global warming in the 1980s and 1990s. These four historical events cry out for more in-depth study to reveal "the moment of impact" between the two disciplines.

Before these points of contact occurred, the broad outline of a legal system for the regulation of the environment was pieced together out of the several centuries' history of our common law legal system.[14] It was followed by the more recent adoption of a system of administrative law primarily to administer the newly emerging welfare state in the 1930s and 1940s.[15] This new administrative law system initially paid little attention to environmental matters. The importance of the fact that the structure and procedures of the legal system were already well institutionalized before ecology took place means that this new science had to fit into an preexisting organization of legal institutions, legislatures, courts and administrative branches, none of which was well adapted to an ecological approach. In fact, most of the current descriptions of environmental law in texts and treatises, after setting forth bold ecologically oriented introductory chapters, promptly return to organizing ecological materials within the preexisting legal categories,[16] thus producing new generations of environmental lawyers who think about our environmental problems with the old preexisting legal categories. [New ecologically oriented law teaching materials and appropriate methods are desperately needed.]

Equally important, the American public culture was shaped by the nineteenth and early twentieth century emergence of a nation committed to voracious economic growth and resource consumption. The grand American "nature thinkers" of the past century – Thoreau, Muir, Leopold, Marsh – were all clearly marginal to the dominant culture of their age. And their views of nature as places to be honored and protected, competed with other views of nature as simply the collective phenomena of the world or the material substrate of all existence – to be manipulated at will.[17] When ecology marched upon the public stage in the mid-twentieth century, there was already lots of competition in the strands of thought about nature and the action within our public culture. That competition continues today with the new fields of genetic and molecular biology. An explanation of the relationships of genetics, ecology and environmental law will be required in the future.

Given our reservations about the significance of any "co-evolution" of ecology and environmental law, our study of the history of these disciplines and their interaction suggests that the 1950s and 1960s, with the first major works of Eugene Odum and Rachael Carson, followed by the first "major" environmental law cases – Scenic Hudson, the Santa Barbara Oil Spill, as well as the Lake Washington work of Edmondson – was the birth of "eco-systemic law." This early history deserves more attention in future volumes, especially to explore the remarkable work of Eugene Odum and his impact upon the environmental use of ecosystemic regimes.[18]

The major attention of our book has been in the period from 1970 to 2000. When studying the period from 1970 to 1990, we found four patterns of relationship between ecology and law to which we have applied a courtship metaphor: the four are "the quarrel," "the courtship," "the shy embrace" and "the marriage." Let us hasten to add that no specific chronological order is posited for these patterns. In fact, these patterns may be simply a useful way to classify a complex set of relationships.

We described a situation in which within some very important areas of environmental law – i.e., air, water, toxics, and land use regulation – the relationship of law and ecology is at best a quarrelsome one; these laws did not originate out of and do not readily admit an ecological framework of thought. The tensions between these media and pollutant oriented laws and ecological science require more study. The major environmental media laws, the Clean Air Act and the Clean Water Act, and pollutant laws, e.g., the Resource Conservation and Recovery Act, do not adopt an explicit ecosystem orientation. Their early formation prior to the full articulation of ecosystem approaches, their public health orientation, and their technology forcing strategies tend to discourage an ecosystem approach. Yet as Eugene Odum noted as early as 1970, pollution laws could easily be formulated and understood in ecosystemic terms.[19]

Despite the failure of these laws to fully embrace an ecosystemic approach, they have slowly moved toward becoming part of ecosystemic regimes. This change has taken place in three ways and is illustrated by the Clean Air Act. First, with the 1977 and 1990 amendments, the Clean Air Act adopted a more ecological approach, at least in some parts. It has recognized the ecological impact of air pollutants and the role of the deposition of pollutants upon ecosystems such as the Great Lakes, other aquatic areas and park ecosystems.[20] The 1990 Act has adopted ecological risk assessment for determining residual risk of toxic pollutants and sought to require assessments of at least some toxic pollutants in terms of the ecosystem pathways and impacts.[21] The 1977 and 1990 Amendments have begun to recognize the importance of air quality districts which are based more upon the air sheds and less upon arbitrary state boundaries.[22]

Table 11.1 HISTORICAL PATTERNS OF RELATIONSHIP BETWEEN LAW AND ECOLOGY

The Quarrel
1. The Clean Air Act
2. The Clean Water Act
3. Resource Conservation and Recovery Act
4. Land Use legislation

The Initial Embrace
1. NEPA
2. Coastal Management
3. Great Lakes Compact
4. Public Trust

The Courtship
1. National Forest Management Act
2. National Parks legislation
3. Endangered Species Act
4. Pesticide legislation

The Marriage
1. Acid Rain legislation
2. Ozone depletion protocol and legislation
3. Global warming protocol
4. Mediterranean legal regime
5. CITES, Convention on International Trade in Endangered Species

Source: Brooks, Jones and Virginia

Not only has the 1990 and earlier reforms placed a more ecological cast upon some parts of Clean Air Act, but the Act has authorized a more ecosystemic management effort, at least in the case of the water areas, Indian lands and national parks.[23] Increasingly, place-based ecosystemic regimes are beginning to look to the control of air pollutants as part of their environmental strategies.[24] Finally and most importantly, air pollution has been linked to acid rain deposition, ozone depletion and global warming. The first two problems, as we have indicated above, have resulted in the forging of connections between global earth systems regimes and the domestic law of air pollution control.[25] A serious approach to global warming will require a similar linkage. Thus, the Clean Air Act and its evolution illustrates a rapprochement between the media-based laws and an ecological approach to the control of pollution.

One may expect a further movement in this direction in the future, not only in the field of air pollution law, but water pollution and solid and hazardous waste pollution as well.

By contrast, NEPA, the Great Lakes Compact, the coastal management program, and the newly rediscovered doctrine of the public trust, exemplify an initial embrace of an ecological perspective. Like many embraces, they may or may not have led to a lasting relationship between the two disciplines. Some histories of these laws have been written,[26] but histories which explore their use (and abuse) of ecology remain to be written. It is altogether possible the too-early joinder of ecology and environmental law has produced illegitimate and malformed offspring. Further examination of a new generation of these laws based upon their early promise and subsequent failure is needed.

A more reliable method of establishing close relations between law and ecology is the slow courtship of ecology and environmental law, in which the national park and forestry laws, endangered species protection, and pesticide laws, were "retrofitted" over time to accept the new ecological insights. This retrofit was, in part, the product of environmental advocacy. An important question here is how successful this retrofit is. Assessments of these retrofits are required.

Finally, a marriage between ecology and environmental law has taken place in the global settings of acid rain control, ozone depletion prevention, the CITES agreements, and steps to curb global warming. As we have indicated above, these international regimes may have established "an experimental jurisprudence" which requires more detailed articulation and possible new applications.

Whether this arguable classification of historical patterns can withstand scrutiny remains to be seen, but it succeeds in provoking a number of inquiries. Why have the media and pollution areas of environmental law been so resistant to ecological insights? Was the initial embrace of ecology in NEPA, coastal management laws and the Great Lakes agreement a wise embrace, or merely a short-lived summer love affair? To mix metaphors, have the laws undergoing courtship by ecology been adequately retrofitted? Or is such a "retrofit" doomed to failure because of initially adopted institutions? And what kind of an ongoing marriage are those laws which appear to have fully if slowly adopted an ecological perspective? What makes for a healthy successful marriage between the two disciplines? By viewing these patterns as hypotheses of historical development, we can begin to reexamine the laws within these patterns and their relationship to ecology.

The Culmination of Ecosystem Regimes

In the 1990s, we have witnessed the culmination of the relations between ecology and environmental law. Not only has conservation biology as a discipline and biodiversity as a concept become an important part of national forest and endangered species management, but major court cases reviewing biodiversity determinations have been decided. The relevant federal agencies have been struggling with appropriate regulations to protect diversity. There is little doubt that attention to biodiversity has led to an intensive relationship between ecology and law. The incorporation of biodiversity within an integrated ecology is a major step in the integration of ecology and law.

On other fronts in the 1990s, EPA and the states have sought to promote the undertaking of ecosystem management. A proliferation of place-based and species-based ecosystem management efforts have been undertaken across the nation, and new efforts to apply an earth systems approach to global warming is also taking place. This legal recognition of ecosystem regimes may be viewed as part of the gradual historic recognition of systems in our urban, economic and environmental life, accomplished primarily through legally authorized planning and regulation.[27]

A history of the relationship of the law to systems thought remains to be written. Since the latest stage in that history is the law of ecosystems, a more systematic collection and description of the current ecosystemic regimes would be valuable.[28] The articulation of regime theory's relationship to ecology and ecosystems has begun, but much work remains.[29] A systematic large-scale canvassing and description of the interdisciplinary frameworks for law and ecology might lay the groundwork for a better assessment of these interdisciplinary frameworks than we have been able to offer in this volume.[30] The time may also have arrived for a collective effort to arrive at a consensus upon an interdisciplinary ecology/law methodology for future environmental regimes.

Forging the Relationship Between Ecology and Law

It is tempting to articulate some master approach to the relationship between ecology and law which would articulate a complete view of the ecological system in question, identify the problems in the functioning of that system, develop a comprehensive plan for resolving those problems, establish a management program for the implementation of the plan, implement the plan, and assess its results. Such an approach has been recommended in recent efforts to define a generic discipline of "ecological management."[31] It has been implemented in the ecologically oriented regulation of selected environmental laws, such as coastal zone management legislation. These approaches are commonly found in the recent proliferating ecological management literature, and have also been vigorously attacked by opponents to ecological management and critics of specific applications of such management efforts.

Our position in this book is that the history of the relations between ecology and law reveals a much more complex relationship between the two disciplines than can be captured by the present paradigms of ecosystem management. The historical approach which we have taken to the relations of law and ecology reveals four major strategies for joining the two disciplines.

The Internal Restructuring of the Law

The problems of relating a synoptic science of ecology to the traditional incremental common law, the legislative legal system, and the more recent administrative law systems were evident in the early attempts to fashion a distinctive environmental law regime. Behind the operation of this legal system may operate a series of background legal principles[32] which may inform the legal reasoning of this field. The public culture of environmentalism may introduce a new more ecological vision of complex interdependency into the more general operation of the law.[33] More specific environmental principles, such as the precautionary principle,[34] may also be operating both tacitly and explicitly. One effort which we did not pursue in detail in this text is the exploration of these principles, their history and relationship to ecology and law.

In Chapter 1, we outlined the dominant ideals paradigm of the modern environmental law regime. This paradigm was based upon a comparative study of western European environmental law regimes. Based upon our history of ecology and environmental law, we are able to indicate the extent to which the ecological vision has affected the dominant paradigm of environmental law. Ecosystemic regimes have had to make their peace with a common law and constitutional system not designed to accommodate an ecological viewpoint.[35] Aside from the obvious difficulty of reconciling our common law private property system, which envisages spatially discrete units of property, in contrast to the interdependent ecosystem envisaged by ecology,[36] other fundamental difficulties in the relationship between law and ecology emerge. Those difficulties include the problem of conducting any unified ecosystem management effort in the face of a legal structure which separates branches (legislative, executive, judicial) and levels (federal, state, and local) of government and pits them against each other. This separation and balance of powers and federalism are based upon "agonistic principles," i.e., principles assuming the desirability for a contest of powers within government to preserve freedom, rather than the unified application of science to preserve or protect nature.[37]

These issues about the relations of our constitutional and common law legal system and their relations to ecology became specific and practically important when the new age of environmentalism began in 1970. At that time, the federal legislature and executive struggled about how they were to organize themselves and their disparate committees and departments to mount an attack on environmental problems. The result was that the U.S. Environmental Protection Agency assumed a part (but not all) of the executive responsibility for environmental protection. Despite this effort, there was no unified organization of the committee structure in Congress.[38] It was an ecologist, Lynton Caldwell, who saw the dilemma facing the effort to reorganize a government based upon contending powers to be compatible with a comprehensive systematic science. He sought to embrace an ecological vision to cover all government activities through the National Environmental Policy Act (NEPA), which envisaged environmental impacts for both legislation and agency actions. Despite this brilliant approach, Congress remained fragmented and the environmental impact statements which NEPA authorized and the agencies completed often conflicted with the previously legally authorized non-environmental missions of the government departments. The result was that federal agencies continued to make decisions without a carefully adopted ecological perspective and often simply adopted routinized environmental impact statements which rationalized their decisions.

Courts similarly struggled with the implications of a more ecological vision. The courts were modeled upon an adversary system composed of a two party, plaintiff–defendant, struggle in which the courts would decide between one or the other party.[39] Initially, courts were tempted to accept a new ecological vision in which the ecosystem would be represented before the court and new procedures would be adopted. This effort to change the court was best exemplified in the struggle over the "standing" of environmental organizations to enter the courts. After an initial broadening of the standing of organizations representing persons and environments suffering diffuse environmental harms indirectly caused by the defendant, the U.S. Supreme Court soon began to restrict access by narrowing the criteria for eligible standing before the courts. Ultimately, the courts did not yield to the temptation, instead making incremental adjustments while refusing to adopt a radical reform of themselves. Similarly, the federal and state legislatures refused to restructure the courts and themselves in light of the environmental challenges.[40] As a consequence, unlike some western European countries, standing of environmental organizations is presently limited to individuals (with the exception of citizen suit provisions).

The limited and incremental adjustments which the federal and state legislatures and the courts made in light of the new ecological vision placed a

heavier burden upon the administrative branch of the federal government as well
as upon the executive branch of state governments to respond to the demands
animated by this ecological vision. The federal executive, after a noble attempt
to engage in comprehensive environmental planning through a newly created
Council of Environmental Quality, largely abandoned that effort.[41] The federal
Environmental Protection Agency and other environ-mentally oriented federal
departments have struggled to reorganize themselves to recognize, at least in
part, a unified ecological perspective.[42] An important part of this reorganization
is the increase in legally authorized plans and planning activities which embrace
ecological methods, concepts and conclusions.[43] Their counterpart state
environmental agencies have also undertaken efforts at "ecological
reorganization."[44]

The early struggle to adjust the realities of the legal system to the vision
and practices of ecology requires much more systematic attention than we have
been able to give in this book. The failure of NEPA and the CEQ, the vanishing
promise of science and environmental courts, the abortive efforts to reorganize
Congress and state legislatures, and the faint imprint of the ecological vision
upon federal and state bureaucracies require a more careful accounting of the
reasons for the failure and its implication for efforts at future reform.[45]

The Internal Restructuring of Ecology

The state of today's environmental law is understood by an analysis of its history
and a study of the incremental changes in the making of individual laws, which
determine our present day environmental law regime. A faint pattern of slow
progress may be discerned from the classic studies of Pound, MacDougal,
Ackerman and Tarlock. However, we have found more progress towards the
establishment of an ecosystemic law.

The movement towards ecosystemic law has been partly stimulated by
the development of ecology itself. Ecology has evolved as an academic
discipline as scientists revise their ideas about how the natural world functions.
Its principles are based upon the development of theory and lead to hypothesis
testing, experimentation, and open debate in the peer-reviewed literature. From
time to time, the restructuring of ecology has occurred in response to pressing
environmental problems, which have in turn have engaged the legal system. In
this way, ecology and environmental law came to know one another and with
time to coevolve and form an ecosystemic regime. These pressing environmental
problems include widely publicized issues such as pesticides and their biological
concentration in the food chain, the impact of acid rain on forests and lakes, the
loss of biodiversity; more specifically the need to protect endangered species,
and the global problems of ozone depletion and global warming.

We have detailed the early historical development of ecology. Ecology has it roots in natural history and systematics and its early history is rich with studies of species distribution and community descriptions. This tradition endures and is central to our understanding of biodiversity. The definition of ecosystem ecology by Eugene Odum, Gene Likens, Herbert Bormann, and others represented one new direction; one focused on the energetics and nutrient cycling dynamics of biological communities and their habitat, i.e., the ecosystem. Eugene Odum and associates began the effort to understand the collective responses and interactions of biological, physical, and chemical systems to human disturbance. Odum outlined the conceptual approach, but it was left to Gene Likens and colleagues to develop the experimental protocols and build the interdisciplinary teams of scientists necessary to study entire ecosystems. The Hubbard Brook ecosystem study remains after 30 years the leading experimental example of this approach and this study continues to inform and influence forest management and acid rain law.

Not only have applications of classic ecology informed environmental law, but environmental law has also stimulated new fields of ecology. Environmentalists early on recognized the power of the Endangered Species Act (ESA) to challenge the development of natural areas as we recount in our description of the famous Snail Darter case. The ESA was a driving force behind the application of ecology to environmental law and it hastened the birth of a new field, Conservation Biology. Michael Soule, E.O. Wilson, Thomas Lovejoy, and many other ecologists interested in species and population level problems came to realize that the protection and management of small populations endangered by human activities would require a new synthesis of knowledge, drawing from ecology, genetics, behavior, ecosystem science, economics, and law. This synthesis is now a distinct discipline with its own professional society. Conservation biology is now serving to bridge a gap that had developed between population ecology and ecosystem ecology Conservation biologists must place the species into its ecosystem, and today most conservation plans can also be viewed as ecosystem management plans which act to provide the necessary conditions for survival of the target species and its associated community.

Conservation biology is not the only new field growing out of environmental protection efforts. Restoration ecology is another such field. The landmark environmental legislation of the 1970s came as a direct response to public demand to halt further damage to our natural environment and the services that it provides. Litigation over these damages pushed ecologists to consider the application of ecological knowledge and theory to the restore damaged ecosystems. It would be ten to twenty years after Earth Day before restoration ecology would be seen as a "respected" and well-supported field in the new ecology. Although the list of damaged ecosystems is long, restoration ecologists have been most active in restoring or reconstructing ecosystems that have high economic value, or those where the disturbance is total and the law requires remedial actions (e.g., strip mined sites). The academic community was slow to acknowledge the growth and merits of restoration ecology because of its intrinsic applied focus. This reluctance has been abandoned with the formation of the Society for Ecological Restoration and the publication in 1990 of the journal Ecological Applications by the Ecological Society of America. Ecology has undergone a significant restructuring since Earth Day. The fields of ecosystem ecology, conservation biology, and restoration ecology are now mainstays of the discipline.

The newest challenges for ecology are at the interface with the social sciences. Herman Daily and Robert Costanza have brokered the engagement of ecology and economics. The International Society for Ecological Econom-ics strives to integrate ecological principles into economic models that focus on sustainability and the preservation of natural capital. This new interest of ecology has many parallels to the longer running relationship between law and ecology. The fields are drawn together through societal pressures to solve problems. At the same time the disciplines have distinct histories and methodologies which pose problems for reaching a new synthesis or regime.

The restructuring of ecology in the context of environmental law can be seen in the emergence of four areas that now receive high interest and funding from environmental management agencies: biogeochemistry of entire ecosystems, conservation biology, restoration ecology, and the interplay of ecology with the social sciences (ecological economics, urban ecology etc.). It is these four major areas and their relationship to environmental law within ecosystemic regimes which should be the focus of future study.

The Establishment of Linkages Between Ecology and Law

The history of ecology and environmental law reveals "linkage persons," "bridge documents," "migratory concepts," and "interdisciplinary conceptual frameworks" for linking the two fields. Here is a brief, and by no means adequate indication of what we are talking about.

A. Linkage Persons. The history of environmental law and ecology is dotted with people who clearly embraced a sensitivity to both law and ecology and their relationships. George Perkins Marsh, Eugene Odum, Rachel Carson, Joseph Sax, John Clark, Ian McHarg, Lynton Caldwell, Robert Keiter, A. Dan Tarlock, John Cairns, and Celia Campbell-Mohn are some of the persons who by virtue of their positions and publications have linked the fields of ecology and law. We have briefly identified these people and highlighted their work, but their work in linking ecology and law deserves more attention and analysis than we have been able to give in our broad history within this volume. We envisage a series of important intellectual biographies of important figures who have dared to bridge the disciplines of law and ecology.

B. Bridge Documents. The fields of ecology and law are joined by certain "bridge documents," documents with low visibility to the public, but which contain both important legal and ecological content. The documents identified in Chapters 5-10 indicate that bridge documents include models, plans, regulations, manuals, UN framework conventions, impact statements, and much more. The importance of these documents for our purposes is that they offer a specific textual focus for legal and ecological considerations coming together in one place. Many of the bridge documents are examples of "low visibility intellectual technology,"[46] developed and applied within academia and the government bureaucracies in an effort to apply one or another aspect of ecology, its methods or conclusions in the regulatory setting. Because these documents are neither pure science nor pure regulation, and because their application is often hidden from public view, their use poses an important challenge both for science and the law. Both science and law must evaluate their use in light of the commons of these two disciplines. It is worth inquiring whether a process of "technology assessment," whether legislative, admin-istrative or judicial, is not needed to assure that the bridges between ecology and environmental law are well made.[47]

Take, for example, a quantitative model, widely used in various environmental regulations.[48] One can take such a model and ask both legal and ecological questions about it. For example do the statutes and regulations authorize the use of the model? Do they govern the content of the model? Do the variables identified in the model match those to be regulated by the statute or regulation? Does the law regulate the development, testing and application of the model? If so, how? On the ecological side of the equation, does the model accurately portray the workings of the ecosystem modeled? Does it contain assumptions? If so, are those assumptions justified? What is the view of the model within the field of ecology? Is it used in research? Has it been modified? Has it been verified? What institutions are available to improve the application of these models? What, if any, is the role of court review of the models? It is important that these bridge documents assume new prominence as objects of the research, study, and teaching of ecological policy and law.

C. Migrating Concepts. In addition to personages, documents, and institutions, shared concepts themselves may link the disciplines. The following is a list of important ecological concepts.

Table 11.2 THE FIFTY MOST IMPORTANT CONCEPTS IN ECOLOGY

The ecosystem	The guild	*r* and *K* selection
Succession	Maximum sustainable yield	Plant animal/coevolution
Energy flow	Population cycles	The diversity/stability hypothesis
Conservation of resources	Predator-prey interactions	Socioecology
Competition	Plant-herbivore interactions	Optimal foraging
Niche	Island biogeography theory	Parasite-host interactions
Materials Cycling	Bioaccumulation in food	Species-area relationships
The community	chains	The ecotype
Life history strategies	Coevolution	Climax
Ecosystem fragility	Stochaastic processes	Territoriality
Food webs	Natural disturbance	Allocation theory
Ecological adaptation	Habitat restoration	Intrinsic regulation
Env'tl heterogeneity	The managed nature reserve	Pyramid of numbers
Species diversity	Indicator organisms	Keystone species
Density-dependent	Competition and the	The biome
regulation	conditions for species exclusion	Species packing
Limiting factors	Trophic level	The 3/2 thinning law
Carrying capacity	Pattern	

Source: J.M. Cherrett, Ed., *Ecological Concepts* (1989), pp. 6-7

These concepts may be adopted within both ecology and law; for example, the concept of *boundary*[49] in both legal and ecological fields. The concepts in both fields may have the same name, but very different meanings within the two fields; this sharing of the name and the difference in meaning stimulates inquiry into the applicability of the concept in both ecology and environmental law. Alternatively, an ecological concept may gain currency in the political culture and hence may become important for both fields. Thus, the concept of *carrying capacity* emerged from biology to capture the attention of the public and hence has migrated into a variety of statutes and regulations.[50] Whether in its travels, the concept has retained similar meanings and, if not, what the scientific and legal implications are from such a change in meaning deserves inquiry. Finally, a third kind of concept is the more technical concept of ecology, which gets adopted in legal regulation. Such concepts, such as diversity[51] or succession[52] are examples. We have discussed at some length the adoption of the diversity concept within selected environmental laws, but by no means have we exhausted the extent to which this concept has entered environmental law. Again, it is important to find careful (perhaps multiple) scientific definitions of these terms, and carefully assess what happens to their meanings as they are adopted in environmental regulation.

We envisage a systematic analysis of shared ecological and environmental law concepts, including a history of their migration between fields. Whether the disciplines of the sociology of knowledge or the history of ideas might be helpful here is an avenue we have not pursued.

D. Interdisciplinary Frameworks. In other research,[53] we have identified seven categories and thirty-six specific interdisciplinary frameworks which have emerged to link ecology and environmental law. The seven categories are as follows:

Table 11.3 CONCEPTUAL FRAMEWORKS

I.   Law and Ecology as Part of More Comprehensive Categories (e.g., science and law).
II. Reconceptualizing in Law and/or Science (e.g., "evolutionary law").
III. Describing the Relationship Between Law, Ecology and Law as Applied Theory (e.g., ecosystem management).
IV. Establishing a Third Mediating Framework (e.g., ecosystem regimes).
V.   Expanding an Existing Third Discipline (e.g., ecological economics).
VI. Mediating by New Concepts (e.g., sustainability).
VII. Ethical Framewoks to Accommodate Ecology and Law.

Emerging Interdisciplinary Frameworks for Law and Ecology (2002)
Source: Brooks, Jones and Virginia

A complete history and analysis of the interdisciplinary efforts seeking to join ecology and law remains to be written. We envisage a more systematic effort in which the relationship of each framework to ecology and law is discussed in detail. Each of these frameworks remains to be fully evaluated in light of our series of criteria designed to assess the extent to which they facilitate appropriate relationships between law and ecology. The criteria we propose include the intellectual clarity (logic, demonstrability), unity, the comprehensiveness, the fruitfulness (of hypotheses, policies), the cost of empirical support, the internal consistency, the compatibility with existing disciplines, the elegance and simplicity, and practicality (normative relevance and accessibility to would-be users). There are, of course, clear tradeoffs between relevance and accessibility to would-be users. There are, of course, clear tradeoffs between the criteria. For example, the comprehensiveness of the theories may conflict with its elegance and simplicity. A comprehensive theory may have high data needs. A simple and elegant theory may be too general to be readily applicable to a given situation. Moreover, not all the criteria may embody desirable traits. Thus, compatibility of a theory to existing disciplines may not reflect proper recognition of the revolutionary quality of the theory. Requiring unity of a theory may not be appropriate at the early stages of a theory when many formulations are attempted.

The Creation of Ecosystemic Regimes

Our history reveals a variety of ecosystemic institutions which play a fundamental role in joining law and ecology together. Some of these institutions are simply "epistemic communities," i.e., informal groups of scientists and government officials who share an ecological agenda. Peter Haas, in his classic study of the Mediterranean and its ecological regime, *Saving the Mediterranean*,[54] identified such a community of marine scientists who promoted an ecological agenda for regulating the pollution of the Mediterranean Sea. A group may be more formally established by means of the ongoing regulation of an ecosystem. Thus, groups of officials are established in various ways as exemplified by the memoranda of agreement in the coastal management program, the restoration area planning process of the Great Lakes, or the assembly of federal officials joined to oversee the Greater Yellowstone Ecosystem. Finally, there are groups who operate as advocates for an ecological position, whether government institutions such as UNEP and the National Research Council, or non-profit advocacy groups. By means of lobbying, citizen action or legal action, these groups seek to promote one or another ecologically defined position.

We have not sought to describe these epistemic communities and organized advocacy groups in our history, nor to profile such groups, their knowledge and adoption of ecology in their work, and their precise role in the policy process is an important task for further research. Especially useful here is Oran Young's notion of a resource regime or ecosystem regime – a cluster of rules and roles which governs a given ecosystem. This regime may include both ecological scientists and environmental lawyers as well as the ecology and law they study and apply. It is now an appropriate time to bring ecologists, environmental scholars and lawyers, regime theorists and practitioners together to explore the interaction of regime theory and law.

The notion of an ecosystem regime may tacitly assume a "public goods" approach to the environment. However, much of the ecosystem is in private hands. Most nations now embrace some system of private real property in which owners can claim rights of occupation, use, and disposal either as a constitutional right and/or by civil or common law. Private property underlies contract law hence promoting markets. There are three major philosophies of private property, Kantian, utilitarian, and classical Aristotelian, each with very different implications for the environmental regulation of such property.[55] The environmentally insensitive occupation and use of property may affect the ecosystem. Various practical ways of limiting the impact of property are to: (1) create private property rights in common property air, water or land; (2) rely upon informal commons controls; (3) establish the land in public trust; (4) acquire the land as public or non-profit property; (5) regulate the land, balancing the ecological and wealth producing aspects of private property.[56] Careful comparative evaluation of these alternative constraints upon private property must be conducted. Various intellectual efforts have been made to reconceptualize private property either through a historical inquiry which purports to find accepted public limits upon property rights, or which "debundles" rights and recovers the loss of property as essentially limited, or places affirmative responsibility upon the property owner to engage in environmental protection, or seeks to condition property as part of community plans and values.[57] This reconceptualization of private property in light of an ecosystemic perspective deserves an organized program of extensive research.

The Focus on Place, Species, and Global Interdependency

The history of the relationship of ecology and environmental law reveals that they are most likely to come together when the public culture is focused upon the value of places or species. The history of efforts to protect the Hudson River and its fish species, the two decade long history of Mono Lake, the fight to protect the fishery resources off the Atlantic coast, the continuing battle to save the Redwoods, the new effort to plan, restore and prevent further harm to the Chesapeake Bay, and Vermont's continuous efforts to protect its unique and beautiful pastoral environment are simply a few of many examples where the love of a place or species has promoted a planning and regulatory effort concentrated upon ecosystems and biodiversity.

Within established environmental programs and laws, since the 1990s, the occasions for the practice of nationwide ecosystems management and biodiversity protection has been predominantly within programs such as the National Forest Management program, the Endangered Species law, and coastal management programs. However, as the table in Chapter 8 indicates, there are a myriad of sub-national efforts. It is no coincidence that these programs are focused upon specific places and/or specific species. To be sure, we have also seen that the Acid Rain, Ozone Depletion and Global Warming programs which are not focused – for the most part – upon specific places or species have adopted a systematic global systems approach. These programs remain the responses to global threats requiring a systematic planning effort; global threats are the third stimulating incentive for an ecosystem approach and we shall discuss this fact below.

A. Sense of Place. The importance of a sense of place is not new. The Indian culture honors place. The early nature visionaries, Thoreau, Muir and Leopold, all grounded their grander environmental visions in their favorite places, i.e., Walden, the Sierras, and the Wisconsin rivers. Much of the literature of nature is a literature of place, and we respond to the portraits of places painted by the words of Wallace Stegner or Peter Matthieson. Recent study of environmental literature and thought has emphasized the importance of specific landscapes within this literature. Planners extending back to Lewis Mumford and Patrick Geddes were place sensitive and their more recent followers such as Kevin Lynch have extended their study of place by developing new concepts to analyze place. Geography and planning has led to an entire collection of literature on place, and the study of place is now enshrined with the term "topophilia."[58] Philosophical literature has not been far behind, with the stimulus of Heidigger's work.[59] Edward Casey has completed two major works on the philosophy of place and geography; the sense of place has developed links to environmental ethics.[60]

Both ecology and conservation biology are place related. The boundaries of ecosystems set the limits of natural places and the distribution of species through space is, in fact, through a limited space. (Space is customarily regarded as relatively unlimited; places have boundaries which contain them and with which we can ordinarily easily identify). The natural places are bounded not only by nature but also often by a human culture. Place and its ecosystem are often inhabited by humans as well, and hence, attention to the ways in which place and ecosystems interact is attention also to a social ecology of which humans are a part. Since we humans are part of places, i.e., we live in places, we experience a sense of place and often we value a place either because we enjoy it, or we interact for our living with it, or we identify ourselves with it or it with us. Our places can become like our extended private property which are expressions of who we are. Once we value our places, place poses ethical issues for us. We may seek to resist others' efforts to change our place or interfere with the relationships we have to our place.

Laws often deal with places, although somewhat clumsily. Thus, the law defines the bounds of our nation and the states which we regard as places important to us.[61] And it often identifies more specific places – rivers, mountains, forests, wetlands – whose boundaries and purposes are both given by nature and defined through ecology and the law. And so the fact that we value places is often translated into environmental law. But the relationship of place to ecology and environmental law is not always a happy one. We may have a strong sense of place which may not coincide with either the legal or ecological boundaries. Our emotional attachments to places may outweigh or blind us to the ecological reality of a place. Ecology is a science; a sense of place is, in part, feeling. Science and feeling don't blend very well. Moreover, science seeks abstract universal laws. Places are particular, with particular histories which are often traced by natural and/or ecological historians. These histories are necessarily specific and particular, not necessarily lending themselves to characterization in science. Finally, a sense of place involves viewing the place, at least in part, in social terms. In fact, it is often the mixture of natural place and human culture which contributes to our valuing the place in question. Thus Vermonters love the mountaintop farms which are now fading from the landscape. Once human culture becomes an important part of a sense of place, the study of place is in part a social science and ethics as well as ecology. We are accustomed to separating natural and social science and often resist mixing the two disciplines. Yet it may be that we require some form of social ecology to understand the relationship between the social culture and the natural ecology of the places we value.

It is this sense of place which stimulates and structures many of the ecosystem management efforts of the 1990s. Thus the efforts to protect the Sierras, the Pine Barrens, the Adirondacks, the coastal areas of our states, Mono Lake, Lake Washington, the Northern Forest, Yellowstone, the New River, the Mediterranean, the English countryside, the Alps, and many others are stimulated by the vivid sense of place which these areas have inspired in their inhabitants and visitors. In our account of place-based ecosystem regimes in Chapter 8, we identify some of the unique legal mechanisms and their bridge documents which link ecology and law. A study of these documents is warranted in the context of further research to pursue in more specific terms how the sense of place and the protection of ecosystems can be joined, and what problems are encountered when the effort to protect them through environmental law and ecosystem management is made.

B. Species. The focus of much of America's nature writing and its environmental law is not a sense of place but rather a beloved species: the snowy egret, the redwood tree, the timber wolf, Bambi. Perhaps such species merely personalize nature, allowing us to better grasp its value. The species becomes a symbolic representative of the ecosystem. From this point of view, the extinction of a species is an easily grasped parable for the threat of more general collapse of our natural world. Endangered species may be the proverbial "canary in the coal mine" of modern industrial and urbanized life. Concentration upon species may also be the environmental equivalent of our nation's commitment to individualist ideals by which we measure the progress of our society. Ecosystems and places represent more communal appeals, while the fate of a species echoes our nation's commitment to the survival, success, and flourishing of individuals or at least individual species.

The Endangered Species Act was one of the earliest mid-twentieth century environmental laws, and one of the few "prohibitory laws" in which the "taking" of a species may be prohibited on pain of criminal penalty. The listing of species required under that law creates a kind of "honor roll" of loved and admired non-human biotic life. The listing of species and the designation of their habitats calls upon the work of biologists, hence perpetuating a long tradition of a discipline which focused upon individual species.

To be sure, ecology and ecosystems lie in the background of the Endangered Species Act. Specific concern with ecosystems is stated at the beginning of the 1973 law, and the historical development of the law has slowly led to increasing concern with the ecology of the habitat in which the species is located.[62]   But the threat of extinction to the species remains the central touchstone of concern for the law. That concern has extended to the administration of other environmental laws which are less individualistic in their orientation. The Wilderness Act, the National Forest Management Act, the National Environmental Policy Act are three of many laws which have also authorized serious legal concern not only about species but also the ecosystem which surrounds them.

The value attributed to species in environmental laws has been described as a recent expression of respect for or rights of individual non-human creatures. Environmental historian Rod Nash, in his *Rights of Nature* has viewed the history of environmental policy as part of the gradual extension of rights in our history. Paul Taylor has articulated a carefully reasoned biocentric individualism in which non-human living things are deemed capable of having a welfare which deserves respect, even if that welfare has to be balanced against human welfare in some cases.[63] Such respect encourages a preservationist ethic of nature and a rule of minimization of environmental harm.

Whether or not such admittedly preservationist and minimal environmental harm approach will eventually carry the day in future environmental policy, the focus upon species need not be a preservationist approach. Thus foresters, fishermen, and farmers may organize their lives and communities around the species whose preservation are not sought, but whose conservation for human use in the future is of deep concern. Thus the cod, swordfish or lobster fished by Atlantic fishermen are the objects of a species based environmental regime of the Fisheries Conservation and Management Act; similarly, selected pines or redwoods within private, state or national forests may be species around which the lives of lumbermen revolve. It is the new ideal of sustainability which presently expresses the value of an ecologically and economically sustainable environment.

The preservationist and conservationist ethics of past generations may be giving way to new concerns about biodiversity and sustainability as guiding ideals of the new millennium. Our history of ecology and environmental law above has touched upon the emergence of these ideals both within ecology and environmental law. As the public culture translates the individualist approach of the preservation of the species into concerns about biodiversity, and conservation becomes reinterpreted as sustainability, subtle changes in the role of both ecology and environmental law may take place. We are now beginning to see case studies which track efforts to preserve and conserve or sustain a viable biodiversity through law and management.[64] The next step will be the drawing of more general conclusions from the studies to trace the precise linkages between biodiversity, ecology and environmental law.

C. *Global Interdependency.* The history of ecology, environmental law and their relations reveals one other major area in which these two disciplines have come together, i.e., the effort to resolve international environmental problems. Acid rain, ozone depletion, global warming, the Great Lakes, the Mediterranean agreements, and new compacts regarding biodiversity protection, including CITES, illustrate these fruitful areas of cooperation for global ecology and environmental law. Of course, not all international environmental arrangements are based upon ecological study, nor does a global ecological perspective necessarily lead to an environmental law regime built upon such a perspective. Nevertheless, it is striking to observe the number of major international environmental arrangements which are the fruit of both an ecological perspective and systematic ecological research. The collection and in-depth study of each of these efforts as examples of the joinder of law and ecology is needed. The reasons for such an emphasis of the joinder of ecology and law at the international level are complex. In some cases, the environmental problem at issue is difficult to define and requires a more systematic inquiry into the sources and nature of the problem at hand leading to the formation of "epistemic communities" of international scientists early in the "problem definition" stage. The nature of the problems themselves as the product of more comprehensive international global processes, i.e., large-scale atmospheric and meteorological processes, encourages a systems approach. The international scope and setting of the problems contributes to the adoption of problem definitions which escape the confines of existing domestic non-ecological regulations which are unable to cope with the broad scope of the problems. The difficulty of defining the problems leads to an extensive planning stage in which problems can be defined in a more comprehensive manner than in cases where the problems are viewed as analogous to problems treated by the existing regulatory system.

The legal structuring of the study and resolution of international environmental problems has led to a three stage approach: first, planning; second, the implementation for resolution of the problems identified in the planning stage; and third, the modification, through scientific feedback, of the implementation regime. The planning stage reflects the ecological study and research in the form of a plan or research conclusions; the implementation stage takes specific conclusions from the first stage and builds a legal and administrative mechanism for addressing the problem. That mechanism itself may not reflect the ecological research which preceded it. Science reasserts itself in the third stage in the effort to evaluate the results and make modifications in the mechanism.

A variety of different ways in which the planning stage is carried out may be found in the history of each of the efforts to resolve international problems, since the planning stage is legally structured in different ways. Similarly, the implementation stage and its relationship to the previous planning may differ and different kinds of implementation may take place.[65] Hence, some implementation, e.g., Great Lakes and the Mediterranean program, have relied upon existing domestic regulatory problems. Acid rain and ozone depletion have added a trading program onto the existing regulatory system. Biodiversity protection appears to be following a unique method of acquisition of biodiverse habitats. In the final stage, the evaluation of these results may be conducted in different ways.

Part of the modern international arena is the rise of the multinational corporation.[66] On the one hand, such corporations may be viewed as exploiters of natural resources ignoring both local and global ecosystems. On the other hand, such corporations provide for the social organization of property, which at least in theory if not practice, permits the possibility of viewing nature to be part of complex relationships.[67] Corporations are now beginning to adopt codes for their practices and products – codes which may begin to offer leverage for the introduction of broader ecological planning as part of their decisionmaking.[68] A study of these codes from an ecological point of view is needed.

The study of international environmental protection regimes is well underway.[69] With the increasing number of international legal regimes and their applications of ecology and earth systems science, the detailed study of their relationship to science and environmental law is needed. Such an inquiry would include careful descriptions of earth systems science and its specific implication for environmental policy. Also, particular importance is the description of the experimental jurisprudence we have described above and an inquiry into the ways in which such an experimental jurisprudence may be strengthened.

The Reconstruction of Environmental Science and Law

The advent of an integrated ecology, the reformation of law to be a proactive discipline, the establishment of bridges between ecology and law, the formation of ecosystem regimes and the new natural values of our public culture laid the basis for a reconstructed environmental sciences and the law. Environmental science is to be organized within the rubric of ecology and its subdisciplines. Environmental law is reconceived in ecological terms and recognized within ecosystemic regimes. The specific format for the study and the construction of an ecological law is illustrated in the following schema. This schema is based upon the recommendation of case-based methods of ecology[70] and the ecology assessment of selected environmental laws.[71]

Table 11.4 LAW AND ECOLOGY: A SCHEMA OF THEIR RELATIONS

1. The Ecosystem and its Setting
   a. An ecological description of the ecosystem
   b. The nesting of the ecosystem in larger natural systems
2. The Public Culture of Place
   a. The cultural perception of the ecosystem
   b. The larger political, social and cultural setting
3. The Political Clustering of Institutions in Relationship to the Ecosystem
4. The Legal Establishment of the Ecosystem Regime Constitutional and statutory enablement at federal and state level
5. The Administration of an Ecosystem Regime
   a. Setting the boundaries
   b. Identifying functions and services of ecosystem
   c. Establishing ecosystem related, other objectives, and their relations
   d. Determining proper ranges and distribution of biotic stock
   e. Determining actual ranges and distribution of biotic stock
   f. Determining flow rates and means of control
   g. Reviewing potential human interventions in ecosystem
   h. Determining generic prohibitions of intervention
   i. Establishing mechanisms for access to ecosystem
   j. Establishing the nature and kind of interventions
   k. Allocation formula for interventions
   l. Permitting, prohibiting or modifying interventions
   m. Monitoring interventions
   n. Prohibiting, modifying or restoring interventions
6. Dispute Resolution Regarding Administration
   a. Enabling mechanisms of dispute resolution
   b. Choice of mechanisms of dispute resolution (negotiation, mediation, court)
   c. Courts
7. Post Legal Activity
   a. Changes in ecosystem, public culture, institutional clustering
   b. New interventions in ecosystem
   c. Administrative actions after dispute
   d. Statutory and constitutional changes in establishing the regime
   e. New court actions
   f. "Outside" assessment

Source: Brooks, Jones and Virginia

The next step both in research and practice is to approach ecology and its applications of environmental law in accord with this schema, at the same time, testing the schema with specific applications.

Conclusion

One of the surprising conclusions we have reached in completing our admittedly broad history of ecology and environmental law is the discovery of the extent to which one form or another of ecology, its methods, concepts and conclusions permeate many parts of environmental law, especially since the mid-1980s. Ecological views have played an important recent role in endangered species legislation, national parks planning, coastal zone management, forestry management, a variety of global environmental programs and many "place based" programs. Even in legal areas more resistant to ecology, such as the Clean Air Act and the Clean Water Act, recent amendments to these laws and/or their administration incorporate ecological notions.

The significant extent of growth of ecology within public policy has been hidden from the general public and environmental policy makers for many reasons. First, as stated above, many of the ecological instruments employed, i.e., the bridge documents, are at a "low visibility" level of regulation, administration and guidance which does not receive general public attention. Second, some of the ecological approaches contained in global planning which relate to ozone depletion or acid rain are part of the "preliminary" planning processes, which are later replaced by international agreements and domestic laws which implement the ecological findings but do not set forth their regulation in ecological terms. A third explanation may rest with the proliferation of place and species based ecological programs: Yellowstone, Lake Tahoe, the Pine Barrens, Snake River, Northern Forest, the Redwood Forest, the Atlantic Marine fishing area, Chesapeake Bay and many others are identified by the place they are located or species they regulate, rather than the fact that they are settings for ecosystem management. (In fact, the advent of place-based ecosystem management raises the difficult question of the relation of place to ecosystem, a problem which both ecologists and environmental law scholars have begun to consider and which we discussed briefly in our last chapter.) Similarly, species related legislation and regulation have stimulated and been stimulated by the entire field of conservation biology. A fourth explanation of the lack of visibility of the rise of ecosystem regimes may be the extent to which the role of ecology is hidden, either due to the application of its specific concepts only, or the replacement of its name "ecology," with other names, i.e., conservation biology or environmental science or earth systems science. The proliferation of ecosystemic regimes in the United States may be due to the flexibility of the federal government structure, the history of past natural resource regimes, the vibrant environmental movement, and the strong non-profit sector. Whether this proliferation of ecosystemic regimes may be found and/or generated elsewhere remains a subject for future speculation.

Despite the proliferation of ecosystemic regimes within the United States, a struggle continues about how nature should be understood and how legal scholarship should be organized. Despite the deep insights of ecology and the comprehensive perspective which it yields, many environmental scientists continue to pursue a reductive scientific approach which fails to yield any central vision of our world. Meanwhile, traditional legal scholars continue to accept uncritically the given legal categories which ignore the gradual knitting together of new webs of law within ecosystem regimes.[72]

Of course the existence of the myriad of ecological laws, regulations, guidances, plans and programs does not establish the desirability of such activities. Dumb ideas may spread as quickly as smart ones, at least in the short term. After all, alchemy and phrenology had their moment of glory in the history of science. But the discovery of the relations between ecology and environmental law does operate to establish the significance of the topic and the importance of inquiring into the relative success of these programs.

Where are we then in our inquiry? Not very far. We have established the importance of the role of ecology in environmental law and, in some cases, identified where environmental law has spurred ecological research. We have identified the historical and present interactions of law and ecology, and arrived at a rough broad typology of their historical relations. We have described, in a variety of brief examples, how some of these relationships play out. We have identified some of the linkage personages, bridge documents, migrating concepts, and interdisciplinary frameworks which are part of the relations of these two disciplines. We have documented the emergence of ecosystem regimes. We have focused our efforts upon the science of ecology and the history of environmental law. We have not plumbed the public culture and its literary expression in the "environmental age" between 1970 and the twenty-first century. We have not reviewed the political structure and its history which underpin the efforts to initiate and maintain ecosystem regimes. We have not discussed ecosystem regime theory in any detail. And we have not reviewed the remarkable flowering of interdisciplinary frameworks and the new environmental ethics. We have not offered a detailed accounting of the signs of a new integrated ecology and the details of its relationship to ecosystem regimes. We leave with a list of undone tasks:

Table 11.5   A SUMMARY OF SELECTED FUTURE DIRECTIONS FOR THE STUDY OF
ECOSYSTEM REGIMES

- Study the competing thought processes in ecology and legal reasoning.
- Study the formulation of background ecologically-oriented legal principles.
- Prepare a more systematic and expanded history of the relations of ecology and environmental law, especially at points of impact.
- Explore the ways in which environmental media laws and pollutant legislation may better reflect an ecological approach.
- Evaluate those laws which have been deliberately designed to facilitate an ecological approach.
- Prepare a detailed history and evaluation of the myriad of interdisciplinary approaches which have sought to unite ecology and environmental law.
- Seek consensus upon an ecology and law methodology to be employed in future regimes.
- Assess the present dominant paradigm of environmental law.
- Evaluate in detail past efforts to reformulate laws to better accommodate the insights of ecology.
- Evaluate the impact of the new developments of ecology for environmental regimes and their laws.
- Conduct intellectual biographies of bridge personnel in law and ecology.
- In-depth study of bridge documents for their ecological and legal content and impact.
- Trace the history of migrating ecological concepts.
- In-depth study and evaluation of each example of interdisciplinary frameworks for their contribution to linking law and ecology.
- Explore the role of "place" and "species" in guiding ecosystems regimes.
- Review the relations of ecology to the public culture of law.
- In-depth study of international and regional efforts to apply earth systems science as experimental jurisprudence.
- Explore the relevance of the "new" environmental ethics to law.
- Develop a curriculum suited to preparing students to function well within ecosystem regimes.

Source: Brooks, Jones and Virginia

We have hinted at the prospect for a new jurisprudence in which environ-mental law is properly viewed as the latest stage in the perennial recognition of one or another form of natural law, extending in history from Aristotle to St. Thomas Aquinas to the natural rights theorists of the Enlightenment to the immediate future of an ecosystemic jurisprudence.[73] This jurisprudence will be described in both scientific and legal detail by the volumes which follow in this series.

Notes

1. We have traced the theory of regimes in Chapter 1 and the emergence of place-based regimes in Chapter 8.
2. The ways in which ecology, at least its ecosystem aspects, was shaped and influenced by systems thought is traced in FRITJOF CAPRA, THE WEB OF LIFE: A NEW SCIENTIFIC UNDERSTANDING OF LIVING SYSTEMS (1996).
3. For a short portrait of American common law, *see* ROSCOE POUND, THE SPIRIT OF THE COMMON LAW (1921).
4. This agenda of ecosystem ecology is set forth in SUCCESSES, LIMITATIONS, AND FRONTIERS IN ECOSYSTEM SCIENCE (Michael L. Pace & Peter M. Groffman eds., 1998). The different scales of study are explored in the concept of hierarchy; *see* TIMOTHY ALLEN & THOMAS STARR, HIERARCHY: PERSPECTIVES FOR ECOLOGICAL COMPLEXITY (1982).
5. *See* DAVID BRAYBROOKE & CHARLES E. LINDBLOM, A STRATEGY OF DECISION (1963).
6. *See* ANN STRONG, PRIVATE PROPERTY AND THE PUBLIC INTEREST: THE BRANDYWINE EXPERIENCE (1975).
7. *See* DONELLA MEADOWS, JOHN RICHARDSON & BEHART BRICKMAN, GROPING THE DARK: THE FIRST DECADE OF GLOBAL MODELING (1982).
8. *See* BRUCE ACKERMAN ET AL., THE UNCERTAIN SEARCH FOR ENVIRONMENTAL QUALITY (1974).
9. *See supra* Chapter 9.
10. *See supra* Chapter 5.
11. The concept of "adaptive planning" has been introduced to provide for a system of plans and their flexible adoption. One of the early efforts at legal authorization of environmental adaptive planning was the Coastal Zone Management Act.
12. One of the authors of this book has explored the different ways in which laws might implement plans, *see* Richard O. Brooks, *The Law of Plan Implementation in the United States*, 16 URBAN LAW ANNUAL 225 (1979).
13. For an account of the evolution of disciplines, *see* STEPHEN TOULMIN, HUMAN UNDERSTANDING (1972).
14. Although it is customary to describe the advent of environmental law as a statutory overlay to the common law system, some authors have discovered a move towards a system vision within the common law itself. It remains to explore the way in which common law court interpretations have directed the course of environmental law.
15. Environmental law may be seen as part of the extension of the welfare state in several ways. First, it may be seen as part of the set of public health laws and health programs expanded in the mid-twentieth century: part of a larger agenda of protecting the vulnerable. *See* ROBERT E. GOODIN, PROTECTING THE VULNERABLE: A REANALYSIS OF OUR SOCIAL RESPONSIBILITIES (1985).
16. One notable exception is the recent text, DAVID HUNTER ET AL., INTERNATIONAL ENVIRONMENTAL LAW AND POLICY (2001).
17. For a discussion of this view of nature in the context of a history of the different views of nature, *see* PETER COATES, NATURE: WESTERN ATTITUDES SINCE ANCIENT TIMES (1998).
18. *See* BETTY JEAN CRAIGE, EUGENE ODUM: ECOSYSTEM ECOLOGIST AND ENVIRONMENTALIST (2001).
19. *See* EUGENE ODUM, FUNDAMENTALS OF ECOLOGY (3rd Ed., 1971).
20. For example, in 1991, the Chesapeake Bay Foundation had uncovered air pollutants as a possible source of Bay pollution and recommended new air controls. *See*

TOM HORTON & WILLIAM EICHBAUM, TURNING THE TIDE: SAVING THE CHESAPEAKE BAY (1991) at 90, 269.

21. *See* 42 U.S.C. 7412(f).

22. *See* 42 U.S.C. 7492(B).

23. *See* 42 U.S.C. 7412(m), 7601(d), 7472.

24. *See infra* Note 20.

25. *See supra* Chapter 10.

26. We have cited these materials in Chapter 4.

27. For an early overview of the law of planning in the United States, *see* Richard Brooks, *Jurisprudence of Planning: Notes on the Outline of Law Required to Support and Control Planners,* 24 CATH. LAW. (1978); Richard Brooks, *The Legalization of Planning Within the Growth of the Administrative State,* 31 ADMIN. L. REV. (1979). For materials on the legal recognition of systems, see: (A) Urban systems: Legislative authorization of community plans [The recognition of a broad planning law in land use was set forth by Donald Hagman]; (B) Resource systems: Natural resource planning boards – 1931 [The history of the Board is set forth in MARION CLAWSON, NEW DEAL PLANNING: THE NATURAL REASONS PLANNING BOARD (1981)]; (C) Economic systems: Economic planning – The Employment Act of 1946 [*See* EUGENE V. ROSTOW, PLANNING FOR FREEDOM (1959)]; (D) Ecological systems: National Environmental Policy Act – 1970 [*See* RICHARD LIROFF, A NATIONAL POLICY FOR THE ENVIRONMENT: NEPA AND ITS AFTERMATH (1976)]; (E) Ecosystems: Ecosystem Management – The Chesapeake Bay Commission – 1978. [*See* TOM HORTON & WILLIAM EICHBAUM, TURNING THE TIDE: SAVING THE CHESAPEAKE BAY.]

28. In our bibliography we have sought to identify some of the principal works, but space constraints have prevented a full accounting.

29. *See* Stephen J. Toope & Jutta Brunée, *Freshwater Regimes: The Mandate of the International Joint Commission,* ARIZ. JOU. OF INTERNAT'L & COMP. LAW at 273 (1998).

30. Because of space constraints, the authors have omitted a chapter on "emerging interdisciplinary frameworks for law and ecology." An independent paper with this title is available from the authors upon request.

31. We have identified and discussed ecological management in *supra* Chapter 8.

32. One such list of principles may be found in international law, HUNTER *supra* note 16.

33. *See* RICHARD GASKINS, ENVIRONMENTAL ACCIDENTS: PERSONAL INJURY AND PUBLIC RESPONSIBILITY (1989).

34. *See* CAROLYN RAFFENSPERGER & JOEL TICHNER, PROTECTING PUBLIC HEALTH AND THE ENVIRONMENT: IMPLEMENTING THE PRECAUTIONARY PRINCIPLE (1999); TOM CHRISTOFFEL & STEPHEN P. TERET, PROTECTING THE PUBLIC LEGAL ISSUES IN INJURY PREVENTION (1993).

35. For a detailed discussion of the general relationship of the constitution to environmental regulations, *see* Richard O. Brooks, *A Constitutional Right to a Healthful Environment,* 16 VT. L. REV. 1063 (1992). *See also* WILLIAM OPFULS & A. STEPHEN BOGAN JR., ECOLOGY AND THE POLITICS OF SCARCITY REVISITED; THE UNRAVELING OF THE AMERICAN DREAM (1992); TIMOTHY BEATLEY & KRISTY MANNING, THE ECOLOGY OF PLACE (1997).

36. There has been an extensive treatment of the relationship of property rights to the environment. Some of these works are cited below. *See infra* notes 55, 56.

37. One interesting effort to unify an ecological perspective, while recognizing the primacy of freedom is MURRAY BOOKCHIN, THE ECOLOGY OF FREEDOM (1982).

38. For a discussion of proposed reorganization of Congress in light of an ecological perspective, *see* EDWIN HAEFELE, REPRESENTATIVE GOVERNMENT AND ENVIRONMENTAL MANAGEMENT (1974).

39. Abraham Chayes has discussed the implication of moving away from the "binary" adversary approach in courts in order to accommodate multiple parties and polycentric legal problems.

40. There was a proposal to create federal environmental court in the 1970s, and some states have created such a court.

41. *See* RICHARD A. LIROFF, A NATIONAL POLICY FOR THE ENVIRONMENT: NEPA AND ITS AFTERMATH (1976).

42. For a discussion of the need to reorganize, *see* Frances H. Irwin, *An Integrated Framework for Preventing Pollution and Protecting the Environment*, 22 ENV'TL L. 1 (1992).

43. *See* JEROME G. ROSE, LEGAL FOUNDATIONS OF ENVIRONMENTAL PLANNING (1983).

44. Several of the states attempted to reorganize along "ecological" lines in the past decade with limited success. *See* Lynda Butler, *State Environmental Programs*, 31 WM & MARY L. REV. 823 (1990).

45. One non-ecological discussion is M.K. LANDRY, MARC J. ROBERTS & STEPHEN R. THOMAS, THE ENVIRONMENTAL PROTECTION AGENCY: ASKING THE WRONG QUESTIONS FROM NIXON TO CLINTON (1994).

46. The concept of "low visibility" refers to the fact that such documents do not have the same public visibility as statutes, although some of them may be publicly reviewed either in courts or through the legislative oversight processes. Thus, quantitative models, risk assessment, and cost-benefit analysis have been reviewed.

47. The now defunct Congressional Office of Technology Assessment performed a review of some intellectual technologies. Or a discussion of intellectual technology, *see* Richard O. Brooks, *Intellectual Technology: The Dilemma of Environmental Law*, 15 RUTGERS COMPUTER & TECH. L. J. 411 (1989).

48. For a brief discussion of models, *see* Chapter 4 *infra*.

49. For one of many discussions of boundary issues, *see* Robert W. Adler, *Addressing Barriers to Watershed Protection*, 25 ENV'TL L. JOU. 973 (1995).

50. Carrying capacity is a particularly important concept in the law pertaining to national parks. *See, e.g.*, 16 U.S.C.A. 79m (2001).

51. For a discussion of diversity, *see supra* Chapter 9.

52. *See, e.g.*, 16 U.S.C.A. 41ohh (2001).

53. *See* R. Brooks, R. Virginia, R. Jones, *Emerging Interdisciplinary Frameworks for Law and Ecology* (unpublished paper, 2002).

54. *See* PETER HAAS, SAVING THE MEDITERRANEAN: THE POLITICS OF INTERNATIONAL ENVIRONMENTAL COOPERATION (1990).

55. For an overview of the different theories of private property, *see* STEPHEN MANZER, A THEORY OF PROPERTY (1990).

56. The literature on the relations of private property to environmental law is extensive. For a good representative article, *see* DAVID W. BROMLEY, ENVIRONMENTAL AND ECONOMY: PROPERTY RIGHTS AND PUBLIC POLICY (1991).

57. Terry Frazier, *Protecting Ecological Integrity Within the Balancing Function of Property Law*, 28 ENV'TL L. JOU. 53 (1998).

58. *See* YI-FU TUAN, SPACE AND PLACE: THE PERSPECTIVE OF EXPERIENCE (1977); Mark Sagoff, *Setting America on the Concept of Place in Environmental Ethics*, 12 J. ENERGY, NAT. RESOURCES & ENVTL.L. 349 (1992).

59. *See* HEIDDEGER, BEING AND TIME (1962).

60.   *See* EDWARD CASEY, THE FATE OF PLACE: A PHILOSOPHICAL HISTORY (1997); GETTING BACK TO PLACE (1993).

61.   Some states, such as Vermont, Maine, Wisconsin, Oregon, and Washington, may have a heightened ecological awareness of their state as an ecological unit.

62.   *See supra* Chapters 5-10 for identification of bridge documents.

63.   *See* PAUL TAYLOR, RESPECT FOR NATURE (1986).

64.   The most comprehensive legal approach to sustainability can be found in CELIA CAMPBELL-MOHN ET AL., ENVIRONMENTAL LAW: FROM RESOURCES TO RECOVERY (1993).

65.   More sophistication in the theory of planning is required both in assessing the planning of ecosystemic regimes and in the construction of new regimes. *See* JOHN FRIEDMAN, PLANNING IN THE PUBLIC DOMAIN: FROM KNOWLEDGE TO ACTION (1987).

66.   *See* MICHAEL HARDT & ANTONIA NEGRI, EMPIRE (2000).

67.   For a sophisticated view of the corporation which may be adaptable to articulating the role of corporations in the environment, *see* CHRISTOPHER STONE, WHERE THE LAW ENDS: THE SOCIAL CONTROL OF CORPORATE BEHAVIOR (1976).

68.   *See* Eric Bregman & Arthur Jacobson, *Environmental Performance Review: Self-Regulation in Environmental Law*, 16 CARDOZO L. REV. 465 (1994).

69.   *See, e.g.*, ORAN YOUNG, INTERNATIONAL GOVERNANCE: PROTECTING THE ENVIRONMENT IN A STATELESS SOCIETY (1994). For a parallel approach, *see* JOHN VOGLER, THE GLOBAL COMMONS: A REGIME ANALYSIS (1995).

70.   *See* K. SHRADER-FRECHETTE & E.D. MCCOY, METHOD IN ECOLOGY: STRATEGIES FOR CONSERVATION (1993).

71.   For one example, *see* NATIONAL RESEARCH COUNCIL ET AL., RESTORATION OF AQUATIC ECOSYSTEMS: SCIENCE, TECHNOLOGY AND PUBLIC POLICY (1992).

72.   A final reason for the lack of public awareness regarding the rise of ecosystemic regimes is the failure of education in ecology and environmental law. Most environmental studies programs have set forth a curriculum composed of a collage of reductive sciences and activist enterprises. Few have organized their curriculum around the science and vision of ecology, and few have been designed to produce ecologically reflective environmentalists. Most environmental law education programs, despite their proliferation, have also failed to grasp the rise of ecosystem regimes, and how these regimes are transforming the subject matter of environmental law. Few have ecologists on faculty, nor require courses in ecology. The "interdisciplinary" environmental law texts are woefully inadequate. *A new set of ecologically oriented basic texts are needed for environmental law courses.* Most of the programs are primarily designed to prepare law students to represent polluters; hence the focus is upon media and toxic pollution laws. *What is needed at this stage of history is the articulation of an ecologically centered curriculum for both environmental studies and environmental law programs.*

73.   LLOYD WEINREB, in his NATURAL LAW AND JUSTICE (1987), offers a dialectical history of natural law.

Bibliography

Note to Reader: The purpose of this Bibliography is not to repeat the variety of references given in the notes, but rather to identify the major works which set forth the history themes and interdisciplinary frameworks that we consider seminal in understanding the relations between law and ecology.

Chapter 1

In this chapter, we set forth the thesis that there is the slow but steady rise of ecosystem regimes, which include a law based upon the developing science of ecology. Such a broad historical generalization is not foreign to historical writing. Thus, the recent publication of Jacques Barzun's *From Dawn to Decadence: 500 Years of Cultural Life – 1500 to the Present* (2000) illustrates such generalization. Since we project that such developments are likely to continue, our approach parallels Paul Kennedy's *Preparing for the Twenty-First Century* (1993). We are aware that such grand histories are suspect to many historians, and our work might be viewed as an example of the enlightenment history assuming the inevitable progress of science and its applications (see Charles Van Doren, *The Idea of Progress* (1967)).

Contained within our writing is the assumption of a gradual change in the values of Americans. Such accounts are parts of world histories, such as J.R. McNeil's recent history, *Something New Under the Sun: An Environmental History of the World* (2000). There are remarkably few major works on the history of American values since deToqueville's *Democracy in America* (1945). However, recently, Michael J. Sandel has offered a law-based philosophical account in *Democracy's Discontent: America in Search of a Public Philosophy* (1996).

One part of public culture and its values is the field of ecological ethics. There has been a literal explosion of attention to this field of inquiry in the past thirty years. Without seeking to cite all the relevant literature, Peter Wenz's *Environmental Justice* (1998) captures the role of the new environmental ethics in the context of traditional ethics, and Bill Duvall and George Sessions' *Deep Ecology: Living as if Nature Mattered* (1985) promotes the new ecosystemic ethics.

Since we believe that ecology is central to our account of the development of environmental law, the definition of ecology is important. This definition is, like most intellectual matters in post modern life, a contested definition. Perhaps a good overall discussion of ecology and its subdivisions is Robert P. McIntosh's *The Background of Ecology: Concept and Theory* (1985). This work is updated in popular ecology texts such as Michael Begon et al., *Ecology: Individuals, Populations and Communities* (1996), and in Mark B. Bush's *Ecology of a Changing Planet* (2000). Many treatments of environmental science give substantial attention to ecology and also touch on law, economics and policy. Examples include *Environment* (1998) by Peter H. Raven, and *Living in the Environment* (2001) by G. Tyler Miller, Jr. The philosophical exploration of the underlying assumptions of ecology is set forth in Andrew Brennan's *Thinking*

About Nature: An Investigation of Nature, Value and Ecology (1988). Attacks on the very notion of an ecology are exemplified by R.H. Peters, *A Critique For Ecology* (1991), and Daniel Botkin, *Discordant Harmonies,* (1990). One way of understanding ecology is through an understanding of its history and development. Such histories of population biology as Sharon E. Kingsland, *Modeling Nature: Episodes in the History of Population Ecology* (1995), general biology [Ernst Mayr, *The Growth of Biological Thought: Diversity, Evolution and Inheritance* (1982)], systems thought [Fritjof Capra, *The Web of Life* (1996)], and ecosystem ecology [Frank Golley, *A History of the Ecosystem Concept in Ecology: More than the Sum of its Parts* (1993)] give accounts of intellectual developments within the field of ecology. But ecology is also part of the broader march of ideas, and several works have sought to put these developments within a larger context, such as Clarence J. Glacken, *Traces on the Rhodian Shore: Nature and Culture in Western Thought From Ancient Times to the End of the Eighteenth Century* (1976), Anna Bramwell, *Ecology in the 20th Century: A History* (1989), Donald Worster, *Nature's Economy, The Roots of Ecology* (1987), Cynthia Eagle Russett, *The Concept of Equilibrium in American Social Thought* (1966), and Peter Coates, *Nature: Western Attitudes Since Ancient Times* (1998).

An important assumption of our discussion is the notion of ecosystem regimes. This concept is an adaption of Oran Young's work, including his *Resource Regimes: Natural Resources and Social Institutions* (1982). Another important tradition of thought in the application of social science concepts to ecosystems is the work of Elinor Ostrom whose book, *Governing the Commons: The Evolution of Institutions for Collective Action* (1990) exemplifies the provocative work done in this area.

Our account of environmental law draws upon many environmental law books. The definitive statement of the field of environmental law is Celia Campbell Mohn et al., *Sustainable Environmental Law* (1998), and there are numerous texts and treatises on the subject. At the international level, Gerd Winter has edited a fine volume, *European Environmental Law: A Comparative Perspective* (1996). Although there are few books which seek to relate the complex fields of ecology and law in a general way, Bruce Ackerman and his colleagues completed an excellent case study in 1974, *The Uncertain Search for Environmental Quality*, whose conclusions reach beyond the specific subject of the Delaware River Basin, offering conclusions about the relations of ecology to law in general.

Our examination of environmental law is in a historical context, and since Anglo-American law is essentially a historically infused subject matter; there are a myriad of historical treatments of American law. We rely, in part, upon the insights of Bruce Ackerman's constitutional law history *We, the People: Foundations* (1991), not in terms of his dualist constitutional theory, but in terms of his recognition of the fundamental importance of the New Deal period, which, in our view, set the administrative structure for environmental law.

These works illustrate the breadth of the assumptions underlying our book. The only works of similar breadth are Yrjo Haila and Richard Levins, *Humanity and Nature, Ecology, Science, and Nature* (1992) and John Dryzek, *Rational Ecology* (1987). Neither book however offers the historical dimension, or a more specific attention to the theory and history of ecology, environmental law and their relations.

Chapter 2

This chapter is devoted primarily to the developments of the nineteenth and early twentieth century in the fields of law and ecology. Much of the law of the nineteenth century was common law, discussed in Norman Cantor's *Imagining the Law: Common Law and the Foundations of the American Legal System* (1997). The specifics of law during that period are well described in Lawrence Friedman's *American Law and Constitutional Order* (1978). The nature of legal thought which dominated the period is discussed in G. Edward White's *Patterns of American Legal Thought* (1977). Law in the nineteenth century, as described in Morton Horwitz, *The Transformation of American Law 1780-1860* (1977) rationalized and supported the economic growth of the era. The environmental costs of this period are well documented in Joseph Petulla's *American Environmental History: The Exploitation and Conservation of American Resources* (1977).

  The conservation movement of the early twentieth century is set forth in Samuel Hays' *Conservation and the Gospel of Efficiency: The Progressive Conservation Movement 1890-1920* (1974). The rise of the welfare state, at least in its legal dimensions, is set forth in G. Edward White's *The Constitution and the New Deal* (2000). Important as well is the growth of instrumental thought in law as discussed in Robert Samuel Summers' *Instrumentalism and American Legal Thinking* (1982), which is reflected, in part, in the growth of administrative law.

  In this chapter, we make mention of the "nature visionaries." Much of the literature related to them is mentioned in the bibliography to Chapter 1. Some of them were "transcendentalists" which are well set forth in Perry Miller's *The Transcendentalists: An Anthology* (1950) and in Peter Wild's *Pioneer Conservationists of Western America* (1979).

  In the Chapter 1 bibliography, we identified many of the histories of ecology. Two such histories bear repeating; namely Sharon E. Kingsland's *Modeling Nature: Episodes in the History of Population Ecology* (1995), since it clearly delineates the early history of population biology, and *Foundations of Ecology* (Leslie A. Real and James H. Brown eds., 1991), which traces the history of ecology through selection of a series of "classic" research articles.

Chapter 3

This chapter reviews the period of the 1950s and 1960s, which was the "seed time" of ecology when ecosystem ecology was definitively formulated and the notion of the ecosystem burst upon the public consciousness. The crucial works are Eugene Odum's *Fundamentals of Ecology* (1953) and Rachael Carson's *Silent Spring* (1962). There have been a variety of biographies written on the lives of both ecologists. The history of ecology and environmental policy in this period is reviewed in histories cited above, as well as Jock Hagen's *An Entangled Bank: the Origins of Ecosystem Ecology* (1992) and Stephen Bocking, *Ecologists and Environmental Politics* (1997). Although the Hubbard Brook experiments took place throughout the 1960s, the book reports of their results did not emerge until the late 1970s with the classic *Patterns and Process in a*

Forested Ecosystem by F. Herbert Bormann and Gene E. Likens (1979) and updated by Likens and Bormann as *Biogeochemistry of a Forested Ecosystem* (1995).

An excellent account of the DDT hearings in Wisconsin, which offers a first hand glimpse of the encounters of law and ecology is Harmon Henkin et al., *The Environment, the Establishment and the Law* (1971). Several accounts of the Hudson River controversy have been written. Allan Talbot's *Power Along the Hudson: The Storm King Case and the Birth of Environmentalism* (1972) is a good brief history. A. Nash et al. have written a comparable history of the Santa Barbara oil spill in *Oil Pollution and the Public Interest: A Study of the Santa Barbara Oil Spill* (1972). One book which captures the excitement of the politics of the era is Charles Reich, *The Greening of America* (1970). In this chapter we provide a brief account of one of the first ecosystem regimes for Lake Washington, whose history is set forth in W.T. Edmundson's *The Uses of Ecology* (1991). We end the chapter by identifying the emerging field of population law. Garett Hardin's *Population, Evolution and Birth Control: A Collage of Controversial Ideas* (1964) and Ann and Paul Ehrlich's *The Population Bomb* (1968) were important writings of the age. The history of the population control movement, including the period of the 1960s, is set forth in Donald Critchlaw, *Intended Consequences: Birth Control, Abortion and the Federal Government in Modern America* (1999).

Chapter 4

This chapter reviews Earth Day, the early 1970s and the initial tensions between the new push for environmental protection and ecology. Although this chapter focuses upon the "environmentalism" which was part of the public culture of the early 1970s, a recent book on the 1970s offers a very different portrait of an emerging new privatism. See Bruce J. Schulman, *The Seventies: The Great Shift in American Culture, Society, and Politics* (2001). Earth Day was heralded with some environmental classics, including Barry Commoner, *The Closing Circle* (1971), D.H. Meadows & D.L. Meadows et al., *The Limits to Growth* (1972), and J.E. Lovelock, *Gaia: A New Look at Life on Earth* (1971). These charismatic statements were routinized in the Environmental Protection Agency, whose history is recounted in Marc K. Landy, Marc K. Roberts, and Stephen Thomas, *The Environmental Protection Agency: Asking the Wrong Questions* (1994). Part of the problem of the tension between environmental protection and ecology lies in the adoption of media specific laws such as the Clean Air Act. See James E. Krier and Edmund Ursin, *Pollution and Policy: A Case Essay on California and Federal Experience with Motor Vehicle Air Pollution* (1977) and Christopher Bailey, *Congress and Air Pollution: Environmental Policies in the U.S.* (1998), the Federal Water Pollution Control Act of 1972, and Robert A Adler, Jessica C. Lindmann, and Dianne M. Cameron, *The Clean Water Act 20 Years Later* (1993).

Similarly, in land use planning, with the exception of the work of Ian McHarg's *Design with Nature* (1969), the predominant land use laws of the early 1970s gave only token attention to ecological considerations. Nevertheless, in the early 1970s, one can find the early beginnings of ecosystem regimes responding to problems of land use. Thus, attention has been given to the Pine Barrens of New Jersey, in *Protecting the*

New Jersey Pinelands: A New Direction in Land Use Management (Beryl Robichaud Collins and Emily W.B. Russell, eds. 1988); to the Chesapeake Bay in Tom Horton and William Eichbaum's *Turning the Tide: Saving the Chesapeake Bay* (1991); to Lake Tahoe in Douglas H. Strong's *Tahoe: An Environmental History* (1984); and to the Northern Forest in Christopher McGrory Klyza and Stephen C. Trombulak's *The Future of the Northern Forest* (1994). These programs were beginning to formulate new "bridge documents" uniting legal regulation and ecological concepts.

Chapter 5

The chapter reviews the early "embrace" of the ecosystemic vision of ecology within environmental law. A good benchmark for the measurement of both the success and failure of these early approaches is offered by John Dryzek's *Rational Ecology* (1987), which seeks to measure what changes in social decisionmaking have to take place to incorporate an ecological view.

The early embrace of ecology is exemplified in the *National Environmental Policy Act*, the *Coastal Zone Management Act*, the effort to clean up Lake Washington, *The Great Lakes Compact*, and the re-emergence of the public trust doctrine. The classic treatment of the National Environmental Policy Act is Lynton K. Caldwell, *Science and the National Environmental Policy Act: Redirecting Policy Through Procedural Reform* (1982). One of the most systematic efforts to apply ecology under the National Environmental Policy Act is the assessment of the Storm King plant on the Hudson River in *Science, Law and the Hudson River Power Plants: A Case Study in Environmental Impact Assessment* (Robert L. Kendall, ed., 1988).

An early ecological approach to lake management was adopted in Lake Washington, and the history of that effort is set forth in W.T. Edmondson, *The Uses of Ecology: Lake Washington and Beyond* (1991). One article which pursues the notion of ecosystem regime as applied to lakes is Jutta Brunnée and Stephen J. Toope, "Environmental Security and Freshwater Resources: Ecosystem Regime Building" 91 *Am. J. Int'l L.* 26 (1997). For one of many accounts of the ecosystemic approach in the Great Lakes, see The Conservation Foundation's Institute For Research on Public Policy, *Great Lakes; Great Legacy* (1990).

The early application of ecology to coastal management is set forth in John Clark's *Coastal Ecosystems: Ecological Considerations For Management of the Coastal Area* (1974). For a more specific application, see Joy R. Brockman "Coastal Ecosystem Protection in Florida" 20 *Nova L. Rev.* 859 (1996).

There is a large legal literature regarding the public trust doctrine, including Joseph Sax's *Mountains Without Handrails, Reflections on the National Parks* (1980). And there is excellent work tracing the development and the application of the concept; see David Slade et al., *Putting the Public Trust Doctrine to Work: The Application of the Public Trust Doctrine to the Management of Lands, Waters, and Living Resources of the Coastal States* (1990); but not the relationship between the ecological aspects of ecosystems and the function of the trust doctrine to protect those ecosystems.

Chapter 6

This chapter identifies the Endangered Species Act, forestry legislation, national park laws and pesticide statutes as illustrating the gradual incorporation of ecological insights. Particularly excellent histories of these laws include Michael Bean and Melanie Rawland, *The Evolution of Wildlife Law* (1997), Charles Wilkinson and H. Michael Anderson, *Land and Resource Planning in the National Forests* (1987), *The Greater Yellowstone Ecosystem: Redefining America's Wilderness Heritage* (Robert Keiter and Mark S. Boyce eds., 1991), and John Wargo, *Our Children's Legacy: How Science and Law Fail to Protect Us From Pesticides* (1996).

Each of these laws may be viewed as part of a broader evolution of public culture which is discussed in the following books: John Passmore, *Man's Responsibility For Nature: Ecological Problems and Western Traditions* (1974); Roderick Nash, *Wilderness and the American Mind* (1967); Robert Pogue Harrison, *Forests, The Shadow of Civilization* (1992); Simon Schama, *Landscape and Memory* (1995); Shepard Krech III, *The Ecological Indian* (1999), Robert McCollough, *The Landscape of Community: A History of Communal Forests in New England* (1995); Samuel Hayes, *Conservation and the Gospel of Efficiency* (1959); and Bill McKibben, *The End of Nature* (1989).

Works which focus upon the efforts to retrofit these laws with ecological insight include: *Ecosystem Management for Parks and Wilderness* (James K. Agee, Daryll R. Johnson eds., 1988); James A. Pritchard, *Preserving Yellowstone's Natural Conditions: Science and the Perception of Nature* (1999); *National Parks and Protected Areas, Keystone to Conservation and Sustainable Development* (James Nelson and Rafal Serafin eds., 1997), and Marcos Kogan, *Ecological Theory and Integrated Pest Management Practice* (1996).

The contributions of ecology to these laws have consisted largely of the development of conservation biology and its focus upon biodiversity. Works include: David Takacs, *The Idea of Biodiversity: Philosophies of Paradise* (1996); *Biodiversity* E.O Wilson ed., 1989); Michael E. Soule and Bruce A. Wilcox, *Conservation Biology: An Evolutionary-Ecological Approach* (1980); and Michael E. Soule ed., *Conservation Biology: The Science of Scarcity and Diversity* (1986). Earlier works include R.F. Dasmann, *Environmental Conservation* (1959) and D.W. Ehrenfeld, *Biological Conservation* (1970).

Chapter 7

This chapter reviews the early history of environmental efforts which were initiated based upon some form of ecology, including a newly emerging earth systems science. The efforts included the laws to control acid rain and ozone depletion, the Mediterranean agreements, and the incipient efforts to control global warming. With the exception of the Mediterranean program, all of these programs deal with air pollution; the best volume on U.S. air pollution law is Arnold Reitze's *Air Pollution Law* (1995). Books dealing with more specific problems include Richard Elliott Benedick, *Ozone Diplomacy: New Directions in Safeguarding the Planet* (1998) and

Peter Haas, *Saving the Mediterranean: The Politics of International Environmental Cooperation* (1990).

The environmental problems of this chapter were long in the making and historical treatments of them include: Gale E. Christianson, *Greenhouse: The 200 Year Story of Global Warming* (1999); Seth Cagin and Philip Dray, *Between Earth and Sky: How CFC's change Our World and Endangered the Ozone Layer* (1993) and Robert Fox, *The Inner Sea: The Mediterranean and Its People* (1993).

The impact of pollutants upon the environments in question is well documented in Gene Likens and F. Herbert Bormann, Robert S. Pierce, John Eaton, Noye Johnson, *Biogeochemistry of a Forested Ecosystem* (1977); James J. MacKenzie and Mohamed T. El-Ashry, *Air Pollution's Toll on Forests and Crops* (1989); William H. Schlesinger, *Biogeochemistry: An Analysis of Global Change* (1997).

The building of the institutions to cope with the international scope of these problems is described in: Roy Gould, *Going Sour: Science and the Politics of Acid Rain* (1985); Frank Greenaway, *Science International: A History of the International Council of Scientific Unions* (1996); Oran Young, *Resource Regimes: Natural Resources and Social Institutions* (1982); and Peter M. Haas, Robert O. Keohane and Marc A. Levy, *Institutions of the Earth: Sources of Effective International Protection* (1993).

Chapter 8

In this chapter, we have traced the development of place based ecosystem regimes which have implemented an adaptive ecosystem management. Two examples of such regimes are the Florida Everglades and Chesapeake Bay programs. The importance of place is discussed in Yi fu Tuan, *Space and Place, The Perspective of Experience* (1977) and Edward S. Casey, *Getting Back to Place: Toward a Renewed Understanding of the Place-World*, (1993). For a pragmatic effort to relate ecology to place, see Timothy Beatley and Kristy Manning, *The Ecology of Place: Planning for Environment, Economy and Community* (1997).

Parts of ecology which are particularly important to place based ecosystem management are landscape ecology. See S.T.A. Pickett and M.L. Cadenasso, "Landscape Ecology: Spatial Heterogeneity in Ecological Systems," 269 *Science* 331 (1995); estuarine science, see *Estuarine Science, A Synthetic Approach to Research and Practice* (John E. Hobbie, ed. 2000); and the notions of ecosystem hierarchy, T.F.H. Allen and Thomas B. Starr, *Hierarchy: Perspectives for Ecological Complexity* (1982); R.V. O'Neill et al, *A Hierarchical Concept of Ecosystems* (1986).

The literature pertaining to ecosystem management is massive. See *Ecosystem Management for Sustainability* (John D. Peine ed., 1999) and Stephen L. Yaffee et al., *Ecosystem Management in the United States* (C.S. Holling, ed., 1996). Adaptive planning is set forth in *Adaptive Environmental Assessment and Management* (1978). Place based ecosystem management efforts are frequently occupied with restoration. For an overview of restoration efforts, see *Environmental Restoration: Science and Strategies for Restoring the Earth* (John J. Berger ed., 1990), Steven M. Davis and John C. Ogden, *Everglades: The Ecosystem and its Restoration* (1994), and *Estuary*

Restoration and Maintenance: The National Estuary Program (Michael J. Kennish, ed., 2000).

For an excellent collection of articles on place based ecosystem management efforts, see *Barriers and Bridges to the Renewal of Ecosystems and Institutions* (Lance Gunderson et al., eds. 1995). For a selection of materials on the Florida Everglades, see David McCalley, *The Everglades: An Environmental History* (1999). In addition to the Chesapeake citation set forth in Chapter 4 above, the following traces its ecological history: Philip D. Curtin, Grace S. Brush and George W. Fisher, *Discovering the Chesapeake: The History of an Ecosystem* (2001).

Chapter 9

Although the notes of earlier chapters identify some of the early works in conservation biology, this chapter discusses more recent developments including the application of island biogeography. See Robert H. MacArthur and Edward O. Wilson, *The Theory of Island Biogeography* (1967); evolutionary biology: Douglas J Futuyma, *Evolutionary Biology* (1997) and for more recent updates of conservation biology, see Gary K. Meefe et al., *Principles of Conservation Biology* (1997).

The recent application of these ecological subdisciplines include endangered species. See National Research Council, *Science and the Endangered Species Act* (1995). On forest management, see Greg D. Corbin, "The United States Forests Service's Response to Biodiversity Science", 29 *Envtl. Law* 377 (1999). Even more specific applications of ecology to aspects of both the Endangered Species Act and other laws is illustrated by such recent works as Peter Kareiva et. al., *Using Science in Habitat Conservation Plans* (1998).

Since much of the very recent work only appears in periodical articles and since we have limited this bibliography to major works, we urge the interested reader to turn to the Chapter endnotes.

Chapter 10

There is a massive literature pertaining to international environmental law problems. Specific works pertaining to the fashioning of international regimes include John Vogler, *The Global Commons: A Regime Analysis* (1995), Elinor Ostrom, *Governing the Commons* (1990) and Oran Young, *International Governance: Protecting the Environment in a Stateless Society* (1994). In the case of some global environmental problems, these regimes are increasingly making use of the newly emerging earth systems science, which is discussed by NASA Advisory Council's *Earth Systems Science, Earth Systems Science Overview: A Program for Global Change (1986),* and *NASA, Exploring Our Home Planet, Earth Science Enterprise Strategic Plan* (2000).

The three major areas of environmental law discussed in this Chapter are: (1) global warming – see David B. Victor, *The Collapse of the Kyoto Protocol and the Struggle to Slow Global Warming* (2001); (2) the CITES – see *Endangered Species, Threatened Convention: The Past, Present and Future of CITES* (Jon Hutton and

Barnabas Dickson eds., 2000) R. van Heijnsbergen, *International Legal Protection of Wild Fauna and Flora* (1997), and (3) ozone depletion – Richard Eliot Benedick, *Ozone Diplomacy: New Directions in Safeguarding the Planet* (1998).

Especially relevant to the CITES issue is the emergence of the "new" non-equilibrium ecology; see Daniel Botkin, *Discordant Harmonies: A New Ecology for the Twenty First* Century (1990). Especially relevant to international law is the growth of the "precautionary principle;" see *Protecting Public Health and the Environment: Implementing the Precautionary Principle* (Carolyn Raffensperger and Joel Tickner, eds., 1999).

Chapter 11

Since this chapter is principally a summary of the entire volume, many of the works cited in the previous footnotes are applicable here, but will not be recited. The conclusion characterizes the general approach of ecology and environmental law as synoptic and incremental as described in David Braybrooke and Charles Lindblom, *A Strategy of Decision* (1963). Many works document the problems of applying a synoptic approach, including Donella Meadows et al., *Groping the Dark: The First Decade of Global Modeling* (1982) and Bruce Ackerman et. al., *The Uncertain Search for Environmental Quality* (1974).

The effort to relate ecology to law is an example of seeking to relate theory to practice and one discipline to another. We have not explored in this volume the complex background problem of the relation of theory to practice. For one recent collection of inquiries on the topic, see *Theory and Practice, Nomos XXXVII* (Ian Shapiro and Judith Wagner DeCew eds., 1995). We have attended the question of relating disciplines in a related unpublished paper, "Emerging Interdisciplinary Frameworks for Ecology and Law" (2002, available on request).

The relating of ecology and law may lead to the reformulation of one or both disciplines. It was Caldwell who sought to rearrange law through the impact assessment as described in Lynton K. Caldwell, *Science and the National Environmental Policy Act* (1982). The reformulation of ecology takes place through the growth of applied fields of ecology including conservation, restoration and coastal ecology. These disciplines are discussed and cited in other chapters. In this chapter, we have sought to identify linkage persons, bridge documents, migrating concepts and regime organizations as the vehicles of linking law and ecology. The persons and their works are cited throughout the book, as are bridge documents. In this chapter, we list the migrating concepts but do not identify the literature around each concept. Finally, we describe a method of approach which links both ecology and law. This method is derived from K.S. Shrader-Frechette and E.D. McCoy, *Method in Ecology: Strategies for Conservation* (1993) and the work of the National Research Council as set forth in *Restoration of Aquatic Ecosystems: Science, Technology and Public Policy* (1992); see also, U.S. GAO, *Ecosystem Management: Additional Actions Needed to Adequately Test a Promising Approach* (1994).

The history of ecology and its relationship to law may be viewed in the context of the entire history of the concept of nature as set forth by Peter Coates in *Nature:*

Western Attitudes Since Ancient Times (1998) and its relationship to law, Lloyd Weinreb, *Natural Law and Justice* (1987).

Index